The Taste of the Town

The Bucknell Studies in Eighteenth-Century Literature and Culture

General Editor: Greg Clingham, *Bucknell University*

Advisory Board: Paul K. Alkon, *University of Southern California*
Chloe Chard, *Independent Scholar*
Clement Hawes, *The Pennsylvania State University*
Robert Markley, *West Virginia University*
Jessica Munns, *University of Denver*
Cedric D. Reverand II, *University of Wyoming*
Janet Todd, *University of Glasgow*

The Bucknell Studies in Eighteenth-Century Literature and Culture aims to publish challenging, new eighteenth-century scholarship. Of particular interest is critical, historical, and interdisciplinary work that is interestingly and intelligently theorized, and that broadens and refines the conception of the field. At the same time, the series remains open to all theoretical perspectives and different kinds of scholarship. While the focus of the series is the literature, history, arts, and culture (including art, architecture, music, travel, and history of science, medicine, and law) of the long eighteenth century in Britain and Europe, the series is also interested in scholarship that establishes relationships with other geographies, literatures, and cultures of the period 1660–1830.

Titles in This Series

Tanya Caldwell, *Time to Begin Anew: Dryden's* Georgics *and* Aeneis

Mita Choudhury, *Interculturalism and Resistance in the London Theatre, 1660–1800: Identity, Performance, Empire*

James Cruise, *Governing Consumption: Needs and Wants, Suspended Characters, and the "Origins" of Eighteenth-Century English Novels*

Regina Hewitt and Pat Rogers, eds., *Orthodoxy and Heresy in Eighteenth-Century Society*

Edward Jacobs, *Accidental Migrations: An Archaeology of Gothic Discourse*

Catherine Jones, *Literary Memory: Scott's Waverley Novels and the Psychology of Narrative*

Sarah Jordan, *The Anxieties of Idleness: Idleness in Eighteenth-Century British Literature and Culture*

Deborah Kennedy, *Helen Maria Williams and the Age of Revolution*

Chris Mounsey, *Christopher Smart: Clown of God*

Chris Mounsey, ed., *Presenting Gender: Changing Sex in Early Modern Culture*

Roland Racesvkis, *Time and Ways of Knowing Under Louis XIV: Molière, Sevigne, Lafayette*

Laura Rosenthal and Mita Choudhury, eds., *Monstrous Dreams of Reason*

Katherine West Scheil, *The Taste of the Town: Shakespearian Comedy and the Early Eighteenth-Century Theater*

Philip Smallwood, ed., *Johnson Re-Visioned: Looking Before and After*

Peter Walmsley, *Locke's* Essay *and the Rhetoric of Science*

Lisa Wood, *Modes of Discipline: Women, Conservatism, and the Novel after the French Revolution*

http://www.departments.bucknell.edu/univ_press

The Taste of the Town

Shakespearian Comedy
and the Early Eighteenth-Century Theater

Katherine West Scheil

Lewisburg
Bucknell University Press
London: Associated University Presses

© 2003 by Katherine West Scheil

All rights reserved. Authorization to photocopy items for internal or personal use, or the internal or personal use of specific clients, is granted by the copyright owner, provided that a base fee of $10.00, plus eight cents per page, per copy is paid directly to the Copyright Clearance Center, 222 Rosewood Drive, Danvers, Massachusetts 01923. [0-8387-5537-2/03 $10.00 + 8¢ pp, pc.]

Associated University Presses
2010 Eastpark Boulevard
Cranbury, NJ 08512

Associated University Presses
16 Barter Street
London WC1A 2AH, England

Associated University Presses
P.O. Box 338, Port Credit
Mississauga, Ontario
Canada L5G 4L8

The paper used in this publication meets the requirements of the American National Standard for Permanence of Paper for Printed Library Materials Z39.48-1984.

Library of Congress Cataloging-in-Publication Data

Scheil, Katherine West, 1966–
    The taste of the town : Shakespearean comedy and the early eighteenth-century theater / Katherine West Scheil.
      p. cm.—(Bucknell studies in eighteenth-century literature and culture)
Includes bibliographical references (p.   ) and index.
   ISBN 0-8387-5537-2 (alk. paper)
    1. Shakespeare, William, 1564–1616—Stage history—1625–1800. 2. Shakespeare, William, 1564–1616—Stage history—England—London. 3. Shakespeare, William, 1564–1616—Adaptations—History and criticism. 4. Theater—England—London—History—18th century. 5. Shakespeare, William, 1564–1616—Comedies. 6. Comedy. I. Title. II. Series.
PR3097 .S34   2003
792.9'5—dc21
                                                2002153081

PRINTED IN THE UNITED STATES OF AMERICA

For my parents, Robert and Janet West
and
For Andrew and William Scheil

All this we must do, to comply with the taste of the town.
—John Gay, *The Beggar's Opera*

The Appetite of the Publick, like that of a fine Gentleman, could only be kept warm by Variety; that let their Merit be never so high, yet the Taste of a Town was not always constant, nor infallible.
—Colley Cibber, *An Apology for the Life of Mr. Colley Cibber*

We have some three or four, as Fletcher, Johnson, Shakespear, Davenant, that have scribled themselves into the bulk of follies and are admired too, but ne'er knew the laws of heroick or dramatick poesy, nor faith to write true English neither.
—Joseph Arrowsmith, *The Reformation*

It is not to the Actor, therefore, but to the vitiated and low Taste of the Spectator, that the Corruptions of the Stage (of what kind soever) have been owing. If the Publick, by whom they must live, had Spirit enough to discountenance and declare against all the Trash and Fopperies they have been so frequently fond of, both the Actors and the Authors, to the best of their Power, must naturally have serv'd their daily Table with sound and wholesome Diet.
—Colley Cibber, *An Apology for the Life of Mr. Colley Cibber*

Contents

Acknowledgments	9
Introduction	13
1. Shakespeare "Made Fitt": Restoration Adaptations of the Comedies	26
2. "Above Ordinary Plays": Shakespearian Comedy, Spectacle, and Music	48
3. "Study [the] Audience as well as the Rules": Shakespeare and Changing Taste in Comedy	87
4. Shakespeare and the Development of the Afterpiece	153
5. Early Georgian Politics and Shakespeare	188
6. Shakespearian Comedy Before Garrick	201
Conclusion	215
Notes	221
Bibliography	288
Index	314

Acknowledgments

THIS PROJECT BEGAN AS A Ph.D. DISSERTATION AT THE UNIVERSITY OF Toronto, and thanks are due to Alexander Leggatt for his generous, wise, and thoughtful guidance, and for his deep understanding of the "mirth and merriment" of comedy "which bars a thousand harms and lengthens life." Brian Corman and Jill L. Levenson gave equally valuable input. The keen critical eye of Robert D. Hume (Pennsylvania State University), the external examiner, helped improve many details, large and small. Jean I. Marsden and Michael Dobson welcomed me into the world of eighteenth-century Shakespearians at an early stage and encouraged my foray into that area of study. Karen Cunningham provided an even earlier inspiration for me to pursue Shakespeare studies.

In the process of revision, several readers offered helpful advice and comments on parts of the manuscript at various stages, particularly Todd Gilman (Sterling Library, Yale University), Timothy Viator, and Richard Proudfoot. Annette Fern at the Harvard Theater Collection has answered many research questions. Tanya Caldwell (Georgia State University) continues to serve as a model for both scholarship and motherhood. Greg Clingham at Bucknell University Press has been especially kind, humane, and encouraging as the manuscript has undergone revision amid various other life events. The comments of the anonymous reader at Bucknell University Press greatly improved the manuscript and helped elucidate the argument throughout. Parts of this book also benefited from seminars at the Shakespeare Association of America annual meetings over the last few years; particular thanks to Lori Newcombe, Fran Teague, Alexander Leggatt, Victoria Hayne, and the participants of those seminars for comments and collegiality. My colleagues at the University of Rhode Island have encouraged the project for several years, particularly Dorothy Donnelly, Stephen Barber, Valerie Karno, and Naomi Mandel. Andrew Scheil has read more versions of this book than I will mention, and must be one of the only medievalists as well versed in Old English as in eighteenth-century adaptations of Shakespeare. His patience, humor, good sense, kindness, and shared love of Shakespeare and related endeavors have shaped this book (and my life) in too many ways to count. Despite this cadre of supporters, readers, and commentators, the errors that remain are my own.

Research for this book has taken place in many libraries, all of which have been generous in their services and working conditions: Robarts Library and Thomas Fisher Rare Book Library at the University of Toronto; the Beinecke and Sterling Libraries at Yale University; at Harvard the Houghton Library, Widener Library, and the Harvard Theater Collection; the Folger Shakespeare Library; in Hartford, Connecticut, the Saint Joseph College Library and Trinity College Library; Wesleyan University Library; and closer to home the libraries at the University of Rhode Island, and The Rockefeller Library and John Hay Library at Brown University in Providence. Grants from the St. Joseph College Faculty Development Fund, the University of Rhode Island Council for Research, the University of Rhode Island Foundation, and the National Endowment for the Humanities/Aston Magna Academy provided funding for various stages of the project.

Parts of Chapter 1 appeared in a slightly different form in *Philological Quarterly* 76 (1997) and in *Restoration: Studies in English Literary Culture 1660–1700* 21 (1997). Chapter 5 grew out of my experience as an NEH fellow at the Aston Magna Academy, "From Handel to Hogarth: The Arts of Georgian England," summer 1997. I am grateful to the Aston Magna organizers and to my fellow participants for their inspiration and assistance. Chapter 5 first saw print in *Shakespeare Survey 51* (1998), reprinted with permission here in a slightly different version.

Finally, this book owes its greatest debt to my family. For my parents and brother, who always have supported and encouraged me, and who continue to nurture a taste for comedy, character, and good nature. For Andrew Scheil, without whom this book, and many of the pleasures of life itself, would not be possible: "So are you to my thoughts as food to life / Or as sweet-seasoned showers are to the ground" (Sonnet 75). And for young William Scheil, who has yet to experience Shakespeare but already knows a lot about comic adaptation: "This fair child of mine / Shall sum my count, and may my old excuse, / Proving his beauty by succession [m]ine" (Sonnet 2). The dedication reflects in small part my gratitude, as Shakespeare's Kate puts it, "too little payment for so great a debt."

The Taste of the Town

Introduction

ON 3 FEBRUARY 1716 *THE DAILY COURANT* PRINTED THE FOLLOWING notice from Lincoln's Inn Fields:

> This present Friday, being the 3d of February, will be presented a Comedy call'd, A Woman's Revenge; or, A Match in Newgate. To which will be added a New Farce, call'd, The Cobler of Preston. The part of the Cobler to be perform'd by Mr. Spiller. With Singing by Mr. Randal. Mrs Fitzgerald, and the Boy. And Dancing by Mr. Shaw, and Mrs. Schoolding.

This advertisement is designed to attract viewers with several enticements: the allure of a "New Farce" would have drawn some spectators, James Spiller was a well-known and well-liked comic actor, music and dance were proven successful accoutrements. The location of Preston would have called to mind the recent events of the Jacobite Rebellion in 1715. Readers of *The Daily Courant* may have even known that both dramatic pieces were written by actor Christopher Bullock of the well-known theatrical family, whose father had been a prominent member of London theaters since the turn of the century. Or they may have been perplexed to find two afterpieces called *The Cobler of Preston* in London theaters this season, the second one by Charles Johnson. Among the many audience members who patronized Lincoln's Inn Fields in 1716, one can imagine a composite group that came to see several of these attractions. This advertisement is a typical document of eighteenth-century theater history, but it holds additional significance. Buried within these entertainments is a comedy of William Shakespeare's, unmentioned in the advertisement. No one came to Lincoln's Inn Fields in February of 1716 to see Shakespeare's *The Taming of the Shrew*, even though Bullock's *The Cobler of Preston* incorporates most of the Induction material.[1] Why was Shakespeare's comic material used in this fashion? What circumstances led to this performance in 1716 and to other similar reworkings of Shakespeare?

Generalizations abound concerning the works of Shakespeare in the period after his death.[2] It has been argued that later writers wanted to "improve" his plays; that subsequent taste mandated their regularization to conform to neoclassical unities; that his plays were reworked to make political points; or even that his texts were changed covertly by playwrights wishing to suppress what they did to Shakespeare.[3] Yet when we examine individual adaptations in detail, these theories do not always suffice and many of the plays do not adhere to a neat formula.

All of Shakespeare's plays were not treated equally, and their diverse history provides a more accurate view of the elements that contributed to the growth of Shakespeare's reputation, and how the comedies in particular fit into the evolution of Shakespeare as the "National Poet."[4] The reputation of Shakespeare the author differs from the reputation of each individual play, and the growth of Shakespeare's reputation was based on a selective group of plays, not on the canon as a whole. The comedies in particular highlight the uneven nature of Shakespeare's reputation, and the selective way his plays were treated. The comedies demonstrate that in many cases, Shakespeare's main function was to provide raw dramatic material that playwrights adapted without hesitation. Despite surrounding rhetoric claiming to elevate Shakespeare, in reality the comic texts themselves were not part of this process of adulation. I would like to suggest through the following chapters that Shakespeare's comedies had a unique history of adaptation and reception, much unlike the tragedies or histories. The adaptations of the comedies were much more extensive and much less tied to Shakespeare's name as author. The plays thus had little to do with his formation as the "National Poet" and functioned more as raw dramatic material, subject to change based on local theatrical conditions.

Recent works have begun to uncover the particular importance of the eighteenth century in the history of Shakespearian reception, through examinations of editions, eighteenth-century literary theory, nationalism, and satire.[5] Generic studies of eighteenth-century drama, and of comedy in particular, have illuminated various patterns in the evolution of comic taste and form,[6] but this is the first study to examine the intersection between eighteenth-century comedy and Shakespeare's comedies on stage from the reopening of the theaters in 1660 until the Licensing Act of 1737.[7]

Adaptations of the comedies have been often criticized for their treatment of Shakespeare and their lack of artistic merit in comparison to their source text. Many scholars are still reluctant to include these adaptations as a valid part of stage history.[8] This book is an argument to see adaptations of Shakespeare from a new angle. We can better understand these texts if we look to the conditions of playwriting in the period and the related circumstances of theatrical practice.[9] We must resist the urge to compare them to Shakespeare's original plays, and take on the harder task of giving them a fair trial within their own theatrical context. Shakespeare was not adapted in isolation of the theater world, and the resultant plays reflect a particular system of artistic production. As we shall see, playwrights of the time reacted much more to local conditions of production (actors, theater facilities, other popular plays) than they did to ideas of how to adapt or appropriate Shakespeare's plays. No play could succeed on the early eighteenth-century stage without attention to performance circumstances, and playwrights' success depended on their ability to entice paying audiences. As a genre, comedy has a need to remain current because of its intimate connection with society. Alexander Leggatt points out that comedy is both "socially aware and highly formalized"—it builds on a social context but also on a longer history of the genre. Social change is part of comedy, and as society's interests and priorities shift, so must comedy.[10]

In the absence of an overarching methodology or ideology about what a Shakespearian comedy *should* look like, or even a sense that there *was* a body of Shakespearian comedies, practical everyday issues related to theaters often took precedence over playwrights' aesthetic ambitions. There was no wholehearted attempt to uniformly alter Shakespeare's plays, and each adaptation arose at a different historical moment, perpetuated by a different adapter for a slightly different audience. These multifarious texts cannot be reduced to a tidy formula that every adapter followed, but this variety is significant in itself—it tells us that early eighteenth-century playwrights and their audiences had few if any expectations about what comprised a Shakespearian comedy, and for the most part had no concern or interest in seeing an original comedy by Shakespeare.[11]

Eighteenth-century critics debated about how to fit Shakespeare into discussions of the rules, producing the concept of "Shakespeare's genius" as an attempt to defend him from the censure of neoclassical critics. On the stage, there was not an established version of any of Shakespeare's comedies, and often wildly different adaptations were accepted as better stage pieces than the Shakespearian original, or even labeled as the original. In the early eighteenth century, the development of Shakespeare's reputation did not rest on the comedies.

In many ways it can be misleading to analyze these plays only as "adaptations of Shakespeare," denoting a primary interest in the Shakespearian text and how it was changed. This approach can produce some false conclusions because it presumes that playwrights reshaped these plays with a main focus on Shakespeare's play, when in fact for many of the comic texts in this period, the Shakespearian play served only as a foundation or skeleton, and was treated in the same way as a play by Fletcher or Massinger. Thus, part of the task of this book will be to ascertain the relative importance of Shakespeare as the author of this comic material, and to point out numerous instances where the success of a comedy and the concerns of a playwright had little to do with Shakespeare. Through such a revision of our ideas of "adaptations of Shakespeare," we can see the reception history of the plays in a more nuanced fashion, particularly in terms of genre. The comedies were not appraised equally to the tragedies and histories, and Shakespeare as a writer of comedy meant something very different from Shakespeare the author of *Hamlet* or *Othello*. In the Restoration and early eighteenth century, there was not a universal attitude to Shakespeare as a playwright, nor were all of his plays viewed in the same light. The comedies were more susceptible to extensive remodeling and often were subsumed by other features of the production, particularly in times when audiences demanded large amounts of music or spectacle.

This book will provide a more specific account of the stages in Shakespeare's rise as the "National Poet" and will show that this progression was by no means unequivocal, steady, or even apparent at all times. Of course, Shakespeare's plays had to be made appealing for a later audience, but what was the relationship between added elements and the Shakespearian source? In many instances, playwrights were not trying to make *Shakespeare* appealing, they were trying to create an appealing *comedy* from an old source, and the fact that this source was Shakespeare was often incidental. In a complex system of theatrical production, the Shakespearian lineage of these comedies was not necessarily an important aspect—Shakespearian comedy did not sell on its own, and audiences sought and appreciated novelty, music, and spectacle far more than they cared who wrote the literary text underneath. In tracing the evolution of Shakespeare into "Shakespeare," the "National Poet," the Bard, or any other adulatory term denoting canonical importance, the comedies in the Restoration and early eighteenth century serve as a corrective to generalizations about Shakespeare's reputation, and encourage us to view attitudes to "Shakespeare" in a context of other factors that made plays successful in particular periods.

Although each chapter discusses why Shakespeare's plays were reshaped to suit particular theatrical seasons, it is worth pausing over some of the broader characteristics of the period that affected artistic production and in turn helped determine how Shakespeare's comedies would be reworked to suit this repertoire. Theatrical offerings were often determined more by the need to please paying audiences than the desire to attain aesthetic goals. Comic actor William Penkethman recognized the power of spectators in a 1706 prologue, proclaiming that "Poets in Prologues, may both Preach and Rail, / Yet all their Wisdom, nothing will avail, / Who writes not up to you, 'tis ten to one will fail." Penkethman spoke from experience that the "thundring plaudit" of audiences "deals out Fame" and "make[s] Plays run;" even the "vainest

Author" must defer to the taste of spectators, and this taste never involved an original Shakespearian comedy in the early eighteenth century.[12] Even at the end of our period, a scene from *The Author's Triumph; or, The Manager Manag'd* (1737) with a group of players in a tavern displays the same priorities of writing for the stage: "Let the scurvy Men of Wit and Learning stick by their Wit and Learning, and starve . . . The Ear and Eye must be delighted, Sir; these People always carry with 'em to a Play—The Understanding's often left at Home" (14–15). Countless plays disappeared from theatrical records after brief appearances, and playwriting was a notably precarious (and rarely lucrative) position—fulfilling the neoclassical unities, perfecting dialogue, crafting political parallels, and weaving thematic resonances were rarely enough to please audiences and merit success.

This situation had less to do with a particular conception of Shakespeare, and more to do with the type of audience and their desires for entertainment. The theater of the Restoration and eighteenth century was shaped by a growing consumer society, and writers frequently employed the commercial metaphor of trade to describe the practice of writing plays according to audience taste.[13] Playwright and theater manager Colley Cibber attests to what he calls the "Necessity of writing": "I may very well be excused in my presuming to write Plays: which I was forced to do for the Support of my encreasing Family, my precarious Income as an Actor being then too scanty to supply it with even the Necessaries of Life." As his number of children increases, so do his plays; "my Muse and my Spouse were equally prolifick; that the one was seldom the Mother of a Child, but in the same Year the other made me the Father of a Play."[14] Cibber may be exaggerating a bit here, but his testimony is borne out by numerous accounts of playwrights who describe how the need to create theatrical success and the reliance on audiences for profit constrained their creative output. The prologue to Elkanah Settle's *The Heir of Morocco* (1682) spells out the monetary incentives for playwrights to please a fickle audience:

> And Poets, we all know, can change like you,
> And are alone to their own Interest true:
> Can Write against all sense, nay even their own;
> The Vehicle, call'd Pension makes it down.
> No fear of Cudgells where there's hope of Bread:
> A well-fill'd Panch forgets a Broken Head.

Settle was particularly concerned with his own survival, but others attest to the financial priorities of authors: "Both Friends and Foes, such Authors make their Game, / Who have your Money, that was all their

Ayme." A passage from *The Gentleman's Journal* (May 1692) similarly describes the financial motivation of writers for the stage:

> Thus 'tis with Poets, much opprest by Need,
> When they leave Nature, 'tis to follow Bread.
> Not to their Judgment, but their Want, we ow[e]
> The many Monsters, they expose to show.
> For he must think most strangely of our Age,
> Who takes his Judgment of it from the Stage. (18)[15]

Of course, prefatory material often involves a certain amount of stock rhetoric and complaint, but the recurrence of statements that stage offerings were guided largely by what would earn money and driven by "Need" from the beginning to the end of our period indicates their basis in the realities of theatrical life. "Who would not then rather Eat by his Nonsense, than Starve by his Wit?" (28), asked a character in Fielding's *The Author's Farce* (1730). With few exceptions, playwrights had to capitulate to the prevailing whims of a marketplace environment and give the public what they demanded, no matter how farcical, ridiculous, or incongruous. As we shall see, unadapted Shakespearian comic material rarely encompassed the right features to suit this public, and his name value held little sway either.

Unfortunately, it was not easy to tap into current taste for entertainment, as John Crowne attests in the epilogue to *Sir Courtly Nice* (1685):

> 'Tis a hard Case, an Audience now to please,
> For every Pallat's spoyl'd with some Disease.
> Poor Plays as fast as Women now decay,
> How often have I heard true wit call'd stuff,
> By Men with nothing in their Brains but Snuff?

Adaptations of the comedies display this wide range of attempts to capture public taste, with no single formula a guarantee of success. It is no surprise that much discussion about the purpose of drama occurred as writers sought to understand aesthetic taste and discover a formula to craft a successful play.[16] In his prologue to *The Constant Couple* (1699), Farquhar mocked these unpredictable and divergent responses: "Why, what your grave Don thinks but dully writ, / His Neighbor i' th' great Wig may take for Wit." Farquhar voices his exasperation at the judgments of contemporary audiences in "A Discourse Upon Comedy": "Now here are a multitude of Criticks . . . and yet every one is a Critick after his own way; that is, Such a Play is best, because I like it. A very familiar Argument, methinks, to prove the Excellence of a Play, and to which an Author wou'd be very unwilling to appeal for his Success: Yet such is the unfortunate State of Dramatick Poetry, that it must submit to such Judgments; and by the Censure or Approbation of such variety it must either stand or fall."[17] If Shakespeare's name was a selling point, these playwrights would have tried to use it.

Farquhar was not alone in his discontent. In Joseph Arrowsmith's *The Reformation* (1673), the Tutor's playwriting method captures the frustration involved in trying to please a multitude: " 'Tis then, when I have writ a Play, I pick some Lady out of general acquaintance, or favourite at the Court, that would be thought a wit, and send it in pretence for to submit it to her judgment. This she takes for such a favour—and raises her esteem so much—she talks of nothing else but Mr. such a ones new Play, and picks out the best on't to repeat, so half the town by this means is engag'd to clap before they come . . . Besides this, I take some half a dozen youngsters of the town, People that pride themselves in one of my nods or a shaking by the hand at the Coffee-house, and let them have a copy of a Song or two, or promise of the Prologue, which does so much oblige, that I have all the faction of the town that makes a noise on my side" (49). The overstated efforts of Arrowsmith's character to ensure theatrical success differ little from other accounts of malicious and intensely negative audience reactions, often delivered at random. In Thomas Durfey's *The Fool Turn'd Critick* (1676), a play is hissed off the stage by an audience member who cannot even remember why he disliked it: "I went to see a Play, and sitting 'mongst the rest in the Wits Corner; I know not what, but somewhat I mislik't, and raised a hiss, which presently was seconded by all the Wits: But to see the poor fellow the Poet, peep out between the Scenes, and shake his empty head, to see his Ten Months labour so rewarded, would have made you die with Laughter, ha, ha, ha" (27). The unpredictable nature of audience reactions is well documented, even if we allow for exaggeration, and the changing composition of audiences throughout the period elicited additional instability in taste for entertainment.[18] When we examine adaptations of the comedies, we must take into account the numerous variables involved in determining a play's success, and the resultant hodge podge of plays created in an attempt to strike the right balance of elements.

Even though the rhetoric of prologues, epilogues, and metadramatic scenes constructed a world where audiences were vicious and fickle to authors, the number of new writers increased in the eighteenth century. The shift in literary culture from the court to the marketplace created opportunities for writers, notably the emergence of a new level of mass authorship characterized as Grub Street. By the second half of the century, Samuel Johnson could describe the climate for writing as "The Age of Authours," which encompassed "men of all degrees of ability, of every kind of education, of every profession and employment" all seeking "the itch of literary praise."[19] As Judith Milhous points out, around the beginning of the eighteenth century, "the recreational efforts of gentleman amateurs and women had a real chance of production" and numerous writers tried their hands at pleasing current audience taste. The lure of success tempted many, as Steele attested, "Nothing can make the Town so fond of a Man as a successful Play." Not everyone welcomed this influx of amateur dramatists; one writer typically lamented, "Wo[e] to us Players, every one turns Poet."[20] One of the central accounts of early eighteenth-century theater, *A Comparison Between the Two Stages* (1702), contains numerous complaints about the state of writing for the stage. Ramble warns that "The Players have all got the itching Leprosie of Scribling" that " 'twill in time descend to the Scene-keepers and Candle-Snuffers." Sullen agrees that "Many a Fellow undertakes to write a Play, when it were much fitter for him to write Journey-work to a Newsmonger, or an Attorney." Accordingly, it is "as common for a Starving young Fellow with an ill Play to put in for a third Night, as now in the commencement of a War, for a ragged Rascal to run into the Service, for the lucre of the King's *Bounty-money*."[21] Third night benefits, a typical mark of preliminary success, did not necessarily indicate literary quality. The poetic achievements of Shakespeare in his comedies were not as highly regarded as other ingredients—most often music and spectacle, or other performative elements. Playwrights were frequently caught at cross-purposes: pleasing current taste did not necessarily involve literary achievement.

Critics of the stage argued that writing suffered from financial, not artistic, incentives. The author of *A Comparison Between the Two Stages* blames the competitive marketplace for the degeneration of poetry: "the Poets have had too great an Encouragement; for 'tis the Profit of the Stage that makes so many Scriblers, and surfeits the Town with new Eighteen-penny Plays" (3). *The English Theophrastus* (1702) similarly states that "The reason we have had so many *ill Plays* of late, is this; The extraordinary *Success* of the worst Performances encourages every Pretender to Poetry to Write; Whereas the indifferent Reception some excellent Pieces have met with, discourages our best Poets from Writing" (4). Not every writer for the stage penned plays only for money, but the financial rewards and possibilities certainly encouraged would-be poets to contribute to the need for new entertainments.

As England grew as a commercial society, the theaters conformed to a system of competition for audiences with increased income and leisure time, and the companies who offered the "products" their consumers desired—whether foreign singers, dancers, actors, or plots—were rewarded with financial success.[22] At the beginning of our period, Dryden admitted that financial priorities often took precedence over aesthetic concerns: "For I confess my chief endeavours are to delight the Age in which I live. If the humour of this, be for low Comedy, small Accidents, and Raillery, I will force my Genius to obey it." Later in his dedication to the *Examen Poeticum* (1693) Dryden voiced a similar opinion: "However it be, I dare establish it for a rule of practice on the stage, that we are bound to please those whom we pretend to entertain; and that at any price, religion and good manners only excepted . . . There is a sort of merit in delighting the spectators, which is a name more proper for them, than that of auditors."[23] Fielding echoes Dryden's sentiment sixty years later in *The Author's Farce* (1730). Marplay (a thinly veiled Cibber) uses the language of mercantile exchange to describe the theater: "But I think it is very hard if a Man who has been so long in a Trade as I have, shou'd not understand the Value of his Merchandize; shou'd not know what Goods will best please the Town" (17). Cibber himself freely admitted that profit played a role in his artistic endeavors: "And however gravely we may assert that Profit ought always to be inseparable from the Delight of the Theatre; nay, admitting that the Pleasure would be heighten'd by the uniting them; yet, while Instruction is so little the Concern of the Auditor, how can we hope that so choice a Commodity will come to a Market where there is so seldom a Demand for it?" (*Apology*, 1:112). Cibber's phraseology underlines the commercial nature of theater in the period, as a market for which he provided commodities to satisfy a demand. Writers did not abandon aesthetic aspects, but had to balance their artistic goals against the desires of the paying populace, which did not include a desire to see unadorned Shakespearian comedy.

Further contributing to the interdependence between theater practitioners and their audiences was the unstable nature of royal support for the theaters.[24] Aside from Charles II, monarchs were ambivalent toward the theaters until the Hanoverians. William and Mary demonstrated minimal support, and Anne was not particularly charitable toward theaters, preferring concerts for her entertainment. Looking back to the eighteenth century, Thomas Carlyle later remarked that literature "was in the very act of passing from the protection of Patrons into that of the Public; no longer to supply its necessities by laudatory Dedications to the Great, but by judicious Bargains with the Booksellers."[25] Forms of art became more dependent on public support that in turn dictated their shape, scope, content, and appearance. As the anonymous author of *Some Thoughts Concerning the Stage in a Letter to a Lady* (1704) points out, "A *Full* House is the very *Life* of the Stage, and keeps it in Countenance, whereas *thin Audiences* would, in time, make it dwindle to nothing."[26] To accurately analyze Shakespearian adaptations, then, we must realize that they were shaped by and crafted for this environment of increased consumerism and financial motivations, or to use J. H. Plumb's phrase, "the way man enjoys himself and the way his enjoyments are exploited."[27] This financial situation affected adaptations of Shakespeare's comedies, as did the monetary motivations of theater managers. The diverse ways these texts were reworked had more to do with satisfying current taste than with reforming the plays to meet a particular conception of Shakespeare as an author.

Various other developments in eighteenth-century culture contributed to this commercial milieu. Beginning in 1702 with the *Daily Courant*, daily newspapers provided a venue to advertise and market theatrical productions.[28] A mere three months after the appearance of the first newspaper, theaters promoted their offerings to a clientele engaged in trade, commerce, and economic endeavors; according to one historian, the *Daily Courant* was "well known and widely read in London" after only a year.[29] Through newspapers, perspective audience members could "comparison shop" and decide which theater to patronize based on the advertised wares. This publicity proliferated to include lengthy descriptions of exotic offerings and unusual amusements printed along with other financial news, contextualizing entertainment amid a variety of products for sale, from books to miracle cures. Theaters could advertise either in newspapers or in bills, which offered the advantage of last-minute changes or specifics. The developing mercantile environment encouraged competition for the consumer pocketbook, and merchants even began to protest posted playbills.[30]

Advertisements relayed the most persuasive information to attract audiences, and they provide important clues about how productions were promoted.[31] For comic adaptations, the Shakespearian content rarely received top billing in advertisements, not because playwrights were attempting to "hide" their source material, but rather because "Shakespeare" did not sell for these early comic endeavors. Title pages for printed plays in the period, another form of promotion in booksellers' shops, rarely enlist "Shakespeare" as one of the selling points for comedy.[32]

Among the most often touted aspects of productions were music, spectacle, and dance, as several chapters will show, and advertisements usually itemized the enticements of various performers in detail.[33] A comment in the *Spectator* (no. 42, 18 April 1711) acknowledges that "the Tailor and the Painter often contribute to the Success of a Tragedy more than the Poet. Scenes affect ordinary Minds as much as Speeches; and our Actors are very sensible, that a well-dress'd Play has sometimes brought them as full Audiences, as a well-written one." Playwrights were not altogether pleased by these proportions; the prologue to Mary

Pix's *The Deceiver Deceived* (1697) decried the "Powderle-Pimp of Dance, Machine and Song" that produced "short Nonsense four hours long." Pix complained that the combination of these various attractions "makes it hard to say, / If Poet, Painter, or Fidler made the Play." The particular playwright was often less important than what he was able to package for an evening's entertainment, and Shakespeare's name held little clout for drawing audiences to comedy. An average playwright such as Christopher Bullock could create a hit like *The Cobler of Preston* with the right combination of plot, actors, music, and accoutrements. Music by a "hot" composer such as Purcell could draw an audience, and the latest dancers from France or Italy could be counted on to attract a crowd. A popular actor could also secure success for a play, as did John Lacy with Sauny in *Sauny the Scott*, and Thomas Doggett as Shylock in *The Jew of Venice*. These actor-driven adaptations relied on the connection between theater personnel and audiences rather than intrinsic elements in the playtexts themselves. In fact, adaptations of the comedies were often crafted by performers such as John Lacy, Christopher Bullock, and Richard Leveridge, who included roles for themselves based on their particular talents, and who were interested in staging a Shakespearian comedy because of its dramatic craftsmanship with little regard for authorship.

Novelty was also an enticement for audiences, and "new" material could derive from earlier texts by Ben Jonson, or Beaumont and Fletcher as well as by Shakespeare.[34] The pursuit of novelty was a larger cultural concern; *The British-Mercury* for 30 July–2 August 1712 describes the "furious Itch of novelty" as an "epidemical Distemper" of the age, reflected in the growth of print culture. Fashion was also a prominent source for content. A character in James Ralph's *The Fashionable Lady; or Harlequin's Opera* (1730), observes that in the theater, "'Tis Fashion only wins the Town, / 'Tis Fashion makes such Stuff go down" (17). Shakespeare was only one ingredient used by later playwrights to appeal to taste, and his name was never sufficient to draw audiences to his comedies without other accoutrements.

The following chapters examine the relationship between Shakespearian comedy and other elements of attraction while keeping an eye on his reputation as author. The comedies on stage reveal a disjunction between ideas of authorship and attitudes to literary texts. Where, if at all, did "Shakespeare" figure in popularity? With the exception of Charles Johnson's *Cobler of Preston* and *Love in a Forest*, every adaptation is by a different playwright, and most are separated by a substantial amount of theatrical change. Each chapter looks at the way the adaptation fits into the contemporary theatrical context: how the choice of cast affected the production, what aspects of theatrical fashion the adapter capitalized on, and what other factors influenced the composition, performance, success, or failure of the play. Admittedly, theatrical failures have the potential to be problematic as evidence, but often these failures can be accounted for by reasons other than playwriting, including casting problems and vagaries of theatrical competition.[35] Too often these plays are studied in isolation of their artistic context, and found "wanting" compared to Shakespeare's originals. If we reserve aesthetic judgment and examine these texts as part of a system of artistic production, we can learn a great deal about who turned to Shakespearian comic material, why they adapted it, and how they reshaped it. The plays were not treated equally, and different playwrights made various choices about adaptation according to a diverse set of variables, including cast, competition, theater facilities, political relevance, and artistic climate.

The opening chapter considers the first adaptations of the comedies produced in the 1660s shortly after the theaters reopened. Sir William Davenant's *The Law Against Lovers*, a combination of *Much Ado About Nothing* and *Measure for Measure*, reflects a burgeoning theatrical climate, and contains the elements which Davenant thought would please early Restoration audiences—novelty, music, dance, and popular cast members. John Lacy's *Sauny the Scott* transforms Shakespeare's *The Taming of the Shrew* into an acting showpiece for Lacy himself in the title role. Lacy's adaptation demonstrates the power a popular actor had over the theatrical offerings, and the lasting success a play can create when it provides such a star role for a comic actor.

The second chapter involves the variations of *The Tempest* in the Restoration, as well as *The Fairy-Queen*, a version of *A Midsummer Night's Dream* with music by Henry Purcell. These adaptations were products of the new Dorset Garden theater, and show the effects a new theatrical facility can have on the creation of plays. The period around the turn of the eighteenth century, the subject of chapter 3, was one of the most difficult times to please audiences. The adaptations written in this climate, Charles Gildon's *Measure for Measure*, George Granville's *The Jew of Venice*, John Dennis's *The Comical Gallant*, and William Burnaby's *Love Betray'd* reflect changes in the nature of comedy and allegiance to older forms of entertainment.

The fourth chapter centers on the two adaptations of the Induction material from *The Taming of the Shrew*, both entitled *The Cobler of Preston*, and Richard Leveridge's anti-Italian opera piece *Pyramus and Thisbe*. These three versions of Shakespeare take the form of the afterpiece, a popular dramatic mode that peaked in 1716 and continued to attract audiences. Charles Johnson's *Love in a Forest*, which combines material from five Shakespearian plays, comprises the fifth chapter and provides insight into the connections between the theater and political concerns.

Chapter 6 considers the effects of print culture on adaptation of the comedies and the creation of a particular artistic climate before the arrival of David Garrick. The Licensing Act of 1737 and the subsequent arrival of Garrick on the London stage shortly thereafter provide an end point to this study, as both the personnel and the performance conditions drastically changed the climate for theater and for Shakespeare.

It seems appropriate to begin this study with the words of Samuel Johnson when he began to reflect on the work of Dryden, known (among other accomplishments) as an adapter of Shakespeare: "To judge rightly of an author we must transport ourselves to his time, and examine what were the wants of his contemporaries, and what were his means of supplying them."[36] We might add to the inquiry on taste, a second task of ascertaining how these adaptations treated Shakespearian material, and how that can contribute to our understanding of Shakespeare's reputation in the Restoration and early eighteenth century. Taken on a case-by-case basis, these plays can provide a composite view of the evolution of Shakespeare's reputation, and how his comic material functioned in the theater and in the public estimation. The following six chapters imitate Johnson's method, and provide a fresh re-evaluation of writers who adapted Shakespeare's comic material in the early eighteenth century, and the role those adaptations played in the construction of Shakespeare as author.

1
Shakespeare "Made Fitt": Restoration Adaptations of the Comedies

After the closing of the theaters in 1642, Shakespeare's plays were not formally divided between Sir William Davenant and Thomas Killigrew until late in 1660. However, performances before this formal division characterize the way that Shakespeare's plays would be used with mirth, spectacle, and pleasure as the guiding factors in comic offerings. Popular actors, favorite plot types or characters, new forms of comedy, or the latest music and dance were frequently added to draw audiences who had no desire to see original Shakespearian comedy. In the late seventeenth century, the precarious nature of theater left little room for concern with promoting the name of Shakespeare or with improving on his creations. The three adaptations in this chapter were inspired by the possibilities of comedy for entertainment, and the choice of Shakespearian play to adapt reflected the fact that these plots and characters were well-constructed stage pieces and required few changes to produce contemporary stageworthy texts. These playwrights relied on Shakespeare's expertise as a theater practitioner but added elements of their own choosing to update comic appeal. Shakespeare was adapted in the early years of the Restoration not because of his name value, but because of his well-crafted theater pieces in a time when few texts were available. It is no accident that those who first turned to Shakespearian comic material, two comic actors and a theater manager, were intimately connected with performance issues rather than literary pretensions.

Bottom the Weaver

The earliest known adaptation of a Shakespearian comedy, the droll *Bottom the Weaver*, illustrates how local theatrical conditions dominated the concerns of performance.[1] First printed in 1661 but acted earlier when the theaters were closed, the short piece *Bottom the Weaver* was "often publikely Acted by some of his Majesties Comedians, and lately, privately presented, by several APPRENTICES for their harmless recreation, with Great Applause," according to the title page. The performative pleasure of the theater is emphasized in this description of a text crafted for "harmless recreation" in both public and private spaces.

The stage history of *Bottom* further illustrates the patterns of performance, revival, and repackaging that recur with the comedies. In 1673, *Bottom the Weaver* was printed by Francis Kirkman in *The Wits*, Part II, a collection of drolls condensed from longer plays. The title page to this compilation promotes its suitability for a variety of performance situations and its ability to incite "the MERRIMENT and DELIGHT of Wise Men, and the Ignorant." This 1673 reprinting notes the versatility of such dramatic texts for staging "in Publique, and Private, In LONDON at BARTHOLOMEW [FAIRES] In the Countrey at other [FAIRES]. In HALLS and TAVERNS. On several MOUNTEBANCKS STAGES, At *Charing Cross*, *Lincolns-Inn Fields*, and other places. BY Several Stroleing PLAYERS, FOOLS, and FIDLERS, And the Mountebancks ZANIES. With loud Laughter, and great Applause." *Bottom* could apparently be acted by almost anyone in just about any type of locale. Langbaine attests that the "Comical part" of *A Midsummer Night's Dream* "used to be acted at *Bartholomew* Fair, and other Markets in the Country by Strolers, under the Title of *Bottom the Weaver*" (*Account*, 460). Local theatrical conditions, namely lack of performance spaces, were surely a factor in the popularity of these portable texts. Kirkman describes *The Wits* as a collection for strollers and performers with limited facilities: "As for those Players who intend to wander and go a stroleing, this very Book, and a few ordinary properties is enough to set them up, and get money in any Town in *England*."[2] This early instance provides a model for how Shakespeare's comedies were often treated—not as masterpieces by an esteemed author, but rather as premade texts to perform with few changes to update them for new audiences and performance spaces.

Robert Cox, a resourceful and resilient comedian who usually acted in his own pieces, was likely the author of this droll. Cox is the first of several actors who employed the performance potential of Shakespeare's comic texts. Langbaine describes Cox as "An Excellent Comedian . . . who when the Ring-leaders of the Rebellion, and Reformers of the Nation suppresst the Stage, betook himself to making Drolls or Farces" (*Account*, 89). When reprinted in 1673, the title page to *The Wits*, Part II notes that the dramatic pieces were "written I know not when, by several Persons, I know not who; But now newly Collected by your Old Friend to please you." The emphasis here is on content, not authorship. If Shakespeare's name could have sold copies or attracted audiences, no doubt it would have been included and even highlighted in this collection.

This earliest adaptation of a Shakespearian comedy demonstrates a typical use of this material—entertainment is the goal, and if the title page can be believed, parts of Shakespeare's play provided "merriment and Delight" for audiences in theaters, taverns, fairs, and halls. *Bottom the Weaver* was attractive to strollers and itinerant players because of its dramatic potential as a portable and entertaining piece regardless of who wrote it. In the late seventeenth century Shakespeare's comic texts were viable due to their dramatic construction, not their derivation, and playwrights found that these source texts worked well in the theater as comic material and could be easily reshaped to accommodate extra elements. We shall see that Shakespeare's comedies were particularly appealing to actors for adaptation because of their well-crafted comic roles. Cox was certainly not the last performer attracted by this aspect.

THE LAW AGAINST LOVERS (1662)

Actors were not the only ones to find attractive comic material in Shakespeare. Theater manager Sir William Davenant's *The Law Against Lovers* (1662) was the first adaptation of Shakespeare performed on the Restoration stage after the reopening of the London theaters. This amalgamation unites Beatrice and Benedick from *Much Ado About Nothing* with Angelo and Isabella from *Measure for Measure*, resulting in a bizarre and fascinating combination. There have been many attempts to explain Davenant's unusual treatment of Shakespeare; most scholars have attributed his changes to either aesthetic or political motivations, but neither reading fits with the plot of the play or provides an adequate explanation for this adaptation.[3] Davenant's changes to Shakespeare were clear and calculated choices made by an experienced theater manager attempting to capture current audience taste for entertainment; the need to create a successful play took precedence over any desire to craft political parallels or improve Shakespeare aesthetically. To understand Davenant's motives in creating *The Law Against Lovers*, we must look to the conditions of theatrical production in the early years of the Restoration. In this environment, it was far more important for Davenant to include elements that attracted new audiences than to fulfill other desires of literary concern. Like Robert Cox, Davenant employed Shakespeare's comic texts for their ready-made possibilities.

In 1660, Shakespeare's plays were divided among Sir William Davenant and Thomas Killigrew, who were to run the Duke's and the King's theaters respectively.[4] As the first adapter of Shakespeare on the Restoration stage, Davenant has been credited with establishing the foundation for how subsequent playwrights would approach Shakespeare's plays. Theater historians have excused Davenant's treatment of Shakespeare by arguing that he was legally required to extensively adapt the old plays in his possession before performing them, resulting in such plays as *The Law Against Lovers*. For instance, John Freehafer asserts that "Davenant was legally obliged to 'reform' those plays, as a prescribed condition for obtaining the right to perform them . . . Whether or not Davenant wished to 'reform' those 'ancient' plays, he bound himself to do so in order to obtain plays his company badly needed."[5] Davenant's warrant demands that he "reform" and "make fit" the plays granted to him before producing them, and several other contemporary theatrical documents show that the requirement to reform and make plays fit for the stage simply means to clean up any obscene passages.[6] In the King's grant of August 1660, both Davenant and Killigrew were forbidden to "at any time Hereafter cause to be acted or represented any Play Enterlude or opera Containing any Matter of Prophanation, Scurrility or Obscenity." They were also commanded to "peruse all playes that haue ben formerly written and to expunge all Prophanesse and scurility from the same, before they be represented or Acted."[7] A similar decree for purging profanity from plays appears in a letter to the Cockpit players on 13 October 1660, and a later document from 1663 issued by the Master of the Revels specifies the removal of profanity before plays could be printed.[8] Legally, Davenant's obligation was to eliminate obscenity; any other changes were optional, not mandatory.

In fact, Davenant did not do a thorough job of excising all risqué elements from *The Law Against Lovers*. For instance, when her young sister Viola asks Beatrice why Julietta is in prison, Benedick answers, "She play'd with a bearded Baby, Mistress, / Contrary to Law."[9] Thus, Davenant was allowed to perform older plays without major changes, as long as he purged the offensive material from them, and he apparently performed several Shakespearian plays in largely unadapted versions in the 1660s, including *Henry VIII*, *King Lear*, and *Twelfth Night*.[10]

If Davenant could perform both *Measure for Measure* and *Much Ado About Nothing* after simply removing any profanity without significant rewriting, why did he apparently not do so? He had to stretch the small number of plays he was granted to fill his first seasons. He only had rights to twenty plays, which was not enough to provide the variety his audiences demanded for a whole season, and he had no extra plays to perform if audiences did not like a particular play.[11] With such a small repertory, Davenant would want to get as much mileage out of each play that he was allowed to stage. The obvious approach would be to perform all of them to have the greatest variety, but we have no evidence that Davenant ever offered *Measure for Measure* or *Much Ado About Nothing* before *The Law Against Lovers* was performed.[12]

A close examination of the theatrical climate that produced *The Law Against Lovers* suggests the motives behind Davenant's adaptation.[13] As the patentholder and "Master and Superior,"[14] Davenant had direct control over the success or failure of the Duke's Company. His main objective was to create a viable play for his newly formed company while adhering to the guidelines established in his theatrical patent, which included access to a limited number of old plays, and a legal requirement to reform obscenity in any of those plays before performing them. If we look at the strategies Davenant used to please audiences, we can see that he chose to emphasize novelty in his theater rather than rely on the reputations of pre-Restoration authors. Instead of cautiously offering a simple performance of the old plays granted to him in his patent, he turned his efforts to new offerings, adding spectacle and novelty to his theater productions. Davenant was intensely conscious of the need to create a successful play, and this imperative took precedence over any desire to create political parallels or correct Shakespeare. Thus, Davenant's primary strategy in crafting *The Law Against Lovers* was not to improve Shakespeare, revive Shakespeare, rewrite Shakespeare, or even acknowledge that he was performing Shakespeare, but rather to act two old plays under a new title, packaging them as a new product and passing them off as his own enterprise. As we saw with *Bottom the Weaver*, Shakespeare's name held little value as a source for comedy, and his texts were chosen primarily for their performance potential.

According to surviving records, *The Law Against Lovers* was first performed in February of 1662.[15] Novelty was a key factor in Davenant's success in the 1660s, and he intended *The Law Against Lovers* to be received as a new play. Various accounts throughout the 1660s testify to the attraction of new plays for audiences. In Davenant's *The Play-house to be Let* (1662), the Player describes the affinity for novelty among London audiences:

> Well, my dear fantastick friends of *London*,
> Who love Novelty, and would scorn to look
> Even on the Moon, but that she changes often
> And becomes new; I hope we shall please you now. (73–4)

On 7 March 1664, Pepys found Lincoln's Inn Fields "very empty, by reason of a new play" at Killigrew's Theatre. In 1667, Pepys again writes, "But to see how Nell cursed for having so few people in the pit was pretty, the other House carrying away all the people at the new play."[16] Indeed, "new" offerings were a trademark of Davenant's. John Downes records that Davenant opened his theater "with the said Plays, having new Scenes and Decorations, being the first that e're were Introduc'd in *England*," and Charles II's 1660 grant to Davenant mentions the "Great expences of Scenes musick and such new Decorations as Haue not bin formerly used."[17] Davenant was adept at making his plays "new" by adding changeable scenery, music, and dance; "new" did not necessarily mean a fresh plot—updated accoutrements would often satisfy.[18]

The first three seasons of the Duke's company further attest to the Restoration audience's interest in new offerings. In the 1660–61 season, Davenant's plays *The Siege of Rhodes*, parts 1 and 2, and *The Wits* were clearly successful, but no examples of older plays from this season were performed with similar results.[19] In the 1661–62 season, performance records at Davenant's theater exemplify a pattern similar to the previous season. Performances of old plays do not survive with as much frequency as new offerings by Davenant.[20] His *Love and Honour* and Cowley's *Cutter of Coleman-Street* were clearly fancied by audiences, again supporting the trend of success based on novelty and connection to Davenant.[21] The 1662–63 season also indicates a similar taste for such offerings at the Duke's Theatre. The two new plays this season, Thomas Porter's *The Villain* and Samuel Tuke's *The Adventures of Five Hours*, were undoubtedly popular.[22] Existing records from 1660–63 indicate that new plays and plays by Davenant were generally successful, while audience preferences are not demonstrable for older plays. Davenant's strategy of offering new plays and his own updated fancy productions was certainly part of the reason for his unexpected success over Killigrew's company. In his prologue to *The Play-house to be Let* (1662), Davenant elucidates his strategy of catering to the spectators who "affect things new."[23] The theatrical climate embraced novel performances, especially with Davenant's style; as an expert theater manager with his finger on the pulse of his audience, these patterns of success would have encouraged Davenant to craft *The Law Against Lovers* as a "new" play of his own, and not as a revival of Shakespeare. Langbaine describes such contemporary playhouse practices of offering something "new" from old material with a new name; playgoers and bookbuyers are "impos'd on by crafty Booksellers, whose custom it is as frequently to vent *old* Plays with *new* Titles, as it has been the use of the Theatres to dupe the Town, by acting old Plays under new Names, as if newly writ, and never acted before."[24]

Surviving performance records also show that Davenant's motives in creating *The Law Against Lovers* had less to do with Shakespeare, and more to do with providing a vehicle for various forms of entertainment involving song, dance, a popular young actress, music, and novelty. Despite the scanty nature of documented performances, enough evidence survives to indicate that Davenant's productions that stressed novelty and music were generally successful while performances of unadorned Shakespeare were not as popular with audiences.[25] In his *An Account of the English Dramatick Poets* (1691), Langbaine attests to the popularity of Davenant's own plays: "To speak of them in general, I need only say, that most of them have appear'd on the Stage with good applause, and have been receiv'd with like success in Print." Langbaine points out that *The Siege of Rhodes* (1656) had been acted before 1660, but was "afterwards enlarged by the Author, and acted with applause at the Duke of York's Theatre in *Lincolns-Inn-Fields*" with the changeable scenery that he made popular (*Account*, 107, 110). A contemporary reference to *The Law Against Lovers* describes Davenant as "a far better Cooke then a Poet" for his ability to "dress" the play.[26] This analogy of Davenant as a "Cook," mixing together various ingredients to create a whole, captures his practice in these early adaptations. His goal was not to be a "poet" in the sense of a literary craftsman perfecting artistic creations. Davenant's purpose in adapting Shakespeare was to concoct a product for consumption based on what he thought would sell, which was not a comedy by Shakespeare.

In addition, Davenant was probably able to pass off *The Law Against Lovers* as his own play because theater audiences would not have recognized the two source plays from Shakespeare. We have no performance records for either *Measure for Measure* or *Much Ado About Nothing* between the reopening of the London theaters and the first performance of *The Law Against Lovers* in 1662. Many seventeenth-century playwrights enjoyed great popularity with readers when the theaters were closed, including Brome, Middleton, Massinger, Shirley, and Davenant himself. The Beaumont and Fletcher 1647 Folio was the most popular dramatic publication during the Interregnum, and numerous Beaumont and Fletcher plays were performed after the theaters reopened in 1660.[27] Shakespeare's plays were printed in Folios in 1632 and 1663, but were not reprinted for reading during the Interregnum except for *The Merchant of Venice* (1652), *Othello* (1655), and *King Lear* (1655).[28] Without evidence of a reading public or performances in the theater, it is highly unlikely that the majority of the 1662 audience would have recognized either *Measure for Measure* or *Much Ado About Nothing* when performed in Davenant's adaptation.[29]

Further evidence points to the obscurity of these now well-known Shakespearian plays in the early 1660s.[30] We have surviving accounts of five audience members who saw Davenant's *The Law Against Lovers* in 1662, but not one of them alludes to Shakespeare, and they all use

Davenant's title when referring to the play. In his diary entry for 18 February 1662, Pepys reports that he saw "*The Law against Lovers*, a good play and well performed, especially the Little Girle's (who I never saw act before) dancing and singing; and were it not for her, the losse of Roxalana would spoil the house." Pepys recognized Moll Davis's performance as Viola (the "Little Girle"), but does not mention any connection to Shakespeare (3:32).[31] John Evelyn records on 18 December 1662: "I saw acted the *Law against Lovers*," but does not associate the play with Shakespeare (3:347). In their diary, travelers Jacques Thierry and Will Schellinks list *The Law Against Lovers* as one of the plays that they saw while in London; although they "judged [it] to be their best play," they did not indicate any relationship between the play and Shakespeare. Edward Browne includes *The Law Against Lovers* in his list of plays seen at Davenant's theater, without identifying it as Shakespeare's.[32] Not one of these eyewitnesses mentions Shakespeare, and they all use Davenant's title to identify the play.

While it is difficult for modern readers to imagine that a Shakespearian play could go unrecognized, other plays of Shakespeare's performed in the 1660s were identified as new plays even with their original titles. In 1661 Pepys calls *Twelfth Night* a "new play" and in 1663 refers to Shakespeare's *Henry VIII* as a new play by Davenant.[33] As the surviving evidence from 1660–63 shows, new plays were more likely to attract an audience than offerings identified as old plays. Even *Hamlet*, perhaps the most popular play of Shakespeare's in all periods, was not a guaranteed success. John Evelyn's November 1661 entry on *Hamlet* is illustrative: "now the old playe began to disgust this refined age; since his Majestie being so long abroad" (3:304). This sentiment may have been part of the impetus for Davenant to offer *The Law Against Lovers* as a new play. Performing a "creation" of his own, despite his small repertory, was apparently a better theatrical strategy than offering two old plays of Shakespeare's.

The printed version of *The Law Against Lovers* contains no evidence to explicitly connect it to Shakespeare (the prologue and the epilogue do not survive), and further suggests that Davenant wanted *The Law Against Lovers* to be considered as his own play.[34] Davenant's works were first collected in a 1673 Folio after his death, put together by his widow Mary Davenant and Henry Herringman. Herringman's address to the reader resolutely declares the originality of the Davenant Folio as "A Collection of all those Pieces Sir William D'avenant ever design'd for the Press; In his Lifetime he often express'd to me his great Desire to see them in One Volume."[35] Herringman emphasizes Davenant's intent to have his work collected and presented as a whole. The plays in the Davenant Folio include his *The Siege of Rhodes*, part 1 and 2, The

Play-house to be Let, *The Unfortunate Lovers*, *The Wits*, and *Love and Honour*. *The Law Against Lovers* is also contained in the Folio, but Davenant's popular adaptations of *Macbeth* and *The Tempest* are not. The integration of *The Law Against Lovers* with his original works in the Folio, and the omission of his other two Shakespearian adaptations demonstrate that Davenant designed and considered (or wanted others to consider) *The Law Against Lovers* as his own play, not as a revised version of Shakespeare.[36] Later dramatic histories attest to the success of this strategy; in *An Account of the English Dramatick Poets* (1691), Gerard Langbaine includes *The Law Against Lovers* in his list of Davenant's own works, but like the Davenant Folio, Langbaine omits *Macbeth* and *The Tempest*. In *Roscius Anglicanus* (1708), prompter John Downes also names *The Law Against Lovers* as one of Davenant's plays, but attributes *Macbeth* and *The Tempest* to Shakespeare (59, 72).

Given that Davenant promoted *The Law Against Lovers* as a new play and chose not to emphasize or even mention its connection to Shakespeare, what did he think would attract audiences? We can look to the popular elements that characterized his performances in the 1650s and early 1660s for similar promotional choices.[37] He had begun to develop his signature performances when the theaters were officially closed, concentrating on medleys of song, music, and spectacle. Productions such as *The First Days Entertainment at Rutland House* (1656) and *The Siege of Rhodes* (1656) established Davenant's trademark of dance, spectacle, and song by such popular composers as Henry Lawes, Henry Cook, Matthew Locke, Charles Coleman, and George Hudson, as well as his success at pleasing audiences with this formula. For *The Siege of Rhodes* (1656), he advertised music from "the most transcendent of *England* in that Art, and perhaps not unequal to the best Masters abroad."[38] As Dryden observes, "It being forbidden him in the Rebellious times to act Tragedies and Comedies . . . he was forc'd to turn his thoughts another way: and to introduce the examples of moral vertue, writ in verse, and perform'd in Recitative Musique."[39] Throughout his career, Davenant relied on this formula to attract and win audiences to his theater.

The Siege of Rhodes has usually been seen as Davenant's underhanded way to sneak in dramatic performances when they were not allowed, but James A. Winn points out that music was perhaps more important for Davenant's productions than the dramatic content and that music was a priority, not a subversive way to perform a play when theaters were closed.[40] In fact, before the theaters closed Davenant had this strategy in mind of presenting an entertainment that incorporated other elements besides a dramatic text. By 1639, he obtained a patent from Charles I to build a theater designed to "gather together, entertain, govern, privelege and keep, such and so many Players and Persons, to exercise Action, musical Presentments, Scenes, Dancing and the like."[41] After the reopening of the theaters, Davenant's focus on novelties including song, dance, and spectacle made him a viable rival to Killigrew.[42] The changes Davenant made in revising *The Siege of Rhodes* for the Restoration stage display the interests and concerns of theater managers in the early 1660s, and *The Law Against Lovers* was part of this production strategy of coupling song and dance with a dramatic piece.[43]

Throughout the Restoration, music increasingly became a vital part of an evening's presentations, and part of the reason for Davenant's success as a theater manager was his ability to synthesize these elements of entertainment within his dramatic works. Davenant's sense of audience taste was prescient; added musical pieces and dances clearly pleased Restoration audiences and would remain in high demand. Pepys attests that Davenant's *Macbeth* is "a most excellent play in all respects, but especially in divertisement, though it be a deep tragedy," later describing it as "a most excellent play for variety" (8:7, 7:423).[44] The prologue to Dryden's *The Wild Gallant* (1663) protests, "your Play is ill design'd, / It should have been but one continued Song, / Or at least a Dance of 3 hours long." Edward Howard similarly complained in the Preface to *Six Days' Adventure* (1671): "Scenes, Habits, Dancing, or perhaps an actress, take more with Spectators, than the best Dramatick wit."[45] Despite various complaints about the intrusion of music into the dramatic text, Davenant had discovered a successful formula for playwriting, which he used when adapting Shakespeare.

The Law Against Lovers reflects this process of craftsmanship. Davenant updates the musical aspects of his play by replacing the Shakespearian songs from both source plays with two new songs, including the ensemble piece "Our ruler has got the vertigo of state."[46] This composition resembles the modern musical cast song, with a stanza for Beatrice, Benedick, Lucio, and Viola to sing their impressions of Angelo's rule and the laws enacted against lovers. "Our ruler has got the vertigo of state" was popular outside the context of the play, and its frequent reprintings affirm Davenant's ability to tap into current audience taste.[47]

Another musical feature was a new song, "Wake All the Dead," designed by Davenant for the popular young actress Moll Davis, who played Davenant's original character Viola, a younger sister to Beatrice. The success of this addition is demonstrated by the fact that Edward Ravenscroft included excerpts from "Wake All the Dead" in his play *The Careless Lovers* (1673).[48] Moll Davis was certainly one of the main attractions of Davenant's theater; Pepys's reaction to *The Law Against Lovers* emphasizes his enjoyment of Davis's (the "Little Girle") dancing and singing. Not to put such alluring material to waste, Davenant also wrote a saraband for Davis to dance with castanets, an entertainment popular with early Restoration audiences.[49]

Davenant's adaptation of *Measure for Measure* and *Much Ado About Nothing* was a calculated and carefully planned production designed to draw audiences to his theater by the enticements of a "new" play, with song, dance, and a popular actress/singer/dancer in several featured capacities. The success of Davenant's theater in the early years of the Restoration was due to his sensitivity to audience taste, as well as his ability to produce plays that catered to current trends in entertainment. *The Law Against Lovers* was packaged as a new play, and according to all surviving accounts, was received as an original play of Davenant's, even meriting a position in the 1673 Folio of his collected works. Such an experienced and successful theater manager recognized that his Shakespearian texts were more useful as raw dramatic material than as plays to promote "by Shakespeare."

Unlike some later adapters, Davenant's use of Shakespeare is unhindered by concerns about Shakespeare's reputation, which in 1662 was no guarantee of theatrical success.[50] In his 1700 adaptation of *Measure for Measure*, discussed in chapter 3, Charles Gildon not only advertises his reliance on Shakespeare, he goes so far as to include Shakespeare himself as part of his play—the ghost of Shakespeare delivers the epilogue, raging because "My Plays, by Scriblers, Mangl'd I have seen." Gildon overtly acknowledges his debt to Shakespeare, but at the same time admits the need to please audiences above all other concerns. The prologue (written by John Oldmixon) opens, "To please this Winter, we all Meanes have us'd; / Old Playes have been Reviv'd, and New Produc'd." Similarly, the prologue also emphasizes the same elements that made Davenant's earlier adaptation successful: "Let neither Dance, nor Musick be forgot." Even though Gildon admits his use of Shakespeare publicly and overtly, he still employs the same recipe for Shakespeare that Davenant had found successful, as the concluding lines of the prologue advertise, " 'Tis *Purcels* Musick, and 'tis *Shakespears* Play." On the title page to Gildon's *Measure for Measure*, both Shakespeare and the musical additions figure prominently: "Written *Originally* by Mr. *Shakespear*: And now very much Alter'd; With *Additions* of several *Entertainments* of *MUSICK*." Unlike Davenant, Gildon does not emphasize his own role as adapter, choosing instead to stress the updating of Shakespeare with the added music of Purcell's *Dido and Aeneas*; in fact, he remarks in the Dedication that the play is "much more *Shakespears* than Mine."

As we shall see in chapter 3, by 1700 the strategy among Shakespearian adapters had shifted from Davenant's covert use of his Shakespearian material, to Gildon's display of Shakespearian origins.[51] By the

1690s, attribution and origin of sources were more prominent concerns, but in 1660 this was not the case, as the differences between Davenant and Gildon's treatment of Shakespeare disclose. *The Law Against Lovers* marks an important moment in the history of Shakespearian reception. In the early 1660s, the pressures of running a successful theater company outweighed any presumptions about improving Shakespeare's plays or using Shakespeare as a selling point. Although nearly impossible for a modern reader or audience to imagine, in the first years of the Restoration it was possible to design a play involving Beatrice, Benedick, Angelo, and Isabella and to claim it as your own. Even a writer who prided himself on his descent from Shakespeare realized that Shakespeare's name value alone would not sell, at least for comedies. Davenant's role as theater manager led him to make choices about his source material, even if from Shakespeare, based on other successful strategies.

Sauny the Scott (1667)

In addition to new plays and musical features, in the newly opened theaters of Restoration London, audiences were often enticed by the opportunity to see a popular actor. The second adaptation of a Shakespearian comedy in the Restoration, actor John Lacy's *Sauny the Scott*, demonstrates the success a stage personality could impart to a dramatic performance. Restoration and early eighteenth-century theaters had a close actor-audience relationship, and plays were written with particular actors in mind who were well-known to the audience.[52] The first of many adaptations of Shakespeare's *The Taming of the Shrew*, John Lacy's play was performed in 1667, printed in 1698, and remained in the theatrical repertoire through the 1720s.[53] Despite the absence of Shakespeare's play from the theater in the period, *Sauny the Scott* has been largely ignored as irrelevant to the stage history of *The Taming of the Shrew* and unworthy of serious study.[54] In addition, most scholarship on the reception history of Shakespeare's play has focused on how different periods have dealt with the disturbing aspects of the shrew-taming plot. John Lacy's purpose in adapting *The Taming of the Shrew* was not primarily to revise the shrew-narrative's sexual politics, but rather to craft a role for his comic talents.[55] Lacy is one of several comic actors who adapted Shakespeare's material for their own performances; Langbaine attests that Lacy was not only a talented actor, "he knew both how to judge and write Plays" (*Account*, 317). Like the early droll *Bottom the Weaver*, the performability of Shakespeare's comic material was the impetus for a comic actor to use a Shakespearian comedy as a basis.

For an audience in the late 1660s, John Lacy's presence in the title role of *Sauny the Scott* would have overshadowed other appeals the play now may have for modern readers; original audiences would have been drawn to the theater simply for a chance to catch the most popular comic actor of the day in a featured part, and Lacy realized that he held greater appeal than did Shakespeare. Lacy was appropriately described by his contemporary Thomas Durfey as the "Standard of true Comedy in our Age" and he takes full advantage of this reputation through his performance as Sauny, Petruchio's servant.[56] Through frequent interaction with the audience, Lacy establishes a comic persona based on contemporary English stereotypes of Scots, pulling the dramatic focus of the play in the direction of his reputation as a skilled comic performer.

As both an actor and a shareholder in Killigrew's company, John Lacy had a vested interest in securing theatrical success. Only Killigrew and Sir Robert Howard held more shares in the King's Company than Lacy, whose personal finances were at stake if he did not produce a successful play. In the "Epistle to the Reader" attached to his play *The Dumb Lady: or, the Farriar made Physician* (1670), Lacy expresses the need to write profitable plays: "I have had my ends upon Poetry, and not Poetry upon me: for if Poetry had gained its ends on me, it had made me mad; but that I having my ends on it appears in my getting money by it, which was shewn plentifully on my Poet's days." Similarly, in the epilogue to his play *The Old Troop* (1664), Lacy affirms that his primary reason for writing plays is to make money from his benefit performances: "My Poets Day I mortgage to some Citt, / At least six Months before my Play is writ." Likewise, Lacy's main purpose in writing *Sauny the Scott* was to earn money for himself and for Killigrew's company, and his play helped ensure the viability of the King's Company shortly after the theaters reopened following the plague in 1665. In the 1665–66 season, the plague curtailed most forms of entertainment in London and the theaters were closed in June of 1665. They reopened in late 1666, and Lacy's *Sauny the Scott: or, The Taming of the Shrew* was performed on 9 April 1667.[57] The King's Company so depended on Lacy's talents to create and perform in successful comedies that his death in 1681 would certainly have weakened the company and may have contributed to the necessary union with the Duke's company the following year.

The first printed edition of the play (in 1698) uses the title *Sauny the Scott: or, the Taming of the Shrew: A Comedy*, written by J. Lacey. The omission of Shakespeare's name on a title page is certainly not unique, but the choice to designate Lacy as the author instead of Shakespeare foregrounds Lacy's connections to the play rather than its Shakespearian origins. Prior to the 1708 edition, which describes the play as "a piece that took its original from the celebrated pen of the famous Shakespeare, and afterwards received its finishing stroke from that ingenious comedian Mr. Lacy, and thereby has acquired the merit of appearing so often on the stage, handed down through so long an age, and even to continue its reputation to the present generation a still darling entertainment," there is no evidence that Restoration audiences distinguished between the original text of Shakespeare and the "finishing strokes" of Lacy, just as they would not have detected Davenant's mixture of two plays.[58] In the early years of the King's Company, Lacy's reputation was more important to advertise than Shakespeare's association with the play.

Indeed, the many laudatory references to Lacy in accounts of the Restoration theater indicate his popularity. For Pepys, Lacy's acting could redeem any performance, as he notes in his diary for 12 June 1663: "saw *The Committee*, a merry but an indifferent play; only Lacy's part, an Irish footman, is beyond imagination" (4:181). Several years later (13 August 1667) Lacy again salvages Howard's play: "I do now find it a very good play and a great deal of good invention in it; but Lacy's part is so well performed that it would set off anything" (8:384). Similarly, Lacy's performance in Shirley's *Love in a Maze* (10 June 1663) was the sole virtue of the play for Pepys: "The play is pretty good, but the life of the play is Lacy's part, the Clowne, which is most admirable" (4:179). Four years later, Pepys reiterates his esteem for Lacy's talents in *Love in a Maze*: "a sorry play, only Lacy's clowne's part, which he did most admirable endeed; and I am glad to find the rogue at liberty again" (8:195–96). Gerard Langbaine is perhaps the most complimentary of Lacy as "A Comedian whose Abilities in Action were sufficiently known to all that frequented the King's Theatre, where he was for many years an Actor, and perform'd all Parts that he undertook to a miracle: insomuch that I am apt to believe, that as *this* Age never had, so the *next* never will have his *Equal*, at least not his Superiour" (*Account*, 317). It was this reputation for comic acting that drew audiences to Lacy's performances, and this was also the aspect he chose to emphasize when adapting Shakespeare's comic material. In *The Taming of the Shrew* Lacy found a dramatic structure ideal for embellishing a Scots character from an already existent minor part.

Lacy's acting ability was complemented by his talents as a dancing master and specialist in comic dialect parts, both of which he employed in *Sauny*.[59] As well as acting, he often danced between acts of plays and most of his own plays, including *Sauny*, end with a dance.[60] Lacy's improvisational talents also were well-known. He was committed to the porter's lodge for acting in Edward Howard's *The Change of Crownes* in 1667, just before *Sauny the Scott* premiered. Although Lacy insisted that

Howard's play was at fault, there is evidence that Lacy was arrested for adding indecent expressions to his role, perhaps similar to the bawdy expressions and improvisations that made his Sauny a memorable character. The audience certainly would have recalled Lacy's recent transgressions mere weeks before he played Sauny.

Fortunately for theater historians, Pepys happened to be in the audience for this first performance and recorded his response: "we saw The Tameing of a Shrew; which hath some very good pieces in it, but generally is but a mean play; and the best part, Sawny, done by Lacy, hath not half its life, by reason of the words I suppose not being understood, at least by me" (8:158). The following season, Pepys also attended a performance of *Sauny the Scott*: "[Mrs. Pepys] and I alone to the King's playhouse and there saw a silly play, and an old one, *The Tameing of a Shrew*" (8:516).[61] Although Pepys uses Shakespeare's title (and Lacy's subtitle) in his diary entries, his comments focus on the comic aspects of Lacy's performance, emphasized by his description of the play as "mean" and "silly." Pepys identifies Lacy as the prominent feature of the play, and his account of Sauny as "the best part" demonstrates the ability of Lacy's character to dominate the play. *Sauny the Scott* proved to be a success not because of its association with Shakespeare, but because it was a dramatic showpiece for the comic talents of this popular actor-turned-playwright.

If we look at the text we can see that Lacy's changes are all related to this strategy. In creating Sauny the Scott, Lacy develops a special relationship with the audience, based on his comic reputation and reinforced through frequent asides and comments to the audience preserved in the printed text. From the first moment he is on stage, Sauny demands the attention of the audience, at times eclipsing the other characters. When Geraldo and Petruchio meet for the first time in the opening scene, Geraldo's first words are to Sauny and not to Petruchio: "How now *Sauny*, What Crying out? Dear *Petruchio*, most wellcome; When came you to Town? What Quarrel is this 'twixt you and *Sauny*?" (4). The primary focus on stage concerns the wrangling between Sauny and Petruchio; the audience is directed to Sauny's physical humor and only secondarily to Petruchio's purpose in coming to London. This type of physical comedy was part of Lacy's typical stage business; he admits in the prologue to *The Old Troop* that he designed the play to please those who "laugh aloud with wide mouth'd grace, / To see Jack Puddings Custard thrown in's face."

Sauny even dominates most of the scenes between Petruchio and Margaret, and his comic antics divert attention from the taming plot. For example, as Margaret protests that Petruchio is sending away the Tailor, Sauny interjects, "Now the Deel's a cruppen untell her Mouth

Sir, you may see a little of his Tail hang out, it looks for aw the world an it were a Sting Sir" (28).[62] Through his comments to the audience, Sauny guides the viewers' reactions to the taming plot, emphasizing Margaret's shrewishness and pointing out the dangers for Petruchio in attaching himself to a shrew. Like the Chorus in a Greek drama, Sauny's constant stream of asides provides an external narrative to the action and establishes a special link with the audience to direct their responses to the taming plot.

In an added scene based on Fletcher's *The Tamer Tam'd*, Margaret stands up to Petruchio when she returns to her father's house. She seems a more outspoken female character, but Lacy reduces this possibility with Sauny's running commentary in the scene:

> *Margaret*. 'Tis very well, you think you are in the Country but you are mistaken, the case is alter'd, I am at home now, and my own disposer; Go swagger at your greazy Lubber there, your Patient Wife will make you no more Sport, she has a Father will allow her Meat and Lodging, and another gaits Chamber-Maid then a *Highlander*.
> *Sauny*. Gud an ye were a top of *Grantham Steple* that aw the Toon may hear what a Scauden Queen ye are, out, out.
> *Petruchio*. Why what's the matter *Peg*? I never saw thee in so jolly a Humour, sure thou hast been Drinking.
> *Sauny*. Gud has she, haud ye tang, ye faw dranken Swine, out, out, out, was ye tak a Drink and nere tak *Saundy* to yee, out, out, out.
> *Margaret*. 'Tis like I have, I am the fitter to talk to you, for no sober Woman is a Companion for you.
> *Petruchio*. Troth thou sayst right, we are excellently Matcht.
> *Margaret*. Well mark the end on't, *Petruchio* prithee come hither, I have something to say to you.
> *Sauny*. De ye nea budge a foot Sir, Deel a my saul bo she'll Scratch your eyn out. (40)

Sauny's commentary constructs a triangle between the three characters, complicating the comic structure of these scenes, and compelling the audience to shift their attention from the taming plot to his bawdy asides, which must have been accompanied by a great deal of physical comedy. Further, his lines emphasize Margaret's shrewishness and deprive her of authority.

In perhaps the most controversial scene of the play, when Margaret submits to Petruchio in the final act, Sauny's reactions dominate the stage, and he even has the final words in this scene, "Shall *Saundy* get her a Bride-Cake, and Brake o'r her Head Sir? and wee's gatt us a good Wadding Dunner" (45). During this key interaction between Petruchio and Margaret, Sauny steals the show and remains the dominant voice on stage. We can see that Lacy's aim was to embellish the low comic potential of the play though his own unique talents, and his changes to Shakespeare's play were in tune with current partiality for this type of bawdy coarse humor in comedies of the late 1660s and early 1670s.[63] Shadwell complained in the preface to *The Humorists* (1671) that "the rabble of little people, are more pleas'd with *Jack Puddings* being soundly kick'd, or having a Custard handsomely thrown in his face, than with all the wit in Plays."

In addition to Sauny's function as a roguish escort through the shrew-taming narrative, Lacy also emphasizes his Scottish attributes, particularly his dialect, as the source of much of his humor. Lacy was a specialist in ethnic stereotypes, and surely would have drawn on this reputation and talent in creating Sauny. He had earlier acted a Welshman in *The Royall King*, the title role in *The French Dancing Master* and the French cook Raggou in his own play *The Old Troop*, and an Irish footman (Teague) in *The Committee*, one of his more famous parts. When expanding the role of Grumio into Sauny, Lacy obviously drew on this proclivity for dialect and ethnic parts as part of his standard comic routine.

Lacy may have needed to perfect his Scottish accent a bit; Pepys admits that he could not understand the words. In the first lines between Petruchio and Sauny, Petruchio tells Sauny to "leave off your *Scotch*, and speak me *English*, or something like it" (4). Lacy's use of this dialect may have been a deliberate method to reinforce contemporary attitudes toward Scots as an unfamiliar, strange, and uncivilized people.

Instead of drawing on one particular theatrical model for Sauny, Lacy employs a pastiche of contemporary English perceptions of Scottish characteristics and habits.[64] Relations between Scotland and England in the late seventeenth century were characterized by a long history of mutual mistrust and animosity, and most Scottish literary characters reflect this sentiment.[65] This view of Scots continued in the eighteenth century; a 1715 diarist writes, "I observe the Scotch are very much employed now at court and in foreign parts by our court. They seem to be men very fit for business, intriguing, cunning, tricking sort of men that have not much honour or conscience, but that are ready to comply with the court in anything."[66] The continued animosity toward Scots may explain the longevity of Lacy's play in the early eighteenth century; it was performed fairly consistently in the first three decades and was reprinted in 1708, 1714, 1731, and 1736.[67]

Lacy would have found much inspiration in numerous anti-Scottish sentiments of his time. John Tatham, who created most of the Lord Mayor's pageants from 1657 to 1664, was renowned for his hatred of Scots and channeled this hostility into his dramatic presentations. Langbaine remarks that if Tatham "was not an Extraordinary Wit, at least he was Loyal in the highest Degree, as may appear by his Plays; and equally hated the *Rump* and the *Scots*." Tatham's tragedy *The Distracted State* (written in 1641 and published in 1651) includes an apothecary with a marked Scottish dialect who tries to poison the King of Sicily. Langbaine comments that "This Play suited well with the Times; and his Hatred to the Scots appears in this play" (*Account*, 502).[68] Tatham's later comedy *The Scots Figgaries: or a Knot of Knaves* (1652) includes the Scotch beggars Jocky and Billy, a Scotch soldier appropriately named Scarefoole, and Folly the Scotch court fool. Jocky opens the play by praising England and denigrating Scotland: "Weele, *Scotland*, weele, tow gaffst me a mouth, but *Anglond* mon find me met; 'tis a geod soile geod feith, an gif aw my Contremon wod plant here, th'od thrive better thon in thair non" (1). Apparently, Tatham's depiction of Scots was realistic; Langbaine affirms that "Most of this Play is writ in the *Scotch* Dialect, and displays them to Life" (*Account*, 503). Tatham's *The Rump* includes a Scottish character named Stoneware, modeled after Scottish statesman Archibald Johnstone, Lord Warriston, who speaks in rough dialect, with coarse qualities similar to Sauny the Scott.[69] *The Rump* was performed and printed in 1660 with a second edition in 1661, "acted many times with great applause" (Langbaine, *Account*, 503) and revised by Aphra Behn as *The Roundheads* (1681). Other contemporary writers also express loathing and revulsion toward this nationality. One particularly disturbing conflation of anti-Scottish sentiments and anti-Semitism occurs in Francis Osborne's play *The True Tragicomedy* (1654), where Stone the fool remarks that "these uncircumcized Scots [are] more nasty and mangy than their ancestors the Jews were ever reported" (1.3.20–21). The widespread and often extreme disdain for the Scottish in the seventeenth century provided ample material for Lacy to draw upon in shaping his portrayal of a Scottish servant.

Specifically, Sauny's characteristics of uncleanness, hunger, incivility, and coarseness derive from contemporary attitudes toward Scots expressed in numerous sources. The account *Scotland Characterised* (1701) describes Scotland as a nation of "Pedantry, Poverty, Brutality, and Hypocrisy." The writer accuses the Scots of "Bringing two of the Plagues of *Egypt* along with them, *viz*. Lice and the Itch; which they have intailed upon their Posterity ever since" (357–58). The English view of Scotland is tidily summarized here:

> To be a Brute's the only Thing in Fashion;
> And Nastiness the Genius of that Nation.
> The Things, that are abominated there,
> Are clean Shirts, Swines-Flesh, and the Common-Prayer. (360)

In *A Modern Account of Scotland* (1670), the author ("an *English* Gentleman") argues that "if the Air was not Pure and well refined by its Agitation, it would be so infected with the Stink of their Towns, and the Steams of the nasty Inhabitants, that it would be pestilential and destructive" (122–23). Scottish houses are described as "seven or eight Stories high, with many Families on one Floor, one Room being sufficient for all Occasions, Eating, Drinking, Sleeping, and Shit—" (123). In these representative accounts, the Scots are viewed by the English as nasty, squalid, and unclean.

Lacy endows Sauny the Scott with these habits of uncleanness and scratching, perhaps also influenced by the Scotch character of Jocky in Tatham's *The Scots Figgaries* (1652), who greets his fellow beggar Billy, "a sud be me Contremon by's scratin an scrubbin" (1). From the beginning to the end of the play, Sauny has a regular routine of "Scratten and Scrubben" (4), probably enacted with exaggerated gestures. The first time Sauny appears on stage, Petruchio remarks, "thou need'st Scrubbing, I'll say that for thee, thou Beastly Knave; Why do ye not get your self Cur'd of the Mange" (4). When Petruchio beats Sauny for not understanding his orders, Sauny turns this physical violence into an opportunity for scratching: "Gude an yeed give *Sawndy* ea bang ar twa mere e that place, for I can ne're come at it to Scrat it me sel Sir ... The Dee'l saw yer Fingers, I may not beat yea o' yee'r e'ne Dunghill, Sir, bot gin I had yea in *Scotland*, I'se ne give yea a Bawbee for your Luggs" (4). Lacy may have capitalized on the characteristics he honed as Sauny in his other roles. Raggou, the French cook in Lacy's *The Old Troop* (1664), is similarly described as a "nasty slovenly rogue" who "stinks above ground" (10). The Lieutenant of his troop tells him, "you are so nasty, no body is able to come near you" (12).

Whenever Sauny is on stage, his gestures draw attention to his uncleanness and his need to scratch, further guiding attention away from the taming plot with this physical humor. In Michael Wright's 1675 portrait of Lacy commissioned by Charles II, Lacy is scratching his left wrist with his right hand.[70] Wright chose to preserve this particular physical action as a memorable trait of Lacy's Scottish character.

Scots were also thought to have voracious and undiscriminating appetites, and Lacy's Sauny is no exception.[71] The author of *A Modern Account of Scotland* describes the "poorer Sort" of Scots as surviving on "Haddock, Whiting, and sowre Milk ... and upon the stinking Fragments that are left at their Laird's Table. Prodigious Stomach, that, like the *Gulon*, can feed on their own Excrements, and strain their Meat through their stomachs, to have the Pleasure of devouring it again!" (127). Sauny exhibits just such an appetite. In Shakespeare's play, when Petruchio arrives at his home, Grumio is late in greeting him because he has been busy getting the servants ready. Here, Sauny's hunger is the excuse for his tardiness, as he tells Petruchio, "Wuns, Sir, Ise be sea hungry, and sea empty, ye may travell quite through me, and nere saw your fingers Sir" (23).

The overall effect of these Scottish stereotypes is to give the play a baseline of lewd and tasteless behavior, often with bawdy overtones.[72] Sauny is cruder than Petruchio in his sexually suggestive and distasteful comments, and he often accompanies Petruchio in sexual and violent threats to Margaret. In the first scene between Petruchio and Margaret, Sauny delivers his crass comments directly to Margaret. Lest audience members focus too much on Petruchio, when Margaret says that Petruchio's appearance turns her stomach, Sauny replies, "Gud an your Stomach wamble to see his *Face*, What will ye dea when ye see his *Arse* Madam." Margaret tries to quell him, but Sauny replies, "S'breed the Deel tak a gripe O yer faw fingers and Driss your Doublat for ye" (11). Sauny offers to teach the other women in the play with his special techniques: "but gin yet let *Sauny* teach 'em? I'se pipe 'em sea Whim—Whum, their Arses shall nere leave giging and joging while their's a Tooth in their head" (9). Lacy's Sauny gives the play a tone of barbarity and disgust, making Petruchio seem almost refined in comparison. Audiences would have been much more horrified and disgusted by Sauny than by anything Petruchio does.

Like Davenant, Lacy's practical experience in the theater seems to have given him a sense of the necessary ingredients for a play's success. In addition to his own comic talents, Lacy also capitalized on a popular plot type, the shrew-taming story. After *Sauny the Scott*, he returned to this enduring plot in *The Dumb Lady* (1670).[73] Other Restoration plays attest to the endurance of this plot type. Actor Thomas Jevon's popular farce *The Devil of a Wife* (1686) involves the taming of a shrew and an abusive cobbler. Peregrine Bertie's reaction attests to the success of Jevon's play: "To day [6 March 1686] is acted Jevarns' new farse; Thursday was the first day. I must confess it is the strangest thinge I ever saw; 'twas mighty full the last time, and to day there is noe getting in."[74] Jevon's play was popular throughout the Restoration and eighteenth century and was reprinted in at least three editions by 1700, later inspiring *The Devil to Pay* (1731), which remained on the stage through the middle of the nineteenth century. Elkanah Settle's *The Siege of Troy* (1707) also contains a shrew-taming narrative, probably influenced by Jevon's play. Settle's droll was popular by 1700, and may have been acted much earlier.[75] Lacy's initial interest in *The Taming of the Shrew* was probably fostered by the potential for success with the plot and the role he could tailor for himself.

Perhaps most persuasive of Lacy's interest in shrew-taming plots is the fact that at the conclusion of *Sauny the Scott*, Lacy points out a connection to one of the most popular shrew-taming plays. Petruchio's concluding lines, "I've *Tam'd the Shrew*, but will not be asham'd/ If next you see the very *Tamer Tam'd*" (48) allude to John Fletcher's *The Woman's Prize, or the Tamer Tam'd* which was performed throughout the Restoration and early eighteenth century.[76] Fletcher's *The Tamer Tam'd* had an obvious influence on Lacy's play, specifically the mock-funeral Petruchio stages for the shrew in *Sauny* as he does for himself in Fletcher's play. No performance records survive for Shakespeare's *The Taming of the Shrew* in the Restoration, but Fletcher's *The Tamer Tam'd* was frequently offered in theaters and was actually performed at the Red Bull two months before Davenant and Killigrew were granted their patents for the reopening of the London theaters in 1660.[77] *Sauny the Scott* may have drawn audiences because of its connections to this popular shrew-taming play; in the later eighteenth century *Sauny the Scott* was performed in conjunction with Fletcher's play.[78]

Lacy's play was one of the more successful adaptations of Shakespearian comedy in the eighteenth century. We can look to its components as indicators of audience taste and as a successful model for adapting Shakespeare: a favorite comic actor in the title part, a proven successful plot type, a stereotypical role that encompassed common English attitudes toward Scots, and various other physical comic antics that do not survive in the printed text, but are captured in a contemporary portrait of Lacy. The buffoonery of Sauny and his many asides establish an actor-audience relationship that shifts the focus of the play toward this comic role and away from the taming plot. As a leading man in Killigrew's company, Lacy would profit from producing new plays, particularly in the first decade of the reopening of the London theaters amid an unstable and erratic theatrical period. Shakespeare's connection to the source play had little selling power, and the text had more appeal as a foundation for these other elements.

Conclusion

Several conclusions can be drawn about the earliest adaptations of Shakespeare's comic material and its importance for later reworkings of these plays. Robert Cox and John Lacy were not the only comic actors interested in good material from the earlier seventeenth century. Most of the major comedians of the eighteenth century tried their hands at Shakespearian comic material, including Jemmy Spiller, William Penkethman, and Thomas Doggett, as subsequent chapters shall show. Davenant's tactics of song, dance, and novelty in *The Law Against Lovers* worked for later successful adaptations of the comedies. These early adaptations also reveal that comedies needed aspects for success other than a Shakespearian pedigree. No bare unadorned or unadapted Shakespearian comedy could entice Restoration and early eighteenth-century audiences. Lacy and Davenant discovered that Shakespeare's comic material was useful as the groundwork for a theatrical offering, but aspects other than Shakespeare's name value—popular actors, music, popular plots, and other "new" elements—were necessary to draw spectators. As the next chapter will show, the need to embellish a bare Shakespearian comic plot only increased in the seventeenth century as theaters began to offer more elaborate and extensive stage productions. Cox's *Bottom the Weaver*, with its emphasis on a bare script and minimal staging requirements, is a far cry from the demands of later seventeenth-century audiences for dramatic offerings, particularly for music and spectacle.

2

"Above Ordinary Plays": Shakespearian Comedy, Spectacle, and Music

"Musick and poetry have ever been acknowledg'd sisters, which walking hand in hand, support each other; As Poetry is the harmony of Words, so Musick is that of Notes: and as Poetry is a Rise above Prose and Oratory, so is Musick the exaltation of Poetry. Both of them may excel apart, but sure they are most excellent when they are joyn'd, because nothing is then wanting to either of their Perfections: for thus they appear like Wit and Beauty in the same Person."[1] Henry Purcell's harmonious and unproblematic description of music and poetry as siblings reveals little of the conflict that besieged this subject during the seventeenth and eighteenth centuries. The relationship between music and drama in the theater was a topic of debate throughout the eighteenth century, and achieving a balance between the two was a fundamental task of playwrights.[2] Of particular concern was the appropriate integration of music with spoken dialogue; the preferred method for English audiences was to separate the musical elements from the dramatic components, as an entertainment for characters in a play, for example. Matthew Locke affirmed that a balance of spoken words and music was "more proper to our [English] genius," and Motteux corroborated that "our English genius will not relish that perpetual Singing," favoring instead "Music and Dancing industriously intermix'ed with Comedy or Tragedy;" Dryden famously described the successful play as "one continued Song, Or at least a Dance of 3 hours long."[3]

The increased desire for music had implications for the shape of dramatic texts, and Shakespeare's comedies were no exception. The most prevalent concern was the dominance of music over drama, as Roger North queried, "how and by what stepps Musick shot up in to such request, as to croud out from the stage even comedy itself, and to sit downe in her place and become of such mighty value and price as wee now know it to be."[4] Complaints about an overabundance of music often took creative forms; a 1676 prologue to Ben Jonson's *Volpone* imagines Jonson's reaction to the dominance of music over his "God-like wit": "Did Ben now live, how would he fret, and rage, / To see the musick-room outvye the stage?" Describing contemporary audiences, the prologue admits that "Yet 'tis too true that most who now are here, / Come not to feast their judgment, but their ear." Music has become "the bus'ness of the theatre," and audiences "judiciously prefer" music rather than the play itself. Any discussion of plays from this period must take into account the "violent inclination in the Towne to follow musick," and the corresponding repercussions for dramatic texts.[5]

What place would Shakespearian comic material have in a climate that valued musical additions? The comedies revived in the later seventeenth century, indeed some of the more successful adaptations, were those that could handle musical additions, namely *The Tempest* and *A Midsummer Night's Dream*. The adaptation of these texts in particular is due to their affinity for music and spectacle. In this chapter, we shall see how the entertainment preferences of late seventeenth-century audiences regarding spoken drama, music, and spectacle, directly affected the reception history of Shakespeare's comedies and helped determine which plays would have a life on stage and which would remain dormant.

Despite complaints from playwrights, theaters provided performance venues for both music and drama, and were able to attract audience members by offering both: "Some come for the play and hate the musick, others come onely for the musick, and the drama is pennance to them, and scarce any are well reconciled to both. M[r]. Betterton (whose talent was speaking and not singing) was pleased to say, that 2 good dishes were better than one, which is a fond mistake, for few are to see 2 at a time of equall choice."[6] Betterton recognized that taste for music would not be easily dispelled, and that theaters must provide what their audiences requested. This equilibrium began to shift in favor of an abundance of music, which satisfied audience demand but proved problematic for drama.

Theatrical productions became more collaborative as these nondramatic elements increased in importance. No longer the sole purview of the playwright, now musicians, composers, dancers, theater managers, and actors all contributed the variety and novelty that the public craved. In his preface to *The Womens Conquest* (1671), Edward Howard describes this melange: "why else are we diverted by Scenes, Machin[e]s, Habits, Jiggs, and Dances; but to give more variety of entertainment to the Spectators?" Shadwell similarly notes the collaborative nature of the Restoration theater: "an ill Play stuff'd full of Songs and Dances" where "the Composer and the Dancing-Master are the best Poets, and yet the unmerciful Scribler would rob them of all the Honour."[7] Disputes over the authorship of Shakespearian adaptations in the later seventeenth century are a result of the complex nature of theater operations. Much scholarly energy has been devoted to discovering the particular contributions of Dryden and Davenant to *The Tempest*, and the 1674 *Tempest* and *The Fairy-Queen* still entice vigorous authorship debate. Yet this avenue can be misleading. As we shall see, these plays were not created solely by individual playwrights, but were a product of many laborers in the theatrical environment all attuned to satisfying paying customers. To focus on determining the name of an "author" is to unjustly privilege the dramatic text over the components preferred by Restoration audiences: the music, scenery, and dances. In a later discussion of the components that make up these "publick Spectacles," George Granville recounts that in addition to the poet, "the Architect, the Painter, the Composer, the Actor, the Singer, the Dancer, &c. have each of them their several Employments in the Preparation, and in the Execution."[8] The more successful Shakespearian comedies in the late seventeenth century were those that could successfully encompass music, spectacle, and drama; each aspect was vital to secure a place in the repertoire.

Financial imperatives still guided entertainment offerings, and pleasing audiences was the priority of theaters, entertainers, and musicians who "soon adapted to new capitalistic marketing principles that rendered establishment of good public relations a pre-condition for success."[9] Dryden lamented the need for fiscal support and its corresponding influence on the type of offerings in a prologue (later printed in the January 1707 *Muses Mercury*):

> Money, the sweet Allurer of our Hopes,
> Ebbs out by Oceans, but comes in by Drops.
> We raise new Objects to provoke Delight,
> But you grow sated at the second sight.

Dryden captures the predicament of entertainers who had to raise "new Objects" for evaluation, but were constrained by financial concerns. The reshaping of Shakespeare's comic material, particularly those plays that could accommodate such additions, took place in direct response to the preferences of paying audiences.

Thus, it was crucial to determine what the public favored, and to advertise and proffer those aspects for consumption. This was not always an easy task, as Cibber attests, "Taste and Fashion with us have always had Wings, and fly from one publick Spectacle to another so wantonly" (*Apology*, 1:95). To facilitate a fresh approach, productions were often adjusted after the discerning reaction of the audience. A description by Thomas Durfey illustrates this process: "tho' my Play might be too long, which is a general fault amongst us, and not to be remedy'd 'till the first day is over, and tho' some Scenes might seem Tedious 'till it was shorten'd, which is allways the Second Days work, yet I had the Confidence to think, that the Variety of a pretty Tale, a good Plot, not very ungratefull Characters, and I am sure very good Musick, both Vocal and Instrumental, with Vaulting, Dancing, and all that I cou'd think of to please, might have oblig'd 'em to a Civil Sufferance, tho' not a liking" (Dedication to *The Banditti*, 1686). Durfey's phrase "all that I cou'd think of" hints at the desperation and anxiety that playwrights must have felt in trying to incorporate ample components of music, dance, and other features. Pieces were often reworked to keep up with the latest fads, and this pattern held true for adaptations of Shakespeare as well. Inclusion of these elements was the primary goal. If we look back to Davenant's *The Law Against Lovers*, which included a variety of strategies—a popular actress, music, dance, and novelty—the plays in this chapter demonstrate a clearer formula for reworking this material around particular additions, several of which Davenant had discovered earlier.

As we saw in the previous chapter, audiences demonstrated a fairly consistent preference for novelty: a play by the latest fashionable author, music by a favorite composer or musician, or a style recently popular from the Continent. One of the earliest dramatic advertisements takes advantage of this taste for new and unique entertainments: "Great preparations are making for a new OPERA, in the play-house in Dorset Garden, of which there is great expectation, the scenes being several new sets, and of a model different from all that have been used in any theatre whatever, being twice as high as any of their former scenes; and the whole decorations of the stage not only infinitely beyond all the Operas ever yet performed in England, but also by the acknowledgement of several gentlemen that have travell'd abroad, much exceeding all that has been seen on any of the Foreign stages" (*The Post-Boy*, 12–15 June 1697). This appetite for novel enticements could be satiated with such extravagant features listed above. "New Plays is still the Cry of the whole Town," proclaimed one 1690 prologue, but "novelty" did not only mean new plays, it also included visual and aural updates to old plays, as Pope mockingly described, "A past, vamp'd, future, old, reviv'd, new piece."[10] Theaters did not necessarily have to provide new dramatic texts as long as they supplied fashionable accoutrements of music, spectacle, and dance to surprise their audiences with fresh productions. The first player in Buckingham's *The Rehearsal* (1671) discovers such a scheme: "The grand design upon the Stage is to keep the Auditors in suspence ... now, here, every line surprises you, and brings in new matter. And, then, for Scenes, Cloaths and Dancing, we put 'em quite down, all that ever went before us: and these are the things, you know, that are essential to a Play." These "essentials" vied with the dramatic text for performance space, and effectively eliminated revivals of comedies that were unable to encompass these features.

The pursuit of novelty and variety led the theaters in new and at times risky directions in order to accommodate fashions; Shadwell describes the scenario in the prologue to *The Squire of Alsatia* (1688), "Then came Machines, brought from a Neighbour Nation, / Oh how we suffer'd under Decoration." By the 1690s, according to Cibber, "Plays of course were neglected, Actors held cheap, and slightly dress'd, while Singers and Dancers were better paid, and embroider'd" (*Apology*, 1:187). The revisions of Shakespeare's comedies in the later seventeenth century grew out of this competitive marketplace where the dramatic text was only one component in a package of entertainments, and the history of Shakespearian adaptation is intimately tied to those plays that could easily accommodate currently popular additions of music and spectacle.

The Tempest (1667)

Given this artistic climate, it is then no surprise that *The Tempest* was the most popular comic text for revival in the late seventeenth century, with its opening shipwreck scene, fantastical characters, and exotic locales, all easily embellished with spectacle and music. John Dryden and Sir William Davenant adapted this material in 1667; the operatic *Tempest* of 1674 solidified the popularity of the play and it remained in the theatrical repertoire until 1769, providing a model for subsequent adaptations of Shakespeare's comic material in its extensive use of music and spectacle. Thomas Duffett cashed in on the success of *The Tempest* with his satirical *The Mock-Tempest* (1674).

Dryden and Davenant were the first to recognize the potential of Shakespeare's play to accommodate these necessary additions, and evidence suggests that the Dryden-Davenant play was a success. It was one of Pepys's favorite plays, which he saw at least eight times. Pepys was not alone in his enchantment with this production; several command performances at the Duke of York's house and at Court (7, 14, 26 November 1667 and 14 March and 13 April 1668) also demonstrate its success. Following its premiere on 6 November 1667 at Lincoln's Inn Fields, the play was so popular that many cast members were long remembered for their roles. The Dryden-Davenant *Tempest* continued to provide stiff competition for new plays like Aphra Behn's *The Forc'd Marriage* (1670), described by Downes as "a good Play and lasted six

Days; but this made its Exit too, to give Room for a greater, *The Tempest*" (*Roscius*, 72). Why was the Dryden-Davenant *Tempest* a "greater" play, and what role did Shakespeare have in its success?

Several scholars have suggested that the popularity of the Dryden-Davenant *Tempest* may derive from political parallels encoded in the action of the play. Eckhard Auberlen sees the work as a "celebration of the restored monarchy." George R. Guffey connects the storm in the opening of the play with London weather in 1667, and ascribes the shift in names of characters to reflect current relations between France, Spain, and England.[11] Nancy Klein Maguire attributes its prosperity to political parallels: "Using a moving target defence, the adaptors camouflaged their meaning by constantly substituting the identifying parallels; in other words, they kept changing the parallels, and later parallels implicitly deny earlier ones. Prospero, for example, clearly paralleling Charles II, also parallels Clarendon, and the audience could read Hippolito as Charles II, the Duke of York, the Duke of Monmouth, or even Charles I." The possibilities for political readings with this loose formula are infinite and their indeterminacy would not have been either effective or influential in drawing crowds for several seasons.[12]

As a government employee, Pepys would be an ideal audience member to draw political connections between contemporaries and characters in a play, but he never records any for *The Tempest*, and his responses to the play focus primarily on its variety and musical elements.[13] Adjusting the plot to accord with contemporary political issues and events was often part of the initial process of making some plays suitable for staging, but the enduring success of *The Tempest*, particularly the later 1674 operatic version, must have appealed to aspects of taste that persisted into the eighteenth century, not to subtle political parallels from the 1670s.

As we saw with Davenant's *The Law Against Lovers*, there is little evidence here to suggest that audiences compared the Dryden-Davenant play to Shakespeare's original.[14] The Dryden-Davenant *Tempest* was not published until 1670, over two years after the premiere, and audiences could not have immediately compared the two versions in print even if they had wanted to.[15] Pepys saw this play more times than any other by Shakespeare, but never made a comparison between the printed *Tempest* and the stage version. Dryden admits at the beginning of his preface that *The Tempest* "was originally *Shakespear*'s," but there was no movement or desire to perform Shakespeare's version of *The Tempest*. Instead of advertising the play as Shakespeare's "original," the title page to the 1670 edition lists no author's name and promotes *The Tempest, or the Enchanted Island* as "a Comedy. As it is now Acted at his Highness the Duke of *York*'s Theatre." Clearly, the printed text capitalized on the novelty of a play that was currently acted on stage, and chose not to highlight its Shakespearian origin as an advertising strategy. To categorize the Dryden-Davenant *The Tempest* as a version closely compared with and consciously preferred to Shakespeare's original would misrepresent how audiences of the late 1660s would have viewed the play. To what, then, can we ascribe the longevity of this play and its lasting influence on eighteenth-century theater?

The features of the Dryden-Davenant *Tempest* match the embellishments and attractions of spectacle, music, and dance that were popular in late seventeenth-century theater, and this formula ensured the play's place on the early eighteenth-century stage. The original text already included much of the stage business that Restoration spectators enjoyed: dances, songs, scenes of discovery, flying, disappearance, and sound effects, with an elaborate banquet scene and masque.[16] Dryden and Davenant employed Shakespeare's framework to support additions and alterations that would expand these elements.

The changes made to Shakespeare's text have been discussed elsewhere; a brief summary of these alterations includes few surprises and many predictable additions of the elements currently popular in theaters. To Shakespeare's eight songs, Dryden and Davenant added three more songs, including "Go thy way," a duet between Ferdinand and Ariel that pleased Pepys, accompanied with dancing by Caliban and the sailors. The second act was supplemented with a masque that resembles Shakespeare's fourth act masque of Juno, Iris, and Ceres. In the third act, "eight fat spirits, with *Cornu-Copia* in their hands" perform a dance, described by Gonzalo as "a Masque of fatten'd Devils, the Borgo-Masters of the lower Region," later burlesqued in *The Rehearsal* (1671).[17] Ariel is given a larger role, accompanied by a companion named Milcha, who ends the play with a dance, and whose presence increased as the play was revised in the later seventeenth century.

Moll Davis, one of Pepys's favorites who had earlier appeared as Viola in Davenant's *The Law Against Lovers*, played Ariel.[18] Pepys again enjoyed Davis's Ariel, and complained when Mrs. Gosnell took over the part: "it is but ill done, by Gosnell in lieu of Mall Davis" (9:422). Dryden and Davenant provide a breeches role with their addition of a new character Hippolito, Prospero's naïve young ward who has never seen a woman, played by Jane Long.[19] Dorinda, who has never seen a man, becomes a younger sister to Miranda, and both Hippolito and Dorinda remained part of the play until Macready's production in 1838. Caliban has a sister named Sycorax (christened "Queen Slobber-Chops" by Trincalo), the object of competition between Trincalo and Stephano. In this version, Prospero resembles "most of the exasperated fathers of Restoration comedy," in his inability to control his daughter and his ward.[20]

The music was a particular fascination, so much so that Pepys wanted to own his own copy. On 7 May 1668 he endeavored to obtain the words and music for the Echo song, "But I did here get [Banister] to prick me down the notes of the Echo in *The Tempest*, which pleases me mightily" (9:189).[21] The popular actor Henry Harris who played Ferdinand supplied Pepys with music to the play: "I to the Duke of York's playhouse and there saw *The Tempest*; and between two acts, I went out to Mr Harris and got him to repeat to me the words of the Echo, while I writ them down, having tried in the play to have wrote them; but when I had done it, having done it without looking upon my paper, I find I could not read the blacklead—but now I have got the words clear; and in going in thither, had the pleasure to see the Actors in their several dresses, especially the seamen and monster, which were very droll. So into the play again" (9:195).[22] Pepys's fascination with the music, song, and variety of *The Tempest* is representative of its critical reception in the late 1660s.

The Dryden-Davenant *Tempest* was one of Pepys's favorite plays, and his reactions offer clues to the play's reception in the late 1660s and to its continued success. When he first mentions *The Tempest* in his entry for 7 November 1667, he identifies it as an old play, without naming either Dryden or Davenant: "Up, and at the office hard all the morning; and at noon resolve with Sir W. Penn to go see *The Tempest*, an old play of Shakespeares, acted here the first day . . . the most innocent play that ever I saw, and a curious piece of Musique in an Echo of half-sentences, the Echo repeating the former half while the man goes on to the latter, which is mighty pretty [Ferdinand's song 'Go thy way']. The play no great wit; but yet good, above ordinary plays. Thence home with W. Penn, and there all mightily pleased with the play" (8:521–22). Pepys attests to the production's success, as he and William Penn were "forced to sit in the side Balcone over against the Musique-room at the Dukes-House" because "the house mighty full, the King and the Court there" (8:521–22).

Pepys's description of *The Tempest* as "above ordinary plays" suggests that Dryden and Davenant sought to construct an offering with features beyond the typical play; the unique music, dances and overall variety were the key to its success.[23] On 3 February 1668, Pepys writes: "after dinner to the Duke of York's House to the play, *The Tempest*, which we have often seen; but yet I was pleased again, and shall be again to see it, it is so full of variety; and perticularly, this day I took pleasure to learn the [tune of the] Seamans dance—which I have much desired to be perfect in, and have made myself so" (9:48). Other plays from the late 1660s contain similar ingredients of variety, music and dance that pleased our diarist; Middleton and Rowley's *The Spanish Gypsies* (7 March 1668) was criticized as, "A very silly play," but praised for its "great variety of dances, and those most excellently done." Pepys continued to return to the theater to see *The Tempest*, and records that even after almost six months, the play "still pleases me mightily" (9:179). Pepys's entry for 13 November 1667 emphasizes the longevity of the play's appeal: "to the Duke of York's House and there saw *The Tempest* again; which is very pleasant, and full of so good variety, that I cannot be more pleased almost in a comedy—only, the seamen's part a little too tedious" (8:527). On 12 December 1667, Pepys writes that he and numerous other theatergoers continued their patronage: "I all alone [saw the play with others and alone] to the Duke of York's House and saw *The Tempest*; which, as often as I have seen it, I do like very well; and the house very full" (8:576). Many Londoners had similar reactions, judging from Pepys's account of the full house.

In addition to extra music and dance, the low comedy in the play is expanded, perhaps to capture some of the same elements that made John Lacy's role as Sauny the Scott so successful a few seasons earlier. Dryden expressed his "disgust of low comedy" in the preface to *An Evening's Love* (1671) but also admitted in "A Defence of an Essay of Dramatique Poesie" (1668), " I confess my chief endeavours are to delight the Age in which I live. If the humour of this, be for low Comedy, small Accidents, and Raillery, I will force my Genius to obey it."[24] In *The Tempest*, Dryden acceded to this "delight." Trincalo, Caliban, and Stephano are here joined by two additional characters, Mustacho and Ventoso for a larger comic ensemble. These roles even became identified with the original actors. Edward Angell was eulogized in his role as Stephano: "Who shall play *Stephano* now? your Tempest's gone, / To raise new Storms i' th' hearts of every one."[25] Cave Underhill acquired the nickname "Prince Trincalo," and later chose *The Tempest* as his benefit in 1702.

We have seen that Restoration spectators did not compare the Dryden-Davenant play to Shakespeare's original, but they did compare it to offerings at the other theater. The two adapters situate their play not as a new adaptation of Shakespeare, but as part of a longer successful dramatic tradition by choosing a plot type popular with audiences, even creating a rivalry between "tempest" plays. The 1667 version of *The Tempest* is often considered the first adaptation of this material, but reworkings of Shakespeare's play actually began with earlier seventeenth-century playwrights; Dryden and Davenant were tapping into material with a history of pleasing audiences. In his 1670 preface, Dryden places his version of *The Tempest* within a context of dramatic raw material that had already been reshaped by contemporaries of Shakespeare. Dryden is concerned to compare Shakespeare's play with the Fletcher-Massinger *The Sea-Voyage*, which "was originally *Shakespear's*: . . . The Play itself had formerly been acted with success in the *Black-Fryers*: and our excellent Fletcher had so great a value for it, that he thought fit to make use of the same Design, not much varied, a second time. Those who have seen his *Sea-Voyage*, may easily discern that it was a Copy of *Shakespear's Tempest*: the Storm, the desart Island, and the Woman who had never seen a Man, are all sufficient testimonies of it." Dryden was right to point out the similarities that audiences may have noted as well. *The Sea-Voyage* (now attributed to Massinger and Fletcher) opens with a ship amid a violent storm at sea, with graphic recreation of the storm and island setting. In both plays, characters on an island observe storms; in Shakespeare's play Prospero directs the storm, and in the Fletcher-Massinger text, Sebastian and Nicusa observe the shipwreck. Like Shakespeare's Miranda, Clarinda has never seen a man. Dryden was clearly aware of this dramatic history and situated his 1667 play in a lineage of *The Tempest* reworkings, appealing to an audience familiar with Fletcher and Massinger.

Just before the Dryden-Davenant version premiered in November, *The Sea-Voyage* was revived by the King's Company on 25 September 1667 as *The Storm*.[26] Pepys describes it as a "new play," but also "a play of Fletcher's." Like *The Tempest*, new did not necessarily mean an original plot. Apparently the play initially attracted a crowd; Pepys describes the theater as "infinitely full, the King and all the Court almost there." He returned to see the play the next day, again admiring "the principal thing extraordinary being the dance, which is very good" (8:450–51).[27] Two songs from the play were reprinted in a later 1673 collection, and *The Sea-Voyage* demonstrates the same dramatic patterns of revision that made the Dryden-Davenant adaptation a success: added song and dance, structured around an exciting shipwreck setting.[28] Pepys writes that the play itself "is but so so methinks; only, there is a most admirable dance at the end, of the ladies in a Military manner, which endeed did please me mightily." As George R. Guffey has pointed out, the production of these plays may also have been prompted by the series of storms that occurred in September of 1667.[29]

Theatrical rivalry further escalated the popularity of the Dryden-Davenant play. In March of 1668, both *The Tempest* (at Lincoln's Inn Fields) and *The Sea-Voyage* (at Bridges) were performed within a few weeks of each other, and additional performances may have occurred for which records do not survive.[30] In May of the same year, both plays were again performed, and Pepys attended both. Competition was clearly a part of this theatrical environment, and audiences were encouraged to compare the offerings at Lincoln's Inn Fields with those of the other theater. In their prologue, Dryden and Davenant call attention to this rivalry: "The Storm which vanish'd on the Neighb'ring shore, / Was taught by *Shakespear*'s Tempest first to roar." Even though both offerings were based on pre-Restoration plays, Dryden and Davenant could claim "novelty" because of their additions, and their prologue boasts "from old *Shakespear*'s honour'd dust, this day / Springs up and buds a new reviving Play." The strategy of comparison encouraged by the pair of adapters worked as a way to distinguish their offering from its competitors. When Pepys attended a performance of *The Storm*, he compared the play unfavorably with *The Tempest*. He writes that he and Mrs. Pepys went "to see *The Storme*; which we did, but without much pleasure, it being but a mean play compared with *The Tempest* at the Duke of York's, though Knipp did act her part of grief very well" (9:133). This competition is further evidence of the influence of contemporary theatrical context on the ways Shakespeare's comedies were adapted. *The Tempest* was part of this rivalry with the King's theater, and was promoted as such.

Dryden and Davenant adapted the play with an eye to what had been done with this material and how to make it "new" for their audience. Dryden's comments in his preface reveal his concern for the theatrical refashioning of source plays. According to Dryden, Davenant also reworked this material in light of what had already been done and what could be adjusted according to current tastes.

The Fletcher-Massinger play was only part of the dramatic context surrounding this adaptation. Adding to *The Tempest* and *The Sea-Voyage*, Suckling's *The Goblins* was performed in the same season (on 21 November 1667) at Bridge's theater in the presence of the King.[31] Dryden specifically comments in his preface that "*Fletcher* was not the only Poet who made use of *Shakespear*'s Plot: Sir *John Suckling*, a profess'd admirer of our Author, has follow'd his footsteps in his *Goblins*; his *Regmella* being an open imitation of *Shakespear*'s *Miranda*; and his Spirits, though counterfeit, yet are copied from *Ariel*." According to Dryden, Davenant's adaptation techniques involved an awareness of this dramatic heritage: "he was a man of quick and piercing imagination, soon found that somewhat might be added to the Design of *Shakespear*, of which neither *Fletcher* nor *Suckling* had ever thought: and therefore to put the last hand to it, he design'd the Counterpart to *Shakespear*'s Plot, namely that of a Man who had never seen a Woman; that by this means those two Characters of Innocence and Love might the more illustrate and commend each other." Further continuing this layered tradition of tempest plays is a 1685 adaptation of *The Sea-Voyage*, entitled *A Common-*

wealth of Women by Thomas Durfey, which purports in its prologue to have "improv'd what *Fletcher* Writ."[32]

Like the later versions of *The Cobler of Preston* (discussed in chapter 4) that participate in a larger tradition of shrew-taming literature, the Dryden-Davenant *Tempest* builds on the plot and characters from an earlier dramatic work, and was only one in a lengthy history of texts fashioned from this material by subsequent theatrical craftsmen. This follows a general pattern we have seen of reworking Shakespeare's comic material according to the local theatrical conditions—other popular plays or plots, theater personnel, and other immediate concerns of the entertainment climate. *Bottom the Weaver* was adapted for theatrical facilities (or lack of) and the type of performers available (strollers and other itinerants), *The Law Against Lovers* was reshaped as a "new play," and *Sauny the Scott* accommodated the talents of its author and performer. Improving a Shakespeare play was still not the concern even for Dryden and Davenant—providing a hit play was the goal.

Dryden and Davenant struck the right balance of variety and contemporary music to please returning audience members such as Pepys, and the durability of Shakespeare's *The Tempest* in all its forms in the Restoration and early eighteenth-century theater was due in part to its suitability for added music and spectacle. Political parallels may have been temporarily relevant, but it was the extratextual features that ensured the longevity of the play. Throughout the Restoration and early eighteenth century, the text of *The Tempest* and the songs from the play were reprinted numerous times.[33] Following Dryden and Davenant's lead, later versions of the play reacted to developments in the London entertainment scene, notably in music and spectacle. We can see the roots of this taste in the Dryden-Davenant play, which helped foster an increasing infatuation with music, dance, and spectacle.

The Operatic Tempest (1674)

Even though the Dryden-Davenant *Tempest* had no problem drawing audiences in the late 1660s, Shakespeare's comic material was soon reshaped to accommodate new possibilities for staging spectacle. Revisions in the 1674 *Tempest* were directly connected to changes in the theatrical climate: new machines and facilities, new possibilities for spectacle, new music, and the need to compete with foreign performers. As we shall see, all of these concerns outweighed any anxiety about changing material that derived from Shakespeare. A new theatrical facility was the impetus to revise *The Tempest*, not a concern related to its original author.

Between 1667 and 1674, many specific changes took place in the London theatrical environment that intensified the need for theater companies to augment the visual and aural components of their offerings. An increased influx of operatic forms of entertainment, concerts, and the new Dorset Garden Theatre built in 1671 transformed the artistic climate. Dorset Garden facilitated a new level of visual components than had previously been possible, creating what Judith Milhous has termed "Dorset Garden spectaculars." Spearheaded by Betterton, these productions involved large casts, significant music, and extensive special effects, costing upward of £3000 to £4000.[34] Because of their impressive stage features, these spectacle-filled English operas such as *The Empress of Morocco* (1673), *The Tempest* (1674), and *Psyche* (1675) were frequently offered as showpiece entertainments for visitors to London, signaling their importance and unprecedented splendor.[35] Downes's comments on *Psyche* are illustrative: "The long expected Opera of *Psyche*, came forth in all her Ornaments; new Scenes, new Machines, new Cloaths, new *French* Dances: This Opera was Splendidly set out, especially in Scenes; the Charge of which amounted to above 800£. It had a Continuance of Performance about 8 Days together, it prov'd very Beneficial to the Company; yet the Tempest got them more Money" (*Roscius*, 75). As we shall see, *The Tempest* "got them more money" and remained in the repertory through the early eighteenth century because it struck the right balance between offering spectacle and controlling costs.

A prologue designed for the 1674 *Tempest* focuses on the attractions of the Dorset Garden spectaculars:

> Then let us laugh; for now no cost wee'l spare,
> And never think we're poor while we your favours share,
> Without the good old Playes we did advance,
> And all ye stages ornament enhance.

This prologue emphasizes the key elements of this offering: financial expenditures to make the audience feel they are being indulged, plus expected injections of music, dancing, and other ornaments. Shakespeare's name is not part of the promotion for this text and was relatively unimportant in selling this comedy. "Good old Playes" have been made new and embellished: "Had we not, for your pleasure found new wayes, / You still had rusty Arras had, & thredbare playes."[36] The "pleasure" and "favour" of the audience are the goals, and if simply reviving an old play of Shakespeare's would have done the trick, no doubt considerable expense would have been spared. Promoting the play as a comedy by Shakespeare would have been a cheaper alternative, but this obviously would not have worked. The epilogue to *The Tempest* underscores the fact that singing, dancing, and ornamentation were the hallmarks of this type of production:

> When you of witt and sence were weary growne,
> Romantick, riming, fustian Playes were showne,
> We then to flying Witches did advance,
> And for your pleasures traffic'd into ffrance.
> From thence new arts to please you, we have sought
> We have machines to some perfection brought,
> And above 30 Warbling voyces gott.
> Many a God and Goddesse you will heare,
> And we have Singing, Dancing, Devils here
> Such Devils, and such gods, are very Deare.
> We, in all ornaments, are lavish growne,
> And like Improvident Damsells of ye Towne,
> For present bravery, all your wealth lay downe.

Quite a bit of "wealth" was required to finance all of these "ornaments" such as the "flying Witches" that adorned the 1672 operatic *Macbeth*. Catering to audience desire was the aim: "To please you, we no Art, or cost will spare," the epilogue concludes. Dorset Garden was willing to go to great lengths for its spectacular performances, encompassing French fads, machines, song, dance, and an array of otherworldly manifestations previously unavailable, and all unrelated to authorship of the source text.

From its first performance in the spring of 1674, *The Tempest* had a solid record of attracting audiences.[37] *The London Stage* records suggest that *The Tempest* was performed regularly from April until mid-May of that season, remained in the theatrical repertoire until Garrick's version of the play in 1756, and was reprinted in 1676 (twice), 1690, 1692, 1695, and 1701.[38] A further measure of success is the number of subsequent productions modeled after *The Tempest*, including *Circe* (1677), *The Lancashire Witches* (1681), *Albion and Albanius* (1685), *Psyche* (1675), and *King Arthur* (1691). Music, dance, and scenic effects were the necessary components according to the formula set up by *The Tempest*'s success.

Music had always been a viable element in Restoration theater, but no performance before the 1674 *Tempest* contained such elaborate visual and aural aspects, driven by new possibilities for spectacle, song, and dance. Roger North noted that public theaters "observed this promiscuous tendency to musick, and . . . [had] taken it into their scenes and profited by it."[39] This second adaptation of *The Tempest* included just such a "promiscuous tendency to music," and exemplified the ability of the stage to profit from musical additions. From the opening stage direction, the play immediately departs from Dryden and Davenant's earlier version: "The Front of the Stage is open'd, and the Band of 24 Violins, with the Harpsicals and Theorbo's which accompany the Voices, are plac'd between the Pit and the Stage."[40] Audiences would have recognized that an extensive musical production was about to occur, one unlike typical plays and strikingly different from its predecessor. It is worth pausing over the attractions of this offering and their significance in the history of adapting Shakespeare.

The 1674 version of *The Tempest* involved many popular figures in music, including singers from the choir of the Chapel Royal, and instrumental music composed by Matthew Locke (Composer in Ordinary to the King), Pelham Humfrey (Master of the Children of the Chapel Royal), John Banister, Giovanni Baptista Draghi (Queen Catherine's organist), James Hart and Pietro Reggio. As the opening stage direction indicates, the orchestra was placed between the pit and the stage, perhaps in imitation of French production practices, with twelve extra violins from the King's Music.[41] Not just any violin players would do, and the instrumentalists were placed front and center, instead of in the usual gallery space above the stage. The King was willing to spare his singers in service of such a production, and an unusual order from Charles II survives that commands Turner, Hart, "or any other Men or Boyes belonging to His Ma[jes]ties Chappell Royall that sing in [the] Tempest at His Royall Highnesse Theatre" to remain in London during the week to perform in the production, and to "performe [the] like Service in [the] Opera in [the] said Theatre or any other thing in [the] like Nature where their helpe may be desired."[42] We can already see that this was no ordinary play; it was a landmark performance unprecedented in English theatre. Advertising the "Shakespearian" origin of the plot was far from a priority in drawing audiences, and much energy instead went into the musical features of this production.

The significance of the songs and masque is reinforced by their publication, the first such libretto designed for use in the theater to capture the memorable musical and scenic elements and allow viewers to relive the performance experience at their leisure.[43] Pepys wanted the words and music to the earlier *Tempest*, and publication of the songs for this later version may have built on an already existent demand for these materials. Roger North expressed his delight that he can now purchase the music and masque from *Psyche* to take home, according it a prized place in his collection: "The masque is also in print, and begins 'Great Psyche,' &c., and the book containing the whole musick of that enterteinement is not unworthy of a place in a *vertuoso's* cabanet."[44] North's enthusiastic view of the music from *Psyche* suggests that *The Tempest* was valued for similar reasons; no one was interested in buying a copy of Shakespeare's play.

With the exception of Draghi's incidental music and dances, the rest of the music from *The Tempest* survived and was frequently reprinted to capitalize on the success of the production. As the play continued to be a regular feature of the repertory, updated music kept the production current.[45] In 1695, for example, the popular composer Henry Purcell may have provided a song "Dear pretty Youth" for a revival which Dorinda (Purcell's favored soprano Letitia Cross) sang over Hippolito's "dead" body.[46] Later, the *Daily Courant* of 13 February 1707 would advertise a return to the original production with "all the Original Flyings and Musick." In addition to the music, the dances were adjusted regularly to accommodate available dancers and fashions.[47] Shakespeare's play remained the foundation, but only served as a delivery system for music and dance.

Complementing the aural aspects, the visual extravaganzas of the production were equally impressive. Unlike the earlier 1667 play, the 1674 text contains elaborate visual and aural details of its scenic extravagance. A brief glance at the first few scenes will provide a sense of the differences from the earlier *Tempest* and the captivating effect these aspects must have had on audiences. As listeners enjoy the opening music, the new frontispiece is revealed: "This Frontispiece is a noble Arch, supported by large wreathed Columns of the *Corinthian* Order; the wreathings of the Columns are beautifi'd with Roses wound round them, and several *Cupids* flying about them. On the Cornice, just over the Capitals, sits on either side a Figure, with a Trumpet in one hand, and a Palm in the other, representing Fame. A little farther on the same Cornice, on each side of a Compass-pediment, lie a Lion and a Unicorn, the Supporters of the Royal Arms of *England*." A perspective scene continues with the requisite tempest: "a thick Cloudy Sky, a very Rocky Coast, and a Tempestuous Sea in perpetual Agitation. This Tempest (suppos'd to be rais'd by Magick) has many dreadful Objects in it, as several Spirits in horrid shapes flying down amongst the Sailers, then rising and crossing in the Air. And when the Ship is sinking, the whole House is darken'd, and a shower of Fire falls upon 'em. This is accompanied with Lightning, and several Claps of Thunder, to the end of the Storm" (1). With the latest technology available at Dorset Garden, this initial montage was an impressive opening of music, movement, and stage magic, quite unlike the 1667 play.

The transition from the shipwreck scene to the second scene between Prospero and Miranda involved an elaborate scene change to a triple perspective: "In the midst of the Shower of Fire the Scene Changes. The Cloudy Sky, Rockes, and Sea vanish; and when the Lights return, discover that Beautiful part of the Island, which was the habitation of *Prospero*; 'Tis compos'd of three Walks of Cypress-trees, each Side-walk leads to a Cave, in one of which *Prospero* keeps his Daughters, in the other *Hippolito*: The Middle-Walk is of a great depth, and leads to an open part of the Island" (5). This "Shower of Fire" was one of the most memorable aspects of the production, as contemporary Ned Ward writes, "This sudden clutter at our Appearance, so surpriz'd me, that I look'd as silly as a *Bumpkin* translated from the *Plough-Tail* to the *Play-House*, when it Rains Fire in the *Tempest*."[48] In just the first two scenes of the production, spectators would have been awed by two impressive visual extravaganzas.

Additional scenes and machines construct a distinct feast for the senses throughout the play, around the framework of Dryden-Davenant dialogue. Select other additions include singing and dancing devils in the second act who join Pride, Fraud, Rapine, and Murder; these devils were placed under the stage, augmenting the melange of musical offerings from unexpected places to surprise the audience with novel components.[49] Ariel's mate Milcha has a larger singing role here, notably in a duet with Ariel ("Dry those eyes") and serves as Ariel's partner for the flying machinery.[50] The elaborate masque of Neptune and Amphitrite in the final act provides a strikingly different conclusion from the Dryden-Davenant version. Visitors to the English stage took special notice of the scenic extravagance in this production: Baron von Schwerin "attended an English play, [*The Tempest*], or the Enchanted Island, which because of the changing of the scenes was well worth seeing."[51]

The collaborative nature of the Restoration theater, with its mixture of drama, music, dance, spectacle, and theater management continues to stimulate scholarly debate about authorship of the 1674 *Tempest*. Although most agree (based on Downes's attribution) that Shadwell is probably the author, the inability of scholars to come to a consensus about attribution is complicated by the many levels of input that produced a Restoration operatic entertainment, and the difficulty of ascribing these aspects to a single individual.[52] The 1674 *Tempest* is more the product of the theatrical environment than the efforts of any one person: actors, musicians, and stage machinery all contributed to the "new wayes" to update a "threadbare play" with masques, songs, flyings, and dancing. Shakespeare's play lay buried well beneath these layers of immediate appeal.

We have seen how the 1674 *Tempest* served as an opportunity to add music and spectacle, and how these attractions were favored by spectators who enjoyed the unexpected and impressive scenic elements. The increasing presence of foreign performers in the seventeenth century provided an additional impetus to craft a successful play, as well as further pressure on native offerings, and *The Tempest* premiered at a time when foreign performers dominated the entertainment scene. The Dorset Garden spectaculars like the updated *Tempest* were part of a larger effort of English drama to compete with foreign performers, a visible presence in London throughout the seventeenth century. The absence of any evidence that Shakespeare served to promote a sense of British drama in these plays indicates that Shakespeare's reputation was not prominent enough to use as a promotional strategy in the 1670s.

According to one estimate, over fourteen French troupes visited England from 1661–88. Encouraged by Charles II, who "had a fancy for a comparison to hear the singers of the severall nations, German, Spanish, Italian, French, and English, performe upon the stage in Whitehall," these imported entertainers challenged theater companies for audiences; as Davenant's Tirewoman remarks, "I like not that these *French* pardonne moys / should make bold with old *England*."[53] During the 1660s and 1670s, French and Italian entertainers played regularly in London, often at the bequest of Charles II. In February 1667 the king placed an order to alter the stage in the theater in Whitehall for French comedians. Later in December of 1667, Henry Savile wrote to the Earl of Rochester concerning the popularity of this group: "I had allmost forgott for another argument to bring you to towne that a French troop of comaedians bound for Nimeguen were by adverse winds cast into this hospitable port and doe act at Whitehall soe very well that it is a thousand pittyes they should not stay, especially a young wench of fifteen, who has more beauty and sweetnesse than ever was seen upon the stage since a friend of ours left it."[54] Even though many of these entertainers had the support of Charles II, they encroached on the territory of native English drama, which often suffered as a result. Dryden was one of the most pointed critics of imported entertainers. In a 1672 prologue he bitterly decried that "A Brisk *French* Troop is grown your dear delight," and the following year denounced the French and Italian performers: "Yet, to our Cost in that short time, we find, / They left their Itch of Novelty behind," lamenting that they "quite Debauch'd the Stage with lewd Grimace."[55] Competition from foreign performers led theater managers to react with similar offerings, resulting in several important productions in the development of English opera. Even though the London stage did not see Italian opera until 1705, there were several French operas performed in the Restoration, and as late as 1704 *The Tempest* may have remained a serious rival for foreign music.[56]

In the season of 1672–73, before the 1674 *Tempest* premiered, the number of foreign performers grew, and this suggests that the play may have been updated as competition.[57] Tiberio Fiorilli (Scaramouche) brought his troupe to court in the spring of 1673 and was given a medal and a chain of gold by Charles II.[58] Scaramouche returned to England in 1675 with great success; Andrew Marvell detailed the positive reception this Italian entertainer received: "*Scaramuccio* acting dayly in the Hall of *Whitehall*, and all Sorts of People flocking thither, and paying their Mony as at a common Playhouse; nay even a twelve-penny Gallery is builded for the convenience of his Majesty's poorer Subjects."[59] Marvell's description of Scaramouche suggests that he diverted playhouse money and patrons. John Evelyn also noted Scaramouche's success and his recent practice of collecting money: "saw the Italian *Scaramucchio* act before the King at *White-hall*; People giving monye to come in, which was very Scandalous, & never so before at Court Diversions: having seene him act before in *Italy* many yeares past, I was not averse from seeing the most excellent of that kind of folly." (*Diary*, 4:75). Foreign entertainments were even more popular in the 1673–74 season prior to *The Tempest*'s appearance. A *Ballet et Musique* was performed this season at court, as was a French opera (probably *Ariadne*) with French dancers and singers. John Evelyn writes that he saw "an *Italian Opera* in musique, the first that had ben in *England* of this kind." Evelyn probably saw a French opera, although he did not realize it, perhaps part of Charles II's efforts for his Royal Academy of Music.[60]

In response, native British entertainers increased their efforts to draw audiences; Humfrey and Betterton had been sent by Charles II to France.[61] John Banister, who wrote music for *The Tempest* and had traveled to France in 1661 to examine their musical practices, battled these Italian and French attractions by offering more concerts of "New Musick" at his "Musick School." Actor Jo Haynes even traveled to France and Italy, reportedly returning to England with continental entertainments, which he put to use in 1677 as Harlequin in Ravenscroft's *Scaramouch a Philosopher, Harlequin a School-Boy, Bravo, Merchant, and Magician*.[62] Thomas Jevon also modeled himself after Italian comedians, in his performance as Harlequin in Mountfort's *Life and Death of Dr. Faustus, with the Humours of Harlequin and Scaramouche* at Dorset Garden in 1686.

In the theaters, numerous comments reflect the turmoil for native playwrights, aptly described by Dryden: "You throw down Plays, / Whilst Scenes, Machines, and empty *Opera's* reign" while "Troops of famisht *Frenchmen* hither drive."[63] Native playwrights did not seem to know how to compete with such offerings. The revamped 1674 *Tempest* was part of the effort to attract customers with surprising novelties and unique features, tailored with these imported fashions in mind.

Further evidence suggests that *The Tempest* was reshaped to compete in this climate. The epilogue from the Egerton MS 2623 promotes *The Tempest* as a production that "for your pleasure traffic'd into ffrance," and Colin Visser notes that the Dorset Garden Theatre was designed with technical resources to imitate French operatic production.[64] In fact, when Locke published his music from *The Tempest* and from *Psyche* in 1675, he labeled it *The English Opera*, stressing the native content of his work. Not everyone had as much faith in the English genius; Locke remarked that "though *Italy* was, and is the great Academy of the World for that Science and way of Entertainment, *England* is not" (preface). Competition between native and foreign entertainments continued through the 1670s. A French character (Monsieur) in the epilogue to Thomas Porter's play *The French Conjurer* from 1677 captures the enduring attraction of these imported acts:

> All my French blood be in a rage.
> Damn d'English Acteur, English Teatre,
> Dere's no such ting as Wit nor Acting dere.
> De Wit, de Sense, de Fame, and de Renown
> Be in de French troop at toder end o' Town.

One commentator criticized a "lamentable ill-acted French Play, when our English actors so much surpass," but could not resist remarking that "the dances and voices were pretty well performed."[65]

The strategy in 1674 was not to promote Shakespeare as a native dramatist, although that would have been a cheap solution, had it been effective. This is a key moment in the development of Shakespeare as the "National Poet." In the 1670s his comic material was more important as a vehicle to support added entertainments, ready-made plots that left theater personnel free to focus on spectacular additions. Shakespeare's name held little clout in the world of competitive entertainments when audiences were drawn to the latest novelty with music and dance regardless of its origin. The monetary investments in these spectacles show the priorities of theater managers—they were only willing to splurge on production elements that were likely to draw audiences. Due to the realities of theatrical competition, an unadorned comedy by Shakespeare was not an adequate draw on its own.

Theaters clearly had to invest money in their productions to compete with foreign attractions, but these funds supported extra-dramatic additions, not the play text itself. These financial expenditures were not wholeheartedly embraced, especially by playwrights concerned primarily with drama. As early as 1664, Richard Flecknoe complained that theaters "for cost and ornament are arriv'd to the heighth of Magnificence; but that which makes our Stage the better makes our Playes the worse perhaps, they striving now to make them more for sight then hearing, whence that solid job of the interior is lost."[66] The preference for sight over poetry only increased. Despite the many admonishments from playwrights and critics about the decline of the English stage due to spectacle and stage business (the "sight" that Flecknoe describes), theaters had to offer performances like the 1674 *Tempest* with more emphasis on sight and sound than on dramatic text. John Crowne described the libretto to his 1674 masque *Calisto* as the "cold lean Carkass of the entertainment;" the heart of these productions resided in the visual and musical elements, not in the "cold lean Carkass" of written language and plot on paper, or the "thredbare playes" that the prologue to the 1674 *Tempest* describes.

Langbaine attests to the successful marketing strategy of this production: "How much this *Opera* takes, every Body that is acquainted with the Theatre knows; and with reason, since the greatest Masters in Vocal Musick, Dancing, and Painting, were concern'd in it" (*Account*, 449–50). Shadwell's *Psyche*, which premiered a year after *The Tempest*, continued this type of entertainment. Like the adapters of Shakespeare's comedies, Shadwell's desire was to appeal to his audience with these various accoutrements to a dramatic text. Langbaine corroborates this view: "But as our Author never valu'd himself upon this Play, so his Design at that time, was to entertain the Town with variety of Musick, curious Dancing, splended Scenes, and Machines; and not with fine Poetry, the Audience being not at leisure to mind the Writing" (*Account*, 449). The attraction of these spectaculars was not the play, the writing, or the "fine Poetry," but the visual and aural elements.[67]

Theaters had to weigh spectacle with cost, and were not always able to find a combination with enough novelty to attract audiences and still turn a profit. *The Tempest* apparently was able to balance production cost against profit, but *Psyche* was not. As one writer noted, "I have often heard the Players cursing at their oversight in laying out so much on so disliked a Play . . . considering how much more they might have expected, had such an Entertainment had that sence in it, that it deserved: and that for the future they expect *The Tempest*, which cost not one Third of *Psyche*, will be in request when the other is forgotten."[68] Downes relates the same estimation that *Psyche* "prov'd very Beneficial to the Company; yet *The Tempest* got them more Money" (*Roscius*, 75). The 1674 *Tempest* seemed to have the perfect mix of spectacle, dance and music to please audiences, yet it could be performed without losing money. Irrespective of literary content, it could please an audience and still keep the company out of the red.

An unusual event in late 1674 and early 1675 provides an additional context for *The Tempest* and suggests ancillary reasons for its hold on audiences. Throughout the late seventeenth century, audiences were fascinated with the scenic aspects of productions, and enjoyed going behind the scenes and venturing on the stage.[69] As late as the 1690s, the prologue to *The Fairy-Queen* pleads, "Pray let our Stage from thronging Beaux be clear," and eventually Queen Anne had to issue proclamations to keep audience members from going backstage.[70] In 1674–75 select Londoners had the chance to become involved in a production first hand. A court performance of John Crowne's masque *Calisto, or the Chaste Nymph* by amateurs and professionals at the Hall Theatre gives us an idea of the popularity of the visual elements that made the 1674 *Tempest* a hit.[71] Designed primarily for Princess Mary and Princess Anne, *Calisto* "effectively dominated court life for as much as six months in 1674 and 1675" and provided an opportunity for spectators to get involved in theater mechanics, to mix with professional singers and dancers, and to work with actor Thomas Betterton.[72] The costumes ordered for this production give some sense of its extravagance. By one estimate, the 161 costumes alone totaled over £5000, and involved ostentatious and extravagant designs.[73]

As well as elaborate garb, Crowne's entertainment included dancing and singing between the five acts. This production would have attracted a great deal of attention, with its numerous rehearsals and performances, and may have been responsible for diverting attention to theatrical production and away from foreign singers. Many Londoners yearned to participate in *Calisto*, as Margaret Blagge's letter to John Evelyn attests: "The play goes on mightyly, which I hoped would never have proceeded farther . . . Would you believe itt, there are some that envy me the honour (as they esteeme it) of acting in this play, and pass malicious Jests upon me."[74] Few citizens could fail to notice this event; Eleanore Boswell maintains that *Calisto* was "probably the most elaborate production staged at Whitehall during the entire Restoration period" because of the extensive preparations involved for staging.[75]

Even though *Calisto* was performed at court, it shared elements and features with successful theatrical productions — spectacular scenery, elaborate and extensive music and dance. To a citizen in 1674, the entertainment scene, both public and private, would have had many similarities in music and scenic extravagance, and the splendors of *Calisto* are certainly reminiscent of the visual components in the 1674 *Tempest*.[76] Though expensive to produce, these performances captivated the public, creating a situation similar to high-budget Hollywood films that compete for special effects and vie for the most spectacular phenomenon. The way Shakespeare's source play was shaped is directly linked to a climate that included imported entertainers, plentiful music and dance, lavish scenes, and overall visual extravagance.

*The Tempest*s of 1667 and 1674 were two drastically different versions of Shakespeare's raw material. Neither one relied on Shakespeare's name value as a selling point, and both emphasized the additions and attractions added to the source play. Despite their radical differences, both Restoration *Tempests* are often yoked into one play, with these important changes elided and the performative aspects of the text ignored.[77] No audience member could mistake one for the other, nor could the theatrical equipment of 1667 satisfy the requirements of the 1674 semi-opera, designed specifically for Dorset Garden. The 1674 version was performed at the rival playhouse, Dorset Garden in March or April of 1674, and Drury Lane was unable to compete with the scenic capacity of this new theater. The audience of 1674 would have certainly noticed the obvious performance differences between the two *Tempests*, let alone the rearranged scenes, added songs, and new masques. Downes categorized these two plays as different productions—he describes the Dryden-Davenant version as "alter'd by Sir *William Davenant* and Mr *Dryden* before 'twas made into an Opera," taking care to note the added innovations in the later text: "*The Tempest, or the Inchanted Island*, made into an Opera by Mr *Shadwell*, having all New in it; as Scenes, Machines; particularly, one Scene Painted with *Myriads* of *Ariel* Spirits; and another flying away, with a Table Furnisht out with Fruits, Sweet meats and all sorts of Viands; just when Duke *Trinculo* and his Companions, were going to Dinner; all things perform'd in it so Admirably well, that not any succeeding Opera got more Money" (*Roscius*, 72–74). The differences between the Restoration versions of *The Tempest* are important in capturing the changes in audience taste and in tracing the responses of theaters to current predilections for entertainment. In fact, audiences would have expected such scenic extravagances from productions staged at Dorset Garden in the 1670s.[78] We cannot overestimate the importance of this theatrical facility for drawing audiences, and for creating expectations for spectacle and visual splendor made possible by its scenic capacity. The venue for these productions was just as important for attracting crowds as their content.

In addition, as Maximillian A. Novak points out, by 1674 Dryden was writing plays for the King's Company, and may not have looked kindly on the spectacle later added to *The Tempest*; in his prologue to the opening of Drury Lane, Dryden writes:

> *French* Machines have ne'r done *England* good:
> I wou'd not prophesie our Houses Fate:
> But while vain Shows and Scenes you over-rate,
> 'Tis to be fear'd———
> That as a Fire the former House o'rethrew,
> Machines and Tempests will destroy the new.[79]

A manuscript version of this prologue found in the Huntington Library clarifies Dryden's meaning in the final line. Virtually identical to the printed copy in all lines save the last, this manuscript's final line reads, "Tempests and Operas will destroy ye New," clearly a dig at the operatic *Tempest*. As Helene Maxwell Hooker has noted, a Restoration audience would have picked up the reference to *The Tempest*, which was either in performance or in rehearsal at the time.[80] Dryden keenly felt the competition engendered by the new "machines" and "shows" added to *The Tempest* at the rival theater and voiced his displeasure.

The evolution of these Restoration versions of Shakespeare's play is important for charting how and why Shakespeare's comic material was reshaped. We can see a clear reaction to increasing audience taste for music and spectacle, as well as a need for a play that could be staged at the new Dorset Garden Theatre and could take advantage of its features. Shakespeare's *The Tempest* provided just such an opportunity for added music and spectacle to a ready-made plot.

Looking back over the two revisions of *The Tempest* in the Restoration, we can draw several conclusions about the use of Shakespeare's comic material. Shakespeare held no name value for audiences in search of spectacular visual and aural elements. Aside from providing a plot suitable for these additions, the two adaptations of *The Tempest* had little to do with Shakespeare per se, and were ultimately connected to and shaped by events in the entertainment climate—foreign competition, developments in theatrical facilities, rival theater offerings, injections of music and dance. It is no accident that the 1674 *Tempest* was the most popular Shakespearian comedy in the Restoration and early eighteenth century, but this record had few connections to its Shakespearian origins or its particular treatment of Shakespeare's poetry.

Duffett's The Mock-Tempest (1674)

In response to the English operas produced at Dorset Garden, the King's Company began to offer a series of plays burlesquing these popular spectacles. Without the facilities to mount competitive spectacular entertainments, the King's Company turned to burlesque as a cheaper way to contend for audiences. Thomas Duffett was the main propagator of such satires as *The Mock-Tempest* and *Psyche Debauched*; his strategy was to provide a bawdy, decadent alternative to some of the most popular current entertainments on the London stage, using the more modest facilities of Drury Lane.

Set in contemporary low-life London, Duffett's *The Mock-Tempest* begins with a storm produced by a mob attempting to destroy a brothel populated by pimps and prostitutes rather than sailors. Here, Stephano becomes Stephania, Mustacho is Moustrappa and Trincalo becomes Drinkallup. Prospero is the warden of Bridewell Prison and Caliban is turned into the pimp Hectorio. Dorinda from the adapted *Tempest* and Miranda are lustful women: Dorinda says to Miranda, "If our fathers don't get us Husbands quickly, wee'l make him lye with us himself, shall we sister?"(13). Ariel's famous song "Where the bee sucks" is transformed into a concluding song:

> Where the good Ale is, there suck I,
> In a Cobblers Stall I lye,
> While the Watch are passing by;
> Then about the Streets I fly,
> After Cullies merrily.
> And I merrily, merrily take up my clo'se
> Under the Watch and the Constable's nose. (55)

Duffett's comic strategy of burlesque relies on an audience familiar with the operatic version of *The Tempest* but not necessarily with Shakespeare's play. Langbaine attests that "The Design of [Duffett's] Play was to draw the Town from the Duke's Theatre, who for a considerable time had frequented that admirable reviv'd Comedy call'd *The Tempest*." Although he attempted to capitalize on the recent success of the latest *Tempest*, the intense popularity of Duffett's play was short-lived: "And the *Mock-Tempest* was a while renown'd; / But this low stuff the Town at last despis'd, / And scorn'd the Folly that they once had priz'd" (*Account*, 177–78). Duffett's play was renowned for its vulgarity, and was "intermixt with so much Scurrility, that instead of Diverting, they offend the modest Mind." Apparently, when *The Mock-Tempest* was performed in Dublin, "several Ladies, and Persons of the best Quality left the House: such Ribaldry pleasing none but the Rabble" (Langbaine, *Account*, 177).[81] Duffett did not aim to burlesque Shakespeare per se (as we have seen, audiences showed little concern with authentic Shakespeare), but rather wanted to mock the conventions of taste that produced the 1674 *Tempest* and create a send-up of a currently popular play to attract spectators who had seen the operatic *Tempest* on stage and would recognize Duffett's travesty.[82] Just as the libretto was sold at performances of the operatic *Tempest*, audience members at *The Mock-Tempest* could also purchase a libretto should they want to memorialize Duffett's ribald humor.[83]

Between 1674 and the next adaptation of Shakespeare's comic material in 1692, *The Fairy-Queen*, Londoners continued to patronize the successful Dorset Garden spectaculars from the Duke's company with

Duffett's burlesques and French entertainers as competition from the King's Company. Exotic amusements still attracted audiences; *The London Gazette* advertised on 1–4 February 1674/5 "A Rare Concert of four Trumpets Marine, never heard before in England." Scaramouche returned to Whitehall, which did not bode well for the playhouses, as one writer notes, "This is not much lik'd by our other players, for it will half break both our houses."[84] Spectacle enticed audiences to productions such as Shadwell's *The Lancashire Witches* (1681), with such features as "several *Machines* of Flyings for the Witches, and other Diverting Contrivances in't" and much success: "all being well perform'd, it prov'd beyond Expectation; very Beneficial to the Poet and *Actors*" (Downes, *Roscius*, 80–81).

After many slim seasons for the King's troupe, the two theatrical companies merged to form the United Company during the 1682–83 season. The details of this period have been recounted elsewhere; a few highlights should serve to contextualize *The Fairy-Queen*.[85] The union produced stability for the theater world, but excluded competition, creating a conservative atmosphere that relied mainly on revivals of old plays. In the preface to *The Treacherous Brothers* (1690), George Powell looks back on the previous decade as a difficult time for new plays: "The Time was, upon the uniting of the two *Theatres*, that the reviveing of the old stock of Plays, so ingrost the study of the House, that the Poets lay dorment; and a new Play cou'd hardly get admittance, amongst the more precious pieces of Antiquity, that then waited to walk the Stage."[86]

Even with the preference for old plays, not a single Shakespearian comedy was adapted until the early 1690s, and then it was not promoted as such. Performances of original comedies were sporadic and infrequent, and this is especially telling in a period when old plays were preferred—the comedies still were not attractive for production as is. A brief account of what *did* seem to attract audiences includes many of the same aspects we have seen already in the late seventeenth century. Foreign entertainers continued to vie with the theater for audiences: Charles II worked to bring a troupe of Italian comedians to London in the 1682–83 season and sent Betterton to France to study opera. Betterton returned with the composer Grabu, who set music for *Valentinian* (1684) and for Dryden's *Albion and Abanius* (1685). In August of 1683, Betterton planned to perform a French opera, apparently at the request of the King.[87] Lord Preston wrote to the Duke of York that Betterton "coming hither [to Paris] some weeks since by his Majesty's command, to endeavour to carry over the Opera, and finding that impracticable, did treat with Monsr Grahme to go over with him to endeavour to represent something at least like an Opera in England for his Majesty's diversion."[88] In 1684 more competition arrived from France, with the Prince of Orange's troupe, managed by François Du Perier "and got the Author great Reputation."[89] In addition to this heavy foreign influence, an unsettled political situation caused by the Exclusion Crisis and the Glorious Revolution was reflected in a fairly conservative decade of erratic theatrical experimentation. Even so, no one used an original Shakespeare comedy as a way to attract audiences.[90]

In this climate dominated by non-native entertainments and limited to only one theater, in the 1690s English composer Henry Purcell helped revive the theater, attaining a "quasi-mythical reputation" for his stage music.[91] Purcell provided music for every new play in the early months of the 1690–91 season; as contemporary Roger North described him, "a greater musicall genius England never had."[92] One of Purcell's more successful endeavors involved music for Betterton's 1690 version of the Massinger and Fletcher *The Prophetess; or, The History of Dioclesian*. *The Prophetess* shares many components with our next adaptation of Shakespearian comedy, but also looks back to several of the features that made *The Tempest* (1674) popular. John Downes describes it as "an Opera, wrote by Mr *Betterton*; being set out with Coastly Scenes, Machines and Cloaths: The Vocal and Instrumental Musick, done my Mr *Purcel*; and Dances by Mr *Priest*; it gratify'd the Expectation of Court and City; and got the Author great Reputation" (*Roscius*, 89). In fact, Betterton commends Purcell's music for *The Prophetess* in the preface to *Amphitryon* (1690), noting that "in whose Person we have at length found an English Man, equal with the best abroad." Purcell's success brought relief to Betterton and other supporters of English entertainment, and his alterations and additions employ the full range of spectacular possibilities at Dorset Garden, including a dance of butterflies, monsters, and a chariot drawn by dragons. The transition of this source play into an opera involved a process similar to what was done with Shakespeare's comedies, and provides a model for the ways old plays of Shakespeare and his contemporaries were refurbished in the last decade of the seventeenth century.[93]

THE FAIRY-QUEEN (1692)

Similar to the revised *The Prophetess* (1690) and the 1674 *Tempest*, the 1692 version of *A Midsummer Night's Dream* (retitled *The Fairy-Queen*) capitalizes even further on the current partiality for music and spectacle, especially in connection with developments in English opera.[94] This adaptation foregrounded Purcell's music and the added visual elements, not its Shakespearian origins; the prologue to the first edition calls attention to the "cost" of the "Scenes, Dress, Dances," also noted by numerous commentators.[95] The impetus for reworking an old source, here a comedy by Shakespeare, derived from a new excitement around Purcell's music and the possibilities for theatrical offerings that could handle heavy musical components.

The play's basis in Shakespeare's *A Midsummer Night's Dream* was not promoted as an enticement for audiences. This was a wise strategy, as Shakespeare's original had not been popular in unadapted form prior to its expansive additions of music and spectacle, and the play was most successful when its comic elements were excerpted and adapted.[96] Pepys records his dissatisfaction at a performance of the full play in 1662, which was saved only by dancing and women, and he famously described Shakespeare's play as "the most insipid ridiculous play that ever I saw in my life. I saw, I confess, some good dancing & some handsome women, which was all my pleasure" (3:208). When revised in the 1690s, the goal was to bring the dramatic text in touch with the taste of the "Age," as the prologue explains, "What have we left untry'd to please this Age, / To bring it more in liking with the Stage?" Purcell's music, not Shakespeare's text, was the key to this strategy.

Contemporary accounts of the play emphasize the appeal of Purcell's contributions, with little mention of Shakespeare's material. In *The Gentleman's Journal* of January 1692, Motteux writes an advance notice for *The Fairy-Queen*, highlighting Purcell's ability to encompass both Italian and French styles: "I must tell you that we shall have speedily a New Opera, wherein something very surprising is promised us; Mr. *Purcel* who joyns to the Delicacy and Beauty of the Italian way, the Graces and Gayety of the French composes the Music, as he hath done for the *Prophetess*, and the last Opera called King *Arthur*, which hath been plaid several times the last Month" (7). Another observer likewise attested to Purcell's appeal: "I have seen much Italian musick. And in all that w[hi]ch ever came or coud come to mr Purcells Sight I never saw anything but what I coud have matchd wth something of his as good att least."[97] Like Shakespeare's *The Tempest*, *A Midsummer Night's Dream* already contained several musical and dance features, and it was a natural choice as a base text to support Purcell's music. Performed by the United Company at Dorset Garden, this was one of the most expensive Dorset Garden spectaculars. Although the preface argues for support of native English entertainment (as discussed below), Shakespeare is not part of that effort, nor is he touted as one of the native aspects of this drama. This omission is significant: Shakespeare as a writer of comedy was not thought of as the "National Poet" in the 1690s.

Purcell had already developed his style of English opera with *The Prophetess* in 1690 and *King Arthur* in 1691 (both with Betterton), which he perfected in *The Fairy-Queen*, devoting the final five years of his life to writing stage music. His *Dido and Aeneas* (with Tate) also entailed the operatic form (discussed in the following chapter as part of Gildon's *Measure for Measure*). *The Fairy-Queen* was first printed in 1692, and a reissued version appeared in 1693, described on the title page as including "Alterations, Additions, and several new SONGS."[98] We know that Purcell provided the music for *The Fairy-Queen*, but the author of the text remains anonymous. Many candidates have been suggested as the textual adapter, including Elkanah Settle, John Dryden, Thomas Betterton (because of his involvement in the other Dorset Garden operas), and actor Jo Haynes.[99] At any rate, Purcell's music was the more important component, and the lack of attribution of the text suggests the relative insignificance of this aspect. As with the 1674 *The Tempest*, *The Fairy-Queen* was a collaborative theatrical enterprise, not the work of one individual.

In the 1690s, debate continued as to whether music should be an integrated part or a separate component of English opera. In his *Gentleman's Journal* of January 1692, Motteux argues that "our English Gentlemen, when their Ear is satisfy'd, are desirous to have their mind pleas'd, and Musick and Dancing industriously intermix'd with Comedy or Tragedy" (8).[100] Even though Motteux acknowledges the English preference for spoken drama ("our English genius will not rellish that perpetual Singing"), he promotes Italian music to his readers, arguing that "since we begin to rellish those entertainments in *England*, I do not doubt but they will make the practice and love of Music more general amongst us" (7, 9). Despite Motteux's encouragement of "perpetual Singing," *The Fairy-Queen* maintains the separation between music and drama, characteristic of developing English opera, with a separate cast of actors and singers. Purcell's music is part of the fairy world, not an integrated aspect of the whole drama, and is concentrated mainly on the fairies and the rustics.[101]

The preface to *The Fairy-Queen* stresses the predominance of its musical components by situating the text within the history of English music drama, looking back to Davenant as the originator of English opera.[102] The author builds on Davenant's plea for the money needed to finance opera, arguing that with sufficient funds, "you might in a short time have as good Dancers in *England* as they have in *France*, though I despair of ever having as good Voices among us, as they have in *Italy*." The preface to *The Fairy-Queen* attempts to channel the fashion for foreign entertainments into patriotic support of a native English product. Perhaps most surprising for modern readers is the fact that the author does not flaunt Shakespeare's name as a nationalistic element. Purcell's music and *The Fairy-Queen*'s place in the history of English opera were important selling factors in the 1690s; Shakespeare provided raw dramatic material, and held little promotional value to either adapter or to intended audience.

According to surviving evidence, *The Fairy-Queen* met audience demands for spectacle and music. It premiered on 2 May 1692, with a performance on 13 June 1692, and one for Queen Mary and her maids of honor on 16 February 1693.[103] In the *Gentleman's Journal* for 14 May 1692, Motteux attests to its immediate popularity because of its music and decorations, "The OPERA of which I have spoke to you in my former, hath at last appear'd, and continues to be represented daily; it is call'd, *The Fairy Queen*. The *Drama* is originally *Shakespears*, the *Music* and *Decorations* are extraordinary. I have heard the Dances commended, and without doubt the whole is very entertaining" (26). Motteux's comment is revealing: Shakespeare's authorship is stated without praise or adulation (unless implicit), whereas the music, decoration, and dances are praised and extolled. The reception history of the music further shows that Purcell's input was the selling point; in 1692, a collection of songs was published from the play in two editions (*Some Select Songs, as they are Sung in the Fairy Queen*), some appearing again in *A Collection of Ayres* (1697) and in *Orpheus Britannicus* (1698, 1702).[104] Publisher Jacob Tonson even began to advertise his printed copy of the play in *The London Gazette* for 5–9 May 1692 before its premiere.

Given the expense of producing *The Fairy-Queen*, it was a considerable stroke of bad luck that the score disappeared shortly after Purcell's death in 1695 and was not recovered until the early part of the twentieth century. This circumstance makes it impossible to determine success, failure, or longevity, but one would suppose that Dorset Garden would have revived this costly production to help recoup expenses, had the score been available. Notices in several papers extending a reward for return of the score point to its importance and value. *The Flying Post* (9–11 October 1701) offered, "Whoever shall bring the said Score, or a true Copy thereof, first to Mr Zachary Briggs, Treasurer of the said Theatre, shall have twenty Guinea's for the same."[105] Apparently, the theater was so intent to retrieve the lost score, that a week later the advertisement was modified to provide a reward for even part of the score: "Whoever first brings the said score, or a true copy thereof . . . shall have 20 Guinea's Reward, or proportionable for any Act or Acts thereof" (*London Gazette*, 16–20 October 1701). The heart of this production was the musical score; Shakespeare's text remained available, but the production was unstageable without its most vital component: Purcell's music.[106]

The Fairy-Queen was the type of production that audiences demanded—visually elaborate and aurally rich—yet enormously costly to produce. The costumes, scenery, and music apparently topped £3,000. As Downes describes it, the production was renowned for its operatic form, its "ornaments," singers and dancers, machines, music, and dances. After these expenses, there was little profit left over for the theater: "The Court and Town were wonderfully satisfy'd with it; but the Expences in setting it out being so great, the Company got very little by it" (*Roscius*, 89).[107] Such productions often stretched the budgets of theaters without providing enough profit; as the preface to *The Fairy-Queen* describes, "what a Sum we must Yearly lay out among Tradesmen for the fitting out so great a work." In light of its unique and costly scenery, it seems likely that *The Fairy-Queen* would have been revived more frequently to take advantage of the expensive preparation, if the score had been available.

A brief summary of the changes made to Shakespeare's play shows that the additions were primarily responses to current taste for music drama.[108] Compared to the other plays in this chapter, *The Fairy-Queen* is the least connected or concerned with the fact that its literary source was a play by Shakespeare. By far the priorities of this production were the lavish spectacular and aural additions. The overall structure is punctuated by four masques, with a fifth masque added to the 1693 printing. Each of these masques is increasingly impressive in scope and extravagance, and clearly provided the substance of the production.

In the first masque of the play, Titania transforms the stage to "*Fairy-Land*"(14), here "*a Prospect of Grotto's, Arbors, and delightful Walks*" (14).[109] As well as this impressive visual display, the masque includes an echo song, a fairy dance, and a song between Night, Mystery, Secresie, and Sleep, concluding with "*A Dance of the Followers of* Night" (18) to please audiences who liked the music Locke composed for the end of *The Tempest* in 1677.[110] Mark A. Radice suggests that Locke's echo song may have been performed with nine separate voices arranged in various sections of the stage, alerting the audience to the wide spectrum of stage space to be employed.[111] But this was only the beginning.

The second masque celebrates Titania's infatuation with Bottom, signified on stage by a bridge made of two dragons with swans in a river below. After much music, the swans change into dancing fairies and dance to a symphony as trees come to life. Just as the audience has digested this spectacle, "Four Savages" chase the fairies away and the masque ends with a dance of Coridon and Mopsa, two rustic lovers (32). The personnel employed for this song were significant components of its appeal. John Reading performed Coridon, and the traditionally ugly shepherdess Mopsa was performed as a cross-dressed part by the countertenor John Pate, who John Evelyn described as "that rare Voice . . . who was lately come from *Italy*, reputed the most excellent singer, ever England had" (*Diary*, 5:289; 30 May 1698).[112] This duet must have been a well-loved component of the production; Purcell published it as a treble clef piece, transposed down from G to F, aimed at women buyers.[113] Audiences would surely have been awestruck by just the first three acts, with the delights of a dragon bridge, swans that turn into fairies, and an elaborate scene change in addition to all of the music and dance.

In the fourth act, Shakespeare's dance is replaced with a masque to celebrate the seasons, in honor of the reconciliation of the Oberon and Titania and inspired by her earlier speech on the seasons (from Shakespeare's 2.1).[114] The masque begins with the requisite ornate visual and musical setting, and employs water and lighting facilities to stage a sunrise coordinated with music, culminating in a fountain at the center of the stage with water rising twelve feet. If the previous act was impressive, the waterworks here were even more breathtaking, and may have called to mind fountains from the fairs, imported here into the theater.[115] While the audience is reveling in the aquatic display, Phoebus appears in a horse-drawn chariot, followed by copious music and dance, capped with what Martin Adams terms "one of [Purcell's] finest instrumental creations," an Italianate symphony. The success of the fourth act masque lasted through the next century with the publication of various pieces.[116] In light of the relative unpopularity of Shakespeare's original play, the accoutrements here clearly overshadowed the skeletal remains of Shakespeare's plot.

To ensure that all appetites were satiated, in the fifth act the fairies present Theseus with another masque "To cure your Incredulity" (47), which must have resonated with the audiences' reaction to the impressive spectacles. This masque is even more ornate and exotic than the previous three (Juno appears in a Machine drawn by Peacocks, who spread their tails to music as Juno sings) and has closer ties to the Stuart masque tradition by involving the stage audience.[117]

The final extravaganza in this production was one of the most striking scenes in Restoration theater, utilizing every facet of the stage to impress. After a dance on a dark stage, suddenly the space is illuminated to reveal an elaborate Chinese garden, with "the Architecture, the Trees, the Plants, the Fruit, the Birds, the Beasts, quite different from what we have in this part of the World" (48), and strange birds fly through the air around a second fountain. Audiences were transported to another world, complete with flora, fauna, fowl, and fountain to satisfy taste for the unusual.[118] What occurs on stage is as exotic as this background, including songs from a Chinese couple, a dance between six monkeys, and Chinese vases containing orange trees rising from below the stage.[119] A *"Grand Dance"* of twenty-four people, several songs, and the arrival of Hymen conclude the piece. These scenes were the clear focus of the entertainment, yet it is worth noting that they involve hardly a word of Shakespeare's text.

The final masque further illustrates the place of Shakespeare in this piece. The scenes, characters, and songs have no connection to Shakespeare's plot of mistaken love in a wood outside of Athens—here the masque was not even inspired by Shakespeare's text, it only acts as entertainment for Theseus. It is safe to say that no audience member went home from this production contemplating the intricacies of Shakespeare's plot or the subtleties of his poetry with so many other distractions. From oriental settings to working fountains, from monkeys to swans, from an Italianate symphony to a cross-dressed duet by popular singers, from the pinching of drunken poets to the arrival of gods in machines, *The Fairy-Queen* sought to satisfy every possible taste except a taste for Shakespeare. A note of desperation comes through in the plethora of ingredients in these productions, an almost frantic grasping at elaborate scene changes, machines, and layers of song and dance to mollify an unpredictable audience who would not have settled for a bare unadorned comedy by Shakespeare. Had the producers thought that attaching Shakespeare's name would attract audience members, they certainly would have promoted the production as such—a much cheaper alternative than adding working fountains and dancing monkeys.

It is difficult to speculate about the long-term success of *The Fairy-Queen* because of several factors in the theatrical environment which affected production runs. In addition to the lost score, *The Fairy-Queen* appeared in the midst of events leading up to the actors' rebellion of 1695, not a particularly stable time.[120] In 1692, Betterton lost his savings in investments, and in 1695 moved to Lincoln's Inn Fields with fellow actors, establishing a second company to compete with Christopher Rich. It is well-known that Betterton's company had better actors, but he no longer had the theatrical facilities to stage his spectacular productions and was forced to scale down his offerings to accommodate Lincoln's Inn Fields theatre. This restriction in facilities had a direct impact on the performance history of works like *The Fairy-Queen* with extensive requirements for staging. Betterton's company had to abandon these elaborate productions and look to other theatrical tactics to attract audiences. In assessing the reception history of *The Fairy-Queen*, we must take into account the circumstances that necessitated an abrupt end to the Dorset Garden spectaculars for Betterton, regardless of audience demands. Even if the score had survived, Betterton could not have offered *The Fairy-Queen* in its full splendor.

We can surmise the importance of this adaptation, however, by its influence on subsequent English operas, including the Purcell/Tate *A New Opera; called Brutus of Alba* (1696), the Purcell/Settle *The World in the Moon* (1697), and the Purcell/Fletcher *The Island Princess* (1699).[121] The author of *A Comparison Between the Two Stages* places *The Fairy-Queen* within this larger history of operatic experiments on the English stage. The character Sullen describes the intricate variety demanded by audiences: "The Actors labour at this like so many Galley Slaves at an Oar, they call in the Fiddle, the Voice, the Painter, and the Carpenter to help 'em; and what neither the Poet nor the Player cou'd do, the Mechanick must do for him: The Town had seen their best at the Drama; and now, I was going to say, the House look'd like a brisk Highway-man, who consults his Perruke-maker about the newest Fashion an Hour before his Execution; this new fangled Invention was a melodious Whim—" (21). Even though Italian opera did not arrive in London until 1705, theater managers' frantic attempts to compete with operatic entertainments show the changeable nature of audiences in the final years of the seventeenth century and the preoccupation with this type of offering. When Ramble asks Sullen, "How? new fangled Mr. *Sullen*? you forget the *Prophetess*, *King Arthur*, and the *Fairy Queen*," Sullen replies, "I remember 'em; and pray are not they new? nay, if you go to the utmost of it's Antiquity, it came from no elder a House than *Davenant*'s, and that's new enough of all Conscience: but as I was saying—the *Opera* now possesses the Stage, and after a hard struggle, at length it prevail'd, and something more than Charges came in every Night: The Quality, who are always Lovers of good Musick, flock hither, and by almost a total revolt from the other *House*, give this new Life, and set it in some eminency above the *New*" (*A Comparison Between the Two Stages*, 21–22). According to the hindsight of this author, these operas were feeble attempts to capture English taste in music as operatic offerings increased their hold on audiences. Samuel Johnson would later describe Italian opera as "an exotick and irrational entertainment, which has been always combated and always has prevailed."[122] In *The Fairy-Queen*, Shakespeare's comic material is a mere skeleton for the large body of musical, visual, and spectacular components to compete in this climate. Shakespeare's name is omitted from the advertisements and promotional materials, and the remnants of his play are overshadowed by the lavish additions to the text. In the Restoration, *A Midsummer Night's Dream* was not a success, and in the 1690s it still could not hold its own without substantial garnishes.

Conclusion

Following *The Fairy-Queen*, theaters continued to offer elaborate productions affixed to the raw material of earlier playwrights' work, and

The Fairy-Queen was part of a larger pattern of adapting older source material for a new theatrical context, a process that involved sources in addition to Shakespeare. The plays of Fletcher in particular rivaled Shakespeare as popular source material, with similar musical and visual accoutrements. One representative example should suffice for illustration. Motteux adapted Fletcher's *The Island Princess* in 1699 and explained his process in his address to "The Reader": "As I found it [*The Island Princess*] not unfit to be made what we here call an Opera, I undertook to revise it, but not as I wou'd have done, had I design'd a correct Play. Let this at once satisfie the Modern Critics, and the Zealous Admirers of Old Plays; for I neither intended to make it regular, nor to keep in all that I lik'd in the Original, but only what I thought fit for my Purpose, and the success has answered my intent, far beyond Expectation." Like the adapters of Shakespeare's *The Tempest* and *The Fairy-Queen*, Motteux aims for theatrical success above all other concerns, clearly disavowing any intent to "make it regular" by conforming to a set of rules. His "Purpose" was to satisfy the taste for music and spectacle, and he achieves this balance by adding an operatic interlude in the fourth act, a musical interlude in the last act entitled "The Four Seasons or Love in Every Age," which was reprinted for separate sale, and additional music by Daniel Purcell, Richard Leveridge, and Jeremiah Clarke.[123]

The title page to his 1699 adaptation highlights the new features: "All the Musical Entertainments and the greatest Part of the Play new, and written by Mr. Motteux." These acclaimed musical parts, not the source play, were the draw for audiences. In his address to the reader, Motteux ascribes the tremendous success "chiefly to the Excellency of the Musical Part" by Daniel Purcell, Clarke, Leveridge, and Pate. Daniel Purcell received much praise for his music; Gildon remarked in his preface to *Phaeton* (1698), "Mr. *Daniel Purcells* Composition in this Play is a certain Proof, that as long as he lives Mr. *Henry Purcel* will never die; or our *English* harmony give place to any of our Neighbours." Motteux included elements that made the earlier *The Fairy-Queen* a success — scenery, song by Pate, music by a Purcell, all in the style of "an opera." The prologue describes the sacrifices necessary on every level to ensure success. The actors even "wave our Pay, / At our own Cost t'adorn these Scenes to day." Motteux employed a methodology similar to what we have seen with *The Fairy-Queen*: an earlier source play used as raw material to support other attractions.

This chapter has shown the need to reassess adaptations of Shakespeare's comedies within the context of theatrical production. Viewed in isolation, these plays may seem bizarre and irrational curiosities, but they were typical offerings of their time. Our interest is peaked because they involve a Shakespearian plot as the source text, but in their own day this held little value or appeal. Shakespeare's comedies were not the only "old plays" that were revamped in the later decades of the seventeenth century. Beaumont and Fletcher plays (especially the latter) were even more popular for adapting in this format, and they show the extent that theaters relied on old plays in new dress.[124] For example, Betterton supplemented Fletcher's *The Prophetess* (1690) with extensive scenes, music, dance, and cost typical of taste in the 1690s. Downes remarks that it was "set out with Coastly Scenes, Machines and Cloaths: The Vocal and Instrumental Musick, done by Mr. *Purcel*; and Dances by Mr. *Priest*; it gratify'd the Expectation of the Court and City; and got the Author great Reputation." In his later estimation of *The Prophetess*, Cibber notes that the revenues did not quite equal expenditures, and that the production "was in Appearance very great, yet their whole Receipts did not so far balance their Expence as to keep them out of a large Debt, which it was publickly known was about this time contracted" (*Apology*, 1:187).

Other Fletcher plays revived in the 1690s were dressed in similar fashion to *The Prophetess* and *The Fairy-Queen*: *The Knights of Malta* (1691) with music by Purcell; *Valentinian* (1694) adapted by Rochester with music and the masque *The Rape of Europa by Jupiter* by Betterton with music by Eccles;[125] *Bonduca* (1695) with music by Purcell, advertised on the title page "With a New Entertainment of Musick, Vocal and Instrumental Never Printed or Acted Before;" *The Pilgrim* (1700) with music by Daniel Purcell, alterations by Vanbrugh, and prologue, epilogue, and masque by Dryden;[126] and *The Mad Lover* (1700) with music by Eccles and the masque *Acis and Galatea* by Eccles and Motteux. These productions resemble the additions appended to Shakespeare's *The Tempest* and *A Midsummer Night's Dream* and show that Shakespeare was reshaped no differently than other "old" dramatic material. For example, the masque added to Fletcher's tragedy *Valentinian*, *The Rape of Europa by Jupiter*, involves the type of stage spectacle that decorated Shakespeare's two comedies. Taking place just after a "Dance of Satyrs," Mercury descends in a chariot drawn by ravens, Jupiter is lowered on an eagle (reminiscent of Shakespeare's *Cymbeline*), with singing and dancing by shepherds, and Europa is discovered "on a Bull's back in the Sea." The changes made to Shakespeare's plays adhered to such typical patterns of popular taste.

These embellishments of Beaumont and Fletcher plays were not received with total acclaim, nevertheless. The author of "The Grove: or, the Rival Muses" (1701) remarks:

> *Motteux*, and *Durfey* are for nothing fit,
> But to supply with Songs their want of Wit.

> Had not the *Island Princess* been adorn'd
> With Tunes, and pompous Scenes, she had been scorn'd.
> What was not *Fletcher's*, no more sense contains
> Than he that wrote the *Jubilee*, has Brains.

These revamped "old plays" (like *The Tempest*) continued to comprise a portion of the repertoire in the early eighteenth century, and were revised according to local theatrical conditions and demands. Fletcher's *The Island Princess* was revived with extra music in 1702, 1703 (for visitors from Spain), and 1706.[127] *The Pilgrim* provided a similar foundation for additions of music and entertainment; *The Post Boy* advertised a benefit performance of the play on 6 July 1700 for Anne Oldfield "Revis'd with Large Alterations, and a Secular Masque. With the Dialogue between the 2 mad Lovers."[128] In 1704 a second benefit performance of the play was performed for the dancer Mrs. Mayers with "a Masque set to Musick by the Famous Mr. Henry Purcell" on 23 March 1704.[129] Like *The Tempest* which changed shape in the late seventeenth century as theater facilities and accoutrements changed, other older plays underwent a similar transformation.

Several key events transpired in the theatrical climate in the years before the next adaptations of Shakespearian comedy in 1700. In the late 1690s productions continued to feature music as a drawing point, including an anonymous reworking of the Dryden/Howard *The Indian Queen* (1695), *Bonduca* (1695) and *A New Opera; called Brutus of Alba* (1696), Durfey's *A New Opera, call'd Cinthia and Endimion* (1697), Settle's *The World in the Moon* (1697), Motteux's *Island Princess* (1699) and Oldmixon's *The Grove* (1700). Betterton imported French entertainers in the late 1690s to draw crowds, and Rich offered productions of opera, reviving *Psyche* and *The Prophetess*, and perhaps even employed Purcell before his death in 1695 to write new music for *The Tempest*.[130] Rich continued to stage extravagant productions at Dorset Garden in the 1690s, vowing to surpass anything yet seen on the English stage and abroad.

Various additional elements of the entertainment scene in the 1690s foreshadow the shape of Shakespearian adaptations in the early eighteenth century. Available theatrical venues affected what theater companies could offer audiences. Without the facilities for the elaborate productions he had mounted at Dorset Garden, Betterton turned to masques by Motteux and Eccles, as well as Dennis's opera *Rinaldo and Armida* (1698).[131] Betterton's company had several actors who were also talented singers, particularly Thomas Doggett and Anne Bracegirdle, and their talents were employed with great success in the early eighteenth century.

Foreign entertainments continued to draw crowds, and theaters had to keep up competitive strategies. Playwrights began to advertise their native English content, as did Settle in the epilogue *The World in the Moon* (1697):

> ... 'tis all home-spun Cloth;
> All from an *English Web*, and *English Growth*.
> But if we'd let it make a costly Dance
> To Paris, and bring home some Scenes from France,
> I'm sure 'twould take: For you, Gadzooks, are civil;
> And wish them well, that wish you at the Devil.

Before 1700, we do not see Shakespeare's name used as native ammunition against imported offerings. "Shakespeare" was not enough to ensure theatrical prosperity without accoutrements, and no Restoration comic adaptation of Shakespeare survived solely because of its "Shakespearian" roots. Indeed, few plays were able to succeed "without scenes and machines;" as one contemporary put it, "the present plays with all that show can hardly draw an audience, unless there by the additional invitation of a Signor Fideli, a Monsieur l'Abbe, or some such foreign regale express'd in the bottom of the bill."[132]

The visual and aural additions to plays discussed in this chapter nurtured a taste for music that may have encouraged Italian opera and eventually created a grim situation for English theater. The versions of *The Tempest* took advantage of current taste for song and spectacle, updating the play with the opportunities for staging provided by the new Dorset Garden theatre. Purcell's *The Fairy-Queen* satisfied audience demand for theatrical offerings that combined drama and song, to compete against a growing partiality for music stimulated by the development of opera and the influx of foreign singers. *The Fairy-Queen*, *The Tempest* and the adaptations with large musical interpolations in the next chapter (*Measure for Measure* and *The Jew of Venice*) all use Shakespearian material in a struggle of English musicians, composers, and dramatists to capture audience taste in music drama, but adapters were seldom concerned with Shakespearian content alone.

In the Restoration, Shakespeare's name value for the comedies held little importance. Beginning with *The Law Against Lovers* and *Bottom the Weaver*, and continuing with *The Fairy-Queen*, these plays attest that Shakespeare's comedies were only valuable as source plays, foundations around which to build theatrical offerings concerned with other elements—usually actors, novelty, music, dance, and spectacle. It is worth pointing out that two of the more successful plays from this era, *The Tempest* and *The Fairy-Queen*, do not even have a definite "author" to ascribe these changes to. Restoration audiences were less concerned with authorial agency, even from Shakespeare, than with production content.

Adaptations of Shakespeare's comic material in the Restoration were governed by the circumstances of theatrical production—popular actors, desire for music, dance, and spectacle—basically, the practical realities of running a successful theater. We cannot separate *what* was done to Shakespeare from *why* it was done, or from the performance conditions and circumstances that necessitated such changes. In many ways it is misleading to look at these plays as adaptations *of* Shakespeare, because to these playwrights, Shakespeare was not the central component of the play. These works were not constructed by what was done *to* Shakespeare, so much as they were texts derived from what was done in addition to using an old play. With the comedies in the Restoration, it mattered little that the old play came from Shakespeare.

3
"Study [the] Audience as well as the Rules": Shakespeare and Changing Taste in Comedy

As THE THEATRICAL CONDITIONS CHANGED IN THE EARLY EIGHTEENTH century, so did the factors affecting the ways Shakespeare's comedies were altered. Four adaptations of Shakespearian comedies took place in the first four years of the eighteenth century, for playwrights a challenging period fraught with complex audience desires and competing distractions from nondramatic offerings; Judith Milhous labels this "the darkest period for the English theatre since the Commonwealth." Moral reformers, described by one contemporary as the "Dread Reformers of an Impious Age, / You awful Catta-nine-Tailes, to the Stage," continued to denounce the theaters, and challenge their position in the culture. "Who of you all can guess a Poet's trouble," Charles Hopkins asked, "Which is in these Religious Days grown double?"[1] Royal support of theaters under Queen Anne was at its lowest point in the Restoration and first three decades of the eighteenth century.[2] In addition to these complications, we have few records of theatrical offerings for the 1701–02 season, making it unusually difficult to draw concrete conclusions about successes and failures.[3]

In order to understand why Shakespeare's comic material was reshaped in particular ways for this audience, we must look to the factors that affected the structure and composition of theatrical offerings overall. At the close of the seventeenth century, Peter Anthony Motteux's prologue to Mary Pix's *The Innocent Mistress* (1697) characterizes this environment of intense competition:

> This season with what Arts both Houses strive,
> By your kind presence, to be kept alive!
> W'have still new things, or old ones we revive;
> We plot, and strive to bring them first o'th' Stage,
> Like wary Pilot for his Weather-gage.
> W'have *Every Act*, and every week a Play;
> Nay, w'have had new ones studied for one Day.

The range of theatrical re-creations enumerated in this prologue, from new to old, alludes to the production strategies necessary in pursuit of public favor: as one contemporary put it, "A *Full* House is the very *Life* of the Stage, and keeps it in Countenance, whereas *thin Audiences* would, in time, make it dwindle to nothing."[4] This *"Full* House" remained elusive yet vital for survival, and comedies by Shakespeare were only offered in versions that were likely to draw a "Full House."

Two theaters competed for audience favor: Drury Lane managed by Christopher Rich, and Lincoln's Inn Fields under the direction of Thomas Betterton.[5] Theaters relied on a public that increasingly veered far away from traditional drama and embraced more music-based offerings, especially opera.[6] Theaters acquiesced to the demands of public taste, yet many playwrights registered resentment and displeasure with competing nondramatic entertainments. Paradoxically, however, as Hume has noted, "until January 1708 virtually all 'opera' performances in London were given under the auspices of the patent theatre companies."[7] Thus, opera received support from the very institution that criticized it the most; apparently many things could be overlooked if a production could pay the bills.

Despite a number of strategies from managers, most dramatic offerings in these early years of the eighteenth century did not please audiences. "I am sure you can't name me five Plays that have indur'd six Days acting," the author of *A Comparison Between the Two Stages* (1702) observed, "for fifty that were damn'd in three" (2). Durfey's epilogue to Robert Gould's *The Rival Sisters* (1695) notes that "Above twice fifty Plays each Year are made, / And of twice fifty Plays scarce five are Play'd." Numerous accounts attest to this erratic environment for plays and lament the power audiences wielded over theaters. The character Frank Wildblood in Elkanah Settle's *The World in the Moon* (1697) captures the image of such capacious audience members: "I never take a turn to a Play, but either just pop in my Head before the Curtain rises, or before it drops again." His companion Ned sympathizes with the theaters and probably voices the opinion of many playwrights: "But why are you so unkind to the Play-houses, especially at this Low-water time with them, to take a turn (as you call it) before the Curtain rises?" (3). Even allowing for some exaggeration from Settle, evidence suggests that many Frank Wildbloods populated audiences and were partly responsible for the fate of many plays. Hume and Scouten have discussed how these "cranky" audiences favored old plays, but condemned new plays of every type, from "tragedy as well as comedy, to humane and reform comedies as well as satiric ones."[8]

Settle's character sketch is corroborated by countless complaints about unpredictable audiences. "Applause does more than doubly pay our pains," wrote one playwright in 1701, "But yet your Tasts so strange of late we find, / New Authors have small hopes to prove you kind."[9] A passage from Motteux's play *Farewel Folly: or, The Younger the Wiser* (1707) similarly describes the fate of plays: "a few Old Plays are applauded, and New ones damn'd in abundance . . . So good Acting being little minded, our Gains decay, and the Audience now make the most sport for one another." Theaters have more new plays "than ever will be launch'd; we have such heaps of Tragedies, Comedies, Farces, Masques, Opera's, and what not, in the House, that we had twenty pounds bidden for 'em by a Grocer and a Pastry Cook." However, there was always the possibility of a hidden success within the heap of rejected plays, as Motteux's Mimic explains, "we have hopes the Town will take 'em off of our hands one time or other; for Plays are like Women and Pictures, there's nothing so ordinary but what some body will like; I have seen the Galleries support a Play against the Boxes, and the Noise of the Footmen impose on the Understanding of their Masters" (15). According to Cibber, "the Appetite of the Publick, like that of a fine Gentleman, could only be kept warm by Variety; that let their Merit be never so high, yet the Taste of a Town was not always constant, nor infallible" (*Apology*, 1:231). Successful plays came from well-known and unknown writers alike, with little predictable audience response. Productions like Motteux's appropriately named hodgepodge *The Novelty* (1697) tried to capture the variety of audience desires with its bizarre combination of "Pastoral, Comedy, Masque, Tragedy, and Farce after the Italian manner," according to its title page. Most participants in London theater during this period would probably have agreed with Charles Johnson's epilogue to Corye's 1704 *The Metamorphosis*: "Keep us but Company when we are Poor, / As better times shall come, we'll quit the Score." The concerns of theaters in the early eighteenth century differ from those of the early Restoration at the beginning of our study. Davenant was concerned to attract an audience; now there is an established audience for theater but it is incredibly hard to please.

In the early years of the eighteenth century, then, there was no clear pattern to predict the success of a production. Countless prefatory remarks express this exasperation: "Each Mind betrays a diff'rent Taste," exclaimed Farquhar, "And ev'ry Dish scarce pleases ev'ry Guest." In his "A Discourse Upon Comedy" Farquhar further delineates the variety of tastes a playwright must please: "The Scholar calls upon us for *Decorums* and *Oeconnomy*; the Courtier crys out for *Wit* and *Purity of Stile*; the Citizen for *Humour* and *Ridicule*; the Divines threaten us for Immodesty; and the Ladies will have an Intreague" (366). Another frustrated playwright asked in 1701, "What must be done to make a Play succeed? / The common Methods are all over try'd."[10] The prefatory verse to Thomas Baker's *Tunbridge-Walks: or, The Yeoman of Kent* (1703) describes the unreceptive and precarious atmosphere:

> 'Tis hard to please, in such a Carping Age,
> When Criticks with such Spleen, Invest the Stage;
> But suddain Death's the Fate of Modern Plays,
> For few we see, are Born to Length of Days.

As we shall see, audiences reacted no differently to Shakespearian content, with the same unpredictable responses, than they did to texts by other authors.[11]

Even the best-known authors were no guarantee of success, as Susannah Centlivre expressed in her preface to *Love's Contrivance* (1703): "Writing is a kind of Lottery in this fickle Age, and Dependence on the Stage as precarious as the Cast of a Die; the Chance may turn up, and a man may write to please the Town, but 'tis uncertain, since we see our best Authors sometimes fail." Paradoxically, public response was so unpredictable that many decided to try their luck at writing plays. Thomas Baker remarked that "a Man that thinks in this Age, to raise his Credit by Writing, exposes his sense by so hazardous an Enterprize, he may as well expect to raise his Means by buying Stock when 'tis got to the highest Value."[12]

This daunting state of affairs apparently did not discourage would-be playwrights: "But now, ev'n from the Court to the Black Guard, / Thro' all degrees of Men starts up a Bard, / The Beau, the Cit, the Lawyer—and the Lord."[13] The preponderance of new and often amateur writers provoked much unpleasant commentary. The author of *The English Theophrastus* (1702) attributes a decline in the quality of plays to an increase in unqualified authors and erratic audience reactions: "The reason we have had so many *ill Plays* of late, is this; The extraordinary *Success* of the worst Performances encourages every Pretender to Poetry to Write; Whereas the indifferent Reception some excellent Pieces have met with, discourages our best Poets from Writing."[14] Many authors decried the lack of aesthetic standards of judgment that allowed these "ill Plays" to succeed regardless of dramatic quality, artistic merit, or authorial achievement. "'Egad, these Times make Poets of us all," remarked Motteux, "for ne're were seen more Scribes, yet less good writing," and in the prologue to Charles Hopkins' *Boadicea* (1697), Betterton deplored, "Wo[e] to us Players, every one turns Poet." John Dennis, the prominent critic and adapter of Shakespeare, was notorious in his condemnation of scribblers.[15] As we shall see, Dennis remained a patriotic supporter of standards for writing, and lamented the decline of the theater and its practitioners. The preponderance of writers in the early eighteenth century is a very different problem from the earlier troubles of the stage: Davenant tried to stretch a limited number of plays, Lacy promoted his own talents, and the operatic adaptations capitalized on theater facilities and staging possibilities. In the early eighteenth century, few writers turned to Shakespeare, and fewer still because they thought audiences would recognize Shakespeare's name.

The "Profit of the Stage" was often the impetus for writers in this consumer climate; as one contemporary writer put it, "the Poets have had too great an Encouragement; for 'tis the Profit of the Stage that makes so many Scriblers, and surfeits the Town with new Eighteen-penny Plays."[16] Actors were also implicated. John Dennis blamed the lack of encouragement for new plays on the financial motives of the players: "Their grand maxim is to gett money, and to sacrifice all things to their Insatiable Avarice. Tis by full House that They Heap up pelf, and as their Houses are always filld by their old plays, They can be noe more by new ones."[17] With profit as the guiding principle, theaters were criticized for catering to audience preferences without regard to the progress of art: "The partiality of the Town makes the Managers of the Theatre in Drury Lane stick to their old Plays," Dennis argues, "and reject all new ones unlesse those which are forcd upon them. For either a new play succeeds or it does not. If it does not succeed, They are sure to have several Thin Houses, of which the other Theatre does not fail to make their Advantage. If it does succeed the whole profits of Three or Four nights goe away to the Authour. Soe that all that is lost to them, besides the expence and pains of getting it up . . . From hence comes their mortal aversion to new plays." Dennis concludes that "if their avarice were not Insatiable," theater managers would encourage new plays (*Works*, 2:279). According to Dennis and many others, financial priorities were detrimental to artistic quality and to the health of dramatic writing; concern for money above aesthetics had implications for Shakespeare's comic material.

Changes in the nature and composition of audiences around the turn of the century made the tasks of playwrights and theater managers even more difficult. Milhous points out that the gradual change in curtain time to 5 or 6 P.M. by 1700 "proves that the theatres were no longer able to rely on a leisured, Court-circle audience. To fill their houses the managers had to attract part of the working populace—people who were occupied in trade until the end of the afternoon."[18] The entertainments offered to this changing audience aimed to satisfy a new type of taste that increasingly involved nondramatic elements. In the adaptations of Shakespeare's comedies discussed in this chapter, we can see that this taste for exotica and novelties extended beyond the traditional five-act play; a comedy by Shakespeare was not enough to succeed.

Even though theater records are sparse for some of the seasons in the early eighteenth century, we can surmise that the two theaters were engaged in stiff competition for these fickle audience members; as Shirley Strum Kenny describes it, a period of "theatrical warfare" began in 1695 when the United Company dissolved.[19] The author of *A Comparison Between the Two Stages* (1702) explains the competitive situation between the talented actors at Betterton's Lincoln's Inn Fields, and the young actors left behind at Drury Lane: "'twas strange that the general defection of the old Actors which left *Drury-lane*, and the fondness which the better sort shew'd for 'em at the opening of their *New-house*, and indeed the Novelty it self, had not quite destroy'd those few young ones that remain'd behind" (7). Betterton could no longer perform his "spectaculars" at Dorset Garden, but the "better sort" of the audience followed their old favorite actors as well as the novelty of a new venue, instead of the dilapidated Lincoln's Inn Fields theater. In 1671, Dorset Garden opened and was constructed to accommodate spectacular entertainments such as *The Tempest*, *Psyche*, and other semi-operas, but was heavily damaged by a storm in 1703 and remained in a state of disrepair. Instead of focussing its energy on plays, Dorset Garden featured such acts as William Joy, "the English Sampson," for a string of unusual performances in the fall of 1699.[20] The ramifications of this theater split for Drury Lane were serious and detrimental: "The disproportion was so great at parting, that 'twas almost impossible, in *Drury-lane*, to muster up a significant number to take in all the Parts of any Play; and of them so few were tolerable, that a Play must of necessity be damn'd that had not extraordinary favour from the Audience: No fewer than *Sixteen* (most of the old standing) went away; and with them the very beauty and vigour of the Stage; they who were left behind being for the most part Learners, Boys and Girls, a very unequal match for them who revolted."[21] If we are to believe the worst, Drury Lane could barely organize a performance with sufficient actors, let alone provide consistent performances from its inexperienced cast. Cibber depicts this period of Drury Lane's history in terms of just such a warfare: "After we had stolen some few Days March upon them, the forces of *Betterton* came up with us in terrible Order: In about three Weeks following, the new Theatre was open'd against us with a veteran Company and a new Train of Artillery; or in plainer *English*, the old Actors in *Lincoln's-Inn-Fields* began with a new Comedy of Mr *Congreve's*, call'd *Love* for *Love*" (*Apology*, 1:196–97).[22] Even allowing for exaggeration in Cibber's reminiscence, the martial language in his description casts this competition as a matter of life or death for the two theaters. Every theatrical offering was important for the welfare and stability of both companies, and the choice to stage a Shakespearian comedy was no exception.

In a telling passage, Cibber describes the dire situation for Drury Lane actors as a "Civil War, of the Theatre!" with thin houses, overpaid actors, and "not half the usual Audiences, to pay them!"[23] This climate was certainly not conducive for playwrights, and Drury Lane was blamed for many theatrical flops. William Walker complained that his play *Victorious Love* (1698) failed because of its venue: "I am blamed for the suffering my Play to be Acted at the Theatre-Royal, accus'd of Foolish Presumption, in setting my weak Shoulders to Prop this Declining Fabrick, and of affronting the Town, in Favouring whom they Discountenance" (preface). Not only were new plays endangered at Drury Lane, works of Shakespeare suffered as well. Cibber remembers "the rude and riotous Havock we made of all the late dramatic Honours of the Theatre! all become at once the Spoil of Ignorance and Self-Conceit! *Shakespear* was defac'd and tortured in every signal Character— *Hamlet* and *Othello* lost in one Hour all their good Sense, their Dignity and Fame" (*Apology*, 1:202). Notably, Cibber names Shakespeare's tragedies as the consummate examples of his works, without as much at stake for the comedies. Even allowing for exaggeration from Cibber, the "Vigorous War" led one writer for Drury Lane to boast that "To please this Audience, we'll no Charges spare," diverting all "New Funds" and "heavy Taxes" to pay dancers and singers, not to encourage new plays.[24]

We can assess the status of Shakespeare's comedies by examining the various strategies Drury Lane and Lincoln's Inn Fields used to attract capricious audience members in this time of intense competition. As Cibber describes it, audiences "so fluctuated from one House to another as their Eyes were more or less regaled than their Ears" (*Apology*, 1:317). This constituency proved difficult to please in the best circumstances. A scene from William Burnaby's play *The Reform'd Wife* (1700) gives us a sense of the challenge involved in trying to attract patrons who vacillated between theaters. Sir Solomon says that if he were to write a play, "I'd have something to divert every Body. I'd have your Atheism to please the Wits—some affectation to entertain the Beaux, a Rape or two to engage the Ladies; and I'd bring in the Bears, before every Act, to secure an interest in the Upper Gallery" (5). Edmund Curll corroborates Burnaby's account of the need for exotic variety, especially with imported entertainments: "About this Time [1698] the *English* Theatre was not only pestered with Tumblers, and Rope-Dancers from *France*, but likewise with Dancing-Masters, Dancing-Dogs; shoals of *Italian* Squallers were daily imported; and the *Drury-Lane* Company almost broke."[25] Such enticements left little room or encouragement for the traditional five-act play that had been the mainstay of patent theaters. Accoutrements were often more important than the plays they accompanied; Cibber comments that in order for theater to survive, it must feed "upon the Trash and Filth of Buffoonery and Licentiousness" and complained that his *Love makes a Man* (1700) "only held up its Head by the Heels of the *French Tumblers*." Another writer lamented that what pleases now "may be perform'd without a writer's Care, / And is the Skill of Carpenter, not Player." Even the work of Shakespeare was insufficient unadorned: "Old *Shakespear's* Days could not thus far Advance, / But what's his Buskin to our Ladder Dance?" A final example illustrates the desperate nature of competition around the turn of the century, which heightened the stakes for new productions: "Get some She-Monster some sixteen Foot high" or "Get some fam'd Opera, any how translated, / No matter, so the t'other House don't get it."[26]

As was the case in the late seventeenth century, foreign entertainers remained an adversary to theaters. Betterton, for example, was diverted from his focus on drama and engaged several performers at costly rates; Downes records that "In the space of Ten Years past, Mr. *Betterton* to gratify the desires and Fancies of the Nobility and Gentry; procur'd from Abroad the best Dances and Singers, as, Monsieur *L'Abbe*, Madam *Sublini*, Monsieur *Balon*, *Margarita Delpine*, *Maria Gallia* and divers others; who being Exorbitantly Expensive, produc'd small Profit to him and his Company, but vast Gain to themselves" (*Roscius*, 96–97).[27] Such attractions sidetracked spectators from traditional five-act offerings; Rowe bemoaned in the epilogue to *The Ambitious Step-mother* (1700), "Must *Shakespear*, *Fletcher*, and laborious *Ben* / Be left for *Scaramouch* and *Harlequin*?" Old standards from Shakespeare, Fletcher, and Jonson were not enough to ensure prosperity, and the loss of even a single dancer could put theaters back in the red. In December of 1699, Vanbrugh writes, "Miss Evans, the dancer at the new playhouse, is dead . . . She's much lamented by the town as well as by the house, which can't well bear her loss, matters running very low with 'em this winter. If Congreve's Play don't help 'em they are undone."[28] A few writers turned to Shakespeare's comedies as ammunition against these exotic entertainers but this was no guarantee of success. "Our Home-spun Authors must forsake the Field," laments the prologue to Edmund Smith's *Phaedra and Hippolitus* (1707), "And Shakespear to the soft Scarlatti yield."[29] Playwrights are notorious for exaggerating complaints against audiences, but the abundance of despairing comments must have had some basis in reality. Shakespeare's comic material provided little assistance against these attractions.

Feeling the financial losses from thin audiences, theater managers began a frenzied attempt to offer anomalous and enticing entertainments, from foreign singers to dancers and animals in hopes of bringing audiences back to the fold. The prologue to Durfey's *The Old Mode and*

3: "STUDY [THE] AUDIENCE AS WELL AS THE RULES" 95

the New (1703) provides a typical expression of the strife between native and foreign offerings:

> If Comick Scenes cou'd please like capring Tricks,
> Or could be sounded with *Italian* Squeaks,
> We might suppose this Play would last six Weeks.
> But since that only can your Mirth provoke,
> And you grow weary of Grimace and Joke,
> We too must try to trafflick cross the Water,
> Five hundred raise for some rare foreign Matter,
> A Portion for an English Farmer's Daughter.

Performances listed in *The London Stage* shows the desperately experimental nature of theatrical offerings in this period. Various entertainments were added to plays in an effort to strike an acceptable balance.

Oldmixon's prologue to *The Governour of Cyprus* (1702) encapsulates this situation:

> Our houses thin apace, our Wares lie dead
> And Fustian quite, or Farce has spoilt the Trade.
> When Cash comes short and we begin to pinch
> Up goes the Boy, the Ladder-dance, and Clinch.

The economic imagery in this passage points to the focus on financial gain and income; "when cash comes short" theaters must respond by offering whatever enticements would draw audiences, regardless of aesthetic value. Both theaters decried this practice of adding features such as the eccentric vocalist/entertainer Mr. Clinch and the fair-derived ladder dance, yet both had to accede to audience demand in order to bring in the necessary funds to survive.[30] The prologue to Mary Pix's *The Double Distress*, performed at Lincoln's Inn Fields in March of 1701, illustrates this method: "Well, we've shew'n all we can to make you easie, / Tumblers and Monkeys, on the Stage to please you." Another contemporary lamented the same year that "Once *Dryden, Otway, Fletcher*, pleas'd the Town; / Now nothing but *The Monkey* will go down."[31] As Dryden described in his 1698 commendatory verses to George Granville, theaters

> ... in Despair their empty Pit to fill
> Set up some Foreign Monster in a Bill:
> Thus they jog on; still tricking, never thriving;
> And Murd'ring Plays, which they miscal Reviving.[32]

Dryden's complaint of the need to "trick" audiences with foreign and exotic entertainments is corroborated by theatrical records.

A look at one season from the early eighteenth century will provide a sense of typical offerings. In 1701–2, Lincoln's Inn Fields promoted the following features, combining old plays with new forms of nondramatic popular entertainments that could better ensure success. *The Country Wife* was paired with "that delightful Exercise of Vaulting on the Manag'd Horse, according to the *Italian* manner." Southerne's *Oroonoko* was performed with "new Musick set to Flutes; and to be perform'd by Mr Bannister and his Son, and others, and some of Mr Weldon's new Songs, perform'd in his last Consort" and dancing by Mrs. Campion with "Vaulting on the Horse." Shadwell's *Bury Fair* publicized singing, dancing, and "the last New Entertainment of Musick, Composed for Flutes on the Stage, by Mr Bannister and his Son, and others." Jonson's *Bartholomew Fair* advertised "Several Extraordinary Entertainments, as will be express'd in the Bills." Ravenscroft's *The London Cuckolds* promised that Penkethman would deliver "the Epilogue upon the Ass" with dances including "a *Scotch Dance* by Mrs Bignell, and a Dance by Monsieur Nevelong [Louis (?) Nivelon] and 8 more, call'd *Dame Ragondes and her 8 Children*; the right *Irish Trot* by Mr. Goodwin." Brome's *Jovial Crew*, which was advertised as "the last time of Acting till after Bartholomew Fair," purported to have the following novelties to lure audiences: "The famous Mr Clench of Barnet will perform an Organ with 3 Voices, the double Curtell, the Flute, and the Bells with the Mouth; the Huntsman, the Hounds, and the Pack of Dogs. With vaulting on the Horse. A Dance between two French-Men and two French-Women, and other Dances. And Monsieur Serene [Sorin] and another Person lately arrived in England [Richard Baxter?], will perform a *Night Scene* by a Harlequin and a Scaramouch, after the Italian manner. And Mr Pinkethman will speak his last new Vacation Epilogue."[33] The sheer number and consistency of references to vaulting on the horse, extraordinary musical feats, outlandish deliveries of epilogues, and wondrous dances sprinkled throughout the bills in this period signal public enthusiasm for such varied and bizarre devices. An unadorned Shakespearian comedy would hold little weight amid other choices for entertainment.

The combinations of entertainments in the theaters closely resemble the victuals offered at Bartholomew Fair in August of 1702, such as the advertisement for Rope Dancing "by the Famous Company of Rope-Dancers, they being the greatest Performers of Men, Women and Children that can be found beyond the Seas, so that the World cannot paralize them for dancing on the Low-Rope, Vaulting on the High-Rope, and for walking on the Slack, and Sloaping Ropes, out-doing all others to that Degree, that it has highly recommended them, both in Bartholomew Fair and May Fair last, to all the best persons of Quality in England. And by all are owned to be the only amasing Wonders of the World, in every thing they do: 'tis there you will see the Italian Scarramouch dancing on the Rope, with a Wheel-barrow before him, with two Children and a Dog in it, and with a Duck on his Head, who sings to the Company and causes much Laughter."[34] The similarities between fair and theater offerings brought these two venues into closer competition for audiences.[35] This rivalry affected the dramatic output of theaters, diverting attention from the traditional five-act play to focus on ephemeral allurements.

In the early eighteenth century, alternative sources of entertainment such as the fairs were often more popular than the theaters, and at times took the lead in charting audience taste.[36] The author of *A Comparison Between the Two Stages* notes that "Very little difference appear'd between [Drury Lane] and the Theatre at the Bear Garden," a venue for entertainment "dedicated originally to Bull-baiting, Bear-baiting, Prize-fighting, and all other Sorts of *Rough Game*."[37] Christopher Rich was particularly susceptible to drawing on the fairs and nondramatic performances for his offerings; Cibber points out that Rich's "Point was to please the Majority, who could more easily comprehend any thing they *saw* than the daintiest things that could be said to them" (*Apology*, 2:6). The physicality of fair entertainments, from tumblers to rope dancers, provided the sufficient stimulation for audiences of the day. If we can believe Cibber, verbal nuances escaped the notice of most spectators, who sought pleasure in extravagant visual delights instead of verbal subtleties. One can easily see how the poetry of Shakespeare would have been a low-ranking priority here. Instead of offering more new plays, theater managers turned instead to these auxiliary entertainments to embellish their dramatic offerings.

Economic realities dictated theatrical offerings, and the reception history of Shakespeare's comedies was shaped by these circumstances. In the first decade of the eighteenth century, Shakespearian comedies are noticeably scarce in the theatrical repertoire.[38] Except for *The Tempest* and *Sauny the Scott*, the other comedies do not appear to have been well-received as either revivals of originals or as adaptations. In fact, the only comedies with recorded performances in the early years of the eighteenth century are *The Merry Wives of Windsor* (Shakespeare's version and John Dennis's *The Comical Gallant*), *Twelfth Night* (as William Burnaby's *Love Betray'd*), *A Midsummer Night's Dream* (as Purcell's *The Fairy-Queen*), *The Tempest* (1674 operatic version), *The Taming of the Shrew* (as *Sauny the Scott*), *Measure for Measure* (Charles Gildon's adaptation), and *The Merchant of Venice* (as George Granville's *The Jew of Venice*).[39] As we shall see in this chapter, none of the four comedies adapted in the early eighteenth century (by Gildon, Granville, Dennis, and Burnaby) was a phenomenal success, but Shakespeare's original comedies were not popular either. In their unadapted form, the comedies suited neither taste for extradramatic entertainments nor for foreign performers, and Shakespeare's name held little clout otherwise.

Lincoln's Inn Fields offered three of the four early eighteenth-century comic adaptations: Gildon's *Measure for Measure* in 1700, Granville's *The Jew of Venice* in 1701, and Burnaby's *Love Betray'd* in 1703. John Dennis's *The Comical Gallant* (1702) was the only adaptation at Drury Lane.[40] In the early 1700s, Rich put on several English operas (*The Prophetess*, *The Island Princess*, *The Tempest*, and *King Arthur*), which seems to have been his strategy, rather than turning to Shakespeare. After these four attempts, there were no new adaptations of Shakespearian comedy until 1716, the subject of chapter 4.

Shakespeare's works as a whole were not in decline, since most of the tragedies and their adaptations enjoyed relative popularity.[41] Audiences seemed to have different expectations for tragedy than for comedy, perhaps because the tragedies are less amenable to additions of extensive spectacle or ladder dances. Comedy, however, has more of a connection with topical events and can handle extra additions; *The Fairy-Queen* discussed in the previous chapter is a case in point. We can look to the adjustments made to Shakespeare's originals for evidence of how the comedies had to be reshaped, and these shifts match other forms of entertainment and comic structures, which had little to do with ideas of how a Shakespeare play (at least, a comedy) should be performed. In the Dorset Garden spectaculars from the previous chapter, Shakespeare's plots provided the basis for visual and aural extravagances, but a bleaker period for English comedy at the turn of the eighteenth century brought modifications necessitated by changes in theatrical facilities. Without Dorset Garden at his disposal, Betterton had to change his performance strategy regardless of audience demand, resulting in musical offerings on a smaller scale, like the masques included with *Measure for Measure*, *The Jew of Venice* and *Love Betray'd*. Changing taste in comedy also affected dramatic output; as comedy shifted toward more humane and amiable models, Dennis and Burnaby adjusted Shakespeare's material to fit these forms. In addition to participating in developing forms of comedy, these plays feature prominent breeches parts: Captain Dingboy in *The Comical Gallant*, Portia in *The Jew of Venice*, and Cesario in *Love Betray'd*, tapping into the same taste we saw earlier for the dancing/singing Moll Davis in *The Law Against Lovers*.[42]

Theatrical warfare, fickle audiences who often preferred rope-dancing to five-act plays, predominant fair entertainments and a growing new contingent of authors provide a necessary context for analyzing the changes made to Shakespearian comedy. These adaptations show both the effect of theatrical changes on Shakespearian comedy around 1700 and what little impact Shakespearian comedy had on the theatrical repertoire, especially compared with earlier plays like the 1674 *Tempest*. *Hamlet* may have held the stage consistently in the late seventeenth and early eighteenth centuries, but no comedy could match that record.

It has often been assumed that eighteenth-century adapters sought to regularize Shakespeare's plays and make them conform to Aristotelian rules, but this is not borne out by evidence from the plays. Concern for rules occupied a growing body of dramatic criticism in the early eighteenth century, but rules were frequently abandoned in dramatic practice, or at least were not a high priority in competing for audiences. As early as the 1660s, disagreement surfaced about the applicability of rules. Sir Robert Howard criticized writers who "have labour'd to give strict rules to things that are not Mathematical." Similarly, Samuel Cobb remarked that "an over-curious Study of being correct, enervates the Vigour of the Mind, slackens the Spirits, and cramps the Genius of a *Free Writer*." Elkanah Settle denounced French authors for cramping the English style with concern for rules: "For as Delight is the great End of Playing, and those narrow Stage-restrictions of *Corneille* destroy that Delight, by curtailing that Variety that should give it us; every such Rule therefore is Nonsense and Contradiction in its very Foundation."[43]

Indeed, writers for the stage in the early eighteenth century recognized audiences' lack of concern for rules. "Now 'tis not Sense, and Wit best entertains," commented Thomas Baker, "Nor what's writ most by Rule, most Favour gains." Susannah Centlivre corroborates the unimportance of rules for theatrical success: "The Criticks cavil most about Decorums, and crie up *Aristotle*'s Rules as the most essential part of the Play; I own they are in the right of it, yet I dare venture a Wager they'll never persuade the Town to be of their Opinion, which relishes nothing so well as Humour lightly tost up with Wit, and drest with Modesty and Air." Humor, wit, variety: all were aspects of comedy preferable to a regularized play. Conscious of the power of audience favor, Thomas Scott advised writers otherwise: "They who pretend to write by Rule, and at the same time hope to divert the Town, will, I fear, have little more than their Labour for their Pains." Farquhar's humorous picture of the scholar writing the perfect regular play according to all the rules, with no music or dance, little substance for the actors, and no variety, ends with the following result for the scholar-playwright: "the *Patentees* rail at him, the Players Curse him, the Town damns him, and he may bury his Copy in *Pauls*, for not a Bookseller about it will put it in Print."[44] Early eighteenth-century audiences would pay for diverting entertainments, but not necessarily for methodical writing. Regularizing Shakespeare's plays to conform to the rules would have been a useless task in light of the relative unimportance of rules compared to other aspects.

What, then, had to be done to craft a successful play? Farquhar posed the same question: "How must this Secret of pleasing so many different Tastes be discovered?" His answer is important for understanding why and how Shakespeare's comedies were adapted; theatrical success ensues "Not by tumbling over Volumes of the Ancients, but by studying the Humour of the Moderns: The Rules of *English* Comedy don't lie in the Compass of *Aristotle*, or his Followers, but in the Pit, Box, and Galleries." A successful comedy caters to current public taste, not rules. As Charles Gildon put it, a successful playwright "must Study his Audience, as well as the Rules."[45]

The adaptations of Shakespeare in the early eighteenth century reflect this mandate to satisfy audiences above and beyond regularizing or adjusting the plays to rules of dramatic writing. Although most of these adaptations were not particularly well-received (with the exception of Granville's *The Jew*), they do show the relative importance (or unimportance) of Shakespeare's name value and the lack of interest in original Shakespearian comedy compared to other components of popular taste. In general, the two earlier adaptations have an increased emphasis on music and spectacle (they both include elaborate masques) in keeping with theatrical trends of the late seventeenth century. The latter two adaptations place less emphasis on entertainments included within the plays (Burnaby's masque is not printed in his text, and Dennis simply embellishes a scene already present in Shakespeare), responding instead to changing taste within the genre of comedy itself. It perhaps was some consolation to the adapters, that no original Shakespearian comedy fared much better than the adapted versions. This period in the history of Shakespeare's reputation illustrates subtle shifts in the construction of the "National Poet" traced by Michael Dobson. In the climate of the early eighteenth-century theater, the comedies were not greeted with overwhelming acclaim, even with Shakespeare's name attached.[46]

Charles Gildon's *Measure for Measure* (1700)

The first adaptation of Shakespearian comic material in the eighteenth century was Charles Gildon's *Measure for Measure, or Beauty the Best Advocate*, presented at Lincoln's Inn Fields in 1700 as part of Betterton's "theatrical warfare" with Drury Lane.[47] The author of *A Comparison Between the Two Stages* (1702) places Gildon's adaptation squarely in the middle of this battle: "Well, this lucky hit of *B[e]tterton's* put *D. Lane* to a non-plus: *Shakespeare's* Ghost was rais'd at the New-house, and he seem'd to inhabit it for ever: What's to be done then?" The strategy of Drury Lane was to counterattack with the works of another old playwright, Ben Jonson: "Then they fell to task on the *Fox*, the *Alchymist*, and *Silent Woman*, who had lain twenty Years in Peace, they drew up these in Battalia against *Harry* the 4th and *Harry* the 8th, and then the Fight began." This climate of warfare and struggle for audience support produced Gildon's adaptation as a strategy to draw audiences. "The Battel continued a long time doubtful, and Victory hovering over both Camps, B[e]tterton Sollicits for some Auxiliaries from the same Author, and then he flanks his Enemy with *Measure* for *Measure*" (26–27). Gildon saw Shakespeare's play as appropriate ammunition in a period that demanded drastic techniques to attract audiences.

Cibber comments in 1701 that the "Complaints, and Hardships of the Stage in general" have caused the stage to be in "need of able Friends" now more than ever. Reformers such as Jeremy Collier contributed to a hostile theatrical atmosphere, and the costly demands of exotic entertainers were a further burden on theaters.[48] Betterton needed a hit play for the survival of his theater, and Gildon needed a hit play for his own survival. One contemporary described Gildon as "the needy *Gil—n*," and his career comprised a series of moderately successful (at best) theater pieces and a number of critical writings, notably in retaliation to Thomas Rymer.[49] Gildon experimented with a variety of play types with little prosperity: *The Younger Brother; or The Amorous Jilt* (1696), a failed adaptation of Aphra Behn's play; *The Roman Bride's Revenge* (1697), a hastily written tragedy; *Phaeton, or The Fatal Divorce* (1698), a classical tragedy; his Shakespeare adaptation *Measure for Measure*, with a modest eight performances; *Love's Victim* (1701), a tragedy and his most successful work; and *The Patriot* (1702), an adaptation of Lee's *Lucius Junius Brutus*. Gildon was often linked to fellow critic and Shakespearian adapter John Dennis, especially in the latter part of his career, and Dennis penned the prologue to Gildon's *The Patriot*.[50] Both writers were satirized in the pamphlet *A New Project for the Regulation of the Stage* (1720) and Aaron Hill's 1716 tragedy *The Fatal Vision* was dedicated to both writers, describing them as "Great in *Knowledge*: Men who, through the Gloom of Fortune's *Shade*, shine out, to the impartial Eye, with native Lustre." Gildon looked to Dennis as his model and called him "my Master."[51]

Like Dennis, Gildon's concern for public taste and aesthetic value is evident in his polemical writings: "for when bad Poets find the highest favour, and the greatest reward, in its consequence it imposes silence upon men of merit in the art, who, unless they can take the same slavish methods to success which the poetasters pursue, they are sure to have their works slighted, if not entirely condemn'd."[52] Gildon realized the power of audience response and its effect on the predicament of literary works; artistic merit was not always rewarded, nor was it necessarily an accurate indicator of theatrical success. Gildon's phrase "th' exactest Play / Must to a long and well writ Bill give Way" aptly describes the priorities of audiences who were drawn to advertised variety, not exactitude of rules.[53]

Because he needed financial stability, Gildon's own writings often respond more to local theatrical conditions than to the aesthetic principles he advocated in his critical writings. Even though he was a firm believer in neoclassical rules, Gildon recognized the need to respond to audience taste, admitting that "an *English* Audience will never be pleas'd with a dry, Jejune and formal Method [that] excludes Variety as the Religious observation of the Rules of *Aristotle* does." Strict adherence to neoclassical rules is associated with dry formality, religious inflexibility, and lack of variety. A writer who will not customize his plays to English tastes "may please himself, but never the public."[54] In keeping with this attitude, Gildon's adaptation of Shakespeare prioritizes popular elements over adherence to rules, a position that may have led him to defend Shakespeare. Had Shakespeare known the rules, Gildon argued, he would have been "a very dangerous rival in Fame, to the greatest Poets of Antiquity."[55]

Writers who professed allegiance to the unities ran into trouble with the works of Shakespeare.[56] Gildon himself was the author of many statements regarding the importance of rules in governing taste, most notably his "Remarks on the Plays of Shakespeare" (1710) appended to Rowe's edition. Here he confesses that "in spite of his known and fisable Errors, when I read Shakespeare, even in some of his most irregular Plays, I am surpriz'd into a Pleasure so great, that my Judgment is no longer free to see the Faults, tho' they are never so Gross and Evident. There is such a Witchery in him, that all the Rules of Art, which he does not observe, tho' built on an equally Solid and Infallible Reason, vanish away in the Transports of those, that he does observe, so entirely, as if I had never known any thing of the Matter" (v). Shakespeare seemed to charm Gildon into abandoning his critical doctrine and defending the Stratford playwright. The debate over Shakespeare's knowledge of the rules involved numerous commentators in the eighteenth century, many of whom agreed with the Duke of Buckingham in his "An Essay Upon Poetry" (1682), that the goal was to "Imitate" the beauties of Shakespeare and Fletcher, and "avoid their faults" (15).[57]

Gildon's work articulates his belief in disciplined writing as a way of cultivating taste in the dramatic arts, but his treatment of Shakespeare repudiates an unqualified commitment to rules in dramatic practice. When he turns to write for the stage, he realizes the constrictions and restraints created by rules that ultimately may not appease audiences, conceding that playwrights must satisfy "the Folly and abandon'd Taste of the Town."[58] As an early biographer described Gildon's career, "Necessity was the first Motive of his venturing to be an Author."[59] The power of paying spectators overrode critical concern for formulaic strictures. Other playwrights realized this issue as well. Farquhar's success with *The Constant Couple: or A Trip to the Jubilee* (1699) provides a useful corrective to overemphasis on rules. Susannah Centlivre attests that "I believe *Mr. Rich* will own, he got more by the *Trip to the Jubilee*, with all its Irregularities, than by the most uniform Piece the Stage cou'd boast of e'er since."[60] Farquhar's prosperity reinforces the importance of popular taste at the expense of strict dramatic formulae.

Adherence to rules failed to guarantee an audience, but Shakespeare's name still had little drawing power either. In his dedication, Gildon promotes his *Measure for Measure* as "much more *Shakespears* than Mine," offering it as "originally" Shakespeare's and now "very much Alter'd," an old play adorned with fresh music and entertainment. In a period when most completely "new" plays failed, it was a wise strategy to advertise this piece as a revamped old play. Even though the ghost of Shakespeare speaks the prologue, the Shakespearian canon was apparently not well-recognized. The advertisement accompanying Gildon's *Love's Victim* (1701) reads, "Measure for Measure a Comedy alter'd from *Beaumont & Fletcher* by Mr. *Gildon*." A second misattribution of the play attests to the lack of familiarity with Shakespeare's oeuvre. A 1706 performance of Gildon's *Measure for Measure* was announced as "Written by the famous Beaumont and Fletcher."[61] Advertisements often differentiated old from new, but dramatic plots, at least of the comedies, were apparently not so recognizable.

Gildon's adaptation has many similarities to other successful theatre pieces. On his title page, Gildon announces his design of combining a Shakespearian comedy with the music of a popular composer: "Written *Originally* by Mr. *Shakespear*: And now very much Alter'd; With *Additions* of several *Entertainments* of *MUSICK*." Most discussions of Gildon's play have focussed on his changes to Shakespeare, but surprisingly little attention has been paid to his use of music: his key strategy for theatrical success. Using Shakespeare's play as a frame, Gildon splits Purcell's opera *Dido and Aeneas* (with a libretto by Nahum Tate) into several masque entertainments for the character of Angelo. This disembodied masque was the main attraction for Gildon's audience as well as the primary impetus for his adaptation—to shape an old play around the type of musical entertainment that would lure audiences.[62]

When he adapted *Measure for Measure*, Gildon followed the pattern of *The Fairy-Queen*, which united a Shakespearian play with Purcell's music, and Ravenscroft's *The Anatomist* (1697), which included Motteux's masque *The Loves of Mars and Venus*. Just before his adaptation of Shakespeare came out, Gildon himself praised *The Anatomist* and was obviously aware of its successful formula: "This play met with extraordinary Success having the Advantage of the excellent Musick of *The Loves of Mars and Venus* perform'd with it."[63]

Not only did Gildon turn to an old play for his work, he also turned to an old musical composition to revamp in a new format. *Dido and Aeneas* was Purcell's only through-composed opera (all dialogue is sung) and has been acclaimed as "the greatest operatic achievement of the English seventeenth century."[64] Its first recorded performance took place in the 1680s at Josias Priest's Chelsea boarding school for girls, although this probably was not the first performance.[65] Priest was an active member of the London theatrical scene as a dancer at Drury Lane; he created the dances for the 1673 *Macbeth* at Dorset Garden, at least one dance for *The Fairy-Queen*, as well as the choreography for Crowne's *Calisto* in 1675.[66]

Purcell's musical piece had appealing features; *Dido and Aeneas* was performed as a separate masque in 1704 (29 January and 8 April) at Lincoln's Inn Fields, and may have even been performed again with *Measure for Measure* in 1706.[67] Gildon's package of entertainment was comprised of pieces culled from various sources, and it actually included little new material. Shakespeare was not the only older source; Nahum Tate's libretto to *Dido and Aeneas* recycles material from his earlier work *Brutus of Alba* (1678), which derives from Virgil's *Aeneid*. Tate's use of Virgil as well as seventeenth-century texts adds another layer to the heritage of plots and characters involved here. In addition to the libretto's roots in earlier sources, Purcell's music also looked backward in its use of traditional English styles for composition.[68] Thus, the whole production of *Measure for Measure* drew on older forms of entertainment, from Shakespeare's source play, to Virgil's poem, to Purcell's traditional English music. Rather than provide a risky entertainment and experiment with something new, Gildon's offering was essentially conservative, drawing on musical and dramatic elements that had already proven successful.

Playwrights were not only willing to cobble together Shakespeare's plays (as did Davenant and later Charles Johnson), they also crossed the bounds of formal entertainments to construct an amalgamation of opera and drama in a single theatrical offering. Gildon's adaptation was written at a time when all-sung opera was practically unknown in London.[69] Playwrights sought ways to include enough music within their dramatic texts to satisfy audiences, but this meant also being careful not to overwhelm dramatic content or action. Thus, Gildon separates dramatic and operatic entertainments in terms of characters and casting (no character or actor from *Measure for Measure* doubles in *Dido and Aeneas*).[70] He integrates *Dido and Aeneas* and *Measure for Measure*, making the musical interpolations reflect the plot of the play. As we shall see, by parceling out *Dido and Aeneas* in three separate entertainments, Gildon uses Angelo's reactions to this opera to provide insight into his character, combining music and drama in an innovative fashion geared to an audience who appreciated both components.

The prologue to Gildon's play, written by John Oldmixon and spoken by Betterton, was designed for an audience that demanded revised old plays and new entertainments but was quick to denounce both:

> To please this Winter, we all Meanes have us'd;
> Old *Playes* have been Reviv'd, and New Produc'd.
> But you, it seems, by *Us*, wou'd not be Serv'd;
> And others Thrive, while we were almost Starv'd.[71]

Oldmixon's prologue reflects the desperate nature of theaters in the early eighteenth century, and points out the current fancy for spectacle, dance and music to which playwrights responded:

> Let neither *Dance*, nor *Musick* be forgot,
> Nor *Scenes*, no matter for the *Sense*, or *Plot*.
> Such things we own in *Shakespears* days might do;
> But then his Audience did not Judge like you.

Oldmixon looks to the past of "Shakespeare's day" as a blissful period when sense or plot supposedly determined artistic success, and not expensive show and spectacle. Oldmixon's statement calls to mind the layers of dance, music, and scenery in *The Fairy-Queen*, Purcell's most elaborate and expensive semi-opera that highlighted the willingness of the United Company to include these elements despite the cost.[72] Regardless of the expense incurred, dance, music, and scenic elements had become prerequisites for audiences. After getting in a dig at Farquhar for his recent success with *The Constant Couple* at Drury Lane, Oldmixon advises playwrights to "Study the *Smithfield-Bards*" to please current audience taste, abruptly adding: "Hold; I forgot the Business of the Day; / No more than this, We, for our Selves, need Say, / 'Tis *Purcels* Musick, and 'tis *Shakespears* Play." This prologue underlines the melange of ingredients aimed at satisfying an even more demanding public; the names of "Shakespeare" and "Purcell" were not enough.

Gildon's epilogue further connected his play to its local theatrical environment. He enlists Shakespeare's ghost to criticize the current state of the theaters: "My *Ghost* can bear no more; but comes to Rage" because "My *Plays*, by *Scriblers*, Mangl'd I have seen; / By Lifeless *Actors* Murder'd on the *Scene*." Writers and actors are condemned, notably the "scriblers," even though as we have seen, "necessity" was "needy" Gildon's own initial motivation to write, and one source describes him as a "Whig scribbler" and hack writer.[73] Nevertheless, his employment of Shakespeare to rehabilitate the stage is an early instance of engaging Shakespeare as an authority on taste who urges,

> Let me no more endure such Mighty Wrongs,
> By *Scriblers* Folly, or by *Actors* Lungs.
> So, late may *Betterton* forsake the *Stage*,
> And long may *Barry* Live to Charm the *Age*.

Shakespeare scorns mistreatment by scribblers or inept actors, and demands high quality treatment for his plays. A recent incident involving David Crauford's *Courtship A-la-mode* in 1700 provides justification for the complaints against the company at Lincoln's Inn Fields. Apparently, Crauford's play spent six weeks in rehearsal and was still not up to par. As he explains in the play's preface, "finding that six or seven people cou'd not perform what was design'd for fifteen," he withdrew it "after so many sham Rehearsals, and in two days it got footing upon the other Stage." Fortunately for Gildon, his play did not receive such treatment; Betterton played Angelo, and Mrs. Bracegirdle played Isabella.[74]

If we are to believe the author of *A Comparison Between the Two Stages*, Betterton approached Shakespeare with almost religious veneration. Seeking to improve his theater's finances, "he enters his Closset, and falls down on his knees, and Prays. O Shakespear, Shakespear! *What have our Sins brought upon us! We have renounc'd the wayes which thou has taught us, and are degenerated into Infamy and Corruption: Look down from thy Throne . . . let thy Spirit dwell with us, . . . let the Streams of thy* Helicon *glide along by* Lincolns-Inn-Fields, *and fructifie our Soil*." After this prayer, "He rose, and rose much comforted: With that he falls to work about his Design, opens the Volume and picks out two or three of *Shakespears* Plays" (25). This amusing scenario accords Betterton more responsibility for reviving Shakespeare than surviving records support. Other than his esteemed Falstaff in *Henry the Fourth*, Shakespeare was not a prominent part of Betterton's comic repertoire at Lincoln's Inn Fields. Although Betterton may have turned to Shakespeare for dramatic inspiration, Gildon's adaptation was one of few performances in the early years of the eighteenth century.

Ben Jonson receives similar treatment by the author of *A Comparison*

Between the Two Stages; Betterton's competitor Rich decides to "pray as well as he" and summons the ghost of Ben Jonson: "with that Mr. R⎯⎯⎯ goes up to the Garret . . . and taking *Ben. Johnson*'s Picture with him, he implores—. *Most mighty* Ben! . . . The Picture seem'd to Nod, which was a token of consent, up he rose, and very devoutly return'd the charitable Image to its place in his own *Theatre*. Then they fell to task on the *Fox*, the *Alchymist*, and *Silent Woman* . . . they drew up these in Battalia against *Harry* the 4th and *Harry* the 8th, and then the Fight began" (26). Shakespeare and Ben Jonson are here accorded equivalent positions in the competition between theaters, though theatrical records do not show that either writer's plays were especially influential.[75] Still, in the early eighteenth century Shakespeare and Jonson began to be used to signify authority aside from their plays' success or failure on stage.

Returning to Gildon's play, we can see that his priority was a theatrical hit, and he looks back to previous stage versions of Shakespeare's play for indications of audience taste. Like the musical and operatic *Tempests* that built on the play's stage history, this version of *Measure for Measure* similarly takes into account how earlier playwrights had adjusted Shakespeare's play, especially Davenant in *The Law Against Lovers*. John Genest notes that "from Davenant Gildon has borrowed whatever suited him, but without any acknowledgment."[76] Gildon's primary motive was to stage a successful production; whether it owed more to Shakespeare or to Davenant was irrelevant to him and to his audience alike.

Following Davenant, Gildon sets *Measure for Measure* in Turin. He removes the *Much Ado About Nothing* material that Davenant had added, except for Balthazar in the first scene, and restores Mariana from Shakespeare's original. The addition of Purcell's opera necessitated trimming elsewhere; thus Gildon shortens Shakespeare's sixteen scenes to nine, and omits the comic characters to make room for the music.[77] A representative example of Angelo's soliloquy at the end of the first act illustrates Gildon's fusion of Shakespeare and Davenant. Gildon combines Davenant's version of the speech:

> I love her virtue. But, temptation! O!
> Thou false and cunning guide! who in disguise
> Of Virtues shape lead'st us through Heaven to Hell.
> No vitious Beauty could with practis'd Art
> Subdue, like Virgin-innocence, my heart. (287)

with Shakespeare's version:

> From thee: even from thy virtue.
> What's this? what's this? Is this her fault, or mine?

> The tempter, or the tempted, who sins most, ha?
> Not she, nor doth she tempt; but it is I
> . . . .
> O fie, fie, fie!
> What dost thou? or what art thou, Angelo?
> Dost thou desire her foully for those things
> That make her good?
>
> (2.2.161–64, 171–74)

The result is an amalgamation of the two:

> What's this I feel? Is it her fault or mine?
> The Tempter, or the Tempted? Who sins most? Ha!
> Not She; nor does She Tempt, but it is I,
> . . . .
> Oh! fie! fie! fie! What dost thou *Angelo*?
> Is it her Virtue, that thou lov'st? oh! no!
> Thou false and deluding Guide, who in Disguise
> Of Virtues shape, leadst us thro' Heav'n to Hell!
> No Vicious Beauty cou'd with Practis'd Art,
> Subdue my Heart like Virgin Innocence. (6–7)

Other adaptations such as the 1674 *Tempest* employ a similar strategy of drawing on a variety of versions in addition to Shakespeare's original play, and the two *Cobler of Preston* afterpieces discussed in the next chapter utilize the same technique of pulling together a number of successful plots to enhance Shakespeare's material from *The Taming of the Shrew*. Restoration and eighteenth-century adaptations of Shakespeare's plays were created within a context of dramatic material that influenced adapters in addition to Shakespeare's works, and Gildon's play corroborates this practice.

The integration of drama and music in Gildon's play makes it one of the most interesting configurations of Shakespearian material. The music is not merely entr'acte filler; it is organic to the plot, facilitating the development of Angelo's character. Gildon restructures the play to focus mainly on Isabella and Angelo, a much darker and more sinister character than in Shakespeare's version, and uses Purcell's opera to explore the pivotal moments for Angelo. Gildon devises a layered visual scene, with the audience viewing *Dido and Aeneas* but also observing Angelo's reaction to this performance.

An additional aspect of Gildon's craft is his inclusion of a performance situation that reconstructs a contemporary reaction to a musical offering. Purcell's music is supposed to inspire reform in Angelo and make him recant his lecherous designs on Isabella's virtue. As we shall see, Purcell's music inspires Angelo in exactly the wrong way and arouses his desire.[78] Through this scenario, Gildon explores the issue of how to control audience reactions, and taps into a contemporary controversy about the corrupting properties of music. In the tract *A Scourge for the Play-Houses: or, the Character of the English-Stage* (1702), Richard Burridge claims that the music of Purcell has the power to lead listeners astray, and his description is strikingly similar to the effect of Purcell's music on Angelo: "*Purcel*'s Train play'd on several sorts of Instruments; whose Mischievous Harmony inspiring the Auditors with Lust, and Imaginations of Visionary Joys, raised such Optious Desires in their roving Thoughts, as made them Mad to run over all the Women in the House" (9). Later reformers developed this idea; Arthur Bedford warns that "Where there are *soft Chromatick Notes joyn'd with a flat Key*, in order to strike gently upon the Passions together with their Strings, they are designed to usher in something that is immodest, or at least to stir up *Lust*."[79] These accounts epitomize the effect of music on Angelo, and Gildon's play enacts this fear of the harmful power of music.

Gildon integrates Purcell's opera to entertain Angelo in the first three acts, followed each time with brief dramatic action, and then an entertainment to conclude the play. The first part of Purcell's opera is inserted at the end of Act 1. After Isabella exits, Angelo tries to get her off his mind with an entertainment: "I'll think no more on't, but with Musick chase / Away the Guilty Image." Angelo tells Escalus, "if your Diversions now are ready / I am dispos'd to see 'em." We then see a grieving Dido, who is consoled to "Banish Sorrow, Banish Care" and takes solace in the reassurance that "The Hero Loves as well as you." Dido laments the "Storms of Care" that "oppress her heart," and Aeneas utters a sentiment reminiscent of Angelo's situation with Isabella: "Some pity on your Lover take" and "defie, / The feeble stroke of Destiny" (7–8). Angelo immediately identifies with Aeneas's plight:

> This Musick is no Cure for my Distemper;
> For, every Note, to my Enchanted Ears,
> Seem'd to Sing only *Isabella*'s Beauty,
> Her Youth, her Beauty, and her Tender Pity
> Combine to ruin me! (9)

As the moral reformers feared, music could corrupt as well as soothe. The masque intended as a diversion for Angelo's desire fails to control his lust and instead kindles his baser instincts.

The next operatic interlude occurs in the second act, after Isabella has refused to submit to Angelo. He tells her, "If you will partake, / Go with me to the Hall, where now they wait me," instructing her to "Consider on it, and at Ten this Evening; / If you'll comply, you'll meet me at the *Opera*" (12–13). Isabella refuses, and Angelo must watch the second entertainment on his own, contemplating her rejection as he observes Dido's fate. Here Gildon inserts the second act of Purcell's opera, with the hunting party, the counterfeit spirit Mercury's order for Aeneas to leave Dido, and Dido's ruin. "The *Spirit* of the *Sorceress* descends to *Æneas* in likeness of *Mercury*," telling him that Jove commands he depart. Aeneas capitulates, "Jove's Commands shall be Obey'd," but laments, "What Language can I try, / My injur'd Queen to pacify?" (14). Aeneas asks, "Ye Sacred Powers instruct me how to choose, / When Love or Empire I must lose" (15), followed by a dance.

Gildon transposes Tate's two scenes in Act 2 of the masque, creating a spectacular scene reminiscent of earlier Dorset Garden extravaganzas: after the dance at the end of the grove scene, Gildon immediately segues to the cave scene, with the cave rising and the witches appearing. His transposition makes perfect sense visually, because this machinery would certainly be more impressive at the end of the scene than in the middle.[80] Gildon changes a dance of Fairies in the 1689 version to a dance of Furies, probably calling to mind the witches that were successful in *Macbeth* and in Shadwell's *The Lancashire Witches* (1681), and also consistent with the more serious tone of *Measure for Measure*.[81]

Angelo confesses that the entertainment has again made his situation worse:

> All will not do: All won't d[i]vert my Pain.
> The Wound enlarges by these Medicines,
> 'Tis She alone can yield the Healing Balm.
> This Scene just hits my case; her Brothers danger,
> Is here the storm must furnish Blest Occasion;
> And when, my Dido, I've Possess'd thy Charms,
> I then will throw thee from my glutted Arms,
> And think no more on all thy soothing Harms. (16)

As the audience must have noticed while watching the production, the entertainment designed as a diversion for Angelo has instead aroused him, and the music becomes a catalyst in the action. Angelo equates Isabella with Dido, and the "Medicines" of the opera have begun to work, only not in the intended fashion. Furthermore, Aeneas's abdication of his commitment to Dido parallels Angelo's treatment of Mariana. While satisfying his audience with musical additions, Gildon also demonstrates the power of music to transform, distract, and convert listeners.

The third entertainment is intended to help Angelo sleep at the end of the third act. Escalus tells him, "My Lord, if we have not tir'd you to day / With our harmonious and officious Love, / I hope you will partake this last Effort, / That may compose your Thoughts for pleasing Slumbers." Angelo replies, still thinking of Isabella's impending arrival: "Let them begin:—No *Isabella* yet?" (26). The stage directions indicate that "*Before 'tis quite done*, Isabella *enters*," presumably at an opportune time in the story. After such distractions as a sailors' dance and a dance of wizards and witches, we encounter the plot to destroy Dido. She reproaches Aeneas, "All that's Good you have forswore. / To your promis'd Empire fly, / And let forsaken *Dido* dye" and vows that "Death is now a welcome Guest" (27–28). Here again the plots collide; as Dido dies of shame at losing her chastity, Isabella is faced with a similar decision. In Gildon's version, Isabella refuses to yield her "honor" to shame, not her "body" as in Shakespeare. This resonates with Dido's situation, and creates sympathy for Isabella as we view the mournful Dido. Angelo's callous reaction to Dido's dilemma makes him all the more reprehensible in this version.

Tate's libretto does not provide a clear exposition of Dido's death, but Price suggests that she enters into "an immoral sexual liaison for which she must ultimately pay." As Harris points out, the moral of *Dido and Aeneas* "is that young girls should not accept the advances of young men no matter how ardent their wooing or how persistent their promises"; Dido must die once she loses her chastity.[82] The juxtaposition of these two plots encourages pity for Isabella, and Angelo appears even more villainous. When the entertainment is over, Angelo immediately addresses her. The last thing on his mind is the slumber the masque was intended to induce, and he can only think of leaving with Isabella as quickly as possible. She must have appeared on stage at the moment Dido spoke of her death, because Angelo's next words are:

> I see my Ev'ning Star of Love appear,
> This is no place to try my last Effort;
> . . . .
> This is no place to hear you; follow me.
> Now my kind Stars assist my fierce Desires
> I ask no other Influence from your fires
> O! Love! how much thy borrow'd shapes disguise,
> Ev'n to themselves, the Valiant and the Wise. (28)

Again, the music fails to put Angelo at rest and instead stimulates his libidinous feelings for Isabella.

In the fourth act, Gildon's Angelo imitates Davenant's character and offers jewels to Isabella, but Gildon's heroine accepts the jewels and gives them to Mariana "as *Mariana*'s due, / And as a proof he cannot sure deny" (30). In the fifth act, Gildon follows Shakespeare's bed trick, but when Mariana accuses Angelo, the Duke asks Mariana to "Produce that Casket" and interrogates Angelo, "Know you, Sir, those Jewels?" The Duke insinuates that he may marry Isabella, "Come hither, *Isabella*. / Your Fryer's now your Prince" (42). He later adds, "Give me your hand, and say you will be mine" (44). Gildon includes a final entertainment at the end of the play, which begins in typical extravagant fashion as *"Phoebus* Rises in his Chariot over the Sea" (45) and includes the variety that so often pleased spectators: a dialogue between shepherds and shepherdesses, a duet between Mars and Peace, morris dancers, a dance between Spring and nymphs, and a concluding dance involving all of the characters. This section is embellished from the 1689 version of *Dido*, and attempts to provide the multiplicity of entertainment that we saw with the Purcell *Fairy-Queen*, concluding with a masque.[83] His use of music to alter a dramatic character is an important change from earlier Shakespearian comedies with music, particularly the recent *Fairy-Queen*, where the characters are not affected by the spectacular entertainments taking place on stage, and there is little connection between the Shakespearian plot and the visual extravaganza. Purcell's music does not alter or influence any of the characters' actions, except to amuse them. In contrast, Gildon uses Purcell's music to incite Angelo, and what takes place in *Dido and Aeneas* affects the outcome of the play.[84] When he adapted Shakespeare's comic material, Gildon recognized the current rage for music and structured his play around musical interludes to satisfy this demand.

Despite Gildon's ingenious melding of music and dramatic text, the records in *The London Stage* include only two performances of Gildon's play between 1700 and 1715.[85] Even with the operatic supplements to *Measure for Measure*, the combination of Shakespeare and Purcell did not produce the prosperity that Gildon should have achieved based on other successful offerings. The probable lukewarm reaction to Gildon's play may illustrate the capricious nature of audiences in the early eighteenth century, and the turbulent relationship between theater and its patrons. Gildon's play remains an important contribution to the reception history of Shakespeare because of its employment of the ghost of Shakespeare as a reformer of theater, its innovative incorporation of music within a dramatic structure, its exploration of prevailing ideas about the power of music to corrupt, its preference for popular elements over rules, and its conglomeration of material from Shakespeare and Davenant.

George Granville, Lord Lansdowne's
The Jew of Venice (1701)

In 1701, George Granville adapted a previously unperformed play, *The Merchant of Venice*, as *The Jew of Venice*, turning it into one of the more popular and enduring versions of Shakespearian comedy in the early eighteenth century. Edmund Curll provides an early account of its positive reception: "Our *excellent Bard* has indeed fared much better under the judicious Pen of Lord *Lansdowne*, whose JEW of *Venice*, preserves all that is valuable in the Original; suffers no Diminution, and is greatly improved."[86] Performance records corroborate Curll's opinion, and as late as 1715, Dudley Ryder, then a student at Middle Temple and later a Chief Justice, lent Granville's play to a friend to read, along with a sermon and Tickell's *Homer*, in exchange for Samuel Clarke's *Scripture Doctrine of the Trinity*.[87] Granville's play is the first adaptation to show clear signs of success since the 1674 *Tempest*.

Why did Granville turn to Shakespeare's play for revision, and what did he find there worth adapting? Granville used several strategies we have seen before to make Shakespearian comedy work on the early eighteenth-century stage, notably enhancing a role for a popular actor and updating it to encompass contemporary stereotypes (like Lacy's *Sauny the Scott*), and developing a musical component resembling the one in the recent *Measure for Measure*.

The Merchant of Venice was not performed in its original form until the later eighteenth century; Granville's adaptation was the only version available on the stage, appearing without Granville's name on the title page.[88] *The Jew of Venice* was one of the few successes for Lincoln's Inn Fields in a season of moderate prosperity. In the 1700–01 season, Betterton took over the company at Lincoln's Inn Fields. Although he apparently found success with new offerings including Granville's *The Jew of Venice*, Rowe's *The Ambitious Step-mother*, and Burnaby's *The Ladies-Visiting Day*, he was barely able to break even; it must have been some consolation that Drury Lane was not in much better shape.[89] Complaints from moral reformers about the stage, coupled with low revenues, created a less-than-welcoming atmosphere for new plays. A 1701 letter from William Morley to Thomas Coke (the Lord Chamberlain) depicts a dire situation: "I believe there is no poppet shew in a country town but takes more money than both the play houses. Yet you wonder that immorality and profaneness should reign so much as it does."[90] Despite the climate, Granville saw several opportunities in his source text for revision in this season, and the play worked on stage because of the talents of actor Thomas Doggett, the revamped role of Shylock as a stock-jobber and more central character in the play, and the additions of music in the form of a masque mixed in with the dramatic text.

Granville was attentive to the power of audience response; a passage from his earlier play *The She-Gallants* (1696) describes a disturbing audience reaction to a new play, even allowing for some exaggeration: "I'll tell you their Method: They spread themselves in Parties all over the House; some in the Pit, some in the Boxes, others in the Galleries, but principally on the Stage; they Cough, Sneeze, talk Loud, and break silly Jests; sometimes Laughing, sometimes Singing, sometimes Whistling, till the House is in an Uproar; some Laugh and Clap; some Hiss and are Angry; Swords are drawn, the Actors interrupted, the Scene broken off, and so the Play's sent to the Devil" (39–40). Granville realized the ability of audiences to control the fate of a play and he conceded, "Ladies and Beaus to please, is all the Task," vowing to "touch every sense and please every palate" by using a variety of stratagems in his dramatic writing.[91] Like Charles Gildon, when Granville turned to Shakespearian comic material as a source text, he kept this priority of pleasing audiences above other concerns.

As we shall see, the changes Granville made to this comic material would have come as no surprise to anyone familiar with the few successes this season. Music and dance continued to have a significant presence, as Granville was well aware: "in vain we write, / Unless the Musick and the Dance invite," he remarked in his epilogue to Boyle's *As You Find It* (1703). In fact, the main competition between the two theaters this season revolved around two semi-operas heavy with music and dance. Betterton offered Motteux's adaptation of Fletcher's *The Mad Lover* with music by Eccles and Daniel Purcell as competition with Drury Lane's *Alexander the Great*, an anonymous adaptation of Lee's *The Rival Queens* (1677) with music by Godfrey Finger and Daniel Purcell (the unpublished text is lost). Betterton's production was a failure, but the fact that theatrical rivalry occurred between semi-operas shows the perseverance of musical entertainment.

Also tapping into the proclivity for music, the old Dorset Garden theater offered a series of concerts and a music competition, which generated much attention and filled the theater, albeit not for a dramatic performance.[92] According to Congreve's description of this "Prize Musick," it must have been one of the central events of the season: "I don't think any one place in the world can show such an assembly. The number of performers, besides the verse-singers [soloists], was 85. The front of the stage was all built into a concave with deal boards; all which was faced with tin, to increase and throw forwards the sound. It was all hung with sconces of wax-candles, besides the common branches of lights usual in the play-houses . . . the whole expence of every thing being defrayed by the subscribers. I think truly the whole thing better worth coming to see than the jubilee."[93] Dorset Garden's musical offerings attracted an impressive crowd, and Betterton would have been interested in staging Granville's play in part because of its musical additions and its suitability for competition this season.

Music was no guarantee of success, however. In May of the 1701 season, the outcome of a major operatic endeavor at Drury Lane demonstrates the unstable audience taste of the period. *The Virgin Prophetess* was an elaborate opera advertised in the *Post-Boy* with much pomp: "Great Preparations have been making for some Months past, for a New Opera to be Acted next Term at the Theatre Royal, which, for Grandeur, Decorations, Movements of Scenes, &c. will be infinitely superior to *Dioclesian*, which hitherto has been the greatest that the English Stage has produced, that probably 'twill equal the greatest Performance of that Kind, in any of the foreign Theatres. The musick is compos'd by the Ingenious Mr Finger, and the Paintings made my Mr Robinson" (14–16 May 1700). Despite its extensive splendor and build up, "this costly Play," as the prologue described it, was a disappointing failure. Nevertheless, Drury Lane's efforts to stage this musical extravaganza show that theater managers still sensed a taste for such entertainments. In fact, scenery and machinery continued to fascinate the public; the *Post Boy* advertisement (and perhaps a disguised puff as well) for *The Virgin Prophetess* included a request that "Persons of Quality not [to] come behind the Scenes, it being otherwise impossible to move the great Changes of them thro' the Play."[94] Although visual components of productions remained of interest, spectators did not always respond consistently, making it difficult to gauge probable successes or failures. The "Prize Musick" at Dorset Garden suggested that aural components pleased audiences, yet *The Virgin Prophetess* failed miserably. Granville penned his adaptation of Shakespeare in this erratic environment.

His cousin Bevil Higgons composed the prologue to *The Jew of Venice*, and here he expresses the friction between an audience that demanded new additions of music and spectacle, and playwrights who were pressured to add or accommodate these elements to their dramatic texts with no guarantee of success. This level of frustration may have led Higgons to invoke both Shakespeare and Dryden as authorial figures to comment on the current state of theater; Higgons must have been inspired by the similar resurrection of the ghost of Shakespeare in the prologue to Gildon's *Measure for Measure*.[95]

In Higgons's prologue, we can sense a growing antagonism between author and audience, which will increase in intensity with John Dennis's adaptation discussed later in this chapter. Here both ghosts chastise the audience with a double-barreled attack. Dryden criticizes the crowd because they "want the nobler Beauties of the Mind." He continues:

> Their sickly Judgments, what is just, refuse,
> And French Grimace, Buffoons, and Mimicks choose;
> Our Scenes desert, some wretched Farce to see;
> They know not Nature, for they taste not Thee.

Dryden's ghost functions as a corrective to audience taste by encouraging them to favor Shakespeare. Shakespeare likewise condemns the audience "whose stupid Souls [Dryden's] Passion cannot move," and labels them "deaf indeed to Nature and to Love." In a period full of repetitive prologues and epilogues that bewail audience taste, this prologue sets up two authoritative voices to chastise audiences, a stronger attack than the more common laments of a contemporary meek playwright bullied by an aggressive audience. It is tempting to imagine that these two ghosts were staged with bloody shirts and ghastly visages (as ghosts often were), but we lack evidence to confirm this.[96]

This spectral Shakespeare endorses Granville's adaptation of a play from Shakespeare's "less polish'd age," and Shakespeare himself even admits the need for improvements to his original:

> These Scenes in their rough Native Dress were mine;
> But now improv'd with nobler Lustre shine;
> The first rude Sketches *Shakespear's* Pencil drew,
> But all the shining Master-strokes are new.

Who would argue with Shakespeare's appraisal of his own play? Shakespeare even addresses critics specifically: "This Play, ye Critics, shall your Fury stand, / Adorn'd and rescu'd by a faultless Hand." Granville himself is "faultless" and his play is thus sanctioned by a voice that took the trouble to arise from the grave for this purpose.

The ghost of Dryden similarly laments his literary status, proclaiming that he "toyl'd in vain for an Ungenerous Age" who "starv'd me living; nay deny'd me Fame, / And scarce now dead, do Justice to my Name." This further carries on the diatribe against current audience taste, insinuating that the preferences of contemporary audiences have caused these two poets to return and rectify this decline. The text does not specify who spoke this prologue, but both Betterton and Verbruggen appeared in the adaptation (as Bassanio and Antonio respectively), and probably took on these two parts in the prologue as well; both had portrayed Shakespeare's ghost in previous incarnations.[97] Bassanio and

Antonio appear in the first scene, and the two actors could easily have made the transition from authorial ghosts to Shakespearian characters between the prologue and the play. As the manager of Lincoln's Inn Fields, Betterton would have taken particular interest in the opportunity to speak directly to the audiences he most desired to reach and to satisfy.

Although prefatory matter often used the rhetoric of "improvement," the more immediate motives derived from economic conditions inherent in attaining theatrical success. In Higgons's prologue, the "lustre" of the freshly "adorn'd" play and its new "shining Master-Stroaks" all trumpet a play newly made. The "fury" of critics aptly captures the response playwrights expected but worked to avoid, and also signals a growing presence of critical writing about art.[98] Shakespeare's name was not enough to sell this production without novelty, popular actors and music. As Granville expressed in his later epilogue to *The British Enchanters*, "in vain we write, / Unless the Music or the Show invite, / Not *Hamlet* clears the Charges of the Night."[99] A Shakespearian comedy without "music" or "show" would not survive.

In his advertisement to the reader, Granville further explains that his source play needed reworking to appease the "Objections" of contemporary audiences: "Alterations have been requisite as to the change of Words, or single Lines, the Conduct of Incidents, and Method of Action throughout the whole Piece, to bring it into the Form and Compass of a Play." Through this process, Granville links his revised version to other dramatic pieces that updated earlier sources, such as Waller's alteration of the Fletcher play *The Maid's Tragedy*, Rochester's updated *Valentinian*, and adapted versions *Troilus and Cressida*, *Timon of Athens*, and *King Lear*.[100] Like Dryden and Davenant, who placed their adaptation of *The Tempest* within a larger context of recycled dramatic material, Granville takes a similar approach and situates his play among the many recent updates of other older texts. Moreover, Granville demarcates additions that he makes to Shakespeare's lines in his text so that "nothing may be imputed to *Shakespear* which may seem unworthy of him." His attitude is one of respect but not undue reverence. Like most playwrights of his day, Granville made a habit of turning to a variety of sources in his career other than Shakespeare, elsewhere drawing on Sedley and Dryden, for example.[101]

With Granville's adaptation, we start to see an acknowledgment of Shakespeare's status as an author, but writers were still not unwilling to rework his comic material. This indicates a separation between the name of Shakespeare and the reality that his unadorned comedies would not work successfully on the stage. Like Gildon, Granville was well aware of the power of his audience, yet like John Dennis he voices his disapproval of their taste and attempts to address potential criticisms and complaints.

The epilogue to Granville's play points out the expense and exertion involved in updating plays for this demanding audience, no doubt to indicate to audiences that great effort has gone into the preceding production, and to increase the pressure on them to approve of the show. Looking back to a previous age when "Plain Beauties" could procure success without the expense required to include "the Varnish and the Dawb of Show," he calls to mind the prologue to Gildon's adaptation and its lament for "Shakespeare's days" when sense and plot mattered. Now theaters labor "At vast Expence . . . to our Ruine, / And court your Favour with our own undoing." This epilogue aims to make the audience suffer some guilt about their demands and to feel sympathy for theater practitioners.

Granville concludes his tirade by shifting the weight of his play onto Shakespeare as a competitive strategy, "'Tis *Shakespear's* Play, and if these Scenes miscarry, / Let *Gormon* take the Stage—or Lady *Mary*." Extravagancies such as Gormon the fighter and Lady Mary the rope dancer, attractions very different in nature from a five-act play, required calculated retaliatory tactics in order to win spectators. Shakespeare is offered as an alternative to these nondramatic entertainers, but it is important to note the disjunction between the rhetoric of Granville's epilogue and his treatment of Shakespeare's comic material in practice—he has no reservations about making major changes to his source play, but tries to invoke the authorial figure of Shakespeare in surrounding material as a shield from criticism for his play.

The changes Granville makes to Shakespeare's *Merchant* have obvious correlations with successful theater offerings of recent seasons. Shaped around two successful actors, the adaptation is buttressed by significant musical components. Granville adds a masque, *Peleus and Thetis* with music by John Eccles, that remained popular through the 1730s, creates a comic Shylock played by the popular actor Thomas Doggett, and crafts a role for actor-manager Thomas Betterton—all strategies that should ensure theatrical success based on previous productions.

The elaborate masque *Peleus and Thetis* provides entertainment for Bassanio, Antonio, and Shylock at the end of the banquet scene. Often omitted from discussions of Granville's play, this masque was clearly an important component to him and to his audience as well, and this opportunity for added entertainment was adjusted as the play was revived throughout the eighteenth century.[102] Just as Gildon used Purcell's opera as entertainment for Angelo in his *Measure for Measure*, Granville separates the characters in his masque from the dramatic action, but includes parallels between the two texts. Covering a variety of topics from the pain of love to jealousy, *Peleus and Thetis* concerns a set of lovers brought together by Jupiter, who impressively enters by descending to "a full Chorus of all the Voices and Instruments" accompanied with thunder to declare, "Presumptuous Mortal hence, / Tremble at Omnipotence" (17).[103] In the tradition of Restoration comedies with interpolated masques, Granville's masque entertains the characters, and the plot resumes when the performance is finished. Granville uses the masque as a way to explain Antonio's melancholy demeanor as the effect of music. Before the masque begins, Antonio confesses, "There sits a Heaviness upon my Heart / Which Wine cannot remove: I know not / But Musick ever makes me thus" (13).[104] Unlike Gildon's Angelo, Antonio's libido is not stimulated, but Granville does acknowledge the possible effects of music on auditors, here with more benign results. Realizing the full potential for profit, Granville included the masque in his *Poems upon Several Occasions*, printed in 1712, 1716, 1721, 1726, and 1732.

Granville's interest in including music is clear and makes sense in this theatrical climate. His main focus, however, was the character of Shylock as a starring role for Thomas Doggett. The play is cropped to nine scenes from the original twenty, but Shylock still appears in five scenes, as he did in the original, resulting in a more compact play with a clear central character.[105] Bassanio becomes a more prominent part for Betterton, and the other suitors are omitted to intensify this focus.

Several additions accommodate these two popular actors with opposing roles. Shylock has a more focussed revenge speech, and Bassanio becomes more heroic. Granville adds a scene to the third act where Shylock visits Antonio in prison and delivers his revenge speech, "To bait Fish withal; if it will feed nothing else, it / Will feed my revenge" (from Shakespeare's 3.1) to Antonio instead of to an audience of Christians, making Antonio the sole recipient of Shylock's venom.[106] In the fourth act, Bassanio acquires Gratiano's speeches and outbursts, and even offers to take Antonio's place: "Here stand I for my Friend. Body for Body / To endure the Torture." He pleads with Shylock to "Practice on Me: Let but my Friend go safe" (389), but Shylock does not accept the exchange. The enlarged roles and the chemistry between these two actors were certainly part of the play's success.

Granville's changes to Shylock have not been without controversy, particularly his reworking of Shylock as a comic stockjobber. As J. Harold Wilson has shown, Shylock is here endowed with "the implications of rascality and ridicule" associated with contemporary stockjobbers.[107] Granville's character is the source of laughter because of his financial practices and his villainy; no jokes are made around his ethnicity or religion, and his toast to money is a humorous attempt to poke fun at his occupation. In the second act banquet scene, Granville emphasizes Shylock's love for money as compared to the desires of the other characters. Antonio toasts to "immortal Friendship,"[108] Bassanio to love and Portia, Gratiano to women, and Shylock to money:

> I have a Mistress, that outshines 'em all—
> Commanding yours—and yours tho' the whole Sex:
> O may her Charms encrease and multiply;
> My Money is my Mistress! Here's to
> Interest upon Interest. (12)

The prologue to the play announces that "To Day we punish a Stockjobbing Jew," and this stereotype provided comic material in other contemporary plays such as Shadwell's 1692 *The Volunteers, or The Stock-Jobbers*. Jews were prominent figures in the financial world of early eighteenth-century London. Legally the number of Jewish stockbrokers was limited to twelve, but there were an unlimited number of stockjobbers who worked independently; one historian estimates that Jews "were a minority of the brokers and jobbers, although quite clearly over-represented in relation to their numbers in London."[109] For Granville, the stage Jew was a figure for comedy based on monetary habits and financial occupations rather than on religion or race.[110]

Like John Lacy's Sauny the Scott discussed in the first chapter, Granville's title character draws on humor rooted in contemporary stereotypes. An account by Ned Ward attests to this image: "There, likewise, were the Lord's vagabonds, the Jews, who were so accursed for their infidelity that they are generally the richest people in all nations where they dwell . . . These, said my friend, are the hawks of mankind, the spies of the universe, subtle knaves and great merchants."[111] A remark by Tom Brown even links Jews and Scots as objects of ridicule: "For your comfort, all our casuists agree that it is no more sin to cheat a Jew than to over-reach a Scot, or to put false dice upon a stock-jobber."[112] Shylock develops a rapport analogous to Sauny's relationship with the audience, based on asides and comments meant to elicit laughter. Not long after his first entrance, Shylock delivers his first digression to the audience, remarking as Antonio enters, "How like a fawning Publican he looks!" (6). The banquet scene provides an opportunity for Shylock to interact with Bassanio and to communicate with the audience in the style of Lacy's character. At one point in the banquet scene, he digresses to the audience, "These two Christian Fools put me in mind / Of my Money: just so loath am I to part with that" (20). Granville omits Shylock's forced conversion to Christianity, which lightens the mood of his play and lessens its potentially dark tone, just as Sauny functioned to detract from the Kate-Petruchio tensions in *Sauny the Scott*.

Another link between Granville's play and Lacy's earlier adaptation is their reliance on comic actors. Granville must have had Thomas Doggett's earlier roles in mind when he turned Shylock into a stockjobber. Doggett had earlier played the stockjobber Colonel Hackwell Senior in Shadwell's *The Volunteers* (1692), and Sancho, a comic Jew in Dryden's *Love Triumphant* (1694);[113] he was an amateur stockjobber himself. Audiences would have associated Doggett's stockjobbing Jew in Granville's comedy with his other roles. This change in *The Merchant of Venice* had virtually nothing to do with Shakespeare's play—it was done in response to the title actor and his talents, in the tradition of Sauny the Scott.

Like Lacy, Doggett was a versatile actor known for his flexibility and comic adaptability. Performances in fairs took advantage of his comic talents, as did strolling.[114] In fact, Ned Ward states that Doggett's fair activities nearly eclipsed his reputation as an actor, and describes the fair, not the stage, as his "proper element": "Having heard much of [Doggett's] fame, who had manfully run the hazard of losing that reputation in the Fair which he had got in the playhouse, and having never seen him in his proper element, we thought the time might not be very illspent if we took a sight of another best show in the Fair (for so they all styled themselves) that we might judge of his performances."[115] In 1697 he was involved with Coysh's strolling company, he was active in the London Fairs around the turn of the century, and even had his own booth at Bartholomew Fair in 1701, the same year he created Shylock in *The Jew*.

Doggett's acting style involved a fresh and daring approach that may have appealed to audiences seeking something different from the usual theatrical performance. Doggett's infamous ad-libbing and comic gagging would have kept an audience alert and anxious for more, and his ability to perform almost anywhere indicates his versatility and talent at improvisation. Immediately after acting Shylock in the 1700–01 season, Doggett returned to strolling again and to the fair. The *Secret Mercury*, (no. 1, 2–9 September 1702) describes a notable performance of Doggett's in a cross-dressed role (probably in *The Distressed Virgin*) at his Bartholomew Fair booth: "The Curtain drew, and discovered a Nation of Beauish Machines, their motions were so starch'd, that I began to question whether I had mistaken myself and Doggets Booth for a Poppet-show; as I was debating the matter, they advanc'd toward the Front of the Stage, and making a Halt, began a Singing so miserably that I was forc'd to tune my own Whistle in Romance . . . At last all the Childish Parade shrunk off the Stage by matter and Motion, and Enter a Hobletihoy of a Dance, and Dogget in an old woman's Peticoats and Red Wastecote, as like Progne Cook as ever Man saw; 'twould have made a Stoick split his Lungs, if he had seen the Temporary Harlot Sing and Weep both at once; a True Emblem of a Woman's Tears!"[116] Doggett's talent at physical comedy was obviously one of the attractions for audiences both at the fairs and at the theaters, and he probably embellished his roles with stage business that no longer survives in the bare scripts, but must have captivated live audiences. Like the Restoration actor John Lacy, Doggett had the ability to develop a pivotal and successful role out of a minor part. Cibber describes his Fondlewife as just such a creation: "This character had been so admirably acted by *Dogget*, that although it is only seen in the Fourth Act, it may be no Dispraise to the Play to say it probably ow'd the greatest Part of its Success to his Performance" (*Apology*, 1:206). As Shylock, Doggett harnessed his ability to draw audiences and steal the show; knowledge of Doggett's reputation is essential for understanding his Shylock.

Although generally played as a tragic figure in most modern productions, Shylock was a comic character in this early version.[117] Granville's adaptation has been criticized for its comic Shylock, but we must remember that audiences had not seen Shakespeare's play and had no preconceived notions about Shylock. It was more important to harness an actor's talents than to adhere to an "authentic Shakespeare," which would not have been either recognized or appreciated by audiences. Given Doggett's career as a comic actor, he would have played Shylock in the comic style for which he was known and respected. A "tragic" Shylock would have been a departure both from his traditional stage roles and from his talent. Contemporaries revered him as a comic actor, and remarked on his lack of aptitude for tragedy. Fellow actor Anthony Aston "found Doggett an honest actor, especially fine in comedy, but hopeless in tragedy, which he seldom essayed."[118] Aston tells of Doggett's failed attempt at a tragic role: "he suffer'd himself to be expos'd, by attempting the serious character of *Phorbas* in *Oedipus*, than which nothing cou'd be more ridiculous—for when he came to these Words—(But, oh! I wish *Phorbas* had perish'd in that very Moment,)—the Audience conceived that it was spoke like *Hob* [from *The Country Wake*] in his Dying-Speech.—They burst out into loud Laughter; which sunk *Tom Dogget*'s Progress in Tragedy from that Time."[119] Doggett seemed incapable of persuading an audience to take him seriously in a tragic role, and apparently just his stage presence elicited laughter: "he was the most faithful, pleasant actor that ever was, for he never deceiv'd his audience, because, while they gaz'd at him, he was working up the joke, which broke out suddenly in involuntary acclamations and laughter"

(*Apology*, 2:317). Audiences expected a comic performance from Doggett, and were unwilling to accept anything else, nor would it have been wise to work against this obvious component of audience appeal.

According to Cibber, Doggett himself was well aware of his affinity for comedy and his unsuitability for tragedy; he "could not with Patience look upon the costly Trains and Plumes of Tragedy, in which knowing himself to be useless, he thought were all a vain Extravagance" (*Apology*, 1:229). Cibber remembers that he "could be extremely ridiculous without stepping into the least Impropriety to make him so. His greatest Success was in Characters of lower Life, which he improv'd from the Delight he took in his Observations of that Kind in the real World." A versatile performer adept at song and dance, in "Humour, he had no Competitor" (*Apology*, 2:159).

A tragic Shylock would have gone against Doggett's talent, reputation, and drawing power as an actor. One of his most successful parts, his Shylock embodied those ingredients of humor that he had honed at the fairs and developed as his trademark. A description from Downes of Doggett's top roles provides further evidence for his comic Shylock: "On the Stage, he's very Aspectabund,[120] wearing a Farce in his Face; his Thoughts deliberately framing his Utterance Congruous to his Looks: He is the only Comick Original now Extant: Witness, *Ben* [Congreve's *Love for Love*], *Solon* [D'Urfey's *The Marriage-Hater Match'd*], *Nikin* [Fondlewife in Congreve's *The Old Batchelour*], The *Jew of Venice*, &c." (*Roscius*, 108). Like Puck and Malvolio, Shylock is one of Shakespeare's comic characters with a potentially dark side; in his rendition, Doggett articulates the purely comic aspects, sidestepping the tragic potential of the character to focus instead on his own talents as a comedian.

Further indication of the play's comic tone in the early eighteenth century can be found in editor Nicholas Rowe's description of the play: "tho' we have seen that Play Receiv'd and Acted as a Comedy, and the Part of the *Jew* perform'd by an Excellent Comedian, yet I cannot but think it was design'd Tragically by the Author."[121] Rowe registers what is perhaps the earliest discomfort with a comic portrayal of Shakespeare's character, yet affirms that the play was both "perform'd" and "receiv'd" as a comedy, as it is advertised on the play's title page. Moreover, Doggett initiated a tradition of comic Shylocks, and the actors who took over the role after him were all prominent comedians: Benjamin Griffin, Anthony Boheme, John Ogden, Walter Aston, and John Arthur.[122]

The patterns of adaptation practiced by Granville served as a model for how to make this material work on the eighteenth-century stage: bring out the comedy and add musical entertainment. Following Doggett's Shylock, the subsequent stage history of the play involves a wide variety of venues and added entertainments, out of sync with the serious nature of the play's twentieth-century reception. By 1711, a performance of *The Jew of Venice* (here with the subtitle *The Female Lawyer*) was advertised for 8 September as a benefit for Mr Teno and Mr Rainton "With Several Songs and Dialogues between the Acts, by Mr. Teno, Mr. Rainton, and a Gentlewoman from London, who never perform'd there before; particularly that Celebrated Dialogue of Tell me Why my Charming Fair, composed by the late famous Mr Henry Purcel; and a Mad Dialogue composed by him: Also several Opera Songs with Instruments."[123] Added songs and dialogues shift Shakespeare's source material further from its tragic overtones.

Comedian William Penkethman's Greenwich Theatre, a site of various low comic and popular entertainments, additionally shaped the reception of *The Jew*, which was performed there in 1711. A highlight from the 1710–11 season provides a taste of this atmosphere. Penkethman offered his "Wonderful Invention," a "surprising and magnificent Machine, call'd the Pantheon, consisting of several curious Pictures and moving Figures; representing the Fabulous History of the Heathen-Gods. The whole contains 14 several Entertainments, and near 100 Figures, besides Ships, Beasts, Fish, Fowl, and other Embellishments, some near a Foot in Height; all which have their respective and peculiar Motions, their Heads, Legs, Arms, Hands, and Fingers artificially moving exactly to what they perform, and setting one Foot before another as they go, like living Creatures."[124]

Penkethman's Greenwich Theatre offered something for every taste, from singing to dancing, Harlequins to tumblers, and the 1711 season included other Shakespearian plays as well: *Hamlet*, *The Jew of Venice* "as it was performed before her Majesty on her birthday at St James," *Timon of Athens, or The Man-Hater* and *King Lear and his Three Daughters*.[125] The other plays advertised at Greenwich this season reflected similar yokings of popular entertainment and dramatic offerings. *Pastor Fido; or, The Faithful Shepherd* included "several Entertainments of Singing and Dancing between the acts. Particularly a Little Girl of five Years old, that Dances with Swords to Admiration," performed on 21 May. *The Jew of Venice* was repeated on 23 August, *Timon of Athens* was performed on 27 August, with advertised music "by the same Masters that perform'd on Thursday last, viz: A Celebrated Concerto, or full Piece compos'd by the famous Albinoni. A Sonata out of the last Works of that great Master Tibaldi. That excellent Piece for the Violin and Flute of Seignior Gasparines."[126] *The Provok'd Wife* was performed 30 August with "the comical Dance of the *Miller and his Wife*," and on 3 September with dancing of "several Comick Entertainments between the Acts, particularly the *Night Scene* of Scaramouch, Harlequin, the

Cooper, his Wife, and others." Etherege's *She Wou'd if She Cou'd* was performed on 13 September "With several entertainments of Dancing by Mr Thurmond Jun. particularly a *Spanish Entry* that he perform'd in the Opera at the Hay-Market last Winter with great Applause. As also that excellent and much admired *Scaramouch*, as it was perform'd by the famous Monsieur du Brill from the Opera at Brussels." Finally that season, *Theodosius* was performed 20 September "With several extraordinary Entertainments of Musick, by those Gentlemen that lately performed on the Stage."[127] Granville's adaptation was integrated into Penkethman's Greenwich Theatre and attracted an audience looking for such assortments of comedy, music, and entertainment outside of the regular season at London theaters. Placing *The Jew of Venice* in these circumstances gives us a more accurate view of how it was received, not as a serious play with tragic elements, but as a comedy amid multifarious exotic offerings to please and entertain.

Subsequent performances of Granville's play at other venues continued this mix of offerings intended to delight and enthrall, without emphasizing the tragic potential of this comedy. In the 1714–15 season, *The Jew of Venice* was revived on 28 February at Lincoln's Inn Fields, advertised "Not Acted these Seven Years," with singing "by Rawlins, who never appeared on the Stage but once, Cook, Jones. Several Songs in Italian and English by the New Girl."[128] It was performed later that season on 22 March, with the afterpiece *The Walking Statue*, complete with singing "By the New Boy" and a "Dialogue between Leveridge and Pack," a flute solo by John Baston, and dancing "By du Pre, Miss Russell, and others." Again that season Lincoln's Inn Fields offered *The Jew of Venice* on 8 July, with dancing by de la Garde and Mrs Bullock with *Scaramouch* "by a Gentleman for his Diversion" as a benefit for Henry Rich, Pit Officekeeper.[129] In the 1715–16 season on 18 November and 20 January Lincoln's Inn Fields staged *The Jew of Venice*, with singing, dancing, and music and on 20 July with *The Cobler of Preston* as an afterpiece at Lincoln's Inn Fields. It was repeated in the 1716–17 season on 16 May at Lincoln's Inn Fields, combined with *The Masquerade; or, An Evening's Intrigue*, a new farce by Benjamin Griffin. *The Jew of Venice* had a long stage life in conjunction with a variety of musical and sensational additions.

In their prefaces, prologues, and epilogues, adapters frequently claim to reform Shakespeare, but this often does not happen in practice. The stage history of Granville's comedy *The Jew* illustrates the consumer-driven focus of adaptation, with a variety of entertainments attached between the acts and at the end of the play, features that de-emphasize close reading of the text and its poetic features.[130] When it was first offered, *The Jew of Venice* included these entertainments in an attempt to please a fickle audience, and soon was featured at the most notable site of low comic entertainment: the fair. By 1719 *The Jew of Venice* was performed, perhaps as a droll, at Southwark Fair. The comic traditions associated with *The Merchant of Venice* were not confined to the eighteenth century; in the nineteenth century, *The Merchant of Venice* productions included dog acts, various acrobats, and other assorted entertainments.[131] Granville's play was printed six times by 1736, and was obviously popular through the first half of the eighteenth century.

The comic Shylock that developed out of Granville's adaptation, based on Doggett's comic talents, should be viewed not as an embarrassing anomaly in the stage history of *The Merchant of Venice*, but rather as a way to make a Shakespearian comedy work on stage, and a window into how Shakespeare was viewed as a writer of comedy in the early eighteenth century.[132] The added masque and the presence of Doggett in the title role were important factors in the play's prosperity. Granville's play premiered in a tumultuous theatrical environment, but remained in the repertoire until Charles Macklin's revival of *The Merchant of Venice* in 1741. Granville may not have planned such a pattern, but *The Jew of Venice* was embraced by the popular performance venues of the fairs, and kept alive in the same manner as the afterpiece adaptations of *The Taming of the Shrew* in 1716, as discussed in the next chapter.

Granville's adaptation met with approval by his contemporary and fellow Shakespeare adapter John Dennis, who endorsed Granville as "him who best understands *Shakespear*, and who has most improv'd him" (*Works*, 2:2). Dennis extended his admiration by dedicating his Shakespearian adaptation and his "Essay on the Genius and Writings of Shakespeare" to his patron Granville, who remained a supporter of Dennis, and in 1711 urged the Lord High Treasurer to provide for him.[133] Dennis wrote to Steele in 1719 that Granville gave him "a Present so noble, as never has been made by a Subject to any Author now living, sufficiently declar'd that what I had writ had not been altogether displeasing to him" (*Works*, 2:173). Granville and Dennis had a relationship based in part on their mutual support for various endeavors such as adapting Shakespeare, which they both undertook with very different methods and results.

John Dennis's *The Comical Gallant* (1702)

The third adaptation of Shakespeare's comic material in the eighteenth century was undertaken by prolific critic John Dennis, who also wrote vehemently about many pressing issues of concern for the theatrical and artistic climate of early eighteenth-century London. Dennis is the first "literary critic" to adapt Shakespearian comic material; to contextualize his adaptation of *The Merry Wives of Windsor* (retitled *The Comical Gallant*), it is important to take into account how his critical outlook would condition his approach to adaptation. Antagonism toward Italian opera, belief in the necessity of rules for creating standards of aesthetic quality, desire to denounce and correct public taste, and awareness of the practical realities of the theater all color Dennis's dramatic writing and affect how he would treat Shakespeare's raw material.

As a critic, Dennis was highly esteemed by many contemporaries who shared his views. Oldmixon labeled him "one of our best Judges" of taste, and Gildon called him "a perfect Critick, and Master of a great deal of Penetration and Judgment." Aaron Hill even remarked to Pope that "none of the *Frailties* of his [Dennis's] *Temper*, any more than the heavy *Formalities* of his *Style*, can prevent your acknowledging, there is often *Weight*, in his *Arguments*; and *Matter*, that deserves Encouragement, to be met with, in his *Writings*." Giles Jacob similarly admired Dennis as "a good Poet, and the greatest Critick of this Age."[134] Despite his critical acumen, Dennis reacted to popular opinion when faced with crafting a play for the public stage, and his work with Shakespeare exposes the connections and disjunctions between literary criticism and literary practice. How did Dennis's decision to adapt a Shakespearian comedy fit with his other agendas as a critic, and how would a seminal figure in the growing area of eighteenth-century literary criticism approach this source material?

In many instances Dennis's critical pronouncements do not always agree with his creative writings, and as we shall see, this was certainly the case with his comic Shakespearian adaptation. Throughout his career, Dennis was a consistent defender of the English stage, and remained an outspoken enemy of Italian opera. After the 1705 arrival of Italian opera in England, Swift, Addison, Gildon, Aaron Hill, and Pope joined Dennis in condemning Italian opera for various reasons, including nationalistic sentiments, fear that English drama would be crowded from the stage, and skepticism about the role of music in reasonable entertainment.[135] Predicting that "the *English* Stage is like to be overthrown" by "those Operas which are entirely Musical," Dennis condemned opera as "a Diversion of more pernicious Consequence, than the most licentious Play that ever has appear'd upon the Stage."[136]

In later writings, Dennis continued to defend the stage against the incipient dangers of this form that privileged sound at the expense of sense. The attention lavished on opera was detrimental to public taste and to poetry, and he warned, "wherever the *Italian Opera* had come, it had driven out Poetry from that Nation, and not only Poetry, but the very Taste of Poetry, and of all the politer Arts."[137] Even at the end of his career, he railed against Italian operas for being "sensual and effeminate, compared to the genuine Drama, and a greater real Promoter of wanton and sensual Thoughts than ever the Drama was pretended to be . . . they have nothing of that good Sense and Reason, and that artful Contrivance which are essential to the Drama."[138] Thus, opera was harmful not only to the artistic world and to drama in particular, but also to the country as a whole through its corruption of English taste.

This nationalistic concern for public taste extended to his dramatic work. To persuade spectators to support drama, Dennis frames his argument against operas in patriotic terms; abolishing the "pernicious Amusement of Operas" is "conducive to the Glory of *England*" and upholds "the Majesty of the *British* Genius."[139] Similarly, the "general ill Taste" of audiences can be traced to "the Effect of the *Italian* Opera," which makes them "as ill-prepar'd to judge of a good Tragedy, as Children that are eating Sugar-plumbs are to taste *Champaign* and *Burgundy*."[140] According to Dennis, support of Italian opera drained sustenance from English drama and corrupted the ability of audiences to judge entertainments.

Public taste is also at fault for supporting "Operas, and Entertainments of Singing and Dancing" that now take up "the room of Dramatick Poems." In a typical passage, he rants that "so many People of great Quality, and of greater Parts, Lovers of their Country, and Encouragers of Art, and of Poetry more particularly, should prove so zealous in the encouraging and promoting Entertainments, which tend so directly to the Detriment of the Publick, to the Detriment of Arts, and especially of expiring Poetry." Dennis's investment in improving taste and expelling foreign opera is clear in his vehement tone. He vows to "defend the *English* Stage" from the "Invasion of Foreign Luxury" that is "pouring in from the Continent" and warns that the all-sung opera "is about to be establish'd in the room of Plays."[141]

An overbalance of excessive "Entertainments of Singing and Dancing" created audiences who "will hardly suffer a Play, that is not interlarded with Singing and Dancing, whereas these are become Theatrical Entertainments, without any thing of the Drama." Fearful that the "interlarded" songs and dances would take over drama, he blames audiences for "utterly neglecting *English* Comedy and Tragedy" in order to "give such Encouragement to Italian *Musick*."[142] Music should enhance, but not dominate drama, and Dennis framed the dilemma in terms of life or death for the theater.

Further extending his quest to improve the aesthetic climate of England, Dennis lambasted the "miserable Taste" of his fellow citizens, predicting that "Tast[e] and Genius daily more and more decline."[143]

Dennis was concerned to rehabilitate this "corrupt" taste, but could not deny its influence on the production of literary texts, even in his own works. Perhaps in a defensive move, Dennis sought to mediate the influence of popular opinion on the success of literary works and tried to discredit artistic judgments from a public whose taste had been corrupted by opera, and who have "drown[ed] their Understandings and debase[d] their Souls" with "unprofitable empty Amusements, or with pernicious Diversions." Dennis's low opinion of the public permeates his critical writings, but also serves as a strategic escape for the possibility of his own artistic failures: "Before a Play can be concluded to be good because it pleases, we ought to consider who are pleased by it, they who understand, or they who do not."[144] Artistic standards are invalidated if they derive from a debased and unprincipled audience.

Despite his diatribes against public opinion, Dennis realized the power of the taste of the town, admitting that "People are always uncertain and fluctuating, and guided by Opinion, and not by Judgment."[145] Of course, if public taste is discredited, this also conveniently places Dennis's works above criticism by spectators. This was no subtlety to Dennis's contemporaries; he was condemned for ransacking "*Bossu* and *Dacier*, to arraign the ill Taste of the Town" after their "fustian Plays" were "damn'd upon the Stage."[146]

Given his outspoken critical pronouncements about declining public taste, Dennis nonetheless felt a responsibility to contribute reasonable entertainments for an insistent public who "must and will have Diversions, . . . if the Government does not take care to provide reasonable Diversions for them, they will not fail to provide such for themselves as are without Reason." The opportunity to provide a "reasonable" diversion compelled Dennis, but the need to cater to public favor prohibited complete artistic freedom. Public opinion was enormously difficult to change; "Men will not be writ out of what they like," he admitted, "nor can they endure that any man should alter their tasts but themselves." Dennis attempted to shape the taste of his contemporaries, even though he avowed that "Fortune enslaves ev'n the Souls of men to opinion."[147]

"Opinion" was a powerful force, especially in the theater, where survival depended on appeasing a paying audience. Vehement condemnations of public taste did not necessarily influence theater patrons whose reactions could decide the fate of a play in an evening. Many fellow playwrights acknowledged this tenet. "However it be," remarked Dryden, "I dare establish it for a rule of practice on the stage, that we are bound to please those whom we pretend to entertain; and that at any price, religion and good manners only excepted." Charles Gildon maintained that a successful playwright "must Study his Audience, as well as the Rules" and Pope observed that "Stage-Poetry of all other is more particularly levell'd to please the *Populace*, and its success more immediately depending upon the *Common Suffrage*."[148] Allowing for Dennis's characteristic exaggeration, he was not alone in his discontent with audience taste; Betterton also deplored "the Depravity of the Taste of the Audience" but according to Gildon, "was oblig'd, on Account of Self-Defence" to comply with his audiences' desires in order to survive.[149] Dissatisfaction with the pressures of writing to satisfy the public and a desire to meet his own aesthetic agendas perhaps led Dennis to "retir[e] from the World" and withdraw from active social organizations in 1705, having written six plays, several critical and political treatises, numerous poems and letters, and a translation of Tacitus. In a somewhat ironic twist of fate, Dennis himself was not immune to the monetary rewards of authorship; due to financial problems, in 1711 he had to embark upon a second phase of writing.[150]

Dennis's dramatic output attests to his belief that a successful writer for the stage must analyze the audience and construct a work to elicit a positive reaction. Many prologues and epilogues claim to "improve" Shakespeare, but in practice these dramatic works usually comply with public opinions rather than critical precepts. This will become evident when we examine Dennis's *The Comical Gallant*, but conformity to public fashion can also be traced in his other dramatic works. Like all writers for the stage, Dennis's success depended on gratifying consumer desires. The need for money often dictated his critical efforts despite his insistence elsewhere on the primacy of artistic standards.

If we compare Dennis's critical writings to his dramatic output, it becomes evident that his own doctrines are frequently not borne out in his dramatic practice. For example, he denounced opera for its reliance on music for primary content, but penned an operatic work himself, *Rinaldo and Armida* (1699). Apparently Dennis's piece met with moderate success; one contemporary recorded in January of 1699: "I never knew a worse Winter only we have had pretty good success in the Opera of Rinaldo and Armida."[151] In his preface to *Rinaldo and Armida*, he concedes the power of the audience and admits that their likes and dislikes must not be ignored: "I should be unpardonably presumptuous, if I should imagine that I could be in the Right, against the Consent of so many Illustrious Assemblies as composed the Audiences of this Tragedy." In his defense, Dennis suggests that he could "retrench that which displeas'd" audiences, and vows to "be a little more cautious the next Time I am to entertain them" (*Works*, 1:196). Dennis's foray into English opera with *Rinaldo and Armida* shows his willingness to cater to current taste and his acknowledgment that if he wishes to "entertain" he must yield to the pleasures of his spectators.

Similarly, concern for the rules of Aristotle were a fundamental part of Dennis's critical oeuvre, yet his priorities shift when he writes for the stage.[152] He remarks in "The Advancement and Reformation of Modern Poetry" (1701) that "There is nothing in Nature that is great and beautiful, without Rule and Order; and the more Rule and Order, and Harmony, we find in the Objects that strike our Senses, the more Worthy and Noble we esteem them" (*Works*, 1:202). In 1695 he likewise expressed his commitment to rules in a letter to Walter Moyle: "a Man may write regularly, and yet fail of pleasing; and . . . a Poet may please in a play that is not regular. But this is Eternally true, that he who writes regularly *ceteris paribus*, must always please more, than he who transgresses the rules."[153] Dennis even went so far as to criticize writers such as Cibber for their lack of standards in dramatic writing: "[Cibber] has been often heard to pronounce . . . that there is a Rule for making a pudding but none for making a play. Why Truly if we consider his manner of making one, we may easily believe that there is noe great Art in the Case."[154] For Dennis the critic, great art followed rules and obeyed order, but Dennis the playwright admitted that both audience desire and the practical concerns of the theater determined success or failure.[155] The intrinsic structure of a dramatic piece was rarely enough to ensure success, as Dennis was well aware, and critical doctrine had little power over a populace easily swayed by spectacle and sound.

Another discrepancy between Dennis's theory and dramatic practice pertains to the influence of actors on drama. He faulted fellow writers because they "adapted their Characters to their Actors" which produces plays of a limited lifespan because "the Lustre of the most shining of their Characters must decay with the Actors, while those of *Sophocles*, *Euripedes*, *Terence*, and *Ben Johnson* will eternally remain."[156] Audiences were often "deluded by the enchanting performance of soe just and soe great an Actour . . . or by the opinion They might have of a celebrated Authour who had pleasd them before."[157] Here as well we can see a gap between Dennis's dramatic writing and his artistic principles. In crafting his play *Liberty Asserted* (1704) Dennis turned to Betterton's acting expertise, thanking him in his preface for "the Hints I received from him, as well as for his excellent Action" (*Works*, 1:324).[158] We can see this practice in his omission of Justice Shallow from the first scene of his version of *The Merry Wives*. Shallow is expunged not for aesthetic reasons, but because Dennis "knew no body who would be capable of Acting that Character, unless those who would be otherwise employed."[159] Thus, part of the play's structure derives from the capacity of the acting company, not from aesthetic reasons independent of performance circumstances. Dennis maintained that artistic works written with immediate stage conditions in mind were less likely to endure, but as we shall see with his adaptation of Shakespeare, he responded to particular theatrical conditions and available personnel.

His only reworking of a Shakespearian comedy, *The Comical Gallant* was printed in May of 1702 with his essay "A Large Account of the Taste in Poetry and the Causes of the Degeneracy of it." Because of his position as a critic and playwright, it is worth pausing over the connections between Dennis's adaptation and the critical essay he published in tandem, described by one scholar as "the first extensive theoretical demonstration of the superiority of humor."[160] Dennis's "Large Account" may have been an angry reaction to the failure of his adaptation, and it demonstrates his preference for low comedy and his appreciation for eccentric characters like Falstaff, integral components in the development of amiable humor.[161] The publication of these two texts together provides an ideal opportunity to compare Dennis's critical dogma with his dramatic practice.

In perhaps a defensive move, Dennis speculates on the decline of comedy, compared to the reign of Charles II, when writers had time to craft comic characters from real life. They were "at leisure to observe their frailties . . . and trace the windings of them up to their very springs. All the sheer Originals in Town were known, and in some measure copied." Dennis traces the problem with contemporary comedy to a busy lifestyle: "great Fools, like great Wits, require leisure and ease to shew themselves" but now "our Poets, for want of Originals are forced to bring Copies, or else to draw after their own Imagination, rather than after the Life, so it has hurt it too indirectly, by the harm which it has done to Playing."[162] Thus, part of the problem with comedy is the scarcity of "Originals" for comic material and the lack of leisure time for playwrights to craft comic characters, perhaps because of a greater need for new plays in a timely fashion. A change in the mindset of audiences toward entertainment also affected their reaction to comedy. Business concerns now interfere with the audience's enjoyment of entertainment, and they are "Too full of great and real events" such as war, employment, and taxes to enjoy "the imaginary" creations of the theater. Also, spectators are too busy to notice a well-crafted play or discern the intricacies of dramatic construction. Spectators "come to a Playhouse full of some business which they have been soliciting, or of some Harangue which they are to make the next day, so that they meerly come to unbend, and are utterly incapable of duly attending to the just and harmonious Symetry of a beautiful design." Thus, Dennis blames the audience for not noticing a well-made play, a conclusion Gildon also voiced a few years earlier. Not content to let an opportunity pass, Dennis took advantage of the possibilities for rehabilitating the stage when he published his play, and he sets up his text as an improvement on the current genre. Readers of Dennis's work were confronted with his critical dogma in connection with his published play and his interpretation of current stage conditions.

Dennis's adaptation of Shakespeare attempts to resolve his concerns about the state of comedy and about the attitude of audiences toward theater, articulated in his "Large Account" and in his other critical writings.[163] Nevertheless, he maintains an awareness of the need to please audiences. In adjusting Shakespeare's original to suit modern fashions, Dennis relied on feedback from friends and "alter'd everything which I dislik'd, and retain'd everything which I or my Friends approved of."[164] Dennis markets *The Comical Gallant* as a play of his own on the title page, simply stating that it is "By Mr *Dennis*," but the prologue opens, "Whate're the Title on our Bills may say, / The merry Wives of *Shakespear* is the Play." Dennis offers *The Comical Gallant* as a correction of Shakespeare's hasty mistakes:

> His haste some errors caus'd, and some neglect,
> Which we with care have labour'd to correct,
> Then since to please we have try'd our little Art,
> We hope you'll pardon ours for *Shakespear*'s part.

As evidence from the play makes clear, however, Dennis did more than he claims here.

If any writer would have liked to pen plays with a sole focus on dramatic theories and rules it would have been Dennis. He was known as a "petulant Critick," proudly nicknamed "The Critic," and depicted in Pope's *Essay on Criticism* (1711) as a staunch advocate of the rules, who concluded that "all were desp'rate Sots and Fools, / That durst depart from *Aristotle*'s Rules" (270–71).[165] Practical realities of writing for the stage tempered his die-hard stance as a critic, especially when he turned to comedy, as he remarks in his "Advertisement to the Reader" in *A Plot, and No Plot* (1697): "regularity in a Comedy, signifies little without Diversion" (*Works*, 1:145).[166] According to Daniel Defoe, Dennis's play *Liberty Asserted* (1704) failed because it lacked "the fashionable Gust to please the Palate of the Town; and all its Regularity of Parts, all its real Beauties of Performance could not supply the Defect."[167] Without this "fashionable Gust," a perfectly written play would likely be condemned. Dennis's stage pieces affirm the need to take into consideration the performance circumstances alongside the artistic ideals of writers for the eighteenth-century stage, particularly with adaptations of Shakespeare.

Dennis's respect for Shakespeare also shaped his attitude to adapting this comic material. Like Gildon, Dennis felt compelled to defend

Shakespeare's failure to observe the rules. His 1712 "Essay on the Genius and Writings of Shakespeare," addressed to fellow adapter George Granville, acclaims Shakespeare as "One of the greatest Genius's that the World e'er saw for the Tragick Stage," but also a writer whose "Faults were owing to his Education, and to the age that he liv'd in." Dennis excuses Shakespeare by asserting that he had no familiarity with Greek or Roman authors and lacked "Time and Leisure for Thought, to have found out those Rules of which he appears so ignorant." With the "Advantage of Art and Learning" Shakespeare would have "surpass'd the very best and strongest of the Ancients."[168] This was an issue that troubled Dennis, as he continued to try to explain and defend Shakespeare. At times he becomes vehement in his patriotic defense of Shakespeare and the English stage: "he who allows that *Shakespear* had Learning and a familiar Acquaintance with the Ancients, ought to be look'd upon as a Detractor from his extraordinary Merit, and from the Glory of *Great Britain*" (*Works*, 2:14). Thus, it is not only wrong to believe that Shakespeare knew the Ancients and disregarded them, it is downright unpatriotic. Dennis explains Shakespeare's faults by asserting that Shakespeare had other "Inconveniencies" that created various errors in his work, due to lack of "time enough to consider, correct, and polish what he wrote, to alter it, to add to it, and to retrench from it," Dennis claims, "nor had he Friends to consult upon whose Capacity and Integrity he could depend" (*Works*, 2:15). Despite Shakespeare's faults, Dennis encouraged authors to imitate his "Beauties" and avoid his "Defects," taking the best from Shakespeare and discarding the faults that resulted from his circumstances of education and writing.

As a writer who "sees [Shakespeare] and reads him over and over and still remains unsatiated," it is natural that Dennis would try his hand at adapting Shakespeare's material (*Works*, 2:17). Shakespeare's characters were a particular item of affection for Dennis, and his choice of *The Merry Wives* to adapt was in part motivated by two aspects: it was one of Shakespeare's more regular plays (and thus may have satisfied Dennis's affinity for rules) and it involved Falstaff, perhaps Shakespeare's most popular comic character.[169] In Lewis Theobald's estimation, "no Man in *England* better understands Shakespeare" than Dennis, and his efforts to adapt this material were balanced between a love for Shakespeare, a desire to establish aesthetic principles, and a patriotic affection for the British stage.[170]

His source play has a fairly steady record of performance in the seventeenth century, but did not peak in popularity until later in the eighteenth century.[171] Downes includes *The Merry Wives* in his list of "Old Plays" that were "Acted but now and then," recording that the play was "very Satisfactory to the Town" (*Roscius*, 25).[172] In the late seventeenth century, the play seems to have been a standard revival that generally received a favorable reception. *The Merry Wives* was one of six command performances at court during the reign of Queen Anne, and later in the eighteenth century it would be praised as "one of the best acting Comedies of Shakespeare . . . replete with character, humour, and incident."[173] *The Merry Wives of Windsor* was successfully revived in the 1720s by Rich at Lincoln's Inn Fields, with James Quin as Falstaff. Quin's input had much to do with the play's success and he kept the play as part of his repertoire until 1751.[174]

The endurance of the play throughout the seventeenth and early eighteenth century owes much to the character of Falstaff, who G. E. Bentley reports was the most well-known character from both Shakespeare and Jonson. Most allusions "reveal an affectionate familiarity with Falstaff which is not generally found in the allusions to other characters." Rowe's comments in his 1709 edition of Shakespeare sustain this admiration: "*Falstaff* is allow'd by every body to be a Master-piece; the Character is always well-sustain'd, tho' drawn out into the length of three Plays."[175]

Falstaff's popularity in the eighteenth century derived mainly from *Henry IV*, especially Betterton's version.[176] A letter from Villiers Bathurst to Arthur Charlett attests to the success of Betterton's Falstaff: "The Wits of all qualities have lately entertained themselves with a revived humour of Sir John Falstaff, in Henry the Fourth, which has drawn all the town more than any new play that has bin produced of late; which shews that Shakespeare's wit will always last: and the criticks allow that Mr. Betterton has hit the humour of Falstaff better than any that have aimed at it before."[177] Unlike the Shylock of Doggett, Dennis's Falstaff had to compete with this other well-known performance of the character. It is likely that Queen Anne's request for a performance at court reflects her appreciation of Falstaff, rather than of *The Merry Wives* itself. In choosing this play to adapt, Dennis wanted to tap into this trend of Falstaffian popularity, and he judiciously adds many references to the *Henry* plays throughout *The Comical Gallant* in hopes of linking his Falstaff to Betterton's successful rendition.[178]

Unfortunately, Dennis may not have had as reliable and competent actor as Betterton. The probable failure of Dennis's play can perhaps be attributed to Betterton's dominance in the role of Falstaff and to the relative ineptitude of George Powell, who most likely played the character in Dennis's play.[179] Powell was not known for his dedication to his craft; Cibber reports that he "idly deferr'd the Studying of his Parts, as School-boys do their Exercise, to the last Day, which commonly brings them out proportionably defective" (*Apology*, 1:240). A contemporary reinforces Powell's reputation as "an idle Fellow, that neither minds his Business, nor lives quietly in any Community." According to John Genest, Powell's Falstaff "was by no means acted to the satisfaction of the audience," perhaps because he planned to mimic Betterton as part of his performance.[180] This would not be the first such occurrence; for a performance of Congreve's *The Old Batchelour* in 1695, Powell planned to play the role of Heartwell himself, and according to Cibber, intended to "mimick *Betterton*, throughout the whole Part" (*Apology*, 1:205). Apparently, this brought a crowd to the theater: "the Curiosity to see *Betterton* mimick'd drew us a pretty good Audience, and *Powel* (as far as Applause is a Proof of it) was allow'd to have burlesqu'd him very well."[181] Powell may have relied on this tactic of imitation if he played Falstaff in Dennis's play; Chetwood records that Powell promised to "perform the part of Sir *John Falstaff* in the manner of that very excellent *English Roscius*, Mr. *Betterton*." In Chetwood's account, Powell "certainly hit his Manner, and Tone of Voice, yet to make the Picture more like, he mimic'd the Infirmities of Distemper, old Age, and the afflicting Pains of the Gout, which that great Man was often seiz'd with." It seems that Powell focussed more on aping Betterton than on enacting the role of Falstaff; Dennis's play may have suffered at the expense of Powell's penchant for imitation and his unwillingness to learn his role.[182]

While Dennis's *The Comical Gallant* is hardly a neglected masterpiece, the theatrical climate in which it was performed makes it no surprise that this play was not a tremendous success—neither were most new plays. Nevertheless, *The Comical Gallant* can tell us much about dramatic texts produced by the pressures of satisfying public taste while balancing critical doctrines. Like fellow adapter George Granville, who reworked *The Merchant of Venice* to focus on Shylock, updating the character with modern stereotypes to suit the performance abilities of a popular actor, Dennis revamps *The Merry Wives* in a similar fashion. His changes to the source play mainly involve the character of Falstaff, obvious in his renaming *The Merry Wives of Windsor* as *The Comical Gallant*.[183] His approach seems wise considering the enthusiasm for Falstaff in the period. As the following section will demonstrate, Dennis makes three types of changes to his title character: shifting the plot in response to changes in comedy, adjusting the piece to suit the availability of an actor to play the starring role, and creating extra scenes to showcase this character.

A number of Dennis's adjustments to Falstaff can be traced to his desire to craft a character that conforms to an emergent comic form which involved greater amiability, gentleness, and tolerance. Several labels have been proposed for this type of comedy; Hume describes it as a compromise between hard and sentimental-exemplary comedy, which he terms "half-heartedly sentimental." In his study on generic change in comedy, Brian Corman divides plays from 1660 to 1710 into punitive comedies, which "depend for their effect on responses to the ludicrous, the ridiculous, or the absurd," associated with the comedies of Jonson; and sympathetic comedies which depend "on the agreeable, the amiable, even what Steele called 'a joy too exquisite for laughter,'" associated with the comedies of Fletcher. In Corman's terminology then, these adaptations of Shakespeare are closer to Fletcher than they are to Jonson.[184]

More specifically, Shirley Strum Kenny pinpoints a transformation in comedy between 1696 and 1707 that produced what she labels "humane comedy," with characters that are "more amiable than their Restoration forebears; heroes and heroines as well as fools are treated with less extravagance, more gentleness and good humor than were their ancestors." Encompassing works by Cibber, Farquhar, Vanbrugh, Congreve, and Steele, humane comedy advocates greater tolerance of characters, a good-natured attitude, and laughter qualified with mercy.[185] In a similar but wider-ranging study of what he terms "amiable humor," Stuart M. Tave explores how the virtues of "good nature" and "good humour . . . promoted the values of cheerfulness and innocent mirth; and . . . restrained raillery, satire and ridicule, the several expressions of 'ill-natured' wit."[186] Tave traces this development to early eighteenth-century debates about the nature and purpose of laughter. The rise in amiable and humane forms of comedy coincides with a growing preference for Shakespeare over Jonson. As G. E. Bentley notes, the last decade of the seventeenth century includes twice as many allusions to Shakespeare as to Ben Jonson.[187]

Dennis's adaptation of *The Merry Wives* reworks Falstaff in light of this shift in contemporary comedy. For instance, Dennis treats him sympathetically by shifting the punishment to Ford at the end of the play.[188] The final scene includes a lengthy reconciliation between Ann Page and her parents, and farcical additions suit the characteristics of humane comedy.[189] Similarly, Dennis's play resolves with the marriage of Fenton and Ann, not the punishment of Falstaff. According to Tave, Falstaff was one of the cornerstones in the developing form of amiable humor. One writer in 1715 attested, "There is a prodigious deal of humour and mirth in the character of Falstaff and it is impossible to read [*The Merry Wives of Windsor*] and not to laugh by one's self." Corbyn Morris's 1744 ebullient description shows the culmination of affection for Falstaff in the later eighteenth century: "it is impossible to *hate* honest *Jack Falstaff* . . . it is impossible to avoid *loving* him; He is the gay, the witty, the frolicksome, happy, and fat *Jack Falstaff*, the most delightful

Swaggerer in all Nature.—You must *love* him for your *own* sake,—At the same time you cannot but *love* him for *his own* Talents; And when you have *enjoy'd* them, you cannot but *love* him in *Gratitude*;—He has nothing to disgust you, and every thing to give you Joy; -His *Sense* and his *Foibles* are equally directed to advance your Pleasure; And it is impossible to be tired or unhappy in his Company."[190] The increase in popularity of Falstaff and *The Merry Wives* during the eighteenth century coincides with the rise in amiable humor, and with what Hume describes as an "increasing sympathy for singularity and eccentricity" which "breeds a gentler view of potential objects of ridicule."[191] Dennis's changes participate in this tradition of affection for Falstaff, and provide the first in a series of sympathetic reinterpretations of the character.[192]

Burnaby's reworking of *Twelfth Night* (discussed later in this chapter) also appeals to this shift in contemporary comedy. Both Shakespearian source plays have punitive elements, such as the harsh treatment of Malvolio in *Twelfth Night* and of Falstaff in *The Merry Wives*, which are either removed completely or softened. Malvolio, a character who is largely responsible for the play's darker tone, is replaced by Taquilet, an innocuous amalgamation of Malvolio and Sir Andrew Aguecheek. Villaretta, the equivalent of Olivia, has a sentimental transformation to good nature that departs from Shakespeare's character.[193] Dennis was not alone in identifying and responding to this shift in comic form.

Dennis capitalizes on the popularity of his central character by adding three new scenes to showcase Falstaff. In the first addition, Falstaff tantalizes a disguised Ford with bawdy details of his wife, bragging that he can be found "two hours hence between a pair of Sheets, at the Bull . . . stretching and panting in expectation of [Mrs. Ford] while she is stripping for the encounter" (17). He provokes Ford with a series of risqué taunts: "Do you fancy *Ford's* wife undressing herself . . . Her Night Gown just slipping off . . . Her under Petticoat falling about her Heels . . . Her Smock-sleeves loose about her Elbows . . . And then her Lilly white Arm stretch'd out, and her milk white Bubbies display'd . . . The Bed-cloaths just turning up . . . And one of the Buxome Legs advanc'd to the Bedstead" (17). Those who assume that Shakespeare's plays were adapted to purge such risqué passages are obviously not familiar with Dennis's additions to *The Merry Wives*, a risky incorporation in light of the activities of moral reformers.[194]

The second Falstaffian addition is a farcical scene with much physical and bawdy comedy involving a new character, Captain Dingboy, played by Mrs. Page in a breeches role. As Falstaff is wooing Mrs. Ford, Mrs. Page (as Captain Dingboy) interrupts and pretends to seduce Mrs. Ford. Falstaff calls Dingboy a "bungling sign-post Picture of man," and Dingboy retorts, "Rumbling Dung-Cart of Butchers Offal, thou Insect magnify'd, that lookst monstrous to the Eye, and to the Mind art Nothing" (23). When Mrs. Page fires a pistol in the air, Falstaff falls and then runs roaring along the stage, the very picture of cowardice. Mrs Ford and Mrs Page coerce him into admitting that he is impotent, and he confesses: "If I have not forgot whether Lust be a pleasure or a pain, I am no two legg'd Creature . . . About two years ago I got to bed to a Cheesemongers Wife, and if I was not canted out of bed by her, and kick'd like a Football for downright Frigidity, may I be beaten, till from Plump *Jack* I dwindle to Poor *John*" (25). This passage calls to mind Falstaff's "banish plump Jack and banish all the world" from *1 Henry IV* (2.4.462). Bringing in additional connections with his character from the *Henry* plays, Falstaff boasts that he was "Pimp in Ordinary to the Royal Family; do you see, *Prince Hall* has sworn me to confine my Talent to that" (26). Falstaff's confession was tailor-made for audience sympathy: "what has happen'd looks like a Judgment upon me. For, what brought thee hither, ask thy self that question, old *Jack*? Why, Vanity, Covetousness and Letchery . . . At the very time that thou hast been yearning to be at performance, thou hast been forc'd in the very face of the party to make a Libel upon thy Impotence" (26).[195] Mrs. Page (as Dingboy) and her servants beat Ford for his jealousy, and the scene ends in a slapstick moment when Ford lunges at Mrs. Page and her wig flies off.

Critics have not looked kindly on Dennis's infusions of farce, but this was a deliberate playwriting technique to take advantage of physical humor around Falstaff and to make his comedy more amiable; Kenny notes that added slapstick was a common ingredient in humane comedy, and Corman points out that in *The Confederacy* (1705) Vanbrugh also uses farce "to soften the impact of punitive comedy by keeping the stakes very low. Farce thus replaces punitive comedy in a theatre where sympathetic comedy becomes humane, exemplary, or sentimental."[196] Consonant with this proclivity for farce, Dennis explains his preference for the Falstaff of *1 Henry IV* and *The Merry Wives* to the Falstaff of *2 Henry IV* because in the latter play "*Falstaffe* does nothing but talk, as indeed he does nothing else in the third and fourth Acts of the first part. Whereas in the Merry Wives, he everywhere Acts . . . 'Tis true, what he says in *Harry* the Fourth is admirable; but action at last is the business of the Stage. The Drama is action itself, and it is action alone that is able to excite in any extraordinary manner the curiosity of mankind" (*Works*, 1:280). Dennis's commitment to action as an important component of drama is borne out in his additional farcical scenes for Falstaff in accord with current trends in comedy.

Dennis continues to exploit the popularity of Falstaff from the *Henry* plays by adding a braggart scene resembling Falstaff's retelling of the

Gad's Hill story. Falstaff recounts to Ford an embellished account of the events at the Bull with Mrs. Ford: "just as we had spoke the Prologue to our Play, and Tory rory was about to begin, there comes me in a swaggerer, a disbanded Officer, with half a dozen swinging Rogues at his Heels; knocks me down flat before I was aware; while his crew of Ragamuffins bound me hand and foot in a trice" (32). Ford's reaction would have called to mind Hal's response to Falstaff's story in *1 Henry IV*. Through such scenes, Dennis employs Falstaff to create farcical action, risque bawdy humor, and braggart characters, enhancing the components that audiences seemed to like in his title character and in comedy itself.

Other changes to *The Merry Wives* reshape Falstaff, accommodate changing comic form, and add music and spectacle. Both Fenton and Ann have much larger roles in Dennis's adaptation; Fenton becomes the nephew of the Fords, which facilitates their aid in his pursuit of Ann. She has made a sacred vow to Fenton, who has convinced Falstaff that Mrs. Page and Mrs. Ford are in love with him.[197] Thus, Fenton induces Falstaff's desire, which exonerates Falstaff from the delusions he has in Shakespeare's play. To increase aural elements, Dennis humorously embellishes Shakespeare's original masquelike scene in Windsor Park. As Hern the Hunter, Falstaff is startled by a *"Terrible Symphony"* (42). Great confusion ensues, the *"terrible Symphony Recommences,"* and the Maskers re-enter with Ford *"in the shape of* Falstaff" (42). A masque occurs here with all of the characters on stage. Ford, instead of Falstaff, is pinched and forced to hear a song that chants "cuff him in Cadence, and kick him in Time" (43), perhaps reminiscent of the drunken poet scene in *The Fairy-Queen*. Ford is punished at the end of the play; Falstaff condemns him as "a Beast of a Husband" and Ford confesses his faults to his wife. As Ford thanks his wife for reforming him, Falstaff interjects comments, making him a party to the rehabilitation of Ford. In Shakespeare's play, Ford is a prominent force in the punishment of Falstaff, but here he plays the husband in need of reform. In the conclusion to Shakespeare's play, most of the characters participate in a lengthy discussion of Falstaff's follies.[198] Falstaff in *The Comical Gallant* receives no such treatment. Instead, Ford is the recipient of all admonishments, and Falstaff is spared any censure.

By aiming the punishment at Ford, Dennis shifts the focus of the play toward the follies of Ford's jealousy and away from Falstaff. Ford is condemned for mistrusting his wife, which for Dennis is more worthy of discipline than Falstaff's harmless escapades. Avon Jack Murphy contends that in changing the ending to punish Ford more severely than Falstaff, Dennis "damages the conclusion" of the play.[199] However, as we have seen, contemporary attitudes toward Falstaff merited such a benign treatment of this popular character. Dennis combines his ideas on comedy with contemporary taste in an effort to please a paying audience, and his adaptation is an important early contribution to what Jeanne Addison Roberts has called "our long-standing uneasiness about what happens to Falstaff."[200]

Increasing his play's wide appeal, Dennis concludes his work with an allusion to contemporary marriage issues, a topic popular with many late seventeenth-century comedies.[201] Fearing that he has upset her parents, Fenton releases Ann from any obligation to him at the end of the play.[202] Page accepts their marriage, and concludes with a didactic address: "a forced Marriage is but a lawful Rape . . . let all men learn from *Fenton's* generous proceeding to avoid the curse that attends a clandestine Marriage, and the dreadful consequence of a Parents just displeasure. / But Heav'n will Crown this Marriage with success, / Which Love and Duty thus conspire to bless" (49). Dennis's play ends with an emphasis on free choice in marriage, leaving Falstaff untouched, unchanged, and unpunished.

Unfortunately, Dennis's play has not received judicious critical treatment. Hume calls Dennis's play "a cloddish and sodden vulgarization" that was "an appeal to popular taste—quite a condescension from Dennis—but it was a flat failure." Spencer labels it "a contemptible compound of farce and smut" and Wheeler states that "Dennis' adaptations, illustrative as they are, survive only as curiosities." In one of the few books devoted to Dennis, Avon Jack Murphy condemns *The Comical Gallant* because Dennis "reworked the comic plot to instruct us about our folly, but at what a price! We have lost all the richness Shakespeare creates when he puts Falstaff into a ritualistic scapegoat role."[203] Dennis's reworkings attempt to capture elements of contemporary comedy and contribute to a tradition of sympathetic treatment of Falstaff. By shifting the ending to feature Ford, Dennis highlights the marital relations in the play to correspond with the concerns of other plays of his time, such as the proviso scene in *The Way of the World*.[204] We may not agree with all of Dennis's changes to the now beloved character, but for an audience in the early eighteenth century, the adaptation had many aspects that should have pleased spectators in a tumultuous season.

Dennis's play was performed at Drury Lane in an atmosphere of much disruption, which no doubt affected its success. We have fewer performance records for the 1701–02 season than for any other season in the eighteenth century; thus all conclusions about successes or failures must remain tentative. In the season when Dennis's *The Comical Gallant* premiered, we only have evidence of sixteen performances of thirteen plays at Drury Lane, but Milhous and Hume estimate that 180 performances actually occurred.[205] Moral reformers continued to badger theaters, and the death of King William closed theaters from 8 March until Anne's coronation on 23 April. A letter from Sir John Percival describes the grim circumstances for theater personnel this season: "None will suffer by the King's death but the poor players, who are ready to starve; neither are they to act till the coronation. One cannot pass by the Play-house now when it is dark but you are sure to be stripped. I accidentally met yesterday the box-keeper, who swore to me he had not drunk all day, for now that they are out of pay, none will trust them so much as for a pot of ale."[206]

Further verification of the forlorn state of theaters comes from an undated petition (Milhous and Hume suggest spring 1702) from Betterton and his actors to Queen Anne asking for the Lord Chamberlain to arrange a union:

> It appears by the Receipts and constant charges of the Theatres for some Years past, that the Town will not maintain two Playhouses.
> That the two Company's have by their bidding against each other for Singers, Dancers &c who are generally strangers, rais'd their Prices so high that both are impoverisht by it, and most of their Profits carry'd away by Forreigners.
> That both Company's have been forc'd for their Subsistance to bring on the Stage Dancers on the ropes, Tumblers, Vaulters, Ladder dancers &c and thereby debas'd the Theatre, and almost levell'd it with Bartholomew ffaire.
> May it therefore please Your Majesty in consideration of the Premises to direct the Right honorable the Lord Chamberlain of Your Majesties houshold to set the Stage upon such a foot, and under such Regulations, that Your Majesties Comedians may be enable'd to Entertain the Town better and that all Irregularitys and Indecency's which have been hitherto complain'd of may hereafter be prevented.[207]

The petition was not granted, but it does provide a glimpse into the conditions of theaters: impoverished because of competition for expensive foreign singers, while desperately integrating dancers, tumblers, and other oddities into the evening's entertainment. This was not a particularly welcoming climate for new offerings.

Despite his desire to shape Shakespeare's play around current directions in contemporary comedy, Dennis was criticized for relying on Shakespeare. In *A Comparison Between the Two Stages*, Ramble argues that Dennis "begins to despair of his own strength, and therefore strikes in with a Confederate: 'Tis compounded of the *Merry Wives* of Windsor, and some Alterations of his own: So much as was *Shakespear*'s was lik'd, but all his own damn'd, and for his sake the whole Play soon afterwards." No evidence exists to corroborate the different reactions to

Shakespeare's material and Dennis's, but the latter's outspoken persona as a critic made his plays an easy target for enemies. The author of *A Comparison Between the Two Stages* snidely remarks that *The Comical Gallant* "dy'd like an Abortive Bastard" and seems to enjoy proclaiming Dennis's failures: "these repeated Disappointments, I hope, have cur'd him of the itch of Play making: Let him stick to his Criticisms and find fault with others, because he does it ill himself" (97). In a season with such a high failure rate for new plays, it is not surprising that Dennis did not find success; neither did most other writers of his day.

Although there is no indication that Dennis's play was anything but a failure, his adaptation helps us better understand the early eighteenth-century theatrical climate and the relationship between critical practice and practical theater. The circumstances of its premiere were not ideal—the theaters had been closed for two months, and audiences were exceptionally inconsistent about their entertainment preferences. It is difficult to judge whether or not Dennis's play may have succeeded with more favorable theatrical conditions, but it seems pointless to conclude that *The Comical Gallant* "could not under the best of circumstances please an audience."[208] Like several adapters before him, notably John Lacy with *Sauny the Scott* and George Granville with *Shylock*, Dennis reworks his source play to focus on a central comic figure, replete with nods to contemporary trends in amiable humor. Dennis includes several devices which had proven successful in other plays: a breeches role, additional farcical scenes, participation in marriage debates, and references to the much-loved Falstaff of the *Henry IV* plays. He also embellishes a masque, which is instrumental in resolving the plot of the play, and which was doubtless more visually spectacular than the skeletal outline on the printed page. For whatever reasons it failed, perhaps due to casting problems with Falstaff, Dennis's play provides useful information about the shifting status of Shakespeare's comic works in the eighteenth century. In the view of one of the most influential and prolific critics of the early eighteenth century, Shakespeare's *The Merry Wives of Windsor* did not have enough emphasis on Falstaff, and did not adequately conform to aspects of amiable humor.

WILLIAM BURNABY'S *LOVE BETRAY'D* (1703)

William Burnaby, a friend of Dennis's, also turned to Shakespeare's material for dramatic use. Burnaby contributed the epilogue to *The Comical Gallant*, and may have joined Dennis in satirizing Sir Richard Blackmore in *Commendatory Verses, on the Author of the Two Arthurs, and the Satyr against Wit* (1700). Burnaby was among the subscribers to

Dennis's *The Grounds of Criticism in Poetry* (1704), and would adapt Shakespearian comedy in a similar manner the following year at Lincoln's Inn Fields. Burnaby chose *Twelfth Night* to rework, a play that had not been staged since the Restoration, and even then without much enthusiasm or promise. In 1669, Samuel Pepys attended a performance of *Twelfth Night*: "To the Duke of York's house, and saw 'Twelfth Night,' as it is now revived; but, I think, one of the weakest plays that ever I saw on the stage."[209] Pepys captures the reaction to Shakespeare's play throughout our period. William Burnaby's 1703 adaptation of *Twelfth Night*, retitled *Love Betray'd*, was as unsuccessful as the revival of Shakespeare's original and has since received little critical attention. The editor of the Arden *Twelfth Night* dismisses William Burnaby's adaptation without even getting his name right, concluding that the play "is of no importance to the history of *Twelfth Night* in the theater . . . though it is of some interest in confirming the un-Shakespearean temper of its time, at least with regard to Shakespearean romantic comedy." F. E. Budd, who edited the only edition of Burnaby's works, apologizes that *Love Betray'd* is "included in the present volume for the sake of completing the edition, not through any mistaken notion of its value." *Love Betray'd* "need be considered only as an instructive failure," and "the best one can do is to find a certain melancholy interest in noting the lines on which Burnaby effected his modernisation and in suggesting causes for its failure."[210]

Despite this reaction, Burnaby's play helps us chart the reception history of Shakespeare's *Twelfth Night*, providing evidence about how the play could work on the eighteenth-century stage, and how Shakespeare's oeuvre was not universally received or appreciated, particularly the comedies. Burnaby was a typical playwright of his day: he was part of the circle at Will's coffeehouse and wrote several plays and epilogues for friends such as Dennis, Centlivre, and Gildon.[211] Even though Burnaby adjusted his Shakespearian adaptation to the current climate for comedy, its failure suggests that Shakespeare's play itself may have been incompatible with contemporary taste.

Love Betray'd was among six new plays offered at Lincoln's Inn Fields in the 1702–03 season. Aside from Baker's *Tunbridge-Walks* and Boyle's *As You Find It*, Hume and Milhous remark that this assortment of plays achieved a mediocre run at best.[212] Existing records for this season show that new plays were not particularly successful, but neither were revived plays. Hume and Scouten conclude that "the percentage of failures [of new plays] was unprecedented in late seventeenth-century drama. No single reason can be given to explain the failures."[213] After its premiere, Burnaby's *Love Betray'd* received a second recorded performance in March of 1705 at Lincoln's Inn Fields as a benefit for Pack (who played Pedro) and Mrs. Bradshaw.[214] Pack's choice of the play for his benefit performance shows that it had some merit, even if it did not draw a respectable crowd for its initial run.

The title page to the first edition of *Love Betray'd* markets it as a play "By the Author of *The Ladies Visiting-Day*." Burnaby's *The Ladies Visiting-Day* (1701) was Betterton's first new comedy at Lincoln's Inn Fields, and the author of *A Comparison Between the Two Stages* reports that is was "very popular" even though "many went to see it that did not like it."[215] Burnaby's decision to highlight the connection to his earlier successful play rather than relying on Shakespeare's name value suggests the relative insignificance of Shakespeare as a writer of comedy.[216] This was probably a wise strategy, considering Pepys's earlier reaction to the original play.

Nevertheless, Burnaby does not hide his use of Shakespeare's material; in the preface to his adaptation, he explicitly acknowledges his debt: "Part of the Tale of this Play, I took from *Shakespear*, and about Fifty of the Lines," which he demarcates in the text. Burnaby shows no desire to conceal his source play, and certainly would have promoted its Shakespearian content if it could help him prosper. Burnaby's prologue overtly proclaims his goal: to make money, even if it means "interlarding" his play with the music and dance that John Dennis (among others) so often criticized: "Our Fiddles, Songs and Dances, are Sham Pleas, / To baffle Justice, and to bring in Fees."

We can see several familiar patterns in the way Burnaby reworks his source play, primarily adding a masque, and reshaping comic characters in response to amiable humor. Neither change proved successful. In his play text, Burnaby specified a masque, but he blames the theater for the poor treatment of this piece: "the House neglecting to have it Set to Musick, the Play came on like a change of Government, the weight of the Calamity fell among the Poor." Although Randy L. Neighbarger erroneously states that "no music was ever written for the masque in the 1703 adaptation of *Twelfth Night*," Burnaby complains that the theater neglected to set the masque to music, not that there never was any music written for the masque. Price suggests that the management "apparently deleted Burnaby's masque against his will, doubtless substituting an already existing entertainment or some less ambitious musical episode so as to risk as little expenditure as possible on this play from a mediocre pen."[217]

At the end of the play, Villaretta (Burnaby's Olivia) introduces the masque "made to Adorn *Cesario's* Nuptials" (60). For an audience expecting an elaborate masque, the meager ending that Lincoln's Inn Fields apparently provided would surely have disappointed. Examples of three other plays from the same season display the wealth of ancillary entertainments that audiences demanded and theater managers offered. A 27 April 1703 performance of Southerne's *Oroonoko* (advertised in *The Daily Courant* for 26 April 1703) included "several Italian Sonatas by Signior Gasperini and others. And a new Entertainment of Instrumental Musick, compos'd by Mr Keller, in which Mr Paisible, Mr Banister and Mr Latour perform some extraordinary Parts of the Flute, Violin, and Hautboy, with several new Dances by Mr Du Ruel, and Mrs Campion. Likewise the famous Mr Evans, lately arriv'd from Vienna (where he had the Honour to perform before Prince Eugene of Savoy, and most of the Nobility of that Court) will Vault on the manag'd Horse, where he lyes with his Body extended on one Hand in which posture he drinks several Glasses of Wine with the other, and from that throws himself a Sommerset over the Horses head, to Admiration."[218] Burnaby's bare play would have paled in comparison to such extravagant and exotic offerings. Similarly, Otway's *The Cheats of Scapin* was performed 30 April 1703 with the following entertainments:

> With several Italian Sonatas by Signior Gasperini and others. And the Devonshire Girl, being now upon her Return to the City of Exeter, will perform three several Dances, particularly her last New Entry in imitation of Madamoiselle Subligni, and the *Whip of Dunboyn* by Mr Claxton her Master, being the last time of their Performance till Winter. And at the desire of several Persons of Quality (hearing that Mr Pinkeman hath hired the two famous French Girls lately arriv'd from the Emperor's Court), They will perform several Dances on the Rope upon the Stage, being improv'd to that Degree, far exceeding all others in that Art. And their Father presents you with the Newest Humours of Harlequin, as perform'd by him before the Grand Signior at Constantinople. Also the Famous Mr Evans lately arriv'd from Vienna, will shew you Wonders of another kind, Vaulting on the Manag'd Horse, being the greatest Master of that kind in the World.[219]

Italian music, unusual dances, foreign rope dancers, imported Harlequins, vaulting on the horse: such offerings created audience expectations for a plethora of impressive and unusual specialties in addition to the five-act play. Further corroborating this taste, a performance of Cibber's *Love's Last Shift* on 18 June 1703 was performed "With an Entertainment of Flute Musick by Mr Bannister and his Son. And also a new piece of Instrumental Musick on the Stage by the best Hands. And the Famous Mr Claxton and his Son will perform *The Highland*, and *The Whip of Dunboyne*. And the Famous Mr Clynch being now in Town, will for this once, at the desire of several Persons of Quality, perform his Imitation of a Organ with 3 Voices, the Double Curtel, and the Bells, the Huntsman with his Horn and Pack of Dogs; All which he performs with his Mouth on the open Stage, being what no man besides himself could ever yet attain to."[220] Clinch's eccentric vocalizations must have been a unique experience, and a bare play like Burnaby's with only two songs and a recycled masque at best would not stand up to the outlandish and extravagant additions to plays that season.

If Betterton did skimp on or even omit the music for Burnaby's masque, it is doubtful that the play would have received any approval from audiences with such a preference for musical entertainments and novelty. Other plays were greeted with a similar cold reception without their musical accessories; the preface to Henry Higden's comedy *The Wary Widdow: or, Sir Noisy Parrat* (1693) claims that the play failed because "The Songs designed were never Set by omission or combination."

The troubled state of the music from Burnaby's masque would have signaled probable disaster for his play. The author of the failed *The Constant Nymph: or, The Rambling Shepheard* (1678) describes what is at stake when a company refuses to spend money on spectacle: "As for Adornments, in Habit, Musick, and Scene-Work, it was Vacation-time, and the Company would not venture the Charge: Though they could not be ignorant, that without such Embellishments, they might, with as much hope to have it take, have presented a Masque as a Pastoral. For, as well the one as the other receives it's Grace, more from Show then Plot; from Novel, and Sprightly Aires and Dances, then curious and busy Intrigues, borrowing more indeed of the Opera then Comedy. Wherefore, in regard to the great Cost in the Presentation of them, they are both of them made almost the peculiar divertisement of Courts, at the Celebration of Marriages, and the like Splendid Entertainments."[221] George Granville tried to prevent a revival of his *The British Enchanters* in 1706 because it was planned without "singing & dancing," for Granville the equivalent of trying to "murder the Child of my Brain." Fortunately, his brother-in-law Sir John Stanley worked for the Lord Chamberlain and was able to intercede; Burnaby was not so lucky.[222] Even a bad performance of music or dance could spoil a play. Durfey blames the failure of his *The Comical History of Don Quixote. The Third Part. With the Marriage of Mary the Buxome* (1696) on weak performances: "The Songish part which I used to succeed so well in, by the indifferent performance the first day, and the hurrying it on so soon, being streightned in time through ill management—(tho extreamly well set to Musick, and I'm sure the just Critick will say not ill Writ) yet being imperfectly performed, was consequently not pleasing; and the Dances too, for want of some good Performers, also disliked" (preface). Musical aspects were in high demand and could make or break a performance, as illustrated by Burnaby's predicament.

Burnaby's other changes to his source play involve reworking the text in accord with amiable humor. Like Dennis's softening of Falstaff's punishment, Burnaby likewise shapes *Twelfth Night* into a kinder, gentler play. Feste is omitted from the play, Duke Orsino becomes Moreno, Olivia is Villaretta, Sir Toby is Drances, and Antonio becomes Rodoregue. Drances is a jolly drunkard who is more benevolent than Sir Toby in Shakespeare's version. Drances comforts Moreno that "grief is never eas'd so well, as when its drown'd" (alluding to Feste's description of Sir Toby as drowned in drink) and, perhaps in reference to Duke Orsino's opening speech in Shakespeare's play, Drances tells him not to sigh because "it has a dead Sound, there's some Musick now in a Hick-up" (8). Sir Toby never consoles Orsino in Shakespeare's play, nor do they discuss women. Burnaby's Drances is a companion to Moreno, advising him that women are "A Country unus'd to War, and easily surpriz'd; but a Widow's a fortify'd Town, that has had Enemies before it, and will never be taken, my Lord, without you bring down the great Guns upon it" (9). In *Twelfth Night*, Orsino and Toby rarely cross paths, and are certainly not comrades. There are three new female characters: Laura is Cesario's servant, Emilia is Villaretta's confidante, and Dromia as an "old Woman" who "is the very Pink of Breeding" (17) in love with Drances (Sir Toby). Malvolio has long been a disturbing component of *Twelfth Night*; Burnaby omits him because he did not fit into the model of amiable humor without significant adjustment.[223]

A new male character named Taquilet combines the roles of Malvolio and Sir Andrew Aguecheek. To further encompass amiability and good nature, Burnaby adjusts the trick that Sir Toby and company play on Taquilet, a simple witless fool who lacks even the professed education of Sir Andrew. The joke that Shakespeare constructs in the letter scene is revealed here in a speech by Drances to Moreno: "I have told the Butler, (who is a very silly Fellow, my Lord,) that my Cousin is in Love with him" (9) and that he has sent for the tailor to make him a gentleman. Taquilet has yet to appear on stage, and the joke is established long before we are given the change to observe the recipient. Shakespeare's Malvolio appears several times before the letter scene occurs, but Burnaby seems reluctant to set up a character for such humiliation. In Burnaby's third act, Emilia, Dromia, and Drances prepare to watch Taquilet. This is the first time that he is on stage, and he is only gulled into thinking that Villaretta is in love with him and thus tries to be a gentleman sans yellow stockings and cross-gartered fashion. In keeping within the bounds of amiable humor, Burnaby includes safeguards to insure that the joke on Taquilet does not go too far, tempering Shakespeare's Malvolio material into a milder version where little damage is done.[224] Like Dennis's treatment of Falstaff, Burnaby's approach to the Malvolio material neutralizes any potentially harsh moments of punishment or reproof.

As we have seen with other dramatists, Burnaby draws on sources in addition to Shakespeare and models parts of his play after Wycherley's *The Plain Dealer*, which had been recently revived.[225] Villaretta (Burnaby's Olivia) resembles Wycherley's Olivia in her wit and "comedy of manners" tone, and Wycherley's Olivia has been traced back to Shakespeare's character of the same name.[226] Burnaby adjusts Wycherley's material (as well as Shakespeare's) to meet changes in comedy around the turn of the century. Villaretta may be a Restoration heroine at first, but her sentimental transformation to good nature reworks older forms of comedy from both Wycherley and Shakespeare, while looking forward to new fashions.[227]

Under Burnaby's revising pen, Villaretta becomes a widow who rejoices in her newfound freedom: "The greatest Happiness of our Lives, is to have got free from the Mens Dominion very early; they are all Tyrants" (2).[228] Similar to Congreve's Millamant, Villaretta is an independent woman who takes pride in scorning her suitors: "I'll treat all Men as I do this Fellow . . . if he has the assurance to write again, I'll have his Ears taken off, and nail'd up in the *Ryalto*" (3). Unlike Shakespeare's Olivia, Villaretta enjoys playing the role of the cruel mistress: "it pleases me to govern him that governs *Venice*" (3). She bluntly advises Moreno to "cease this whining Entertainment, and when we meet, let us have no Speeches with Sighs at the end of 'em . . . No bleeding Heart, soft Sonnet, purling Streams, nor such like melancholy Things" (7).

Symbolic of the way comedy itself was turning, Villaretta converts from a sharp-tongued heroine to a disciple of amiability. She begins the play harshly satirizing men, but ends up promoting good nature in the mode of amiable humor. In contrast to some of her cruel lines at the beginning of the play, she advocates kindness after Cesario rejects her:

> Satyr, *Emilia*, is the Vice of Wit, as Bullying is of Courage; the Love it abuses, wou'd teach it to be Gentle! Good-natured! Kind! Sincere—! That only Cordial-drop that sweetens Life, and gives us Joys which are ally'd to Heaven.
>
> *For all we know of what they do above,*
> *Is that they Sing, and that they Love.* (31)

Emilia is surprised at Villaretta's metamorphosis and highlights the change in this character, lest the audience fail to notice: "You that use to laugh at all Lovers, to become one!" (31).[229]

The unpopularity of the Viola/Cesario character in the eighteenth century may be responsible for the poor reception of *Love Betray'd*. G. E. Bentley has shown that in this period Viola is "mentioned so seldom as to seem unknown," and would not have attracted a following. Casting choices may have also affected the play; Anne Bracegirdle, an actress known for her breeches roles, is listed for the part of Villaretta, but Cesario was played by a lesser known actress, Mrs. Prince.[230] Bracegirdle earlier played Portia in Granville's *The Jew of Venice* (1701), Isabella in Gildon's *Measure for Measure* (1700), Millamant in *The Way of the World* (1700), and Fulvia in Burnaby's *The Ladies' Visiting Day*. She would have been the obvious choice to play Viola/Cesario, and her absence in the role may have been instrumental in the play's failure. Shakespeare's other cross-dressed heroines were not particular favorites either—*The Merchant of Venice* was reworked by Granville around Shylock, not Portia, and *As You Like It* was not even staged until the 1720s.

Poor performance records from the period prevent any clear conclusions about the play's failure, but casting choices and lack of music were surely partially responsible. The lack of a central comic character may also have precluded the play's success. Malvolio was unsuitable for contemporary comic preferences, and even Olivia had to be softened. Production problems with the masque also complicate our assessment of the play's success, as does Burnaby's choice of a source play, which did not accommodate extensive music in the manner of *A Midsummer Night's Dream* and *The Tempest*.

Conclusion

The four adaptations around the turn of the century did not fare as well as some of the Restoration versions. Both *Sauny the Scott* and the 1674 *Tempest* remained in the theatrical repertoire well into the mid-eighteenth century, but aside from the moderate success of Granville's *The Jew of Venice*, none of the early eighteenth-century adaptations prospered. Written within four years of each other, the adaptations in this chapter include multiple strategies to achieve theatrical success. The two earlier plays, Gildon's *Measure for Measure* and Granville's *The Jew of Venice* look back to plays like the 1674 *Tempest* and *The Fairy-Queen*, while Dennis's *The Comical Gallant* and Burnaby's *Love Betray'd*, written only a few years later, look forward to shifting trends in comedy itself. From the additions of entertainment to the treatment of comic material, this variety is emblematic of the status of the theaters in the early 1700s, as sites of theatrical warfare, intense competition, and fairly consistent audience dissatisfaction. All four adaptations utilize some of the aspects that had worked on stage before, whether a popular actor, a masque, or added musical entertainment. As the prologue to Gildon's adaptation advised, no adapter "Let neither *Dance*, nor *Musick* be forgot." The position of Shakespearian comedy in the early eighteenth century repertoire was by no means stable. Moreover, the inability of playwrights to discover the formula for another hit play like the 1674 *Tempest* suggests that Shakespeare's comic material was not a natural fit for taste around 1700. In fact, in 1705, A. Chaves in the epilogue to *The Cares of Love* records little potential for Shakespeare and other earlier writers:

> Old *Shakespear*'s *Genius Now* is laid aside,
> And *Johnson*'s Artful Scenes in vain are try'd;
> *Otway* and *Wytcherley*, tho' Bards Divine,
> Whose Nervous *Passion*, *Wit* and *Humour* shine,
> To empty Benches to *Our* Cost we Play:
> To Sense *too* Faithful, thus *We* lose our Pay.

Shakespeare's comedies were not the only dramatic pieces that found little success in this period. As we shall see in the next chapter, it was not until a decade later when the form of the afterpiece provided a structure in which Shakespeare's comic material could prosper, but this was due more to literary form than to interest in Shakespearian content.

We can draw several conclusions about the ways Shakespeare's comedies were adapted in the first few years of the eighteenth century. First, the comedies fared no better or worse than any other comedies in this period—they were neither more nor less popular. It was difficult for any play to succeed on the early eighteenth-century stage, so we cannot ascribe the lack of success here to Shakespearian origin. We must also acknowledge the possibility that adaptations of Shakespeare's comic material occurred at random; this chapter in particular illustrates the lack of cohesion among adapters. Gildon, Granville, Dennis, and Burnaby were a diverse group of playwrights of vastly different experiences, abilities, and agendas, with little in common. Gildon was a struggling writer who later developed critical writing on Shakespeare in connection with Rowe's edition of 1709 and his own *The Complete Art of Poetry* in 1718, discussed further in chapter 6. Granville was a writer with perhaps the most financial security of this group, yet his adaptation was the most successful. Dennis was well-known as a critic and his approach to adapting a Shakespearian comedy encompassed this mindset, at least when he packaged his play for print. William Burnaby, like Gildon, was also a struggling writer who recently had a hit play with *The Ladies' Visiting-Day* shortly before he adapted *Twelfth Night*. What, then, can we say about these four adaptations? Gildon's *Measure for Measure* and Granville's *The Jew of Venice* did not have the same production problems as the latter two plays, and both perhaps focussed more on production issues (how to include and stage a masque, and how to accommodate a starring comic actor) than the later two plays, which were more concerned with comic form than performance circumstances. Both Dennis and Burnaby experienced serious problems in production—Dennis's lead actor likely did not deliver a competent performance as Falstaff, and Burnaby's masque apparently did not receive adequate treatment by Betterton.

It is also possible that the lukewarm reception of these adaptations (with the exception of Granville's play) may have discouraged other playwrights from turning to Shakespeare's comedies as sources; the next adaptations did not appear for thirteen years after Burnaby's play, and these pieces (discussed in the next chapter) were truncated portions of the comedies, not full-scale adaptations of five-act plays. After Burnaby's *Love Betray'd*, the next five-act adaptation of a comedy did not take place for twenty years. There is no concrete evidence as to why Shakespeare's comedies were left largely untouched, and we cannot even say for sure that the reception of plays like Burnaby's had anything to do with playwrights' lack of interest in Shakespearian comedy as source material. The following chapter will examine how Shakespearian comedy did work on the eighteenth-century stage, in a very different format from what we have seen so far.

4
Shakespeare and the Development of the Afterpiece

In the seasons between Burnaby's *Love Betray'd* (1703) and the appearance of the next set of comic adaptations in 1716, London theatres went through significant changes that affected the ways Shakespeare's comic material was used.[1] Theaters continued to wrestle with the balance between music and spoken drama; a brief account of this history will sketch the subsequent climate for plays in the first two decades of the eighteenth century, and may suggest why Shakespeare's comedies were not appealing as source material. Two major figures in this period, Drury Lane manager Christopher Rich and architect/playwright Sir John Vanbrugh, further shifted theaters toward music and spectacle, and we can ascribe the lack of interest in Shakespeare's comic material in part to the strategies of these two powerful managers. Cibber describes Rich's priorities: "to account for this Disregard to his Actors, his Notion was that Singing and Dancing, or any sort of Exotick Entertainments, would make an ordinary Company of Actors too hard for the best Set who had only plain Plays to subsist on" (*Apology*, 1:335). Rich's preference for singing, dancing, and exotic entertainments did not bode well for drama. Theaters often focused on operatic competition, and Vanbrugh's various negotiations to secure his monopoly on opera perhaps diverted attention from more traditional comic material. In addition, the Dorset Garden Theatre, site of the most extravagant productions, was no longer in a usable condition in the first few years of the eighteenth century. In 1703, Vanbrugh planned to unite both companies by building a new theater, and his Haymarket theater opened with a concert in late 1704 despite incomplete facilities.[2] By 1705 he was able to convince Betterton's company to move to the Haymarket, but Rich refused to unite his company with Vanbrugh's. Both troupes performed plays and operas in the 1705–06 season, and as Judith Milhous has noted, between 1704 and 1706 they seemed to reach a noncompetitive agreement.[3] As we will see, the priorities of theater managers involved opera, with an eventual generic separation between venues; neither circumstance was conducive to staging a comedy by Shakespeare.

The story of the first performance of Italian opera in London has been recounted elsewhere in detail; for our purposes a short summary will provide the necessary background for subsequent Shakespearian adaptations. In a quintessential example of theatrical rivalry, Thomas Clayton's *Arsinoe*, intended to "introduce the Italian manner of Musick on the English stage," was written for the Haymarket, but Christopher Rich finagled the opera for Drury Lane in 1705.[4] *Arsinoe* was a tremendous success, and provided "just the right bastardization of opera with which to initiate London audiences."[5] This first Italian opera demonstrates the unpredictable nature of audience response; one scholar has described the music as "verg[ing] on the incompetent—phrases that go nowhere, arias that begin and end in different keys for no apparent reason, meandering melodies with no shape or form." Indeed, a contemporary even condemned Clayton's piece as "the Hospital of the old Decrepid Italian Opera's . . . a filthy Fardle of old *Italian* airs."[6] Nevertheless, *Arsinoe* seemed to please audiences. Dennis's warnings about the decline of public taste may not have been that far from the mark.

After losing *Arsinoe* to Drury Lane, Vanbrugh did not find it easy to introduce Italian opera at his own venue. Congreve's epilogue to Greber's *Gli Amori d'Ergasto* (*The Loves of Ergasto*) lays out Vanbrugh's strategy for this first offering:

> This Day, without Presumption, we pretend
> With Novelty entire you're entertain'd;
> For not alone our House and Scenes are new,
> Our Song and Dance, but ev'n our Actors too.

The familiar selling point of "Novelty" is prominent here, but Congreve expresses optimism that "Sound and Show" will not be the standard components: "In time we may regale you with some Sense, / But that, at present, were too great Expence." However, by the end of 1705, Congreve withdrew from Vanbrugh's project, as he explained in a letter, "I have quitted the affair of the Hay-market. You may imagine I got nothing by it."[7]

A calamitous scramble took place in opening the Haymarket theater, and signs of Vanbrugh's imminent failure were evident from the opening performance.[8] Downes describes the reaction to Vanbrugh's production of *The Loves of Ergasto*: "And upon the 9th, of *April* 1705. Captain *Vantbrugg* open'd his new Theatre in the *Hay-Market*, with Foreign Opera, Perform'd by a new set of Singers, Arriv'd from *Italy*; (the worst that e're came from thence) for it lasted but 5 Days, and they being lik'd but indifferently by the Gentry; they in a little time marcht back to their own Country." This led to productions of old plays for the rest of their new season. Downes reports that "The first Play Acted there, was *The Gamester*. Then the *Wanton Wife*. Next, *Duke and no Duke*. After that, *She wou'd, if She Cou'd*; and half a Score of their old Plays, Acted in old Cloaths, the Company brought from *Lincolns-Inn-Fields*. The Audiences falling off extremly with entertaining the Gentry with such old Ware, whereas, had they Open'd the House at first, with a good new *English* Opera, or a new Play; they wou'd have preserv'd the Favour of Court and City, and gain'd Reputation and Profit to themselves" (*Roscius*, 99–100). Old plays must have seemed a safer strategy, but they certainly did not provide the excitement or novelty that audiences anticipated.

The 1705–6 season brought more stable competition between the theaters, especially with operas. Vanbrugh offered three new operatic productions: Granville's *The British Enchanters* was very popular; but *The Temple of Love* by Motteux with music by Saggioni and Durfey's *The Wonders in the Sun; or, The Kingdom of the Birds* were failures. Many earlier semi-operas were revived this season, including *The Tempest*. Had the score to *The Fairy-Queen* been available, it seems likely that it would have been offered this season as well. Vanbrugh's company advertised a revival of Dryden's *The Spanish Fryar* to open the 1706–07 season "Without Singing or Dancing" (14 and 15 October 1706), but a prologue by Vanbrugh from 1706 protests that theaters still must "feed those Damn'd Dragoons of Song and Dance."[9] Drury Lane offered *Camilla* in English and continued to offer *Arsinoe*. Rich also reopened Dorset Garden and in the 1706–07 season began to import castrati.[10] Meanwhile, Vanbrugh kept seeking a monopoly on theatrical entertainments, especially those with music.

The Union of 1708 gave Vanbrugh what he wanted: the sole right to perform operas at the Haymarket (although without the right to perform plays), and Rich was left with both acting companies and the rights to perform plays but not music, thus halting the competition between theaters in terms of dramatic offerings. This genre separation proved to be Vanbrugh's undoing and drastically changed the possibilities for entertainment.[11] Not only were operas expensive to produce, Vanbrugh could only legally perform Italian opera, and Rich could not legally perform music. The combination of drama and music that audiences seemed to enjoy was now impossible to procure. As Milhous and Hume conclude, semi-opera was "driven from the stage—not by changing audience taste but by the Lord Chamberlain's edict." Rich could not perform semi-operas because he could not do the music, and Vanbrugh had no acting company.[12] Vanbrugh's ideas of how to allocate performance material and space determined the course of English opera, and in turn influenced the history of eighteenth-century theater. The practical conditions of theaters and legal agreements determined the course of entertainment offerings, regardless of aesthetic or artistic concerns, and this situation must be acknowledged when we look at the reception history of Shakespeare.

Vanbrugh's account of his experience with opera provides an apt summary of the influential factors in early eighteenth-century London theaters. Audiences demonstrated a desire for extravagance and novelty, but their preferences were inconsistent, at times unpredictable, and often impossible to satisfy. Vanbrugh laments, "I lost so Much Money by the Opera this Last Winter, that I was glad to get quit of it; And yet I don't doubt but Operas will Settle and thrive in London." Although he continued to be optimistic about opera, among the reasons he identifies for his loss were financial expenditures encouraged by the Lord Chamberlain "Upon a Supposition that there wou'd be Immence gain, Oblig'd us to Extravagant Allowances; An Other thing was, That the Towne having the Same Notion of the Proffits, wou'd not come into Any Subscription." Vanbrugh was not the only one who felt opera would succeed; apparently the Lord Chamberlain agreed. Like many fellow playwrights, Vanbrugh blames his failure on audiences: "That tho' the Pitt and Boxes did very near as well as usuall the Gallery People (who hitherto had only throng'd out of Curiosity, not Tast) were weary of the Entertainment: so that Upon the Whole, there was barely Money to Pay the Performers & Other daily Charges."[13] It must have been exasperating to try to please spectators attracted by curiosity, not taste, who soon lost interest. Vanbrugh's description calls to mind Dennis's admonitions of popular taste, and helps fill in the picture of audiences around this time. Old plays were not likely to last long with spectators seeking the unusual or exotic, yet new offerings rarely met with much acclaim either.

"Our stage is in a very indifferent condition," wrote one contemporary in 1706. "There has been a very fierce combat between the Haymarket and Drury Lane, and the two sisters, Music and Poetry, quarrel like two fishwives at Billingsgate . . . Though Farquhar meets with success, and has the entire happiness of pleasing the upper gallery, Betterton and Wilks, Ben Jonson and the best of them, must give place to a bawling Italian woman, whose voice to me is less pleasing than merry-andrew's playing on the gridiron. 'The Mourning Bride,' 'Plain Dealer,' 'Volpone,' or 'Tamerlane,' will hardly fetch us a tolerable audience, unless we stuff the bills with long entertainments of dances, songs, scaramouched entries, and what not."[14] Addison corroborates this taste in 1711: "At present, our Notions of Musick are so very uncertain, that we do not know what it is we like; only, in general, we are transported with any thing that is not *English*: So it be of a foreign Growth, let it be *Italian*, *French*, or *High-Dutch*, it is the same thing" (*Spectator*, no. 18, 21 March 1711). Even standbys by Ben Jonson or Congreve and solid performances by beloved actors such as Betterton and Wilks were not enough to overcome the charms of foreign singers and entertainers or establish a solid audience base. Clearly spectators were attracted by the new, the exotic, the unusual, not the familiar, predictable, and well-known standards of the stage.

Rich remained an intolerable manager for actors to work under, and in 1709 the Lord Chamberlain ordered Rich to cease performances at Drury Lane, and the Haymarket became the only venue for both plays and operas.[15] Drury Lane was later reopened by William Collier, and then managed by Wilks, Cibber, and Doggett beginning in 1710. The fortunes of Drury Lane improved throughout this period, especially in comedy. With a roster of such well-known comedians as Dicky Norris, William Bullock, William Penkethman, and Jo Haynes, Drury Lane became the top company for comedy. As Farquhar attests, "the *Theatre Royal* affords an excellent and compleat set of Comedians."[16] After the death of Queen Anne in 1714, the actors were able to replace Collier with Richard Steele. That same year, Lincoln's Inn Fields opened under the direction of John Rich, and provided competition once again with Drury Lane.

When George I appointed Steele as governor of Drury Lane in 1714, many had high hopes for his ability to reform the stage. "It were to be wished our Stage was chaster," wrote one contemporary, "and I cannot but hope, now it is under Mr. *Steele's* Direction, that it will mend."[17] Despite his plans to reform Drury Lane and his distaste for "nonrational" entertainments, the opening of Lincoln's Inn Fields under Rich at the end of that year compelled Steele to offer entertainments to compete with his rival.[18] In a letter to Lord Stanley, Steele points out the need to satisfy the taste of the town: "I lay in my Claim to endeavour at pleasing the King, within the Powers He has given me, by representations of all Kinds as the Fashion, or Genius of the times, with regard to the true interest of the publick, shall present me with Opportunity."[19] The practical necessity to draw audiences with enticing entertainments outweighed the desire to reform the stage. Cibber, also an experienced theater manager, justifies this simultaneous presentation and condemnation of these entertainments: "I did it against my Conscience! and had not Virtue enough to starve by opposing a Multitude that would have been too hard for me"(*Apology*, 2:182). John Rich had the same philosophy and "knew that to be successful plays needed powerful patrons more than powerful lines."[20] Cibber referred to Rich's new theater as the "Enemy" and the actors who joined Rich were thus "Deserters."

Whatever newfangled offering Lincoln's Inn Fields provided, "it could not be safe for us, wholly to neglect it" (*Apology*, 2:169). Lincoln's Inn Fields and Drury Lane engaged in a particularly notable competition in 1716 around the afterpiece, a brief comical entertainment involving singing and dancing that followed a mainpiece. When theatrical competition resumed in the 1714–15 season, so did the demand for more dramatic pieces, and thus Shakespearian comedy reentered the repertoire.

In the second decade of the eighteenth century, the theatrical climate was still unreceptive to new plays. John Dennis complained about the "mortal aversion to new Plays" because "the partiality of the Town makes the Managers of the Theatre in Drury Lane stick to their old Plays, and reject all new ones unlesse those which are forcd upon them."[21] The epilogue to *Sir Walter Raleigh* (1719) expresses surprise that even two new plays premiered that season: "What! two New Plays! and those at once appear! / Sure, Authors fancy this a thriving Year!" George I was a much-needed supporter of theater, but he favored Italian opera and farce, and developed a taste for pantomine as well.[22] Hence, it is not surprising that no mainpiece adaptations of Shakespeare's comedies were written in the twenty years between 1703 and 1723, and Shakespeare's original comedies were not viable as five-act offerings either.

This period of theater history is enormously complex, but a few points should be stressed for the purposes of this study.[23] Italian opera gained in popularity after its 1705 debut, and for brief intervals provided direct competition with drama. During this period when Vanbrugh tried to run an opera company, and Drury Lane was silenced, there seemed little impetus to revive Shakespearian comedies, as there was only one company acting plays for the majority of the time. Farquhar advanced the view that competition was good for theaters: "If we grow one, then Slav'ry must ensue / To Poets, Players, and, my Friends, to you."[24] This certainly was true for Shakespearian comedy; theater practitioners rarely turned to Shakespearian comedy in periods of little or no theatrical rivalry. It is no coincidence that shortly after Lincoln's Inn Fields opened and a new form of comedy emerged, we see the resurgence of comic adaptations to provide more material for entertainment, this time within the framework of the afterpiece. This chapter will show that afterpieces were a cost-effective and relatively safe way to experiment with audience taste and offer tidbits to entice a variety of audience members, without the effort that a five-act play entailed. Thus, it should come as no surprise that the Shakespearian comic material chosen for these afterpieces consisted of brief comical pieces that could stand alone: namely the Induction material from *The Taming of the Shrew* and the Pyramus and Thisbe section of *A Midsummer Night's Dream.*

The afterpiece and multiple bill tradition arose as a result of rivalry between the new theater at Lincoln's Inn Fields and the older Drury Lane theater.[25] Colley Cibber corroborates this: "After this new Theatre had enjoy'd that short Run of Favour which is apt to follow Novelty, their Audiences began to flag: But whatever good Opinion we had of our own Merit, we had not so good a one of the Multitude as to depend too much upon the Delicacy of their Taste: We knew, too, that this Company, being so much nearer to the City than we were, would intercept many an honest Customer that might not know a good Market from a bad one; and that the thinnest of their Audiences must be always taking something from the Measure of our Profits" (*Apology*, 2:171–72). The highly successful afterpiece peaked in the 1715–16 season and provided a successful venue for three reworkings of Shakespearian comic material. The two *Cobler of Preston* afterpieces were instrumental in establishing this dramatic form as part of the double bill formula. The five-act play that modern scholarship privileges was not necessarily the main attraction for eighteenth-century audiences; it was the entire package that appealed to the current taste for variety.

The afterpiece allowed for additional song and dance in an evening's bill, and five-act plays would also contain these elements. John Rich, newly ensconced at Drury Lane, is credited with establishing this entertainment package.[26] A typical theatrical offering, for example, at Lincoln's Inn Fields for 18 November 1715 included a performance of Granville's adaptation *The Jew of Venice*, singing ("By Randal and the Boy"), music ("A flute solo by John Baston"), dancing (by "de la Garde, Thurmond Jr, Shaw, Mrs Bullock, Mrs Cross") and the afterpiece *The Petticoat Plotter.*[27] The afterpiece was only part of the variety that often overwhelmed and exhausted spectators; one audience member wrote in 1716 that the afterpiece "was diverting enough but the whole diversion lasted so long that it tired us."[28]

The subsidiary position of the afterpiece has caused it to be overlooked in most studies of Shakespearian performance history, but this marginality is important in evaluating the status of the comedies in the early eighteenth century.[29] According to surviving performance records, Shakespeare's comedies were not viable as five-act plays in the first few decades of the eighteenth-century theater. In fact, in these adaptations Shakespeare is not the primary attraction at all, but is part of a large body of the dramatic heritage, as Christopher Bullock phrased it, the "old plays." Playwrights did not prioritize Shakespeare's name value or authenticity as highly as they did other aspects when crafting these afterpieces.[30]

Three of the earliest afterpieces succeeded not because of their Shakespearian material, but because of this novel format; *"Novelty,* Sir, is *Wit;* for *Wit* at best without *Novelty,* will signify nothing in this Town," wrote one 1714 observer.[31] In *The Cobler of Preston* (1716), Charles Johnson incorporates references to the recent Jacobite Rebellion of 1715. In a competitive piece of the same title, Christopher Bullock interweaves popular music and plot types, while Richard Leveridge uses the form to satirize the current popularity of Italian opera in *Pyramus and Thisbe.* It is no coincidence that the three authors of concern for this chapter were all intimately involved in the entertainment world of early eighteenth-century London, and their plays were responses to events of the contemporary moment rather than attempts to create enduring dramatic masterpieces.[32]

Charles Johnson's *The Cobler of Preston* (1716)

The prolific playwright Charles Johnson wrote seventeen plays in the first three decades of the eighteenth century. Although they have received little critical attention, Johnson's works expose the practical strategies of a dramatist who diligently offered London audiences a play almost every season. Johnson was infamous for his plagiarism, and most of his plays are derived from other sources; Christopher Bullock criticized Johnson for "diverting the *Town* with other People's Writings, and endeavouring to acquire the Name of a *Poet* by transcribing from other *Men's Plays.*"[33] Johnson used Shakespearian material as the basis for two plays, the 1716 afterpiece *The Cobler of Preston* discussed in this chapter, and the 1723 play *Love in a Forest,* which will occupy the next chapter. Both adaptations were written in times of social turmoil as responses to specific historical conditions; Johnson turned to Shakespeare as source material only under particular circumstances. We can see a new sense of Shakespeare's "authority" with Johnson—he was the first playwright to invoke Shakespeare's authorial status in connection with the comedies, in part because his motivations were highly political.

As a regular at Button's Coffee House, Johnson circulated among the Whig literati of the early eighteenth century. In the opening lines to *Umbra* (1714), Pope identifies Johnson as one of "Button's Wits," and the anonymous pamphlet *Characters of the Times* (1728) describes him as "Famous for many Years for writing a Play every Season, and for being at Button's every Day."[34] Johnson's association with Button's would have kept him in touch with the political discussions of the day, as coffeehouses were central disseminators of newspapers and periodicals;

the *Freeholder's Journal* of 18 May 1723 described, "The Crowd of *Papers* that incumber the Town, and make the Tables of the *Coffee-House* look like the Counter of a *Pamphlet-shop*."[35] Since both Drury Lane and Button's were Whig strongholds, it is not surprising that Johnson's dramas would express Whig sentiments, often vehemently anti-Jacobite in nature. A passage from Christopher Bullock's *Woman Is a Riddle* attests to the fragile balance between addressing contemporary issues and offending those of other political parties: "In short, the old Plays are so curtail'd for fear of giving Offence to Parties, that if *Shakespear*, *Fletcher*, and *Johnson* were alive, they'd hardly believe their Productions legitimate; and for New Plays, there can be none worth seeing, since the Viciousness of the Age has beat out Satyr's *tripple* row of Teeth by a kind of general Consent."[36]

Throughout his career, Johnson maintained the view that theater should support the government. In the preface to *The Force of Friendship* (1710), Johnson urges that the stage become, "as it certainly may be, both Ornamental and Useful to the Government" and yearns for the Ancient theater, where a poet "taught nothing that contradicted the Constitution he liv'd under, or the Religion of his Country, and those knowing People found their Morals improv'd, their Manners polish'd, and their Judgment strengthen'd by the reasonable and noble Entertainment of the Theater." His adaptations of Shakespeare most clearly articulate this mingling of entertainment with pro-government propaganda.

Although he only uses Shakespearian material as the source for two of his plays, Johnson often expressed his reverence for Shakespeare as the standard toward which he should strive. In the prologue to his popular comedy *The Wife's Relief: or, the Husband's Cure* (1712), Johnson commends Shakespeare's "unique genius":

> Bright Fancy, Learning, Language, Wit, and Art,
> Each in the labour'd Scene shou'd claim a Part,
> But Partial Nature lavishly bestows
> On One, what wou'd Inrich Ten Thousand Brows;
> Or 'tis with Labour she creates a Son
> Like *Shakespear*; therefore never Form'd but One:
> He sham'd the Stage of *Athens* and of *Rome*,
> And starv'd the whole *Dramatick* World to come.
>   Well therefore may our Author own his Fears
> To tread, where *Avon's* Swan so oft appears . . .

Similarly, he describes Shakespeare as the measure of proper taste in the prologue to *The Masquerade* (1719): "Good Sense still triumphs on the *British* Stage: / *Shakespear* beholds with Joy his Sons inherit / His good old Plays, with good old *Bess*'s Spirit," and in the preface to the *Tragedy of Medæa* (1731) Johnson refers to Shakespeare as an "inimitable and immortal Genius" who clearly represented a position of power and stability in a dramatic world that was fickle and uncertain toward its playwrights.[37]

As Michael Dobson has shown, the early eighteenth century was a pivotal point in the growth of Shakespeare's reputation as the "National Poet," but Charles Johnson is the first playwright to wholeheartedly use Shakespeare's comic material for overt political purposes.[38] Johnson turned to Shakespeare twice in his career to sanction the political opinions expressed in his plays, and helped contribute to Shakespeare's ascendance as a symbol of British nationalism. Earlier adapters used Shakespeare's comic texts as their own (Davenant), privileged the musical additions (Purcell) or highlighted components of their dramatic package other than Shakespeare; Johnson marks an upward shift in Shakespeare's reputation, but his practical use of the comic material remains unencumbered by this new attitude to Shakespeare's name value. Johnson's aim was to effect political change rather than reform Shakespeare's material.

The afterpiece *The Cobler of Preston* (1716) is his most overtly political play, written just after the Jacobite Rebellion in 1715, and set in Preston, the site of the first battle between the King's army and the Jacobite rebels in November of that year. Johnson reshapes the Sly Induction material from *The Taming of the Shrew* to make the cobbler Kit Sly a Jacobite supporter.[39] The prologue, delivered by Drury Lane co-manager Robert Wilks, sets the play clearly within the context of the Jacobite Rebellion, and the failure of the Jacobite plot is blamed for any weaknesses in Johnson's plot: "If he wants Plot, consider, Sirs, he draws / These Scenes, from the *worst Plot* that ever was." The opening lines "Names that could never rise to *Epic* Verse, / May furnish out a *Ballad*, or a *Farce*" describe rebels as unheroic, but point out their suitability for a farce: "Our Author has a Comick Rebel stole / To make you Mirth; a drinking, noisy Fool." He reduces the historical plot to a comic impulse: "—But—may this Plot, and every Plot hereafter, / Produce but little Bloodshed, and much Laughter."

In Shakespeare's *The Taming of the Shrew*, the motives of the Lord in tricking Sly are "pastime passing excellent" (1.1.67) and "sport" (1.1.91), whereas in Johnson's adaptation, Sly is duped as a punishment for his political views. In his inebriated state at the beginning of the afterpiece, Sly confesses his Jacobite leanings: "Huzza, Huzza, a *Mackentosh*, a *Mackentosh*; there is something now so couragious, as it were, in the very Sound of his Name -You are sure he wears Wiskers, as soon as you hear him mention'd—I must be a Rebel, and I will be a

Rebel—I never saw a finer Army of Sportsmen in my Life—Hawks, Halloo my brave Boys—O'd, here is my Guard, and this will I stand, do you see, firm to the Cause, to the last Drop of Eale in Squire *Carbuncle's* Cellar" (1–2).[40] Sly's use of the Tory cry "Huzza" and his veneration of the Scottish rebel William McIntosh, who was captured at Preston, would have been overt signals of his political stance. Johnson's play opens with Sly returning from an alehouse, a location often associated with rebellion.[41] The lord, appropriately named Sir Charles Briton, describes Sly as "the greatest Politician, and the great Sot in our Parish . . . His Head is perpetually confounded with the Fumes of Ale and Faction" and he has "laid aside cobling of Shoes, to mend our Constitution" (3). As part of Sly's taming, Sir Charles plans to "take this Opportunity to punish him a little, and practise upon him for our Diversion" (4).

At the end of the first act, Sly is extremely intoxicated in the house of Sir Charles and is unable to contain his Jacobite passions: "Rumps and Round-Heads, Rumps and Round-Heads! I'll be a Rebel, down with the Rump, down with the Rump; and yet I do not Rebel, look'ee because I hate the Government—but because there should be no Government at all" (23).[42] In contrast to Sly's characterization as a misguided Jacobite, Sir Charles Briton flaunts his Englishness: "In the mean time let us not forget the Surloin of Beef I order'd to be ready by Three. That will be the chief of your Dinner, Mr. *Jolly*, with a Flask of spritely *Burgundy*, to drink his Majesty's Health, and all the Royal Family" (24). Johnson's audience would have recognized the references to roast beef and toasts to the King as symbols of Sir Charles's Hanoverian loyalty. At the end of the play, Sir Charles advises Sly to "Learn to Cobble thy Shoes, and let the Commonwealth alone" (45). Sly is punished for his political leanings and forced to swear allegiance to King George I. Barely three months after the Jacobite Rebellion of 1715, Johnson reworks a Shakespearian source into the framework of a comic afterpiece, gently guiding his audience on the proper way to respond to this political upheaval by condemning Jacobitism and endorsing the Hanoverian monarchy. His concerns went beyond creating a successful play.

Johnson's play is important for its place in the history of *Shrew* adaptations, but it has additional significance previously unnoticed by scholars. One of the earliest commentators on the play, John Genest, suggested that "it seems probable that some Cobler had made himself conspicuous at Preston in the time of the rebellion," but more recent scholars have dismissed this possibility, concluding that Johnson simply "borrowed the drunkard and his adventures from *The Taming of the Shrew* and at least one idea from Jevon's play about a cobbler . . . it will scarcely be necessary to go searching for historical Jacobite cobblers."[43] However, as the following evidence will show, Johnson based his character on a historical source which lends further significance to his text. Johnson's Kit Sly is modeled after Colonel John Hewson, a one-eyed cobbler in the mid-seventeenth century who joined Cromwell's army. Cromwell promoted Hewson to the rank of Colonel, made him a lord and appointed him governor of Ireland after he led a foot regiment of troops.[44] Hewson is infamous for attempting to suppress a rioting group of London apprentices in 1659, which resulted in several deaths and much bloodshed. The parallels between the story of Hewson and the cobbler character are numerous, and Johnson looks back to this Civil War figure as a way of linking rebellious Jacobites to previous failures in the history of English rebellions.

Johnson was not the first to appropriate the figure of Hewson for dramatic purposes. John Tatham's play *The Rump* (1660) emphasizes Hewson's one eye, and his actions in the apprentices' uprising. Tatham's play is representative of the satiric literature on Hewson as a cobbler who has risen above his station and betrayed his trade. Aphra Behn's comedy *The Round-heads* (1682), based on Tatham's play, gives Hewson a more central role. Behn uses the roundheads as a warning against rebels involved in the Exclusion Crisis and Popish Plot of the 1680s.[45]

In *The Cobler of Preston*, Charles Johnson devises a similar use for this historical figure, following in the tradition of Tatham and Behn. Johnson's Kit Sly shares several characteristics with the Civil War colonel and the associated satiric literature. As well as his plot of the rebellious cobbler tamed into obedience, Johnson's *The Cobler of Preston* includes a frontispiece engraving of a cobbler swinging a club and spilling a vessel of liquor. The motto below the cobbler, "Ne Sutor ultra Crepidam," let the shoemaker stick to his business, appears in several other contexts relating to Colonel Hewson, and further connects Johnson's character to this historical figure.[46] The title page to the pamphlet "Colonel Huson's (Or the Cobler's) Confession, In a Fit of Despair" (1659), purportedly "Taken in Short-and by the Pen of a Ready-Writer," contains the same motto, along with the phrase, "The Devil would be Gods Ape." Indeed, Hewson's proud rise to power from cobbler to lord, encapsulated in this motto, was the subject of much derision. A stanza from the song "The Bloody Bed-roll, or Treason displayed in its Colours" attests to this frequent depiction:

> Make room for one-eyed HEWSON,
> A *Lord* of such account,
> 'Twas a pretty Jest

> That such a Beast
> Should to such honour mount.
> When *Coblers* were in fashion,
> And *Nigherds* in such grace;
> 'Twas sport to see
> How PRIDE and he
> Did justle for the Place.[47]

This motto of the cobbler rising above his station occurs throughout the satirical literature on Hewson and supplies the motivation for punishing the cobbler in Johnson's play.

Physical taming is an additional link between anti-Jacobite and Civil War literature and often exposes intense hostility; Johnson's play is no exception. As part of the Lord's torment of Sly, the Spanish Doctor describes his plan to remove part of Sly's brain: "It will be proper therefore to shave your Head—After which we will make a Couple of Blisters incisional in the Nape of your Neck, which will occasion a plentiful Evacuation, and draw down the Humours from the *Pia Mater* of your Brain; which Dreins must be kept open by two small Ventages, that may not improperly be called Back-Doors in your Body" (39). This violent treatment of Sly resembles the punishments designed for Hewson in the 1656 pamphlet *The Out-Cry of The London Prentices for Justice to be Executed upon John Lord Hewson; with Their desires and Proposalls touching his Arraignment, as also A Hue-and-cry, or Proclamation*. After detailing Hewson's ambition and insolence, the writer underscores the lowly origins of "Hewson the Cobler, lately Hewson the Colonel." The writer imagines that Hewson will "cry Jumps up and down the streets, and old Shooes and Boots, to humble his haughty spirit, and make him the fitter for Execution." Then, he will be pilloried and have as many rotten eggs thrown at him "as he hath sowed stitches in Shooes or Boots," followed by stoning and boring "through the Tongue for his wicked perjuries." Hewson will hang at Tilburn "as long as Shooe-making is used in *London*" (5). The pamphlet continues to describe how Hewson's hide will be pierced, his skin stretched, his good eye given to Milton, his skull scraped and used as a drinking bowl, and his bones picked over. The closing "Hue-and-Cry" further emphasizes Hewson's rank, "He was one of the Nations grand Infectors: / Was made a Lord, a Colonell, Prince, what not?" Hewson undergoes a much more violent punishment than Kit Sly does in Johnson's play. This especially harsh pamphlet ends with a version of the motto on Johnson's frontispiece: "What can be Registred of's former fame, / But that he was *Sutor ultra Crepidam*" (7). In Johnson's play as well as in the texts on Hewson, the insolent cobbler-turned-lord is punished for straying from his vocation.

To ensure that his audience has understood the evils of rebellion, Johnson's Sly reforms after he is threatened with torture. "I am not the Person you take me for; I am but a Cobler," he pleads, "Oh, spare my Life, Captain, and I'll Peach; I'll tell you the whole Plot" (42–43). After a bit of physical taming, Sly confesses his transgressions in detail, "I was drawn away, as they [say], to Drink your Jacobite Papish Healths; which I did at first for the Love of the Beer only, as I am a Christian . . . Then, when I was very Boosie, I used to leave my Stall, and go a Rioting . . . then we did beat and knock down all People who were soberly disposed: and we did likewise most abominably disuse both the King and the Parliament" (44). In a straightforward didactic moment, Sly promises to amend his life and agrees to "learn to Cobble thy Shoes, and let the Commonwealth alone" (45).

Johnson incorporates this moral in his afterpiece, punctuated by a masque that is not described in the text, but that probably featured Sly's reform. At the end of the masque, Sir Charles reminds Sly to "Mend thy Life and thy Shoes. Be courteous to thy Customers, and mannerly to thy Superiors. Live soberly, and be a good Christian. And remember you are obliged to me for bringing you to the Knowledge of your self" (46). Sly vows to "mix Loyalty with my Liquor" (47) and the play ends with the patriotic lines:

> Our Squire, for Kit, may by himself Rebel,
> To his mad Politicks I bid Farewel.
> Henceforth I'll never Rail against the Crown,
> Nor swallow Traytors Healths, in Bumpers down;
> Nor sham Pretences of Religion forge,
> But with true Protestants cry, Live King GEORGE.

Johnson lessens the seriousness of Sly's confession by keeping it within the genre of the comic afterpiece and infusing the piece with other distractions discussed later in this chapter. The final words of the play reinforce the authority of King George and highlight the follies of a reformed Jacobite cobbler modeled after a defeated Roundhead.

The epilogue to *Hewson Reduc'd, or, The Shoomaker return'd to his trade* (1661) contains a similar message for Hewson to return to his cobbling and leave politics alone. The Shoemaker confesses:

> If Bungler-like my Work be brought to end,
> I'le be a *Cobler*, who ye know may mend.
> Next time I hope my Work shall be more meet,
> Now I have learnt the length of all your feet:
> But if in Workmanship I do excell,
> I know your bounty, ye will pay me well.

> Or else I'le trust, and book't at your Commands,
> So that ye will subscribe it with your Hands.

Like Kit Sly, in this text Hewson humbly returns to cobbling and disavows politics.

The final speech of Johnson's Sly resembles the confessions of Colonel Hewson noted above, but is also characteristic of other anti-Jacobite literature in the period. In particular, the final scene of John Philips's play *The Pretender's Flight, or, A Mock Coronation*, the sequel to *The Earl of Mar Marr'd* (1715), was offered in 1716 and must have resonated with Johnson's play. Philips's play concludes with the following didactic lines:

> Let this Example be a Warning to Posterity.
> For all Rebellions, wheresoe'er they tend,
> Bad in their Cause, are fatal in their End;
> They fix that Pow'r they're striving to o'erthrow,
> As shaken Trees more strongly rooted grow.
> And may all Politicks that come from *Rome*
> Fall like this last, and meet an equal Doom. (39)

Although Sly's final speech has a much lighter tone, it expresses similar views of the futility of rebellion, akin to the "fatal" rebellion symbolized by Colonel Hewson.

In addition to the references to the Jacobite Rebellion and the similarities with Colonel Hewson, Johnson adds comical devices to the play to ensure that it met current proclivities for comedy. He creates the role of the Spanish Doctor, who is played by Sir Charles in disguise. When Sly argues that he should be allowed to go to bed with his lady, the doctor rapidly (as the stage directions indicate) warns him: "indeed your Blood must be gently temper'd by degrees, the possession of a Woman now wou'd cause a Tumefaction, which wou'd occasion an Inflammation, which might increase to a Conflagration, and thereby give Birth to a Schirrification, which must end in a Mortification, which is properly speaking, a Dissolution of Action, in consequence whereof the Springs of Life stand still—the Vulgar call it Death" (15–16). This quick verbal delivery, similar to the later patter songs of Gilbert and Sullivan, was part of the humor of Johnson's piece.

By embellishing the farcical aspects of his play, Johnson aligns his work with the current fondness for this action-filled form of comedy, as earlier articulated in Dennis's *The Comical Gallant*.[48] To increase his quotient of farce, Johnson doubles the transformation plot in his second act by exchanging Sir Charles's butler for the cobbler. In a comic repetition of the Sly scene, the drunken Butler in the cobbler's clothes raises his head and shouts kitchen commands instead of references to the rebellion, "Dick, Dick! Lay the Cloath—whet the Knives: I cannot come; I am busie, very busie—" (25). Supplementing the transformation of the Butler, Johnson repeats the trick played on Sly, an aspect of his play often criticized but well within the repetitive nature of farce and no doubt aimed at a fondness for this type of comedy.[49]

As part of his attempt to appeal to continuing desire for music with drama, Johnson augments his play with music, some of which is related to this cobbler tradition. A sung dialogue between a cobbler and his wife, "Goe, goe; you vile Sot!" (18) in the middle of the play, encapsulates many of the common themes in texts about Hewson and Jacobites. At the end of the song, the cobbler vows to *"new-vamp the State; / The Church I'll translate; / Old Shoes are no more worth the mending"* (19). This popular Jacobite ballad was frequently reprinted in anthologies of the period, including the 1726 collection *The Hive: A Collection of the Most Celebrated Songs*.[50] Johnson even includes a dance in his afterpiece, during which an inebriated Sly blurts out his Jacobitism: "Dub—Rub, Dub a Dub! Rumps and Round-Heads, Rumps and Round-Heads! I'll be a Rebel, down with the Rump, down with the Rump" (23).[51] Johnson employed anti-Jacobite propaganda with song and dance to unite his aims of political change and theatrical success.

Despite the potential for somber moments in its moralizing conclusion and in the inclination to tame Sly, the tone of Johnson's play remains light and humorous, especially with the frequent interjections of song, dance, and a masque. By relying on the comic reaction to laugh and forgive, Johnson achieves a benign but direct treatment of a political issue of his day, contained within the lighthearted style of the afterpiece. Johnson found a ready-made plot in Shakespeare's Induction to *The Taming of the Shrew*, onto which he could graft references to Hewson, the cobbler-turned-lord/politician, and allude to contemporary rebellious Jacobites as well. This politically charged afterpiece held the stage for at least fourteen performances (twelve of those performances in February), and probably would have been more popular without the competition from Christopher Bullock's farce of the same title, surreptitiously put on at Lincoln's Inn Fields two weeks before Johnson's play premiered. Johnson certainly lost profits in the theater due to competition from Bullock's farce, but Johnson's version was favored by the reading public; it was reprinted in eight editions throughout the eighteenth century, including three in 1716.[52] The popularity of Johnson's play in print signals the potentially successful recipe of combining Shakespearian material with current political events in 1715–16. His concern was to capitalize on a newly popular dramatic form and educate his audience about rebellion in the process. The Shakespearian content of his afterpiece is an incidental factor to his main motives. Any added value that the name "Shakespeare" provided to Johnson's cause was supplemental, not integral, to his anti-Jacobite aim.

CHRISTOPHER BULLOCK'S *THE COBLER OF PRESTON* (1716)

The significance of Johnson's conglomerate of song, dance, politics, and farce is evident in the fact that rival theater Lincoln's Inn Fields offered a play of the same title by Christopher Bullock as competition. Bullock and his father William left Drury Lane to join John Rich's company at Lincoln's Inn Fields in 1714 and must have enjoyed competing with their former theater. Christopher began writing plays in 1715 with an afterpiece *The Slip*, taken from Middleton's *A Mad World My Masters*; and continued with *A Woman's Revenge* (based on Marston's *The Dutch Courtezan* and Behn's *The Revenge: or a Match in Newgate*) in 1715, *The Cobler of Preston*, *The Adventures of Half an Hour* and *Woman Is a Riddle* in 1716; followed by *The Per-Juror* in 1717 and *The Traytor* in 1718.[53] Like Johnson, Bullock was a prominent figure in eighteenth-century theater. Most of his plays included parts specifically crafted for himself and for other family members, and he was influential in shaping the theater scene of his day. At the end of the 1716–17 season, with Theophilus Keene he took over management of Lincoln's Inn Fields from Rich, but died an early death in 1722 when he was in his early 30s.[54] As an actor, playwright, and later co-manager of Lincoln's Inn Fields, Bullock was acutely conscious of strategies to attract paying audiences; his afterpiece *The Cobler of Preston* was written at the height of his career, and demonstrates his ability to construct a piece tailored to acting possibilities, popular source plays, and comic techniques.

We have seen that writers turned to Shakespearian comedy as a source for a variety of reasons: politics, opportunities to add music and spectacle to a preexisting framework, suitable roles for actors, etc. Bullock's *The Cobler of Preston* adds another motivation to this list: pure theatrical competition. Bullock turned to Shakespeare as a source primarily because a writer from the rival theater had done so.

If we can believe his own testimony, Bullock knew that Johnson was using Shakespeare for political reasons, specifically in favor of Hanoverian Whigs. He remarks that he "did hear, there was a *Farce* in Rehearsal at *Drury-lane Theatre*, call'd the *Cobler* of *Preston*, and that it was taken from the foremention'd Play of *Shakespear's*." In the preface to his version of *The Cobler of Preston* (1716), Bullock further attests that Johnson's play "was penn'd for the particular Service of a *Party*." An oft-repeated theater story maintains that actor Jemmy Spiller, who played Toby Guzzle (Bullock's Kit Sly) at Lincoln's Inn Fields, stole Johnson's *The Cobler of Preston* from William Penkethman, who was to perform the title role at Drury Lane.[55] Spiller's biographer recounts that Penkethman and Spiller, "who had with an equal Warmth the Honour and Interest of the *British Stage at Heart*, soon gave up the Animosities that generally arise between the Comedians of Rival Theatres, and enter'd into a free, and entirely mirthful Conversation." However, Spiller's competitive nature took over: "He meditated the Dishonour of the man he convers'd with, and taking the Advantage which he had waited for, of Mr. *Pinkethman's* being overtaken with Liquor, without any Regard to the Laws of Society, Honesty and Justice, stole the Part of the *Cobler* out of his Pocket, and discharging . . . the Reckoning, took his Leave of the Tavern, left his Brother *Pinkethman* drunk and asleep."[56]

In the spirit of theatrical rivalry, Spiller immediately delivered his "Prize" to Christopher Bullock, who "embraced Mr. *Spiller* and his invaluable *Piece of Theft*, with all the Transports that naturally arise in a truly Poetical Bosom on such an Occasion." Realizing his good fortune, Bullock "instantly fell to work, and by the Hints given him by *Pinkethman's* Part of the *Cobler*, was able to bring upon the Stage a Farce of the same Title as Mr. *Johnson's*, a Fortnight before the *other House* could present theirs, through the above-mentioned Advantage taken of Mr. *Pinkethman* by Mr. *Spiller*, the former not being able to recover his Part, tho' he used the greatest Application in less than that Time" (22–23).[57] If this contemporary account is to be believed, Bullock's dramatic efforts were inspired solely by his competitive desire to provide a successful form of entertainment within a short period of time, and this pattern certainly fits his practice of composition.

Even if this story is exaggerated, nevertheless it exposes the reputation for competition between theaters and comic actors in the early eighteenth century. In addition, Shakespeare's *The Taming of the Shrew* may have been recognizable to the Bullocks from their experience with *Sauny the Scott*. Christopher had played Tranio and his father played Sauny; perhaps their roles in *Sauny* sparked their interest in the Sly material omitted from Lacy's play. Bullock was a crafty and resourceful actor/playwright who was prepared to go to great lengths to ensure his success. He seemed to thrive in the competitive theater world, and his compositions resulted from discoveries as to how he could win audiences from the rival theater. His *Cobler* is a case in point.

The prologue to John Philips's *The Pretender's Flight* (1716), attests that this publicized "Cobbler" competition was a successful technique to attract audiences:[58]

> I HEAR Alarms, and bloody Wars begin,
> 'Twixt haughty *Drury-Lane*, and *Lincoln's Inn*,
> Advertisements against Advertisements are toss'd,
> Bills fight with Bills, and clash on ev'ry Post;
> *Coblers* of *Preston* like two *Socia's* Rise,
> So like—they might deceive their Author's Eyes . . .

Philips's analogy of warfare seems a bit harsh compared to the more dire rivalry at the beginning of the eighteenth century. In 1716 competition seems to have been part of the theatrical system rather than the grim life or death association between theaters that occurred earlier in the century. Bullock apologized to the managers of rival Drury Lane theater for his theft, but he justified his actions as part of the mutual combat: "my Endeavours to support its *Interest* shou'd be urg'd against me for a *Crime*, since what I have done, was ever practis'd when there were *Two Companies*, tho' never till now thought *Injustice*, it being only look'd on, as intercepting of *Ammunition* going to the *Enemy*, and afterwards employing it *against them*" (ix). Bullock's language underlines his primary aim: to provide fresh "Ammunition" against the "Enemy" theater in the spirit of friendly competition, not to create a dramatic masterpiece. It is worth noting that Bullock had particular reasons for appeasing Drury Lane co-manager Robert Wilks: Bullock was married to Wilks's daughter Jane Rogers. Bullock's hastily written piece provided over a week of profits in the theater before Johnson's adaptation appeared on 3 February 1716. According to his preface, Bullock began composing the play on Friday morning 20 January, finished the following Saturday, and the next Tuesday (24 January) the play was performed. This intensely competitive strategy had been successfully used elsewhere, such as Drury Lane's usurpation of *Arsinoe* in 1705. Bullock's enterprising reaction was ideal preparation for his stint as co-manager of Lincoln's Inn Fields. As such, his managerial position also affected how he would approach source material: his priorities were financial and practical, not artistic or aesthetic.

Financial success was certainly his primary motive, and Bullock was willing to employ any technique that would aid him in this goal, including suggestive (false) advertising about political content. We can assess the relative importance of Shakespeare's name value amid other possible ways to attract audiences. Bullock and Spiller, his lead actor, had previously capitalized on their political leanings and certainly realized the potential draw of this component. Akerby records that Bullock's *The Per-juror* was "acted in Opposition to the *NONJUROR*" written by Cibber. Spiller "bore a considerable Part, and spoke a Prologue to it, which gave Mr. *Cibber* and the *Court-Party* no small Chagrin. No Body will wonder if this *Farce* had a considerable Run, to very large Audiences of Persons who went under the Censure of being disaffected to the Government, since Mr. *Spiller* was the Comedian, who, next to the *Party-Jokes* in it, gave, by his Performance, a Life and Spirit to it" (25).[59] Bullock's play and Spiller's performance promised political content and first-rate comic acting—a combination they would repeat in *The Cobler of Preston*. Spiller and Bullock's coup over Johnson was also a triumph for their political views, but they were more concerned with using the theater to provide comic entertainment rather than serious political content. According to a contemporary account of these events, Bullock "always prided himself upon his Attachment to the Principles of *Toryism*, not only robb'd the above-mention'd ingenious Mr. *Charles Johnson* of great Part of the large Profits which he expected from the Run of a *Farce*, which was wrote, so much to the Support, and Defence of the H——r *Succession*, but wrote his own Farce, call'd *The Cobler of Preston*, likewise in quite another Manner, turning into Burlesque and Ridicule all Mr. *Johnson's* Thoughts and Designs, and giving Spirit to that Party which Mr. *Johnson* had rendred contemptible and Spiritless." Spiller's theft was motivated by party interests; he "not only knew his Brother *Pinkethman* to be a fervent Friend to the *Interests* of his late M——y, and his Administration, but was satisfied that his Patron, Mr. *Bullock*, for whose Sake and Interest he was guilty of so felonious an Act, as picking Mr. *Pinkethman's* Pocket, was a Person whose Hopes depended entirely on the Favour of a contrary *Party*."[60] The attitudes of these adapters toward Shakespeare was secondary to their more crucial goals of competition and success, and was encouraged by the contrasting political views of actors and theaters.[61] Leo Hughes observes that "the decade following 1713 was more heavily marked by political activity in the theater than was any other since the sixteen-eighties."[62]

Of course, one cannot be too serious about using farce to make a political comment, as Bullock himself points out: "these Gentlemen, I am afraid, did not think they were at the same time Satyrizing the said Party, when they gave out that a Farce was to defend their Proceedings" (vii).[63] Bullock realizes the comedy inherent in the use of farce for political commentary and ultimately privileges entertainment over politics, arguing that the theater should not stoop to further political quarreling: "Wit must sure be at a low Ebb, which can only be supported by one *Party* for railing at another; and how beneath the Dignity of a *Theatre* such sort of writing is, I leave to the Determination of the *Unbyas'd*" (vii-viii). Even though he goaded audiences with hints of political content (which he did not pursue), Bullock complained about the infiltration of politics into the theater. In his *Woman Is a Riddle* (1716), the prologue states, "But now you [critics] judge from Passion, not from Reason; / All Wit's thought Factious, and all Satyr—Treason." Similarly, in the prologue to his *The Per-juror* (1717) delivered by Spiller, Bullock taunted audiences, "All you that come, expecting *Party-Wit*, / As sure as you're alive now, you are all bit" and proclaimed that "Politicks we cautiously disclaim."

The contrast between Bullock's and Johnson's treatment of the same material illustrates Bullock's philosophy. Johnson used theater (and secondarily Shakespeare) to make a specific political point, and believed that theater should function as a support to the government. Bullock, on the other hand, emphasized the pleasure and entertainment inherent in comedy, and felt that the business of theater (and the value of Shakespeare's comic material as well) was to entertain, not convert, and that politics did not have a place in comedy. Bullock's focus was on crafting parts for his ensemble of comic actors, and Shakespeare's Induction scene provided an ideal framework. The drunken Toby Guzzle suited Spiller as a title role, and Dame Hackett and Toby's wife, Dorcas, were perfect for two cross-dressed male actors with several slapstick quarreling scenes. Shakespeare's plot also proved amenable for the addition of an underplot for Bullock and his father.

In *The Cobler of Preston*, Bullock welcomes the opportunity in his prefatory material to ridicule Johnson's politics, but his primary aim is comic entertainment, and he abandons political significance in the text of his afterpiece. Although his play is set in Preston, Bullock assures that "we've no Plot / But what Old *Shakespear* made—to ridicule a Sot."[64] Despite the political teaser in his title, his adaptation primarily draws on comic actors, musical elements, and shrew-taming/transformation plots proven popular with his audience, without political commentary. This strategy successfully established his afterpiece in the theatrical repertoire, and it remained popular for several decades because of his comic devices and his reluctance to engage in the minutiae of contemporary politics.

The combination of comic actors at Lincoln's Inn Fields in 1716 particularly fostered successful farces, and Bullock would have had this in mind when deciding what source material to adapt for this group. Leo Hughes points out that Christopher Bullock, William Bullock, James Spiller, and Benjamin Griffin "with some assistance from the rest of the troupe, played a number of old and new farces, more in fact than any other company had ever offered."[65] Toby Guzzle, the equivalent of Shakespeare's Sly, was played by James (Jemmy) Spiller, who specialized in over-the-top comic parts, frequent pantomimes, entracte dances, and prologues and epilogues often delivered while riding on an ass: Bullock found in Shakespeare a perfect part for Spiller's talents.

Spiller had just moved to Lincoln's Inn Fields in 1715 and must have been a hot attraction. According to his biographer, "into whatever Place he came, or in whatever Play he acted, he was, at all Times, the Life of the Performance, and the greatest Support of the *Company.*" Spiller was lauded for his comic talent, as one commentator wrote, "In such repute was Spiller held as a comedian, when he was only 23 years of age, that, we are told, plays were written expressly to bring him forward on the stage."[66] John Rich apparently had high regard for Spiller and paid for his burial "in a very decent manner."[67] Bullock's admiration for Spiller is apparent in the dedication of his play *A Woman's Revenge* (1715) to "my merry friend and brother comedian, Mr. James Spiller" and his praise of Spiller's "good performance in this farce." Bullock's match of part to actor was a success: Toby Guzzle was one of Spiller's most popular parts, and Bullock's play was revived as a benefit for Spiller in 1720. Spiller only had sight in one eye; his line "I am no Rogue, but honest *Toby Guzzle,* the one-ey'd Cobler of *Preston*" (4) shows his ability to capitalize on this physical characteristic.[68]

Along with his physical aptness, Spiller also had firsthand experience with the drunkenness required for the part of Toby Guzzle, and Bullock may have incorporated Spiller's reputation for drinking into the character for additional contemporary relevance. One account of Spiller's career attests that his "talents for low wit were not more notorious than his love for the bottle; in which last there is great reason to suppose, he was rivalled by his wife."[69] Bullock employs this reputation of Spiller right away; his afterpiece opens with a drunken Toby Guzzle explaining to his wife, Dorcas, that he was drinking "special Ale" at Dame Hacket's. He promises his wife Dorcas that he will mend his ways; after singing a few drunken songs, Guzzle falls asleep and is carried into the lord's place (here Sir Jasper).

In addition to taking advantage of Spiller's talents, Bullock also reworked his comic material for two other actors, John Hall and Benjamin Griffin, creating several scenes for this cross-dressing duo. Hall played Dame Hacket as a cross-dressed part; known as "Fat Hall," he frequently acted Falstaff in *Henry IV* on stage as well as at Southwark Fair, where he ran a booth in the 1720s.[70] Griffin, a short and lean comedian who specialized in skirts parts (Mrs. Fardingale in *The Funeral* and the Old Woman in *Rule a Wife and Have a Wife*), took the part of Guzzle's wife, Dorcas. Griffin's cross-dressing talents were certainly one of the attractions of this afterpiece; he also played the role of Mother Griffin in Bullock's *A Woman's Revenge,* which was often paired with *The Cobler of Preston* as a double bill, featuring Spiller and Christopher and William Bullock as well. Like Hall, Griffin acted at the fairs and later in his career operated a booth at Bartholomew Fair. The visual contrast between the fat Hall and the slim Griffin, much like the later success of Laurel and Hardy, provided much of the physical comedy in Bullock's adaptation, especially the skirmishes between Dorcas and Dame Hacket. Early in the play, after Guzzle has been taken away, Dorcas confronts Dame Hacket. Alluding to *The Taming of the Shrew*, Dame Hacket threatens Dorcas, "if [Toby] comes to my House again, I'll comb his Head with a three-footed Stool" (6).[71] Dorcas challenges, "I'll trounce you for keeping my Husband from me, you may have murder'd him for ought I know, you Whore" (7). Scenes of men playing quarreling women were a common feature of popular literature, and this quibbling scene must have been one of the most amusing.[72] This feature also calls to mind the type of physical comedy that the earlier comedians Lacy and Doggett were known for. It is worth noting also that Shakespeare's cross-dressed heroines (particularly Rosalind and Viola) were not particular attractions in these plays; cross-dressed men pleased audiences much more than cross-dressed women.

Bullock creates a second scene to feature these actors, where both "women" think that Sly is a Justice of the Peace and approach him for arbitration. This effectively shifts the focus of the play away from the trick played on the cobbler to the humorous fight between his wife and Dame Hacket. Dorcas implores Sly: "I am, so please you, a poor Cobler's Wife of *Preston*, my Husband, this wicked Woman has taken from me; he was once an honest Man, and liv'd in Peace, and Love with me for Fifteen Years, but falling into the Company of that lewd Woman, she has seduc'd him, and drawn him into her Snare, from his Home, and from me his Wife" (14). Dame Hacket's accusations are equally comical: "This false Woman has most wickedly abus'd me, defam'd me to the World, to ruin me, and spoil my Reputation, she has call'd me Whore" (13).

Eventually, Dorcas recognizes Guzzle and Dame Hacket joins her in condemning the cobbler. Guzzle threatens to tame both women, "They are scolding Queans, and let 'em be *whipt*, or carry 'em to the *Ribble* and duck 'em—I'll try if I can tame you" (15). The scene descends into a slapstick quarrel between the three characters, two of them cross-dressed men, and avoids the potential seriousness of a taming scene. As we have seen, John Lacy used a similar technique to defuse the shrew-taming material with his character Sauny the Scott. In the final scene of the play, Bullock continues to feature these two actors. Dame Hacket and Dorcas curse Guzzle and imagine how they might torment him to get their revenge. Dame Hacket proposes to "run an Awl in his Buttocks, the first time I lay my Eyes on him a Dog-Whelp" (19). In a reverse of the traditional taming scene, the two women beat Guzzle with sticks until he takes out his strap in retaliation. The three of them agree to "shake Hands, laugh at all that has happen'd, and drown Animosities in a dozen of Ale" (20). Bullock ends his farcical piece with a truce offered by Guzzle: "Ads *foot*, give me thy *Hand*, let all Quarrels cease / And when we are a bed, we'll sign the Peace" (21). Bullock's play is a far cry from the didactic political ending of Johnson's text. Focussing on the talents of his troupe of comic actors, Bullock crafts his afterpiece around low comic gagging.

In addition to casting choices, familiar plots and farcical scenes, popular music was part of Bullock's successful formula. A few specific examples should suffice. Guzzle breaks into song spontaneously throughout the play, singing snatches from well-known ballads such as "A Mournful Ditty of the Lady Rosamund":

> When as King *Henry* rul'd the Land,
> The Second of that Name,
> Besides the Queen, he dearly lov'd
> A fair and comely Dame. (4)

Most audience members would have recognized this ballad; it was reprinted in numerous contemporary anthologies of songs, and dates from the early seventeenth century.[73] Bullock incorporates Guzzle's intoxication into his musical interludes. As he begins to sing another well-known lyric, "My Lodging it is on the cold Ground, / And very hard is my Fare," he interrupts, "The Unkindness of—Hic—my Dear,—/ where's this Ale" (4).[74] Guzzle's drunken renditions of popular songs resemble John Gay's later use of popular ballads in *The Beggar's Opera* (1728). Additional music and dance occur throughout the afterpiece, concluding with a dialogue sung by Richard Leveridge and Mrs. Fitzgerald, "Since Times are so Bad."[75]

To top off his comic piece, Bullock adds an original underplot for himself and his father to perform, clearly based on a popular formula of actor and text, designed specifically to "please some friends" and "draw the vulgar in" (preface). The Bullocks had performed many comic roles together, and audiences would have recognized this comic team. The underplot involves a cuckolding plot and long-enduring character types. Toby Guzzle acts as a judge for Grist the Miller (played by William Bullock), who has cuckolded Snuffle the Puritan, played by his son Christopher. The Miller confesses that "Master *Snuffle's* Wife and I have been very great, and for that matter—so has my Wife and Master *Snuffle* . . . if I have *expounded* in his *Pulpit*—he has *held forth* in my *Hopper*, and there's an end on't" (16–17).[76] This plot continues with much amusing banter between the group of actors.

Together with his incorporation of popular music, Bullock's use of this typical plot with standard stock comic characters designed for three popular actors was part of his performance-based method to "draw the vulgar in" and please audiences. The ridiculous skirmishes between Dame Hacket and Dorcas Guzzle, played by two popular male actors, the frequent songs and dances, and the comical fabliau relayed by Grist the Miller and Snuffle the Puritan all helped secure a prominent position for Bullock's adaptation within the developing genre of the afterpiece.

Bullock's pirated text encouraged an atmosphere of competition and enticed audiences to the theaters, as corroborated by the prologue to Philips's *The Pretender's Flight* quoted earlier. In addition, advertisements for both afterpieces promoted them as "new farces," and no advertisement highlights or even names the Shakespearian content. The puff from *The Daily Courant* for 3 February 1716 exemplifies the strategy Bullock used to promote his afterpiece: "*A Woman's Revenge*; or, *A Match in Newgate*. To which will be added a New Farce, call'd, The Cobler of Preston. The part of the Cobler to be perform'd by Mr. Spiller. With Singing by Mr. Randal, Mrs Fitzgerald, and the Boy. And Dancing by Mr. Shaw, and Mrs. Schoolding." The comic actor, the "New Farce" and the accoutrements are the selling points. The notice from 27 January 1716 similarly elaborates on the elements of music and dance: "At the Theatre in Lincoln's-Inn-Fields, this present Friday, being the 27th of January, will be performed a Play call'd, The Fatal Marriage; or, The Innocent Adultery. To which will be added a New Farce call'd, The Cobler of Preston. With several Entertainments of Singing and Dancing, (viz.) A Cantata by Mrs. Fitzgerald; A Sollo on the Violin by Mr. Clodio; And several Entertainments of Dancing my Monsieur de la Garde, Mr. Shaw, Mrs. Bullock, and Mrs Schoolding." The novelty of the play, the popular comedian Jemmy Spiller, and the attractions of song and dance are marketed, but not the Shakespearian content. As Drury Lane began to advertise its version of *The Cobler of Preston*, the descriptions of music and dance continue. *The Daily Courant* from 10 February 1716 is illustrative: "*The Tender Husband*, To which will be added a New Farce, call'd, The Cobler of Preston. With Dancing by Mons. Dupre, Mons. Boval, Mons. Dupre, jun., Mrs. Santlow and Miss Younger." The advertisements never mention Shakespeare, but repeatedly highlight the farcical aspects, the popular actors, singers, and dancers, always labeling the play "new."

As we have seen, Charles Johnson's afterpiece was initially a response to the Jacobite rebellion, and Bullock's piece began life as a competitor to Johnson. Yet the endurance of both texts in the theatrical repertoire suggests other reasons for their continued success. In the Induction material to *The Taming of the Shrew*, Johnson and Bullock found a plot that seemed ready-made for early eighteenth-century taste, even though their end-products were very different.[77] Shrew-taming and transformation plots were common in plays of the period, and must have been part of the attraction to Shakespeare's original play, as they were for John Lacy in *Sauny the Scott*. Both *Cobler* adaptations show traces of other shrew-taming and transformation plots besides Shakespeare's text, and were part of a wider commentary on taming and rebellion on the eighteenth-century stage.

Actor Thomas Jevon's *The Devil of a Wife* (1686) influenced both *Coblers of Preston*. Jevon's farce involves a cobbler convinced that he is a lord, and a shrew, Lady Lovemore, who is treated as a commoner. Sly's violent relationship with his wife in Johnson's afterpiece resembles Jevon's cobbler Jobson, and the initial scene of Bullock's *Cobler* is similar to Jevon's opening, where Jobson, "A Psalm-singing Cobler," tells his wife that he is determined to go to the ale house and drink. When she challenges him, he rants, "How now, Brazen-Face do you speak ill of the *Government*? I am King in my own House, and this is Treason against my Majesty" (1).[78] Jevon's play premiered in 1686, and was revived in July of 1715 at Lincoln's Inn Fields, less than a year before the premiere of both *Coblers*. In 1716, Jevon's play was paired with Bullock's *The Cobler of Preston* as an afterpiece on many occasions. Although no cast is listed for these performances, later notices list Jemmy Spiller in the role of Jobson, and it is likely that he performed both cobbler characters in these double bills. Later in the same season, Jevon's play was performed with Lacy's *Sauny the Scott*. The overabundance of taming stories suggested that this topic appealed to eighteenth-century audiences who may have particularly liked a double bill on this theme.

Bullock and Johnson rely on material from Jevon's *The Devil of a Wife* and allude to other anti-Jacobite plays such as *The Pretender's Flight*. Elkanah Settle's droll *The Siege of Troy* (1707), popular at Bartholomew Fair, also contains comic scenes that are based on the shrew-taming story, as does Bullock's own farce *The Adventures of Half an Hour* (1716).[79] Steele's *The Tatler* of 30 September 1710 features a shrew-taming story that involves the marriage of a father's youngest daughter to a man notable for killing his horse when it stumbled at an inopportune moment, and a test of several wives by their husbands. There were several contemporary variations on the dream-play, including Griffin's afterpiece *The Humours of Purgatory* and Nahum Tate's *A Duke and no Duke* (1685). These various shrew-taming and transformation narratives show a proclivity for these plots in the early eighteenth century. As Christopher Bullock explains, Shakespeare was only part of the "old plays" available for use: "I hope I may be allow'd (without Offence) to take *Shakespear's Tinker of Burton-Heath*, and make him the *Cobler of Preston*, as well as another; for no single Person has yet pretended to have a

Pattent for plundering Old Plays, how often soever he may have put it in practice."[80] These *Cobler* plays capitalize on a much larger and richer tradition of transformation, rebellion, and taming narratives beyond Shakespeare's text.[81]

Both 1716 versions of *The Cobler of Preston* had a lasting impact on later shrew-taming and cobbler texts. This plot remained in fashion for most of the eighteenth century, as exemplified by the farcical opera *The Merry Cobler: Or, the Second Part of The Devil to Pay* (1735) by Charles Coffey, based also on Jevon's *Devil of a Wife*.[82] The plot revolves around Jobson the Merry Cobler, and Sir John Loverule, a worthy Country Gentleman, with his wife Lady Loverule, "much alter'd for the better." Here, Jobson engages in violent taming of his wife by strapping her, "This is the sov'reign Pill, / If she's proud and scorning, / Cures her of every Ill, / Taken Night and Morning" (3). Coffey's piece involves shrew-taming and substantial music and was even translated into German in 1743. This opera shows the influence of Jevon's play and contains the motto associated with Hewson and Johnson's cobbler on the title page, *Ne Sutor untral Crepidam*.

Further continuing the popularity of shrew-taming plots is painter James Worsdale's *A Cure for a Scold*, a ballad opera performed at Drury Lane in February 1735. The prologue patriotically claims to "revive" Shakespeare's play "to instruct us how to wive." Worsdale intersperses Shakespeare's shrew-taming plot with ballads on the subject, clearly an appeal to the music-centered offerings that had become popular in the second two decades of the century. Worsdale's piece is essentially a conservative offering, hearkening to an older popular plot type augmented with song.[83]

The 1749 burletta *The Jovial Cobler, or, A Light Heart's better than a Heavy Purse* also resembles *The Cobler of Preston* plots. This version opens with a cobbler's stall on one side of the stage, and Sir Walter Wealthy's house on the other side. The cobbler Gabriel Nightengale begins the play by singing, which wakes Sir Walter, and his wife Lady Wealthy rants, "This Cobler now has nothing else to think on, / But sing all Day, and every Night to drink on" (8). When Gabriel is asked to come before Sir Walter because of his incessant singing, he breaks into song:

> Come all fellow Coblers and listen to me,
> I'll shew you how those of superior Degree,
> Are nothing but Coblers, no better than we,
> Both High and Low in this agree.
> 'Tis here fellow Cobler, and there fellow Cobler,
> Still patching and mending d'ye see.
> The Patriot so great when the Nation's wore out,

With Economy's Leather he heel taps it stout,
And tho' but a Cobler, he makes a great Rout.
Both High and Low, &c. (9).

The Jovial Cobler continues the tradition of the singing cobbler from Bullock, and the title signals its distance from Johnson's didactic cobbler text. These later versions of the cobbler story and shrew-taming plot embellish their sources with additions of music in line with the two 1716 afterpieces. Initially inspired the Jacobite Rebellion and by theatrical competition, the *Cobler* plays were popular on the stage and in print. Both adapters hit the mark with a comic form that appealed to audiences irrespective of current politics or theatrical squabbles, harnessing music and plots with an enduring ability to satisfy taste.

In 1716, Shakespeare's comic material provided an ideal basis for these two afterpieces. The Induction from *The Taming of the Shrew* was a brief stand-alone comic plot, suitable for two very different end products, one related to anti-Jacobite concerns, and the other connected to the possibilities for comic roles to suit his acting company as well as to incorporate popular music. Neither adapter turned to this material with the primary aim of improving or even adapting Shakespeare.

Richard Leveridge's *The Comick Masque of Pyramus and Thisbe* (1716)

A third afterpiece from this season used Shakespearian comic material as a basis, here the Pyramus and Thisbe section from *A Midsummer Night's Dream*. Like the Induction from *The Taming of the Shrew*, this material was a short independent interlude, a ready-made plot for embellishment, specifically with the reaction of a popular English singer to the invasion and predominance of Italian opera and singers. Richard Leveridge used Shakespeare's comic material to satirize Italian opera in his afterpiece *The Comick Masque of Pyramus and Thisbe*. Not unlike John Dennis, Leveridge aspired to reform public taste and direct it away from opera. Dennis turned to critical prose as his medium, and Leveridge employed the dramatic form of the afterpiece as a method of comment. Leveridge was a popular bass singer who composed songs for the theater, including music for *Macbeth* in 1702, and participated in many of the earliest English operas, such as *Arsinoe* in 1705. He established a niche as Hecate in *Macbeth* for almost fifty years, did some moonlighting for the opera company at the Queen's theater at the Haymarket, and moved to Rich's theater in 1714. Leveridge specialized in entracte songs and songs within plays, and popularized many of the patriotic songs that he wrote, including "The Roast Beef of Old England" and "In Praise of Old English Brown Beer," and he published several collections of his songs.[84] Like Charles Johnson, Leveridge also ran a coffee house at Covent Garden and was a well-known figure in the eighteenth-century theatrical world.[85] Charles Gildon's praise of Leveridge stresses his native roots in opposition to foreign competitors: "scarce any Nation has given us, for all our Money, better Singers, than Mrs *Tofts* and Mr *Leveridge*, who yet being of our own Growth, maintain but a second or third Character among worse Voices."[86]

Though he was known as "the Father of the English Stage" in his retirement, Leveridge's career began to wane as the popularity of Italian opera singers grew in the early eighteenth century.[87] To craft a burlesque of Italian opera, Leveridge turned to Shakespeare's "Pyramus and Thisbe" material, a piece easily adaptable to the current situation with opera and also amenable to additions of music and song. The success of Gay's recent 1715 afterpiece *The What D'Ye Call It: A Tragi-Comi-Pastoral Farce*, which mocks every variety of play, certainly influenced Leveridge, and he may have seen an opportunity for a similar burlesque using Shakespeare's play as a base.[88] Leveridge staged his piece as a benefit performance for himself, and it served as a means to personally express his sentiments against this foreign fad in a format that took advantage of his musical talents. As early as 1705, writers were complaining about foreign taste. The epilogue to *The Amorous Miser; or the Younger the Wiser* (1705) laments that "The golden Days of Wit / When English Humour, English Hearts cou'd please" are gone, and "Foreign Whims" and "Foreign Tricks" are all the rage. Leveridge yearns for a return to native English entertainments, and espouses a patriotic nostalgia we also see in the prologue to Gay's 1717 play *Three Hours After Marriage*:

> How shall our author hope a gentle Fate,
> Who dares most impudently—not translate.
> It had been civil in these ticklish Times,
> To fetch his Fools and Knaves from foreign Climes;
> Spaniards and French abuse to the World's End
> But spare old England, lest you hurt a Friend.

Like Gay, Leveridge reacts against foreign entertainments, specifically their influence on music.

Similar to the advertisements for the two *Cobler of Preston*s, Leveridge's afterpiece boasted "all New Musick . . . both Vocal and Instrumental" as an attraction to audiences on the title page. The entertainment and variety of the piece are promoted as its selling points: "As Diversion is the Business of the Stage, 'tis Variety best contributes to that Diversion. The Reader therefore, or *Auditor rather*, tho' the severest Critick, 'tis hoped will accept of the following *Entertainment*." Here opera is the object of burlesque; it has been "chiefly regaled with high *Recitative* and *Buskin* Airs" but in "this Exotick Essay" he has "endeavoured the quite Reverse of those *exalted Performances*."[89] As Johnson used Shakespeare's tinker to ridicule rebellion, so Leveridge employs Shakespearian material to deride Italian opera. "If the first *Founders*, the *Italians*, in the Grandest of their *Performances*, have introduced *Lions*, *Bears*, *Monkies*, *Dragons*, &c. as their *Doughty Fables* require," poses Leveridge, "I know no Reason why I may not turn *Moonshine* into a *Minstrel*; the *Lion* and *Stone Wall* into *Songsters*; and make them as Diverting as a Dance of *Chairs* and *Butterflies* have been in one of our most Celebrated *British* Entertainments."[90] Leveridge's send up of Italian opera parallels Shakespeare's mockery of amateur acting. Aspiring to poke fun at the absurdities of Italian opera that threatened his own popularity, he draws on a formula for comedy derived from Shakespeare: "From that Immortal Author's Original, I have made bold to Dress out the same in Recitative, and Airs, after the present *Italian* Mode, hoping I have given it the same Comical Face, though in a Musical Dress."[91]

Leveridge found little he needed to change in his source plot, and his major effort was to supplement the comic text with music. These musical additions were highlighted as the substance of the work, and he advertised the libretto for *Pyramus and Thisbe* at the first performance to capitalize on the aural features.[92] This mixture of music and Shakespeare hearkens back to the strategy used in the 1674 *Tempest*, the 1692 *Fairy-Queen*, and Charles Gildon's *Measure for Measure*. Leveridge does not include either his or Shakespeare's name on his title page—his priority was music.[93]

Instead of presenting *Pyramus and Thisbe* to an audience of Athenians, Leveridge instead creates Mr. Semibreve, the composer of the work, and the afterpiece is performed for Semibreve's friends Crotchet and Gamut. The plot of a rehearsal play-within-a-play resembles Gay's recent *The What D'Ye Call It* (1715) as well as the perennially successful burlesque *The Rehearsal*. The cast is separated according to music and drama, with dramatis personae played by actors, and *personaggi* played by singers.

Leveridge's afterpiece featured many of the same actors as Bullock's *The Cobler of Preston*, produced three months earlier at Lincoln's Inn Fields, and he may well have wanted to re-create an ensemble rapport between these short comic pieces. The popular actor Jemmy Spiller (who played Toby Guzzle in Bullock's *The Cobler of Preston*) took the part of Bottom, and Leveridge himself was Pyramus. William Bullock, Sr., who played Grist the Miller, performed Peter Quince. Hildebrand

Bullock, the brother of Christopher and son of William, played Flute, and Thisbe was performed by Pack, who frequently sang women's parts opposite Leveridge. W. R. Chetwood, in his *A General History of the Stage* (1749), remembered that Pack "first came upon the Stage as a Singer; and being, as they say, a *smock-fac'd Youth*, used to sing the Female Parts in Dialogues with Mr *Leveridge*, who has so many Years charm'd with his manly Voice" (208). The comic rapport between Leveridge and Pack must have been one of the selling points of the afterpiece for contemporary audiences.[94]

The musical embellishments to Leveridge's source play maintain the humor of the original and provide a well-integrated musical commentary on the dramatic plot. For instance, after Leveridge delivers the prologue to the play-within-the play, he includes an extra song that captures the rustic simplicity of the original plot:

> Yet I see some Critick Faces,
> That will say, the Author's Noodle
> Is grown frantick, soft or addle;
> But no matter if it please ye,
> At their Thoughts he will be easy:
> So he bid me when he sent me,
> Say his Hopes were to content ye,
> And that you should not repent ye
>
> . . . .
>
> So to Night with something Airy,
> Let not our good Will miscarry,
> We intend to make you Merry. (5–6)

Perhaps punning on the good "Will" Shakespeare, the prologue concludes that "The Singers [instead of Shakespeare's "Actors"] are at hand, and by their show / You shall know all, that you are like to know" (6). Semibreve corrects the Prologue's singing: "Hold, hold, Mr. *Prologue* I would have it / With a falling Cadence as thus— / You shall know all, that you are like to know" (6). Leveridge capitalizes on his own well-known voice here, having Semibreve correct him in an amusing scene where he could take advantage of his reputation for comic effect. Leveridge's ridicule of extravagant singing continues with a dig at the irrational nature of Italian opera. When Crotchet asks, "I wonder whether the *Lion* be to sing?" Semibreve replies, "Never wonder at that, for we that have Study'd the *Italian Opera* may do any thing in this kind" (9).[95] Similarly, Crotchet describes Pyramus's death, "I'll assure you the Man died well, like a Hero in an *Italian Opera*, to very good Time and Tune" (12). The financial motivations of Italian opera do not escape critique; when Pyramus discovers Thisbe's bloody mantle, Semibreve comments on his fiscal concerns: "If this won't fetch a Subscription, I'll never pretend to Compose *Opera*, or *Mask* again, while I live" (12).

The conclusion to Leveridge's piece further burlesques the conventions of Italian opera, with all of the characters alive at the end. Gamut protests that Pyramus and Thisbe cannot sing the epilogue because they are dead, but Semibreve responds that this is no problem for audiences accustomed to operatic irrationalities: "Pho, pho, d'ye think the Audience suppose them to be Dead? that's a Jest indeed. — I think it is better to make 'em rise and sing the Epilogue, and go off by themselves, than to have Three of Four dirty Property Fellows come and carry 'em off" (14). Even Pyramus finds this a bit of a stretch for his imagination, as he admits, "'tis a New thing, / To make the Dead get up and sing" (14), but realism obviously is not a priority here.

As Charles Johnson hoped to squelch any rebellious tendencies in 1716 Londoners, Leveridge aimed to mock fickle audience taste for foreign opera over native English music, particularly the implausible plots, extravagant singing, and financial goals of Italian opera.[96] Pyramus's concluding verses, "All are Wise, / And feign wou'd rise / To Pow'r and Riches" (15), call attention to Leveridge's goal of pleasing audiences, and also suggest a predicament similar to Dennis's — Leveridge wants to provide pleasing entertainment, yet he does not agree with current taste, especially for opera.

Unfortunately, none of Leveridge's music for *Pyramus and Thisbe* survives, but the script clearly shows his intent to poke fun at the art form that had nearly cost him his career. As a native English vocalist, Leveridge had a personal stock in the success or failure of Italian singers, and chose to use his benefit performance to combat these foreign competitors with the successful formula of mixing substantial music with his dramatic text, and promoting these musical additions as a drawing point for audiences. Leveridge's dramatic and musical achievements extended beyond the immediate concerns of 1716, and influenced later adapters of the Pyramus and Thisbe material, particularly Lampe's 1744 burlesque *Pyramus and Thisbe*.

A fourth farce from the 1716 season at Lincoln's Inn Fields, William Taverner and Dr. Browne's *Everybody Mistaken: A Farce*, unfortunately was not printed, but apparently had several similar aspects to other reworkings of Shakespearian comic material this season. *The London Stage* records only three performances of this piece, which involved *The Comedy of Errors* and a new masque entitled *Presumptuous Love*.[97] The masque does survive, with a relationship between the character Mopsa and her husband, Damon, that resembles other shrew-taming plots. Damon, played by Richard Leveridge, is teased for having "a Scold for your

Wife" (19), and this plot would have been right at home with many of the other shrew-taming texts of the season.

In addition to the shrew-taming resonances in the masque, even without the text of the mainpiece we can draw a few preliminary conclusions based on the authors and on contemporary responses to the performance. Both Taverner and Browne were hack writers, the type of scribblers condemned in the epilogue to Gildon's *Measure for Measure*. Taverner wrote a few minor plays that are largely forgotten, and Browne was a physician who was convicted of libel twice in 1706. Reminiscent of "needy Gildon," Browne is described as "as a mere tool of the booksellers," "always needy," and "an industrious writer."[98] Taverner and Browne adopt an older formula of combining Shakespearian comic material with a masque, resembling earlier adaptations by Granville and Burnaby from the turn of the century, but this did not capture current taste as Bullock, Johnson, and Leveridge were able to. This adaptation had perhaps the shortest life, probably because it was out of step with more profitable ways to rework a Shakespearian comic source.

Conclusion

We can draw several conclusions about the ways Shakespearian comic material was adapted in 1716. The pieces discussed in this chapter were written by practical men of the theater: Johnson was a seasoned playwright, Bullock was an actor-playwright-manager, and Leveridge was active in the London entertainment scene for over fifty years, writing and singing his own popular pieces as well as performing in pantomime and opera. It is thus understandable that these three adaptations in particular would have a close affinity with immediate concerns in eighteenth-century theaters. The success of these pieces owed more to the form of the afterpiece than to the Shakespearian content. In the middle years of the eighteenth century, audiences demanded more than a Shakespearian pedigree for their comic enjoyment, and the comedies were treated no differently than works by the minor Restoration dramatist Thomas Jevon: for use as plot material. The Induction to *The Taming of the Shrew* supplied a plot type popular with audiences, appropriate for adding music and dance with timely political relevance. Shakespearian material existed in these pieces within a heritage of English forms of entertainment—songs, shrew-taming and transformation plots, farce, and popular actors—and was unencumbered by later concerns to improve and elevate his plays. The three comic adaptations that did not disappear from the repertory in this period, Granville's *The Jew of Venice,* Lacy's *Sauny the Scott,* and the operatic *Tempest* have similarities to the entertainments in these three adaptations: *The Tempest* had spectacular stage effects and music, *The Jew of Venice* had a lengthy masque, and *Sauny the Scott* contains the comic role of Sauny as well as music and dance. The 1716 afterpieces were successful not because they were based on Shakespeare, but because they reconfigured this popular plot type in connection with other successful material.

 The differences between Bullock's and Johnson's treatment of the Sly material can be traced to their contrasting positions in the eighteenth-century theater world. Johnson was a Hanoverian with strong anti-Jacobite politics derived in part from his social interaction with other Whigs at Button's Coffee House and at Drury Lane. Johnson saw the theater as an extension and support of the government, and he espoused a more political role for theater. Thus, his adaptation of Shakespeare invoked a political message. Bullock, on the other hand, as a member of a prominent family of comic entertainers active in the fairs and theaters since the turn of the century, valued theater for its potential entertainment value. As an eventual co-manager of Lincoln's Inn Fields, Bullock was acutely aware of what audiences responded to. Also, Bullock was an experienced actor who performed in his own plays, including *The Cobler of Preston.* He approached Shakespeare's material as an actor, entertainer, and soon-to-be theater manager. Johnson approached the same material as a diligent playwright with political interests, but no practical experience from a performance standpoint. This crucial difference can account for the diverse treatment of Shakespeare's comic material by these two playwrights in the same season. Leveridge's reworking of Shakespeare can likewise be tracked to his individual circumstances as a popular singer whose career was jeopardized by taste for foreign entertainments.

 In the second decade of the eighteenth century, as interest in literary criticism of Shakespeare increased, his comedies on the stage continued to provide raw material for farcical entertainments with little regard for aesthetic perfection or permanence.[99] The name of Shakespeare is more prominent in the prefatory material to these plays, but Shakespeare's comic texts remained fair game for extensive reworking with little regard for keeping them intact. Even in 1716, performance conditions and opportunities remain important influences, as they were almost seventy years earlier with *Bottom the Weaver* in our first discussion of Shakespearian comic material. This 1716 revival occurred only because playwrights found two brief comic pieces that could be easily embellished and reworked, not because of any intrinsic interest in Shakespeare as a writer of comedies. Adaptations of the comedies in 1716 continue to foreground performance aspects—actors, singers, and comic gagging—

and were revised according to the context of other popular comic forms, not according to ideas of what a comedy by Shakespeare should look like.

We saw in this chapter how Charles Johnson used Shakespearian material for political purposes, and we can begin to see the seeds of his next adaptation of Shakespeare here. Johnson saw potential for invoking the authority of Shakespeare, though again this notion remained separate from the idea of Shakespeare as the author of sacrosanct inviolable texts. At the same time that Shakespeare's comedies provided foundations for afterpiece plots with little concern for reforming or perfecting the Stratford poet, his works were increasingly the subject of interest in a growing body of literary and textual criticism. Charles Gildon's 1710 "Shakespeare's Life and Works," appended to Rowe's edition, and John Dennis's essay "On the Genius and Writings of Shakespear" (1711) were among the early critical studies of Shakespeare, and the poet also became a subject for discussion in *The Tatler* and *The Spectator*. The next chapter discusses how this developed alongside the practical realities of running successful theaters, and the impact of these circumstances on Shakespeare's comedies.

5
Early Georgian Politics and Shakespeare

FOLLOWING THE THREE 1716 AFTERPIECES, THE NEXT ADAPTATION OF Shakespearian comic material did not surface until seven years later, from the familiar pen of Charles Johnson.[1] In the previous chapter, we saw how Johnson employed Shakespearian material in *The Cobler of Preston* to satirize Jacobites. Later in his career, Johnson turned to Shakespeare again to craft an adaptation with a more subtle political relevance. *Love in a Forest* (1723) centers on *As You Like It* with additions from *Richard II*, *Love's Labour's Lost*, *Twelfth Night*, *Much Ado About Nothing*, and *A Midsummer Night's Dream*. None of the plays that Johnson included had been performed regularly; his selection of source material was motivated by concerns other than stage popularity.[2]

In 1722 Sir John Vanbrugh wrote to Jacob Tonson, "With all this encouragement from the Towne, not a fresh Poet Appears; they are forc'd to Act round and round upon the Old Stock, though Cibber tells me, 'tis not to be conceiv'd, how many and how bad Plays, are brought to them."[3] As Vanbrugh's comments indicate, the situation in the 1720s was dismal for new plays.[4] Theaters were reluctant to offer new plays because of the immense cost involved in mounting a fresh offering: actors had to learn new parts but received no compensation, and theaters had to pay author's benefits for new plays. This chapter examines the circumstances that would encourage a playwright to offer a new production in such an unreceptive environment, and that might persuade a theater to put on a new play as well, specifically one based on Shakespeare. To understand the impetus behind Charles Johnson's adaptation, we must look to the political and cultural context of the 1720s, particularly the circumstances surrounding the Black Act of 1723.[5]

As we saw in the previous chapter, Johnson often relied on other sources for his plays, but he only turned to Shakespearian comedy twice, both times when he wrote plays with political messages. Even though Johnson shows little regard for the integrity of his Shakespearian source in either play, he did seem to recognize that the name of Shakespeare was beginning to hold some authority in the early eighteenth century, and that Shakespeare could be useful for more than raw dramatic material. Although this did not affect the way Johnson treated Shakespeare's texts, it does signal a wider development of Shakespeare's reputation, albeit not necessarily based on appreciation for the comedies.

Johnson was the first adapter to use Shakespeare for overt political purposes related to the Jacobite rebellion and the celebration of George I in *The Cobler of Preston*. A second set of political and social circumstances incited him to turn to Shakespeare again for dramatic material and for authorization of his work. A brief summary of the political climate in the early 1720s will help explain why Johnson reworked Shakespeare in this particular manner in 1723. The wave of Jacobite activity from the 1715 rebellion, which culminated in the 1720s, has been described as the "most widespread and the most dangerous" period of Jacobitism.[6] The Atterbury plot revived concerns of Jacobitism, the bursting of the South Sea Bubble in 1720 encouraged hopes of a Stuart restoration, and the activities of the Blacks, a group of mischievous pseudo-criminals, were a growing concern. The circumstances preceding the Black Act of 1723 figure prominently in the political context of *Love in a Forest*, and for Johnson they provided an incentive that outweighed the many impediments to writing a new play. In the early 1720s there was much anxiety about the Blacks and the actions that would be taken against them, even though the Black Act did not receive final royal assent until May of 1723.

Most accounts of the Blacks emphasize their dangerous potential, their crimes against the forest, and their status as gentry. One of the earliest descriptions of the Blacks occurs in a proclamation of George I from *The London Gazette* of 22–26 March 1720. The forest had long been considered the property of the king, and hunting rights in the forests belonged to royalty, based on a tradition of enforcing a property qualification for hunters.[7] The King refers to an earlier act against hunting in the night, and then rails against "divers Persons in great Numbers, some with painted Faces, some with Visors, and otherwise disguised, to the Intent they should not be known, riotously, and in manner of War arrayed, [who] had oftentimes then of late hunted as well by Night as by Day, in divers Forests, Parks, and Warrens in divers Places of this Realm, by Colour wherof had ensued great and heinous Rebellions, Insurrections, Riots, Robberies, Murders, and other Inconveniencies." His complaints extend beyond simple poaching, and involve accusations of more serious activity. Warning that such actions would now be considered felonies, he cites the example of "divers Persons, amounting to the Number of fourteen Men on Horseback, all armed with Guns, and some with Pistols, and two Footmen with a Greyhound, [who] did, in a violent and outragious Manner, on the two and twentieth Day of February last past, at Four of the Clock in the Afternoon, come into Bigshot-walk in Finchamsted Bailiwick in our Forest of Windsor, with their Faces blacked and disguised, some with Straw Hats and other deformed Habits, and did there pursue and shoot at our Red Deer, and did continue Hunting there till after Six a Clock, in which time they did kill four Deer there, three of which they carried away whole, and did cut off the Haunches of the fourth, and left the rest of the Carcase, and did terrifie and threaten the Keeper of our said Walk to shoot him, if he offered to come near them." Emphasizing their illegality and irresponsibility, George vows that "a speedy and effectual Stop may be put to all such outragious Practices," and offers a reward of £100 for the apprehension of any offenders. This Royal Proclamation, which preceded the Black Act, warns that the actions of the Blacks will lead to "great and heinous Rebellions, Insurrections, Riots, Robberies, Murders, and other Inconveniencies" that must be contained. The description provides specific graphic details of the reckless treatment of the deer, and similar depictions of poachers would later appear in Charles Johnson's *Love in a Forest* in 1723. Thus, as early as February of 1720, the government was taking action against what it labeled as dangerous activities by the Blacks, and urged further control of this group's operations.

Later accounts of the Blacks argue more emphatically for government intervention, and provide further details about this group's affairs. A description of the Blacks in Waltham-Chace printed in *The London Journal* of 10 November 1722 identifies them as gentry, and aims "to check the Insolence of a Set of Whimsical Gentlemen who have of late started up to make their Will a Law in the Neighborhood where they live." The forest, which is "well stock'd with Deer" now is "infested by a Body of artificial Negro's, (vulgarly called *The Blacks of Waltham:*) They are well arm'd and mounted, and the better to disguise themselves, black their Faces, &c. and seem to pay a sort of Obedience to one who stiles himself John, King of the Blacks." The dangers of this organization are apparent in their leadership and their weapons. The writer underscores their menacing and malevolent intents: "At their first Appearance 'twas believ'd they only propose to command this Chace, which they do when they please, and carry off what Deer is kill'd at Noon-Day, in Defiance of all Opposers, the keepers with their Quarter-Staves being unable to contend with Men arm'd with Carbines and Pistols. This dusky Tribe presume to punish all who dare to give an Information against any Deer Stealer." As the Proclamation by King George had earlier done, this account describes the Blacks as violent, rebellious, wanton poachers with little regard for authority.

The London Journal further illustrates the upper-class status of the

Blacks with the following anecdote. A ranger's widow received a reward for informing on a Deer Stealer, "upon which the smutty Chief, attended by some of his Black-Guard, came up to the Lodge, and with abusive language, threatned to burn the House in case she did not refund; adding, that they were Gentlemen, and were determined to do Justice: The good Woman undauntedly reply'd, that Gentlemen would scorn to insult her after that manner, and that therefore she believ'd them to be worthless Fellows, and would not return the Money; immediately their Captain drew off his black Glove, and exposed a fine white Hand, at the same time asking, whether she thought it had been ever used to hard Labour, or belong'd to a sorry Fellow?" The noble status of this group emerges clearly here, and their wide-ranging transgressions warrant immediate retribution: "it is hoped Means will be found to bring them to a deserved Punishment, since their Insolence is become intolerable; for with their lawless Authority, they interfere in most Disputes that happen. Most of our neighbouring Gentleman have been insulted by them." The writer gives several other instances of altercations between citizens and the Blacks: the group wreaked havoc on the trees of a certain gentleman after a dispute about his timber, and a similar argument with a woman over a church pew resulted in the Blacks cutting down trees in front of her house and defacing her garden. The Blacks again intervened in a quarrel between a farmer and a doctor who refused to pay for the hay he had ordered because it was damaged by rain. *The Daily Journal* of 13 January 1722 reflects the increasing legal concern over the Blacks: "The Justices of the Peace for the County of Essex have detained most of the Inhabitants about Epping Forest, to prevent their farther Hostilities on the Game in the said Forest."

As we shall see, Charles Johnson crafted *Love in a Forest* amid this climate of fear and unease. *The London Journal* of 22 December 1722, barely two weeks before Johnson's adaptation was performed, recounts that the Waltham Blacks "still continue to go on in the lawless Manner which they have heretofore done; that they have at several Times cut down, and bark'd 600 Trees belonging to one Gentleman, and *King John* has, by Letter, threaten'd several others: So mischievous are these *masked Gentry*, that where 50 Deer used to be seen in a Herd on the Chace, there is now scarce Half a score." As the Blacks continue their forest depredations and persist in their intimidations, the call for government intervention becomes more acute. *The London Journal* proclaims, "Their Insolence is become insupportable, and the Country Gentlemen are about to Petition the Parliament for Redress."

Johnson's adaptation was performed and printed in January of 1723, when references to the Blacks increasingly filled the newspapers. *The*

Daily Journal of 24 December 1722 contains the following story of the Blacks' violence: "On Thursday Night last a lamentable Misfortune happen'd at Hackwood Park in Hampshire, a Seat of the Duke of Bolton's, where the Keepers apprehending that some Deer-stealers were in the Park, alarm'd the House, calling all the Servants to their Assistance; amongst the rest the Confectioner to the Family ran to their Aid, when one of the Park-keepers mistaking him for a Thief, discharged the Blunderbuss against him, loaded with sixteen Balls, which tore the unhappy Person all to pieces." What began as poaching ended with an unexpected death, due to the unpredictable nature of the Blacks' insurgencies and the potential for their mischief to escalate.

Within a few days of the 9 January premiere of *Love in a Forest*, *The Weekly Journal: or, British Gazetteer* reported on 5 January that "The Person who stiles himself King of the Blacks with his Company, still continues to commit fresh Disorders, and 'tis said they have murder'd some Persons who boasted that they knew and would discover some of the Company. 'Tis believ'd that their Violences will shortly be laid before the Parliament." Similar to the earlier anecdotes of the Blacks, this report stresses their capacity for murder, and the much-anticipated intervention of Parliament. Johnson's play coincided with these accounts; *The Daily Journal* of 22 January 1722–23 describes the activities of the Blacks: "Complaint haveing been made to his Majesty of a Set of People who style themselves the *Blacks of Waltham*, and have a Person at their Head called *King John*, who ride about the County of Southampton in disguise, committing great Depredations on the Estates and Persons of his Majesty's Liege Subjects; a Proclamation is order'd to the Press for the discovering and seizing the said *King John* and his Accomplices, in order to their being brought to answer for their unlawful Practices."[8] On the same page, an advertisement for Johnson's *Love in a Forest* appears. The forest setting emphasized the contemporary relevance of Johnson's play, and the activities of the Blacks and the subsequent response of the Whig government are crucial for understanding the genesis and context of this adaptation.

Regardless of what actually happened in the forests, the public perceived the situation as an emergency that could escalate into heinous crimes, and thus must be contained.[9] In May of 1723 the Hanoverian government enacted the Black Act, which made it a felony to enter a forest under disguise or with a blackened face and to hunt, wound, or steal deer. It was a capital offense if the deer were taken from the King's forest, and the act transformed a number of other criminal offenses into capital crimes.[10] However, the events of the early 1720s complicate the motives behind the Black Act and point to concerns other than simply preserving the forests from poachers. In particular, the episodes related

5: EARLY GEORGIAN POLITICS AND SHAKESPEARE   193

to Jacobitism in the 1720s figure prominently in the course of the government's actions concerning the forests.[11] Aftereffects of the Jacobite conspiracy known as the Atterbury Plot were still resonant, since conspirator Christopher Layer was not hanged until May of 1723. The newspapers of late 1722 and early 1723 regularly discuss Bishop Atterbury's arrest and exile, as well as Layer's imprisonment and impending execution. The Black Act was part of the Hanoverian government's effort to maintain control of disruptive social influences. This oppressive law was an essential component in consolidating Robert Walpole's influence, and coincided with his rise to power.[12] In turn, Johnson's *Love in a Forest* also had wider appeal as an anti-Jacobite text in the tradition of this earlier *The Cobler of Preston*.

As numerous historians have pointed out, Walpole's real fear was Jacobitism, not the Blacks. Several anti-Catholic measures were instigated in the early 1720s, including the suspension of habeas corpus and a fine for Roman Catholics. The Black Act itself has connections to Jacobitism because the Blacks were involved with the Atterbury plot.[13] The Dutch envoy L'Hermitage reported in 1723 that Sir Henry Goring, a central figure in the Atterbury Plot, "had formed a company out of the Waltham Blacks for the Pretender's service." According to L'Hermitage, Walpole's discovery of this connection between the Blacks and Jacobitism "led to the bringing of the Waltham Black Act into Parliament."[14]

A Jacobite broadside found in the state papers for the day Christopher Layer was arrested (18 September 1722) further associates the deer poachers with Jacobitism. Entitled "The Hunting of the Newfound *Dear* with its Last Legacy," this text casts King George I as a "beast that's come from Dover / And some call it a Deer" who will be hunted:

> And when that we do chase him,
> And dress him fit for the Spit,
> We will make the best of his Carcass
> We will not waste a Bit.

The poem details how various parts of the King's body will be distributed, including his hide to "make / A presbyterian Jump," and even his "excrement will serve / To dung some _____ Land." Two triumphant stanzas conclude the poem by pledging to give the King's horns "to some honest Tory" who will "blow the tidings to the Man / That's O're the Raging Sea":

> And you that will come to this feast,
> Come let's goe chase the Dear,

> For Hunting it is a pleasant sport
> Fit for a Lord or Peer.[15]

The deer hunters in this poem are Jacobite Lords, and their prey is not a deer, but rather the King. The antagonism between the government and the Blacks, with their links to Jacobitism, became the subject for literary use in this broadside. As we shall see, Charles Johnson's adaptation *Love in a Forest* involves a similar employment of this conflict for dramatic material.

The Black Act had lasting ramifications for the history of English criminal law, and many historians have debated whether the act was a direct response to the forest activities, or a method of government repression. E. P. Thompson maintains that it was not the deer-stealing actions of the Blacks, but instead the challenge to authority that led to this law. John Broad argues that the Black Act "together with the Riot Act of 1715 provided the Whigs with a machinery for law and order which could be operated in the interests of the establishment."[16] Government control of the forests was not universally agreed upon as the best solution to the situation, and there was not unequivocal support for government intervention. Many local inhabitants saw this intrusion as disrupting the age-old methods of maintaining relationships between gentry and forest residents. In fact, the vicar of Winkfield, Reverend Will Waterson remarked that *"Liberty* and *Forest Laws* are incompatible."[17] Thus, Charles Johnson had a compelling reason to craft a new play around *As You Like It*, in order to justify the Hanoverian government's intervention in the forests. His adaptation would have been attractive to Drury Lane because of its pro-Hanoverian stance, a characteristic mode of that theater.[18]

Johnson's advertising strategy differs significantly from earlier adaptations of Shakespearian comic material, and marks a new juncture in Shakespeare's reputation. Johnson's name never appears in promotions for the play, and Shakespeare assumes a more prominent position as the author. Johnson accentuates the Shakespearian pedigree of *Love in a Forest* even though the piece is promoted as a "new play." *The Daily Post* of 9 January advertised "a Comedy, call'd *Love in a Forest*, Alter'd from the Comedy, call'd *As you Like it*. Written by Shakespear." *The Daily Journal* for January 1723 similarly did not include Johnson's name in the advertisements: "a New Comedy, call'd, *Love in a Forest*. As it is alter'd from Shakespear's Comedy, call'd, *As you like it*." The advertisements for *Love in a Forest* deliberately focus on Shakespeare as the drawing point, not Johnson. We have seen that all previous adapters of the comedies promoted components other than Shakespeare — William Burnaby's revamped *Twelfth Night*, for instance, was advertised as a work by the author of *The Ladies' Visiting-Day*, and Davenant's *The Law Against Lovers* was passed off as his own play—but with Johnson's second reworking, we can see an increase in the value of Shakespeare's name.

In Shakespeare's *As You Like It*, Johnson found material that was relevant to this political situation.[19] Even by simply renaming the play *Love in a Forest*, Johnson called to mind the troubling events that precipitated the Black Act; John Loftis points out that the practice of titling plays in reference to current affairs was not uncommon, even if the contents of the play did not bear out the political implications in the title.[20] Additionally, the advertisement in *The Evening Post* for the printed version of *Love in a Forest* includes the epigraph printed on the title page of the first edition, "Nostra nec erubuit Sylvas habitare Thalia" [Our comic muse (Thalia) did not blush to live in the Woods].[21] This phrase links Johnson's comic endeavor to the current events in the English woods and overtly locates his dramatic efforts in the scene of contemporary legal, social and political strife.

Many aspects of *As You Like It* conveniently parallel the forest controversy, and it is easy to see why Johnson turned to this source material. Even though Duke Senior and his followers remain poachers in both the original play and the adaptation, Duke Senior expresses reservations about their activities. For instance, in Johnson's 2.1 (as in Shakespeare's), Duke Senior remarks:

> Come, shall we go and kill us Venison?
> And yet it irks me, the poor dapple Fools,
> Being native Burghers of this Desart City,
> Shou'd, in their own Confines, with forked Heads,
> Have their round Haunches goar'd. (22)

This reflection echoes the descriptions of the activities of the Blacks, such as the *London Gazette* (22–26 March 1720) account of three deer "which they carried away whole, and did cut off the Haunches of the fourth, and left the rest of the Carcase." For Johnson, this reference to slaying deer in their own territory was ideal for strengthening sentiment against the Blacks, and reinforcing the need to protect the forest from such encroachments.

Several of Johnson's changes to *As You Like It* further promote government intervention in the forests, but perhaps the most significant shifts occur in the character of Jaques. Adding components of Benedick from *Much Ado About Nothing* and Berowne from *Love's Labour's Lost* to Jaques, Johnson creates a more sympathetic character. Jaques falls in love with Celia despite his admonishments about marriage—a far cry from the cynical, solitary character in Shakespeare's play, and Jaques and Celia are allotted almost equal time to Rosalind and Orlando. Other changes to Jaques condemn the Blacks' depredations. In Johnson's adaptation, Jaques delivers the First Lord's speech on the wounded stag, from 2.1:

> To Day, my Lord of *Amiens*, and myself,
> Lay in the Shade of an old Druid Oak,
> Whose antique venerable Root peeps out
> Upon the Brook that brawls along this Wood,
> To which Place, a poor sequestred Stag,
> That from the Hunter's Aim had ta'en a Hurt,
> Did come to languish; and indeed, my Lord,
> The wretched Animal heav'd forth such Groans,
> That their Discharge did stretch his leathern Coat
> Almost to bursting, while the big round Drops
> Cours'd one another down his innocent Nose
> In piteous Chace; and thus the hairy Fool
> Stood on the extreamest Verge of the swift Brook,
> Augmenting it with Tears. (22–23)

This sympathetic portrait of the wounded deer surely would have resonated with Johnson's audience when similar events were happening in the English forests.[22] By giving this speech to Jaques (a major character transformed into a sympathetic lover) instead of to the First Lord (a minor character), Johnson creates a spokesman who generates sympathy for the Whig government's actions against the Blacks.[23]

At the end of the same scene, Jaques delivers a further moralization (which is relayed secondhand by the First Lord in Shakespeare's version): "Are we not all Usurpers, Tyrants, worse, / To fright these Animals and kill them thus / In their assign'd and native Dwelling-Place." In Shakespeare's play, at the end of this speech, Duke Senior says to the Second Lord, "Show me the place [where you left Jaques]. / I love to cope him in these sullen fits, / For then he's full of matter" (2.1.67–69). Johnson changes the Duke's lines so that he becomes a companion of Jaques in the contemplation of the wounded deer: "Shew me this Place, / There will we sweetly moralize together, / And make our Contemplations give at once / Delight and Use" (23). Instead of observing Jaques, Duke Senior here joins in his compassion, again questioning the unequivocal acceptance of poaching in which he participates. It is likely that members of Johnson's audience would have picked up on this sympathetic musing, increasing support for government intervention in the forests.

Casting choices further solidified Johnson's political aims, particularly with Colley Cibber in the role of Jaques. Cibber was a prominent Hanoverian supporter: he had recently dedicated his anti-Jacobite play *The Non-Juror* to the King, netting £200 in royal favor, and subsequently became Poet Laureate in 1730.[24] At Drury Lane, Cibber's Jaques would have added support for the actions of the Hanoverian government. The role of Jaques was expanded not only to tailor a part for Cibber, but also to provide a prominent advocate for government control of the forests. The fact that Johnson included an appropriate political role for Cibber must have helped persuade Drury Lane to stage the play in a time when few new plays were mounted.

Johnson also makes changes to Shakespeare's play to comment on the Foresters, who were responsible for patrolling the forests. In his version of Shakespeare's 4.2, Johnson clearly delineates the Foresters from the Lords. In Shakespeare's play, the Lord is referred to as "Forrester," whereas Johnson makes the Forester a separate character. The song "What shall he have that killed the deer?" is sung in Shakespeare's version by the Lord, but Johnson specifies that the Forester, not the Lord, sings it.[25] Johnson capitalizes on current events taking place in the forests, creating a musical comment on poaching sung by Foresters. His use of Shakespeare to sanction the repressive government actions resulting in the Black Act of 1723 follows in the pattern of his earlier *Cobler* afterpiece, creating a second reworking of Shakespearian comedy with an anti-Jacobite aim.

The final words of Johnson's play appear to contradict the pastoral substance of his drama, as they posit preference for the city above the country. The epilogue questions the virtues of the country, lest the pastoral setting of *Love in a Forest* be mistaken for an approval of Tory country values over Whig support for the city. The epilogue criticizes the "*Country* Spouse, and Rural 'Squire" who are "Dirty and dull; ——— to every Pleasure lost" in favor of "The circulating Pleasures of the Town" that are "By regular and virtuous Laws refin'd." Not only does Johnson conclude his drama by favoring the city over the country, he includes a comment on the need for "virtuous laws" to refine the structure of civilized life, as the laws governing the forest intended. This characteristic Whig statement about the virtues of city life is a fitting conclusion to Johnson's reworking of Shakespeare.[26]

Johnson makes several structural changes to *As You Like It*, aside from interpolations from the Shakespearian canon and alterations to address contemporary politics. He omits Touchstone, Audrey, Phoebe, and William and combines the characters of Corin and Silvius into one smaller role. The rustics from *A Midsummer Night's Dream* enter in the final act of the play to perform an interlude entertainment while Ganymede changes to re-enter as Rosalind. Audiences may have recognized this popular source, which endured from Cox's Commonwealth droll *Bottom the Weaver* to Leveridge's more recent *Pyramus and Thisbe*, as a crowd-pleasing and accommodating text.

Johnson creates a set piece with this material by using well-known comic actors who performed only in this brief interlude. Pyramus was played by William Penkethman, described as "[the Flower of] *Bartholomew*-Fair, and the Idol of the Rabble. A fellow that over-does every thing, and spoils many a Part with his own stuff."[27] John Downes recorded that Penkethman "has gain'd more in Theatres and Fairs in Twelve Years, than those that have Tugg'd at the Oar of Acting these 50" (*Roscius*, 108). Penkethman acted Pyramus in Leveridge's *Pyramus and Thisbe* in September of 1723 at his Richmond theatre and must have been well-known in the popular role. The other actors in Johnson's mock play were similarly associated with fairs and low entertainments, including Thomas Wilson as the Lion and John Ray as Moonshine, who debuted as a singer at Southwark Fair in 1721.[28] Josias Miller was Thisbe, and Dicky Norris played Wall, both of whom shared booths with Penkethman at Bartholomew and Southwark Fairs. With this entertainment, Johnson capitalized on the comic ensemble acting of this group, in effect incorporating an afterpiece into his play based around successful comic characters and material. It is worth noting that Shakespeare's cross-dressed heroine Rosalind was not of particular interest in this adaptation. Jaques is the spokesperson for Johnson's views, not Rosalind, and Johnson does little to highlight or feature this now popular cross-dressed part.

While Johnson's play is certainly interesting for its use of Shakespeare, it is also an important document in the history of political performances at Drury Lane. Johnson's unusual dedication of the play to the Freemasons, of which he was a member, is the earliest evidence of the Masonic influence on a specific play.[29] Harry William Pedicord had identified William Chetwood's 1730 opera *The Generous Freemason; or, The Constant Lady, with the Comic Humours of Squire Noodle and his Man Doodle* as the earliest Masonic theatre piece, but Johnson's dedication shows Masonic activity in the London theaters at least seven years earlier.[30] Although Johnson's play was performed at a Whig theater and published by a Whig publisher, Johnson dedicates it to the Freemasons. As Paul Monod has recently argued, the Freemasons in England had a long history of association with the Stuart family, and thus with Jacobitism, a link that Johnson would certainly want to avoid.[31] Why would Johnson choose this group for his dedication, especially in light of his earlier *The Cobler of Preston*, which vehemently denounced Jacobitism shortly after the Rebellion of 1715?

The answer lies in the status of the Freemasons at the particular time of Johnson's adaptation. In 1717, the Grand Lodge was created, centralizing four London Lodges. Between the establishment of the Grand Lodge and 1723, five Grand Masters were elected, including the first noble Grand Master, John Duke of Montagu in 1721.[32] Philip, Duke of Wharton (1698–1731) was named the Grand Master of the Grand Lodge in 1722–23. Wharton had Jacobite sympathies, beginning with his controversial marriage to the daughter of a Tory general, and his encounter with The Pretender during his Grand Tour in 1716. The Duke of Wharton was later involved in the Atterbury Plot in 1722, and Wharton's Jacobitism is evident in his *True Briton* of 1723–24.[33] Wharton still maintained his Jacobite leanings as Grand Master, and had Jacobite songs played at his inauguration. Wharton was removed as Grand Master in 1723 and later formed the Gormogans, a new society claiming to exclude George I.[34]

Thus, by dedicating a Whig play to the Freemasons Johnson announces the legitimacy of the society as a result of the impending removal of Wharton in 1723. James Anderson's *Constitutions* of the Freemasons were also published in the same year; Johnson's dedication coincides appropriately with the publication of the first history of the Freemasons. In fact, the *Constitutions* were advertised in *The Daily Journal* for 25 January 1722–23, in the same issue with an advertisement for *Love in a Forest*. Johnson's inclusion of the mechanics from *A Midsummer Night's Dream* may also allude to the Freemasons. In the first act of *Love in a Forest*, Charles the Duke's Fencer announces that "the very Mechanicks, and Labourers in this Handicraft leave every Day their Occupations, and this populous City of *Liege*, and flock to visit their exil'd Sovereign, as they call him" (5).[35] Johnson employs Shakespeare to show approval for the Freemasons at a crucial point in their growth as a Hanoverian Whig institution.[36]

The success of *Love in a Forest* attests to Johnson's ability to speak to current events through Shakespeare and to craft a new offering in a difficult season. *Love in a Forest* was performed at least six times, including two author's benefits for Johnson.[37] *The London Post* for 14 January 1723 attests to the popularity of Johnson's benefit performance on 11 January, with "as numerous an Audience as has for this great while been seen; not only the Boxes, Pit and Galleries, but the Stage too being crowded with Spectators."[38] Lincoln's Inn Fields used a variety of Shakespearian plays to compete against Johnson, but for some reason did not mount any of the plays in Johnson's adaptation. For the second performance of *Love in a Forest* (10 January), Lincoln's Inn Fields offered *Julius Caesar*, *1 Henry IV* the next night, and on 14 January *Measure for Measure*. The final performance of *Love in a Forest*, another benefit for Johnson, took place on 15 January opposite a performance of *Othello* at Lincoln's Inn Fields. Compared to other adaptations of Shakespearian comedies in the early eighteenth century, *Love in a Forest* was certainly not a failure. It is unclear why its popularity waned after six performances; perhaps theatergoers preferred the Shakespearian offerings of Lincoln's Inn Fields over Johnson's adapted conglomeration. The competition strategy of Lincoln's Inn Fields relied mainly on the tragedies and histories; both were more popular than the comedies in our period. Johnson was eager to capitalize on the timely relevance of his play, and most likely published it as its run was ending. *The Evening Post* advertised the printed edition of *Love in a Forest* for sale first in the 15–17 January issue, and continued to promote the printed play for the rest of the month as anxiety over the Blacks increased.[39]

By presenting *Love in a Forest* as a rescued play of Shakespeare's, Johnson taps into the cultural resonance of the developing "National Poet," at a time when many of Shakespeare's plays were revived.[40] His prologue opens, "In Honour to his Name, and this learn'd Age, / Once more your much lov'd SHAKESPEAR treads the Stage." Johnson attaches his play to Shakespeare's growing reputation, claiming that he has "refin'd" "Another Work from that great Hand."[41] Shakespeare's "sacred Truths" buttress Johnson's pro-Whig comments on the forest and sanctity of its inhabitants. By "giv[ing] the Stage, from SHAKESPEAR one Play more," he claims only to "tune the sacred Bard's immortal Lyre," applying Shakespeare's views to the policies of the Hanoverian government. Like many adapters of the comedies, Johnson has more deference for Shakespeare's name than for his comic texts, and he engaged in a process of significant revision and compilation.

Charles Johnson maintained a position in the theatrical repertoire with a play almost every season for three decades and often incorporated contemporary social and political concerns into his plays. Johnson's appropriation of Shakespearian material at two points of political tension was an integral part of Drury Lane's pro-Hanoverian stance, and no doubt helped get his plays performed. With *Love in a Forest*, on the surface his aim is to present a timeless literary masterpiece retrieved from oblivion and rescued from obscurity, while unconditionally reworking numerous Shakespearian texts without reservation. Johnson both invites and shields his play from political application, offering the retitled work as a teaser to those who might be interested in such a reading. He gives Shakespeare a more prominent position in his prefatory material than we have seen in previous adaptations, and his adulation in his prologue departs from earlier attitudes to Shakespearian comedy. As the next chapter will show, Johnson certainly had no qualms about making major changes to his source plays, yet he was the most overt comic adapter to employ Shakespeare's name value.

6
Shakespearian Comedy Before Garrick

DAVID GARRICK'S ARRIVAL ON THE LONDON STAGE HAS USUALLY BEEN considered a major point of transformation for adaptations of Shakespeare. However, several important changes in the methods of and attitudes to adaptation in the two decades before Garrick's debut provided an ideal climate for his treatment of Shakespeare. We have already seen the effects of actors on the plays (John Lacy and Thomas Doggett), the influence of theater facilities on the 1674 *Tempest*, and the impact of a composer like Henry Purcell on *The Fairy-Queen*. In the 1720s and 1730s a new dynamic began to transform the ways Shakespeare's comedies were reshaped: reading Shakespeare and appreciation for his plays as printed texts.

The effects of reading Shakespeare can be seen in *Love in a Forest* and the subsequent adaptations of the comedies in the 1720s and 1730s. Beginning with Charles Johnson in 1723, playwrights tended to approach Shakespeare more as readers, and not so much as writers looking for raw dramatic material to accommodate actors or music. Johnson, for example, had a wide knowledge of the Shakespearian canon, especially unperformed plays, which he was able to draw on when writing his adaptation. As we shall see, other adaptations of the 1720s and 1730s show an interest in Shakespeare's comedies as texts, and even depend on a reading knowledge of both adapter and audience member.

The previous chapter demonstrated that *Love in a Forest* was inspired by the events surrounding the Black Act and the potential for the theater to comment on current events. Yet the play also marks a new phase in Shakespearian reception. Playwrights are as concerned with the page as they are with the stage, and also presume an audience who would appreciate both. Johnson's *Love in a Forest* derives from six Shakespearian plays that had not been performed regularly, and in some cases not at all. His familiarity with these plays had to come from reading them; he was the first adapter to appropriate Shakespeare based on a thorough reading knowledge.[1] Editions, periodicals, commonplace books, and other works designed for readers reshaped the climate for adaptations of the comedies.[2]

In the first three decades of the eighteenth century, even though Shakespeare's comedies were not all particularly successful on stage, his texts received more attention as reading material. Rowe's editions of 1709 and 1714, and Pope's edition of 1725 allowed playwrights and audience members to look at Shakespeare in new ways that previously had not been available.[3] The growing demand for editions in the early eighteenth century reflected an increase in stage popularity and in critical writings on the plays.[4] By 1719, according to one contemporary, a play "must please the Readers as well as the Hearers" in order to "gain an establish'd fame and reputation." Within fifty years, criticism likewise had transformed the reading public: "Criticism, which was formerly the great business of a scholar's life," remarked Joseph Priestly, "is now become the amusement of a leisure hour."[5]

The development of taste was a concern with John Dennis earlier in the eighteenth century, and editors of Shakespeare began to take up this cause, particularly Pope. The lack of guidance provided by the prefatory material in Rowe's edition suggests that refinement of public taste was not a predominant goal of his project. In fact, he specifically refuses to "enter into a Large and Compleat Criticism upon Mr. *Shakespear*'s Works" or "prescribe to the Tastes of other People."[6]

Rowe's 1709 readers were on their own to sort out Shakespeare's beauties from his faults. Pope's audience of 1725, however, received specific guidance about Shakespeare's poetry. Instead of leaving issues of taste to the reader, Pope could not resist "mention[ing] some of [Shakespeare's] principal and characteristic Excellencies, for which (notwithstanding his defects) he is justly and universally elevated above all other Dramatic Writers." Not content to let readers judge Shakespeare's poetry for themselves, Pope infamously relegates passages "which are excessively bad" to "the bottom of the page" and distinguishes "some of the most shining passages" with "comma's in the margin, and where the beauty lay not in particulars but in the whole, a star is prefix'd to the scene."[7] The reader of Pope's edition cannot escape the visual guidance provided by his system of "pointing out an Authors excellencies." The topical indexes to Pope's edition also contributed to the breakdown of Shakespeare's plays into individual passages for admiration and contemplation outside of the context of the plays.

Pope's 1725 edition was followed by Lewis Theobald's reply, *Shakespeare Restored* (1726) and his 1733 edition; the work of Pope and Theobald solidified interest in Shakespeare's texts as printed matter to be explicated on the page within the confines of the study. The well-known correspondence between these two editors in the 1720s signifies an unprecedented concern with close reading of Shakespeare's plays as printed texts.[8] By 1728, Pope mocked the obsessive interest in editing Shakespeare:

> Pains, Reading, Study, are their just Pretence,
> And all they want is Spirit, Taste, and Sense.
> *Commas* and *Points* they set exactly right;
> And 'twere a Sin to rob them of their *Mite*.
> Yet ne'er one Sprig of Laurel grac'd those Ribbalds,
> From slashing B[entle]y down to pidling *Tibbalds*:
> Who thinks he *reads* when he but *scans* and *spells*,
> A Word-catcher, that lives on Syllables.
> Yet ev'n this Creature may some Notice claim,
> Wrapt round and sanctify'd with *Shakespeare's* Name . . .[9]

Punctuation, scanning, and spelling are all aspects of a printed text, not a theatrical performance, and Pope's target is Shakespeare on the page. The impetus to establish an authentic text initiated by these early editors began to affect the stage, culminating in Garrick's advertised revivals of Shakespeare's original plays. Shakespeare was no longer just raw material for playwrights to reshape—he had a growing presence outside the boundaries of the theater with a public who began to read his works.

In the first few decades of the eighteenth century, excerpts from Shakespeare began to be commonly used to provide apt poetic descriptions and examples in a variety of print formats, from commonplace books to periodicals. Both the *Tatler* and the *Spectator* employed Shakespeare's poetry in this fashion. George Winchester Stone, Jr., notes that Steele often "seems to write an article solely to quote an appealing Shakespearian passage" and explicate it in his quest to educate readers.[10] Steele's use of Shakespeare to illustrate a moral precept is typical of the way the Stratford poet's words functioned outside of theatrical adaptation and performance.[11] By the 1720s, the use of Shakespeare for illustrative quotation was widespread and rarely relied on a theatrical context.[12]

The detachment of Shakespearian material from the domain of the plays was also encouraged by poetical commonplace books, which were enormously popular in the early eighteenth century.[13] The best-known, and most widely read was Edmund Bysshe's *The Art of English Poetry*. Initially printed in 1702, *The Art of English Poetry* went through nine editions before 1740. Bysshe's method of organization "inserts" passages of Shakespeare and other writers into a new context according to the "Subject" of the reader's "Thought," not the context of the original work, with the passages presented "as naked, and stript of superfluities" as possible. Within Bysshe's collection, Shakespeare exists as the author of poetical beauties arranged topically, not the originator of plots and characters for the stage, and his poetry was intermingled with that of other writers. Shakespeare was not so much the author of good stageworthy comic parts, like Bottom, Pyramus, and Shylock—here the emphasis is on poetic beauty, completely divorced from stage success or performativity. It is likely that most eighteenth-century playwrights encountered these commonplace books; Bysshe's *The Art of English Poetry* went through seven editions by 1724, for example.[14] Most literati of the later eighteenth century including Samuel Johnson, Oliver Goldsmith, Samuel Richardson, Horace Walpole, William Oldys, and Henry Fielding owned copies, and Hogarth's "Distressed Poet" (1736) labors to write poetry next to an open copy of Bysshe.[15]

The popularity of commonplace books continued in the early eighteenth century. The anonymous *Thesaurus Dramaticus* appeared the year after *Love in a Forest*, and was based on the dramatic selections from Bysshe.[16] This collection includes most of Shakespeare's plays, even those not performed regularly on the stage; the compiler had little regard for stage popularity or for originality.[17] The work privileges passages "within the Bounds of the Tragic Muse," even though it includes excerpts from several comedies. The anonymous compiler was motivated both by a patriotic impulse to defend and celebrate British theater, as well as concern for public taste. Shakespeare is a part of this nationalistic endeavor designed for individual readers, but only as one of many native writers valued for words over characters, for moral reflections over plot. The vogue for commonplace books in the 1720s is evident by the competition that occurred when the *Thesaurus Dramaticus* was printed. In 1724, new editions of Gildon's *The Laws of Poetry* and Bysshe's *The Art of English Poetry* were produced to compete with the *Thesaurus Dramaticus*. The following year Pope's edition of Shakespeare was printed, further enlarging the scope of Shakespeare in print. Editions, periodicals, and commonplace books shaped the reception history of Shakespeare in many significant ways before Garrick's arrival.[18]

We can see how the climate for Shakespeare has changed over twenty years with an example from Charles Gildon. Shakespeare provides a considerable proportion of selections in Charles Gildon's 1718 *The Complete Art of Poetry*. Gildon's first foray with Shakespeare focussed on musical additions without much concern for textual purity. At the turn of the century, he reworked Shakespeare's *Measure for Measure* mainly to incorporate Purcell's *Dido and Aeneas*, and even combined Shakespeare with Davenant's earlier adaptation of the play. By 1718 he approaches Shakespeare differently, with a new respect for Shakespeare's texts and their integrity, and for Shakespeare as a poet, not just a source of raw dramatic material.

Gildon had earlier applied his critical faculties to Shakespeare in his essay "Remarks on the Plays of Shakespear," included with Rowe's edition, where he denoted the beauties of each play.[19] Gildon continued this impetus in his 1718 work, avowing "to give the Reader the great *Images* that are to be found in those of our Poets, who are truly great, as well as their Topics and Moral Reflections." Shakespeare looms large here, and Gildon is convinced that the Stratford poet's "charms" will "touch the Soul of any one who has a true Genius for Poetry, and by Consequence enlarge that Imagination which is so very necessary for all Poetical Performances."[20] Gildon's reading practice is to "go through" Shakespeare, presumably looking for "the great Images" and "Charms" to "touch the Soul" of his readers and prospective poets.

Shakespeare is a particularly prominent part of this collection; a section of the sixth part of Gildon's work is devoted to "*Shakespeariana*; or the most beautiful Topicks, Descriptions, and Similes that occur throughout all *Shakespear*'s Plays." In this separate section of excerpts arranged by play, Gildon praises the writer he had earlier adapted: "Finding the Inimitable *Shakespear* rejected by some Modern Collectors for his Obsolete Language, and having lately run over this great Poet, I could not but present the Reader with a Specimen of his Descriptions, and Moral Reflections, to shew the Injustice of such an Obloquy. I might have been more large, for he abounds in Beauties; but these are sufficient to evince the Falsehood of their Imputation" (1:304).[21] Gildon is not reading with an eye to improving Shakespeare; his design is to skim the poetry for "specimens" of poetic beauty and taste. As an adapter, Gildon did not have the freedom to shape Shakespeare's material independent of the requirements for stage success. As a compiler of poetic beauties later in his career, however, Gildon could have free reign in his treatment of Shakespeare, with little concern for variables associated with audiences, actors, or theatrical conditions. Shakespeare no longer provides just plots and characters; he is now a source for descriptions and "Moral Reflections" as well, and his place in these commonplace books is separate from his reputation on stage. Plays are included that were not popular on the stage, and popular stage plays are not necessarily prominent.

If we turn back for a brief moment to *Love in a Forest*, we can see how this climate would affect adaptations of the comedies before Garrick revived them. There is no evidence that Charles Johnson used a specific commonplace book as a direct source for *Love in a Forest*, but the type of passage he cribs from Shakespeare and his willingness to borrow affirm a similar philosophy of excerpting, selecting, and combining relevant passages with little regard for original contexts.[22] In his prologue, Johnson apologizes for his "Honest Zeal" in approaching Shakespeare "with Pain, and Care." He uses a Shakespearian play (*As You Like It*) as a framework supplemented with relevant sections from other plays, as if he had read through Shakespeare looking for moral precepts or exemplary lines, drawing on Shakespeare's "Beauties" to supplement his own writing. This reading practice resembles the method used by authors of commonplace books or periodicals, as well as by Pope in selecting passages to demarcate for his readers' taste.

A brief discussion of Johnson's method of adapting Shakespeare will display his unique technique as well as the influence of Shakespeare in print and as a writer of poetical beauties. Johnson's changes to *As You Like It* fall into two main categories: new material written by Johnson, and material added from the Shakespearian canon. Several previous adapters had used more than one Shakespearian play: Davenant's *The Law Against Lovers* (1662) amalgamated *Measure for Measure* with *Much Ado About Nothing*, but both plays were among the few Shakespearian originals granted to Davenant in his theatrical patent. Colley Cibber's *Richard III* (1700) includes passages from *Richard II*, *Henry IV*, *Henry V*, and *Henry VI*; all of these history plays were performed on the stage from 1660–1700 and probably would have been familiar to Cibber from his experience in the theater. The crucial difference between Johnson's *Love in a Forest* and previous Shakespearian adaptations combining two or more plays is that Johnson assembles his Shakespearian material from plays that had not been performed regularly, and in some cases not at all. His knowledge of the canon came from reading.

A few select examples should sufficiently illustrate Johnson's technique. In the first occurrence, Johnson combines passages from *Richard II*, *Much Ado About Nothing*, and *As You Like It* to create a more formal scene for the battle between Charles the wrestler and Orlando. Charles expresses his reason for fighting with excerpts from Bolingbroke's speech to Richard II (1.1) when he charges Mowbray with treason:

> Now young Orlando do I turn to thee,
> And mark my Greeting well, for what I speak
> My Body shall make good upon this Earth,
> Or my divine Soul answer it in Heaven.
> Thou art a Traitor and a Miscreant,
> And wish (so please my Sovereign) e're I move,
> What my Tongue speaks, my right drawn sword may prove. (10)

Orlando responds with Mowbray's reply,

> Let not my cooler Words accuse my Zeal,
> 'Tis not the Trial of a Woman's War,

> The bitter Clamour of two eager Tongues,
> Can arbitrate this Cause between us two,
> The Blood is hot that must be shed for this. (10–11)

This interjection of material from *Richard II* elevates the tone and seriousness of this moment in the play while maintaining its Shakespearian flavor. Later in this scene, Charles taunts Orlando with a combination of lines from Antonio and Leonato from the final act of *Much Ado About Nothing* (5.1.76, 84): "Come, Sir, I'll whip you from your foining Fence, / Spight of your May of Youth and Bloom of Blood" (11). Audiences may not have recognized the specific Shakespearian material here, but Johnson maintains authentic Shakespearian dialogue without the risk of writing new and perhaps inferior verse.

In the previous chapter, we have seen that the modified character of Jaques was one of Johnson's major changes to his source. In crafting this character, Johnson uses material from Shakespeare, not external additions such as ideas of stockjobbers or Scots as earlier adapters did with Shylock and Sauny the Scott. A new scene between Jaques and Orlando illustrates this method with material from 3.2. of *As You Like It* where Orlando tells Jaques of his love for Rosalind. At this moment in the scene, Johnson inserts a version of the dialogue between Don Pedro and Benedick in the first act of *Much Ado About Nothing*. Orlando accuses Jaques of being "an obstinate Heretick in the Despight of Beauty, and the whole Female World."[23] Jaques's reply would be familiar to any reader of *Much Ado*: "That a Woman conceiv'd me I thank her: That she brought me up I likewise give her my most hearty Thanks; but that I will have a Recheate winded in my Forehead all Women shall pardon me: Because I will not do them the wrong to mistrust any, I will trust none." Further fusing Jaques with Benedick, Johnson gives his character Benedick's speech protesting marriage: "The Savage Bull may [bear the Yoak], but if ever the sensible *Jaques* does, pluck off the Bull's Horns and set them in my Forehead, and let me be vilely painted, and in such great Letters as they write, Here are Horses to be let; let them signify under my Sign, Here liveth *Jaques* the marry'd Man" (34–35). When merged with Benedick, Jaques becomes a witty lover rather than a melancholy solitary figure, and Orlando becomes a matchmaker and advocate for love in the tradition of Don Pedro. Even though *Much Ado* was rarely performed, Johnson was very familiar with these now famous characters, and could conceive of mixing them together. It is uncertain whether or not an audience would recognize this material, but we can at least conclude that Johnson knew the Shakespearian canon well enough to imagine combining these character to achieve his desired result.

Yet Johnson's method did not only involve assimilating two comic characters; he also included components of Touchstone from *As You Like It* and Berowne from *Love's Labour's Lost* when reworking Jaques. In a soliloquy after Celia departs, Jaques confesses (like Benedick in 2.3) that he is "in Love, horribly, strangely in Love!" and fears that he will be "the Jest of the World, I shall have Quirk and Witticisms broke on me innumerable,—Because I have railed on Marriage:—Why—Appetites alter, and one may love in his Age, I hope, what he cou'd not endure in his Youth." This new Jaques also has Touchstone's fear of cuckoldry (from 3.3): "wou'd my Mistress marry me, which bears a Question likewise, we have here no Temple but the Wood, no Assembly but horned Beasts,—Horns,—Aye, they may be a Wife's Dowry, 'tis plain they can not be a Man's own getting;—And yet the noblest married Man hath them as huge as the Rascal;—Is a Batchelor, therefore, more honourable than a Husband?" (41). Johnson's Jaques is a composite lover fashioned from a catalogue of Shakespearian love scenes and characters, constructed from authentic Shakespearian dialogue.

A final infusion from Berowne of *Love's Labour's Lost* (3.1 and 4.3) completes this character. Jaques tells Rosalind that he comes "in the Name of that wimpled, whining, purblind, wayward Boy; Regent of Rhiming, Lord of folded Arms, anointed Sover[ei]gn of Sighs and Groans, Don *Cupid*—!" (44) and confesses his lovesick state: "Prithee do not laugh at me, aye, I wou'd have a Woman—A Thing that is like a *German* Clock, always repairing—Ever out of Tune—Yes I am shot—Thumpt with the Boy's Bird-bolt under the Left Pap" (44). Jaques becomes an amalgamation of Shakespearian lovers derived from highlights from several plays. The way Johnson reworked Jaques shows his familiarity with comedies that had not been staged with any frequency, and he knew the plays well enough to cobble together bits and pieces from various speeches.

A concluding example will extend Johnson's range of reference. To generate additional dialogue between Rosalind/Ganymede and Orlando, Johnson turns to the exchange between Duke Orsino and Viola in *Twelfth Night* (2.4) for fodder. Rosalind tells Orlando, "Too well I know what Sort of Faith we Men to Women owe, my Father had a Daughter lov'd a Man; as it might be, perhaps, were I a Woman, I might Love you." Predictably, in response to Orlando's question "And what is her History?" she responds, "A Blank, she never told her Love, but let Concealment, like a Worm i'th Bud, feed on her Damask Cheek, she pined in Thought; and with a green and yellow Melancholly, she sat like Patience on a Monument, smiling at Grief—" (48). Shakespeare's oeuvre acts as a commonplace book for Johnson, providing passages for use in appropriate moments.

Johnson obviously knew Shakespeare's comedies well enough to cull passages from four of them (*As You Like It, A Midsummer Night's Dream, Love's Labour's Lost*, and *Much Ado About Nothing*) as well as from *Richard II*. Most of these plays had not been performed regularly, but a careful reader of Shakespeare could piece them together. It is unclear how many audience members, if any, actually recognized these bits of Shakespeare (no firsthand evidence survives), but readers would have found it difficult to separate Johnson's work from Shakespeare. Johnson does not use quotation marks to differentiate his text from Shakespeare's, and synthesizes Shakespeare's words with his own in an indistinguishable fusion.[24]

In *The Cobler of Preston* (1716), Johnson did not advertise his reliance on Shakespeare either, and was frequently accused of plagiarism.[25] In *Love in a Forest*, Johnson acknowledges due respect to Shakespeare in his prologue and dedication, but does not employ any system of separation between his own writing and the passages he excerpts from Shakespeare. For a reading audience, Johnson's adaptation can be deciphered only by those with an extensive knowledge of Shakespeare. For a theatrical audience, Johnson's play shows no seams between his work and Shakespeare's, and an audience with solely theatrical knowledge probably would not recognize the main play or the interpolated passages.

Before we turn to the remaining adaptations in the early eighteenth century, it is worth pausing over the significance of Johnson's adaptation technique in *Love in a Forest*, and the related influence that reading Shakespeare had on adaptation. By reworking the play primarily by adding more Shakespearian material, the end result is still a "Shakespearian" play in the sense that Johnson tries to maintain Shakespearian dialogue, albeit from several different plays. Earlier adaptations showed little or no concern with the source of added material—Lacy's Scottish stereotypes, Bullock's added underplot, or the masques appended to *The Fairy-Queen*, for example. It must have been important to Johnson to maintain a "Shakespearian" flavor to his play, and this concern with preserving Shakespeare's words is something we have not seen before 1723, but will characterize subsequent adaptations in the 1720s and 1730s.

Other Adaptations of Shakespeare

The few comic adaptations between the time of *Love in a Forest* and Garrick's arrival on the London stage reflect this shift to greater cognizance of Shakespeare's comedies as textual entities, not just as raw dramatic material. The last three adaptations before Garrick are significant for their relative lack of concern for popular actors, additions of music, or other pressures from the stage. These three plays were influenced by developments in Shakespeare plays as printed texts—editions, interest in textual issues, and the growth of a reading public. We can also trace the development of a new audience for Shakespearian comedies, not as performance pieces with the comic gagging of John Lacy or Thomas Doggett, but instead as written examples of Shakespeare's poetry.

In terms of their position in the overall repertoire, theatrical offerings in the decade before the Licensing Act of 1737 are conservative, hearkening back to older plays for their models. The climate for new plays in the 1730s was risky at best, and complaints recurred that "Farce and Pantomimes have taken place of *Shakespear* and *Otway*; and the *Players* have destroy'd that Taste they did not understand."[26] Adaptations in this last period break no new ground in terms of their form, but continue to indicate a new attitude to Shakespeare based on increased reading knowledge of the plays and a development of interest in textual matters.

The stage and the page became more entertwined as editions of Shakespeare and their surrounding commentaries promoted an awareness of the plays as printed texts.[27] Interest in Shakespeare's original plays began before Garrick's debut on the English stage; he "simply rode the wave of the rapidly increasing popularity of William Shakespeare" and capitalized on the preference for originality.[28] Garrick would claim to be restoring Shakespeare's authentic texts to the stage, a concept only available once authenticity became a valued consideration—we can see this develop before Garrick.[29]

Lewis Theobald exemplifies this new preoccupation with Shakespeare on the page as well as with stage performances. In his 1733 edition of Shakespeare, Theobald often consulted adaptations of Shakespeare's plays to see how an adapter dealt with a problematic passage, and his knowledge of the theater aided him in explicating Shakespeare's texts.[30] When he wrote for the stage, Theobald capitalized on the growing concern for Shakespeare's plays as written texts. Claiming to have found a lost play by Shakespeare, Theobald labeled his *Double Falshood* (1728) as "Written Originally by *W. SHAKESPEARE*; And now Revised and Adapted to the Stage By Mr. THEOBALD, the Author of *Shakespeare Restor'd*." The combination of an original Shakespearian play with the stamp of Theobald as restorer of Shakespeare's texts highlights this interest. In the printed edition Theobald draws attention to his role as editor and caretaker of Shakespeare's texts, describing himself as "an *Editor*, not an *Author*."

Theobald thought audiences would be interested in a theater piece because of its textual origins, and he presents his work as a "lost manuscript" of Shakespeare's.[31] In the preface to the second edition of the play (1728), Theobald specifically refers to his plan of "restoring SHAKESPEARE from the numerous Corruptions of his Text" and vows that nothing will "prevent me from putting out an *Edition* of *Shakespeare*." Though not specifically an adaptation of a single Shakespeare play, Theobald's tragicomedy has hints of *1 Henry IV*, *Hamlet*, *Troilus and Cressida*, and *Romeo and Juliet*; his method of composition resembles the technique used by Charles Johnson in *Love in a Forest*, combining echoes of many Shakespearian texts rather than revamping a single play.[32] The prologue to Theobald's play praises the "Beauties" that Shakespeare "alone could write," evoking the view of Shakespeare that derives from printed texts, not from the stage.

Theobald was right about the textual interest in Shakespeare. The *Evening Journal* (14 December 1727) touted it as "an original play of William Shakespear's" and observed that "the Audience was very numerous and the most remarkable Attention through the whole." His play lasted for thirteen performances with three author's benefits, and Brean S. Hammond points out that "press interest in this production went well beyond what was usual in the period."[33] Theobald capitalized on the attention to his project; he received "the extraordinary sum of one hundred guineas" for the copyright of the play, and it was revived in 1741 to "Benefit the last Editor of Shakespear."[34] Jacob Tonson was probably behind the offer for copyright, and he continued his commitment to Shakespeare in print by publishing six "new" plays by Shakespeare in 1734–35.[35] The *Double Falshood* continued through three editions as late as 1767, and *The Gazetteer* proclaimed in 1770 (26 March): "a new edition of this supposed relick of the immortal Shakespeare, was published on Saturday last." Pope's taunts in The *Grub-street Journal* (11 November 1731) further emphasize the interest in printed texts related to Theobald's play with a mock bill "against the importation or sale of any book pretended to be written by a dead author" and a denunciation of anyone who "affix[es] the name of William Shakespeare, alias Shakespear, to any book, pamphlet, play, or poem, hereafter to be by him, or them, or any person for him, or them, written, made, or devised." A poem "The Modern Poets" printed soon after in The *Grub-street Journal* characterizes Theobald as a poet with a "tortur'd brain" who "pores o'er Shakespear's sacred page" and then resolves "I'll write—then—boldly swear 'twas Shakespear wrote." We can trace connections between Theobald's play and Johnson's *Love in a Forest* in their concern with Shakespeare's plays as written texts. Johnson displayed the results of an adapter widely read in Shakespeare, and Theobald saw the opportunity for crafting a play based on a "newly discovered" text and the chance to profit from printing his play. Of course, Theobald's best-known work with Shakespeare is his edition of 1733, but his interest in Shakespeare's written word began earlier with *Double Falshood*, where he combined concern with Shakespearian texts and writing for the stage.

The last two comic adaptations before Garrick continue this pattern of growing influence from aspects of Shakespeare in print. An unusual adaptation from 1737 was inspired by the latest textual work on Shakespeare as well as a recent translation of Molière. The 1732 translation of Molière by James Miller and Henry Baker led to Miller's interest in combining the two writers,[36] and his adaptation *The Universal Passion* mixed material from *Much Ado About Nothing* with bits from *Twelfth Night* and *Two Gentlemen of Verona*, added to selections from Molière's *Princess d'Elide*.[37] This piece premiered at Drury Lane on 28 February 1737, mere months before the Licensing Act of 1737.[38] Miller linked his play to the theatrical environment, and created a comic character Joculo (based on Molière's Moron) as a role for the popular comedian Theophilus Cibber. Five added songs (written by Miller) featured the character Liberia, Miller's equivalent of Beatrice, played by Mrs. Clive. Miller's dedication speaks of "the extraordinary kind Reception which this Performance has met with from the Town," and the play received ten performances in the 1736–37 season with two more in the 1740–41 season. Unlike previous responses to adaptations, Miller's audience demonstrated their familiarity with Shakespeare's texts by identifying his borrowings from Shakespeare and Molière. A letter to the *Daily Journal* (5 March 1737) criticized him for "altering Names in *Shakespeare*," combining characters, shifting scenes, and producing a play "most miserably *hacked* and *defaced*" by "cruel, as well as *unskilful*, Hands." Despite the accusations of careless hack work, Miller attended to the latest textual advancements by using Theobald's edition, paying particular attention to Theobald's emendations when crafting his play. Miller's *The Universal Passion* demonstrates this dual concern that we saw with Charles Johnson, of crafting a stageworthy play while responding to interest in Shakespeare's plays as printed texts.[39]

The last pre-Garrick comic adaptation focuses solely on Shakespeare on the printed page, and was not even designed for stage performance. *The Modern Receipt* (1739) is a closet version of *As You Like It*, which author John Carrington describes in his preface as "the Product of a few leisure Hours, designed only for my private Amusement, and never intended to be made Publick in any Shape whatever." The study was both the inspiration and the destination for this text, the first such comic adaptation created without regard for the theater. If we recall the emphasis on performance aspects for all previous comic adaptations, we can sense a significant shift in emphasis from the stage to the page.

Carrington takes advantage of this and markets his adaptation as a dramatic commonplace book, a potpourri of literature to be consulted in the study.[40] "It has been a very common Remark of the Alterers, and Imitators of *Shakespeare*," he remarks, "that they have grossly neglected his Beauties, and too frequently copied, or reserved his Deformities. I have endeavoured to avoid this Imputation as much as possible; and if, at least, I have omitted any of his most shining Passages, I will ingenuously confess it to be owing to my Want of Judgement in distinguishing them" (preface). This statement echoes the remarks of compilers of Shakespearian quotations, who sifted his works for beauties and moral precepts. Carrington even employs Pope's phrase to describe Shakespeare's "most shining passages" when describing his reading practices. He acknowledges the need for "Judgement" in evaluating Shakespeare, a practice also promoted by Pope's edition and by commonplace books that collected Shakespeare's "beauties" as examples of taste, designed for reading and contemplation. Performance and theatrical context are no longer requisite determining factors in the shape of adaptations, and the study now provides an alternative venue for production.

The climate for Shakespeare has changed significantly over seventy years. Beginning in 1723 with Charles Johnson's *Love in a Forest*, playwrights began to think of Shakespeare's plays in ways conditioned by print culture. Characters and speeches had unusual portability, and Shakespeare provided sources for moral exempla on particular topics available for consultation outside the theater. The plethora of available Shakespearian material in print, from editions to commonplace books, sustained this type of private reading and intellectual exercise, without the need for performance or theatrical success. Editions encouraged a focus on textual issues and a concern for authenticity unlike the climate in the Restoration and early eighteenth century, which privileged stage practice over textual integrity. Current editorial work influenced stage versions of the plays, and stage actors in turn promoted the industry of Shakespeare studies.[41] Reading Shakespeare was the starting point for Garrick's stage productions; in addition to his well-known contributions to stage versions of Shakespeare, Garrick had one of the largest collections of English drama and helped Edward Capell collect texts of Shakespeare for his 1768 edition.[42] The intersection of print culture, scholarship, and theater in the mid-eighteenth century shows a change in adaptation methods toward a text-based paradigm and away from a performance-based approach. The climate for adapting Shakespeare had already shifted before Garrick began his work; he was simply perceptive enough to capitalize on an already growing theatrical trend.[43] The contributions of Garrick—restoring Shakespeare's original plays to the stage and reviving an "authentic" Shakespeare—depended on this receptive environment already created in the 1720s and 1730s.

Conclusion

In March of 1737, the *Daily Journal* printed the following passage from a letter:

> His Love of altering shews itself with the same Delicacy in shifting the Scene from Messina to Genoa; for I believe no one Person in the Audience could find any Reason for it: But this, it seems, is called altering Shakespeare, changing the Names of the Drama, and Scene of Action; leaving out one or two characters necessary to the Fable, and adding one that has nothing to do with it. His Usage of Benedick is abominable . . . The Under-plot of making Benedick and Beatrice in love with each other, as well as the principal Part of the Fable that relates to Claudio and Hero, he has indeed condescended to preserve; and to these scenes, mangled as they are, and the excellent Performance of Actors in general, must be attributed the Town's Indulgence in seeing Shakespeare, whom they would not suffer to be murdered in the Person of King John, most miserably hacked and defaced (notwithstanding the Act against Maiming, &c.) by more cruel, as well as unskilful, Hands.

Philo-Shakespear, as the author signed him or herself, was responding to *The Universal Passion*, an adaptation of *Much Ado About Nothing* by clergyman James Miller, which was successfully performed at Drury Lane that spring.[1] The reaction of this self-proclaimed "lover of Shakespeare" tells us several important things about the overall development of Shakespeare's reputation with regard to the comedies in the early eighteenth century.

Not only did Philo-Shakespear recognize Miller's source play, he took great pains to point out the particular changes made to Shakespeare. Modifications in location and title, small shifts in character structure, and omissions of minor cast members are enough to merit the angry and lengthy missive. The 1737 writer calls Miller's treatment of Shakespeare "abominable," condescending, "unskilful"; and Shakespeare's material is maimed, "miserably hacked and defaced." No reaction this severe greeted earlier comic adaptations. In fact, Philo-Shakespear's tone sounds remarkably like George C. D. Odell and Hazelton Spencer, the still influential commentators of the early twentieth century, who were horrified at the treatment of Shakespeare's texts by "depredators," "tamperers," "violent alterers," and "impudent improvers." We can trace this attitude back to the mid-eighteenth century and the influence of print culture, when a definitive shift occurred in attitudes to Shakespeare's texts exemplified by Philo-Shakespear, unlike the freedom engendered by the dominance of performance in the Restoration and earlier eighteenth century.

As well as indicating a transition in attitudes to Shakespeare's plays, particularly the comedies, Philo-Shakespear's letter also marks the year of a major change in the operations of London theaters, and provides a logical stopping point for this study. Three months after the premiere of *The Universal Passion* in February of 1737, the House of Commons considered a bill that would affect London theaters until the 1960s.[2] The *Daily Post* of 23 May 1737 summarized the issue: "a Bill is ordered into Parliament for suppressing the great Number of Play-Houses . . . so justly complained of, and for the future no Persons shall presume to Act any Play, &c. without first obtaining a Licence from the Lord Chamberlain of his Majesty's Houshold for the Time being, any Persons acting without such Licence to be deemed Vagrants and Punished as such, according to the Act of the 12th of Queen Anne." Limiting theatrical competition to only two patent theaters, Drury Lane and Covent Garden, discouraged new plays as well as competition among several theaters. If we remember the circumstances surrounding the inception of *The Cobler of Preston* in the opening anecdote to this book, we can better understand the ramifications of this act. Bullock's play, as we saw in chapter 4, was generated from theatrical competition, and the 1730s in particular were an apex of theater rivalry, with as many as five major venues offering enticements for audiences (Covent Garden, Drury Lane, Goodman's Fields, the Little Haymarket, and Lincoln's Inn Fields). The abrupt end to this atmosphere of variety drastically changed the conditions for new plays and for theatrical offerings overall. In the words of one scholar, "the damage to drama and theatre is incalculable."[3] The effects of the Licensing Act roughly coincide with the arrival of David Garrick on the London stage, and Garrick's treatment of Shakespeare deserves its own examination elsewhere.

Specific conclusions have been drawn in each chapter about particular adaptations; a few main threads concerning the unique reception history of the comedies and the wider significance of this study may be mentioned here. Each play was intimately connected with the production process, from available and popular actors, musicians, and dancers, to possibilities in theatrical facilities. Performance opportunities often affected which plays were staged: what could be performed in the new Dorset Garden theater, which plays would suit the acting abilities of particular actors or groups of actors, or which plays could accommodate additional music and spectacle. Various competitive tactics also encouraged the staging of particular plays to best compete with foreign entertainments or with offerings at rival theaters. Shakespeare was not a significant component in these strategies, nor was his name necessarily connected with those plays offered as native competition; no Restoration or early eighteenth-century comedy survived or succeeded because of its connection to Shakespeare. Political events could spawn a production, but the stage life of a play depended on capturing elements of popular taste that endured beyond immediate topical concerns. Popular plot types recur in comedies, a characteristic of the genre itself but also one that affected which plays were revived—shrew-taming, transformation, and tempest plots were especially attractive in this period. Low comedy was alluring and was often expanded in these plays—the success of the Bottom/Pyramus and Thisbe plot from *A Midsummer Night's Dream*, the physical and exaggerated humor of Lacy as Sauny the Scott and Doggett as Shylock, added low comedy to *The Tempest* with Stephano and Trinculo, Bullock's *The Cobler of Preston* with its farcical underplot.

Other external factors also determined the ways Shakespeare was adapted, particularly editions and treatment of Shakespeare's material in other forms of print culture. Changes in dramatic and generic form often influence plays as well. The role of the actor as adapter also shifted over the course of our period. The comedies remained a domain to showcase male actors and even for cross-dressed male actors, but not for actresses. Late seventeenth- and early eighteenth-century comic actors like Lacy or Cox reworked Shakespeare with their own talents in mind, whereas Garrick's approach privileged the text over his own performance. Garrick did not feel at liberty to remake and claim Shakespeare's comedies as his own, as did earlier writers and actors.

Several sections of this book have illustrated the disjunction between theory and practice in adapting Shakespeare—writers often had to abandon aesthetic concerns in favor of audience preferences in entertainment: audience power defeated the rules every time. Even Davenant chose performance aspects over authorship, despite his claim to Shakespeare's lineage. At the end of our period, reading knowledge of Shakespeare and proliferation of Shakespeare in print created a separation between text and the theatrical/performance context that presaged thinking of Shakespeare's plays as a whole, a body of work by a specific author, rather than raw material available for adaptation according to genre.

In general, Shakespeare's comedies were a blank slate for most of the early eighteenth century. Grumio from *The Taming of the Shrew* could become a Scottish servant who steals the show because the audience had no preconceived ideas about the focus or content of Shakespeare's play. Davenant could bring together *Much Ado About Nothing* and *Measure for Measure* as a new play, Shylock could become a stockjobber and Christopher Sly could be a Jacobite cobbler. The tragedies were of course adapted, but not in this wholesale fashion. Hamlet never became a Whig, and though Lear and Cordelia remain alive in Nahum Tate's version, they are not transformed into stockjobbers, mixed in with characters from other Shakespeare plays, or given a particular ethnicity or comic stereotype. Shakespeare's tragedies were not treated as raw material to the extent that the comedies were, and thus they helped form Shakespeare's reputation much more than the comedies did. The development of Shakespeare's status as the "National Poet" was more generically based than has been previously noted—the genres of tragedy and history rather than comedy comprised the plays of note, and there was a significant difference in reception and treatment of plays of different genres.

The type of playwright who turned to Shakespeare's comic material tells us much about the process of dramatic composition and the practical realities of writing for the stage. With the exception of Dryden and Davenant, no major successful comic playwright turned to Shakespearian comic material as a primary source in the eighteenth century. Not one play by Farquhar, Steele, Congreve, Gay, Vanbrugh, Etherege, Wycherley, Centlivre, Behn, Cibber, or Fielding is based on a Shakespearian comedy. The writers who did employ comic material of Shakespeare's were often influential members of the theatrical community: John Lacy, Richard Leveridge, Christopher Bullock, and Charles Johnson all had a significant effect on London entertainments. But the combination of a successful prominent comic dramatist and a Shakespearian comedy did not occur in this period. Perhaps the most prudent conclusion to draw pertains to the canonical status of these adaptations. Often consigned to the "minor play" category of drama, with interest to few but specialists, these adaptations have taken a minor role both in theater history and in studies of Shakespearian reception history. Had one of the above-named playwrights undertaken an adaptation of *Twelfth Night* or *Much Ado About Nothing*, we may have a different conception of the place of Shakespeare in the repertoire of the early eighteenth century.[4]

Nevertheless, a diverse group of writers did turn to Shakespeare's comedies as sources. This group has few things in common, but that in itself is significant. All types of writers in the early eighteenth-century theater approached Shakespearian comedy with few reservations about his reputation or the integrity of his comic texts: playwrights involved in theater management (Davenant, Bullock), struggling but persistent writers trying to craft a hit play (Burnaby, Gildon, Johnson), actor-performer-playwrights who saw the opportunity for a workable comic role in a play by Shakespeare (Bullock, Lacy, Leveridge), a literary critic (Dennis) who sought to reconcile his dramatic works with his critical agendas, and even "authorless" pieces, *The Fairy-Queen* and the operatic *Tempest*, with no certain authorial figure at work. The tragedies, in contrast, received more attention from more serious and accomplished playwrights, with more of a sense that they were adapting a Shakespeare play and not just using his material as a source. Compared to comic adapters, the roster of writers who took on Shakespeare's histories and tragedies as sources includes fewer minor writers and more laureates and authors with literary aspirations—Colley Cibber's *Richard III*, Nahum Tate's *King Lear*, Nicholas Rowe's *Jane Shore* "Written in imitation of Shakespeare's style," just to name a few. The tragedies were not reshaped with such a direct connection to practical performance issues of theater, perhaps because comedy is more attuned to the popular, the fad, the moment, and it needs to be updated more so than tragedy. Comedy can be a more actor-driven genre, with space for improvisation and ad-libbing that promotes a more fluid text such as those by John Lacy, Thomas Doggett, and the Bullocks. Comedy is also aligned with entertainment more so than tragedy, with a basis in popular forms which is more amenable to additions. Furthermore, most of the tragedies were stageable basically "as is," particularly *Othello* and *Hamlet*, and needed much less adjustment (Davenant's *Macbeth* is an exception). *King Lear* was reworked by Nahum Tate, but primarily to change the ending, not to add significant music and spectacle.

Just as the playwrights who did not turn to Shakespeare's comedies as sources can tell us much about the ways eighteenth-century authors thought about these works, so can the types of things that were not of interest. Shakespeare's comedies were appealing for very different reasons than in the last two centuries. No adaptation in the Restoration or early eighteenth century centered on the female roles in these plays. Shakespeare's heroines, particularly Rosalind, Viola, and Portia, so often the focus of the comedies in the last two centuries, held little interest for audiences or playwrights, even in the very period when actresses were first introduced to the English stage. Despite the availability of actresses, these plays were not revived or staged successfully because of their strong roles for women.

The ways Shakespeare's comic material was shaped were in response to a number of dynamics, not just a single author's idea of the perfect Shakespeare play. The primary factors were the practical realities of early eighteenth-century theater: how to attract a paying audience, how to combine drama and music, how to harness the talents of actors, how to utilize stage facilities, how to compete with rival theaters and offerings. All of these aspects were capable of outweighing any conception of "Shakespeare." Not until Shakespeare in print becomes a substantial presence do we see an interest in originality. Davenant could get away with combining two plays as a new one, but James Miller's *The Universal Passion* provoked an angry letter when he merely made a few minor adjustments. Miller's audience of 1737 knew their Shakespeare; Davenant's audience of 1662 did not.

Shakespeare's name was rarely used in connection with the comedies, not because of any desire to "hide" what the particular adapter had done to his material, but rather as a result of how to market, advertise, and publicize a play. In the competitive theatrical conditions that characterized most of the period of this study, playwrights were eager to use any strategy that would attract an audience, and worried more about the success of their play than how they used a source text from Shakespeare. Writers for the early eighteenth-century stage did not have the luxury to discard or discount an aspect of their plays that might sell. Shakespeare's name was thus of little value for comic entertainment. Rarely were Shakespeare's comic plays viewed as more than raw dramatic material, "old plays" to rework for new tastes by particular playwrights at specific moments. This book will have fulfilled one of its goals if readers are left with a sense of the variety and vast differences between adaptations of Shakespeare in the Restoration and eighteenth century, and are thus reluctant to dismiss these plays as "failed improvements" or curiosities consigned to dramatic oblivion. The business of theater, to entertain, has always been a determining factor in theatrical offerings, and Shakespeare's plays were no exception. Early eighteenth-century comic adaptations of Shakespeare could take a line from Gay's *The Beggar's Opera* as their motto: "All this we must do, to comply with the taste of the town."

Notes

INTRODUCTION

1. The specific circumstances that led to Bullock's piece will be discussed in more detail in chapter 4. Bullock provides a brief nod to "Old *Shakespear*" in the prologue. Quotations from prologues, epilogues, prefaces, and other eighteenth-century texts are from the first London edition unless otherwise noted.

2. Christopher Spencer's otherwise excellent introduction to *Five Restoration Adaptations of Shakespeare* (Urbana: University of Illinois Press, 1965) exhibits this tendency to draw broad generalizations about adaptations. He claims that Restoration and eighteenth-century adapters "were interested in the sense of harmony and pattern and consistency and order that they felt art should have" (11); the adaptations "emphasize permanent patterns of human relationships with less attention to the depths of individual experience" (12); the characters "tend to become generalized as the adapter fits them into his mould, where they serve the stronger interests of moral clarity, of easily understandable motivation, of sharpened comparison, or simply of balance and unity" (12). Other oversimplifications recur in standard works. Brian Vickers generalizes that "the period from the 1690s to the 1730s is one in which the theoretical system of Neoclassicism was applied with energy and with few reservations." *Shakespeare: The Critical Heritage* (London: Routledge and Kegan Paul, 1974), 2:1. While some of these generalizations may hold true for some of the adaptations, changing theatrical fashions and audience preferences must be accounted for in the changes made to Shakespeare by these playwrights. John Lacy's *Sauny the Scott*, a Restoration adaptation that Spencer omits from his study, exemplifies the problems with this approach: none of these generalizations accounts for Lacy's embellishment of the character of Sauny as an acting showpiece for his comic talents, as we shall see in chapter 1.

3. Some of the earliest critics of the adaptations, George C. D. Odell and Hazelton Spencer, promoted these views, which remain influential. In *Shakespeare Improved: The Restoration Versions in Quarto and on the Stage* (Cambridge: Harvard University Press, 1927), Spencer sees each adaptation as a failed attempt to improve Shakespeare: "The Restoration adapter was not trying to *restore* his text, the professed aim of the long line of later tamperers, but to *improve* it" (145). Spencer's attitude toward the adaptations is one of dismay and revulsion. A few examples should suffice: Charles Gildon's *Measure for Measure* "has the sole merit of being less violently altered from Shakespeare's comedy than was D'Avenant's version" (335); Granville is an "impudent improver" whose changes to *The Merchant of Venice* are "outrageous garbling" and "the merest pandering to a ridiculous fashion of the moment," with "abominably garbled dialogue" (340–44); John Dennis's adaptation of *The Merry Wives* is "frightfully mutilated" (347) and "a contemptible compound of farce and smut" (349); the Dryden-Davenant *Tempest* is "wretched stuff" (201) that "ruined Shakespeare's play," and this adaptation is "the worst, as it was the most successful" (203). Odell, in *Shakespeare from Betterton to Irving*, 2 vols. (1920; reprint, New York: Dover Publications, 1966), begins his study of "dep-

redators" with Davenant, who "set a despicable fashion to future generations of dramatists and versifiers" with his "stage perversions of Shakespeare" (1:24). Odell concludes that reading these adaptations "is like an attempt to see beloved features through a mist or in encircling gloom. Literally, Shakespeare is 'smeared over' by the inferior stuff so proudly vaunted by the perpetrators. It is almost like a rouged corpse—a thing too ghastly to conceive of" (1:79). A few representative examples show how pervasive this denunciation has been: Alan Brissenden calls Charles Johnson's *Love in a Forest* a "gallimaufry" that Johnson "plundered" from Shakespeare. *As You Like It* (Oxford: Oxford University Press, 1994), 51–52. Howard S. Collins, in an otherwise sympathetic study of Davenant, *The Comedy of Sir William Davenant* (The Hague: Mouton, 1967) remarks that "on the whole any serious comparison with the originals illustrates beyond doubt that one may tamper with Shakespeare, but one cannot better him" (140).

4. Michael Dobson's *The Making of the National Poet: Shakespeare, Adaptation and Authorship 1660–1769* (Oxford: Clarendon, 1992) traces the rise of Shakespeare as the national poet in the eighteenth century, through a selective study of representative texts to illustrate his argument, but not a comprehensive examination of all adaptations.

5. Jean I. Marsden points out in the introduction to *The Appropriation of Shakespeare: Post-Renaissance Reconstructions of the Works and the Myth* (Hemel Hempstead: Harvester Wheatsheaf, 1991), that critics are increasingly looking at Shakespeare's plays "as part of an historical context" (5), but these studies rarely venture beyond either the Renaissance or the twentieth century. Marsden's *The Re-imagined Text: Shakespeare, Adaptation, and Theory in the Restoration and Eighteenth Century* (Lexington: University Press of Kentucky, 1995) integrates a broad study of Shakespearian adaptations in connection with developments in eighteenth-century literary theory, to show how ideas of criticism and literary theory influenced adaptation. In *Shakespeare Verbatim* (Oxford: Clarendon, 1991), Margreta de Grazia examines the importance of Malone's 1790 edition and its emphasis on authenticity. Jonathan Bate's *Shakespearean Constitutions: Politics, Theatre, Criticism 1730–1830* (Oxford: Clarendon, 1989) has brought to light the role of caricature and other forms of satire in appropriating Shakespeare's plays for various political and ideological agendas in the late eighteenth century. See also Stanley Wells, ed., *Shakespeare Survey 51: Shakespeare in the Eighteenth Century* (Cambridge: Cambridge University Press, 1998) and Sandra Clark's introduction to *Shakespeare Made Fit: Restoration Adaptations of Shakespeare* (London: Dent, 1997). Michael Dobson provides an overview of eighteenth-century adaptations in his essay, "Improving on the Original: Actresses and Adaptations," in Jonathan Bate and Russell Jackson, eds., *Shakespeare: An Illustrated Stage History* (Oxford: Oxford University Press, 1996), 45–68.

6. Among the important genre studies are the following: Robert D. Hume, *The Development of English Drama in the Late Seventeenth Century* (Oxford: Clarendon, 1976); Eric Rothstein and Frances M. Kavenik's *The Designs of Carolean Comedy* (Carbondale and Edwardsville: Southern Illinois University Press, 1988); and Brian Corman's *Genre and Generic Change in English Comedy 1660–1710* (Toronto: University of Toronto Press, 1993). Derek Hughes's *English Drama 1660–1700* (Oxford: Clarendon, 1996) builds on Hume's 1976 study and focuses on "recurrent and interacting motifs" as well as "social, political, and philosophical influences" on drama (vi). Laura Brown's *English Dramatic Form 1660–1760: An Essay in Generic History* (New Haven: Yale University Press, 1981) examines "the best works" from the period because "they are more representative of their genre and of their period than minor or average works" and "come closer to fulfilling the potential of their form. They grasp the realities of their age more fully, and they embody its concerns and contradictions more completely" (xiv). As will become evident throughout this book, I disagree with Brown's unexamined category of "best works" as well as her dismissal of average or minor works without regard to the processes that form canons of taste.

7. Adaptations of Shakespearian tragedies have generally received more critical attention than the comedies have. George C. Branam's *Eighteenth-Century Adaptations of Shakespearean Tragedy* (Berkeley: University of California Press, 1956) examines the alterations of tragedies but devotes little attention to theatrical context aside from general statements such as, "The large theater of Garrick's day lacked the intimacy of Shakespeare's stage: a spectator's attention was more likely to wander if action or argument became complex or subtle" (171–72). Two early studies establish some preliminary connections between Restoration comedy and earlier comedies. Arthur Gewirtz's *Restoration Adaptations of Early 17th Century Comedies* (Washington, D.C.: University Press of America, 1982) is limited to chapters on Davenant's use of farce and theatrical elements, and a thematic chapter on "libertine naturalism." Gunnar Sorelius's *"The Giant Race Before the Flood": Pre-Restoration Drama on the Stage and in the Criticism of the Restoration* (Stockholm: Uppsala, 1966) considers adaptations of a wide range of seventeenth-century plays, not just those of Shakespeare. Gewirtz and Sorelius provide a foundation for this type of study, but both are limited in what they say about Shakespeare.

8. For instance, H. J. Oliver asserts in the Oxford edition of *The Taming of the Shrew* (Oxford: Clarendon, 1982) that Lacy's *Sauny the Scott* is interesting "only in the contrast its vulgarity provides with Shakespeare's Elizabethan directness and in the examination of the possible reasons for retaining some Shakespearian phrases and not others" (66). Oliver similarly appraises both *The Cobler of Preston* afterpieces: "neither of the plays adds anything to our understanding of Shakespeare" (67). Tori Haring-Smith remarks, in her stage history of *The Shrew*, that after the Renaissance "the next two hundred and fifty years of the stage history of *The Taming of the Shrew* have remarkably little to do with Shakespeare." *From Farce to Metadrama: A Stage History of "Taming of the Shrew" 1594–1983* (London: Greenwood Press, 1985), 9. Ann Thompson omits any mention of the two *Cobler of Preston* plays in her Cambridge edition of *The Shrew* (Cambridge: Cambridge University Press, 1984), as do Graham Holderness and Bryan Loughrey in their edition of *A Pleasant Conceited Historie, Called The Taming of a Shrew* (Hemel Hempstead: Harvester Wheatsheaf, 1992). T. W. Craik, the editor of the Arden *Twelfth Night* (London: Methuen, 1975), dismisses William Burnaby's *Love Betray'd* (which he attributes to Charles Burnaby) as "of no importance to the history of *Twelfth Night* in the theater (most of Shakespeare's design being changed beyond recognition), though it is of some interest in confirming the un-Shakespearean temper of its time, at least with regard to Shakespearean romantic comedy" (lxxx).

9. Dobson attests that "Restoration and eighteenth-century rewritings of Shakespeare's plays . . . have attracted little sustained or sympathetic critical attention: in fact they have inspired such horror among Shakespeareans that to wish to look into them at all may seem perverse." *The Making of the National Poet*, 9.

10. Alexander Leggatt, *English Stage Comedy 1490–1990: Five Centuries of a Genre* (London: Routledge, 1998), 2, 7–9.

11. In constructing a theatrical context for these plays, I have drawn on the methodology of Robert D. Hume and Judith Milhous, most recently articulated in Hume's *Reconstructing Contexts: The Aims and Principles of Archaeo-Historicism* (Oxford: Oxford University Press, 1999), where he provides a theorized methodology "to reconstruct past events and viewpoints, and to use our constructions in aid of contextual interpretation" (45). Through a series of articles, books, archival work, and revisions of *The London Stage*, Hume and Milhous provide the framework for this type of study. See particularly Milhous and Hume, *Producible Interpretation: Eight English Plays 1675–1707* (Carbondale and Edwardsville: Southern Illinois University Press, 1985), and Hume, *The Development of English Drama*. The approach of Peter Holland's *The Ornament of Ac-*

tion: Text and Performance in Restoration Comedy (Cambridge: Cambridge University Press, 1979) has also influenced my study.

12. William Penkethman, prologue to Susannah Centlivre's *The Basset-Table* (1706). Paul Trolander and Zeynep Tenger point out that "while critical discourse emphasized the centrality of the poet as a judge of literary production, economic forces of the marketplace located critical authority in a public sphere accessible to both producers and consumers of performances and texts." "Criticism Against Itself: Subverting Critical Authority in Late-Seventeenth-Century England," *Philological Quarterly* 75 (1996): 311–38.

13. Much work has been done on the developing consumer society of the eighteenth century. Lee Davison, Tim Hitchcock, Tim Keirn, and Robert B. Shoemaker examine the role of commercial forces on English society in the early eighteenth century in *Stilling the Grumbling Hive: The Response to Social and Economic Problems in England, 1689–1750* (New York: St. Martin's Press, 1992), xvi–xxviii. Christopher Pye discusses the relationship between theater and economics in "The Theater, the Market, and the Subject of History," *ELH* 61 (1994): 501–22. John Brewer and Roy Porter's edited collection *Consumption and the World of Goods* (London: Routledge, 1993) includes a variety of discussions about the consumer culture in the eighteenth century. See particularly the introduction to this volume and Jean-Christophe Agnew's review of scholarship in "Coming up for air: consumer culture in historical perspective," 19–39 (originally printed in *Intellectual History Newsletter* 12 [1990]: 3–21). John Brewer's *The Pleasures of the Imagination: English Culture in the Eighteenth Century* (New York: Farrar Straus Giroux, 1997) provides a general discussion of how the arts became more commercial and less courtly in the eighteenth century. Douglas Bruster argues that the Elizabethan playhouse was a place of business, and suggests the need to examine the material conditions of the theater. *Drama and the Market in the Age of Shakespeare* (Cambridge: Cambridge University Press, 1992). Other works to consult include Jean-Christophe Agnew, *Worlds Apart: The Market and the Theater in Anglo-American Thought, 1550–1750* (Cambridge: Cambridge University Press, 1986); Ann Bermingham and John Brewer, eds., *The Consumption of Culture 1600–1800* (London: Routledge, 1995), particularly Bermingham's introduction (1–20).

14. Colley Cibber, *An Apology for the Life of Mr. Colley Cibber*, ed. Robert W. Lowe. (1888; reprint, New York: AMS Press, 1966), 1:264. Subsequent references to Cibber's *Apology* are cited parenthetically in the text.

15. Epilogue to John Banks's *Vertue Betray'd: or, Anna Bullen* (1682); the anonymous "An Epistolary Essay to Mr. Dryden upon his *Cleomenes*" in *The Gentleman's Journal* (May 1692). Shirley Strum Kenny provides an excellent discussion of the issues of profit and the business of theater in "Theatre, Related Arts, and the Profit Motive: An Overview," in Shirley Strum Kenny, ed., *British Theatre and the Other Arts, 1660–1800* (Washington, D.C.: Folger Books, 1984), 15–38. Prologues and epilogues can be notoriously exaggerated; throughout this book I have tried to corroborate statements in prefatory material with additional references and theatrical context to ensure their reliability.

16. For a discussion of the development of aesthetics in the eighteenth century, see Paul Mattick Jr., ed., *Eighteenth-Century Aesthetics and the Reconstruction of Art* (Cambridge: Cambridge University Press, 1993) and Marsden, *The Re-Imagined Text*. John Guillory critiques the concept of "aesthetic" value and examines the connections between aesthetic and economic discourse in *Cultural Capital: The Problem of Literary Canon Formation* (Chicago: University of Chicago Press, 1993), especially chapter 5. B. Sprague Allen's *Tides in English Taste (1619–1800): A Background for the Study of Literature*, 2 vols. (Cambridge: Harvard University Press, 1937) remains an invaluable work for period taste in the arts.

17. "A Discourse Upon Comedy, In Reference to the English Stage. In a Letter to a Friend." In *Love and Business* (1701). George Farquhar, *The Works of George Farquhar*, ed. Shirley Strum Kenny (Oxford: Clarendon, 1988), 2:366.

18. See the work on heterogeneous eighteenth-century audiences by Milhous and Hume in *Producible Interpretation: Eight English Plays 1675–1707* and *The Rakish Stage: Studies in English Drama, 1660–1800* (Carbondale and Edwardsville: Southern Illinois University Press, 1983), 11. For discussions of audiences, see Emmett L. Avery, "The Restoration Audience," *Philological Quarterly* 45 (1966): 54–61; Harold Love, "Who were the Restoration Audience;" and Arthur H. Scouten and Robert D. Hume, "'Restoration Comedy' and its Audiences, 1660–1776," both in *The Yearbook of English Studies* 10 (1980): 21–44 and 45–69; Leo Hughes, *The Drama's Patrons: A Study of the Eighteenth-Century London Audience* (Austin: University of Texas Press, 1971); Harry William Pedicord, *The Theatrical Public in the Time of Garrick* (1954; reprint, Carbondale: Southern Illinois University Press, 1966). Hume summarizes many of the debates on the Restoration audience in *The Development of English Drama*, 23–28.

19. Samuel Johnson, *Adventurer* 115, 11 December 1753. See Pat Rogers, *Grub Street: Studies in a Subculture* (London: Methuen, 1972); Robert Lewis Collison, *The Story of Street Literature: Forerunner of the Popular Press* (London: Dent, 1973); Paula McDowell, *The Women of Grub Street: Press, Politics, and Gender in the London Literary Marketplace 1678–1730* (Oxford: Clarendon, 1998). Brean S. Hammond provides an excellent discussion of writing conditions in *Professional Imaginative Writing in England, 1670–1740 "Hackney for Bread"* (Oxford: Clarendon, 1997). Claudia Thomas discusses the image of the hack in "Pope and His *Dunciad* Adversaries: Skirmishes in the Borders of Gentility," in James Gill, ed., *Cutting Edges: Postmodern Critical Essays on Eighteenth-Century Satire* (Knoxville: University of Tennessee Press, 1995), 275–300.

20. Judith Milhous, *Thomas Betterton and the Management of Lincoln's Inn Fields 1695–1708* (Carbondale and Edwardsville: Southern Illinois University Press, 1979), 98; "Mr. Steele's Apology (1714)," in Sir Richard Steele, *Tracts and Pamphlets by Richard Steele*, ed. Rae Blanchard (Baltimore: Johns Hopkins University Press, 1944), 339; prologue to Charles Hopkins's *Boadicea* (1697).

21. Staring B. Wells, ed., *A Comparison Between the Two Stages* (Princeton: Princeton University Press, 1942), 16, 92. Subsequent references are cited in the text by page number.

22. This situation of consumption and demand in eighteenth-century theaters parallels what Neil McKendrick calls "the commercialization of society," which encouraged the creation of "new and improved species and exciting novelties with which to delight the eye, to exhibit one's taste and to assert one's wealth. The avowed intention was to proclaim one's ability constantly to improve on the old and the inherited, and of course, to swell the demand for what was new and exciting and modern." Of course, as McKendrick notes, the *"desire* to consume" was nothing new, but "the *ability* to do so" was a more recent development, and underlines the connections between theater and economic conditions. Neil McKendrick, John Brewer and J. H. Plumb, eds., *The Birth of a Consumer Society: The Commercialization of Eighteenth-Century England* (Bloomington: Indiana University Press, 1982), 2. For a critique of McKendrick, see Ben Fine and Ellen Leopold, "Consumerism and the Industrial Revolution," *Social History* 15 (1990): 151–79.

23. "A Defence of an Essay of Dramatique Poesie" (1668), in John Dryden, *The Works of John Dryden*, ed. Edward Niles Hooker et al., 20 vols. (Berkeley and Los Angeles: University of California Press, 1956-), 9:7. Subsequent passages from Dryden's works are taken from this edition. *Examen Poeticum* (1693), John Dryden, *Essays of John Dryden*, ed. W. P. Ker (Oxford: Clarendon, 1926), 2:7. Later in the century,

James Ralph remarked that "The Writer has three Provinces. To write for Booksellers. To write for the Stage. To write for a Faction in the Name of the Community." *The Case of Authors* (1758), 19. In *The Commercialisation of Leisure in Eighteenth-century England* (University of Reading, 1973), J. H. Plumb discusses the development of theater as one of several "festivals of leisure" that arose due to increased leisure and commercialization (11) and traces a similar growth in music between 1660 and 1760.

24. See Louis D. Mitchell, "Command Performances During the Reign of Queen Anne," *Theatre Notebook* 24 (1970): 111–17; and "Command Performances During the Reign of George I," *Eighteenth-Century Studies* 7 (1974): 343–49. Mitchell concludes that after James II's patronage, theaters lacked royal support until George I and his successors gave "a new life to the theatre" (347). For further discussion of the Hanoverian court and the arts, see John M. Beattie, *The English Court in the Reign of George I* (Cambridge: Cambridge University Press, 1967), 257–78. Theaters were at their lowest ebb during the reign of Queen Anne; Calhoun Winton makes the argument that William and Anne may have even hindered the progress of theater. See "The London Stage Embattled: 1695–1710," *Tennessee Studies in Literature* 19 (1974): 9–19. Deborah C. Payne points out that in the Restoration "patronage came to constitute the very infrastructure of the theatrical system." "Patronage and the Dramatic Marketplace under Charles I and II," *Yearbook of English Studies* 21 (1991): 138. According to Jennifer Thorp, patronage of dance also shaped artistic production. "Your Honor'd and Obedient Servant: Patronage and Dance in London c.1700–1735," *Dance Research* 15 (1997): 84–98. See also Michael Foss, *The Age of Patronage: The Arts in England 1660–1750* (London: Hamish Hamilton, 1971); Paul J. Korshin, "Types of Eighteenth-Century Literary Patronage," *Eighteenth-Century Studies* 7 (1973–74): 453–73; and Dustin Griffin's *Literary Patronage in England, 1650–1800* (Cambridge: Cambridge University Press, 1996). Alvin Kernan points out that print "created the conditions that eventually separated the writer from the patron, and the social order he represented, by providing writers with a new way of earning a living—writing for a reading public." *Printing Technology, Letters and Samuel Johnson* (Princeton: Princeton University Press, 1987), 102–103.

25. *Fraser's Magazine* 5 (1832): 396–98.

26. Emmett L. Avery, ed., *Some Thoughts Concerning the Stage in a Letter to a Lady* (1704; Los Angeles: Augustan Reprint Society, 1947), 8. Calhoun Winton suggests that the author may be Queen Anne. "The London Stage Embattled," 19n.

27. Plumb, *The Commercialisation of Leisure in Eighteenth-century England*, 20.

28. As John Brewer has pointed out, early newspapers "taught precisely those virtues and values which were necessary for survival in an economically expansive though debt-ridden society." "Commercialization and Politics," in *The Birth of a Consumer Society*, 217. James R. Sutherland discusses the impact of newspapers in "The Circulation of Newspapers and Literary Periodicals, 1700–30," *The Library* 15 (1934): 110–24. See also Michael Harris, "London Printers and Newspaper Production During the First Half of the Eighteenth Century," *Journal of the Printing Historical Society* 12 (1977–78): 33–51.

29. Sutherland, "The Circulation of Newspapers," 110.

30. See "Advertising," in Emmett L. Avery and Arthur H. Scouten, introduction to *The London Stage* 1:lxxv–lxxviii and Emmett L. Avery, "Advertising," in introduction to *The London Stage* 2:lxxxix–xcv.

31. Franklin B. Zimmerman has detailed the role of the public music concert in securing the success of musicians within this climate in "The Court Music of Henry Purcell," in Robert P. Maccubbin and Martha Hamilton-Phillips, eds., *The Age of William III and Mary II* (Williamsburg, Va.: College of William & Mary, 1989), 312.

32. See Robert D. Hume's appendix of title pages in "Before the Bard: 'Shakespeare' in Early Eighteenth-Century London," *ELH* 64 (1997): 69–75.

33. Randy L. Neighbarger describes the role of music in adaptations but too often oversimplifies these texts. *An Outward Show: Music for Shakespeare on the London Stage, 1660–1850* (Westport, Conn.: Greenwood Press, 1992). Moira Goff provides an overview of the popularity of dancing on the stage in the early eighteenth century in "'Actions, Manners, and Passions': entr'acte dancing on the London stage, 1700–1737," *Early Music* 26 (1998): 213–28.

34. Adaptation of Beaumont and Fletcher is discussed in Arthur Colby Sprague, *Beaumont and Fletcher on the Restoration Stage* (Cambridge: Harvard University Press, 1926) and John Harold Wilson, *The Influence of Beaumont and Fletcher on Restoration Drama* (1928; reprint, New York: Haskell House Publishers, 1969). Robert Gale Noyes examines the performance history of Ben Jonson's plays in *Ben Jonson on the English Stage, 1660–1776* (Cambridge: Harvard University Press, 1935). For an excellent general summary of adapting earlier dramatic material, see Paulina Kewes, *Authorship and Appropriation: Writing for the Stage in England, 1660–1710* (Oxford: Clarendon, 1998). Gunnar Sorelius's *"The Giant Race Before the Flood": Pre-Restoration Drama on the Stage and in the Criticism of the Restoration*, Arthur Gewirtz's *Restoration Adaptations of Early 17th Century Comedies*, and David Paxman's "The Burden of the Immediate Past: The Early Eighteenth Century and the Shadow of Restoration Comedy," *Essays in Literature* 17 (1990): 15–29, also provide general considerations of this material. Laura Rosenthal points out that "we would be hard pressed . . . to find a playwright in this period who repeated nothing from the past." *Playwrights and Plagiarists in Early Modern England* (Ithaca: Cornell University Press, 1996), 1.

35. Hume and Scouten discuss the complex reasons for theatrical failures in "'Restoration Comedy' and its Audiences," 57–65. We must not summarily attribute every theatrical failure to bad playwriting without further investigation.

36. Samuel Johnson, "Dryden," in *Lives of the English Poets*, ed. George Birkbeck Hill (Oxford: Clarendon, 1905), 1:411.

Chapter 1. Shakespeare "Made Fitt"

1. *Bottom the Weaver* contains the Bottom material from *A Midsummer Night's Dream*, omits the lovers, and makes only brief references to Oberon, Titania, and Puck. The first part of James Shirley's masque *The Triumph of Beauty* is based on *A Midsummer Night's Dream* and was probably designed for amateur performance after 1642. Shirley's play includes a rustic named Bottle who plans to entertain Prince Paris with his group of shepherds, but the entertainment turns out to be just a dance. Shirley borrowed from numerous sources in his work, mainly conventional devices and plots "with probably no reference to any single earlier play." Robert Stanley Forsythe, *The Relations of Shirley's Plays to the Elizabethan Drama* (New York: Columbia University Press, 1914), 148. Gerard Langbaine notes that Shirley "has imitated *Shakespear*, in the Comical part of his *Midsummer Night's Dream*; and *Shirley*'s Shepherd's *Bottle*, is but a Copy of *Shakespear's Bottom, the Weaver.*" *An Account of the English Dramatick Poets* (London, 1691), 485. Subsequent references to Langbaine's work are cited parenthetically in the text. See also Dale B. J. Randall, *Winter Fruit: English Drama 1642–1660* (Lexington: University Press of Kentucky, 1995), 147–56.

2. John James Elson, ed., *The Wits or, Sport upon Sport* (Ithaca: Cornell University Press, 1932), 270.

3. A. D. Harvey asserts that Davenant "may be counted amongst the Bard's least sensitive adapters" and condemns his "radical structural vandalism" of Shakespeare's plays. "Virginity and Honor in *Measure for Measure* and Davenant's *The Law Against Lov-*

ers," *English Studies* 75 (1994): 123–32. Similarly, N. W. Bawcutt remarks that "the effect of Davenant's alterations is to reduce Shakespeare's play to a meaningless jumble." William Shakespeare, *Measure for Measure*, ed. N. W. Bawcutt (Oxford and New York: Oxford University Press, 1991), 26. Others have proposed various political reasons for Davenant to combine these two plays in such a fashion. Hughes describes *The Law Against Lovers* as a play about "the re-establishment of legitimate rule." *English Drama 1660–1700*, 35. Dobson maintains that Davenant's adaptation is a "royalist drama" that "wishes to erase" all of the "crimes, discomforts, and civil strife" of the Commonwealth period. *The Making of the National Poet*, 35. Nancy Klein Maguire connects the play to the Restoration political climate, arguing that Davenant "perhaps to stabilize the new regime, stresses that obligations are based on accepted duties rather than on personal loyalty." *Regicide and Restoration: English Tragicomedy 1660–1671* (Cambridge: Cambridge University Press, 1992), 79. Davenant specifically creates a familial relationship between Angelo, Beatrice, and Benedick, promoting a conflict on a personal level and actually testing obligations based on these loyalties. Also, in Davenant's version the unrest is resolved not with the return of the Duke, but rather with the military actions of Benedick against Angelo.

4. Gunnar Sorelius discusses this division in "The Rights of the Restoration Theatrical Companies in the Older Drama," *Studia Neophilologica* 37 (1965): 174–89. Davenant had rights to Shakespeare's *The Tempest, Measure for Measure, Much Ado About Nothing, Romeo and Juliet, Twelfth Night, Henry VIII, King Lear, Macbeth,* and *Hamlet*. Mary Edmond provides a summary of Davenant's connections to earlier acting traditions in *Rare Sir William Davenant* (New York: St. Martin's Press, 1987), 140–41.

5. John Freehafer, "The Formation of the London Patent Companies in 1660," *Theatre Notebook* 20 (1965): 27.

6. Davenant's warrant states that he presented "a proposition of reformeinge some of the most ancient Playes that were playd at Blackfriers and of makeinge them, fitt, for the Company of Actors appointed vnder his direction and Com[m]and." L.C. 5/137, 343–4, in Allardyce Nicoll, *A History of English Drama 1660–1900* (Cambridge: Cambridge University Press, 1952–59), 1:352–53. *Measure for Measure* and *Much Ado About Nothing* are among the plays granted to Davenant.

7. N. W. Bawcutt, ed., *The Control and Censorship of Caroline Drama: The Records of Sir Henry Herbert, Master of the Revels 1623–73* (Oxford: Clarendon, 1996), 228.

8. Master of the Revels Sir Henry Herbert reminds the troupe to "bringe or sende to me All such old Plaies As you doe Intende to Acte at the saide playhouse, that they may be reformed of Prophanes & Ribaldry, at your perill." Ibid., 235. I have expanded the abbreviations. The 1663 document demands that "all prophanenes, oathes, ribaldry, and matters reflecting vpon piety, and the present governement may bee obliterated, before there bee any action [vpon] in a publiq[ue] Theatre." The document adds that plays must be purged of "all vnsauoury words, & vnbecomming expressions, (not fitt to bee lycenced in a Christian Commonwealth)." Ibid., 271–72.

9. Davenant, *The Works of Sir William Davenant* (London, 1673), 284. Hazelton Spencer's observation is obviously misguided: Davenant "might almost be called a prude. He took quite seriously the injunction of the royal patent to purge the old plays of scurrility" (*Shakespeare Improved*, 137).

10. Gunnar Sorelius, "The Early History of the Restoration Theatre: Some Problems Reconsidered," *Theatre Notebook* 33 (1979): 59.

11. Milhous, *Thomas Betterton*, 18–19.

12. According to *The London Stage*, no performance records of either play survive from this period. A few scattered references to the two plays exist, but there is no evidence of performance or popularity around 1660. Charles H. Shattuck notes a prompt-

book from the First Folio "marked in the early seventeenth century" of *Measure for Measure* performed in England, c. 1640, but this is no indication that the play was performed after the closing of the theaters. *The Shakespeare Promptbooks: A Descriptive Catalogue* (Urbana and London: University of Illinois Press, 1965), 269.

13. Most scholarship on *The Law Against Lovers* deals with the differences between Davenant's play and Shakespeare's; see Mongi Raddadi's *Davenant's Adaptations of Shakespeare* (Stockholm: Uppsala, 1979) and Rudolf Stamm, "Sir William Davenant and Shakespeare's Imagery," *English Studies* 24 (1942): 65–79, 97–116. The theatrical history behind Davenant's adaptation has largely been overlooked. In *The Comedy of Sir William Davenant*, Collins states that Davenant "wanted to ally two well-known Shakespeare plots" (147), but neither Shakespearian play had been performed since the reopening of the theaters, and would not have been well-known to a theatre audience in 1662.

14. Davenant's "Articles of Agreement" with the players at the Cockpit uses this phrase to describe his position. See Bawcutt, *The Control and Censorship of Caroline Drama*, 240 and Milhous, *Thomas Betterton*, 9–10.

15. Jacques Thierry and Will Schellinks attended the first performance on 15 February 1662, Pepys saw the play on 18 February, and John Evelyn recorded a performance on 17 December 1662. References to Evelyn's diary are taken from John Evelyn, *The Diary of John Evelyn*, ed. E. S. De Beer, 6 vols. (Oxford: Clarendon, 1955), and cited by volume and page in the text. An additional performance survives from Edward Browne's 1662 list of plays seen while in London (W. W. Greg, "Theatrical Repertories of 1662," in J. C. Maxwell, ed., *W. W. Greg: Collected Papers* [Oxford: Clarendon, 1966], 44–47). In *The London Stage*, William Van Lennep notes that "Browne's date of '1662' is apparently not to be taken literally, for his list includes plays beyond 1662, extending so far as *The Playhouse To Be Let*, which was apparently first acted in the summer of 1663, and *The Stepmother*, which apparently was first acted in the early autumn of 1663. Other plays on his list were acted in 1661 but may, of course, have been performed in 1662 as well," 1:36. Robert D. Hume argues that "the chronological limits [of the plays on Browne's list] are the spring of 1661 (probable) to October-November 1663 (definite)." See "Dr Edward Browne's Playlist of '1662': A Reconsideration," *Philological Quarterly* 64 (1985): 76.

16. Samuel Pepys, *The Diary of Samuel Pepys*, ed. Robert Latham and William Matthews, 11 vols. (London: Bell and Hyman, 1970–83), 5:77; 8:463. Subsequent references to Pepys are cited by volume and page number in the text.

17. John Downes, *Roscius Anglicanus* (1708), ed. Judith Milhous and Robert D. Hume (London: The Society for Theatre Research, 1987), 51; Bawcutt, *The Control and Censorship of Caroline Drama*, 227. Subsequent references to Downes are cited by volume and page number in the text.

18. Robert D. Hume and Alfred Harbage point out that most "newly written" plays in the early 1660s (like *The Law Against Lovers*) are actually reworkings of older plays that were repackaged. Hume, "Securing a Repertory: Plays on the London Stage, 1660–65" in Antony Coleman and Antony Hammond, eds., *Poetry and Drama 1570–1700: Essays in Honour of Harold F. Brooks* (London: Methuen, 1981) and Harbage, "Elizabethan-Restoration Palimpsest," *Modern Language Review* 35 (1940): 287–319. Hume discusses the varieties of comedy in the early years of the Restoration in "Diversity and Development in Restoration Comedy 1660–1679," *Eighteenth-Century Studies* 5 (1972): 365–97. As he points out, many adaptations of Molière also appeared in the early years of the Restoration (381). See also John Wilcox, *The Relation of Molière to Restoration Comedy* (1938; reprint, New York: Benjamin Blom, 1964).

19. For example, we have records of one performance of Fletcher's *The Mad Lover*,

three performances of Massinger's *The Bondman*, one performance of Fletcher's *Rule a Wife and Have a Wife*, and one performance of Shakespeare's *Hamlet* for the 1660–61 season. See *The London Stage* for complete data. However, John Downes's comment that "No succeeding Tragedy for several Years got more Reputation, or Money to the Company than this" (*Roscius*, 52) complicates the assessment of *Hamlet*'s popularity. See Evelyn's comment on *Hamlet* cited elsewhere in this chapter.

20. *The London Stage* records for 1661–62 include one performance of Shakespeare's *Twelfth Night*, one performance of *Hamlet*, two performances of the Fletcher/Rowley *The Maid in the Mill*, and three performances of Massinger's *The Bondman*, which was probably more successful than the number of performances indicates, as Killigrew offered it the same season to compete with Davenant.

21. *Cutter of Coleman-Street*, Cowley's revamping of *The Guardian* (1642), was performed at least six times, and *Love and Honour* at least four times. Pepys comments on the popularity of *Love and Honour* (2:200, 201.)

22. Ten performances of *The Villain* are documented for this season, and thirteen performances of *The Adventures of Five Hours* are recorded. In contrast, Webster's *The Duchess of Malfi* and Shakespeare's *Twelfth Night* only had one performance each, with two performances of *Hamlet*. John Evelyn comments on the popularity of Tuke's *The Adventures of Five Hours*: "I went to see Sir S. Tuke's (my kindsmans) Comedy acted at the Duke's Theater, which so universaly tooke as it was acted for some weekes every day, & was believed would be worth the comedians 4 or 5000 pounds" (3:350). Although Evelyn's assertion of the company's earnings is certainly exaggerated, his statement of the play's popularity is corroborated by Pepys, who relates his experience of arriving at the theater early for *The Adventures of Five Hours*, but not getting a good seat because the theater was so full (4:8).

23. *The Works of Sir William Davenant*, 67.

24. Gerard Langbaine, *Momus Triumphans: or, The Plagiaries of the English Stage* (1688), preface.

25. Such conclusions must be offered with some reservation. As Hume points out, in the first few seasons of the Restoration theater, "in all probability the Duke's Company did perform a number of plays of which we have no record." "Securing a Repertory: Plays on the London Stage 1660–5," 170 n. 16.

26. A letter in verse which Leslie Hotson dates from late 1662 survives with a reference to *The Law Against Lovers* as a new play, combined from two older plays. Shakespeare's name is not mentioned:

> Then came the Kn*igh*t agen with his Lawe
> Ag*ain*st Lovers the worst that ever you sawe
> In dressing of w*h*ich he playnely did shew it
> Hee was a far better Cooke then a Poet
> And only he the Art of it had
> Of two good Playes to make one bad . . .

The letter writer concludes, "And these are all the new playe wee have had." See Leslie Hotson, *The Commonwealth and Restoration Stage* (Cambridge: Harvard University Press, 1928), 345–47. Although we cannot conclude that the initial run was successful, a later eighteenth-century account reports that *The Law Against Lovers* "met with great success." David Erskine Baker, *Companion to the Playhouse* (1764), revised and expanded as *Biographia Dramatica; or, a Companion to the Playhouse*, ed. Stephen Jones. (1812; reprint, London and New York: AMS Press, 1966), 2:364.

27. Louis B. Wright, "The Reading of Plays during the Puritan Revolution," *Huntington Library Bulletin* 6 (1934): 73–108, and Paulina Kewes, "'Give me the Sociable

Pocket-Books . . .'" Humphrey Moseley's Serial Publication of Octavo Play Collections," *Publishing History* 38 (1995): 5–21. See also Arthur Colby Sprague, *Beaumont and Fletcher on the Restoration Stage* and W. W. Greg, "The Printing of the Beaumont and Fletcher Folio of 1647," *The Library* 2 (1922): 109–15.

28. James Gellert points out that the First and Second Folio were the sources Davenant used for *The Law Against Lovers*, not the quarto versions of the plays as argued by Hazelton Spencer. See "The Source of Davenant's *The Law Against Lovers*," *The Library* 8 (1986): 355.

29. Thirty years after *The Law Against Lovers* was performed, Langbaine identifies Davenant's sources for the play (*Account*, 109).

30. In his survey of Shakespeare's reputation in the seventeenth century, Gerald Eades Bentley concludes that in the Restoration "one is at once struck with the obscurity of Shakespeare's heroines as compared with their vogue in the nineteenth and twentieth centuries. Only Desdemona and Ophelia seem to have made any impression worth mentioning. Lady Macbeth and Cleopatra, Beatrice, Portia, Rosalind, Miranda, Viola, Perdita, Imogen, and Cordelia are mentioned so seldom as to seem unknown." *Shakespeare and Jonson: Their Reputations in the Seventeenth Century Compared* (Chicago: University of Chicago Press, 1945), 1:128.

31. In contrast, Pepys uses Shakespeare's title when referring to John Lacy's adaptation of *The Taming of the Shrew*, retitled *Sauny the Scott* (1667). Pepys writes that he saw "The Tameing of a Shrew; which hath some very good pieces in it, but generally is but a mean play; and the best part, Sawny, done by Lacy, hath not half its life, by reason of the words I suppose not being understood, at least by me" (8:158).

32. Ethel Seaton, *Literary Relations of England and Scandinavia in the Seventeenth Century* (Oxford: Clarendon, 1935), 335; Greg, "Theatrical Repertories of 1662," 47.

33. On 10 December 1663 he expects to see "a rare play to be acted this week of Sir William Davenant's, the story of Henry the 8th with all his wifes" (4:411) and later on 24 December of the same year he writes about the "goodness of the new play of Henry the 8th" (4:433). Pepys identifies *Twelfth Night* as a "new play" in his entry of 11 tember 1661 (2:177).

34. Authors' names did not appear in the playbills at this time; see Emmett L. Avery, "The Dramatists in the Theatrical Advertisements, 1700–1709," *Modern Language Quarterly* 8 (1947): 448–54.

35. *The Works of Sir William Davenant* (London, 1673).

36. Deborah C. Payne discusses Davenant's self-conscious fashioning of his career and concern to establish himself as a professional and an innovator in "Patronage and the Dramatic Marketplace under Charles I and II," *Yearbook of English Studies* 21 (1991): 151.

37. Charles Gildon's use of *The Law Against Lovers* in his 1700 adaptation *Measure for Measure, or Beauty the Best Advocate* (London, 1700) testifies to the influence of Davenant's version on the stage history of the play, discussed in more detail in chapter 3. As John Genest writes, "from Davenant Gildon has borrowed whatever suited him, but without any acknowledgment." *Some Account of the English Stage from 1660 to 1830*. (Bath: H.E. Carrington, 1832), 2:221. Subsequent references to Genest are cited parenthetically in the text. Gildon advertises the play on the title page as "now very much Alter'd; with *Additions* of several *Entertainments* of Musick." The detachment of Shakespeare's name from the play is still evident in the early eighteenth century; a 1706 performance of Gildon's play was advertised as "Written by the famous Beaumont and Fletcher" (*The London Stage* 2:124).

38. "To the Reader," *The Siege of Rhodes* (London, 1656). Mary Edmond attests that "the importance of Sir William Davenant's contribution to the musical life of Commonwealth London has been greatly under-valued." *Rare Sir William Davenant*, 127.

39. "Of Heroique Playes," Dryden, *Works*, 11:9.

40. The original music for *The Siege of Rhodes* is lost. James A. Winn, "Heroic Song: A Proposal for a Revised History of English Theater and Opera, 1656–1711," *Eighteenth-Century Studies* 30 (1996–97): 114.

41. Thomas Rymer, *Foedera, conventiones, literae, et cujuscunque generis acta publica* (London: A. & J. Churchill, 1704–35), 377–78. For further discussion of Davenant's 1639 plans, see John Freehafer, "Brome, Suckling, and Davenant's Theater Project of 1639," *Texas Studies in Literature and Language* 10 (1968): 367–83.

42. Milhous explains, "All the adjuncts to a bare script—scenery, dance, music—had put the Duke's Company ahead and forced Killigrew to scramble to keep up." *Thomas Betterton*, 25.

43. Winn remarks that "the process of revision, which probably continued for several years, moved *The Siege of Rhodes* toward the form later called semiopera, with episodes of song and dance alternating with scenes of spoken dialogue." "Heroic Song," 121.

44. Winn discusses Davenant's ability to add music and spectacle, "economically recycling his own materials while indicating his awareness of the tastes of the Restoration audience." Ibid., 121.

45. Curtis A. Price concludes, "between 1660 and about 1705 scarcely a play was mounted that was not accompanied by vocal and instrumental music—often in abundance—newly composed by the best masters." "Music as Drama," in Robert D. Hume, ed., *The London Theatre World* (Carbondale and Edwardsville: Southern Illinois University Press, 1980), 210; Dryden, *Works*, 8:5.

46. Oddly, Edward A. Cairns asserts that Davenant "had not 'dressed' [*The Law Against Lovers*] in his usual popular fashion: there are no musical interludes, dances or other entertainments," adding: "audiences who had seen his 'operatic' *Macbeth* produced the same month, with mysterious dances of magic and actually flying witches, must have been disappointed with a straightforward production." *Charles Gildon's Measure for Measure, or Beauty the Best Advocate: A Critical Edition* (New York and London: Garland, 1987), 6–7.

47. The song was reprinted four times in *The New Academy of Complements, Erected for Ladies, Gentlewomen, Courtiers, Gentlemen, Scholars, Souldiers, Citizens, Country-men, and all persons* in 1669, 1671, 1681, and 1684. Sophia B. Blaydes and Philip Bordinat, *Sir William Davenant: An Annotated Bibliography 1629–1985* (New York and London: Garland, 1986), 72–75.

48. Further evidence of Davis's popularity is her song "My lodging it is on the Cold Ground" from Davenant's play *The Rivals*, which was so well-known that it was parodied by her rival Nell Gwyn in James Howard's *All Mistaken*, performed as early as 1665. Robert D. Hume, "Dryden, James Howard, and the Date of *All Mistaken*," *Philological Quarterly* 51 (1972): 422–29.

49. Curtis A. Price lists several other plays from 1660–1675 that include dances with castanets. *Music in the Restoration Theatre, With a Catalogue of Instrumental Music in the Plays 1665–1713* (Ann Arbor, Mich.: UMI Research Press, 1979), 257 n. 73.

50. Hume has recently discussed this in "Before the Bard: 'Shakespeare' in Early Eighteenth-Century London," especially the Appendix. For an earlier discussion of this material, see Katherine West (Scheil), "'All this we must do, to comply with the taste of the town': Shakespearian Comedy and the Early Eighteenth-Century Theatre," Ph.D. diss., University of Toronto, 1995.

51. Paulina Kewes argues that beginning in the 1690s, "the emergent preoccupation with the integrity and legitimacy of source materials reflects a new perception of the complex network of relationship, links, and affinities between old texts and new

ones," as articulated in Langbaine's *Momus Triumphans* (1688) and *An Account of the English Dramatick Poets* (1691). "Gerard Langbaine's 'View of *Plagiaries*': The Rhetoric of Dramatic Appropriation in the Restoration," *Review of English Studies* 48 (1997): 2–3. Rosenthal's *Playwrights and Plagiarists in Early Modern England* similarly locates concern with authorship in the 1690s.

52. See Holland, *The Ornament of Action* and Milhous and Hume, *Producible Interpretation: Eight English Plays 1675–1707*.

53. As late as 1716, new music was still being written for *Sauny the Scott*; Richard Leveridge set "When Sawney First Did Woe Me." See Neighbarger, *An Outward Show: Music for Shakespeare on the London Stage, 1660–1830*, 269.

54. Tori Haring-Smith, in her study of the performance history of *The Taming of the Shrew* remarks that Restoration and eighteenth-century adaptations "have remarkably little to do with Shakespeare." *From Farce to Melodrama*, 9. In the Oxford edition of *The Taming of the Shrew* (Oxford: Clarendon, 1982), H. J. Oliver states that "interest [in *Sauny the Scott*] today can be only in the contrast its vulgarity provides with Shakespeare's Elizabethan directness and in the examination of the possible reasons for retaining some Shakespearian phrases and not others" (66). Graham Holderness and Bryan Loughrey quickly jettison *Sauny the Scott* with a single reference in their discussion of the stage history of the *Shrew* plays, but manage to misdate Lacy's play and attribute the later adaptation *Catherine and Petruchio* to "Edward" Garrick, not David. *A Pleasant Conceited Historie, Called The Taming of a Shrew*, 28.

55. See works by Odell (*Shakespeare from Betterton to Irving*) and Spencer (*Shakespeare Improved*) for act-by-act plot summaries of *Sauny the Scott*. The major differences from Shakespeare can be summarized as follows: Petruchio's servant Grumio becomes Sauny, Gremio is renamed Woodall, Hortensio is Geraldo, Lucentio is Winlove, Vincentio is renamed Sir Lyonel Winlove, Biondello becomes Jamy, and Katherina is renamed Margaret. Cynthia M. Tuerk suggests that "Kate" is renamed "Margaret" in Lacy's play in reference to Margaret Cavendish, but Lacy's renaming is probably an allusion to Fletcher's heroine Maria in *The Tamer Tam'd*. "The Duchess of Newcastle and John Lacy's *Sauny the Scot*," *Notes and Queries* 42 (1995): 450–51. Lacy sets the play in London and omits the Sly Induction scenes. Lacy's Margaret is more outspoken than Katherina, and has a tumultuous relationship with Bianca. Margaret's tormenting scenes are intensified from Shakespeare: she is not only deprived of sleep and food, but Petruchio also makes her smoke a pipe and drink excessively. At the end of the play, Margaret warns Bianca about the dangers of men, standing up to Petruchio's demands even when he stages a mock funeral for her. Lacy's Margaret has a brief speech on a woman's duty to her husband, and Petruchio ends the play with a reference to taming the tamer, a nod to Fletcher's play. Sandra Clark provides one of the best discussions of *Sauny the Scott* in *Shakespeare Made Fit: Restoration Adaptations of Shakespeare*, xlvi-lii. See Susan Staves, *Players' Scepters: Fictions of Authority in the Restoration* (Lincoln: University of Nebraska Press, 1979) for a brief mention of domestic relations in *Sauny the Scott* (133–34). Rothstein and Kavenik also note in passing that Lacy's *Sauny the Scott* exemplifies "how peremptory in Carolean Comedy such an equalizing treatment of male and female leads is, for this play adapts the most famous, or glaring, example of masculine triumph disguised as 'nature' in Elizabethan comedy, Shakespeare's *The Taming of the Shrew*." Lacy "turns into madcap farce his predecessor's lesson about the order of nature" but they conclude that "such a denouement remains very much atypical." *The Designs of Carolean Comedy*, 30.

56. Prologue to *Sir Hercules Buffoon* (1684). Some scholars unfamiliar with *Sauny the Scott* have assumed that Sauny is a combination of Grumio from *The Shrew* and Sander from *A Shrew* (see Holderness and Loughrey above), but Lacy's changes to the Grumio

character do not correspond to Sander. Aside from being an embellished servant role, which Lacy was known to create in his other plays, there are no significant similarities between Sander and Sauny.

57. An entry in *The Dramatic Records of Sir Henry Herbert* for October 1664 records a "Re[vived] Play Taminge [the] Shrew," which may mean that *Sauny the Scott* was performed four years earlier (Bawcutt, *The Control and Censorship of Caroline Drama*, 283–84).

58. James Maidment and W. H. Logan, eds., *The Dramatic Works of John Lacy, Comedian* (London: H. Southeran, 1875), 316.

59. John Aubrey asserts that Ben Jonson "took a catalogue from Mr Lacy (the player) of the Yorkshire dialect. 'Twas his hint for clownery to his comedy called *The Tale of a Tub*. This I had from Mr Lacy." John Aubrey, *Brief Lives*, ed. Richard Barber (Suffolk: Boydell Press, 1982), 180.

60. Describing a performance of Corneille's *Horace*, Pepys states: "this the third day of its acting—a silly Tragedy; but Lacy hath made a farce of several dances, between each act, one. But his words are but silly, and invention not extraordinary as to the dances" (9:420). Pepys remarks that a 1669 performance of Brome's *A Jovial Crew* was "ill acted to what it was heretofore in Clun's time and when Lacy could dance" (9:411–12).

61. Pepys uses the term "silly play" also to describe Richard Rhodes's *Flora's Vagaries*: "to the King's House, and there, in one of the upper boxes saw *Flora's vagarys*, which is a very silly play, and the more, I being out of humour, being at a play without my wife" (9:78).

62. Lacy may have recycled this line; Drench the farrier has a similar line in *The Dumb Lady*: "a woman has no tongue, they'r tongues in mens mouths, but they'r call'd stings in women" (14).

63. Hume concludes that the comedies of the late 1660s are "markedly low in tone," with prominent "farce and knockabout" and blatant indecency ("Diversity and Development in Restoration Comedy," 383). See also Leo Hughes, "Attitudes of Some Restoration Dramatists Toward Farce," *Philological Quarterly* 19 (1940): 268–87.

64. There were Scottish characters in earlier plays, such as Jamy in Shakespeare's *Henry V*, but most of these plays had not been performed regularly. In his survey of Scottish, Welsh, and Irish characters in English drama, J. O. Bartley attests that "Sauny has no predecessor." *Teague, Shenkin, and Sawney: Being an Historical Study of the Earliest Irish, Welsh and Scottish Characters in English Plays* (Cork: Cork University Press, 1954), 154.

65. See William Ferguson, *Scotland's Relations with England: A Survey to 1707* (Edinburgh: John Donald Publishers, 1977) for an in-depth discussion of particular historical events and their effects on Anglo-Scottish relations before the Union of 1707. For history of relations between England and Scotland after the Union of 1707, see Linda Colley, *Britons: Forging the Nation 1707–1837* (New Haven: Yale University Press, 1992), 117–22. Other useful histories of Scotland and England in the late seventeenth century include Wallace Notestein, *The Scot in History* (1946; reprint, Westport, Conn.: Greenwood Press, 1970) and R. A. Houston and I. D. Whyte's introductory chapter to *Scottish Society 1500–1800* (Cambridge: Cambridge University Press, 1989).

66. Dudley Ryder, *The Diary of Dudley Ryder, 1715–1716*, ed. William Matthews (London: Methuen, 1939), 88. For anti-Scots sentiment in the civil war, see the ballads "Newes from New-castle," "Good Newes from the North," and "A true Subjects wish," which vowed to "Tame these proud outdaring Scots." All three ballads, c. 1640, are included in Hyder E. Rollins, ed., *Cavalier and Puritan: Ballads and Broadsides Illustrating the Period of the Great Rebellion 1640–1660* (New York: New York University Press, 1923).

67. A promptbook from the 1731 edition survives, probably from a 1735 performance. See Edward A. Langhans, *Eighteenth-Century British and Irish Promptbooks: A Descriptive Bibliography* (New York: Greenwood Press, 1987), 104.

68. See also Kenneth Richards, "The Restoration Pageants of John Tatham," in David Mayer and Kenneth Richards, eds., *Western Popular Theatre* (London: Methuen, 1977), 49–73, and John Patrick Montaño, "The Quest for Consensus: The Lord Mayor's Day Shows in the 1670s," in Gerald Maclean, ed., *Culture and Society in the Stuart Restoration* (Cambridge: Cambridge University Press, 1995), 31–51.

69. Randall, *Winter Fruit*, 301–302. See also Virgil Joseph Scott, "A Reinterpretation of John Tatham's *The Rump: or the Mirrour of the Late Times*," *Philological Quarterly* 24 (1945): 114–18.

70. There has been considerable scholarly debate about which three characters are represented in this portrait. In his diary, John Evelyn states that Wright's best picture is "*Lacy* the famous *Rossius* or Comedian, whom he has painted in three dresses, a Gallant, a Presbyterian Minister, and a *Scots* highlander in his plod [plaid]" (3:338–39). In the notes to Evelyn's diary, E. S. De Beer identifies the three characters as "Mounsieur Device in *The Country Captain* . . . Scruple in *The Cheats* . . . Sauny in *Sauny the Scott: or, the Taming of the Shrew*" (3:338 n. 7). Although the *Biographical Dictionary* asserts that the roles in the Wright portrait "seem to be Parson Scruple in *The Cheats*, Galliard in *The French Dancing Master*, and Monsieur De Vice in *The Country Captain*," the entry gives no reasons for this interpretation, and no evidence to discount the Scottish character as a representation of Sauny the Scott. Philip H. Highfill, Jr., Kalman A. Burnim, and Edward A. Langhans, eds., *A Biographical Dictionary of Actors, Actresses, Musicians, Dancers, Managers and Other Stage Personnel in London, 1660–1800*, 16 vols. (Carbondale and Edwardsville: Southern Illinois University Press, 1973–93), 9:104. Subsequent references are cited by volume and page number. Charles W. Cooper argued that the 1675 portrait is a copy of an earlier picture of Lacy from 1662 also by Michael Wright ("The Triple-Portrait of John Lacy," *PMLA* 47 [1932]: 759–65), but as Gunnar Sorelius contends, because the picture is explicitly dated 1675 and Lacy's costume agrees with that date, there is "no longer any reason not to identify the character with Teague or Sauny, roles that we know that Lacy performed and was famous for." "The Early History of the Restoration Theatre: Some Problems Reconsidered," 56. Jocelyn Powell persuasively argues that the portrait shows Lacy as "the coarse and foolish Sawney in *Sawney, the Scot*, his own adaptation of *The Taming of the Shrew*, as the fastidious Scruple in *The Cheats*, and the snide Galliard in *The Variety*." Powell notes "Sawney's gesture of pinching at his scrofulous wrist" and explains that "Scrofula was a traditionally Scottish disease (the consequence, it was supposed, of their barbarous diet) and much coarse humour is got from this affliction in the course of the comedy." *Restoration Theatre Production* (London: Routledge, 1984), 104. This gesture specifically matches performance antics of Sauny the Scott, as does his costume. See also J. O. Bartley, "Irish, Welsh and Scottish Stage Costume Before the Interregnum," *Theatre Notebook* 5 (1950): 64.

71. Lacy may have recycled this trait in a later character: Raggou in *The Old Troop* also provides for his large appetite. He carries meat in one sleeve of his jacket for himself and oats in another sleeve for his horse; he remarks, "Begar, dis sleeve be my Stabla, dere by good Oata for mine Arse: and dis sleeve be my Kitchin, dere be meat for my self" (20). As with Sauny's dirty appearance, this is the source of much amusing stage business in the play; the Captain remarks to Raggou that his "sleeves stink abominably" (20).

72. Lacy endows Drench in *The Dumb Lady* (acted by 1670) with similar bawdy characteristics. Disguised as a physician, he asserts, "I must see [the Nurse's] breasts, it is the Doctors duty to look to the Nurses milk" (18). He advises a seaman's wife who

complains of problems having children, "come i' th' evening to me, after a glass of Wine I may have something to help thee" (31). Later, an apprentice confides that his lady has been "so troubled with these frights since my Master's absence, that I have never had a good nights rest since he went; for she'll come in her sleep, and throw her self upon my bed; and then I lye as still as can be, and then she rises like a mad woman, and throws all the clothes off, and makes such work with me, that I'm ashamed your worship should know it" (32–33). Drench's solution to the apprentice is, "I know her disease, commend me to thy Mrs; and tell her, because I'll make a perfect cure on't, I'l come and lye in the next room to her my self, and thou shalt go into the Garet again" (33). Scottish literature has a long history of fascination with sex, women, and marriage. See Jenny Wormald, *Court, Kirk, and Community: Scotland, 1470–1625* (Toronto: University of Toronto Press, 1981), 30.

73. In Lacy's *The Dumb Lady*, Isabel, the wife of Drench the farrier, arranges to have him beaten at the beginning of the play, but he retaliates by committing her to Bedlam to be tamed; he tells the arresting officers that "you'l find a damn'd scould of her" (55), and they assure him, "O, Sir, we that can tame mad folks, can tame a scould, I warrant you" (55).

74. *The London Stage*, 1:348.

75. Leo Hughes notes a 1703 edition in the Huntington Library that includes the phrase "often acted with great applause." *A Century of English Farce* (Princeton: Princeton University Press, 1956), 216.

76. A performance of *The Taming of the Shrew* is listed for the 1633–34 season at court: "On tusday night at Saint James, the 26th of Novemb. 1633, was acted before the King and Queene, The Taminge of the Shrew. Likt.'" The subsequent entry shows that Shakespeare's play and Fletcher's *The Tamer Tam'd* played off of each other as late as 1633: "On thursday night at St. James, the 28 of Novemb.1633, was acted before the King and Queene, The Tamer Tamd, made by Fletcher. Very well likt." Bawcutt, *The Control and Censorship of Caroline Drama*, 185.

77. Sprague, *Beaumont and Fletcher on the Restoration Stage*, 8. Pepys saw *The Tamer Tam'd* on 30 October 1660, which he described as "a very fine play" that was "very well acted" (2:145) and also saw a performance on 31 July 1661 that was "well done" (1:278). *The Tamer Tam'd* was also put on twice for the King on 9 November 1668 at Court and at Drury Lane on 8 December 1674. See *The London Stage*, 1:148, 225.

78. Records in *The London Stage* indicate that *Sauny the Scott* endured in London theaters through the middle of the eighteenth century. Many records survive of performances of Fletcher's *Tamer Tam'd* in the Restoration as well. Margaret Maurer raises the possibility that Lacy's play may have influenced Nicholas Rowe's 1709 edition of Shakespeare. "The Rowe Editions of 1709/1714 and 3.1. of *The Taming of the Shrew*," in Joanna Gondris, ed., *Reading Readings: Essays on Shakespeare Editing in the Eighteenth Century* (Madison, N.J.: Fairleigh Dickinson University Press, 1998), 244–67.

Chapter 2. "Above Ordinary Plays"

1. Henry Purcell, dedication to *The Vocal and Instrumental Musick of the Prophetess, or the History of Dioclesian* (1691). Curtis A. Price says that Dryden wrote this, but Purcell signed it. See *Henry Purcell and the London Stage* (Cambridge: Cambridge University Press, 1984), 264–65.

2. Theater pieces with extensive musical scores are problematic to categorize. Roger North was the first to coin the term "semi-opera" for dramas with substantial music (also called "dramatic operas") but this terminology is notoriously unstable.

North's label appeared long after the inception of this type of entertainment. *Roger North on Music*, ed. John Wilson (London: Novello, 1959). Peter Anthony Motteux, himself a creator of these music dramas, observed in his prologue to *The Loves of Mars and Venus* (1696), that few could agree on what opera was: "And what we call a Masque some will allow / To be an Opera, as the World goes now." For a review of the meanings of "opera" in the period, see Howard Mayer Brown's entry in Stanley Sadie, ed., *The New Grove Dictionary of Opera* (London: Macmillan, 1992), 3:671–75. Robert D. Hume provides a cogent discussion of terminology in "Opera in London, 1695–1706," in *British Theatre and the Other Arts, 1660–1800*, 69. Many scholars have addressed the relationship between music, drama, and theater, including Todd S. Gilman, "*The Beggar's Opera* and British Opera," *University of Toronto Quarterly* 66 (1997): 539–61, and "Augustan Criticism and Changing Conceptions of English Opera," *Theatre Survey* 36 (1995): 1–35; Robert D. Hume, "The Sponsorship of Opera in London, 1704–1720," *Modern Philology* 85 (1988): 420–32; Price, *Henry Purcell* and "Music as Drama" in Robert D. Hume, ed., *The London Theatre World, 1660–1800* (Carbondale and Edwardsville: Southern Illinois University Press, 1980), 210–35, and *Music in the Restoration Theatre*; Milhous, *Thomas Betterton*; Eugene Haun, *But Hark! More Harmony: The Libretti in English of the Restoration Opera* (Ypsilanti: Eastern Michigan University Press, 1971); Robert Etheridge Moore, *Henry Purcell and the Restoration Theatre* (London: Heinemann, 1961); W. J. Lawrence, "Music and Song in the Elizabethan Theatre" and "The Mounting of the Carolan Masques" in *The Elizabethan Playhouse and Other Studies* (Stratford-upon-Avon: Shakespeare Head Press, 1912). For discussion of the development of semi-opera, see also Edward J. Dent, *Foundations of English Opera : A Study of Musical Drama in England During the Seventeenth Century* (Cambridge: Cambridge University Press, 1928); Richard Luckett, "Exotick but Rational Entertainments: The English Dramatic Operas," in Marie Axton and Raymond Williams, eds., *English Drama: Forms and Development* (Cambridge: Cambridge University Press, 1977), 123–41.

3. See Moore, *Henry Purcell and the Restoration Theatre*, 30–31. Motteux passage from *The Gentleman's Journal*, January 1692, 5. Dryden, prologue to *The Wild Gallant* (1663).

4. Wilson, *Roger North*, 302.

5. Prologue printed in Robert Gale Noyes, "A Manuscript Restoration Prologue for *Volpone*," *Modern Language Notes* 42 (1937): 198–200; Wilson, *Roger North*, 353. Ben Jonson's relationship with Inigo Jones comes to mind here, in the struggle between poetry and visual/aural elements.

6. Wilson, *Roger North*, 273.

7. Shadwell, preface to *The Sullen Lovers* (1668).

8. George Granville, preface to *The British Enchanters* (London, 1710).

9. Franklin B. Zimmerman, "The Court Music of Henry Purcell," in Robert P. Maccubbin and Martha Hamilton-Phillips, eds., *The Age of William III and Mary II* (Williamsburg, Va.: College of William and Mary, 1989), 312.

10. Mountfort's prologue to Powell's *The Treacherous Brothers* (1690); *The Dunciad* Book I, line 238. *The Poems of Alexander Pope*, ed. John Butt (London: Methuen, 1963). According to Pepys, actors insisted on a higher fee for new plays than for revivals. Henry Harris "demanded £20 for himself extraordinary there, [more] then Batterton or anybody else, upon every new play, and £10 upon every Revive," which Davenant refused to give him (4:239).

11. Eckhard Auberlen, "*The Tempest* and the Concerns of the Restoration Court: A Study of *The Enchanted Island* and the Operatic *Tempest*," *Restoration* 15 (1992): 71–88; George R. Guffey, "Politics, Weather, and the Contemporary Reception of the Dryden-Davenant *Tempest*," *Restoration* 8 (1984): 1–9.

12. Nancy Klein Maguire, *Regicide and Restoration: English Tragicomedy, 1660–1671* (Cambridge: Cambridge University Press, 1992), 132. As Hume points out, "a message sufficiently secret to be beyond recrimination is not likely to be very clear, let alone effective," and "one cannot readily imagine the actor-sharers of the company agreeing to invest staggering sums of money in something that was not intended to retain its appeal for many years." "The Politics of Opera in Late Seventeenth-Century London," *Cambridge Opera Journal* 10 (1998): 25, 20. Matthew W. Wikander suggests interesting political possibilities for some of the differences between Shakespeare's version and the Dryden-Davenant version, but does not acknowledge the realities of theatrical competition or the dramatic climate. "'The Duke My Father's Wrack': The Innocence of the Restoration *Tempest*," *Shakespeare Survey* 43 (1991): 91–98. For a line-by-line comparison between the Dryden-Davenant *Tempest* and Shakespeare's *The Tempest*, see Raddadi, *Davenant's Adaptations of Shakespeare*, Appendix II and Chapter 6. Maximillian E. Novak provides an excellent discussion of the differences between Dryden-Davenant's plot and Shakespeare's in Dryden, *Works*, 10, 319–43. Derek Hughes discusses the Dryden-Davenant *Tempest* in terms of thematic revisions, particularly the idea of the stranger, in *English Drama 1660–1700*, 49–55.

13. In contrast, Pepys picked up political references in other plays; for instance, he remarks about Edward Howard's *The Usurper* (1668), "A pretty good play in all but what is designed to resemble Cromwell and Hugh Peters, which is mighty silly" (9:381).

14. In an often-cited article, Katharine Eisaman Maus erroneously focuses on whether a Restoration audience would have "preferred the revised version of *The Tempest*" to Shakespeare's play. "Arcadia Lost: Politics and Revision in the Restoration *Tempest*," *Renaissance Drama* 13 (1982): 201. It was not until Charles Gildon's "Remarks on the Plays of Shakespear," published in conjunction with Rowe's 1709 edition, that Shakespeare's *The Tempest* was formally evaluated in comparison to the adapted versions.

15. The 1673 Davenant Folio omits *Hamlet*, *Macbeth*, *The Tempest, or The Enchanted Island*, and *The Rivals*, but includes *The Law Against Lovers*, as discussed in the previous chapter. *The Tempest* was included in Dryden's *Works* in 1701, and may have been considered one of his own plays by then.

16. Many have discussed the attribution of various aspects of this adaptation to Dryden and Davenant. See, for example, Spencer, *Five Restoration Adaptations of Shakespeare*, 16–22 and Novak, ed., Dryden, *Works*, 10:322. Novak points out that Dryden probably defended Davenant because of recent critics such as Richard Flecknoe, and may have exaggerated Davenant's role in the adaptation. Novak argues that Dryden had a greater role in the adaptation because the play is listed with Dryden's plays but is excluded from the 1673 Davenant Folio (which includes *The Law Against Lovers*). However, the Davenant Folio does not include his adaptation of *Macbeth*, which Davenant composed single-handedly. Both Shakespearian adaptations were not included with Davenant's works probably because he still considered them as Shakespeare's, whereas he tried to pass off *The Law Against Lovers* as his own play (as discussed in the previous chapter.)

17. Bayes remarks that "all these dead men you shall see rise up presently, at a certain Note . . . and fall a Dancing." The men "dance worse than the Angels in Harry the Eight, or the fat Spirits in *The Tempest*, I gad" (19).

18. See John Harold Wilson, *All The King's Ladies: Actresses of the Restoration* (Chicago: University of Chicago Press, 1958), 140, 166.

19. Dryden credits Davenant with the addition of Hippolito; Arthur H. Nethercot notes that Davenant's earlier *The Platonick Lovers* (1636) contains a character named Gridonel who has never experienced women or sex. *Sir William Davenant: Poet Laureate*

and *Playwright-Manager* (Chicago: University of Chicago Press, 1938), 399–400. Auberlen sees Hippolito as an influence on Celadon in Dryden's *Secret Love* (1667), and suggests that Miranda, Dorinda, and Hippolito are precursors of Margery Pinchwife in *The Country Wife* (1675), Miss Prue in Congreve's *Love for Love* (1695) and Hoyden in Vanbrugh's *The Relapse* (1697). "*The Tempest* and the Concerns of the Restoration Court," 71–88.

20. Novak, ed., Dryden, *Works*, 10:341. Jack M. Armistead points out that Prospero reflects "fresh assumptions about the dynamics of human history and about the definition of human competence in relation to Providential decree." "Dryden's Prospero and his Predecessors," *South Atlantic Review* 50 (1985): 23–33.

21. Pepys does not comment on the fact that the echo song is not in Shakespeare; either he did not know the Shakespearian original that well, or he did not think it worth distinguishing the two. Echo songs had been popular throughout the century. Campion's 1607 *The Lord Hayes' Masque* includes a chorus "in the manner of an Echo, seconded by the cornets, then by the consort of ten, then by the consort of twelve, and by a double chorus of voices standing on either side, the one against the other, bearing five voices apiece, and sometimes every chorus was heard severally, sometimes mixed, but in the end all together."

22. Harris gives Pepys the music to his echo song that he sings with Ariel; the music was by John Banister and Pelham Humfrey. See W. J. Lawrence, "Purcell's Music for *The Tempest*," *Notes & Queries* II (1904): 164–65. See also William Van Lennep, "Henry Harris, Actor, Friend of Pepys," in M. St. Clare Byrne, ed., *Studies in English Theatre History in Memory of Gabrielle Enthoven* (London: Society for Theatre Research, 1952), 9–23.

23. Pepys was often taken with unique music. At a performance of the Dekker and Massinger *The Virgin Martyr*, he writes, "but that which did please me beyond any thing in the whole world was the wind-musique when the Angell comes down, which is so sweet that it ravished me; and endeed, in a word, did wrap up my soul so that it made me really sick, just as I have formerly been when in love with my wife" (9:94).

24. Dryden, *Works*, 10:202–13, 9:7. Hume points out the proclivity for this type of low comedy in the 1660s in "Diversity and Development in Restoration Comedy 1660–1679," 388. Rothstein and Kavenik discuss the relationship between the "low" and "high" plot in *The Tempest*. *The Designs of Carolean Comedy*, 85–107.

25. "An Elegy Upon that Incomparable *Comedian*, Mr. Edward Angell," repr. in *A Little Ark*, ed. G. Thorn-Drury (London: P.J. & A.E. Dobell, 1921), 38–39.

26. For similarities between Shakespeare's *The Tempest* and *The Sea-Voyage*, see Daniel Morley McKeithan, *The Debt to Shakespeare in the Beaumont-and-Fletcher Plays* (Austin, n.p. 1938). Rothstein and Kavenik compellingly argue that Dryden and Davenant revised Shakespeare's play "along fletcherian [*sic*] lines for the Carolean public." *The Designs of Carolean Comedy*, 86.

27. *The London Stage* (1:118) also lists a performance of *The Sea-Voyage* on 27 September for the King.

28. "Hark the storm grows" by Robert Smith and "Cheer up my mates" by Pelham Humfrey were printed in *Choice Songs and Ayres*, The First Book, 1673.

29. Guffey discusses the tempestuous weather in "Politics, Weather, and the Contemporary Reception of the Dryden-Davenant *Tempest*," 6–8.

30. Novak suggests that Killigrew put on *The Sea-Voyage* after hearing that Dryden and Davenant were revising *The Tempest*. See Dryden, *Works*, 10:320–21.

31. *The London Stage*, 1:124. See Ruth Wallerstein, "Suckling's Imitation of Shakespeare," *Review of English Studies* 75 (1943): 290–95.

32. Durfey's play was perhaps revived in 1690–91; see *The London Stage*, 1:386.

Langbaine describes this play as *"Fletcher's Sea-Voyage* reviv'd, with the Alteration of some few Scenes; tho' what is either alter'd or added may be as easily discern'd from the Original, as Patches on a Coat from the main Piece" (*Account,* 180). Like Shakespeare's original play, *The Sea-Voyage* was also augmented throughout the period with additions of music. Wilson has detailed the various permutations and combinations of Beaumont and Fletcher plays in the Restoration in *The Influence of Beaumont and Fletcher on Restoration Drama.*

33. The Dryden-Davenant version was first printed in 1670. A second and third edition appeared in 1676, a fourth in 1690, a fifth in 1692, a sixth in 1695, and a seventh in 1701, as well as in Congreve's edition in Dryden's *Dramatick Works* (1717). See Novak, ed., Dryden, *Works,* 10: 493. *Windsor-Drollery* (1672) reprinted the echo song that Pepys enjoyed. The *Dialogue between Cupid and Bacchus* was added in 1707 and a "Grand Devil's Dance" was added in 1727 *(The London Stage,* 2:136 and 2:927). In the later eighteenth century, *The Tempest* continued its influence: an early novel entitled *The Force of Nature; or the Loves of Hippollito and Dorinda. A Romance* (1720) draws on the new characters from the Dryden-Davenant version. See Charles C. Mish, "An Early Eighteenth-Century Prose Version of *The Tempest,*" in *British Theatre and the Other Arts, 1660–1800,* 237–56. Mish concludes that since the book was printed by provincial printers, it was intended as a chapbook, and "its readers would probably be people who had never been in a theatre or in London and were probably innocent of any knowledge of Shakespeare's or anybody else's *Tempest*" (240). *The Tempest* has also been cited as a possible source for Defoe's *Robinson Crusoe.* John Robert Moore, "*The Tempest* and *Robinson Crusoe,*" *RES* 21 (1945): 52–56. *The Tempest* had a long history as a Christmas revival pantomime, and was performed in 1749 at Bartholomew Fair (*Daily Advertiser,* 23 August 1749). For the history of *The Tempest* in the later eighteenth century, see Michael Dobson, "'Remember/First to Possess His Books': The Appropriation of *The Tempest,* 1700–1800," *Shakespeare Survey* 43 (1991): 99–107.

34. See Judith Milhous, "The Multimedia Spectacular on the Restoration Stage," in *British Theatre and the Other Arts,* 42, and *Thomas Betterton,* 45–48; Hume, *The Development of English Drama,* 206, and "The Nature of the Dorset Garden Theatre," *Theatre Notebook* 36 (1982): 99–109. Additional works on Dorset Garden include Edward A. Langhans, "A Conjectural Reconstruction of the Dorset Garden Theatre," *Theatre Survey* 13 (1972): 74–93; Robert D. Hume, "The Dorset Garden Theatre: A Review of Facts and Problems," *Theatre Notebook* 33 (1979): 4–17; Richard Leacroft, *The Development of the English Playhouse* (Ithaca: Cornell University Press, 1973); and Diana de Marly, "The Architect of Dorset Garden Theatre," *Theatre Notebook* 29 (1975): 119–24.

35. For example, the *Post Boy* advertised on 13–15 January 1698: "'Tis said that this day will be Acted, at the Theatre in Dorset Garden, the Opera, called Prophetess or Dioclesian, at the Request of a Nobleman; they will not tell us who, but we presume for the Entertainment of a very great Foreigner." The recipient was the Czar of Muscovy. Actress Nell Gwyn attended the theater regularly, but only sat in Charles II's box once, for the opening night of *Psyche.* William Van Lennep, "Nell Gwyn's Playgoing at the King's Expense," *Harvard Library Bulletin* 4 (1950): 405–408.

36. BL Egerton MS 2623 contains this manuscript prologue and epilogue to *The Tempest.* Prologue and epilogue are transcribed by Christopher Spencer in *Five Restoration Adaptations,* 408, 412–13 and W. J. Lawrence, "'Did Thomas Shadwell Write an Opera on 'The Tempest'?" in *The Elizabethan Playhouse and Other Studies,* 200–202. Brian Corman and Todd S. Gilman summarize issues related to dating this prologue and epilogue in "The Musical Life of Thomas Shadwell," *Restoration* 20 (1996): 160–61. Lawrence argues that Shadwell wrote both for the 1674 *The Tempest* as a rebuttal to Dryden's prologue and epilogue written for the opening of the new theater in March of 1674. "Did Thomas Shadwell Write an Opera on 'The Tempest'?," 193–206.

37. John Downes dates the first performance in 1673, but most scholars agree that he is mistaken, and date the first performance in March or April of 1674.

38. See Dryden, *Works*, 10:493. Shakespeare's original play was revived briefly before Garrick's version, but this "original" included a "Musical Entertainment (compos'd by Arne) of Neptune and Amphitrite." See *The London Stage*, 3:121–25, and George Winchester Stone, Jr., "Shakespeare's *Tempest* at Drury Lane During Garrick's Management," *Shakespeare Quarterly* 7 (1956): 1. Garrick's version included parts from the Dryden-Davenant *The Tempest*, the 1674 operatic *The Tempest*, and 32 various songs. See also George R. Guffey, *After The Tempest* (Los Angeles: William Andrews Clark Memorial Library, 1969), xv-xviii.

39. Wilson, *Roger North*, 306.

40. Mark A. Radice suggests that the use of a pit orchestra was necessitated by the elaborate flying machines in this production of *The Tempest*. "Sites for Music in Purcell's Dorset Garden Theatre," *The Musical Quarterly* 81 (1997): 438. Price notes that the setup probably took place in an understage room. *Music in the Restoration Theatre*, 85. Jocelyn Powell captures the 1674 *Tempest* in a detailed reconstruction of the production in chapter 4 of *Restoration Theatre Production*.

41. See William Barclay Squire, "The Music of Shadwell's Tempest," *Musical Quarterly* 7 (1921): 565–78. Radice suggests that this arrangement may have been in imitation of French or continental practice. "Sites for Music," 437.

42. Nicoll, *History of English Drama*, 1:356.

43. Milhous, "The Multimedia Spectacular," 43; Charles Haywood, "*The Songs & Masque in the New Tempest*: An Incident in the Battle of the Two Theaters, 1674," *Huntington Library Quarterly* 19 (1955): 40. McManaway suggests that this libretto was designed for use in the theater by the audience and as a memento of the performance for later recollection; this was the first instance of a libretto intended primarily for the theater, not for a reading public. "Songs and Masques in the *Tempest*." *Theatre Miscellany*, Luttrell Society Reprints, No. 14 (Oxford, 1953), 133.

44. Wilson, *Roger North*, 307.

45. McManaway has detailed the proliferation of songs in the 1674 *Tempest*, including one song, "Dorinda Lamenting the loss of her Amintas" that appears in two song books but not in any version of the play, and involves a character not listed in the play as well ("Songs and Masques," 139). Franklin B. Zimmerman provides a digest of the music (which he obviously considers as Purcell's) in *Henry Purcell 1659–1695: An Analytical Catalogue of His Music* (New York: St. Martin's, 1963). See also Neighbarger, *An Outward Show: Music for Shakespeare on the London Stage, 1660–1830*, 26–38.

46. Moore argues that Purcell composed most of the music for the 1674 *Tempest*. *Henry Purcell and the Restoration Theatre*, 188–203. See Roger Fiske, *English Theatre Music in the Eighteenth Century*, 2d ed. (Oxford: Oxford University Press, 1986), 29–31, for a discussion disputing Purcell's authorship. Further discussion of the music can be found in G. Thorn-Drury, "Some Notes on Dryden," *Review of English Studies* 1 (1925): 327–30, and "Shadwell and the Operatic Tempest," *Review of English Studies* 3 (1927): 204–208. Additional debate concerning Purcell's authorship of music for *The Tempest* occurs in Margaret Laurie, "Did Purcell set *The Tempest*," *Proceedings of the Royal Musical Association* 90 (1963/4): 43–57, and W. J. Lawrence, "Purcell's Music for *The Tempest*," *Notes and Queries* 11 (1904): 164–65.

47. In *The English Opera* (1675), Matthew Locke published his music to *The Tempest*, but left out "the Tunes of the Entries and Dances in the *Tempest* (the Dancers being chang'd)" (preface).

48. *The London Spy* (1700), 3.

49. The stage direction indicates *"Another flourish of Voyces under the Stage"* (27). See Radice, "Sites for Music," 441–42.

50. Flying characters had been part of English theater in the earlier seventeenth century, but the possibilities for flight were more sensational with the machinery of Dorset Garden. See Andrew Gurr, *The Shakespearian Stage: 1574–1642* (Cambridge: Cambridge University Press, 1970), 125.

51. *The London Stage*, 1:216.

52. The authorship debate about this play has been recounted on several occasions. The text of the 1674 version is based on the Dryden-Davenant text. Shadwell contributed at least one song, and has been proposed as the author of the operatic version itself, in particular by prompter John Downes. "Arise ye subterranean winds" is ascribed to Shadwell in *Songs Set by Signior Pietro Reggio* (1680), pt. II, 12–13. See McManaway, "Songs and Masques," 138. The prologue and epilogue in Egerton MS 2623 are also attributed to Shadwell. For Shadwell's authorship, see Corman and Gilman, "The Musical Life of Thomas Shadwell," 151–53; Judith Milhous and Robert D. Hume, "Attribution Problems in English Drama, 1660–1700," *Harvard Library Bulletin* 31 (1983): 32–33; Michael W. Alssid, *Thomas Shadwell* (New York: Twayne, 1967); and Don R. Kunz, *The Drama of Thomas Shadwell* (Salzburg: Institut für englische Sprache und Literatur, 1972). Even though he describes Downes's work as "the old story of a senile memory with nothing to check its vagaries," Lawrence argues for Shadwell's authorship in "Did Thomas Shadwell Write an Opera on 'The Tempest'?," 193–206. Betterton managed several of the Dorset Garden "spectaculars," including *The Tempest*, which has been attributed to him. Charles E. Ward argues for Betterton's authorship in "*The Tempest*: A Restoration Opera Problem," *ELH* 13 (1946): 119–30. After comparing the 1670 and 1674 versions of *The Tempest*, Guffey comes to perhaps the most bizarre verdict: "of the forty-three substantial cuts made in the 1670 copy (passages of two to thirty-two lines in length), only two run over from the bottom of one page to the top of the next. It would appear then, that the physical nature of the book itself partly influenced the revisers, that they were, to a degree, unconsciously drawn to the middle of pages as they worked." *After the Tempest*, ix–x. It is hardly likely that such an enduringly successful play was created by excising random passages that occur in the middle of pages. Guffey's other conclusions seem the most persuasive in light of the long stage history of the play: "That Shadwell was responsible for all the changes made in 1674 is unlikely... the operatic *Tempest* probably was the creation of a number of hands" (*After* ix). William M. Milton expressed a similar view that it is pointless to search for a single "author" amid so many contributors. "*Tempest* in a Teapot," *ELH* 14 (1947): 207–18. For a summary of the authorship debate concerning the 1674 *Tempest*, see Novak, ed., Dryden, *Works*, 10:324–25; Spencer, *Five Restoration Adaptations*, 18–20; and Guffey, *After the Tempest*, xxi n20.

53. Wilson, *Roger North*, 350–51. See Margaret Mabbett, "Italian Musicians in Restoration England (1660–90)," *Music & Letters* 67 (1986): 237–47. Foreign entertainers have a long history of performing in England, which W.J. Lawrence discusses in "Early French Players in England," in *The Elizabethan Playhouse and Other Studies*, 126–56. Sybil Rosenfeld provides a detailed record of foreign troupes in *Foreign Theatrical Companies in Great Britain in the 17th and 18th Centuries* (London: The Society for Theatre Research, 1955). Davenant, *The Play-house to Be Let*, 68. Roger North noted, "during the first years of Charles II all music affected by the *beau-mond* run into the French way; and the rather, because at that time the master of the Court musick in France... had influenced the French style by infusing a great portion of the Italian harmony into it; whereby the Ayre was exceedingly improved." For Charles, English music "brought up the 'rere'" (Wilson, *Roger North*, 350, 300).

54. *The London Stage*, 1:266.

55. Prologue to *Arviragus* Reviv'd (1672); "Epilogue to the University of Oxford," 1673. In Dryden, *Works*, 1:145, 147–48.

56. For the number of French troupes, see Madam Horn-Monval, "French Troupes in England During the Restoration," *Theatre Notebook* 7 (1953): 81–82. Richard Luckett discusses the attraction of Italian and French offerings in "Exotick but Rational Entertainments: The English Dramatick Operas," 123–41. For French operas performed, see Gilman, "Augustan Criticism," 31n. Hume points out the rivalry between *The Tempest* and opera in "The Nature of the Dorset Garden Theatre," 104.

57. For example, on 17 December 1672 a troupe of French comedians obtained permission to import their property and they stayed until 19 August 1673. Judith Milhous and Robert D. Hume, eds., *The London Stage 1660–1800, Part 2: 1700–1729. A New Version*, 202, in the Harvard Theatre Collection, Harvard University. I have used this version wherever possible.

58. See Eleanore Boswell, *The Restoration Court Stage (1660–1702)* (Cambridge: Harvard University Press, 1932), 117–18; Nicoll, *History of English Drama*, 1:253 and Ifan Kyrle Fletcher, "Italian Comedians in England in the 17th Century," *Theatre Notebook* 8 (1954): 86–91.

59. 24 July 1675. *The Poems and Letters of Andrew Marvell*, ed. H. M. Margoliouth, 3rd ed. (Oxford: Clarendon, 1971), 2:342.

60. Evelyn, *Diary* 4:30 (5 January 1673/74). See Luckett, "Exotic but Rational Entertainments." French operas were performed frequently in the 1670s. Pierre Danchin, "The Foundation of the Royal Academy of Music in 1674 and Pierre Perrin's *Ariane*," *Theatre Survey* 25 (1984): 55–66.

61. According to the *Biographical Dictionary*, Betterton traveled to France in 1662, 1669, or 1671.

62. Fletcher, "Italian Comedians," 89–90.

63. "Prologue on the Opening of the New House" (1674), Dryden, *Works*, 1:149.

64. Colin Visser, "French Opera and the Making of the Dorset Garden Theatre," *Theatre Research International* 6 (1981): 163. Andrew R. Walkling also remarks that "the example of *Calisto* shows that French culture was the order of the day at court in the mid-1670s." "Masque and Politics at the Restoration Court: John Crowne's *Calisto*," *Early Music* 24 (1996): 52.

65. See Lawrence, "Early French Players in England," 147.

66. "A Short Discourse of the English Stage," in J. E. Spingarn, ed., *Critical Essays of the Seventeenth Century* (Bloomington: Indiana University Press, 1957), 2:95.

67. Corman and Gilman argue that "no dramatist or composer is more important in determining the course of English opera and musical theatre in the late seventeenth century" than Shadwell. Their article provides a discussion of the influence of *Psyche* as well. "The Musical Life of Thomas Shadwell," 149–64.

68. Preface to Settle's *Ibrahim* (1677).

69. See Leo Hughes, *The Drama's Patrons: A Study of the Eighteenth-Century London Audience*.

70. See Cibber, *Apology*, 1:235n.

71. Dent discusses the connections between English music and amateurs, especially in court masques. *Foundations of English Opera*, 78. Pepys records how his wife's maid Mary remembers parts from masques from her school days (26 April 1663). See Nicoll, *History of English Drama*, 1:357–58. Boswell in *The Restoration Court Stage* provides a lengthy discussion of *Calisto*; see 178–227.

72. Walkling, "Masque and Politics at the Restoration Court: John Crowne's *Calisto*," 28. Walkling provides an excellent in-depth summary of this production and its important impact on London society.

73. Boswell, *The Restoration Court Stage*, 216.

74. John Evelyn, *The Life of Mrs. Godolphin*, ed. Samuel Lord Bishop of Oxford

(New York: D. Appleton, 1847), 52. See Walkling, "Masque and Politics at the Restoration Court: John Crowne's *Calisto*" for discussion of *Calisto*'s popularity and importance.

75. Boswell, *The Restoration Court Stage*, 208.

76. Sybil Rosenfeld says that *Psyche* was as elaborate, and "for the first time rivalled those [spectacles] of the court masques." *A Short History of Scene Design in Great Britain* (Oxford: Basil Blackwell, 1973), 53.

77. For instance, Katharine Eisaman Maus opens her article on the "Restoration *Tempest*" as follows: "The most popular play on the Restoration stage was *The Tempest*, as revised by John Dryden and William D'Avenant in 1667" (189), and erratically notes that "the script of the operatic *Tempest* differs little from the Dryden-D'Avenant play" (192). If Shadwell was in fact the author of the 1674 version, his notoriously rocky relationship with Dryden makes this conflation of the two versions even more erroneous. The tendency of scholars like Maus to ignore the musical differences between these versions may be attributed to the way they have been published; Andrew Pinnock laments that (and this would hold true for *The Tempest* as well), "None of the Purcell dramatic operas has yet been published in a complete scholarly edition—with all the words (the 'play' part), all the music fitted in where it belongs, and a full critical apparatus." "Play into opera: Purcell's *The Indian Queen*," *Early Music* 18 (1990): 4.

78. Hume, "The Nature of the Dorset Garden Theatre," 103.

79. Dryden, *Works*, 10:324, 1:150. For discussion of other possible references of these final lines, especially to the newly revised *Macbeth*, see McManaway, "Songs and Masques," 140–41.

80. Helene Maxwell Hooker, "Dryden's and Shadwell's *Tempest*," *Huntington Library Quarterly* 6 (1943): 224–28.

81. Derek Hughes calls Duffett's burlesques "the bawdiest plays to appear on the Restoration stage." *English Drama 1660–1700*, 136.

82. Stanley Wells, "Shakespearian Burlesques," *Shakespeare Quarterly* 16 (1965): 49–62.

83. Charles Haywood, "*The Songs & Masque in the New Tempest*," 39–56. A quarto survives in the Huntington library.

84. *The London Stage*, 1:234.

85. See Hume, *The Development of English Drama*, 360–62 and Milhous, *Thomas Betterton* among others.

86. *The London Stage: A New Version*, 316.

87. John Harold Wilson, "More Theatre Notes from the Newdigate Newsletters," *Theatre Notebook* 16 (1961/62): 82.

88. *The London Stage*, 1:323. See W. J. Lawrence, "Early French Players in England," 149, and Nicoll, *History of English Drama*, 1:253n.

89. *The London Stage: A New Version*, 382.

90. See Hume, *The Development of English Drama*, 340–79; Hume, "Opera in London, 1695–1706"; and Maguire, *Regicide and Restoration*.

91. Zimmerman, "The Court Music of Henry Purcell," 311.

92. Wilson, *Roger North*, 307.

93. The Dryden-Robert Howard *The Indian Queen* (1664) was also revived in 1695, with added spectacle and music by Purcell, which Price describes as "the most brilliant operatic scene in a late seventeenth-century English play" ("Music as Drama," 220).

94. The title resonates with several similar titles from the period, including Robert Howard and Dryden's *The Indian Queen* (1664), *The Maiden Queen* (Dryden's *Secret Love*), *The Island Queens* (1684), and Lee's *The Rival Queens* (1677). Musical features abound: Titania falls asleep to a lullaby "You spotted snakes" in 2.2 and awakens to "The ousel

cock" and "The finch, the sparrow, and the lark" sung by Bottom in 3.1; the first scene of act four includes instrumental music and a dance between Oberon and Titania; in Act 5 the final words of Oberon may have included song and/or dance. See Harold F. Brooks's discussion of the play's musical elements in *A Midsummer Night's Dream* (London: Methuen, 1979), cxx–cxxv.

95. Moore explains that "what swept the audience away was downright bedazzlement, the splendour of the scenes and machines in conjunction with lavish costumes and large musical effects." *Henry Purcell and the Restoration Theatre*, 120–21. Roger Savage argues that Purcell attempted to replace elements of Shakespeare's text with updated components. "The Shakespeare-Purcell *Fairy Queen*: A Defence and Recommendation," *Early Music* 1 (1973): 201–21. Trevor R. Griffiths accepts Savage's argument, concluding that *The Fairy-Queen* attempted "to provide acceptable contemporary equivalents for aspects of Shakespeare's work which were considered to be obsolescent or unsuitable and did so by using the allegorical pageantry associated with opera to cope with the staging problems posed by the plays supernatural characters." *A Midsummer Night's Dream*, Shakespeare in Production (Cambridge: Cambridge University Press, 1996), 13. Most scholars have considered the semi-opera, if at all, only as a corrupted version of Shakespeare's play. Dent dismisses it as "a barbarously mutilated version" of Shakespeare's play (*Foundations of English Opera*, 216), Hume similarly labels it "a mangled version" (*The Development of English Drama*, 209) and Gunnar Sorelius refers to it as a "rigmarole" (*The Giant Race Before the Flood*, 165). Hazelton Spencer concludes that the scenic and musical "embellishments . . . do not call for serious criticism" because they do not pertain to Shakespeare (*Shakespeare Improved*, 323–24). In *Our Moonlight Revels: "A Midsummer Night's Dream" in the Theatre* (Iowa City: University of Iowa Press, 1997), Gary Jay Williams argues that *The Fairy-Queen* was intended as a tribute to Queen Mary and tries to connect the first performances of the semi-opera with significant events for William and Mary. Although Purcell's piece opened soon after their fifteenth wedding anniversary and William's birthday, no references in advertisements or prefatory material survive to link *The Fairy-Queen* to William and Mary.

96. See Griffiths, *A Midsummer Night's Dream*, 10–14. Shakespeare's play provided a source for the Commonwealth droll *Bottom the Weaver*, and Charles Johnson would later incorporate this in *Love in a Forest*, discussed in chapter 5. See G. Blakemore Evans, *Shakespearean Prompt-Books of the Seventeenth Century* (Charlottesville: Bibliographical Society of the University of Virginia, 1960), vol. 3, and Charles H. Shattuck, *The Shakespeare Promptbooks: A Descriptive Catalogue* (Urbana: University of Illinois Press, 1965) for early promptbooks.

97. These annotations appear on the copy of Raguenet's *Comparison between the French and Italian Musick* (1709) at Cambridge. Richard Luckett suggests the author may be William Corbett. "Exotick but rational entertainments," 140 and .n29.

98. Bruce Wood and Andrew Pinnock persuasively suggest that there is only one edition of *The Fairy Queen*, and that the 1693 version was a corrected copy. "*The Fairy Queen*: A Fresh Look at the Issues," *Early Music* 21 (1993): 45–62.

99. Price, *Henry Purcell*, 321–22. For further discussion of *The Fairy-Queen* authorship, see Milhous and Hume, "Attribution Problems," 15, and David Dyregrov, "Jo. Haines as Librettist for Purcell's The Fairy Queen," *Restoration and Eighteenth-Century Theatre Research* 7:2 (1992): 29–54. F. C. Brown argues for Settle's authorship in *Elkanah Settle: His Life and Works* (Chicago: University of Chicago Press, 1910), 96–97.

100. Lucyle Hook has detailed Motteux's importance in the late seventeenth- and early eighteenth-century world of music and theater in "Motteux and the Classical Masque," in *British Theatre and the Other Arts, 1660–1800*, 105–15.

101. Price argues that *The Fairy-Queen* actually was a "jolting detour on the road to

pure opera" because it "encouraged the separation rather than the integration of music and spoken dialogue." *Henry Purcell*, 357. For an extended analysis of the music in *The Fairy-Queen*, see Price, *Henry Purcell* 320–57; Martin Adams, *Henry Purcell: The Origins and Development of his Musical Style* (Cambridge: Cambridge University Press, 1995), 310–20; Luckett, "Exotic but Rational Entertainments." Savage offers a defense of *The Fairy-Queen* in production, calling it a "*summa* of English theatre arts in the 17th century" because it combines "the popular tradition of speech, rapid action, psychology and bare boards, and the courtly tradition of elaborate song and dance, allegory and spectacle." "The Shakespeare-Purcell *Fairy Queen*," 205. W. Moelwyn Merchant discusses the stage directions and scenery of *The Fairy-Queen* in "'A Midsummer Night's Dream': A Visual Re-creation," in John Russell Brown and Bernard Harris, eds., *Early Shakespeare. Stratford-upon-Avon Studies* 3 (London: Edward Arnold, 1961), 165–85.

102. See Gilman, "Augustan Criticism," 14. *The Siege of Rhodes* was not called an opera by Davenant. See Donald J. Grout, *A Short History of Opera*, 2d ed. (New York: Columbia University Press, 1965), 136. Others have traced elements of *The Fairy-Queen* to earlier dramatic traditions. Savage connects the masques in *The Fairy-Queen* with Jacobean masques, and reminds us that none of *The Fairy-Queen*'s "masquing devices were joltingly new in Purcell's time. Boorish figures of fun who blunder into fairy rings and are pinched black and blue for their pains also have a Shakespearean precedent in Falstaff of *The Merry Wives*." "The Shakespeare-Purcell *Fairy Queen*," 215–16.

103. Rob Jordan suggests that *The Fairy-Queen* may have had three additional performances: 14 February 1693, 25 February 1693, and early March 1693. "An Addendum to *The London Stage 1660–1700*," *Theatre Notebook* 47 (1993): 74. Wilson note a reference to Princess Anne attending *The Fairy-Queen* on 11 June 1692. "More Theatre Notes from the Newdigate Newsletters." See Eric Walter White, "Early Theatrical Performances of Purcell's Operas, With a Calendar of Recorded Performances, 1690–1710," *Theatre Notebook* 13 (1958): 51.

104. An additional copy of some of the music survives in a manuscript in the British Council Library. See Price, *Henry Purcell*, 331–36 for a discussion of all surviving copies of music and text.

105. *The London Stage: A New Version*, 43. This advertisement also appeared in *The London Courant* and *The London Gazette*. Price discusses this Purcell manuscript, which was found in 1900 in the library of the Royal Academy of Music. See *Henry Purcell*, 329–36.

106. Scant theater records show a performance of one act of the play at a concert on 1 February 1703, and of the Dance of the Four Seasons as an afterpiece to a play (6 June 1704).

107. Narcissus Luttrell records that *The Fairy-Queen* "exceeds former playes: the clothes, scenes, and musick cost 3000£." *A Brief [Historical?] Relation of State Affairs, September 1678 to April 1714* (Oxford: Oxford University Press, 1857), 2:435. W. J. Lawrence points out that Carolan masques cost between £5,000 and £20,000 and were rarely performed more than twice ("The Mounting of the Carolan Masques," 100). For further discussion of the music in *The Fairy-Queen*, see Neighbarger, *An Outward Show: Music for Shakespeare on the London Stage, 1660–1830*, 38–43.

108. The difficult relationship between Oberon and Hipployta and Theseus and Titania is omitted, perhaps to avoid showing an unflattering relationship between monarchs. See Williams, *Our Moonlight Revels*, 47, and Paul Dunkin, "Issues of the Fairy Queen," *Library* 26 (1946): 297–304. The 1693 version adds a scene of low comedy with music in the first act, where Titania orders any mortal to be tormented who enters her lair. One of three drunken poets is captured by the fairies and pinched as a punishment for his bad poetry. The drunken poet was probably a reference to either Settle or

Durfey, as both stuttered, and Durfey may have even played the role himself to earn money. Wood and Pinnock argue for Durfey in *"The Fairy Queen*: A Fresh Look at the Issues," 47–49. See also Price, *Henry Purcell*, 337. The pamphlet *Wit for Money: or, Poet Stutter* (1691) mocks Durfey's speech defect. To further highlight the comic aspects of the piece, the Pyramus and Thisbe material is moved from the final act to the third act, to serve as a comic centerpiece in the midst of the operatic material. This added scene derives from Suckling's play *The Goblins*, which also influenced *The Tempest*. Dent, *Foundations of English Opera*, 226. Wood and Pinnock identified the Suckling source in *"The Fairy Queen*: A Fresh Look at the Issues," 47. The song "The Plaint" was added as well in 1693, probably to suit a popular singer. I have reversed italics in lengthy stage directions from *The Fairy-Queen*.

109. Price describes this as "one of the greatest scenes in opera." *Henry Purcell*, 341. Williams argues that this setting resembles William and Mary's gardens at Hampton Court (*Our Moonlight Revels*, 48). See also B. Sprague Allen's chapter "The Prospect, the Flower-Garden, and the Stage-Garden in the Seventeenth Century" in *Tides in English Taste* (Cambridge: Harvard University Press, 1937), 1:124–33. The last scene in Settle's *The World in the Moon* (1697) resembles this garden setting, with "a Prospect of Terras Walks on Eight several Stages mounted one above another . . . On Thirty Two Pedestals are planted Sixteen Golden Flower-Pots, and Sixteen Statues of Gods and Goddesses . . . Through the center, and advancing Twenty Four Foot high, is an Ascent of Marble Steps."

110. Adams, *Henry Purcell* 76, 145; Price, *Henry Purcell*, 343.

111. Radice, "Sites for Music," 444.

112. An edition of the song between Mopsa and Coridon denotes that John Pate sang the part "in Woman's Habit" with the bass John Reading. See Zimmerman, *Henry Purcell*, 629. Reading continued his association with *A Midsummer Night's Dream*—he played Moonshine in Leveridge's *Pyramus and Thisbe* in 1716. Both Reading and Pate were involved in a Jacobite riot at the Dog Tavern, Drury Lane, in 1695. Presumably the two collaborated in more than song. See *Biographical Dictionary*, 11: 234–35.

113. See Wood and Pinnock, *"The Fairy Queen*: A Fresh Look at the Issues," 49–50.

114. Price describes this as "the most cerebral music of the score—or of any of the major stage works." *Henry Purcell*, 349.

115. This fountain may have been functional, as other fountains at the fairs involved similar hydraulic equipment. See McManaway, "The Renaissance Heritage of English Staging (1642–1700)," in Richard Hosley, Arthur C. Kirsch, and John W. Velz, eds., *Studies in Shakespeare, Bibliography, and Theater* (New York: Shakespeare Association of America, 1969), 237.

116. Adams, *Henry Purcell*, 75, 147–51, 311. Adams describes this masque as having "a far wider range of styles, textures and techniques than any earlier grouping of comparable size, be it in the odes or on the stage" (75).

117. See Price, *Henry Purcell*, 327. Dent discusses the influence of the seventeenth-century court masque on English opera in *Foundations of English Opera*, 18–41. The device of Juno's appearance was also used by Dryden in *Albion and Albanius* (1685).

118. Here in the 1693 version, Oberon requests the song "O let me weep," which was probably inserted to accommodate a popular singer (Dent, *Foundations of English Opera*, 226). Price concurs (*Henry Purcell*, 353–54). Williams notes (53–54) that the Chinese garden may have been painted by Robert Robinson, who was famous for his *chinoiserie* painting. B. Sprague Allen discusses the English fashion with oriental art in *Tides in English Taste*, 192–217.

119. This resembles the final act of the Purcell/Betterton *The Prophetess* and its symbolic orange trees associated with William and Mary. See Williams, *Our Midnight Revels*,

55–57. For further discussion of the symbolism of this scene, see Savage, "The Shakespeare-Purcell *Fairy Queen,*" 217 n.35 and Moore, *Henry Purcell and the Restoration Theatre,* 128–29; Zimmerman, *Henry Purcell,* 198–99.

120. Milhous provides a detailed account of events leading up to the actors' rebellion in *Thomas Betterton,* 52–55.

121. Fiske discusses the similarities between *The Fairy-Queen* and subsequent English operas in *English Theatre Music in the Eighteenth Century,* 8–25.

122. Samuel Johnson, "Hughes," in *Lives of the English Poets,* ed. George Birckbeck Hill (Oxford: Clarendon, 1905), 2:160.

123. The *Post Boy* for 7–9 February 1699 advertised "This Day is Publish'd, The Words of a New Interlude, called, the Four Seasons . . . and of all the Musical Entertainment in the new Opera, called the Island Princess, or the Generous Portuguese. Performed at the Theatre Royal."

124. See Sprague's detailed history of Beaumont and Fletcher's plays and their adaptations on the Restoration stage in *Beaumont and Fletcher on the Restoration Stage.* Sprague ignores many of the musical additions to the plays, in favor of detailing the plot changes, but at the expense of recounting some of the most popular added elements. For example, Sprague remarks about *The Pilgrim,* "Dryden furnished a prologue, an epilogue, and a Secular Masque, but these in no way concern us" (248) even though these elements are the items highlighted on the title page to *The Pilgrim.* See also Wilson, *The Influence of Beaumont and Fletcher on Restoration Drama.*

125. Rochester's attitude toward his source material is especially cavalier; in the prologue to *Valentinian,* he remarks:

> Fam'd and substantial Authors give this Treat,
> And 'twill be solemn, Noble all and Great.
> Wit, sacred Wit, is all the bus'ness here,
> Great *Fletcher,* and the Greater *Rochester.*
> Now name the hardy Man one fault dares find,
> In the vast Work of two such Heroes joyn'd.

126. In later performances, *The Pilgrim* provided opportunities for comic gagging, as did many of Shakespeare's comedies (*Sauny the Scott* and *The Cobler of Preston,* for instance). *The Pilgrim* also had additional farcical aspects added, a technique often practiced by these Shakespeare adapters. In his "Essay on the Art, Rise, and Progress of the Stage," Gildon states, "*Beaumont* and *Fletcher* have perform'd abominably in his Mad-House in the *Pilgrim,* and our Modern Alterer of that Play has increas'd his Absurdities." *The Works of Mr. William Shakespear,* (1710), 7: xxxiv. The title page to *The Pilgrim* describes it as "Written Originally by Mr. Fletcher, and now very much Alter'd, with several Additions. Likewise A Prologue, Epilogue, Dialogue and Masque, written by the late Great Poet Mr. Dryden, just before his Death, being the last of his Works" (1700).

127. See Sprague, *Beaumont and Fletcher on the Restoration Stage,* 86.

128. *The London Stage,* 1:531.

129. *The London Stage: A New Version,* 154.

130. See Hume, "Opera in London, 1695–1706," 72. Moira Goff points out that Betterton employed dancers from the Paris Opéra in the late 1690s. "'Actions, Manners, and Passions': entr'acte dancing on the London stage, 1700–1737," *Early Music* 26 (1998): 215. See also Milhous, *Thomas Betterton,* 134–35. Rich's advertisement for *The World in the Moon* in the *Post-Boy* of 12–15 June 1697 highlights the extravagance of Dorset Garden that continued in the 1690s: "the Scenes being several new Sets and of a model different from all that have been used in any Theatre whatever, being twice as

high as any of their former Scenes. And the whole Decoration of the Stage not only infinitely beyond all the Opera's ever yet performed in England, but also by the acknowledgement of several Gentlemen that have travell'd abroad, much exceeding all that has been seen on any of the Foreign Stages."

131. See Hume, "Sponsorship of Opera," 422.

132. *Historia Histrionica*, ed. R. W. Lowe, in *An Apology for the Life of Colley Cibber* (London, 1889).

CHAPTER 3. "STUDY [THE] AUDIENCE AS WELL AS THE RULES"

1. Robert D. Hume makes this point at length in "Jeremy Collier and the Future of the London Theater in 1698," *Studies in Philology* 96 (1999): 480–511. Milhous, *Thomas Betterton*, 113. Prologue to Vanbrugh's *The False Friend* (1702); Charles Hopkins, epilogue to *Boadicea* (1697). Vanbrugh attests that because theaters are in "a feeble State," they "cannot well afford to Love or Hate, / So shou'd not meddle much in your Debate" (prologue to *The False Friend*). See Joseph Wood Krutch for a summary of objections to drama and theater in the late seventeenth century. *Comedy and Conscience after the Restoration* (1924; 2nd ed. New York: Columbia University Press, 1949) and Aubrey Williams's article "No Cloistered Virtue: Or, Playwright versus Priest in 1698," *PMLA* 90 (1975): 234–46.

2. Louis D. Mitchell, "Command Performances During the Reign of George I," 343–49, especially his table on p. 348. Mitchell also discusses Anne's lack of patronage in "Command Performances During the Reign of Queen Anne."

3. The theaters had been closed from 8 March through 23 April in 1702 for the death of King William, and reopened on 25 April with Queen Anne's coronation concert. Unless otherwise noted, the performance information in this chapter is taken from the Draft of the Calendar for Volume 1, 1700–1711 of *The London Stage 1660–1800, Part 2:1700–1729. A New Version*, ed. Judith Milhous and Robert D. Hume, in the Harvard Theatre Collection, Harvard University.

4. *Some Thoughts Concerning the Stage in a Letter to a Lady* (London, 1704), 8. Reprinted in *Essays on the Stage*, No. 2, ed. Emmett L. Avery (Los Angeles: Augustan Reprint Society, 1947).

5. The history of theater from the mid-1690s through the early eighteenth century has been recounted elsewhere in depth. See Judith Milhous and Robert D. Hume, *Vice Chamberlain Coke's Theatrical Papers 1706–1715* (Carbondale and Edwardsville: Southern Illinois University Press, 1982); Milhous, *Thomas Betterton*; Hume, "The Sponsorship of Opera in London, 1704–1720," *Modern Philology* 85 (1988): 420–32, *Development of English Drama*, and "Opera in London, 1695–1706."

6. See Lorenzo Bianconi and Thomas Walker, "Production, Consumption and Political Function of Seventeenth-Century Opera," in *Studies in Medieval and Early Modern Music*, ed. Iain Fenlon, *Early Music History* 4 (Cambridge, 1984), 209–96.

7. Hume, "The Sponsorship of Opera," 420.

8. "'Restoration Comedy' and its Audiences, 1660–1776," *The Yearbook of English Studies* 10 (1980), 57. See also Milhous, *Thomas Betterton*, 164, and Leo Hughes, *The Drama's Patrons: A Study of the Eighteenth-Century London Audience*.

9. Prologue to Thomas Baker's *The Humour of the Age* (1701).

10. Prologue to Farquhar's *The Inconstant* (1702); Prologue to Catharine Trotter's *Love at a Loss* (1701). See "A Discourse Upon Comedy, In Reference to the English Stage," in *Love and Business* (London, 1702), in *The Works of George Farquhar*, ed. Shirley Strum Kenny (Oxford: Clarendon, 1988).

11. Paulina Kewes demonstrates the predominance of post-Restoration works in the theatrical repertoire of the early eighteenth century; eighteenth-century dramatists surpassed Shakespeare in popularity. See the chapter entitled "The Canon" in *Authorship and Appropriation: Writing for the Stage in England 1660–1710* (Oxford: Clarendon, 1998), 180–224.

12. Dedication to *The Humour of the Age* (1701).

13. Durfey's epilogue to Gould's *The Rival Sisters*. The prologue to Doggett's *The Country-Wake* (1696) refers to "wretched Scriblers." Motteux, in his prologue to Ravenscroft's *The Anatomist* (1697), complains that a "dull Scribbler (to our Cost we knew it) / Writes a damn'd Play, and is misnam'd a Poet." His epilogue to the same play asserts that fear of criticism kills "our trembling Scribblers." Similarly, Thomas Scott denounced the "Scribling Wretch" who the audience should use "roughly, nip him in the Bud, / He'll grow too sturdy if he's not withstood" (epilogue to *The Mock-Marriage* [1696]).

14. *The English Theophrastus: or The Manners of the Age* (London, 1702), 4. See also Claudia Thomas's discussion of "scriblers" in "Pope and his *Dunciad* Adversaries: Skirmishes on the Borders of Gentility," in *Cutting Edges: Postmodern Critical Essays on Eighteenth-Century Satire*, ed. James E. Gill (Knoxville: University of Tennessee Press, 1995), 275–300.

15. Motteux from his epilogue to Ravenscroft's *The Anatomist* (1697). All critical works of John Dennis are cited by volume and page number from Edward Niles Hooker, ed., *The Critical Works of John Dennis*, 2 vols. (Baltimore: Johns Hopkins University Press, 1939–43). Reference quoted here is from Dennis, *Works*, 2:lxiii.

16. Preface to *A Comparison Between the Two Stages*. Staring B. Wells persuasively argues that Gildon is not the author in "An Eighteenth-Century Attribution," *JEGP* 38 (1939): 233–46. "Do you not wonder, Sirs, in these poor Days, / Poets should hope for Profit from their Plays?" asks the prologue to Charles Hopkins's *Boadicea* (1697). They "Dream of a full Third Day, nay good sixth Night," but may not receive it "Especially considering how they Write."

17. Dennis, *Works*, 2:279.

18. Milhous, *Thomas Betterton*, 77. See Milhous's cogent discussion of the changing audience in *Thomas Betterton*, 75–79. Hume points out that theater "in Williamite London" was "a disreputable entertainment for a shrinking elite that had lost its court patronage. Few people attended the theater and few bought published plays." "Jeremy Collier and the Future of the London Theater in 1698," 508.

19. Shirley Strum Kenny's "Theatrical Warfare, 1695–1710," *Theatre Notebook* 27 (1973): 130–45, provides the background for this section. Milhous notes a period of truce between 1702 and 1705, when both theaters sought to attract different audiences. *Thomas Betterton*, 164–65.

20. *The London Stage*, 1:518, 520.

21. *A Comparison Between the Two Stages*, 7. The young age of the Drury Lane company eventually worked to their advantage. As Cibber writes, "*Betterton's* People (however good in their Kind) were most of them too far advanc'd in Years to mend; and tho' we in *Drury-Lane* were too young to be excellent, we were not too old to be better" (*Apology*, 1:302).

22. See also the anonymous *She Ventures and He Wins* (1696) and *Bonduca* (1696), Thomas Southerne's *Oroonoko* (1696), and Motteux's *The Loves of Mars and Venus* (1696) for more references to warfare. Even with this competition for audiences, evidence survives of mixed cast performances, including one of *The Merry Wives of Windsor* in 1704.

23. Farquhar describes the "present Politicks o' th' Stage' as a 'Battle held with bloody Strife'" in "A *Prologue* on the propos'd Union of the two Houses," in Pierre

Danchin, *The Prologues and Epilogues of the Restoration 1660–1700*. 7 vols. (Nancy: Publications de l'Université de Nancy, 1981–88), 1:43–44.

24. Richard Estcourt, epilogue to Motteux's *Camilla* (1709).

25. Edmund Curll, *The Life of That Eminent Comedian Robert Wilks, Esq.* (London, 1733),

26. Curll, *The Life of That Eminent Comedian Robert Wilks*, 8; *Apology*, 1:288; Cibber, preface "To the Reader," *Ximena* (1719); Prologue to Steele's *The Funeral* (1702); Motteux, epilogue to *The Temple of Love* (1706).

27. Farquhar comments that "Vast sums of Treasure too we did advance / To draw some mercenary Troops from *France*" to please audiences. "A *Prologue* on the propos'd Union of the two Houses," in Danchin, *The Prologues and Epilogues of the Restoration 1660–1700*, 1:43–44.

28. See *Court and Society from Elizabeth to Anne. Edited from the Papers at Kimbolton*, ed. W. D. Montagu, Seventh Duke of Manchester (London: Hurst and Blackett, 1864), 2:55. Price describes the theatrical conditions around the turn of the eighteenth century: "playwrights and managers exploited native as well as foreign singers and dancers in the great battle for audiences, a bitter competition that nearly caused the collapse of the English theatre" ("Music as Drama," 211).

29. Addison wrote the prologue to Smith's play, and also tried to profit from opera this same year with *Rosamond*, which was a failure. In addition to competition from foreign entertainers, new developments in theater facilities were geared toward opera, not drama—the Haymarket Theatre built in 1705 was designed solely for operas.

30. In *Memoirs of Bartholomew Fair* (London: Chapman and Hall, 1859) Henry Morley refers to "JAMES MILES from *Sadler*'s Wells at *Islington*, who performed at his establishment" such entertainments as "a Young Woman who dances with the Swords and upon the ladder, with that Variety, that she challenges all her Sex to do the like" (350).

31. Epilogue to Thomas Baker's *The Humour of the Age* (1701).

32. "To Mr. Granville, on his Excellent Tragedy, call'd *Heroick Love*," prefixed to Granville's *Heroick Love* (1698). Farquhar writes, "about two years ago, I had a Gentleman from France that brought the play-house some fifty audiences in five months" (preface to *The Inconstant*, 1702).

33. *The London Stage*, 2:43; 62–63; 22.

34. *The London Stage*, 2:1:64.

35. See Sybil Rosenfeld, *The Theatre of the London Fairs in the Eighteenth Century* (Cambridge: Cambridge University Press, 1960), Richard Altick, *The Shows of London* (Cambridge, Mass.: Belknap Press, 1978), and Ricky James, *Learned Pigs and Fireproof Women* (New York: Villard Books, 1986).

36. See Leo Hughes, *A Century of English Farce* (Princeton: Princeton University Press, 1956), 216.

37. *A Comparison Between the Two Stages*, 7; *Aesop at the Bear-Garden: A Vision By Mr. Preston* (London, 1715), 33. Wells notes that the "Bear Garden" may refer either to the location on the Bankside or to Hockley-in-the-Hole (*A Comparison Between the Two Stages*, 120).

38. In contrast, G. E. Bentley points out that Jonson's comedies *Volpone*, *The Alchemist*, *The Silent Woman*, and *Bartholomew Fair* were frequently performed. *Shakespeare and Jonson: Their Reputations in the Seventeenth Century Compared* (Chicago: University of Chicago Press, 1945), 1:117–18.

39. See also Charles Beecher Hogan, *Shakespeare in the Theatre 1701–1800*, 2 vols. (Oxford: Clarendon, 1952) for specific performance data.

40. Louise Jaquelyn Weeks examines these four adaptations "in depth with regards

to the adapters' own critical beliefs as shown in their criticism and as manifested in their other plays" (4), but disregards the theatrical and performance context for these adaptations. "Shakespeare as adapted: *Measure for Measure, or, Beauty, the Best Advocate, Love Betray'd, The Jew of Venice,* and *The Comical Gallant*" (Ph.D. diss., University of Mississippi, 1988).

41. George C. Branam discusses adaptations of the tragedies in *Eighteenth-Century Adaptations of Shakespearean Tragedy*.

42. Cesario and Portia are not new parts (the breeches elements are not developed beyond Shakespeare's originals, except in their use of actresses), but Captain Dingboy (a breeches role for Mrs. Page) in *The Comical Gallant* is Dennis's original version of this popular device. Marsden points out the prevalence of breeches parts in the Restoration and eighteenth century. *The Re-Imagined Text*, 30. For further discussion of the effect of actresses, see Katharine Eisaman Maus, "'Playhouse Flesh and Blood': Sexual Ideology and the Restoration Actress," *ELH* 46 (1979): 595–617.

43. Sir Robert Howard, "To the Reader," *The Great Favourite, or The Duke of Lerma* (1668); Samuel Cobb, "A Prefatory Discourse" to "A Discourse on Criticism and the Liberty of Writing," in *Poems on Several Occasions* (1707); Elkanah Settle, *A Farther Defence of Dramatick Poetry* (1698), 33. See also Farquhar's discussion in "A Discourse Upon Comedy." Farquhar mockingly describes England as "an ignorant, self-will'd, impertinent Island, where let a Critick and a Scholar find never so many irregularities in a Play, yet five hundred saucy People will give him the Lie to his Face, and come to see this wicked play Forty or Fifty times in a Year" (383). Cibber's epilogue to *The Non-Juror* (1718) denounces writing that adheres to "Time, Place, Action, Rules by which Old Wits / Made Plays, as – – –Dames do Puddings, by Receipts." The prologue to Thomas Killigrew's *Chit-Chat* (1719) taunts, "Where is the Order, Method, the Design, / And all that makes a well-wrogt *Drama* shine," answered thus: "Why, if [the author's] Conduct merits not Applause, / Consider, Sirs, they are your Lives he draws." The epilogue repeats the point that the scenes are "Loose and irregular" because "it is your Lives he drew." See the response in *Critical Remarks on the Four Taking Plays of This Season . . . by Corinna* (1719), 53.

44. Thomas Baker, prologue to *The Humour of the Age* (1701); Susannah Centlivre, preface to *Love's Contrivance* (1703); Thomas Scott, preface to *The Mock Marriage* (1696); Farquhar, "A Discourse Upon Comedy" (1701), 367–69. Hooker notes that "enthusiasm for the rules was a comparatively recent thing in England" in the late seventeenth century, and confines their height of popularity to 1674–1692 (Dennis, *Works*, 2:lxxx). Not everyone agreed that rules should be a secondary concern. Catharine Trotter contended that "If the Drammatick rules were justly observ'd, the Stage would soon retrieve that Credit which the abuses of it has I fear with too great reason lost, and be again a useful Entertainment." For the growth of critical writings on drama, see Krutch, *Comedy and Conscience After the Restoration*, 48–71; Paul Trolander and Zeynep Tenger, "Criticism Against Itself: Subverting Critical Authority in Late-Seventeenth Century England," *Philological Quarterly* 75 (1996): 311–38.

45. Farquhar, "A Discourse Upon Comedy," 380; Gildon, preface to *Love's Victim* (1701). "'Tho I did not observe the Rules of *Drama*," remarks Susannah Centlivre in her preface to *Love's Contrivance* (1703), "I took particular Care to dress my Thoughts in such a modest Stile, that it might not give Offence to any." See also Oldmixon, *Reflections on the Stage* (1699), 169.

46. *The Making of the National Poet*. The one exception is *The Tempest*, which remained popular and influenced other plays, but this had little to do with its Shakespearian origin.

47. The date of the premiere is unknown, but the play was printed in 1700 and the prologue refers to "this Winter"—the editors of *The London Stage* suggest February of 1700 for the first performance.

48. Dedication to Cibber's *Love Makes a Man*. As Hume has shown, Collier's threat was to the status of theater. See "Jeremy Collier and the Future of the London Theatre in 1698." Calhoun Winton has detailed the circumstances of theater reformers in "The London Stage Embattled: 1695–1710," *Tennessee Studies in Literature* 19 (1974): 9–19. The operatic *Tempest* was the victim of one such attack. When the play was revived during a storm in 1703, Arthur Bedford, rector of St. Nicolas, Bristol preached: "*God was pleased to shew us, the 26th of November following, that he would not be mock'd*, by visiting us with . . . a storm of Wind," *Serious Reflections on the Scandalous Abuse and Effects of the Stage: In a Sermon Preach'd at the Parish-Church of St. Nicolas in the City of Bristol, on Sunday the 7th Day of January, 1704/05* (Bristol: W. Bonny, 1705), 18. See also *A Representation of the Impiety and Immorality of the English Stage* (London, 1704), in Augustan Reprint Society Series Three: Essays on the Stage, No. 2, ed. Emmett L. Avery (Los Angeles: Augustan Reprint Society, 1947), which admonished theaters who "within a few Days after we felt the late dreadful Storm, entertain their Audience with the ridiculous Representation of what had fill'd us with so great Horror in their Plays call'd *Macbeth* and the *Tempest*, as if they design'd to Mock the Almighty Power of God, *who alone commands the Winds and the Seas, and they obey him*" (5).

49. The reference to "needy Gildon" occurs in the lines prefixed to the anonymous *Animadversions on Mr. Congreve's Late Answer to Mr. Collier* (1698). For further discussion of Gildon's critical criteria, see Paulina Kewes, *Authorship and Appropriation*, 218–21. Edward A. Cairns argues that "Gildon was not merely scribbling for the crowd, nor was his purpose simply to outdo Davenant. He was, in 1700, deeply in the midst of a struggle toward a coherent critical position from which he could write." *Charles Gildon's Measure for Measure, or Beauty the Best Advocate: A Critical Edition* (New York: Garland, 1987), 9. Within the context of the struggling theaters, 1700 seems hardly the time to work out critical precepts on the stage. The stakes were high, and neither company could afford to allow playwrights to gratify their personal critical aims at the expense of the company's welfare. Gildon noted that "The Managers of our Stage have been all along afraid of reforming the Stage lest they shou'd run any Hazzard of a Bad Audience" ("Essay on the Art, Rise, and Progress of the Stage").

50. Gildon addressed his "Essay at a Vindication of Love in Tragedies" to Dennis. For further references to the relationship between Dennis and Gildon, see Gildon's *Miscellaneous Letters and Essays* (1694), 64; *Lives and Characters of the English Dramatick Poets* (1698), 38; Rowe, *The Works of Mr. William Shakespear* (1710), 7:xliv; *The Complete Art of Poetry* (1718), 1:191; *The Post-Man Robb'd of His Mail* (1719), 112–13; *The Laws of Poetry* (1721), 61 and 121. Also *The Complete Art of Poetry* (1718), 1:iii, for the idea that Dennis and Gildon met daily.

51. Letter dated 11 August 1721. See *Works*, 2:374.

52. *The Laws of Poetry* (London, 1721), 39. See also *The Post-Man Robb'd of his Mail*, 109–13; 212–19, 265.

53. Prologue to Charles Boyle's *As You Find It* (1703).

54. Charles Gildon, "To My Honoured and Ingenious Friend Mr. Harrington, for the Modern Poets Against the Ancients," in his *Miscellaneous Letters on Several Subjects* (1694), 209–24; preface to *Love's Victim* (London, 1701).

55. "An Essay on the Art, Rise, and Progress of the Stage in Greece, Rome, and England," in Nicholas Rowe, ed., *The Works of Mr. William Shakespear* (London: 1709–10), 7:iii. See this essay for further comments on Shakespeare.

56. See Marsden, *The Re-Imagined Text*. Other writers such as John Dennis and Aaron Hill agreed that rules were important.

57. Gildon used a similar phrase to describe his revision of Langbaine's *An Account of the English Dramatick Poets*. In *The Lives and Characters of the English Dramatick Poets*, Gildon "endeavour'd to avoid [Langbaine's] Faults, and preserve his Beauties." In his *Miscellaneous Letters and Essays* (1694), Gildon states that he withheld his vindication of Shakespeare because he was waiting for Dennis's efforts, but now writes "since I find some build an Assurance on this *General Silence* of all the Friends of *Shakespeare*." Gildon defends Shakespeare for not following the rules (64, 92). Similarly, Catharine Trotter praised Shakespeare even though he did not observe the rules: "The inimitable *Shakespear* seems alone secure on every side from an attack, (for I speak not here of Faults against the Rules of Poetry, but against the natural Genius) he had all the Images of nature present to him, Study'd her thoroughly, and boldly copy'd all her various Features, for tho' he has chiefly exerted himself on the more Masculine Passions, 'tis as the choice of his Judgment not the restraint of his Genius, and he seems to have design'd those few tender moving Scenes he has giv'n us, a proof he cou'd be every way equally Admirable" (dedication to *The Unhappy Penitent* [1701]).

58. Duke of Buckingham, "An Essay Upon Poetry" (1682). Later in his career, Gildon dealt with contemporary issues in criticism in *The Complete Art of Poetry* (1718). Cairns provides a survey of Gildon's critical precepts in the introduction to *Measure for Measure*.

59. Langbaine, *Account*, 175. See also *A Letter to A.H. Esq. Concerning the Stage* (1698), 19, regarding Gildon's writing for money.

60. Preface to *Love's Contrivance* (1703). The *Muses Mercury* of May 1707 praised Farquhar's comedies for being "rather above the Rules than below them" and for having "a certain Air of *Novelty* and *Mirth*, which pleas'd the Audience every time they were represented." As Kenny notes, Farquhar "scorned the Rules by which other playwrights wrote, and yet audiences, crude and uncultivated as they were, scrambled to the theatre to make his 'farce' the most popular new play ever." "Theatrical Warfare," 138.

61. *The London Stage*, 2:1:124.

62. In *Henry Purcell and the London Stage*, Price speculates that Betterton had somehow obtained the rights to *Dido and Aeneas*, since it was the only Purcell work that Drury Lane did not revive in the decade after Purcell's death. Price explains that after Purcell's death, the rights to his works remained with Drury Lane, and Betterton was able to secure the rights to only *Dido and Aeneas* for Lincoln's Inn Fields (*Henry Purcell*, 234). Many have questioned why Gildon chose Shakespeare's play as the vehicle for Purcell's work. Price argues that the extravaganza *A New Opera; called, Brutus of Alba: or, Augusta's Triumph* (1696) was the inspiration for Gildon's play because of the similarities in the two works: "in both an absent ruler appoints a deputy whom he suspects of hypocrisy and corruption in order to expose him. Asaracus in *A New Opera* and Angelo in *Measure for Measure* preach sexual morality while trying to ravish honourable women. Angelo threatens to execute Isabella's brother unless she satisfies his lust; Asaracus compromises Amarante by making her appear unvirtuous. And in both works, masques are offered as parables to reform the villains" (*Henry Purcell*, 235). In *Henry Purcell's Dido and Aeneas* (Oxford: Clarendon, 1987), Ellen T. Harris points out that *Dido and Aeneas* would have been one of the easier operas to condense and adapt to a different venue because it "is conceived on a small scale for what must have been a small, private audience. It is short and demands less in the way of vocal technique than the later works, and its orchestra consists only of strings, whereas the dramatic operas include beautiful and effective writing for woodwinds and trumpet" (7). Harris adds that it also "lacks scenic displays and stage machinery" (9).

63. Gildon, *The Lives and Characters of the English Dramatick Poets* (1699), 115.

64. Harris, *Henry Purcell's Dido and Aeneas*, 3. Harris discusses the connections to seventeenth-century masques on pages 7–9 and 69–70.

65. This was not an isolated occurrence; Duffett and Banister's *Beauties Triumph* was acted at a "New Boarding-School for Young Ladies and Gentlewomen" in the location of Priest's school in 1676. In all probability these performances were more common than surviving records indicate, and may have been revivals of pieces written earlier. See Price, *Henry Purcell*, 225–26. It is also possible that Richard Leveridge, the popular bass and author of *Pyramus and Thisbe* (discussed in chapter 4) may have revamped *Dido and Aeneas* in 1708. See Milhous and Hume, *Vice Chamberlain Coke's Theatrical Papers*, 82. Much controversy surrounds the contested first performance date and venue of *Dido and Aeneas*. See Harris, *Henry Purcell's Dido and Aeneas*, 4–10, for a summary of this debate; Harris places the first performance in April of 1689. Richard Luckett discusses the relationship between *Dido and Aeneas* and John Blow's *Venus and Adonis*, also performed at Josias Priest's boarding school in Chelsea, in "A New Source for *Venus and Adonis*," *The Musical Times* 80 (1989): 76–79. Price enumerates the musical similarities between these two pieces in *Henry Purcell*, 245–47. For additional discussion of both the date of composition and the first performance, see Bruce Wood and Andrew Pinnock, "'Unscarr'd by turning times'?: the Dating of Purcell's *Dido and Aeneas*," *Early Music* 20 (1992): 372–90. Price replies to Wood and Pinnock in "*Dido and Aeneas*: Questions of Style and Evidence," *Early Music* 22 (1994): 115–25.

66. Jennifer Thorp raises the possibility that Josias Priest (the dancing-master) and Joseph Priest (the choreographer) were not the same person, as both names appear in the historical records of the seventeenth century. See "Dance in late 17th-century London: Priestly muddles," *Early Music* 26 (1998): 198–210.

67. See Eric Walter White, "New Light on *Dido and Aeneas*," *Henry Purcell 1659–1695: Essays on His Music*, ed. Imogen Holst (London: Oxford University Press, 1959), 18; Price, *Henry Purcell*, 242, and Harris, *Henry Purcell's Dido and Aeneas*, 48. *Dido and Aeneas* was revived with Ravenscroft's *The Anatomist* and the *Masque of Mars and Venus* 29 January 1704 at Lincoln's Inn Fields and on 8 April 1704 with *The Man of Mode*. See *The London Stage: A New Version*, 140, 158.

68. Price discusses Tate's use of Virgil in *Henry Purcell*, 226–29. Harris considers the similarities between *Dido* and other seventeenth-century plays in *Henry Purcell's Dido and Aeneas*, 24–33, and the relationship between *Dido* and traditional English styles on 96–101.

69. Charles II saw some opera at court, but the only all-sung English opera in the public theaters was *Albion and Albanius* (1685).

70. See Price, "Music as Drama," 224. For a proposed cast of *Dido and Aeneas*, see White, "New Light on *Dido and Aeneas*," 33–34. Gildon reduces the original number of dances, but Harris suggests that many dances may remain hidden within the music. *Henry Purcell's Dido and Aeneas*, 64–68.

71. Dennis similarly denigrates the taste of the audience in his "Large Account of the Taste in Poetry and the Causes of the Degeneracy of it" prefixed to *The Comical Gallant*: "the *English* were never sunk so miserably low in their taste, as they are at present." He criticizes those who favor "Tumbling and Vaulting and Ladder Dancing, and the delightful diversions of *Jack Pudding*." See Leo Hughes, *The Drama's Patrons* for a lengthy discussion of audience taste and behavior.

72. Hume suggests that Oldmixon's opera *The Grove* provided competition for *Measure for Measure* in early 1700, but this seems unlikely since Oldmixon wrote the prologue to Gildon's play ("Opera in London," 74–75).

73. *Dictionary of National Biography* 7:1226. Claudia Thomas provides an excellent discussion of the difficult politics involved in labeling writers "hacks" or "scriblers." "Pope and His *Dunciad* Adversaries: Skirmishes on the Borders of Gentility."

74. Shortly after *Measure for Measure* was performed, Verbruggen accused Betterton, Barry, and Bracegirdle of skimming profits from Lincoln's Inn Fields. See Milhous, *Thomas Betterton*, 161–64.

75. See Noyes, *Ben Jonson on the English Stage, 1660–1776*.

76. Genest, *Some Account* 2:221. In particular, Gildon enlarges the scene between Claudio and Isabella in Act 3, using some of Davenant's material, and adds another scene between these two characters at the beginning of Act 4, which is also based on Davenant. In his edition of Gildon's adaptation, Cairns provides an outline of Gildon's changes to Shakespeare (43–58).

77. Claudio and Julietta are secretly married, which invalidates their crime from Shakespeare's play. Genest describes Gildon's fifth act as "sadly mutilated" (2:222), and Isabella's character is not as venerated as in Gildon's source play. Isabella tells the Duke that Angelo promised to marry her, but Angelo does not confirm this. Angelo has already married Marianna, and Isabella's complaint seems pointless.

78. As Price points out, "instead of being morally instructed or even moved by the tragedy, [Angelo] sees *himself* as Aeneas, an anti-heroic perversion of Virgil's protagonist" (*Henry Purcell*, 237). Harris makes a similar point in *Henry Purcell's Dido and Aeneas*, 33.

79. *Serious Reflections on the Scandalous Abuse and Effects of the Stage: In a Sermon Preach'd at the Parish-Church of St. Nicolas in the City of Bristol, on Sunday the 7th Day of January, 1704/5* (Bristol: W. Bonny, 1705), 28. For additional discussion of the effect of moral reformers on the early eighteenth-century theater, see Winton, "The London Stage Embattled."

80. See White, "New Light on *Dido and Aeneas*," 23–24. The cave scene ends with the direction, "At the end of the Dance Six *Furies* sink. The four open the Cave fly up." This would involve a trap door and flying, not included in the 1689 libretto due to the limited range of stage possibilities at Priest's school.

81. Spencer, *Five Restoration Adaptations of Shakespeare*, 14–16, and Price, *Henry Purcell*, 231–32.

82. Price, *Henry Purcell*, 238; Harris, *Henry Purcell's Dido and Aeneas*, 17.

83. See Harris, *Henry Purcell's Dido and Aeneas*, 58–59.

84. Price points out a further relationship between *Measure for Measure* and *Dido and Aeneas*: "[Escalus] has arranged a performance of the little opera as an apologue to show Angelo the possible consequences of enforcing too zealously a law against nature. Aeneas is thus meant to represent Claudio, and Dido the violated Julietta. The allegory implies an interpretation of the central ambiguity of *Dido and Aeneas* in direct opposition to almost all modern criticism: in the new context, the lovers have committed a sin punished by the havoc wrought when the Sorceress tricks Aeneas into abandoning the queen. Angelo acknowledges the design, but instead of being morally instructed or even moved by the tragedy, he sees *himself* as Aeneas, an anti-heroic perversion of Virgil's protagonist" (*Henry Purcell* 236–37).

85. This may be because its major musical aspects were not particularly flattering to a monarchy. Price explains the potential unflattering parallels in the *Dido and Aeneas* story: "Aeneas, legendary great-grandfather of Brutus the founder of Albion, leaves his beloved queen and sails across the sea to liberate a foreign land and establish a new kingdom. A cynic might therefore have seen in the Trojan prince William of Orange, the dour and reluctant hero, preparing to leave Holland for his destiny in England. But then Dido would symbolize Mary, a linkage that Tate surely wanted to avoid, cautionary tale or no." Price argues that in order to "disengage Queen Mary from a symbolic link with Queen Dido," Tate had to make "major changes of plot, motivation, and characterization" (*Henry Purcell* 229–30).

86. *The Life of that Eminent Comedian Robert Wilks, Esq* (London, 1733), 43. Politics may have also had a hand in the play's preliminary success; Richard Braverman has argued that *The Jew of Venice* "expressed support for a Jacobite succession at a critical juncture, the interim between the death of Princess Anne's son and William's heir, the Duke of Gloucester (July, 1700), and the passage of the Act of Settlement (May 1701)." "Politics in Jewish Disguise: Jacobitism and Dissent on the Post-Revolutionary Stage," *Studies in Philology* 90 (1993): 347–70. This may have been part of the initial resonance of the play, but its enduring reputation on the stage in the first four decades of the eighteenth century points to factors other than immediate political concerns of 1701.

87. Dudley Ryder, *The Diary of Dudley Ryder 1715–1716*, ed. William Matthews (London: Methuen, 1939), 114. For printings of *The Jew of Venice*, see Spencer, *Five Restoration Adaptations of Shakespeare*, 464–68.

88. Based on his index to *The London Stage*, Ben Ross Schneider, Jr., argues that "*The Merchant of Venice* was the most popular Shakespearean comedy of the 18th century (if we exclude *The Merry Wives* as a farce)" (116), but the play did not become popular until the 1740s when Macklin revived the original version. The history of *The Merchant of Venice* does include some nontheatrical references. Thomas Jordan's ballad *The Forfeiture*, included in his 1664 *A Royal Arbor of Loyal Poesie*, refers to the pound of flesh, and the play was one of the few quarto versions issued during the seventeenth century (in 1637 and 1652).

89. Few records survive from either theater this season. At Lincoln's Inn Fields, we know of seventeen performances of fifteen plays, seven of them new, but Milhous and Hume estimate that the company performed "upwards of 180 times (or more) before its even less documented summer season" (*The London Stage: A New Version*, 5). In addition to the three moderately successful new plays, Betterton premiered Motteux's *The Mad Lover* (an operatic adaptation of Fletcher containing two masques), Pix's *The Double Distress* and *The Czar of Muscovy*, Gildon's *Love's Victim*, and the anonymous *The Gentleman Cully*. Drury Lane under Christopher Rich had a similar season, though more records of performances there survive. Christopher Rich remained in charge at Drury Lane, but Milhous and Hume estimate that only a third of performances from Drury Lane appear in records (3). We have evidence of sixty-nine performances of thirty-six plays, ten of them new: Centlivre's *The Perjured Husband*, Trotter's *Love at a Loss*, Cibber's *Love Makes a Man*, Trotter's *The Unhappy Penitent*, adaptation of Lee: *Alexander the Great* (20 February), Baker's *The Humour of the Age*, anonymous adaptation of Shirley's *Like to Like*, Farquhar's *Sir Harry Wildair*, Settle's *The Virgin Prophetess* and Durfey's *The Bath*.

90. *The London Stage*, 2:1.

91. "An Essay Upon Unnatural Flights in Poetry;" Preface to *The British Enchanters* (1710), in *Poems on Several Occasions* (London, 1716), 121.

92. In his introduction to Eccles's score of *The Judgment of Paris* (Tunbridge Wells: R. Macnutt, 1984) Richard Platt say that the "Prize Musick" was staged. Hume lists it as a concert performance in his "The Politics of Opera."

93. Congreve's letter from Wilson, *Roger North*, 312 n.68.

94. Performance information in this paragraph is from *The London Stage: A New Version*, 27.

95. Granville had allotted the profits of his play to Dryden, who died before the play was performed, so his son was accorded the receipts. The 1713 London edition of Granville's *Three Plays* notes that "The Profits of this Play were given to Mr. *Dryden*'s Son" (prologue).

96. A 1709 inventory of theatrical furniture from Christopher Rich included the

following: "A *Suit of Cloaths* for a GHOST, *viz.* A bloody *Shirt*, a *Doublet* Curiously pinked, and a *Coat* with three great Eyelet-Holes upon the Breast." Edmund Curll, *The Life of That Eminent Comedian Robert Wilks, Esq*, 52.

97. Verbruggen played Shakespeare's ghost in the prologue to Gildon's *Measure for Measure* and Betterton acted Shakespeare's ghost in the prologue to Dryden's *Troilus and Cressida* (1679).

98. See Kewes, *Authorship and Appropriation*, and Marsden, *The Re-Imagined Text*.

99. Granville, *Poems on Several Occasions* (1716), 107. Danchin notes that an earlier version of this epilogue appeared with *As You Find It. The Prologues and Epilogues of the Restoration 1660–1700*, (1:312–14).

100. Elizabeth Handasyde discusses Waller's influence on Granville: "From Waller he borrowed his manner, his metaphors, and even his phrases. He imitated him in the choice of his rhythms and metres, in the themes of his poems, and in the lightness of his handling." *Granville the Polite: The Life of George Granville Lord Lansdowne, 1666–1735* (London: Oxford University Press, 1933), 19.

101. Ibid., 33–53. Kewes rightly points out that adapters of Shakespeare also revised other source plays: "Davenant also reworked French and Spanish plays; Dryden adapted Sophocles, Corneille, and Molière, and in the last year of his life contributed a masque to a revival of Fletcher's *The Pilgrim;* Cibber altered Corneille, Fletcher, Lee, and many others; Dennis modified Tasso and Euripides; Gildon remodeled Euripides, Quinault, and Lee; D'Urfey rewrote several plays by Fletcher and one by Chapman; Crowne Anglicised Seneca, Racine, and the Spanish *No puede ser*" (*Authorship and Appropriation*, 90).

102. The 1736 edition of Granville's play replaces the masque with the direction, "Here to be a complete Concert of Vocal and Instrumental Musick, after the *Italian* Manner." *The Genuine Works in Verse and Prose of the Right Honourable George Granville Lord Lansdowne* (London, 1736), 3:133. *Peleus and Thetis* appears in the first volume with Granville's poetry. His later semi-opera *The British Enchanters* includes a closer correlation between the music and the dramatic action; see Price, "English Traditions in Handel's *Rinaldo*," in *Handel Tercentenary Collection*, ed. Stanley Sadie and Anthony Hicks (Ann Arbor, Mich.: UMI Research Press, 1987), 122, and Todd S. Gilman, "Augustan Criticism and Changing Conceptions of English Opera," *Theatre Survey* 36 (1995): 25–29.

103. Braverman connects this masque allegorically with political events around the turn of the century. See "Politics in Jewish Disguise," 360–64.

104. Ben Ross Schneider, Jr., points out that music is the mysterious source of Antonio's sadness. "Granville's *Jew of Venice* (1701): A Close Reading of Shakespeare's *Merchant*," *Restoration* 17 (1993): 128–29.

105. William S. E. Coleman has pointed out that even though Granville trims the number of scenes, the result is to strengthen the character of Shylock as the central role. "Post-Restoration Shylocks Prior to Macklin," *Theatre Survey* 8 (1967): 20. Catherine A. Craft discusses similarities between Granville's characters and the stage types of "the lover, the lady, and the villain" in "Granville's *Jew of Venice* and the Eighteenth-Century Stage," *Restoration and Eighteenth-Century Theatre Research* 2 (1987): 38–54.

106. Handasyde argues that Granville's object was to "shift the sympathy of the audience from Shylock to his victim Antonio. By omitting the scene with Tubal he left the Jew's malignant cruelty without its explanation, and also left Antonio's misfortunes to burst without preparation on the audience." *Granville the Polite*, 61.

107. J. Harold Wilson, "Granville's 'Stock-Jobbing Jew,'" *Philological Quarterly* 13 (1934): 5. Schneider remarks that the "prejudice against Shylock in both original and adaptation is ethic, not ethnic" ("Granville's *Jew of Venice*," 119). According to Defoe,

by 1724 stockjobbing was "so vast in its extent, that almost all the men of substance in England are more or less concerned in it." *A Tour Through the Whole Island of Great Britain* (London, 1724–26), 1: 336.

108. Craft argues that Granville emphasizes the theme of friendship throughout the play. Schneider also addresses this topic, pointing out that the interpolated masque "gives Granville a chance to write on the sky, in explicit terms, what he considers to be the play's moral message": friendship and love. "Granville's *Jew of Venice*," 117.

109. Harold Pollins, *Economic History of the Jews in England* (Madison, N.J.: Fairleigh Dickinson University Press, 1982), 56–60, at 57. For Jews in the history and literature of the eighteenth century, see Montagu Frank Modder, *The Jew in the Literature of England to the End of the Nineteenth Century* (Philadelphia: The Jewish Publication Society of America, 1939); Cecil Roth, *A History of Jews in England* (Oxford: Oxford University Press, 1949), 194–95; R. D. Barnett, "Anglo-Jewry in the Eighteenth Century," in V. D. Lipman, ed., *Three Centuries of Anglo-Jewish History* (Cambridge: W. Heffer, 1961), 45–68; Thomas W. Perry, *Public Opinion, Propaganda, and Politics in Eighteenth-Century England: A Study of the Jew Bill of 1753* (Cambridge: Harvard University Press, 1962); David S. Katz, *The Jews in the History of England 1485–1850* (Oxford: Clarendon, 1994), 190–239; John Gross, *Shylock: Four Hundred Years in the Life of a Legend* (London: Chatto & Windus, 1992); Frank Felsenstein, *Anti-semitic Stereotypes: A Paradigm of Otherness in English Popular Culture, 1660–1830* (Baltimore: Johns Hopkins University Press,1995); Natalie Zemon Davis, "Religion and Capitalism Once Again? Jewish Merchant Culture in the Seventeenth Century," *Representations* 59 (1997): 56–84; James Shapiro, *Shakespeare and the Jews* (New York: Columbia University Press, 1996).

110. R. D. Barnett notes that "it was as merchants that they [Jews] were best known" ("Anglo-Jewry in the Eighteenth Century," 45). Jews met in a corner of the Royal Exchange known as "Jews' Walk"; *Spectator* no. 1 (1 March 1711) comments, "I have been taken for a Merchant upon the *Exchange* for above these ten Years, and sometimes pass for a *Jew* in the Assembly of Stock-Jobbers at *Jonathan's*" coffee house. Felsenstein contends that Granville's character as a stockjobber "is more a petty dealer who has overreached himself, a comic villain to be scorned and ridiculed by the audience, than a fiendish agent nurturing murderous instincts akin to those of the medieval theological stereotype of the Jew." *Anti-semitic Stereotypes*, 166.

111. Ned Ward, *The London Spy*, ed. Arthur L. Hayward (London: Cassell, 1927), 57–58.

112. Tom Brown, *Amusements Serious and Comical*, ed. Arthur L. Hayward (London: Routledge, 1927), 200.

113. See Abba Rubin, *Images in Transition: The English Jew in English Literature 1660–1830* (Westport, Conn.: Greenwood Press, 1984), 50–53. For various sides of the debate surrounding Doggett's portrayal of Shylock, see Frederick T. Wood, "*The Merchant of Venice* in the Eighteenth Century," *English Studies* 15 (1933): 209–18; Wilson, "Granville's 'Stock-Jobbing Jew'"; Coleman, "Post-Restoration Shylocks"; Craft, "Granville's *Jew of Venice* and the Eighteenth-Century Stage"; Schneider, "Granville's *Jew of Venice*"; Spencer's introduction to *Five Restoration Adaptations of Shakespeare* and M. M. Mahood's introduction to *The Merchant of Venice* (Cambridge: Cambridge University Press, 1987).

114. Robert D. Hume and Judith Milhous discuss Doggett's activities with his strolling company in "Thomas Doggett at Cambridge in 1701," *Theatre Notebook* 51 (1997): 147–65.

115. *Biographical Dictionary*, 4:446.

116. *The London Stage: A New Version*, 65.

117. Many scholars have been reluctant to accept this, but the evidence is over-

whelming. A. C. Sprague, in *Shakespeare and the Actors: The Stage Business in His Plays (1660–1905)* (Cambridge: Harvard University Press, 1948), asserts that if Doggett played Shylock as "a merely farcical character . . . the part was of course misinterpreted, just as it has been misinterpreted over and over again in the present century. What cannot be too strongly emphasized, however, is that the production of 1701 was a revival of a quite unfamiliar play. *The Merchant of Venice* had been unacted since the Restoration—perhaps for a long time before that." Sprague confidently concludes that "Doggett may have established a tradition. He was not following one" (19). Similarly, Hazelton Spencer states that although Doggett may have played Shylock as a comic character, "let me reiterate that the absence of any record of performance for the hundred years previous would nullify any effort to use the Granville *Jew* as evidence concerning Elizabethan interpretation of the rôle" (*Shakespeare Improved*, 343). Coleman epitomizes this reluctance in his argument that early eighteenth-century actors "performed the role non-tragically" ("Post-Restoration Shylocks," 18). Wilson discusses the relationship between a comic Shylock and Shakespeare's original creation in "Granville's 'Stock-Jobbing Jew," 1–15. Spencer pointed out that "Granville's Jew was surely comic" (*Five Restoration Adaptations of Shakespeare*, 30), but a recent book on the history of Shylock rigorously assaults a comic version of Shylock. In *Shylock: Four Hundred Years in the Life of a Legend*, Gross chastises Granville for his adaptation: "His alterations killed most of the poetry; his additions, where they were not merely trite, introduced a note of awesome vulgarity." Gross adds that "the chief victim in this last respect was Shylock . . . this is not a Shylock who was likely to inspire much fear. He is primarily a figure of fun, and his antics, divorced from any serious purpose on the author's part, belong in the never-never world of pantomime." Gross provides an additional jab at Granville's version of the play: "If Granville had in fact turned Shylock into a jobber, *The Jew of Venice* would have been even more grotesque than it is, but at least it would have gained in interest as a historical document. Instead, he was content to make him a clown" (92–93).

118. *Biographical Dictionary*, 4:450.

119. Anthony Aston, *A Brief Supplement to Colley Cibber, Esq; His Lives of the late Famous Actors and Actresses*, appended to Cibber, *Apology*, 2:309.

120. He "acted with his face more than was usual" (Downes, *Roscius*, 108 n.393).

121. Nicholas Rowe, "Some Account of the Life, &c. of Mr. Wm. Shakespear," in *The Works of Mr. William Shakespear*, 1:xix–xx. An earlier Jewish character in Thomas Jordan's ballad "The Forfeiture" (c.1644) was possibly comic. See Felsenstein, *Antisemitic Stereotypes*, 163. A later stage account records that the "celebrated Doggett performed the *Jew* almost in the style of broad farce." William Cook, *Memoirs of Charles Macklin, Comedian* (London, 1804), 90.

122. For further discussion of these comic actors, see Coleman, "Post-Restoration Shylocks," 17–36. The tradition that Doggett established becomes even clearer when Charles Macklin performed Shylock in the 1740s. Toby Lelyveld states that when Macklin "announced his intention to depart from the comic tradition that had been established by way of the Granville version of *The Merchant of Venice*, the play had been off the boards for more than two years. He encountered nothing but derision and discouragement on the part of his colleagues at the Drury Lane. They believed that a serious treatment of Shylock would be only an arrogant and presumptuous display." The stage history of Jews also indicates the influence of Granville's comic Shylock: "Following in the spirit of the tradition that was established by Granville's *The Jew of Venice* was a host of plays that depicted the Jew unfavorably, in the second half of the eighteenth century. The stage-Jew was irredeemably evil and miserly until after the Restoration. He then evolved into a less obnoxious type; but he was still caricatured and

ridiculed. He had been a villain; he now became funny. It was this characterization that stubbornly persisted throughout the eighteenth century." Toby Lelyveld *Shylock on the Stage* (London: Routledge, 1960), 21, 33.

123. *The London Stage: A New Version*, 646.

124. *The London Stage*, 2:1:234.

125. See Sybil Rosenfeld, *Strolling Players and Drama in the Provinces* (Cambridge: Cambridge University Press, 1939), 270.

126. The "Thursday last" would be the 23 August performance of *The Jew of Venice*.

127. *The London Stage*, 2:637, 645, 646, 647.

128. Braverman argues that Granville's play "draws on anti-semitic tradition to set out the conflict over the succession as a conflict of two very different futures for England. Shylock may not be at the center of Granville's adaptation, but the mercantile values he represents are, and on that account the play exploits the fear of the moneyed interest as a threat to aristocratic blood, a threat that can be held in check only by restoring the genealogical values that will assuredly flow from a Jacobite succession" ("Politics in Jewish Disguise," 351). *The Jew of Venice* may have been revived in this season because of the Jacobite Rebellion of 1715.

129. *The London Stage*, 2:348; 2:362.

130. Andrew Pinnock points out that the adapter of the operatic *Indian Queen* "made no attempt to put the critical principles of his own age into practice" and "threw out material fundamental to an understanding of the plot" and kept only "the poetical highlights." Nevertheless, the piece remains "a perfectly efficient vehicle" for Purcell's music. See "Play into opera: Purcell's *The Indian Queen*," *Early Music* 18 (1990): 17.

131. See Lelyveld, *Shylock on the Stage*, 115.

132. Granville's play has not been well-received by later generations. To protect his readers from Granville, Jay L. Halio refuses to cite any of Granville's lines in his edition of *The Merchant of Venice* (Oxford: Clarendon, 1993): "While much of Shakespeare's verse remains, much is changed, as the example shows (in deference to the reader's sensibility I refrain from quoting verse that is utterly Granville's)" (62). Lelyveld similarly states that "Granville interpolates scenes, omits characters, improvises dramatic incidents, jumbles Shakespeare's poetry with his own doggerel. So indiscriminating is his tampering, that the resultant perversion has only the merest resemblance to its original" (*Shylock on the Stage*, 15).

133. An entry in the *Calendar of Treasury Papers, 1708–1714* for 29 August 1711 reads: G. Granville to the Lord [High Treasurer]. Recommends Mr. John Dennis, the bearer, to his Lordship for assistance and reminds his Lordship of the assurance given him [Mr. Granville] that he [the bearer] shold be made easy" (*Works*, 1:506).

134. Oldmixon, *Poems on Several Occasions* (London, 1696), preface; Gildon, *Lives and Characters of the English Dramatic Poets*, entry for Dennis; Hill to Pope, 10 February 1731, in *The Correspondence of Alexander Pope*, ed. George Sherburn. (Oxford: Clarendon, 1956), 3:175; Giles Jacob in *An Historical Account of the Lives and Writings of our Most Considerable English Poets* (London, 1720), 2:257. Dennis was a formidable personality; Pope describes him as staring *"Tremendous*! With a threatning Eye; / Like some *fierce Tyrant* in *Old Tapestry*!" ("Essay on Criticism," lines 586–87).

135. Dennis's "Essay on the Opera's After the Italian Manner" (1706), penned four years after his adaptation of *The Merry Wives of Windsor*, is his most extended objection against this foreign invader, written in reaction to the opening of the Haymarket theater in 1705, its production of operas, and the public support these entertainments received. *In Tatler* no. 4 Steele describes Dennis as a critic driven to lunacy by Italian opera. In his *Short View of Tragedy* (1693), Rymer denounced opera as a "conspiracy against Nature and good Sense. 'Tis a Debauch the most insinuating and the most pernicious."

Addison voiced his objections in *The Spectator* nos. 5, 13, 18, 29. Gildon reacted against opera in his *The Life of Mr. Thomas Betterton* (1710), 143–44, 167–74 and *The Complete Art of Poetry* (1718), 1:203–205. See also Nicoll, *A History of Early Eighteenth-Century Drama*, 225–37.

136. *Works*, 1:382–83; *The Dunciad*, Book IV, note 45. For discussion of Dennis's views on opera within the context of other contemporary critical comments, see Gilman, "Augustan Criticism." David Wheeler provides a limited discussion of some of Dennis's critical theories and his dramatic practice in "Eighteenth-Century Adaptations of Shakespeare and the Example of John Dennis," *Shakespeare Quarterly* 36 (1985): 438–49.

137. "Reflections on An Essay Upon Criticism" (1711), in *Works*, 1:396.

138. "The Stage Defended" (1726), *Works*, 2:301. Todd S. Gilman discusses Dennis's vilification of Italian opera in connection with British attacks on the castrati in "The Italian (Castrato) in London," in *Genre, Nationhood, and Sexual Difference*, ed. Richard Dellamora and Daniel Fischlin (New York: Columbia University Press, 1997), 49–70.

139. "Essay on the Opera's," *Works*, 1:390–91. Other contemporary texts offered similar patriotic views and stressed their native roots. The epilogue to Settle's *The World in the Moon* (1697), for example, claimed to be "All from an English Web, and English Growth." Dobson traces Shakespeare's role in this growing nationalism in *The Making of the National Poet*.

140. "Remarks upon Cato," 1713; *Works*, 2:44.

141. Dennis, *Works*, 1:384–85. Hooker points out that "the immediate cause of his attack upon the opera . . . was the new policy of the Haymarket theater, which had opened in 1705" (Dennis, *Works*, 1:521).

142. "Essay on the Opera's" (*Works*, 1:386).

143. "Reflections on An Essay Upon Criticism," (1711), (*Works*, 1:410). In his "Large Account" Dennis concluded that "the *English* were never sunk so miserably low in their taste, as they are at present" (*Works*, 1:289).

144. "Large Account" (*Works*, 1:287); letter "To Richard Norton of Southwick," 10 August 1708 (*Works*, 2:393). Cibber's catering to public taste made him a particular enemy of Dennis.

145. "Large Account" (*Works*, 1:287).

146. *Letters of Wit, Politicks, and Morality* (1701), 221.

147. *Works*, 1:382; 1:49; 1:287.

148. W. P. Ker, *The Essays of John Dryden* (Oxford: Clarendon, 1926), 2:7. Gildon, preface to *Love's Victim*. Pope from "Preface of the Editor," *The Works of Shakespear* (London, 1725), 1:v.

149. Charles Gildon, *The Life of Mr. Thomas Betterton*, 142–43, 155. See also Nicoll, *A History of Early Eighteenth-Century Drama*, 8–25, and Tom Brown, *Collection of Original Letters on Several Occasions*, in *Works* (1710), 2:246.

150. Dennis, *Original Letters*, 2 vols. (London, 1721), 1:46. See *Works* 2:xxiv, n.80 for Hooker's discussion of Dennis's "retirement." In "Notes on the Life of John Dennis" (*ELH* 5 [1938]: 211–17), Fred S. Tupper speculates that Dennis's work as a notary public may have entangled him in financial difficulties around 1711.

151. *The London Stage*, 1:505–507. Like many members of his audience, Dennis acknowledged the power of music, "There is no Man living who is more convinc'd than my self of the Power of Harmony, or more penetrated by the Charms of Musick. I know very well that Musick makes a considerable Part both of Eloquence and of Poetry; and therefore to endeavour to decry it fully, would be as well a foolish, as an ungrateful Task, since the very Efforts which we should make against it, would only serve to declare its Excellence" ("Essay on the Operas," *Works*, 1:385).

152. See *Works*, 2:lxxxv, for Hooker's in-depth discussion of Dennis and the rules.

153. *Works*, 2:386. Dennis continued to discuss the merits of rules in works such as his "The Causes of the Decay and Defects of Dramatick Poetry" (1725).

154. "The Causes of the Decay and Defects of Dramatick Poetry" (1725) (*Works*, 2:281).

155. Letter to Walter Moyle (*Works*, 2:386). Dennis made other exceptions to the rules; Milton's *Paradise Lost* earned his respect even though Milton did not adhere to the rules. Dennis praised *Paradise Lost* as "the greatest Poem that ever was written by Man" (*Works*, 1:351).

156. "Reflections Critical and Satyrical, Upon a Late Rhapsody, Call'd, An Essay upon Criticism" (1711) (*Works*, 1:418).

157. "The Causes of the Decay and Defects of Dramatick Poetry" (1725); (*Works*, 2:277).

158. In the dedication to *The Distress'd Innocence* (1691), Settle also thanked Betterton "for his several extraordinary Hints to the heightning of my best Characters." Dennis was on friendly terms with William Penkethman and he wrote several letters in support of Penkethman. See Dennis, *Original Letters*, 1:21–25 and 152–53.

159. "Large Account," in *Works*, 1:281.

160. Stuart M. Tave, *The Amiable Humorist: A Study in the Comic Theory and Criticism of the Eighteenth and Early Nineteenth Centuries* (Chicago: University of Chicago Press, 1960), 110.

161. Dennis argues that "'tis among People of the lower sort, that by the means of Passion and Humour, nature appears so admirably conspicuous in all her Charming diversities: Since therefore Humour is the chief business in Comedy after the Fable . . . it is very plain that low Characters are more proper for Comedy than high ones, and that low Comedy is to be preferred to the high" (*Works*, 1:282–83). See Tave, *Amiable Humorist*, 110–18, for a discussion of the difference between humor and wit.

162. David Paxman states that "Even authors who did not write humors comedy moaned about the dearth of novel fools" (18) and "complaints about the depletion of originals became more frequent and more pointed at the beginning of the eighteenth century" (19). "The Burden of the Immediate Past: The Early Eighteenth Century and the Shadow of Restoration Comedy," *Essays in Literature* 17 (1990): 15–29.

163. He justifies the need for his adaptation because the original was written at the command of Queen Elizabeth and was composed by Shakespeare in fourteen days. This alone makes it in need of improvement according to Dennis; "in so short a time as this Play was writ, nothing could be done that is perfect." However, Dennis is the only source of this story, as Dobson points out, and may have manufactured it to justify his adaptation (*The Making of the National Poet*, 147n.). Jeanne Addison Roberts states that Dennis's story has survived "probably because it so neatly accounts for the startling change in the circumstances of Falstaff, the presence of the characters from the histories in what otherwise seems a contemporary domestic comedy, and for the signs of haste throughout the play." *Shakespeare's English Comedy: The Merry Wives of Windsor in Context* (Lincoln: University of Nebraska Press, 1979), 49. Dennis's tale has provoked some humorous responses; Hartley Coleridge, in his 1851 "Notes on Shakespeare," remarks: "That Queen Bess should have desired to see Falstaff making love proves her to have been, as she was, a gross-minded old baggage." *Essays and Marginalia* (London: Edward Moxon, 1851), 2:133.

164. "Large Account," *Works*, 1:281–82.

165. The phrase "petulant Critick" comes from *A Comparison Between the Two Stages*, 176. Boyer called him "a *Giant-Wit*, and a *Giant-Critick*." See preface to *Achilles: or, Iphigenia in Aulis* (1700).

166. Elsewhere Dennis voiced a flexible attitude about rules; in "The Grounds of Criticism in Poetry," he remarks, "When . . . we have laid down the Rules, we come briefly to examine, Whether those Rules are always to be kept inviolable; and if they are not, in what parts, and by whom, they may be alter'd" (*Works*, 1:331). Dennis praises Milton's poetry for being not so much "against the Rules, as it may be affirmed to be above them all" (*Works*, 1:333). In "The Impartial Critick," Dennis admits that "things which succeeded very well with the Ancients, . . . would yet be very ill receiv'd amongst us, upon the account of the difference of our Religion, Climate, and Customs" (*Works*, 1:12).

167. *A Review of the State of the English Nation* vol. 3, no. 96 (10 August 1706).

168. *Works*, 2:4. Dennis esteemed Ben Jonson's *Volpone*, *The Alchemist*, and *Epicoene* as "incomparably the best of our Comedies; and they are certainly the most regular of them all" (*Works*, 2:196). Ben Jonson provides evidence that "it was the Opinion of the greatest of all our Comick Poets, That the Rules were absolutely necessary to Perfection" (*Works*, 2:196). Dennis did criticize Jonson; see *Works*, 2:cxxxiii.

169. Dennis says of Shakespeare's characters: "He has for the most part more fairly distinguish'd them than any of his Successors have done" (*Works*, 2:4).

170. *Shakespeare Restored* (1726), 181.

171. *The Merry Wives of Windsor* was included in the list of plays performed at the Red Bull in 1660, and later performed at Vere Street on 9 November 1660. See Bawcutt, *The Control and Censorship of Caroline Drama* and Downes, *Roscius*, 111. See Pepys's comments on the play for 5 December 1660 (1:310), 25 September 1666 (2:185), and 15 August 1667, where he remarks that the play "did not please me at all—in no part of it" (8:386). According to the records in *The London Stage*, from 1660 through the 1716/17 season, *The Merry Wives* was only performed eleven times. Milhous and Hume assert that *The Merry Wives* probably "was in the repertory at both theatres" from 1700–1706 (*Roscius*, 97 n.345). Rob Jordan lists an additional performance in 1698–99. "An Addendum to *The London Stage 1660–1700*," *Theatre Notebook* 47 (1993): 75. However, in *Shakespeare in the Theatre 1701–1800*, Charles B. Hogan lists *The Merry Wives* as the fifth most popular Shakespearian play in the period from 1701–1750, with only *1 Henry IV*, *Othello*, *Macbeth*, and *Hamlet* receiving more performances. *The Merry Wives* was the most popular comedy in the period from 1701–1750, but it did not become popular until the 1720s; from 1720 through 1750 it was performed several times every year. Nancy A. Mace provides an in-depth study of the popularity of *The Merry Wives* throughout the eighteenth century, especially in relation to actor James Quin in "Falstaff, Quin, and the Popularity of *The Merry Wives of Windsor* in the Eighteenth Century," *Theatre Survey* 31 (1990): 55–66.

172. In *The Gentleman's Journal* (January 1692), Motteux notes that "*The Merry Wives of Windsor*, an Old Play, hath been reviv'd, and was play'd the Last Day of the Year" (56).

173. Mrs. Griffith, *The Morality of Shakespeare's Drama Illustrated* (1775; reprint, New York: Augustus M. Kelley, 1971), 127. See Louis D. Mitchell, "Command Performances During the Reign of Queen Anne," 114. Downes records a command performance on 23 April 1705 or 1706, with Betterton as Falstaff, Doggett as Sir Hugh, Penkethman as Caius, and Anne Bracegirdle as Mrs. Ford (*Roscius*, 98). Hume and Milhous note that Vanbrugh performed the play on 23 April 1705 as a possible "warm-up for a court performance later that evening" (*Roscius*, 98n.). See also *The London Stage: A New Version*, 161 and 221.

174. See Mace, "Falstaff, Quin," 63–64.

175. Bentley, *Shakespeare and Jonson* 1:122. Bentley states that most allusions to Falstaff are "passing references obviously intended to enlighten the reader by a comparison

or to amuse him by reminding him of the escapades or characteristics of Shakespeare's fat knight" (1:121). He also records two anonymous almanacs of 1674 and 1681 which list Falstaff's birthday (2:5, 6). Rowe passage from "Some Account of the Life, &c. of Mr. Wm. Shakespear," in *The Works of Mr. William Shakespear*, 1:xvii. Gildon also praised *The Merry Wives* as an admirable specimen of comedy, "before the Learned *Ben Johnson*, for no Man can allow any of *Shakespear's* Comedies, except the *Merry Wives of Windsor*." *The Life of Mr. Thomas Betterton* (1710), 173.

176. Hume calls Betterton's *Henry IV* not an adaptation, but "merely a players' quarto with some cuts," which included making the rebels unattractive, playing down Henry's status as an usurper, cutting the churchmen out of the rebels' plot, and deleting profanity so that Betterton could "anticipate political and moral objections" (*The Development of English Drama*, 441). Avon Jack Murphy states that Dennis's timing was right in adapting this play because "the original enjoyed great popularity, as did the Falstaff of the Henry IV plays" (*John Dennis* [Boston: Twayne, 1984], 83).

177. *The London Stage*, 1:523.

178. The Falstaff of *The Merry Wives* has been associated with Jonsonian comedy. The editors of Jonson's works remark that "To pass from the Falstaff of Eastcheap to the Falstaff of Windsor is in some sense to pass from Shakespearean to Jonsonian comedy." *Ben Jonson*, ed. C. H. Herford, Percy and Evelyn Simpson (Oxford: Clarendon, 1925), 2:73.

179. See Milhous, *Thomas Betterton*, 147.

180. *A Comparison Between the Two Stages*, 106; Genest, *Some Account*, 2:250. Harry Gilbert Paul suggests that Bullock may have played Falstaff. *John Dennis; His Life and Criticism* (New York: Columbia University Press, 1911), 40 n.25.

181. Cibber, *Apology*, 1:207. Powell's first recorded performance at Lincoln's Inn Fields is not until 19 May 1701 in the title role of *King Lear*, but it is unclear when Powell left Drury Lane (*Biographical Dictionary*, 12:111). While at Lincoln's Inn Fields, he played the role of Ford in *The Merry Wives* in 1703–04, in a performance with actors from both houses. He had earlier played Fenton at a Drury Lane production in the 1690s.

182. W. R. Chetwood, *A General History of the Stage* (London, 1749), 155. *The Spectator* no. 346 (7 April 1712) describes Powell in 1712: "The haughty *George Powell* hopes all the Good-natured Part of the Town, will favour him whom they Applauded in *Alexander*, *Timon*, *Lear*, and *Orestes*, with their Company this Night, when he hazards all his Heroick Glory for their Approbation in the humbler Condition of honest *Jack Falstaff*" (3:291). There were other instances of actors attempting to usurp Betterton's role. Cibber relates that Estcourt annotated his copy of the part of Falstaff with "Notes and Observations upon almost every Speech of it, describing the true Spirit of the Humour, and with what Tone of Voice, Look, and Gesture, each of them ought to be delivered" (*Apology*, 1:115).

183. Six new plays were among the lot at Drury Lane: Steele's *The Funeral* (a success), Bevill Higgons's *The Generous Conquerour* (a failure), Burnaby's *The Modish Husband* (few performances), Vanbrugh's *The False Friend* (its run was cut short because Cibber was injured, but it was performed four nights), Farquhar's *The Inconstant*, an adaptation of Fletcher's *The Wild Goose Chase* (six nights, sparsely attended), and Dennis's *The Comical Gallant*. Records survive for more than one performance of only four plays, Rowe's *Tamerlane*, Wycherley's *The Country Wife*, Steele's *The Funeral*, and Jonson's *Bartholomew Fair*. *The Funeral* (1701) was one of the few successful comedies in this period, perhaps because it combines a number of strains of popular plot aspects as well as amiable comic tendencies that Steele would later develop in *The Conscious Lovers* (Hume, *The Development of English Drama*, 440).

184. Hume, *The Development of English Drama* 435; Corman, *Genre and Generic Change*, 10–11. See Hughes and Scouten in "'Restoration Comedy' and its Audiences," 56. For additional discussion of the change in comedy, see John Harrington Smith, "Shadwell, the Ladies, and the Change in Comedy," *Modern Philology* 46 (1948): 22–33, and *The Gay Couple in Restoration Comedy* (Cambridge: Harvard University Press, 1948). David Wheeler examines the effect of Dennis's dramatic theory on *The Comical Gallant*, remarking that he "transforms a comedy of language into a comedy of situation," but disappointingly concludes that Dennis's adaptations "survive only as curiosities." "Eighteenth-Century Adaptations of Shakespeare," 446, 449.

185. Shirley Strum Kenny, "Humane Comedy," *Modern Philology* 75 (1977): 30, 35.

186. Tave, *Amiable Humorist*, viii.

187. Bentley, *Shakespeare and Jonson* 1:75.

188. Mace asserts that audiences were unhappy with Dennis because he "shifted the focus away from their favorite character. Significantly, Dennis's revision was the only attempt to adapt this play in the eighteenth century; others probably knew that any alteration of the play would reduce Falstaff's presence and spell disaster with playgoers." See "Falstaff, Quin," 62.

189. See Kathleen M. Lynch, "Thomas D'Urfey's Contribution to Sentimental Comedy," *Philological Quarterly* 9 (1930): 249–59.

190. *The Diary of Dudley Ryder, 1715–1716*, 104. Corbyn Morris, "An Essay Towards Fixing the True Standards of Wit, Humour, Raillery, Satire, and Ridicule. To which is Added, an Analysis of the Characters of An Humourist, Sir *John Falstaff*, Sir *Roger De Coverly*, and Don *Quixote*" (London, 1744), 29.

191. Robert D. Hume, "The Multifarious Forms of Eighteenth-Century Comedy," in *The Stage and the Page: London's "Whole Show" in the Eighteenth-Century Theatre*, ed. George Winchester Stone, Jr. (Berkeley: University of California Press, 1981), 10.

192. Dennis articulated his views on good nature on several occasions. See for example his letter "To Mr. Bradley" from 20 March 1720/21 (*Works*, 2:412–13), and "Remarks on Prince Arthur" (1696) (*Works*, 1:48–49).

193. Alden T. and Virginia Mason Vaughan note a similar trend in eighteenth-century representations of Caliban: "Caliban's relative insignificance to eighteenth-century productions is understandable. Though the audience enjoyed the seamen's music and antics, Caliban did not fit well with the age's notions of comedy ... Caliban's grotesque deformities were not the proper vehicle for good-natured wit; his natural folly was inappropriate to an art form that dealt with manners and artificial follies." *Shakespeare's Caliban: A Cultural History* (Cambridge: Cambridge University Press, 1991), 178.

194. Dennis was a central figure in refuting Collier and his followers, particularly his work *The Usefulness of the Stage*. See *Works*, 1:467, for discussion of Dennis's role. Murphy also attacks Dennis for the "most outrageous addition" of Falstaff "explicitly detail[ing] how [Mrs. Ford] bares herself," which Hazelton Spencer refers to as "unquotable" (*Shakespeare Improved*, 347). Murphy condemns Dennis: "if he expects us to find such lines humorous, Dennis has misgauged our relish for low comedy" (*John Dennis*, 85).

195. Edward Niles Hooker writes that in Charles Johnson's 1710 farce *Love in a Chest*, "The main incident of the farce, in which Faschinetti, the unwelcome wooer, is maliciously concealed in a chest by Theresa and later carried in the chest and presented to his wife, was probably suggested by the *Merry Wives of Windsor*." "Charles Johnson's *The Force of Friendship* and *Love in a Chest*: A Note on Tragicomedy and Licensing in 1710," *Studies in Philology* 34 (1937): 408 n.3.

196. Kenny, "Humane Comedy," 40–41; Corman, *Genre and Generic Change*, 114. See Murphy, *John Dennis*, 85, for criticism of Dennis's use of farce.

197. Wheeler states that "though Fenton is often in the background of the play, in Dennis' version he is at least nominally in control of the whole plot through his schemes and his intermediaries. The play thus becomes a convoluted intrigue like many of the Restoration comedies to which we are accustomed" ("Eighteenth-Century Adaptations of Shakespeare," 445). Roberts has a much harsher view of Dennis's changes: Dennis "greatly expands [Ann Page's] role and ruins the play" (*Shakespeare's English Comedy*, 71).

198. Falstaff admits that he has overreached, and is taunted by "one that makes fritters of English" (5.5.143). Mrs. Page tells him, "do you think . . . that ever the devil could have made you our delight?" (5.5.146–50). Ford calls him a "hodge-pudding" and "a bag of flax" (151); Page says he is "Old, cold, wither'd, and of intolerable entrails" (153–54). After everyone has insulted him, Falstaff says, "Well, I am your theme, You have the start of me, I am dejected. I am not able to answer the Welsh flannel; ignorance itself is a plummet o'er me. Use me as you will" (5.5.161–64). Page smoothes things over and tells Falstaff to "be cheerful, knight. Thou shalt eat a posset to-night at my house, where I will desire thee to laugh at my wife, that now laughs at thee" (5.5.170–72).

199. Murphy, *John Dennis*, 84.

200. Roberts, *Shakespeare's English Comedy*, xii.

201. The marriage concerns of Dennis's ending have a long stage history. See Glenn H. Blayney, "Enforcement of Marriage in English Drama (1600–1650)," *Philological Quarterly* 38 (1959): 461. Hume states that "Carolean comedies almost invariably attack arranged marriage of convenience and uphold the virtues and attractions of freely chosen marriage for love" (*The Rakish Stage*, 184).

202. Although Roberts argues that in *The Comical Gallant* the "lovers return from their elopement unmarried to seek their parents' permission," it is only Ann who seeks parental approval. Mrs. Ford is his aunt, but Fenton's parents are not part of the play. *Shakespeare's English Comedy*, 82–83.

203. Hume, *The Development of English Drama*, 441; Spencer, *Shakespeare Improved* 349; Wheeler, "Eighteenth-Century Adaptations of Shakespeare," 449; Murphy, *John Dennis*, 85. Some of the earliest commentators also condemned Dennis; in *A Comparison Between the Two Stages* (1702), Ramble asks Sullen if he has heard "any thing of a Comedy of *Dennis*'s here this Winter?" Ramble tells him that his "borrow'd" play was "damn'd" (97). Marsden gives a more reasonable summation of Dennis's play: "a critic's ideal of drama does not always make a good play." *The Re-Imagined Text*, 56.

204. See Robert D. Hume, "Marital Discord in English Comedy from Dryden to Fielding," *Modern Philology* 74 (1977): 248–72.

205. *The Comical Gallant* was printed May 19. In their article "Dating Play Premieres from Publication Data, 1660–1700," *Harvard Library Bulletin* 22 (1974), Milhous and Hume conclude that by the 1690s, the time between performance of a play and its publication is usually a month (395). Kenny asserts that in the 1700s, "the usual time lapse shrank yet again" and she concludes that "a common spread of slightly more than two weeks" was the norm. "The Publication of Plays," in *British Theatre and the Other Arts, 1660–1800*, 313. William J. Burling states that "Dennis' play is assigned by *The London Stage* to May 1702" (2:19), but Paisible's airs for this comedy were advertised in the *Post-Boy* for 11–13 December 1701, pushing the date of premiere back at least to early December and possibly even earlier. William J. Burling, "British Plays, 1697–1737: Premieres, Datings, Attributions, and Publication Information," *Studies in Bibliography* 43 (1990): 173. Hume and Milhous date the first performance of Dennis's play in late February according to their revision of *The London Stage*.

206. *The London Stage: A New Version*, 55.

207. Ibid., 38.

208. Murphy, *John Dennis*, 86.

209. *Diary*, 9:421. Downes records a Restoration performance of *Twelfth Night* with a cast of Betterton as Sir Toby, Harris as Sir Andrew, Fool by Underhill, Malvolio by Mr. Lovel, Olivia by Ann Gibbs. "All the Parts being justly Acted Crown'd the Play" (*Roscius*, 54). The role of Viola/Cesario is noticeably missing.

210. Editor T. W. Craik states, "In 1703 Charles Burnaby published his *Love Betray'd: or, the Agreable [sic] Disapointment[sic]*." *Twelfth Night*, ed. J. M. Lothian and T. W. Craik (London: Methuen 1975), lxxx. William Burnaby, *Dramatic Works*, ed. F. E. Budd (London: E. Partridge, 1931), 100, 76, 97.

211. See *Letters of Wit, Politicks and Morality* (1701), 216, 220. See also *Poems on Affairs of State*, ed. Frank H. Ellis (New Haven: Yale University Press, 1970), 6:702.

212. *The London Stage: A New Version*, 70. Lincoln's Inn Fields offered twenty mainpieces in twenty-seven performances, and one afterpiece (Motteux's *Acis and Galatea*), for about 150 performances total. Lincoln's Inn Fields put on six new plays: Centlivre's *The Heiress*, Oldmixon's *The Governour of Cyprus*, Burnaby's *Love Betray'd*, an anonymous adaptation of Randolph's *The Fickle Shepherdess* by all women, Charles Boyle's *As You Find It*, and Rowe's *The Fair Penitent*.

213. Hume and Scouten, "'Restoration Comedy' and its Audiences," 67.

214. *The London Stage: A New Version*, 211.

215. *A Comparison Between the Two Stages*, 96. See Milhous, *Thomas Betterton*, 144. Burnaby's *The Ladies' Visiting-Day* provided a third of the material (along with his *The Reform'd Wife* [1700] and Centlivre's *Love at a Venture* [1706]) for Cibber's *The Double Gallant*. As Corman states, Cibber had "the good taste to recognize that there was much of value in Burnaby's plays, despite the audiences' neglect of them" (*Genre and Generic Change*, 116).

216. Avery points out that "whereas Jonson's name appears in the advertisements for each of his plays then active, Shakespeare's name tends to be attached only to his less well-known plays . . . Actually, Shakespeare's name seems to be attached to only four plays: *Richard III, Cymbeline, Titus Andronicus*, and *Macbeth*." "The Dramatists in the Theatrical Advertisements, 1700–1709," 449–50. Avery concludes that "the managers apparently used Shakespeare's name mainly to link a less familiar play with the spectator's presumed knowledge of the dramatist's more popular pieces" (450).

217. Neighbarger, *An Outward Show: Music for Shakespeare on the London Stage, 1660–1830*, 59. Price, *Restoration* xix. Kenny details other instances of Betterton's "incompetence" when he was appointed theatrical manager in 1700 ("Theatrical Warfare" 139–40).

218. *The London Stage: A New Version*, 95.

219. Ibid., 96.

220. Ibid., 104.

221. Dedication to *The Constant Nymph: or, The Rambling Shepherd*, Written by a Person of Quality (1678).

222. Granville complains that "the Players in the Hay-market have put forth Bills for acting the British Enchanters to morrow without singing & dancing mauger the necessity thereof, which I can deem no other than a design to murder the Child of my Brain." Milhous and Hume, *Vice Chamberlain Coke's Theatrical Papers*, 15.

223. *Twelfth Night*, and the Malvolio material in particular, have often been linked to the comedies of Ben Jonson, and Burnaby may have excluded this Jonsonian character because of a growing preference for Shakespeare over Ben Jonson around the turn of the century. See G. E. Bentley, *Shakespeare and Jonson*. In their article "Jonsonian Elements in the Comic Underplot of *Twelfth Night*," Paul Mueschke and Jeannette Fleisher

state that Shakespeare's "indebtedness" to Jonson consists of "the strikingly similar relationship between Sir Toby and Sir Andrew and that of the Jonsonian victimizer and gull" and "Shakespeare's adaptation of the Jonsonian 'humour' character in Malvolio." *PMLA* 48 (1933): 722. The editors of Jonson's works state that "the baiting of the surly Morose, who abhors revelry, has a parallel in the baiting of Malvolio for his puritan rigour towards the lovers of cakes and ale. The story of Malvolio is itself somewhat Jonsonian in conception." *Ben Jonson*, ed. C. H. Herford, Percy and Evelyn Simpson (Oxford: Clarendon, 1925), 2:75.

224. Similar checks are also included in Congreve's *The Old Batchelour*. Brian Corman remarks that "the young wits have their laugh at [Heartwell's] expense, but Bellmour will not let it go beyond that" (*Genre and Generic Change*, 53).

225. *The Plain-Dealer* appears frequently in surviving notices, even during seasons with few records. The revised *London Stage* lists performances in November 1700, January 1701, October 1702, and February and November 1704, and February 1705. Wycherley's reputation held strong in the early eighteenth century. On 1 October 1701 Wycherley's *The Country Wife* was advertised as "Written by the most Ingenious William Wycherly Esq." (*The London Stage: A New Version*, 42). One of Dennis's models was Wycherley's *The Plain Dealer* (see his "Large Account," *Works*, 1:283) and he praises this play in "The Advancement and Reformation of Modern Poetry" (1701) for its variety of characters and "exact Imitation of Nature" (*Works*, 1:225, 283). Burnaby's earlier play *The Ladies' Visiting Day* derives from Wycherley's *The Country Wife*; Wycherley seemed to be a frequent source for Burnaby.

226. See Norman Suckling, "Moliére and English Restoration Comedy," *Restoration Theatre*. Stratford-upon-Avon Studies 6 (London: Edward Arnold, 1965), 105. Budd remarks that Villaretta is "a typical wealthy widow of the comedy of manners type, rejoicing in her newly-found liberty and freely bandying cynical remarks on husbands with her woman, Emilia." Burnaby, *Dramatic Works*, 97.

227. Kewes argues that the reception of drama after the Restoration was "more appreciative of contemporary achievement than has been realized. The new generation of playwrights—Dryden, Otway, Lee, Behn, Shadwell, and, later, Congreve, Vanbrugh, and Farquhar—enjoyed a high reputation. Their plays proved enduringly popular on the stage and won critical acclaim when printed" (*Authorship and Appropriation*, 181).

228. This scene is one of female companionship and raillery against men, similar to Kate and Bianca in the last act of Lacy's *Sauny the Scott*. In Lacy's play, Margaret advises Bianca: "there's no trusting these Men: Thy temper is soft and easy, thou must Learn to break him, or he'll break thy heart" (39). The opening of act two of *The Plain Dealer* also resembles Burnaby's initial scene. Wycherley's Olivia exclaims, "Ah, cousin, what a world 'tis we live in! I am so weary of it" (2.1.1). Eliza replies, "I must confess I think we women as often discover where we love by railing, as men when they lie by their swearing; and the world is but a constant keeping gallant, whom we fail not to quarrel with when anything crosses us, yet cannot part with't for our hearts"(2.1.8–12). When asked what she thinks of a "rich young husband," Olivia replies, "O horrid! Marriage! What a pleasure you have found out! I nauseate it of all things" (2.1.52–54).

229. Here Emilia sings the second Eccles' song in Burnaby's play. The first occurs in the beginning of act two as Cesario sings Eccles' "If I hear Orinda swear" to Moreno. Burnaby's play also includes act music by William Corbett; see Price, *Music in the Restoration Theatre*, 191.

230. Bentley, *Shakespeare and Jonson* 1:128. Pat Rogers names Nell Gwyn, Elizabeth Barry, Anne Bracegirdle, and Mrs. Mountfort as popular breeches actresses. "Most actresses given the opportunity to take a prominent breeches role were young, instantly identifiable by the audience, and familiar in the stock female repertoire." "The Breeches

Part," in *Sexuality in Eighteenth-Century Britain*, ed. Paul-Gabriel Boucé (Manchester: Manchester University Press, 1982), 249, 256. Elizabeth Howe (who attributes *Love Betray'd* to Charles Burnaby), mistakenly lists Anne Bracegirdle's part (Villaretta) as a breeches role. *The First English Actresses: Women and Drama, 1660–1700* (Cambridge: Cambridge University Press, 1992), 183. F. E. Budd reassigns the roles of Villaretta to Mrs. Barry, Caesario to Mrs. Bracegirdle, and Emilia to Mrs. Prince (Burnaby, *Dramatic Works*, 338, 448).

Chapter 4. Shakespeare and the Development of the Afterpiece

1. For detailed discussions of this period, see Thomas McGeary, "Thomas Clayton and the Introduction of Italian Opera to England," *Philological Quarterly* 77 (1998): 171–86; Gilman, "Augustan Criticism and Changing Conceptions of English Opera"; Fiske, *English Theatre Music in the Eighteenth Century*, 1–66; Hume, "The Sponsorship of Opera" and "Opera in London, 1695–1706;" J. Merrill Knapp, "Eighteenth-Century Opera in London before Handel, 1705–1710," in *British Theatre and the Other Arts*, 92–103; Milhous and Hume, eds., *Vice Chamberlain Coke's Theatrical Papers, 1706–1715*; Milhous, *Thomas Betterton*, 151–221; Curtis A. Price, "The Critical Decade for English Music Drama, 1700–1710," *Harvard Library Bulletin* 26 (1978): 38–76; Philip Olleson, "Vanbrugh and Opera at the Queen's Theatre, Haymarket," *Theatre Notebook* 26 (1972): 94–101; Daniel Nalbach, *The King's Theatre, 1704–1867* (London: Society for Theatre Research, 1972); K. G. Ruttkay, "The Critical Reception of Italian Opera in England in the Early Eighteenth Century," *Studies in English and American Philology* 1 (1971): 93–169; Donald C. Mullin, "The Queen's Theatre, Haymarket: Vanbrugh's Opera House," *Theatre Survey* 8 (1967): 84–105; Ronald C. Kern, "Documents Relating to Company Management, 1705–1711," *Theatre Notebook* 14 (1959–60): 60–65.

2. See Judith Milhous, "The Date and Import of the Financial Plan for a United Theatre Company in P.R.O. LC 7/3," *Maske und Kothurn* 21 (1975): 81–88; *Thomas Betterton*, chapter 7; Milhous and Robert D. Hume, "The Drury Lane Actors' Petition of 1705," *Theatre Notebook* 39 (1985): 62–67.

3. Milhous, *Thomas Betterton*, 159.

4. Preface to *Arsinoe*, in Charles Burney, *A General History of Music*, ed. Frank Mercer, (1935; reprint New York: Dover, 1957), 2: 655. Milhous and Hume promote the view that Rich stole the opera from Vanbrugh, but Thomas McGeary suggests that Clayton may have arranged for the production at Drury Lane because the Haymarket was not ready in time. See "Thomas Clayton and the Introduction of Italian Opera to England," 173; Judith Milhous, "New Light on Vanbrugh's Haymarket Theatre Project," *Theatre Survey* 17 (1976): 153; Hume, "The Sponsorship of Opera," 423.

5. Milhous, "New Light on Vanbrugh's Haymarket Theatre Project," 153.

6. Knapp, "Eighteenth-Century Opera in London before Handel, 1705–1710," 94–95; "A Critical Discourse on Opera's and Musick in England" (1709), 65, 68. The sets for *Arsinoe* were done by Sir James Thornhill, discussed by Graham Barlow in "Sir James Thornhill and the Theatre Royal, Drury Lane, 1705," *Essays on the Eighteenth-Century English Stage*, ed. Kenneth Richards and Peter Thomson (London: Methuen, 1972), 179–93.

7. *William Congreve: Letters and Documents*, ed. John C. Hodges (New York: Harcourt, Brace and World, 1964), 38.

8. See Milhous, "New Light on Vanbrugh's Haymarket Theatre Project," 153–54.

9. Prologue in Shirley Strum Kenny, "A Broadside Prologue by Farquhar," *Studies in Bibliography* 25 (1972): 183.

10. See Gilman, "The Italian (Castrato) in London."

11. *The London Stage: A New Version*, 371.

12. Milhous and Hume, *Vice Chamberlain Coke's Theatrical Papers*, xxii. As Gilman points out, "if it had not been for the forced genre division—thanks to which English semi-opera effectively was put out of business as its unique performance requirements collided with managerial agreements and an official order—English semi-opera probably would have continued to flourish." "Augustan Criticism," 18.

13. Milhous and Hume, *Vice Chamberlain Coke's Theatrical Papers*, 112–13. Vanbrugh lists a fourth reason for his lack of success—he had to rely on managers to look after his theater.

14. Percy Fitzgerald, *A New History of the English Stage* (London, 1882), 1: 240.

15. For a detailed discussion of theatrical conditions between 1708 and 1713, see Hume, "The Sponsorship of Opera," 426–32.

16. Preface to *The Constant Couple*.

17. *The Diary of Mary Countess Cowper, Lady of the Bedchamber to the Princess of Wales, 1714–1720*, ed. Spencer Cowper (London: John Murray, 1865), 46–47, entry for 15 February 1715.

18. Steele's patent included an obligation to reform the stage. For Steele's efforts at reforming Drury Lane, see John Loftis, *Steele at Drury Lane* (Berkeley: University of California Press, 1952). Steele was actually offered the post by Lord Lansdowne, author of *The Jew of Venice*. Loftis contends that Lansdowne may have offered Steele the position in order to support a fellow playwright, even though he and Steele were political opponents. Denise Elliott Shane discusses Rich's role in this competition in "John Rich and the Reopening of Lincoln's Inn Fields," *Theatre Notebook* 42 (1988): 23–34. Calhoun Winton surveys the reform movement after George I's accession in "Sentimentalism and Theater Reform in the Early Eighteenth Century," in *Quick Springs of Sense: Studies in the Eighteenth Century*, ed. Larry S. Champion (Athens: University of Georgia Press, 1974), 97–112.

19. *The Correspondence of Richard Steele*, ed. Rae Blanchard (London: Oxford University Press, 1941), 112. For contemporary criticism of these entertainments, see Emmett L. Avery, "The Defense and Criticism of Pantomimic Entertainments in the Eighteenth Century," *ELH* 5 (1938): 127–45.

20. Paul Sawyer, "John Rich's Contribution to the Eighteenth-Century London Stage," in *Essays on the Eighteenth-Century English Stage*, ed. Kenneth Richards and Peter Thomson (London: Methuen, 1972), 97.

21. "The Causes of the Decay and Defects of Dramatick Poetry, and of the Degeneracy of the Publick Taste" (1725), Dennis, *Works*, 2:278.

22. Mitchell, "Command Performances During the Reign of George I."

23. Milhous and Hume provide a helpful chart for the shifts in London theater management and offerings from 1705–1715 in *Vice Chamberlain Coke's Theatrical Papers*, xix-xx.

24. Farquhar, "A *Prologue* on the propos'd Union of the two Houses," (1701–2), Danchin, *The Prologues and Epilogues of the Restoration 1660–1700*, 1:43–44.

25. Kevin Pry, "Theatrical Competition and the Rise of the Afterpiece Tradition 1700–1724," *Theatre Notebook* 36 (1982): 21–27. Richard Bevis point out the role of competition in the development of the afterpiece in his introduction to *Eighteenth-Century Drama: Afterpieces* (London: Oxford University Press, 1970). For a history of the evolution of the afterpiece, see Philip K. Jason, "The Afterpiece: Authors and Incentives," *Restoration and Eighteenth-Century Theatre Research* 12 (1973): 1–13 and "The

Afterpiece: Origins and Early Development," *Restoration and Eighteenth-Century Theatre Research* series 2, 1 (1986): 53–63; Leo Hughes, "Afterpieces: Or, That's Entertainment," in George Winchester Stone, Jr., ed., *The Stage and the Page: London's "Whole Show" in the Eighteenth-Century Theatre* (Berkeley: University of California Press, 1981), 55–70.

26. Sawyer calls Rich "an afterpiece-man" because of his penchant for this form in pantomimes, coronations, and ballad opera. "John Rich's Contribution to the Eighteenth-Century London Stage," 93.

27. *The London Stage*, 2:377. Richard Steele's Sensorium project created a similar variety for private audiences. Steele planned a series of evenings in the great room in York Buildings, comprised of poetry, music, lectures, scientific experiments, and artwork. A prologue to the evening's events from 1715 captures the variety of Steele's event: "To please you here shall different ages strive, / New Arts shall flourish, and the Old revive." Steele's *Town Talk*, no. 7 (27 January 1715–16).

28. *The Diary of Dudley Ryder 1715–1716*, 241. Ryder specifically refers to Bullock's *The Cobler of Preston* afterpiece.

29. These afterpieces have been largely ignored in performance histories of Shakespeare's plays. Tori Haring-Smith sums up the overall critical opinion when she asserts that versions of *The Taming of the Shrew* in the Restoration and eighteenth century "have remarkably little to do with Shakespeare." *From Farce to Metadrama*, 9. In the Oxford edition of *The Taming of the Shrew* (Oxford: Clarendon, 1982), H. J. Oliver concludes that "neither of the plays adds anything to our understanding of Shakespeare" (67). In her edition of *The Taming of the Shrew* (Cambridge: Cambridge University Press, 1984), Ann Thompson does not mention either version of *The Cobler of Preston*, and neither does Sylvan Barnet in his performance history of *The Taming of the Shrew* (ed. Robert Heilman [New York: Penguin Books, 1966], 213–23.) Although they pay close attention to the Sly material in their discussion of *A Shrew* and *The Shrew*, Graham Holderness and Bryan Loughrey omit *The Cobler of Preston* in their discussion of the stage history of the *Shrew* plays. *The Taming of A Shrew* (Hemel Hempstead: Harvester Wheatsheaf, 1992). Scholars have treated Leveridge's afterpiece in the same way as the two *Cobler of Preston* adaptations. In his edition of *A Midsummer Night's Dream* (Cambridge: Cambridge University Press, 1984), R. A. Foakes gives no mention of Leveridge's *Pyramus and Thisbe* in his section "The Play on the Stage," though he does state generally that various "operatic adaptations of the play, or parts of it, were staged in the eighteenth century" (13).

30. The climate seems to have been different for Shakespeare as a writer of tragedy. Nicholas Rowe's *The Tragedy of Jane Shore. Written in Imitation of Shakespear's Style* (1714) suggests that Shakespeare had a higher reputation as a tragic writer. The prologue similarly extols Shakespeare:

> In such an Age, Immortal Shakespeare wrote,
> By no quaint Rules, nor hampering Criticks taught;
> With rough, majestick Force he mov'd the Heart,
> And Strength, and Nature made amends for Art.
> Our humble Author does his Steps pursue,
> He owns he had the mighty Bard in View;
> And in these Scenes has made it more his Care
> To rouse the Passions, than to charm the Ear.

31. *A New Rehearsal, or Bays the Younger* (London, 1714), 40. This dialogue was published anonymously, but has been attributed to Charles Gildon.

32. Jason remarks that "the production of afterpieces fell more and more into the

hands of theatre professionals" as opportunities to showcase their acting skills. "The Afterpiece: Authors and Incentives," 3.

33. Preface to *The Cobler of Preston* (London, 1716), viii. *The Successful Pyrate* was adapted from Lodowick Carlell's *Arviragus and Philicia*, *The Victim* derives from Jean Racine's *Iphigénie*, *The Cobler of Preston* is taken from Shakespeare's *The Taming of the Shrew*, *The Sultaness* is adapted from Racine's *Bajazet*, *The Masquerade* derives from Molière's *Dom Garcie* and Shirley's *The Lady of Pleasure*, *Love in a Forest* is adapted from Shakespeare's *As You Like It* with additions from *Richard II*, *Much Ado About Nothing*, *Twelfth Night*, *Love's Labour's Lost*, and *A Midsummer Night's Dream*; *The Village Opera* is based on Florent Dancourt's *Le Galant jourdinier* and Alain-René Lesage's *Crispin rival de son maître*; *Medæa* derives from classical sources; *The Ephesian Matron* is probably from Louis Fuzélier's *La Matron d'Ephese*. *The Force of Friendship*, *Love in a Chest*, *The Generous Husband*, *The Wife's Relief*, *The Country Lasses*, *The Female Fortune-Teller*, and *Caelia* do not have identified sources. See William J. Burling, "Charles Johnson." *Dictionary of Literary Biography*, vol. 84, ed. Paula R. Backscheider (Detroit: Gale Research, 1989). Although *Love in a Chest* and *The Force of Friendship* have echoes from Shakespearian plays, neither uses Shakespeare as a direct source. See Edward Niles Hooker, "Charles Johnson's *The Force of Friendship* and *Love in a Chest*: A Note on Tragicomedy and Licensing in 1710," *Studies in Philology*, 34 (1937): 407–11.

34. *Characters of the Times; or, an Impartial Account of the Writings, Characters, Education, &c. of several Noblemen and Gentlemen, libell'd in a preface to a late Miscellany Publish'd by P___PE and S_____FT*, Reprinted in *Popeiana* (New York and London: Garland Press, 1975), 7:19.

35. Appropriately, Johnson opened his own tavern in Covent Garden after retiring from the stage.

36. Christopher Bullock, *Woman Is a Riddle* (1716), 3. John Loftis has detailed the influence of politics on theaters in this period in *The Politics of Drama in Augustan England* (Oxford: Clarendon, 1963), 63–93.

37. For example, the preface to Johnson's *Tragedy of Medæa* (1731) attacks critics who "cabal together before-hand, they meet over their Coffee, and deliberately resolve to assassinate the future Piece, without having read or seen it, if the Author does not happen to be of their Faction." Johnson again turns to Shakespeare for guidance: "Now I will venture to say that if half a Score only of these ingenious Criticks had attended the dramatical Performances of *Shakespeare*, when they first appeared, in the Manner, and with the same Candor and Humanity, with which they prosecuted *Medæa*, his Works must have sunk under their Prejudice; and the World would have been rob'd, by a few malevolent and ignorant half Wits, of the Labours of that inimitable and immortal Genius. And this I only mention to shew how impossible it is that any, even the best dramatick Entertainment, should live under such Treatment." For further discussion of the practice of cabals, see Leo Hughes, *The Drama's Patrons: A Study of the Eighteenth-Century London Audience*, 54–55.

38. Dobson, *The Making of the National Poet*.

39. Other cobbler figures occur in Interregnum literature. See Charles Read Baskervill, *The Elizabethan Jig and Related Song Drama* (1929; reprint, New York: Dover Publications, 1965), 324. "The Cobbler's Jig" first appeared in the seventh edition of *The Dancing Master* (1686). A. E. H. Swaen, "The Cobbler's Jig," *Shakespeare Jahrbuch* 46 (1910): 122–24. Chappell records that cobblers were known for their singing ability. *Popular Music of Olden Time; A Collection of Ancient Songs, Ballads, and Dance Tunes, Illustrative of the National Music of England* (London: Cramer, Beale, and Chappell, 1859), 1:98. Another use of the cobbler material occurs in the 1716 *New and Curious School of Theatrical Dancing*, ed. Cyril W. Beaumont (New York: Dance Horizons, 1966), where Grego-

rio Lambranzi cites two dances to be performed by cobblers. Although these dances were performed on the continent, Emmett L. Avery suggests that they may have been performed in England. "Dancing and Pantomime on the English Stage, 1700–1737," *Studies in Philology* 31 (1934): 424.

40. Roger North remarks "So at all the Tory Healths, as they were called, the Cry was reared of *Huzza*! Which, at great and solemn Feasts, made no little Noise, and gave Advantage to the *Whigs*, that liked not such Music, to charge the *Tories* with Brutality and Extravagance." *Examen: or, An Enquiry into the Credit and Veracity of a Pretended Complete History* (London, 1740), 617. "A Congratulatory Poem on the Whigs' Entertainment" (c. 1682) describes a Tory extremist, "No northern healths would with *huzzas* be crowned, / No loyal *dammes* therre would rend the ground." *Poems on Affairs of State* 3:177.

41. See Anthony Fletcher, *Reform in the Provinces: The Government of Stuart England* (New Haven: Yale University Press, 1986), 229–52; Peter Clark, "The Alehouse and the Alternative Society," in *Puritans and Revolutionaries*, ed. Donald Pennington and Keith Thomas (Oxford: Clarendon, 1978), 47–72, and *The English Alehouse: A Social History, 1200–1830* (London: Longman, 1983). Clark points out that during the Civil War, "local authorities were anxious to prevent alehouses becoming social and political flashpoints in the critical economic conditions of the late 1640s . . . Their reports to London demonstrate that action against alehouses was a high priority, partly because of the fear that they were hidey-holes of royalist traitors" (177).

42. The doctrine of nonresistance was often seen as a smokescreen for Jacobitism, thus the reference to "sham Pretenses of Religion." See *Poems on Affairs of State* 7:408. Steven N. Zwicker remarks that "Passive obedience was a banner that flew high over the camp of nonjurors and Jacobites; it was an idiom of considerable moral capital and authority." *Lines of Authority: Politics and Literary Culture 1649–1689* (Ithaca: Cornell University Press, 1993), 177. See also J. P. Kenyon, *Revolution Principles: The Politics of Party, 1689–1720* (Cambridge: Cambridge University Press, 1977), 61–101. Passive obedience, or nonresistance, was also associated with belief in Divine Right, most vocally supported by High Churchman Henry Sacheverell who denounced rebellion with the power of the church. Belief in divine right brought suspicions of Jacobitism. See *Poems on Affairs of State* 7:349–50, 408. Benjamin Hoadly avows that for Jacobites "*Non-resistance*" means "to damn the *Revolution.*" *The Jacobite's Hopes Reviv'd by our Late Tumults and Addresses* (1710), 8–9. Sly's speech mocks these ideas, in his insistence on abolishing any government.

43. Genest, *Some Account*, 2:576; Leo Hughes and Arthur H. Scouten, *Ten English Farces* (Austin: University of Texas Press, 1948), 146.

44. Hewson's name appears on two broadsheets that list those responsible for the trial and execution of Charles I, *The Black Remembrancer* (1661) and *The Great Memorial* (1660). For discussion of these documents, see Jonathan Sawday, "Re-Writing a Revolution: History, Symbol, and Text in the Restoration," *The Seventeenth Century* 7 (1992): 171–99.

45. Other texts connected the Civil War with the Popish Plot and Exclusion Crisis. See, for example, "A Loyal Satire Against Whiggism" (1682), *Poems on Affairs of State* 3:358–65. The narrator cautions against "The hellish principles of forty-one" and "another bloody massacre" (lines 124, 134). Another poem from 1682, "Satire, or Song" warns of a "forty-one again." *Poems on Affairs of State* 3:383–86, line 10. Shadwell's poem "The Protestant Satire" (1684) tells of "the dang'rous tracks of Forty-one," see *Poems on Affairs of State* 3:511–40, line 341.

46. This phrase comes from an incident involving the fourth-century painter Apelles. When a cobbler criticized the appearance of shoes in a painting by Apelles, Apelles

replied with this motto. Leo Hughes discusses this portrait in "Doggett Dancing the Cheshire Round?" *Theatre Notebook* 7 (1952–3): 12–14.

47. This song "The Bloody Bed-roll, or Treason displayed in its Colours" appears in the collection *The Rump*, part I (1662), 347–48. Hewson's pride and his one-eyed appearance are also prominent features in the song "The Gang or the Nine Worthies and Champions, Lambert, &c.," in *The Rump*, part II, (1662), 106.

48. Richard Bevis notes the popularity of farce in this period in his introduction to *Eighteenth-Century Drama: Afterpieces*, ix–xii.

49. John Genest remarks that Johnson "has contrived very badly in making the trick be played on Sly a second time—more especially as Sly is sober, when the servants find him in his stall." *Some Account*, 2:576. Tori Haring-Smith also criticizes Johnson for making Sly go through the transformation of cobbler to Lord twice, "Merely repeating the plot in this way does not improve it." *From Farce to Metadrama*, 12.

50. Baskervill notes that the ballad "seems to be at least early enough to reflect the resurgence of Catholic hopes in the reign of James II. It was probably written before 1682, for Hickes's *Grammatical Drollery* of that year contains a song . . . that offers a coarse parallel" (*The Elizabethan Jig*, 65 n. 1).

51. Sly's cry "Down with the Rump" was typical of Jacobites; see Paul Klebér Monod, *Jacobitism and the English People, 1688–1788* (Cambridge: Cambridge University Press, 1989), 52–53.

52. Editions were printed in Dublin in 1725 and 1767, and three editions were printed in London in 1775, 1817, and 1838 as part of *Cumberland's British Theatre*.

53. Bullock apparently had little regard for issues of authorship; according to Samuel Johnson, Bullock's play *Woman Is a Riddle* was written by Savage, but Bullock rewrote it, passed it off as his own, and "allowed the unhappy author no part of the profit." "Savage," in *Lives of the English Poets*, ed. George Birkbeck Hill (Oxford: Clarendon, 1905), 2:330.

54. Sawyer discusses Bullock's term as manager and the competitive theatrical environment in "John Rich's Contribution to the Eighteenth-Century London Stage," 88–89.

55. The story is recounted in George Akerby, *The Life of Mr. James Spiller, the Late Famous Comedian* (London, 1729), and in Samuel Ireland, *Graphic Illustrations of Hogarth* (London, 1794). Hughes and Scouten are skeptical of this story, but it fits with other activities of Spiller and Bullock (*Ten English Farces*, 147). Loftis takes the story seriously, admitting the possibility for exaggeration. See *The Politics of Drama*, 69–70.

56. Akerby, *The Life of Mr. James Spiller*, 22–23.

57. In his *Graphic Illustrations of Hogarth*, Ireland relates a version of the same story that he probably derived from Akerby's *Life*: "SPILLER was not only the rival of Pinkethman; but, we are told, he once picked his pocket, when asleep, at the Gun Tavern Billingsgate, of his part, the character of the cobler, written for him by Johnson, and which he was then studying." Ireland adds that "With this treasure Spiller hastened to his friend Bullock, the comedian, and Manager of Lincoln's Inn Fields theatre; who was likewise an author. Bullock received him graciously, and without scruple applied the theft to his own use, by preparing a piece on the same subject, called, the Cobler of Preston; and this he was enabled to produce a fortnight before the other house could prepare their drama for the stage" (1:64–65).

58. *The Cobler of Preston* was not the only play that came between Johnson and Bullock. Genest remarks that in the farce *The Slip*, Bullock "takes the robbery from Middleton, as Charles Johnson does in the Country Lasses, and retains that part of the original Comedy, about the pretended players, which Johnson omits . . . it does not appear whether C. Bullock was, or was not, aware of Johnson's play—but he certainly played him a slippery trick as to the Cobler of Preston." *Some Account*, 2:566–67.

59. Drury Lane Theatre was Hanoverian and anti-Jacobite, while Lincoln's Inn was a Tory theater with possible pro-Jacobite leanings. See Loftis, *The Politics of Drama*, 63–65.

60. Akerby, *The Life of Mr. James Spiller*, 24–25.

61. Other writers eschewed politics; John Dennis deliberately chose to align himself with neither Whigs or Tories and preferred to remain neutral; he wrote in his preface to *Liberty Asserted* (1704) that "to declare for the Publick against Parties is to make no Friends" (*Works*, 1:322).

62. Hughes, *The Drama's Patrons*, 57.

63. Leo Hughes notes that the term farce "was used more than once by bitter rivals as a means of dismissing with a scornful gesture the literary works of an enemy." See "The Early Career of Farce in the Theatrical Vocabulary," *University of Texas Studies in English* 20 (1940): 89.

64. Dobson notes Bullock's "desire to embarrass Johnson" (*The Making of the National Poet*, 111). See also Loftis, *The Politics of Drama*, 71.

65. Leo Hughes, *A Century of English Farce* (Princeton: Princeton University Press, 1956), 186.

66. Akerby, *The Life of Mr. James Spiller*, 7; Ireland, *Graphic Illustrations of Hogarth*, 1:67.

67. Akerby, *The Life of Mr. James Spiller*, 47.

68. Coincidentally, Hewson, the cobbler who provided a source for Johnson's afterpiece, also had only one eye.

69. Ireland, *Graphic Illustrations of Hogarth*, 1:71. Ireland refers to an engraved benefit ticket that featured Spiller and his wife "both in a state of intoxication," but W. J. Lawrence argues that "Ireland errs very flagrantly in assuming that the features of this benefit ticket afford another illustration of Spiller's audacious habit of flaunting his vices before the public. So far from being depicted in their private capacities, the actor and actress were here represented in the parts played by them in *The Cobler of Preston*." "A Player-Friend of Hogarth," *The Elizabethan Playhouse* (Stratford: Shakespeare Head Press, 1913), 218. However, the only surviving benefit ticket of Spiller's is the one engraved by Hogarth, which only shows Spiller, not apparently intoxicated, but handing out tickets for a benefit. Lawrence gives no reference for this mysterious benefit ticket.

70. *Biographical Dictionary*, 7:26–27.

71. *The Taming of the Shrew* 1.1.62–65.

72. Baskervill traces the domestic brawl as dramatic material to the eighteenth century (*The Elizabethan Jig*, 201–205).

73. Rollins reports that this ballad was entered into the Stationers' Register on 1 March 1675, but Francis Oscar Mann asserts that it was printed in Thomas Deloney's *The Garland of Good Will* of 1631, and "the earliest known copy of this ballad is that added to the 1607 edition of *Strange Histories*." See Hyder E. Rollins, *An Analytical Index to the Ballad Entries (1557–1709) in the Register of the Company of Stationers of London* (Chapel Hill: University of North Carolina Press, 1924), 159, and Francis Oscar Mann, ed., *The Works of Thomas Deloney* (Oxford: Clarendon, 1912), 563. In 1708, "A New Ballad, To the Tune of Fair Rosamund" appeared, possibly by Arthur Mainwaring. See *Poems on Affairs of State*, 7:306–16. Frank Ellis points out that Deloney's ballad "was set to the tune of *Flying Fame*, which is probably an earlier name for the famous tune of *Chevy Chase*. Deloney's ballad, in its turn, supplied a new name for the old tune, and several ballads in the seventeenth and eighteenth centuries . . . call for the tune of *Fair Rosamund*" (*Poems on Affairs of State*, 7:307). See also Claude M. Simpson, *The British Broadside Ballad and Its Music* (New Brunswick: Rutgers University Press, 1966), 96–99; Thomas Wright, ed., *Political Ballads: Published in England During the Commonwealth* (Lon-

don: Percy Society, 1841), 1:65, for a song with Hewson; W. Walker Wilkins, *Political Ballads of the Seventeenth and Eighteenth Centuries* (London, 1860); J. O. Halliwell, *A Catalogue of An Unique Collection of Ancient English Broadside Ballads* (London: Chiswick Press, 1856); Hyder Rollins, *Cavalier and Puritan: Ballads and Broadsides Illustrating the Period of the Great Rebellion 1640–1660* (New York: New York University Press, 1923).

74. This pastoral lyric appeared frequently in the eighteenth century, and was used earlier by Davenant in *The Rivals* (1668). See Baskervill, *The Elizabethan Jig*, 210, and Chappell, *Popular Music of Olden Time*, 2:525–30, for the history of this ballad.

75. "Since Times are so Bad," a duet, appeared in Durfey's *The Comical History of Don Quixote*, part II (1694).

76. Millers, Puritans, and cuckoldry were well-worn subjects in jigs and ballad literature. The interpolated farcical story in Bullock's afterpiece also resembles the seventeenth-century jig "Singing Simpkin," with its concerns of adulterous wives deceiving their husbands with hidden lovers. Baskervill records that "the earliest extant text of 'Singing Simpkin' in English is that in Robert Cox's *Actaeon and Diana*, published near the middle of the seventeenth century. Cox could not have written the jig nor even recast it radically, for the version in *Engelische Comedien und Tragedien* of 1620 corresponds usually line for line to Cox's version" (*The Elizabethan Jig*, 235; see also 278–81).

77. Bevis notes that this is characteristic of the afterpiece: "the art of the afterpiece is stereotypic . . . A very few plots and character-types serve as the constants in an equation whose variables are the particular situations and incidents . . . which the individual playwright invents." *Eighteenth-Century Drama: Afterpieces*, xiii.

78. Since the Exclusion Crisis, it was an act of loyalty to the King to get drunk on English Ale. See David Allen, "Political Clubs in Restoration London," *The Historical Journal* 19 (1976): 570.

79. In this farce by Bullock, the character of Mr. Tagg (played by Pack), expresses the impossibility of taming his wife: "Well, if ever I get home again, I'll make an Oath never to watch my Wife more, let her do what she will, go where she will, with whom she will: For I find she will have her Will, let me say or do what I will" (38).

80. Christopher Bullock, *The Cobler of Preston* (1716), vii.

81. Charles Johnson's play does not include any prefatory material besides the prologue; his debt to Shakespeare remains unacknowledged, even on the title page. Dobson has argued that Johnson "wishes actively to suppress this piece of information in the interests of Shakespeare's authorial honour" (*The Making of the National Poet*, 122). However, Johnson also relies (without acknowledgment) on other sources for material in his adaptation, such as Thomas Jevon's *The Devil of a Wife*. Johnson's omission of Shakespeare should be seen within the context of his failure to indicate *any* of his sources.

82. *The Devil to Pay* was first presented in 1731; Fiske calls it "the second most successful ballad opera of the century" (*English Theatre Music in the Eighteenth Century*, 112).

83. Unfortunately, the music for Worsdale's piece is lost, but the printed play lists twenty-three songs. Roger Fiske details the "boom in ballad operas" in the 1730s in *English Theatre Music in the Eighteenth Century*, 103–14. Hume discusses the popularity of farcical ballad opera afterpieces in *Henry Fielding and the London Theatre, 1728–1737* (Oxford: Clarendon, 1988), 109–10.

84. Neighbarger points out that Leveridge set "When Sawny First Did Woe Me" for a 1716 performance of Lacy's *Sauny the Scott* at Lincoln's Inn Fields. *An Outward Show: Music for Shakespeare on the London Stage, 1660–1830*, 269.

85. Baldwin and Wilson suggest that his coffeehouse provided Leveridge with "an alternative source of income should his theatre company collapse." "Richard Leveridge, 1670–1758," *The Musical Times* 111 (1970): 893. Pack later ran a tavern near the Hay-

market to "retrieve his circumstances as happily as his humorous Friend Dick Leveridge has done" (*Weekly Journal or Saturday's Post* 11 August 1722).

86. Gildon, *The Life of Mr. Thomas Betterton*, 156–57.

87. *The Daily Advertiser* 26 October 1751. The entry for Leveridge in the *New Grove Dictionary of Music and Musicians*, ed. Stanley Sadie (London: Macmillan, 1980), 10:701–702 provides background for Leveridge. Olive Baldwin and Thelma Wilson supply details of Leveridge's career in "Richard Leveridge, 1670–1758." His career was revived in the 1720s with pantomimes under Rich.

88. Gay's afterpiece shows traces of Shakespeare; the title alone calls to mind Polonius's speech in 2.2. of *Hamlet* describing the actors, and the play-within-a-play structure resembles *A Midsummer Night's Dream*, to which Gay refers in his preface.

89. For further discussion on Leveridge's play as a burlesque, see Peter Elfed Lewis, "Richard Leveridge's *The Comick Masque of Pyramus and Thisbe*," *Restoration and Eighteenth-Century Theatre Research* 15 (1976): 33–41.

90. In the third act of *The Prophetess* (1690), the scene is "a Room, Chairs in it, the Hangings and Figures Grotesk." Later, "the Figures come out of the Hangings and Dance: And Figures exactly the same appear in their places: When they have danc'd a while, they go to sit on the Chairs, they slip from 'em, and after joyn in the Dance with 'em" (36). In the Fourth act, "the Prophetess waves her wand, the Termes leap from their Pedestalls, the Building falls, and the Termes and Cupola are turn'd into a Dance of Butterflies" (47).

91. The entry for Leveridge in the *Biographical Dictionary* summarizes his plight: "English opera after the Italian manner was something he evidently could manage well enough, but with the growing number of imported singers and their ability to offer operas in Italian, Leveridge's career as a serious opera singer withered" (9:264–65).

92. At the 11 April 1716 opening of *Pyramus and Thisbe*, Leveridge advertised, "The Books of the Masque are just printed for W. Mears . . . and sold by him, and at Mr Leveridge's in Tavistock-street" (*The London Stage*, 2:397).

93. As Lewis points out, *Pyramus and Thisbe* is "primarily a dramatic burlesque; the fact that it is also a Shakespearean adaptation is of secondary importance." "Richard Leveridge's *The Comick Masque of Pyramus and Thisbe*," 33.

94. Baskervill notes that in *The Island Princess*, Leveridge and Pack sang a dialogue between a clown and his wife that "was popular enough to be advertised by title in 1710 as an interact piece at Haymarket by Doggett and Leveridge, with *The Old Bachelor* on 6 July, and with *Hamlet* on 26 July. Motteux had introduced a somewhat similar dialogue into his *Love's a Jest* of 1696 (Act II)" (*The Elizabethan Jig*, 174).

95. Lewis points out that Leveridge's Lion, while based on Shakespeare's character, "is aimed specifically at the lion in Mancini's opera, *Hydaspes*, made notorious by Addison's ridicule in *The Spectator* No. 13 (Thursday, 15 March, 1711)." "Richard Leveridge's *The Comick Masque of Pyramus and Thisbe*" (38).

96. Pyramus ends the masque with some closing lines taken partly from Feste's final song in *Twelfth Night* with possible resonances from Rosalind's epilogue to *As You Like It*:

> Say, Ladies—I've a Boon to ask,
> That you wou'd smile—and then,
> Bow round to all the Gentlemen,
> And beg that they too wou'd consent,
> To like this little Amusement;
> And in return, our Thanks we'll pay
> With Strife to please you Day by Day,
> And wish all you in Love—may be,
> As I to *Thisbe*—she to me. (15)

97. *The London Stage* lists performances on 10, 12, and 13 March 1716 (2:392). Although Genest lists *Everybody Mistaken* as "Never acted," he remarks that "this piece is said to have been in 3 acts—it is supposed not to have been printed—the Masque of Presumptuous Love seems to have been introduced in it—this contemptible masque is on the story of Ixion and Juno—it consists of airs and recitative—and was acted 3 times" (*Some Account*, 2:585).

98. *Dictionary of National Biography*, 3:51.

99. Marsden's chapter, "The Beginnings of Shakespeare Criticism," in *The Re-Imagined Text* discusses the proliferation of critical works on Shakespeare in the early eighteenth century.

CHAPTER 5. EARLY GEORGIAN POLITICS AND SHAKESPEARE

1. Paul Sawyer points out that although *The Merry Wives of Windsor* "almost triples the frequency of any other Shakespearean play" in the 1720s, Shakespeare's plays were not very popular without accoutrements of pantomime and other forms of entertainment. "The Popularity of Shakespeare's Plays, 1720–21 through 1732–33," *Shakespeare Quarterly* 29 (1978): 427–30. He provides an excellent discussion of entertainments that drew audiences in this period in "The Popularity of Various Types of Entertainment at Lincoln's Inn Fields and Covent Garden Theatres, 1720–1733," *Theatre Notebook* 24 (1970): 154–63. See also Arthur H. Scouten, "Shakespeare's Plays in the Theatrical Repertory When Garrick Came to London," *University of Texas Studies in English* (1944): 257–68, and "The Increase in Popularity of Shakespeare's Plays in the Eighteenth Century: A *Caveat* for Interpreters of Stage History," *Shakespeare Quarterly* 7 (1956): 189–202.

2. From 1700, *Richard II* was performed only as Lewis Theobald's adaptation in 1719, 1720, and 1721, but Theobald does not include any of the speeches from *Richard II* that Johnson uses. *A Midsummer Night's Dream* was performed only as *The Fairy-Queen* and as Richard Leveridge's *Pyramus and Thisbe* in 1716 and 1717. *Much Ado* was performed in its original version only three times in 1721. *Twelfth Night* was seen only as William Burnaby's *Love Betray'd* in 1703 and 1705. *Love's Labour's Lost* and *As You Like It* were not performed at all. With the exception perhaps of Theobald's *Richard II*, none of these plays was a regular offering in the London theaters in this period.

3. *The Complete Works of Sir John Vanbrugh*, ed. Geoffrey Webb (London: Nonesuch Press, 1928), 4:146, letter from 18 June 1722.

4. Robert D. Hume notes that "neither Drury Lane nor Lincoln's Inn Fields had been particularly receptive to new plays after 1714, despite the reestablishment of competition, which historically had encouraged the staging of fresh fare." *Henry Fielding and the London Theatre 1728–1737*, 14–15.

5. Most scholarship on *Love in a Forest* has not been kind to the play. M. Maurice Shudofsky, in an otherwise appreciative article on Johnson, calls *Love in a Forest* "a miserable perversion" (157n.) and remarks that "Pot-pourris like *Love in a Forest* do not make pleasant reading, but they go far in explaining why early eighteenth-century drama rarely rises above mediocrity." "Charles Johnson and Eighteenth-Century Drama," *English Literary History*, 10 (1943): 131–58; 134. Although Edith Holding claims to look at "the literary, political, and theatrical context" surrounding *Love in a Forest*, she does not make any connections with the Black Act of 1723 and anti-Jacobitism. See "*As You Like It* Adapted: Charles Johnson's *Love in a Forest*," *Shakespeare Survey* 32 (1979): 38.

6. Monod, *Jacobitism*, 11.

7. See P. B. Munsche, *Gentlemen and Poachers: The English Game Laws 1671–1831*

(Cambridge: Cambridge University Press, 1981), 3, 5. Munsche points out that according to the Game Act of 1605, deer or rabbit hunters had to have an income of at least £40 from land, or £200 worth of goods. Munsche also defines "game" as "hares, partridges, pheasants and moor fowl" because "only these animals were accorded protection under what eighteenth-century Englishmen called the game laws."

8. *The Weekly Journal: or, British Gazetteer* for 26 January carried the same anecdote.

9. E. P. Thompson, *Whigs and Hunters: The Origin of the Black Act* (New York: Pantheon Books, 1975), 190–91.

10. See Pat Rogers, "The Waltham Blacks and the Black Act," *The Historical Journal*, 18 (1974): 465–86.

11. Monod, *Jacobitism*, 116.

12. Thompson, *Whigs and Hunters*, 197.

13. Eveline Cruickshanks and Howard Erskine-Hill, "The Waltham Black Act and Jacobitism," *Journal of British Studies*, 24 (1985): 358–65.

14. Ibid., 365.

15. This broadside appears in John Broad, "Whigs and Deer-Stealers in Other Guises: A Return to the Origins of the Black Act," *Past and Present*, 119 (1988): 56–72, at 69–70.

16. Thompson, *Whigs and Hunters*, 191; Broad, "Whigs and Deer-Stealers," 58.

17. Thompson, *Whigs and Hunters*, 49.

18. Loftis, *The Politics of Drama*, 63–65.

19. Earlier in his career, Johnson had links to prominent Whigs concerned with maintaining the forests. Johnson dedicated his play *The Country Lasses* (1715) to Thomas Pelham-Holles, Earl of Clare, who was appointed the steward of Sherwood Forest and Folewood Park in 1714 by George I. Sarah Churchill, Duchess of Marlborough and ranger of Windsor Great and Little Parks, was also a patron of Johnson's (his 1714 play *The Victim* was dedicated to her).

20. Loftis, *The Politics of Drama*, 71 n.1. Loftis points out that "the trick of presenting plays with politically suggestive titles was used more than once by Lincoln's Inn Fields, whose dramatists might deplore the intrusion of party into drama but were none the less aware of their audiences' preferences," such as Benjamin Griffin's suggestively titled play *Whig and Tory* (1720), which was targeted "to arouse the expectation of party clamour that the author had no intention of satisfying."

21. Johnson's epigraph comes from Virgil's sixth eclogue, and was also used by Ben Jonson as the epigraph for the unfinished *The Sad Shepherd: or, a Tale of Robin-Hood*.

22. Johnson's former patron Sarah, Duchess of Marlborough experienced a similar situation in Windsor Forest. See Thompson, *Whigs and Hunters*, 41.

23. Genest remarked that giving Jaques this speech was "an improvement which is still retained on the stage." *Some Account*, 3:101.

24. Loftis, *Politics of Drama*, 72.

25. Neighbarger points out that Henry Carey's setting of this song survives as "The Hunstman's Song" in two prints and was performed on its own on 12 May 1724. *An Outward Show: Music for Shakespeare on the London Stage, 1660–1830*, 93.

26. For further discussion of the political issues behind town and country, see Loftis, *The Politics of Drama*, 116.

27. *A Comparison Between the Two Stages*, 106.

28. *Biographical Dictionary*, 12:267.

29. The *Daily Post* for 15 January advertised *Love in a Forest* "For the Benefit of the Author, a Free-Mason." Johnson's dedication is reprinted in *Early Masonic Pamphlets*, ed. Douglas Knoop, Gwilym P. Jones, and Douglas Hamer (Manchester, 1945).

30. See Henry William Pedicord, "White Gloves at Five: Fraternal Patronage of

London Theatres in the Eighteenth Century," *Philological Quarterly* 45 (1966): 270–88; "Masonic Theatre Pieces in London 1730–1780," *Theatre Survey* 25 (1984): 153–66; and "George Lillo and 'Speculative Masonry,'" *Philological Quarterly* 53 (1974): 401–12.

31. Monod, *Jacobitism*, 300, 305. Monod points out that the story of Hiram Abiff, the central Masonic mystery, can be read allegorically as endorsing the return of the Stuarts from exile.

32. T. O. Haunch, "The Formation: 1717 to 1751," in A. S. Frere, ed., *Grand Lodge 1717-1967* (Oxford, 1967), 47–91. Paul Monod's work provides background for this section on Jacobites and Freemasons.

33. Paul Monod, "The Politics of Matrimony: Jacobitism and Marriage in Eighteenth-Century England," in *The Jacobite Challenge*, ed. Eveline Cruickshanks and Jeremy Black (Edinburgh, 1988), 30; Eveline Cruickshanks, "Lord North, Christopher Layer and the Atterbury Plot: 1720–23," in *The Jacobite Challenge*, 99; Monod, *Jacobitism*, 29.

34. Monod, *Jacobitism*, 301.

35. Holding, "*As You Like It* Adapted," 43.

36. See Margaret Jacob, *The Radical Enlightenment: Pantheists, Freemasons and Republicans* (London: George Allen & Unwin, 1981). The Forum in *Eighteenth-Century Studies* 33 (2000) includes a discussion of scholarship on freemasons, as does Steven C. Bullock's "Initiating the Enlightenment?: Recent Scholarship on European Freemasonry," *Eighteenth-Century Life* 20 (1996): 80–92.

37. *The London Stage* lists performances for 9, 10, 11, 12, 14, and 15 January. According to a statement in *The British Journal* for 5 January 1723, *Love in a Forest* was to have premiered on 2 January, but was delayed because of the illness of Mrs. Younger: "Mr. *Johnson*'s new Play, alter'd from Mr. *Shakespear*'s, *As you like it*, was not play'd at the Old House on *Wednesday*, as intended, by Reason of Mrs. *Younger*'s Indisposition, who was to bear a principal Part in that Performance." *The Daily Journal* of 1 January carries a similar advertisement. The only cast list is printed with the first edition of *Love in a Forest*, and does not include Mrs. Younger. Elizabeth Younger played such parts as Margery Pinchwife in Wycherley's *The Country Wife*, Sylvia in Farquhar's *The Recruiting Officer*, and Desdemona in *Othello*. There are only four parts for women in Johnson's play: Rosalind, Celia, Hymen, and Thisby. Mrs. Younger probably was to play either Rosalind or Celia, the two main parts for women.

38. *The London Stage*, 2:704.

39. This was advertised in the 19–22 January, 22–24 January, and 24–26 January issues. *The British Journal* carried advertisements for the printed play in the 26 January, 2 February, and 9 February issues. *The Daily Post* advertised the printed edition 16, 19, 21, 22, and 23 January. *The Daily Journal* advertises the printed play 22–26 January.

40. Sawyer, "The Popularity of Shakespeare's Plays," 427–30.

41. Aaron Hill's adaptation of *Henry V* from the same year (1723) also reveals a similar use of Shakespeare for political purposes. In the preface, Hill encourages his audience to support his play, and triumph over French entertainments, just as Henry V was able to defeat the French.

Chapter 6. Shakespearian Comedy Before Garrick

1. A similar movement happens later in the 1730s with the Shakespeare Ladies' Club, a group of women who promoted performances of earlier playwrights including Shakespeare. Many of the plays they requested had not been performed; their knowledge was based on reading the plays. See Katherine West Scheil, "'Rouz'd by a Wom-

an's pen': The Shakespeare Ladies' Club and Reading Habits of Early Modern Women," *Critical Survey* 12 (2000): 106–27.

2. Print culture has received a great deal of attention among recent scholars. For one of the best discussions of this topic in the eighteenth century, see Alvin Kernan, *Printing Technology, Letters & Samuel Johnson* (Princeton: Princeton University Press, 1987). Kernan points out that around the turn of the eighteenth century "printing began to affect the structure of social life at every level" (48). See also Terry Belanger, "Publishers and writers in eighteenth-century England," in Isobel Rivers, ed., *Books and their Readers in Eighteenth-Century England* (London: St. Martin's Press, 1982), 5–25. Shirley Strum Kenny remarks that print "allowed the theatre to be sold for home consumption in many forms." "Theatre, Related Arts, and the Profit Motive: An Overview," in *British Theatre and the Other Arts, 1660–1800*, 17.

3. Eighteenth-century editions of Shakespeare have been discussed in depth elsewhere; see Arthur Sherbo, *The Birth of Shakespeare Studies: Commentators from Rowe (1709) to Boswell-Malone (1821)* (East Lansing, Mich.: Colleagues Press, 1986); Peter Seary, *Lewis Theobald and the Editing of Shakespeare* (Oxford: Clarendon, 1990); Arthur Brown, "The Great Variety of Readers," *Shakespeare Survey* 18 (1965): 11–22; R. B. McKerrow, "The Treatment of Shakespeare's Text by his Earlier Editors, 1706–1768," British Academy Shakespeare Lecture, 1933; repr. in *Studies in Shakespeare*, ed. Peter Alexander (London, 1964), 103–31; R. F. Jones, *Lewis Theobald. His Contribution to English Scholarship With Some Unpublished Letters* (New York, 1919); and the collection edited by Joanna Gondris, *Reading Readings: Essays on Shakespeare Editing in the Eighteenth Century* (Madison, N.J.: Fairleigh Dickinson University Press, 1998).

4. Brian Vickers discusses the growth of critical interest in Shakespeare in his introduction to *Shakespeare: The Critical Heritage Volume 2, 1693–1733* (London: Routledge and Kegan Paul, 1974). Marsden's *The Re-Imagined Text* provides a lengthy discussion of the growth of criticism and the shift in emphasis from stage to page. Kernan points out that in the eighteenth century, "criticism and textual scholarship were encouraged . . . by the increasing availability of different printed texts and the ideals of accuracy that print technology and the comparison of a number of texts made possible" (*Printing Technology, Letters*, 14). Julie Stone Peters remarks that Congreve's "move from work for the active stage in the seventeenth century to work on editions and on his own library in the eighteenth century parallels this shift in the idea of the drama" from performance to print. *Congreve, the Drama, and the Printed Word* (Stanford: Stanford University Press, 1990), 73–74.

5. *Critical Remarks on the Four Taking Plays of this Season*, 12; Joseph Priestly, *An Essay on a Course of Liberal Education for Civil and Active Life* (London,1765), 23. Priestly adds that "a hundredth part of the time which was formerly given to criticism and antiquity is enough, in this modernized age, to gain a man the character of a profound scholar" (23). Kernan sees the development of criticism as "a standard literary genre" as part of a "general transformation to a print culture." *Printing Technology, Letters*, 49.

6. *The Works of Mr. William Shakespear* (London, 1709), 1:xv, xvi. The most Rowe offers readers is to "observe some of those Things I have been pleas'd with in looking him over." John Butt discusses Pope's desire to thoroughly give an account of Shakespeare's merits and faults which could not be done in a brief preface. *Pope's Taste in Shakespeare* (London: Oxford University Press, 1936), 5. Butt calls Pope "the best example to be found of a cultured reader selecting passages without either deference to tradition or reaction against it" (6).

7. Pope, Preface to *The Works of Shakespear* (1725), 1:ii, xxii, xxiii. See Butt, *Pope's Taste in Shakespeare*; Seary, *Lewis Theobald and the Editing of Shakespeare*; and Peter Dixon, "Edward Bysshe and Pope's 'Shakespear,'" *Notes and Queries* 209 (1964): 292–93.

Dixon argues that "the correspondences between Pope and Bysshe do at least indicate that Pope's taste in Shakespeare was not quite the unique thing that it has sometimes been thought" (293). In "Pope's Shakespeare" (*JEGP* 63 [1964]: 191–203), Dixon concludes that "of the passages and scenes admired by Pope (there are more than 160 of them) just over half had been admired by one or more of his predecessors" (197). See also Simon Jarvis, *Scholars and Gentlemen: Shakespearian Textual Criticism and Representations of Scholarly Labour, 1725–1765* (Oxford: Clarendon, 1995), 11–12 and 43–62. Aaron Hill describes Barton Booth's acting as a type of selective process of highlighting beauties and minimizing faults: he would gloss over "with a kind of Negligence, the Improprieties in a part he acted; while on the contrary, he would dwell with Energy upon the Beauties, as if he exerted a latent Spirit, which had been kept back for such an Occasion, that he might alarm, waken, and transport, in those Places only, where the Dignity of his own good Sense could be supported with that of his Author." W. R. Chetwood, *A General History of the Stage* (1749), 94. Butt notes that Pope may have been influenced by this style (*Pope's Taste in Shakespeare*, 14).

8. For further discussion of the editing quarrels between Pope and Theobald, see Seary's thorough reevaluation of Theobald, especially Chapter 6. As Seary explains, "the most obvious difference between Theobald and Pope is that Theobald is much more consistent in his desire to reproduce what Shakespeare had written (as opposed to what, perhaps, he ought to have written)" (*Lewis Theobald and the Editing of Shakespeare*, 68). Kernan provides a helpful discussion of Pope's objection to "the inevitable consequences of print" in *Printing Technology, Letters*, 8–16.

9. "An Epistle from Mr. Pope, To Dr. Arbuthnot," in *The Poems of Alexander Pope*, ed. John Butt (London: Methuen, 1963), 603.

10. George Winchester Stone, Jr., "Shakespeare in the Periodicals, 1700–1740: A Study of the Growth of Knowledge of the Dramatist in the Eighteenth Century," part 1, *Shakespeare Quarterly* 2 (1951): 224–25.

11. Addison and Steele were not the only writers excerpting Shakespeare to illustrate concepts for imitation. In his *Censor* (2 May 1715), Theobald praises Shakespeare: "What admirable Thoughts of Morality and Instruction has he put in Lear's Mouth on the Growling of the Thunder and Flashes of Lightning." Similarly, in a letter of 11 December 1724 to William Cranstoun, James Thomson alludes to Shakespeare's *As You Like It*: "Witt and beauty this join'd would be as Shakespear has it making honey a sauce to sugar." *James Thomson (1700–1748) : Letters and Documents*, ed. Alan Dugald McKillop (Lawrence: University of Kansas Press, 1958), 2. Touchstone's line is "for honesty coupled to beauty is to have honey a sauce to sugar" (3.3.30–31). When reading *Busirus, King of Egypt*, "Corinna" noted that "this merry Speech . . . puts me in Mind of a Speech of *Owen Glendower*, in *Shakespear's Henry the Fourth*" (*Critical Remarks on the Four Taking Plays of this Season*, 60–1).

12. See Scott Black, "Social and Literary Form in the Spectator," *Eighteenth-Century Studies* 33 (1999): 21–42.

13. Poetical commonplace books and miscellanies have a long history aside from their popularity in the early eighteenth century. See Arthur E. Case, *A Bibliography of English Poetical Miscellanies, 1521–1750* (Oxford: Oxford University Press, 1935) and Sister Joan Marie Lechner, *Renaissance Concepts of the Commonplaces* (New York: Pageant Press, 1962). Shakespeare appeared in collections of quotations in the early seventeenth century, including John Bodenham's *Belvedere, or the Garden of the Muses* (1600) and Poole's *The English Parnassus* (1657). See John Munro, *The Shakspere Allusion-Book: A Collection of Allusions to Shakespeare from 1591–1700* (London: Humphrey Milford, 1932), 2:478–79. A few early commonplace books include Shakespeare. See James G. McManaway, "Excerpta quaedam per A.W. adolescentem," in T. P. Harrison, Archibald A.

Hill, Ernest C. Mossner, and James Sledd, eds., *Studies in Honor of DeWitt T. Starnes* (Austin: University of Texas Press, 1967), 117–29, and G. Blakemore Evans, "A Seventeenth-Century Reader of Shakespeare," *Review of English Studies* 21 (1945): 271–79.

14. A. Dwight Culler, "Edward Bysshe and the Poet's Handbook," *PMLA* 63 (1948): 861. Editions were printed in 1702, 1705, 1708, 1710, 1714, 1718, 1724, 1725, 1737, and 1762. The 1708 edition was a significant expansion. In *The Laws of Poetry* (1721), Bysshe's influential work is condemned as "a book too scandalously mean to name, which, by the arts of the *booksellers* concern'd, has spread, by many editions, thro' all *England*, and corrupted, or at least continu'd the corruption of the young readers and lovers of poetry" (72).

15. Culler, "Edward Bysshe and the Poet's Handbook," 864. Gildon criticized Bysshe's work in a mock-passage: "I have myself perus'd great Part of this ridiculous Author, and he had almost provok'd me into a *Writer*, to vindicate the Honour of the *Art* I admire, from the shameful Ignorance of a little *Pretender*." *The Complete Art of Poetry* 1:92.

16. The *Thesaurus Dramaticus* came out in a second and enlarged edition entitled *Beauties of the English Stage* in 1737. Thomas Jefferson used the *Thesaurus Dramaticus* for his own literary commonplace book. Douglas L. Wilson, "Thomas Jefferson's Early Notebooks," *William and Mary Quarterly* 42 (1985): 433–52.

17. Many adaptations are also included: Dryden's *All for Love*, Sedley's *Antony and Cleopatra*, Otway's *Caius Marius* (*Romeo and Juliet*), Granville's *The Jew of Venice*, Tate's *King Lear* and *The Ingratitude of a Commonwealth* (*Coriolanus*), Aaron Hill's *Henry V*, Cibber's *Richard III*, Dryden's *Troilus and Cressida*, Dryden's *The Tempest*, and Shadwell's *Timon of Athens*. Otway's *Caius Marius* and Dryden's *All for Love* have more than twice as many quotations as any of Shakespeare's original plays; stage success and authenticity have little bearing on this anthology.

18. Margreta de Grazia has traced connections between Shakespeare and public taste in "Shakespeare in Quotation Marks," in *The Appropriation of Shakespeare: Post-Renaissance Reconstructions of the Works and the Myth* (Hemel Hempstead: Harvester Wheatsheaf, 1991), 57–71, and *Shakespeare Verbatim: The Reproduction of Authenticity and the 1790 Apparatus* (Oxford: Clarendon, 1991).

19. See Alfred Jackson, "Rowe's Edition of Shakespeare," *The Library*, 4th series, 10 (1930): 455–73. Peter Dixon discusses Gildon's method in "Pope's Shakespeare," *JEGP* 63 (1964): 194–97.

20. Charles Gildon, preface to *The Complete Art of Poetry* (London, 1718).

21. Gildon's collection is a precursor to William Dodd's 1752 *The Beauties of Shakespear*, which remained popular through the nineteenth century. See Jonathan Bate, *Shakespeare and the English Romantic Imagination* (Oxford: Clarendon, 1989), 30, 200, and Taylor, *Reinventing Shakespeare*, 91, 108.

22. The passages Johnson excerpts are not included in collections by Bysshe or Gildon.

23. Don Pedro's line is: "Thou wast ever an obstinate heretic in the despite of beauty" (1.1.234–35).

24. Several earlier adapters used quotation marks or other methods (albeit sporadically) to indicate Shakespearian material, notably George Granville in *The Jew of Venice* (1701) and William Burnaby in *Love Betray'd* (1703). In his 1700 adaptation of *Richard III*, Colley Cibber deliberately used italics to distinguish between his words and Shakespeare's to avoid the "danger of the Reader's mistaking any of my lines for *Shakespeare's*." C. J. Mitchell discusses the growth of quotation marks toward the end of the eighteenth century. "Quotation Marks, National Compositorial Habits and False Imprints," *The Library*, 6th series, 5 (1983): 359–84.

25. In the pamphlet *Critical Remarks on the Four Taking Plays of this Season* (1719),

written by "Corinna, a Country Parson's Wife," Johnson's play *The Masquerade* is "said to be written by an old Stager" whose "Name I find to several other Plays, much of the same Value and Merit, and as much his; for I don't remember one of them that is not stoln from other Authors except his *Iphigenia or Victim*." (49). See also Bullock's preface to *The Cobler of Preston* (1716).

26. *A Proposal for the Better Regulation of the Stage*, in *The Gentleman's Magazine* (1732), 2:566. See Hume, *Henry Fielding*, 31, for further discussion of this climate.

27. Dobson describes this as "a new emphasis on the textuality of drama." *The Making of the National Poet*, 113.

28. Ibid., 159; Arthur H. Scouten, "Shakespeare's Plays in the Theatrical Repertory When Garrick Came to London," *University of Texas Studies in English* (1944): 268.

29. See Stephen Orgel, "The Authentic Shakespeare," *Representations* 21 (1986): 1–25; de Grazia, "Shakespeare in Quotation Marks," 57–71, and *Shakespeare Verbatim*; Mark Rose, "The Author as Proprietor: Donaldson v. Becket and the Genealogy of Modern Authorship," *Representations* 23 (1988): 51–85, and *Authors and Owners: The Invention of Copyright* (Cambridge: Harvard University Press, 1993).

30. As Seary points out, Theobald did "not wish to improve Shakespeare," and his "emendations are the result of a conscientious endeavour to recover an authorial reading." Seary recounts Theobald's connections with the London theaters: starting in 1715, Theobald "acquired a familiarity with the ways of the theatre and with the treatment and appearance of dramatic manuscripts. Both were of incalculable importance in Theobald's conjectural emendations of Shakespeare. Because of this expertise he was able, with a preciseness available to few other editors, to strip away the veil of print and imagine the nature of the manuscript before a compositor, as well as the kind of misreadings such a manuscript might induce" (*Lewis Theobald and the Editing of Shakespeare*, 19).

31. As early as 1715, Theobald attempted to imitate Shakespeare in his *The Cave of Poverty. A Poem. Written in Imitation of Shakespeare*. See Seary, *Lewis Theobald and the Editing of Shakespeare*, 17.

32. According to Seary, the general opinion is that Theobald "did indeed possess manuscripts of a play that he initially believed to be by Shakespeare." See his Appendix C to *Lewis Theobald and the Editing of Shakespeare*, for further discussion of the play. Kenneth Muir suspects that "some scenes in *Double Falsehood* look as though they were manufactured by Theobald, with a copy of Shakespeare's works open in front of him." *Shakespeare as Collaborator* (London: Methuen, 1960), 151–54. For further discussion of the relationship between *Cardenio* and *Double Falsehood*, see Muir's introduction to the Cornmarket Press edition of *Double Falsehood* (London, 1970) and John Freehafer, "*Cardenio*, By Shakespeare and Fletcher," *PMLA* 84 (1969): 501–13.

33. Brean S. Hammond, "The Performance History of a Pseudo-Shakespearean Play: Theobald's Double Falshood," *British Journal for Eighteenth-Century Studies* 7 (1984): 49–60, at 50. Hammond discusses performances of the play in the later eighteenth century.

34. *The London Stage*, 3:917.

35. Seary, *Theobald and the Editing of Shakespeare*, 25–26, 135n. Seary notes that Jacob Tonson was probably behind the offer for copyright; Tonson published *The Tragedy of Locrine* (1734), *The London Prodigal* (1734), *The History of Sir John Oldcastle* (1734), *Pericles* (1734), *The Puritan: Or, the Widow of Watling-Street* (1734), and a *Yorkshire Tragedy* (1735). The Tonson-Walker copyright war of 1734–35 affected the availability of Shakespeare in print; Arthur H. Scouten estimates that "115 different separate printings of all thirty-seven plays" appeared in 1734 and 1735. "The Increase in Popularity of Shakespeare's Plays in the Eighteenth Century: A *Caveat* for Interpreters of Stage

History," *Shakespeare Quarterly* 7 (1956): 197. See also Giles E. Dawson, "The Copyright of Shakespeare's Dramatic Works," *University of Missouri Studies* 21 (1946): 30.

36. See Joseph E. Tucker, "The Eighteenth-Century English Translations of Molière," *Modern Language Quarterly* 3 (1942): 83–103, and L. P. Goggin, "Fielding and *The Select Comedies of Mr. De Molière*," *Philological Quarterly* 31 (1952): 344–50. Tucker remarks that "one can see a very close connection between [Miller's] interest in translating Molière and the plays he wrote for production on the stage" (87). Fielding also relied on this new translation, and his adaptation of *The Miser* was favorably received in 1733; Miller's concern with social and moral instruction in his plays provided a model for Fielding. See Hume, *Henry Fielding*, 191. Goggin points out Fielding's textual focus: "it is probable that he compared his adaptations" and "invited his readers to do so as well" (344).

37. For a detailed analysis of Miller's use of Shakespeare and Molière, see Powell Stewart, "An Eighteenth-Century Adaptation of Shakespeare," *University of Texas Studies in English* 12 (1932): 98–117.

38. Brought before the House of Commons on 20 May, the Licensing Act became law on 21 June and took effect on 24 June 1737. See Thomas Lockwood, "Fielding and the Licensing Act," *Huntington Library Quarterly* 50 (1987): 379–93.

39. See Stewart, "An Eighteenth-Century Adaptation of Shakespeare," 104. Charles Washburn Nichols reproduces the letter from Philo-Shakespear in "A Reverend Alterer of Shakespeare," *MLN* 44 (1929): 30–32.

40. Dobson points out that "this play is the first closet adaptation of Shakespeare" designed to "compete solely against printed editions of *As You Like It*" (*The Making of the National Poet*, 132).

41. Cecil Price remarks that Garrick "made some effort to restore Shakespeare's lines to texts that had been partly stripped of them, though where he thought a scene needed improvement, he supplied new lines himself. He collected early and very rare editions, lent them to scholars at work on the texts, and finally left them to the British Museum" (*Theatre in the Age of Garrick* [Oxford: Basil Blackwell, 1973], 3). Although Pepys collected plays, there is no indication that he viewed them as serious literary scholarship; he traded up his copy of the First Folio for a later Folio.

42. Stone and Kahrl summarize Garrick's role: "in his collecting, and studies, and patronage, his friendships with the leading dramatic scholars of his day, Garrick emerges as a cultivated scholar himself, with a deep understanding of dramatic poetry, an eclectic collector of early English drama, a tireless restorer of the text both on the stage and in the literature of the drama, a patron of letters with some historical perspective" (198–99). For further discussion of Garrick's role in eighteenth-century Shakespearian scholarship, see the chapter "The Literary World of Scholarship" in George Winchester Stone, Jr., and George M. Kahrl, *David Garrick: A Critical Biography* (Carbondale and Edwardsville: Southern Illinois University Press, 1979), 165–99. Stone and Kahrl attest that Garrick "assembled and used the largest collection of English drama either written, produced, or published before 1600. With his private means he patronized the editing, writing, and publishing of a number of significant and influential books on the history of English drama" (166). Garrick and Capell had a close association, and Capell "obtained all the recent editions, the folios, and all the known quartos, except six" for his 1768 edition of Shakespeare, which Garrick sponsored (174). Stone and Kahrl stress the importance of textual studies for Garrick's approach to Shakespeare: "Garrick very early began to *read* Shakespeare, and to see tremendous possibilities, not only for acting parts in the plays, but for fresh approaches to the texts of most of them" (248).

43. Arthur H. Scouten demonstrated that unadapted Shakespearian plays in-

creased in popularity several seasons before Garrick came to the London stage. "Shakespeare's Plays in the Theatrical Repertory When Garrick Came to London," *University of Texas Studies in English* (1944): 257–68, and "The Increase in Popularity of Shakespeare's Plays in the Eighteenth Century: A *Caveat* for Interpretors of Stage History," *Shakespeare Quarterly* 7 (1956): 189–202.

Conclusion

1. As we saw in the previous chapter, Miller combined Shakespeare's play with Molière's *Princess d'Elide*.

2. The patent monopoly lasted until 1843, and 1968 marked the end of the Lord Chamberlain's role in censorship. For an overview of the theatrical conditions leading up to the Licensing Act, see Hume, *Henry Fielding*, 2–19, and *The Rakish Stage*, 308–11. For a detailed analysis of the Licensing Act, see Vincent J. Liesenfeld, *The Licensing Act of 1737* (Madison: University of Wisconsin Press, 1984) and Liesenfeld's edited collection *The Stage and the Licensing Act 1729–1739* (New York: Garland, 1981).

3. Hume, *Henry Fielding*, 253, and 104–10. In a later work, Hume describes the effects of the Licensing Act: "the generic and theatrical results of the 1737 act were indeed catastrophic: noncompetition, generic stasis, and growing elephantiasis of the patent theaters as they expanded their capacity to accommodate the growing population of a booming city." "Jeremy Collier and the Future of the London Theater in 1698," 511. For further discussion of these issues in connection with Licensing Act, see Loftis, *The Politics of Drama*, 128–53.

4. The overabundance of scholarship on the Dryden-Davenant *Tempest* and the 1674 version testifies to this effect. As Michael Dobson puts it, hack work should not be discarded: "the fact that many adaptations of Shakespeare were undoubtedly written quickly with the sole aim of catering lucratively to popular taste may, indeed, make them more useful indicators of contemporary beliefs and assumptions than some of the self-consciously 'higher' literary forms criticism has traditionally privileged" (*The Making of the National Poet*, 6).

Bibliography

Adams, Martin. *Henry Purcell: The Origins and Development of His Musical Style*. Cambridge: Cambridge University Press, 1995.

Addison, Joseph, Richard Steele, et al. *The Tatler*. Edited by Donald F. Bond. 5 vols. Oxford: Clarendon, 1965.

Agnew, Jean-Christophe. "Coming Up for Air: Consumer Culture in Historical Perspective." *Intellectual History Newsletter* 12 (1990): 3–21.

———. *Worlds Apart: The Market and the Theater in Anglo-American Thought, 1550–1750*. Cambridge: Cambridge University Press, 1986.

Akerby, George. *The Life of Mr. James Spiller, the Late Famous Comedian*. London, 1729.

Allen, B. Sprague. *Tides in English Taste (1619–1800): A Background for the Study of Literature*. 2 vols. Cambridge: Harvard University Press, 1937.

Allen, David. "Political Clubs in Restoration London." *The Historical Journal* 19 (1976): 570–84.

Alssid, Michael W. *Thomas Shadwell*. New York: Twayne, 1967.

Altick, Richard. *The Shows of London: A Panoramic History of Exhibitions, 1600–1862*. Cambridge, Mass.: Belknap Press, 1978.

Animadversions on Mr. Congreve's Late Answer to Mr. Collier. London, 1698.

Armistead, Jack M. "Dryden's Prospero and his Predecessors." *South Atlantic Review* 50 (1985): 23–33.

Arrowsmith, Joseph. *The Reformation*. London, 1673.

Auberlen, Eckhard. "*The Tempest* and the Concerns of the Restoration Court: A Study of *The Enchanted Island* and the Operatic *Tempest*." *Restoration* 15 (1992): 71–88.

Aubrey, John. *Brief Lives*. Edited by Richard Barber. Suffolk: Boydell Press, 1982.

The Author's Triumph; or, The Manager Manag'd. London, 1737.

Avery, Emmett L. "Dancing and Pantomime on the English Stage, 1700–1737." *Studies in Philology* 31 (1934): 417–52.

———. "The Defense and Criticism of Pantomimic Entertainments in the Eighteenth Century." *ELH* 5 (1938): 127–45.

———. "The Dramatists in the Theatrical Advertisements, 1700–1709." *Modern Language Quarterly* 8 (1947): 448–54.

———. "The Restoration Audience." *Philological Quarterly* 45 (1966): 54–61.

Backscheider, Paula R., ed. *The Dictionary of Literary Biography*. Detroit: Gale Research, 1989.

Bader, A. L. "The Modena Troupe in England." *Modern Language Notes* 50 (1935): 367–69.

Baker, David Erskine. *Companion to the Playhouse* (1764), revised and expanded as *Bio-*

graphia Dramatica; or, a Companion to the Playhouse. Edited by Stephen Jones. 1812. London and New York: AMS Press, 1966.

Baker, Thomas. *The Humour of the Age.* London, 1701.

———. *Tunbridge-Walks: or, The Yeoman of Kent.* London, 1703.

Baldwin, Olive, and Thelma Wilson. "Richard Leveridge, 1670–1758." *The Musical Times* 111 (1970): 592–94, 891–93, 988–90.

Banks, John. *Vertue Betray'd: or, Anna Bullen.* London, 1682.

Barlow, Graham. "Sir James Thornhill and the Theatre Royal, Drury Lane, 1705." In *Essays on the Eighteenth-Century English Stage.* Edited by Kenneth Richards and Peter Thomson. London: Methuen, 1972. 179–93.

Barnett, R. D. *Anti-Semitic Stereotypes: A Paradigm of Otherness in English Popular Culture 1660–1830.* Baltimore: Johns Hopkins University Press, 1995.

———. "Anglo-Jewry in the Eighteenth Century." In *Three Centuries of Anglo-Jewish History,* Edited by V. D. Lipman. Cambridge: W. Heffer, 1961. 45–68.

Bartley, J. O. "Irish, Welsh and Scottish Stage Costume Before the Interregnum." *Theatre Notebook* 5 (1950): 61–64.

———. *Teague, Shenkin, and Sawney: Being an Historical Study of the Earliest Irish, Welsh and Scottish Characters in English Plays.* Cork: Cork University Press, 1954.

Baskervill, Charles Read. *The Elizabethan Jig and Related Song Drama.* 1929. New York: Dover Publications, 1965.

Bate, Jonathan. *Shakespeare and the English Romantic Imagination.* Oxford: Clarendon, 1986.

———. *Shakespearean Constitutions: Politics, Theatre, Criticism, 1730–1830.* Oxford: Clarendon, 1989.

———, and Russell Jackson, eds. *Shakespeare: An Illustrated Stage History.* Oxford: Oxford University Press, 1996.

Bawcutt, N. W., ed. *The Control and Censorship of Caroline Drama: The Records of Sir Henry Herbert, Master of the Revels 1623–73.* Oxford: Clarendon, 1996.

Beattie, John M. *The English Court in the Reign of George I.* Cambridge: Cambridge University Press, 1967.

Bedford, Arthur. *Serious Reflections on the Scandalous Abuse and Effects of the Stage: In a Sermon Preach'd at the Parish-Church of St. Nicolas in the City of Bristol, on Sunday the 7th Day of January, 1704/05.* Bristol: W. Bonny, 1705.

Behn, Aphra. *The Round-heads.* London, 1682.

Belanger, Terry. "Publishers and Writers in Eighteenth-Century England." In *Books and their Readers in Eighteenth-Century England.* Edited by Isobel Rivers. London: St. Martin's Press, 1982.

Bentley, Gerald Eades. "John Cotgrave's English Treasury of Wit and Language and the Elizabethan Drama." *Studies in Philology* 40 (1943): 186–203.

———. *Shakespeare and Jonson: Their Reputations in the Seventeenth Century Compared.* Chicago: University of Chicago Press, 1945.

Bermingham, Ann, and John Brewer, eds. *The Consumption of Culture 1600–1800.* London: Routledge, 1995.

Bevis, Richard. *Eighteenth-Century Drama: Afterpieces.* London: Oxford University Press, 1970.

Bianconi, Lorenzo, and Thomas Walker. "Production, Consumption and Political Function of Seventeenth-Century Opera." In *Studies in Medieval and Early Modern*

Music. Edited by Iain Fenlon, *Early Music History* 4. Cambridge: Cambridge University Press, 1984. 209–96.

Black, Scott. "Social and Literary Form in the *Spectator*." *Eighteenth-Century Studies* 33 (1999): 21–42.

Blake, William. *The Poetry and Prose of William Blake*. Edited by David V. Erdman. New York: Doubleday, 1965.

Blaydes, Sophia B. and Philip Bordinat. *Sir William Davenant: An Annotated Bibliography 1629–1985*. New York and London: Garland, 1986.

Blayney, Glenn H. "Enforcement of Marriage in English Drama (1600–1650)." *Philological Quarterly* 38 (1959): 459–72.

Boswell, Eleanore. *The Restoration Court Stage (1660–1702)*. Cambridge: Harvard University Press, 1932.

Boyle, Charles. *As You Find It*. London, 1703.

Branam, George C. *Eighteenth-Century Adaptations of Shakespearean Tragedy*. Berkeley: University of California Press, 1956.

Braverman, Richard. "Politics in Jewish Disguise: Jacobitism and Dissent on the Post-Revolutionary Stage." *Studies in Philology* 90 (1993): 347–70.

Brewer, John and Roy Porter, eds. *Consumption and the World of Goods*. London: Routledge, 1993.

Brewer, John. *The Pleasures of the Imagination: English Culture in the Eighteenth Century*. New York: Farrar Straus Giroux, 1997.

Bristol, Michael. *Shakespeare's America, America's Shakespeare*. London: Routledge, 1990.

Broad, John. "Whigs and Deer-Stealers in Other Guises: A Return to the Origins of the Black Act." *Past and Present* 119 (1988): 56–72.

Brown, Frank Clyde. *Elkanah Settle: His Life and Works*. Chicago: University of Chicago Press, 1910.

Brown, Arthur. "The Great Variety of Readers." *Shakespeare Survey* 18 (1965): 11–22.

Brown, Laura. *English Dramatic Form, 1660–1760: An Essay in Generic History*. New Haven: Yale University Press, 1981.

Brown, Tom. *Amusements Serious and Comical*. Edited by Arthur L. Hayward. London: Routledge, 1927.

Bruster, Douglas. *Drama and the Market in the Age of Shakespeare*. Cambridge: Cambridge University Press, 1992.

Buckingham, George Villiers, Second Duke of. *The Rehearsal*. London, 1672.

Bullock, Christopher. *The Adventures of Half an Hour, a Farce*. London, 1716.

———. *The Cobler of Preston*. London, 1716.

———. *The Per-juror*. London, 1717.

———. *Woman Is a Riddle*. London, 1716.

———. *A Woman's Revenge*. London, 1715.

Bullock, Steven C. "Initiating the Enlightenment?: Recent Scholarship on European Freemasonry." *Eighteenth-Century Life* 20 (1996): 80–92.

Burling, William J. "British Plays, 1697–1737: Premieres, Datings, Attributions, and Publication Information." *Studies in Bibliography* 43 (1990): 164–82.

———. "Charles Johnson." *Dictionary of Literary Biography*, vol. 84. Edited by Paula R. Backscheider. Detroit: Gale Research, 1989.

———. *A Checklist of New Plays and Entertainments on the London Stage, 1700–1737*. Madison, N.J.: Fairleigh Dickinson University Press, 1993.

Burnaby, William. *Dramatic Works*. Edited by F. E. Budd. London: E. Partridge, 1931.

———. *The Ladies Visiting-Day*. London, 1701.

———. *Love Betray'd*. London, 1703.

———. *The Reformed Wife*. London, 1700.

Burney, Charles. *A General History of Music*. Edited by Frank Mercer. 2 vols. 1935. Reprint, New York: Dover, 1957.

Burridge, Richard. *A Scourge for the Play-Houses: or, the Character of the English-Stage*. London, 1702.

Butler, Martin. *Theatre and Crisis, 1632–1642*. Cambridge: Cambridge University Press, 1984.

Butt, John. *Pope's Taste in Shakespeare*. London: Oxford University Press, 1936.

Bysshe, Edward. *The Art of English Poetry*. London, 1702.

Carrington, James. *The Modern Receipt: or, A Cure for Love*. London, 1737.

Case, Arthur E. *A Bibliography of English Poetical Miscellanies, 1521–1750*. Oxford University Press, 1935.

Centlivre, Susannah. *The Basset-Table*. London, 1706.

———. *Love's Contrivance*. London, 1703.

Chappell, William. *Popular Music of Olden Time; A Collection of Ancient Songs, Ballads, and Dance Tunes, Illustrative of the National Music of England*. 2 vols. London: Cramer, Beale, and Chappell, 1859.

Characters of the Times; or, an Impartial Account of the Writings, Characters, Education, &c. of several Noblemen and Gentlemen, libell'd in a preface to a late Miscellany Publish'd by P___PE and S_____FT, Reprinted in *Popeiana*. New York and London: Garland Press, 1975.

Chartier, Roger. *The Culture of Print: Power and the Uses of Print in Early Modern Europe*. Translated by Lydia G. Cochrane. Princeton: Princeton University Press, 1987.

———. *The Order of Books*. Translated by Lydia G. Cochrane. Palo Alto: Stanford University Press, 1994.

Chaves, A. *The Cares of Love*. London, 1705.

Chetwood, William Rufus. *A General History of the Stage*. London, 1749.

Cibber, Colley. *An Apology for the Life of Mr. Colley Cibber*. Edited by Robert W. Lowe. 1888. Reprint, New York: AMS Press, 1966.

———. *Love Makes a Man*. London, 1700.

Clark, Peter. "The Alehouse and the Alternative Society." In *Puritans and Revolutionaries*. Edited by Donald Pennington and Keith Thomas. Oxford: Clarendon, 1978. 47–72.

———. *The English Alehouse: A Social History, 1200–1830*. London: Longman, 1983.

Clark, Sandra, ed. *Shakespeare Made Fit: Restoration Adaptations of Shakespeare*. London: Dent, 1997.

Coffey, Charles. *The Merry Cobler: Or, the Second Part of The Devil of Pay*. London, 1735.

Coleman, Antony, and Antony Hammond, eds. *Poetry and Drama 1570–1700: Essays in Honour of Harold F. Brooks*. London: Methuen, 1981.

Coleman, Edward D. *The Jew in English Drama: An Annotated Bibliography*. New York: New York Public Library, 1938–40.

Coleman, William S. "Post-Restoration Shylocks Prior to Macklin." *Theatre Survey* 7 (1966): 17–36.

Colley, Linda. *Britons: Forging the Nation 1707–1837*. New Haven: Yale University Press, 1992.

Collins, Howard. *The Comedy of Sir William Davenant*. Paris and The Hague: Mouton, 1967.

Collison, Robert Lewis. *The Story of Street Literature: Forerunner of the Popular Press*. London: Dent, 1973.

Colonel Huson's (Or the Cobler's) Confession, in a Fit of Despair. London, 1659.

A Comparison Between the Two Stages. Edited by Staring B. Wells. Princeton: Princeton University Press, 1942.

Congreve, William. *William Congreve: Letters and Documents*. Edited by John C. Hodges. New York, 1964.

The Constant Nymph: or, The Rambling Shepheard. London, 1678.

Cook, William. *Memoirs of Charles Macklin, Comedian*. London, 1804.

Cooper, Charles W. "The Triple-Portrait of John Lacy." *PMLA* 47 (1932): 759–65.

Corman, Brian. *Genre and Generic Change in English Comedy 1660–1710*. Toronto: University of Toronto Press, 1993.

———, and Todd S. Gilman. "The Musical Life of Thomas Shadwell." *Restoration* 20 (1996): 149–64.

Corye, John. *The Metamorphosis*. London, 1704.

Cowper, Mary Countess. *The Diary of Mary Countess Cowper, Lady of the Bedchamber to the Princess of Wales, 1714–1720*. London, 1864.

Craft, Catherine A. "Granville's *Jew of Venice* and the Eighteenth-Century Stage." *Restoration and Eighteenth-Century Theatre Research* 2 (1987): 38–54.

Crauford, David. *Courtship A-la-mode*. London, 1700.

Critical Remarks on the Four Taking Plays of this Season. London, 1719.

Crowne, John. *Sir Courtly Nice*. London, 1685.

Cruickshanks, Eveline, and Howard Erskine-Hill. "The Waltham Black Act and Jacobitism." *Journal of British Studies* 24 (1985): 358–65.

Culler, A. Dwight. "Edward Bysshe and the Poet's Handbook." *PMLA* 63 (1948): 858–85.

Curll, Edmund. *The Life of That Eminent Comedian Robert Wilks, Esq*. London, 1733.

Danchin, Pierre. "The Foundation of the Royal Academy of Music in 1674 and Pierre Perrin's Ariane." *Theatre Survey* 25 (1984): 55–66.

———. *The Prologues and Epilogues of the Restoration 1660–1700*. 7 vols. Nancy: Publications de l'Université de Nancy, 1981–88.

Darnton, Robert. *The Great Cat Massacre and Other Episodes in French Cultural History*. New York: Basic Books, 1984.

Davenant, William. *The Law Against Lovers*. 1673. Intro. A. M. Gibbs. London: Cornmarket Press, 1970.

———. *The Play-house to be Let*. London, 1662.

———. *The Works of William Davenant*. London, 1673.

Davis, Natalie Zemon. "Religion and Capitalism Once Again? Jewish Merchant Culture in the Seventeenth Century." *Representations* 59 (1997): 56–84.

Davison, Lee, Tim Hitchcock, Tim Keirn, and Robert B. Shoemaker. *Stilling the Grum-*

bling Hive: The Response to Social and Economic Problems in England, 1689–1750. New York: St. Martin's Press, 1992.

Defoe, Daniel. *A Tour Through the Whole Island of Great Britain.* London, 1724–26.

De Grazia, Margreta. "Shakespeare in Quotation Marks." In *The Appropriation of Shakespeare: Post-Renaissance Reconstructions of the Works and the Myth.* Edited by Jean I. Marsden. Hemel Hempstead: Harvester Wheatsheaf, 1991. 57–71.

———. *Shakespeare Verbatim: The Reproduction of Authenticity and the 1790 Apparatus.* Oxford: Clarendon, 1991.

Deloney, Thomas. *The Works of Thomas Deloney.* Edited by Francis Oscar Mann. Oxford: Clarendon, 1912.

De Marly, Diana. "The Architect of Dorset Garden Theatre." *Theatre Notebook* 29 (1975): 119–24.

Dennis, John. *The Comical Gallant.* 1702. London: Cornmarket Press, 1969.

———. *The Critical Works of John Dennis.* Edited by Edward Niles Hooker. 2 vols. Baltimore: Johns Hopkins University Press, 1939–43.

———. *Original Letters.* London, 1721.

Dent, Edward J. *Foundations of English Opera: A Study of Musical Drama in England During the Seventeenth Century.* Cambridge: Cambridge University Press, 1928.

De Quehen, A. H. "*The Silent Woman* in the Restoration." In *Craft and Tradition: Essays in Honour of William Blissett.* Edited by H. B. de Groot and Alexander Leggatt. Calgary: University of Calgary Press, 1990. 137–46.

Dixon, Peter. "Edward Bysshe and Pope's 'Shakespear.'" *Notes and Queries* 209 (1964): 292–93.

———. "Pope's Shakespeare." *JEGP* 63 (1964): 191–203.

Dobson, Michael. *The Making of the National Poet: Shakespeare, Adaptation and Authorship 1660–1769.* Oxford: Clarendon, 1992.

———. "'Remember/First to Possess His Books': The Appropriation of *The Tempest*, 1700–1800." *Shakespeare Survey* 43 (1991): 99–107.

Doggett, Thomas. *The Country-Wake.* London, 1696.

Downes, John. *Roscius Anglicanus.* Edited by Judith Milhous and Robert D. Hume. London: The Society for Theatre Research, 1987.

Dryden, John. *Essays of John Dryden.* Edited by W. P. Ker. Oxford: Clarendon, 1926.

———. *The Works of John Dryden.* Edited by Edward Niles Hooker et. al. 20 vols. Berkeley and Los Angeles: University of California Press, 1956–.

———, and William Davenant. *The Tempest, or the Enchanted Island.* London, 1670.

Duffett, Thomas. *The Mock-Tempest.* London, 1674.

Durfey, Thomas. *The Banditti.* London, 1686.

———. *The Comical History of Don Quixote. The Third Part. With the Marriage of Mary the Buxome.* London, 1696.

———. *The Fool Turn'd Critick.* London, 1676.

———. *The Old Mode and the New.* London, 1703.

Dunkin, Paul. "Issues of the Fairy Queen." *The Library* 26 (1946): 297–304.

Dyregrov, David. "Jo. Haines as Librettist for Purcell's *The Fairy Queen.*" *Restoration and Eighteenth-Century Theatre Research* 7 (1992): 29–54.

Earle, Peter. *The Making of the English Middle Class: Business, Society and Family Life in London, 1660–1730.* Berkeley: University of California Press, 1989.

Edmond, Mary. *Rare Sir William Davenant*. New York: St. Martin's Press, 1987.

Eisenstein, Elizabeth L. *The Printing Press as an Agent of Change: Communication and Cultural Transformation in Early-Modern Europe*. 2 vols. Cambridge: Cambridge University Press, 1979.

Elson, John James, ed. *The Wits or, Sport upon Sport*. Ithaca: Cornell University Press, 1932.

The English Theophrastus: or, The Manners of the Age. London, 1702.

Evans, G. Blakemore. "A Seventeenth-Century Reader of Shakespeare." *Review of English Studies* 21 (1945): 271–79.

———. *Shakespearean Prompt-Books of the Seventeenth Century*. 6 vols. Charlottesville: Bibliographical Society of the University of Virginia, 1960.

Evelyn, John. *The Diary of John Evelyn*. Edited by E. S. De Beer. 6 vols. Oxford: Clarendon, 1955.

———. *The Life of Mrs Godolphin*. Edited by Samuel Lord Bishop of Oxford. London, 1847.

The Fairy-Queen. London, 1692.

Farquhar, George. *The Constant Couple*. London, 1699.

———. *The Inconstant*. London, 1702.

———. *The Works of George Farquhar*. Edited by Shirley Strum Kenny. Oxford: Clarendon, 1988.

Felsenstein, Frank. *Anti-Semitic Stereotypes: A Paradigm of Otherness in English Popular Culture, 1660–1830*. Baltimore: Johns Hopkins University Press, 1995.

Ferguson, William. *Scotland's Relations with England: A Survey to 1707*. Edinburgh: John Donald Publishers, 1977.

Fielding, Henry. *The Author's Farce*. London, 1730.

Fine, Ben, and Ellen Leopold. "Consumerism and the Industrial Revolution." *Social History* 15 (1990): 151–79.

Finlayson, Iain. *The Scots: A Portrait of the Scottish Soul at Home and Abroad*. New York: Atheneum, 1987.

Firth, C. H. and R. S. Rait, eds. *Acts and Ordinances of the Interregnum 1642–1660*. London: HMSO, 1911.

Fiske, Roger. *English Theatre Music in the Eighteenth Century*, 2d ed. Oxford: Oxford University Press, 1986.

Fitzgerald, Percy. *A New History of the English Stage*. London, 1882.

Fletcher, Anthony. *Reform in the Provinces: The Government of Stuart England*. New Haven: Yale University Press, 1986.

Fletcher, Ifan Kyrle. "Italian Comedians in England in the 17th Century." *Theatre Notebook* 8 (1954): 86–91.

Fletcher, John. *The Woman's Prize, or the Tamer Tam'd*. Edited by George B. Ferguson. The Hague: Mouton, 1966.

Forsythe, Robert Stanley. *The Relations of Shirley's Plays to the Elizabethan Drama*. New York: Columbia University Press, 1914.

Foss, Michael. *The Age of Patronage: The Arts in England 1660–1750*. London: Hamish Hamilton, 1971.

Freehafer, John. "Brome, Suckling, and Davenant's Theater Project of 1639." *Texas Studies in Literature and Language* 10 (1968): 367–83.

———. "*Cardenio*, By Shakespeare and Fletcher." *PMLA* 84 (1969): 501–13.
———. "The Formation of the London Patent Companies in 1660." *Theatre Notebook* 20 (1965): 6–30.
Gay, John. *Three Hours After Marriage*. London, 1717.
———. *The What D'Ye Call It*. London, 1715.
Gellert, James. "The Source of Davenant's *The Law Against Lovers*." *The Library* 8 (1986): 351–57.
Genest, John. *Some Account of the English Stage from 1660–1830*. 10 vols. Bath: H. E. Carrington, 1832.
Gewirtz, Arthur. *Restoration Adaptations of Early 17th Century Comedies*. Washington, D.C.: University Press of America, 1982.
Gildon, Charles. *Charles Gildon's Measure for Measure, or Beauty the Best Advocate*. Edited by Edward A. Cairns. New York and London: Garland, 1987.
———. *The Complete Art of Poetry. In Six Parts*. 2 vols. London, 1718.
———. *The Life of Mr. Thomas Betterton*. London, 1710.
———. *The Lives and Characters of the English Dramatick Poets*. London, 1699.
———. *Love's Victim*. London, 1701.
———. *Measure for Measure. Or, Beauty the Best Advocate*. 1700. London: Cornmarket Press, 1969.
———. *Miscellaneous Letters and Essays*. London, 1694.
———. *Phaeton*. London, 1698.
———. *The Post-Man Robb'd of His Mail*. London, 1719.
Gilman, Todd S. "Augustan Criticism and Changing Conceptions of English Opera." *Theatre Survey* 36 (1995): 1–35.
———. "*The Beggar's Opera* and British Opera." *University of Toronto Quarterly* 66 (1997): 539–61.
———. "The Italian (Castrato) in London." In *Genre, Nationhood, and Sexual Difference*. Edited by Richard Dellamora and Daniel Fischlin. New York: Columbia University Press, 1997. 49–70.
Goff, Moira. "'Actions, Manners, and Passions': Entr'acte Dancing on the London Stage, 1700–1737." *Early Music* 26 (1998): 213–28.
Goggin, L. P. "Fielding and *The Select Comedies of Mr. De Molière*." *Philological Quarterly* 31 (1952): 344–50.
Goldgar, Bertrand A. *Walpole and the Wits: The Relation of Politics to Literature, 1722–1742*. Lincoln: University of Nebraska Press, 1976.
Goldsmith, Oliver. *New Essays by Oliver Goldsmith*. Edited by R. S. Crane. Chicago: University of Chicago Press, 1927.
Gondris, Joanna, ed. *Reading Readings: Essays on Shakespeare Editing in the Eighteenth Century*. Madison, N.J.: Fairleigh Dickinson University Press, 1998.
Gould, Robert. *The Rival Sisters*. London, 1695.
Granville, George. *The British Enchanters*. London, 1710.
———. *The Genuine Works in Verse and Prose of the Right Honourable George Granville Lord Lansdowne*. London, 1736.
———. *Heroick Love*. London, 1698.
———. *The Jew of Venice*. London, 1701.
———. *Poems on Several Occasions*. London, 1716.

―――. *The She-Gallants*. London, 1696.

―――. *Three Plays, Viz. The She-Gallants, A Comedy. Heroick-Love, A Tragedy. And The Jew of Venice, A Comedy*. London, 1713.

Greg, W. W. "The Printing of the Beaumont and Fletcher Folio of 1647." *The Library* 2 (1922): 109–15.

―――. "Theatrical Repertories of 1662." In *W. W. Greg: Collected Papers*. Edited by J. C. Maxwell. Oxford: Clarendon, 1966. 44–7.

Griffin, Benjamin. *Whig and Tory*. London, 1720.

Griffin, Dustin. *Literary Patronage in England, 1650–1800*. Cambridge: Cambridge University Press, 1996.

Griffith, Elizabeth. *The Morality of Shakespeare's Drama Illustrated*. 1775. Reprint, New York: Augustus M. Kelley, 1971.

Griffiths, Trevor R. *A Midsummer Night's Dream*. Shakespeare in Production. Cambridge: Cambridge University Press, 1996.

Gross, John. *Shylock: Four Hundred Years in the Life of a Legend*. London: Chatto and Windus, 1992.

Grout, Donald J. *A Short History of Opera*. 2d ed. New York: Columbia University Press, 1965.

Guffey, George R. *After the Tempest*. Los Angeles: William Andrews Clark Memorial Library, 1969.

―――. "Politics, Weather, and the Contemporary Reception of the Dryden-Davenant *Tempest*." *Restoration* 8 (1984): 1–9.

Guillory, John. *Cultural Capital: The Problem of Literary Canon Formation*. Chicago: University of Chicago Press, 1993.

Gurr, Andrew. *The Shakespearian Stage: 1574–1642*. Cambridge: Cambridge University Press, 1970.

Halliwell, J. O. *A Catalogue of An Unique Collection of Ancient English Broadside Ballads*. London: Chiswick Press, 1856.

Hammond, Brean S. "The Performance History of a Pseudo-Shakespearean Play: Theobald's Double Falshood." *British Journal for Eighteenth-Century Studies* 7 (1984): 49–60.

―――. *Professional Imaginative Writing in England, 1670–1740: "Hackney for Bread."* Oxford: Clarendon, 1997.

Handasyde, Elizabeth. *Granville the Polite: The Life of George Granville Lord Lansdowne, 1666–1735*. London: Oxford University Press, 1933.

Harbage, Alfred. "Elizabethan-Restoration Palimpsest." *Modern Language Review* 35 (1940): 287–319.

―――. *Sir William Davenant: Poet Venturer 1606–1668*. Philadelphia: University of Pennsylvania Press, 1935.

Haring-Smith, Tori. *From Farce to Metadrama: A Stage History of "Taming of the Shrew" 1594–1983*. London: Greenwood Press, 1985.

Harris, Ellen T. *Henry Purcell's Dido and Aeneas*. Oxford: Clarendon, 1987.

Harris, Michael. "London Printers and Newspaper Production During the First Half of the Eighteenth Century." *Journal of the Printing Historical Society* 12 (1977–78): 33–51.

Harvey, A. D. "Virginity and Honor in *Measure for Measure* and Davenant's *The Law Against Lovers*." *English Studies* 75 (1994): 123–32.

Haun, Eugene. *But Hark! More Harmony: The Libretti in English of the Restoration Opera.* Ypsilanti: Eastern Michigan University Press, 1971.

Haunch, T. O. "The Formation: 1717 to 1751." In *Grand Lodge 1717–1967.* Edited by A. S. Frere. Oxford, 1967. 47–91.

Haywood, Charles. "*The Songs & Masque in the New Tempest*: An Incident in the Battle of the Two Theaters, 1674." *Huntington Library Quarterly* 19 (1955): 39–56.

Hewson Reduc'd, or, The Shoomaker Return'd to His Trade. London, 1661.

Higden, Henry. *The Wary Widdow: or, Sir Noisy Parrat.* London, 1693.

Highfill, Philip H., Jr., Kalman A. Burnim, and Edward A. Langhans, eds. *A Biographical Dictionary of Actors, Actresses, Musicians, Dancers, Managers and Other Stage Personnel in London, 1660–1800.* 16 vols. Carbondale and Edwardsville: Southern Illinois University Press, 1973–93.

Hill, Aaron. *The Fatal Vision.* London, 1716.

Hoadly, Benjamin. *The Jacobite's Hopes Reviv'd by our Late Tumults and Addresses.* London, 1710.

Hodgdon, Barbara. *The Shakespeare Trade: Performances and Appropriations.* Philadelphia: University of Pennsylvania Press, 1998.

Hogan, Charles Beecher. *Shakespeare in the Theatre 1701–1800.* 2 vols. Oxford: Clarendon, 1952.

Holderness, Graham, and Bryan Loughrey, eds. *A Pleasant Conceited Historie, Called The Taming of a Shrew.* Hemel Hempstead: Harvester Wheatsheaf, 1992.

Holderness, Graham. *The Shakespeare Myth.* Manchester: Manchester University Press, 1988.

Holding, Edith. "*As You Like It* Adapted: Charles Johnson's *Love in a Forest.*" *Shakespeare Survey* 32 (1979): 37–48.

Holland, Peter. *The Ornament of Action: Text and Performance in Restoration Comedy.* Cambridge: Cambridge University Press, 1979.

Hook, Lucyle. "Motteux and the Classical Masque." In *British Theatre and the Other Arts, 1660–1800.* Edited by Shirley Strum Kenny. Washington, D.C.: Folger Books, 1984. 105–15.

Hooker, Edward Niles. "Charles Johnson's *The Force of Friendship* and *Love in a Chest*: A Note on Tragicomedy and Licensing in 1710." *Studies in Philology* 34 (1937): 407–11.

Hooker, Helene Maxwell. "Dryden's and Shadwell's *Tempest.*" *Huntington Library Quarterly* 6 (1943): 224–28.

Hopkins, Charles. *Boadicea.* London, 1697.

Horn-Monval, Madam. "French Troupes in England During the Restoration." *Theatre Notebook* 7 (1953): 81–82.

Hotson, Leslie. *The Commonwealth and Restoration Stage.* Cambridge: Harvard University Press, 1928.

Houston, R. A., and I. D. Whyte. *Scottish Society 1500–1800.* Cambridge: Cambridge University Press, 1989.

Howard, Edward. *Six Day's Adventure.* London, 1671.

———. *The Womens Conquest.* London, 1671.

Howe, Alan. "English Actors in Paris during the Civil Wars: Samuel Speede and the Prince of Wales's Company." *The Seventeenth Century* 14 (1999): 130–42.

Howe, Elizabeth. *The First English Actresses: Women and Drama, 1660–1700.* Cambridge: Cambridge University Press, 1992.

Hughes, Derek. *English Drama 1660–1700*. Oxford: Clarendon, 1996.

Hughes, Leo, and Arthur H. Scouten. *Ten English Farces*. Austin: University of Texas Press, 1948.

Hughes, Leo. "Afterpieces: Or, That's Entertainment." In *The Stage and the Page: London's "Whole Show" in the Eighteenth-Century Theatre*. Edited by George Winchester Stone, Jr. Berkeley: University of California Press, 1981. 55–70.

―――. "Attitudes of Some Restoration Dramatists Toward Farce." *Philological Quarterly* 19 (1940): 268–87.

―――. *A Century of English Farce*. Princeton: Princeton University Press, 1956.

―――. "Doggett Dancing the Cheshire Round?" *Theatre Notebook* 7 (1952–3): 12–14.

―――. *The Drama's Patrons: A Study of the Eighteenth-Century London Audience*. Austin: University of Texas Press, 1971.

―――. "The Early Career of Farce in the Theatrical Vocabulary." *University of Texas Studies in English* 20 (1940): 82–95.

Hume, Robert D. "Before the Bard: 'Shakespeare' in Early Eighteenth-Century London." *ELH* 64 (1997): 41–75.

―――. *The Development of English Drama in the Late Seventeenth Century*. Oxford: Clarendon, 1976.

―――. "Diversity and Development in Restoration Comedy 1660–1679." *Eighteenth-Century Studies* 5 (1972): 365–97.

―――. "The Dorset Garden Theatre: A Review of Facts and Problems." *Theatre Notebook* 33 (1979): 4–17.

―――. "Dr. Edward Browne's Playlist of '1662': A Reconsideration." *Philological Quarterly* 64 (1985): 69–81.

―――. "Dryden, James Howard, and the Date of *All Mistaken*." *Philological Quarterly* 51 (1972): 422–29.

―――. *Henry Fielding and the London Theatre 1728–1737*. Oxford: Clarendon, 1988.

―――. "Jeremy Collier and the Future of the London Theater in 1698." *Studies in Philology* 96 (1999): 480–511.

―――. "Marital Discord in English Comedy from Dryden to Fielding." *Modern Philology* 74 (1977): 248–72.

―――. "The Multifarious Forms of Eighteenth-Century Comedy." In *The Stage and the Page: London's "Whole Show" in the Eighteenth-Century Theatre*. Edited by George Winchester Stone, Jr. Berkeley: University of California Press, 1981. 3–32.

―――. "The Nature of the Dorset Garden Theatre." *Theatre Notebook* 36 (1982): 99–109.

―――. "Opera in London. 1695–1706." In *British Theatre and the Other Arts, 1660–1800*. Edited by Shirley Strum Kenny. Washington, D.C.: Folger Books, 1984. 67–91.

―――. "The Politics of Opera in Late Seventeenth-Century London." *Cambridge Opera Journal* 10 (1998): 15–43.

―――. *The Rakish Stage: Studies in English Drama, 1660–1800*. Carbondale and Edwardsville: Southern Illinois University Press, 1983.

―――. *Reconstructing Contexts: The Aims and Principles of Archaeo-Historicism*. Oxford: Oxford University Press, 1999.

―――. "A Revival of *The Way of the World* in December 1701 or January 1702." *Theatre Notebook* 26 (1971): 30–36.

―――. "Securing a Repertory: Plays on the London Stage, 1660–65." In *Poetry and*

Drama 1570–1700: Essays in Honour of Harold F. Brooks. Edited by Antony Coleman and Antony Hammond. London: Methuen, 1981. 156–72.

———. "The Sponsorship of Opera in London, 1704–1720." *Modern Philology* 85 (1988): 420–32.

———, ed. *The London Theatre World.* Carbondale and Edwardsville: Southern Illinois University Press, 1980.

———, and Judith Milhous. "Thomas Doggett at Cambridge in 1701." *Theatre Notebook* 51 (1997): 147–65.

Ireland, Samuel. *Graphic Illustrations of Hogarth.* London, 1794.

Jackson, Alfred. "Rowe's Edition of Shakespeare." *The Library* 4th series 10 (1930): 455–73.

Jacob, Giles. *An Historical Account of the Lives and Writings of our Most Considerable English Poets.* London, 1720.

Jacob, Margaret. *The Radical Enlightenment: Pantheists, Freemasons and Republicans.* London: George Allen & Unwin, 1981.

James, Ricky. *Learned Pigs and Fireproof Women.* New York: Villard Books, 1986.

Jarvis, Simon. *Scholars and Gentlemen: Shakespearian Textual Criticism and Representations of Scholarly Labour, 1725–1765.* Oxford: Clarendon, 1995.

Jason, Philip K. "The Afterpiece: Authors and Incentives." *Restoration and Eighteenth-Century Theatre Research* 12 (1973): 1–13.

———. "The Afterpiece: Origins and Early Development." *Restoration and Eighteenth-Century Theatre Research* series 2, 1 (1986): 53–63.

Jevon, Thomas. *The Devil of a Wife.* London, 1686.

Johns, Adrian. *The Nature of the Book: Print and Knowledge in the Making.* Chicago: University of Chicago Press, 1998.

Johnson, Charles. *The Cobler of Preston.* London, 1716.

———. *The Country Lasses.* London, 1715.

———. *The Force of Friendship.* London, 1710.

———. *Love in a Forest.* London, 1723.

———. *The Masquerade.* London, 1719.

———. *The Tragedy of Medæa.* London, 1731.

———. *The Victim.* London, 1714.

———. *The Wife's Relief: or, the Husband's Cure.* London, 1712.

Johnson, Samuel. *Lives of the English Poets.* Edited by George Birkbeck Hill. 3 vols. Oxford: Clarendon, 1905.

Jones, Robert F. *Lewis Theobald. His Contribution to English Scholarship with Some Unpublished Letters.* New York: Columbia University Press, 1919.

Jordan, Rob. "An Addendum to *The London Stage 1660–1700.*" *Theatre Notebook* 47 (1993): 62–75.

Jordan, Thomas. *A Royal Arbor of Loyal Poesie.* London, 1664.

The Jovial Cobler, or, A Light Heart's better than a Heavy Purse. London, 1749.

Katz, David S. *The Jews in the History of England 1485–1850.* Oxford: Clarendon, 1994.

Kenny, Shirley Strum. "A Broadside Prologue by Farquhar." *Studies in Bibliography* 25 (1972): 179–85.

———. "Humane Comedy." *Modern Philology* 75 (1977): 29–43.

———. "Perennial Favorites: Congreve, Vanbrugh, Cibber, Farquhar, and Steele." *Modern Philology* 73 (1976): S4–S11.

———. "The Publication of Plays." In *British Theatre and the Other Arts, 1660–1800*. Edited by Shirley Strum Kenny. Washington, D.C.: Folger Books, 1984. 309–36.

———. "Theatre, Related Arts, and the Profit Motive: An Overview." In *British Theatre and the Other Arts, 1660–1800*. Edited by Shirley Strum Kenny. Washington, D.C.: Folger Books, 1984. 15–38.

———. "Theatrical Warfare, 1695–1710." *Theatre Notebook* 27 (1973): 130–45.

———, ed. *British Theatre and the Other Arts, 1660–1800*. Washington, D.C.: Folger Books, 1984.

Kenyon, J. R. *Revolution Principles: The Politics of Party 1689–1720*. Cambridge: Cambridge University Press, 1977.

Kern, Jean B. *Dramatic Satire in the Age of Walpole 1720–1750*. Ames: Iowa State University Press, 1976.

Kern, Ronald C. "Documents Relating to Company Management, 1705–1711." *Theatre Notebook* 14 (1959–60): 60–65.

Kernan, Alvin. *Printing Technology, Letters and Samuel Johnson*. Princeton: Princeton University Press, 1987.

Kewes, Paulina. *Authorship and Appropriation: Writing for the Stage in England, 1660–1710*. Oxford: Clarendon, 1998.

———. "Gerard Langbaine's 'View of *Plagiaries*': The Rhetoric of Dramatic Appropriation in the Restoration." *Review of English Studies* 48 (1997): 2–18.

———. "'Give me the Sociable Pocket-Books . . .': Humphrey Moseley's Serial Publication of Octavo Play Collections." *Publishing History* 38 (1995): 5–21.

Killigrew, Thomas. *Chit-Chat*. London, 1719.

Knight, Charles A. "Bibliography and the Shape of the Literary Periodical in the Early Eighteenth Century." *The Library* 8 (1986): 232–48.

Knoop, Douglas, Gwilym P. Jones, and Douglas Hamer, eds. *Early Masonic Pamphlets*. Manchester, 1945.

Korshin, Paul J. "Types of Eighteenth-Century Literary Patronage." *Eighteenth-Century Studies* 7 (1973–4): 453–73.

Kowaleski-Wallace, Elizabeth. *Consuming Subjects: Women, Shopping, and Business in the Eighteenth Century*. New York: Columbia University Press, 1997.

Krutch, Joseph Wood. *Comedy and Conscience After the Restoration*. 1924. Reprint, New York: Russell and Russell, 1967.

Kunz, Don R. *The Drama of Thomas Shadwell*. Salzburg: Institut für englische Sprache und Literatur, 1972.

Lacy, John. *The Dramatic Works of John Lacy, Comedian*. Edited by James Maidment and W. H. Logan. London: H. Sotheran, 1875.

———. *The Dumb Lady: or, the Farriar Made Physician*. London, 1670.

———. *The Old Troop*. London, 1664.

———. *Sauny the Scott. Or, the Taming of the Shrew*. 1698. London: Cornmarket Press, 1969.

———. *Sir Hercules Buffoon*. London, 1684.

Lambranzi, Gregorio. *New and Curious School of Theatrical Dancing*. 1716. Edited by Cyril W. Beaumont. New York: Dance Horizons, 1966.

Langbaine, Gerard. *An Account of the English Dramatick Poets*. Oxford, 1691.

———. *Momus Triumphans: or, The Plagiaries of the English Stage*. London, 1688.

Langhans, Edward A. "A Conjectural Reconstruction of the Dorset Garden Theatre." *Theatre Survey* 13 (1972): 74–93.

———. *Eighteenth-Century British and Irish Promptbooks: A Descriptive Bibliography*. New York: Greenwood Press, 1987.

Laurie, Margaret. "Did Purcell Set *The Tempest*." *Proceedings of the Royal Musical Association* 90 (1963/4): 43–57.

Lawrence, W. J. "A Player-Friend of Hogarth." *The Elizabethan Playhouse*. Second series. Stratford-upon-Avon: Shakespeare Head Press, 1913.

———. "Did Thomas Shadwell Write an Opera on 'The Tempest'?" In *The Elizabethan Playhouse and Other Studies*. Stratford-upon-Avon: Shakespeare Head Press, 1912. 193–206.

———. "Early French Players in England." In *The Elizabethan Playhouse and Other Studies*. Stratford-upon-Avon: Shakespeare Head Press, 1912. 126–56.

———. "Music and Song in the Elizabethan Theatre" and "The Mounting of the Carolan Masques." In *The Elizabethan Playhouse and Other Studies*. Stratford-upon-Avon: Shakespeare Head Press, 1912.

———. "Purcell's Music for *The Tempest*." *Notes and Queries* 11 (1904): 164–65.

Leacroft, Richard. *The Development of the English Playhouse*. Ithaca: Cornell University Press, 1973.

Lechner, Sister Joan Marie. *Renaissance Concepts of the Commonplaces*. New York: Pageant Press, 1962.

Leggatt, Alexander. *English Stage Comedy 1490–1990: Five Centuries of a Genre*. London: Routledge, 1998.

Lelyveld, Toby. *Shylock on the Stage*. London: Routledge, 1960.

A Letter to A.H. Esq. Concerning the Stage. London, 1698.

Leveridge, Richard. *The Comick Masque of Pyramus and Thisbe*. 1716. London: Cornmarket Press, 1969.

Lewis, Peter Elfed. "Richard Leveridge's *The Comick Masque of Pyramus and Thisbe*." *Restoration and Eighteenth-Century Theatre Research* 15 (1976): 33–41.

Liesenfeld, Vincent J. *The Licensing Act of 1737*. Madison: University of Wisconsin Press, 1984.

———, ed. *The Stage and the Licensing Act 1729–1739*. New York: Garland Press, 1981.

Locke, Matthew. *The English Opera*. London, 1675.

Lockwood, Thomas. "Fielding and the Licensing Act." *Huntington Library Quarterly* 50 (1987): 379–93.

Loftis, John. *The Politics of Drama in Augustan England*. Oxford: Clarendon, 1963.

———. *Steele at Drury Lane*. Berkeley: University of California Press, 1952.

The London Stage 1660–1800, Part 2: 1700–1729. A New Version. Edited by Judith Milhous and Robert D. Hume, in the Harvard Theatre Collection, Harvard University.

The London Stage 1660–1800. Edited by William Van Lennep, Emmett L. Avery, Arthur H. Scouten, George Winchester Stone, Jr., and Charles Beecher Hogan. 5 parts, 11 vols. Carbondale: Southern Illinois University Press, 1960–68.

Love, Harold. "Who Were the Restoration Audience?" *Yearbook of English Studies* 10 (1980): 21–44.

Luckett, Richard. "Exotick but rational entertainments: The English dramatick operas." In *English Drama: Forms and Development*. Edited by Marie Axton and Raymond Williams. Cambridge: Cambridge University Press, 1977. 123–41.

———. "A New Source for *Venus and Adonis*." *The Musical Times* 80 (1989): 76–79.

Luttrell, Narcissus. *A Brief [Historical?] Relation of State Affairs, September 1678 to April 1714*. Oxford: Oxford University Press, 1857.

Lynch, Kathleen M. "Thomas D'Urfey's Contribution to Sentimental Comedy." *Philological Quarterly* 9 (1930): 249–59.

Mabbett, Margaret. "Italian Musicians in Restoration England (1660–90)." *Music & Letters* 67 (1986): 237–47.

Mace, Nancy A. "Falstaff, Quin, and the Popularity of *The Merry Wives of Windsor* in the Eighteenth Century." *Theatre Survey* 31 (1990): 55–66.

Maclean, Gerald, ed. *Culture and Society in the Stuart Restoration*. Cambridge: Cambridge University Press, 1995.

Maguire, Nancy Klein. *Regicide and Restoration: English Tragicomedy 1660–1671*. Cambridge: Cambridge University Press, 1992.

Marsden, Jean I. *The Re-Imagined Text: Shakespeare, Adaptation, and Eighteenth-Century Literary Theory*. Lexington: University Press of Kentucky, 1995.

———, ed. *The Appropriation of Shakespeare: Post-Renaissance Reconstructions of the Works and the Myth*. Hemel Hempstead: Harvester Wheatsheaf, 1991.

Marvell, Andrew. *The Poems and Letters of Andrew Marvell*. Edited by H. M. Margoliouth. 3d ed. Oxford: Clarendon, 1971.

Mattick, Paul, Jr., ed. *Eighteenth-Century Aesthetics and the Reconstruction of Art*. Cambridge: Cambridge University Press, 1993.

Maurer, Margaret. "The Rowe Editions of 1709/1714 and 3.1. of *The Taming of the Shrew*." In *Reading Readings: Essays on Shakespeare Editing in the Eighteenth Century*. Edited by Joanna Gondris. Madison, N.J.: Fairleigh Dickinson University Press, 1998. 244–67.

Maus, Katharine Eisaman. "Arcadia Lost: Politics and Revision in the Restoration *Tempest*." *Renaissance Drama* 13 (1982): 189–209.

———. "'Playhouse Flesh and Blood': Sexual Ideology and the Restoration Actress." *ELH* 46 (1979): 595–617.

Mayer, David, and Kenneth Richards, eds. *Western Popular Theatre*. London: Methuen, 1977.

McDowell, Paula. *The Women of Grub Street: Press, Politics, and Gender in the London Literary Marketplace 1678–1730*. Oxford: Clarendon, 1998.

McGeary, Thomas. "Thomas Clayton and the Introduction of Italian Opera to England." *Philological Quarterly* 77 (1998): 171–86.

McKeithan, Daniel Morley. *The Debt to Shakespeare in the Beaumont-and-Fletcher Plays*. Austin, 1938.

McKendrick, Neil, John Brewer, and J. H. Plumb. *The Birth of a Consumer Society: The Commercialization of Eighteenth-Century England*. Bloomington: Indiana University Press, 1982.

McKerrow, R. B. "The Treatment of Shakespeare's Text by his Earlier Editors, 1706–1768." British Academy Shakespeare Lecture, 1933. Rpt. in *Studies in Shakespeare*. Edited by Peter Alexander. London, 1964. 103–31.

McManaway, James G. "Excerpta quaedam per A.W. adolescentem." In *Studies in*

Honor of DeWitt T. Starnes. Edited by T. P. Harrison, Archibald A. Hill, Ernest C. Mossner, and James Sledd. Austin: University of Texas Press, 1967. 117–29.

———. "The Renaissance Heritage of English Staging (1642–1700)." In *Studies in Shakespeare, Bibliography, and Theater*. Edited by Richard Hosley, Arthur C. Kirsch, and John W. Velz. New York: Shakespeare Association of America, 1969. 233–39.

———. "Songs and Masques in the *Tempest*." *Theatre Miscellany*, Luttrell Society Reprints, no. 14. Oxford, 1953. 69–96.

Merchant, W. Moelwyn. "'A Midsummer Night's Dream': A Visual Re-creation." In *Early Shakespeare*. Edited by John Russell Brown and Bernard Harris. *Stratford-upon-Avon Studies* 3. London: Edward Arnold, 1961. 165–85.

The Merry Conceited Humours of Bottom the Weaver. Edited by Stanley Wells. 1661. London: Cornmarket Press, 1970.

Milhous, Judith. "An Annotated Census of Thomas Betterton's Roles, 1659–1710." Part One. *Theatre Notebook* 29 (1975): 33–43.

———. "An Annotated Census of Thomas Betterton's Roles, 1659–1710." Part Two. *Theatre Notebook* 29 (1975): 85–94.

———. "The Date and Import of the Financial Plan for a United Theatre Company in P.R.O. LC 7/3." *Maske und Kothurn* 21 (1975): 81–88.

———. "The Multimedia Spectacular on the Restoration Stage." In *British Theatre and the other Arts, 1660–1800*, ed. Shirley Strum Kenny. Washington, D.C.: Folger Books, 1984. 41–66.

———. "New Light on Vanbrugh's Haymarket Theatre Project." *Theatre Survey* 17 (1976): 143–61.

———. *Thomas Betterton and the Management of Lincoln's Inn Fields 1695–1708*. Carbondale and Edwardsville: Southern Illinois University Press, 1979.

———, and Robert D. Hume, "Attribution Problems in English Drama, 1660–1700." *Harvard Library Bulletin* 31 (1983): 5–39.

———. "Dating Play Premieres from Publication Data, 1660–1700." *Harvard Library Bulletin* 22 (1974): 374–405.

———. "The Drury Lane Actors' Petition of 1705." *Theatre Notebook* 39 (1985): 62–67.

———. "New Light on English Acting Companies in 1646, 1648, and 1660." *Review of English Studies* 42 (1991): 487–509.

———. *Producible Interpretation: Eight English Plays 1675–1707*. Carbondale and Edwardsville: Southern Illinois University Press, 1985.

———. *Vice Chamberlain Coke's Theatrical Papers 1706–1715*. Carbondale and Edwardsville: Southern Illinois University Press, 1982.

Miller, James. *The Universal Passion*. 1737. London: Cornmarket Press, 1969.

Milton, William M. "*Tempest* in a Teapot." *ELH* 14 (1947): 207–18.

Mish, Charles C. "An Early Eighteenth-Century Prose Version of *The Tempest*." In *British Theatre and the Other Arts, 1660–1800*. Edited by Shirley Strum Kenny. Washington, D.C.: Folger Books, 1984. 237–56.

Mitchell, C. J. "Quotation Marks, Compositorial Habits, and False Imprints." *The Library*, 6th series 5 (1983): 359–84.

Mitchell, Jim. "The Spread and Fluctuation of Eighteenth-Century Printing." *Studies in Voltaire and the Eighteenth Century* 230 (1985): 305–21.

Mitchell, Louis D. "Command Performances During the Reign of George I." *Eighteenth-Century Studies* 7 (1974): 343–49.

― ― ―. "Command Performances During the Reign of Queen Anne." *Theatre Notebook* 24 (1970): 111–17.

Modder, Montagu Frank. *The Jew in the Literature of England to the End of the Nineteenth Century*. Philadelphia: The Jewish Publication Society of America, 1939.

A Modern Account of Scotland. London, 1670.

Monod, Paul Klebér. *Jacobitism and the English People, 1688–1788*. Cambridge: Cambridge University Press, 1989.

― ― ―. "The Politics of Matrimony: Jacobitism and Marriage in Eighteenth-Century England." In *The Jacobite Challenge*. Edited by Eveline Cruickshanks and Jeremy Black. Edinburgh, 1988.

Montagu, W.D., Seventh Duke of Manchester, ed. *Court and Society from Elizabeth to Anne. Edited from the Papers at Kimbolton*. 2 vols. London: Hurst and Blackett, 1864.

Montaño, John Patrick. "The Quest for Consensus: The Lord Mayor's Day Shows in the 1670s." In *Culture and Society in the Stuart Restoration*. Edited by Gerald Maclean. Cambridge: Cambridge University Press, 1995. 31–51.

Moore, John Robert. "*The Tempest* and *Robinson Crusoe*." *Review of English Studies* 21 (1945): 52–56.

Moore, Robert Etheridge. *Henry Purcell and the Restoration Theatre*. London: Heinemann, 1961.

Morley, Henry. *Memoirs of Bartholomew Fair*. London: Chapman and Hall, 1859.

Morris, Corbyn. "An Essay Towards Fixing the True Standards of Wit, Humour, Raillery, Satire, and Ridicule. To which is Added, an Analysis of the Characters of An Humourist, Sir *John Falstaff*, Sir *Roger De Coverly*, and Don *Quixote*." London, 1744.

Motteux, Peter Anthony. *Camilla*. London, 1709.

― ― ―. *Farewel Folly: or, The Younger the Wiser*. London, 1707.

― ― ―. *The Loves of Mars and Venus*. London, 1696.

― ― ―. *The Novelty*. London, 1697.

Mueschke, Paul, and Jeannette Fleisher. "Jonsonian Elements in the Comic Underplot of *Twelfth Night*." *PMLA* 48 (1933): 722–40.

Mui, Hoh-Cheung, and Lorna H. Mui. *Shops and Shopkeeping in Eighteenth-Century England*. London: Routledge, 1989.

Muir, Kenneth. *Shakespeare as Collaborator*. London: Methuen, 1960.

Mullin, Donald C. "The Queen's Theatre, Haymarket: Vanbrugh's Opera House." *Theatre Survey* 8 (1967): 84–105.

Munro, John. *The Shakspere Allusion-Book: A Collection of Allusions to Shakespeare from 1591–1700*. 2 vols. London: Humphrey Milford, 1932.

Munsche, P. B. *Gentlemen and Poachers: The English Game Laws 1671–1831*. Cambridge: Cambridge University Press, 1981.

Murphy, Avon Jack. *John Dennis*. Boston: Twayne, 1984.

Nalbach, Daniel. *The King's Theatre, 1704–1867*. London: Society for Theatre Research, 1972.

Neighbarger, Randy L. *An Outward Show: Music for Shakespeare on the London Stage, 1660–1830*. Westport, Conn.: Greenwood Press, 1992.

Nethercot, Arthur H. *Sir William Davenant: Poet Laureate and Playwright-Manager*. Chicago: University of Chicago Press, 1938.

Nichols, Charles Washburn. "A Reverend Alterer of Shakespeare." *MLN* 44 (1929): 30–32.

Nicoll, Allardyce. *A History of English Drama 1660–1900*. 6 vols. Cambridge: Cambridge University Press, 1952–59.

Nilan, Mary Margaret. "The Stage History of *The Tempest*: A Question of Theatricality." Ph.D. diss., Northwestern University, 1967.

North, Roger. *Examen: or, An Enquiry into the Credit and Veracity of a Pretended Complete History*. London, 1740.

———. *Roger North on Music*. Edited by John Wilson. London: Novello, 1959.

Notestein, Wallace. *The Scot in History*. 1946. Rpt., Westport, Conn.: Greenwood Press, 1970.

Noyes, Robert Gale. *Ben Jonson on the English Stage, 1660–1776*. Cambridge: Harvard University Press, 1935.

———. "A Manuscript Restoration Prologue for *Volpone*." *Modern Language Notes* 42 (1937): 198–200.

Odell, George C. D. *Shakespeare from Betterton to Irving*. 2 vols. 1920. New York: Dover Publications, 1966.

Oldmixon, John. *The Governour of Cyprus*. London, 1702.

———. *Poems on Several Occasions*. London, 1696.

———. *Reflections on the Stage*. London, 1699.

Olleson, Philip. "Vanbrugh and Opera at the Queen's Theatre, Haymarket." *Theatre Notebook* 26 (1972): 94–101.

Orgel, Stephen. "The Authentic Shakespeare." *Representations* 21 (1988): 1–25.

Osborne, Francis. *The True Tragicomedy*. London, 1654.

The Out-Cry of the London Prentices for Justice to be Executed . . . London, 1656.

Paul, Harry Gilbert. *John Dennis: His Life and Criticism*. New York: Columbia University Press, 1911.

Paxman, David. "The Burden of the Immediate Past: The Early Eighteenth Century and the Shadow of Restoration Comedy." *Essays in Literature* 17 (1990): 15–29.

Payne, Deborah C. "Patronage and the Dramatic Marketplace under Charles I and II." *Yearbook of English Studies* 21 (1991): 137–52.

Pedicord, Henry William. "George Lillo and 'Speculative Masonry.'" *Philological Quarterly* 53 (1974): 401–12.

———. "Masonic Theatre Pieces in London 1730–1780." *Theatre Survey* 25 (1984): 153–66.

———. *The Theatrical Public in the Time of Garrick*. Carbondale: Southern Illinois University Press, 1966.

———. "White Gloves at Five: Fraternal Patronage of London Theatres in the Eighteenth Century." *Philological Quarterly* 45 (1966): 270–88.

Pepys, Samuel. *The Diary of Samuel Pepys*. Edited by Robert Latham and William Matthews. 11 vols. London: Bell and Hyman, 1970–83.

Perry, Thomas W. *Public Opinion, Propaganda, and Politics in Eighteenth-Century England: A Study of the Jew Bill of 1753*. Cambridge: Harvard University Press, 1962.

Peters, Julie Stone. *Congreve, the Drama, and the Printed Word*. Stanford: Stanford University Press, 1990.

Philips, John. *The Pretender's Flight, or, A Mock Coronation*. London, 1716.

Pinnock, Andrew. "Play into Opera: Purcell's *The Indian Queen*." *Early Music* 18 (1990): 3–21.

Pix, Mary. *The Deceiver Deceived*. London, 1697.

―――. *The Double Distress*. London, 1701.

―――. *The Innocent Mistress*. London, 1697.

Plumb, J. H. *The Commercialisation of Leisure in Eighteenth-Century England*. University of Reading, 1973.

Poems on Affairs of State: Augustan Satirical Verse, 1660–1714. 7 vols. New Haven: Yale University Press, 1963–75.

Pollins, Harold. *Economic History of the Jews in England*. Madison, N.J.: Fairleigh Dickinson University Press, 1982.

Pope, Alexander. *The Correspondence of Alexander Pope*. Edited by George Sherburn. Oxford: Clarendon, 1956.

―――. *The Poems of Alexander Pope*. Edited by John Butt. London: Methuen, 1963.

―――. *The Works of William Shakespeare*. 6 vols. London, 1725.

Porter, Roy. *English Society in the Eighteenth Century*. 1982. London: Penguin, 1990.

Porter, Thomas. *The French Conjuror*. London, 1677.

Powell, George. *The Treacherous Brothers*. London, 1690.

Powell, Jocelyn. *Restoration Theatre Production*. London: Routledge, 1984.

Price, Cecil. *Theatre in the Age of Garrick*. Oxford: Basil Blackwell, 1973.

Price, Curtis A. "The Critical Decade for English Music Drama, 1700–1710." *Harvard Library Bulletin* 26 (1978): 38–76.

―――. "*Dido and Aeneas*: Questions of Style and Evidence." *Early Music* 22 (1994): 115–25.

―――. "English Traditions in Handel's *Rinaldo*." In *Handel Tercentenary Collection*. Edited by Stanley Sadie and Anthony Hicks. Ann Arbor, Mich.: UMI Research Press, 1987.

―――. *Henry Purcell and the London Stage*. Cambridge: Cambridge University Press, 1984.

―――. "Music as Drama." In *The London Theatre World*. Edited by Robert D. Hume. Carbondale and Edwardsville: Southern Illinois University Press, 1980. 210–35.

―――. *Music in the Restoration Theatre, with a Catalogue of Instrumental Music in the Plays 1665–1713*. Ann Arbor, Mich.: UMI Research Press, 1979.

Priestly, Joseph. *An Essay on a Course of Liberal Education for Civil and Active Life*. London, 1765.

Pry, Kevin. "Theatrical Competition and the Rise of the Afterpiece Tradition 1700–1724." *Theatre Notebook* 36 (1982): 21–27.

Pye, Christopher. "The Theater, The Market, and the Subject of History." *ELH* 61 (1994): 501–22.

Raddadi, Mongi. *Davenant's Adaptations of Shakespeare*. Stockholm: Uppsala, 1979.

Radice, Mark A. "Sites for Music in Purcell's Dorset Garden Theatre." *The Musical Quarterly* 81 (1997): 430–48.

Ralph, James. *The Case of Authors*. London, 1758.

―――. *The Fashionable Lady; or Harlequin's Opera*. London, 1730.

Randall, Dale B. J. *Winter Fruit: English Drama 1642–1660*. Lexington: University Press of Kentucky, 1995.

Ravenscroft, Edward. *The Anatomist*. London, 1697.

A Representation of the Impiety and Immorality of the English Stage (1704). In Augustan

Reprint Society Series Three: Essays on the Stage, No. 2. Edited by Emmett L. Avery. Los Angeles: Augustan Reprint Society, 1947.

Richards, Kenneth. "The Restoration Pageants of John Tatham." In *Western Popular Theatre*. Edited by David Mayer and Kenneth Richards. London: Methuen, 1977. 49–73.

Rivers, Isabel, ed. *Books and their Readers in Eighteenth-Century England*. New York: St. Martin's Press, 1982.

Roberts, Jeanne Addison. *Shakespeare's English Comedy: The Merry Wives of Windsor in Context*. Lincoln: University of Nebraska Press, 1979.

Rogers, Pat. "The Breeches Part." In *Sexuality in Eighteenth-Century Britain*. Edited by Paul-Gabriel Boucé. Manchester: Manchester University Press, 1982. 244–58.

———. *Grub Street: Studies in a Subculture*. London: Methuen, 1972.

———. "The Waltham Blacks and the Black Act." *The Historical Journal* 18 (1974): 465–86.

Rollins, Hyder E. 'The Commonwealth Drama: Miscellaneous Notes." *Studies in Philology* 20 (1923): 52–69.

———. "A Contribution to the History of English Commonwealth Drama." *Studies in Philology* 18 (1921): 267–333.

———, ed. *An Analytical Index to the Ballad Entries (1557–1709) in the Register of the Company of Stationers of London*. Chapel Hill: University of North Carolina Press, 1924.

———. *Cavalier and Puritan: Ballads and Broadsides Illustrating the Period of the Great Rebellion 1640–1660*. New York: New York University Press, 1923.

Rose, Mark. "The Author as Proprietor: Donaldson v. Becket and the Genealogy of Modern Authorship." *Representations* 23 (1988): 51–85.

———. *Authors and Owners: The Invention of Copyright*. Cambridge: Harvard University Press, 1993.

Rosenfeld, Sybil. *Foreign Theatrical Companies in Great Britain in the 17th and 18th Centuries*. London: The Society for Theatre Research, 1955.

———. *A Short History of Scene Design in Great Britain*. Oxford: Basil Blackwell, 1973.

———. *Strolling Players and Drama in the Provinces*. Cambridge: Cambridge University Press, 1939.

———. *The Theatre of the London Fairs in the Eighteenth Century*. Cambridge: Cambridge University Press, 1960.

Rosenthal, Laura J. *Playwrights and Plagiarists in Early Modern England: Gender, Authorship, Literary Property*. Ithaca: Cornell University Press, 1996.

Roth, Cecil. *A History of Jews in England*. Oxford: Oxford University Press, 1964.

Rothstein, Eric, and Frances Kavenik. *The Designs of Carolean Comedy*. Carbondale and Edwardsville: Southern Illinois University Press, 1988.

Rowe, Nicholas. *The Tragedy of Jane Shore*. London, 1714.

———, ed. *The Works of Mr. William Shakespear; in Six Volumes*. London, 1709.

Rubin, Abba. *Images in Transition: The English Jew in English Literature 1660–1830*. Westport, Conn.: Greenwood Press, 1984.

Rule, John. *Albion's People: English Society, 1714–1815*. London: Longman, 1992.

———. *The Vital Century: England's Developing Economy, 1714–1815*. London: Longman, 1992.

Ruttkay, K. G. "The Critical Reception of Italian Opera in England in the Early Eighteenth Century." *Studies in English and American Philology* 1 (1971): 93–169.

Ryder, Dudley. *The Diary of Dudley Ryder, 1715–1716.* Edited by William Matthews. London: Methuen, 1939.

Rymer, Thomas. *Foedera, conventiones, literae, et cujuscunque generis acta publica.* 20 vols. London: A. & J. Churchill, 1704–35.

Sadie, Stanley, ed. *The New Grove Dictionary of Opera.* 4 vols. London: Macmillan, 1992.

Savage, Roger. "The Shakespeare-Purcell *Fairy Queen*: A Defence and Recommendation." *Early Music* 1 (1973): 201–21.

Sawday, Jonathan. "Re-Writing a Revolution: History, Symbol, and Text in the Restoration." *The Seventeenth Century* 7 (1992): 171–99.

Sawyer, Paul. "John Rich's Contribution to the Eighteenth-Century London Stage." In *Essays on the Eighteenth-Century English Stage.* Edited by Kenneth Richards and Peter Thomson. London: Methuen, 1972.

— — —. "The Popularity of Shakespeare's Plays, 1720–21 through 1732–33." *Shakespeare Quarterly* 29 (1978): 427–30.

— — —. "The Popularity of Various Types of Entertainment at Lincoln's Inn Fields and Covent Garden Theatres, 1720–1733." *Theatre Notebook* 24 (1970): 154–63.

Scheil, Katherine West. "'Rouz'd by a Woman's pen': The Shakespeare Ladies' Club and Reading Habits of Early Modern Women." *Critical Survey* 12 (2000): 106–27.

Schneider, Ben Ross, Jr. "Granville's *Jew of Venice* (1701): A Close Reading of Shakespeare's *Merchant*." *Restoration* 17 (1993): 111–34.

Scotland Characterised. London, 1701.

Scott, Thomas. *The Mock-Marriage.* London, 1696.

Scott, Virgil Joseph. "A Reinterpretation of John Tatham's *The Rump: or the Mirrour of the Late Times.*" *Philological Quarterly* 24 (1945): 114–18.

Scouten, Arthur H. "The Increase in Popularity of Shakespeare's Plays in the Eighteenth Century: A *Caveat* for Interpreters of Stage History." *Shakespeare Quarterly* 7 (1956): 189–202.

— — —. "Shakespeare's Plays in the Theatrical Repertory When Garrick Came to London." *University of Texas Studies in English* (1944): 257–68.

— — —, and Robert D. Hume. "'Restoration Comedy' and its Audiences, 1660–1776." *The Yearbook of English Studies* 10 (1980): 45–69.

Seary, Peter. *Lewis Theobald and the Editing of Shakespeare.* Oxford: Clarendon, 1990.

— — —. "Lewis Theobald, Edmond Malone, and Others." In *Reading Readings: Essays on Shakespeare Editing in the Eighteenth Century,* ed. Joanna Gondris. Madison, N.J.: Fairleigh Dickinson University Press, 1998.

Seaton, Ethel. *Literary Relations of England and Scandinavia in the Seventeenth Century.* Oxford: Clarendon, 1935.

Serious Reflections on the Scandalous Abuse and Effects of the Stage: In a Sermon Preach'd at the Parish-Church of St. Nicolas in the City of Bristol, on Sunday the 7th Day of January, 1704/5. Bristol, 1705.

Settle, Elkanah. *A Farther Defence of Dramatick Poetry.* London, 1698.

— — —. *The Heir of Morocco.* London, 1682.

— — —. *The Siege of Troy.* London, 1707.

— — —. *The World in the Moon.* London, 1697.

Shadwell, Thomas. *The Humorists.* London, 1671.

— — —. *Ibrahim.* London, 1677.

———. *The Squire of Alsatia*. London, 1688.

———. *The Sullen Lovers*. London, 1668.

———. *The Volunteers, or The Stock-Jobbers*. London, 1692.

Shakespeare, William. *As You Like It*. Edited by Alan Brissenden. Oxford: Oxford University Press, 1994.

———. *Measure for Measure*. Edited by N. W. Bawcutt. Oxford and New York: Oxford University Press, 1991.

———. *The Merchant of Venice*. Edited by Jay L. Halio. Oxford: Clarendon, 1993.

———. *A Midsummer Night's Dream*. Edited by Harold F. Brooks. London: Methuen, 1979.

———. *A Midsummer Night's Dream*. Edited by R. A. Foakes. Cambridge: Cambridge University Press, 1984.

———. *The Taming of the Shrew*. Edited by Ann Thompson. Cambridge: Cambridge University Press, 1984.

———. *The Taming of the Shrew*. Edited by Robert Heilman. New York: Penguin Books, 1966.

———. *The Taming of the Shrew*. Edited by H. J. Oliver. Oxford: Clarendon, 1982.

———. *Twelfth Night*. Edited by J. M. Lothian and T. W. Craik. London: Methuen 1975.

Shane, Denise Elliott. "John Rich and the Reopening of Lincoln's Inn Fields." *Theatre Notebook* 42 (1988): 23–34.

Shapiro, James. *Shakespeare and the Jews*. New York: Columbia University Press, 1996.

Shattuck, Charles H. *The Shakespeare Promptbooks: A Descriptive Catalogue*. Urbana and London: University of Illinois Press, 1965.

Sheffield, John, Duke of Buckingham. *The Laws of Poetry*. London, 1721.

Sherbo, Arthur. *The Birth of Shakespeare Studies: Commentators from Rowe (1709) to Boswell-Malone (1821)*. East Lansing, Mich.: Colleagues Press, 1986.

Shudofsky, M. Maurice. "Charles Johnson and Eighteenth-Century Drama." *ELH* 10 (1943): 131–58.

Simpson, Claude M. *The British Broadside Ballad and Its Music*. New Brunswick, N.J.: Rutgers University Press, 1966.

Smith, Edmund. *Phaedra and Hippolitus*. London, 1707.

Smith, John Harrington. *The Gay Couple in Restoration Comedy*. Cambridge: Harvard University Press, 1948.

———. "Shadwell, the Ladies, and the Change in Comedy." *Modern Philology* 46 (1948): 22–33.

Some Thoughts Concerning the Stage in a Letter to a Lady. London, 1704. Reprinted in *Essays on the Stage*, No. 2. Edited by Emmett L. Avery. Los Angeles: Augustan Reprint Society, 1947.

Sorelius, Gunnar. "The Early History of the Restoration Theatre: Some Problems Reconsidered." *Theatre Notebook* 33 (1979): 52–61.

———. *"The Giant Race Before the Flood": Pre-Restoration Drama on the Stage and in the Criticism of the Restoration*. Stockholm: Uppsala, 1966.

———. "The Rights of the Restoration Theatrical Companies in the Older Drama." *Studia Neophilologica* 37 (1965): 174–89.

Spencer, Christopher, ed. *Five Restoration Adaptations of Shakespeare*. Urbana: University of Illinois Press, 1965.

Spencer, Hazelton. *Shakespeare Improved: The Restoration Versions in Quarto and on the Stage*. Cambridge: Harvard University Press, 1927.

Spingarn, J. E., ed. *Critical Essays of the Seventeenth Century*. Bloomington: Indiana University Press, 1957.

Sprague, Arthur Colby. *Beaumont and Fletcher on the Restoration Stage*. Cambridge: Harvard University Press, 1926.

———. *Shakespeare and the Actors: The Stage Business in His Plays (1660–1905)*. Cambridge: Harvard University Press, 1944.

Squire, William Barclay. "The Music of Shadwell's Tempest." *Musical Quarterly* 7 (1921): 565–78.

Stamm, Rudolf. "Sir William Davenant and Shakespeare's Imagery." *English Studies* 24 (1942): 65–79, 97–116.

Staves, Susan. *Players' Scepters: Fictions of Authority in the Restoration*. Lincoln: University of Nebraska Press, 1979.

Steele, Richard. *The Correspondence of Richard Steele*. Edited by Rae Blanchard. London: Oxford University Press, 1941.

———. *The Funeral*. London, 1702.

———. *The Tatler*. Edited by Donald F. Bond. 3 vols. Oxford: Clarendon, 1987.

———. *Tracts and Pamphlets by Richard Steele*. Edited by Rae Blanchard. Baltimore: Johns Hopkins University Press, 1944.

Stewart, Powell. "An Eighteenth-Century Adaptation of Shakespeare." *University of Texas Studies in English* 12 (1932): 98–117.

Stockwell, La Tourette. *Dublin Theatres and Theatre Customs*. New York: Benjamin Blom, 1968.

Stone, George Winchester, Jr. "Shakespeare in the Periodicals, 1700–1740: A Study of the Growth of Knowledge of the Dramatist in the Eighteenth Century." Part 1, *Shakespeare Quarterly* 2 (1951): 221–31.

———. "Shakespeare in the Periodicals, 1700–1740: A Study of the Growth of Knowledge of the Dramatist in the Eighteenth Century." Part 2, *Shakespeare Quarterly* 3 (1952): 313–28.

———. "Shakespeare's *Tempest* at Drury Lane During Garrick's Management." *Shakespeare Quarterly* 7 (1956): 1–7.

Stone, George Winchester, Jr., ed. *The Stage and the Page: London's "Whole Show" in the Eighteenth-Century Theatre*. Berkeley: University of California Press, 1981.

———, and George M. Kahrl. *David Garrick: A Critical Biography*. Carbondale and Edwardsville: Southern Illinois University Press, 1979.

Suckling, Norman. "Moliére and English Restoration Comedy." *Restoration Theatre*. Stratford-upon-Avon Studies 6. London: Edward Arnold, 1965. 93–107.

Sutherland, James R. "The Circulation of Newspapers and Literary Periodicals, 1700–30." *The Library* 15 (1934): 110–24.

Swaen, A. E. H. "The Cobbler's Jig." *Shakespeare Jahrbuch* 46 (1910): 122–24.

Tatham, John. *The Distracted State*. London, 1651.

———. *The Rump*. London, 1660.

———. *The Scots Figgaries: or a Knot of Knaves*. London, 1652.

Tave, Stuart M. *The Amiable Humorist: A Study in the Comic Theory and Criticism of the Eighteenth and Early Nineteenth Centuries*. Chicago: University of Chicago Press, 1960.

Taylor, Gary. *Reinventing Shakespeare: A Cultural History from the Restoration to the Present*. London: The Hogarth Press, 1990.

The Tempest. London, 1674.

Theobald, Lewis. *The Cave of Poverty. A Poem. Written in Imitation of Shakespeare*. London, 1715.

———. *Double Falshood: or, The Distrest Lovers*. 1728. London: Cornmarket Press, 1970.

———. *Shakespeare Restored*. London, 1726.

Thesaurus Dramaticus. 2 vols. London, 1724.

Thomas, Claudia. "Pope and his *Dunciad* Adversaries: Skirmishes on the Borders of Gentility." In *Cutting Edges: Postmodern Critical Essays on Eighteenth-Century Satire*. Edited by James E. Gill. Knoxville: University of Tennessee Press, 1995. 275–300.

Thompson, E. P. *Whigs and Hunters: The Origin of the Black Act*. New York: Pantheon Books, 1975.

Thomson, James. *James Thomson (1700–1748): Letters and Documents*. Edited by Alan Dugald McKillop. Lawrence: University of Kansas Press, 1958.

Thorn-Drury, G. "Shadwell and the Operatic *Tempest*." *Review of English Studies* 3 (1927): 204–208.

———. "Some Notes on Dryden." *Review of English Studies* 1 (1925): 327–30.

———, ed. *A Little Ark*. London: P. J. and A. E. Dobell, 1921.

Thorp, Jennifer. "Dance in late 17th-century London: Priestly muddles." *Early Music* 26 (1998): 198–210.

———. "Your Honor'd and Obedient Servant: Patronage and Dance in London c.1700–1735." *Dance Research* 15 (1997): 84–98.

Trolander, Paul, and Zeynep Tenger. "Criticism Against Itself: Subverting Critical Authority in Late-Seventeenth Century England." *Philological Quarterly* 75 (1996): 311–38.

Trotter, Catharine. *Love at a Loss*. London, 1701.

———. *The Unhappy Penitent*. London, 1701.

Tucker, Joseph E. "The Eighteenth-Century English Translations of Molière." *Modern Language Quarterly* 3 (1942): 83–103.

Tuerk, Cynthia M. "The Duchess of Newcastle and John Lacy's *Sauny the Scot*." *Notes and Queries* 42 (1995): 450–51.

Tupper Fred S. "Notes on the Life of John Dennis." *ELH* 5 (1938): 211–17.

Vanbrugh, Sir John. *The Complete Works of Sir John Vanbrugh*. Edited by Geoffrey Webb. London: Nonesuch Press, 1928.

———. *The False Friend*. London, 1702.

Van Lennep, William. "Henry Harris, Actor, Friend of Pepys." In *Studies in English Theatre History in Memory of Gabrielle Enthoven*. Edited by M. St. Clare Byrne. London: Society for Theatre Research, 1952. 9–23.

———. "Nell Gwyn's Playgoing at the King's Expense." *Harvard Library Bulletin* 4 (1950): 405–8.

Vaughan, Alden T., and Virginia Mason Vaughan. *Shakespeare's Caliban: A Cultural History*. Cambridge: Cambridge University Press, 1991.

Vickers, Brian, ed., *Shakespeare: The Critical Heritage 1623–1800.* 6 vols. London: Routledge, 1974–81.

Visser, Colin. "French Opera and the Making of the Dorset Garden Theatre." *Theatre Research International* 6 (1981): 163–71.

Walker, William. *Victorious Love.* London, 1698.

Walkling, Andrew W. "Masque and Politics at the Restoration Court: John Crowne's *Calisto.*" *Early Music* 24 (1996): 27–62.

———. "Political Allegory in Purcell's 'Dido and Aeneas.'" *Music & Letters* 6 (1995): 540–71.

———. "Politics and the Restoration masque: the case of *Dido and Aeneas.*" In *Culture and Society in the Stuart Restoration.* Edited by Gerald Maclean. Cambridge: Cambridge University Press, 1995.

Wallace, John M. "Dryden and History: A Problem in Allegorical Reading." *English Literary History* 36 (1969): 265–90.

———. "'Examples Are Best Precepts': Readers and Meanings in Seventeenth-Century Poetry." *Critical Inquiry* 1 (1974): 273–90.

Wallerstein, Ruth. "Suckling's Imitation of Shakespeare." *Review of English Studies* 75 (1943): 290–95.

Walpole, Horace. *The Letters of Horace Walpole.* Edited by Paget Toynbee. Oxford: Oxford University Press, 1904.

Ward, Charles E. "*The Tempest*: A Restoration Opera Problem." *ELH* 13 (1946): 119–30.

Ward, Ned. *The London Spy.* Edited by Arthur L. Hayward. New York, 1927.

Weeks, Louise Jaquelyn. "Shakespeare as Adapted: *Measure for Measure, or, Beauty, the Best Advocate, Love Betray'd, The Jew of Venice,* and *The Comical Gallant.*" Ph.D. diss., University of Mississippi, 1988.

Wells, Stanley. "Shakespearian Burlesques." *Shakespeare Quarterly* 16 (1965): 49–62.

———, ed. *Shakespeare Survey 51: Shakespeare in the Eighteenth Century.* Cambridge: Cambridge University Press, 1998.

Wells, Staring B. "An Eighteenth-Century Attribution." *JEGP* 38 (1939): 233–46

West, Katherine [Scheil]. "'All this we must do, to comply with the taste of the town': Shakespearian Comedy and the Early Eighteenth-Century Theatre." Ph.D. diss., University of Toronto, 1995.

Wheeler, David. "Eighteenth-Century Adaptations of Shakespeare and the Example of John Dennis." *Shakespeare Quarterly* 36 (1985): 438–49.

White, Eric Walter. "Early Theatrical Performances of Purcell's Operas, With a Calendar of Recorded Performances, 1690–1710." *Theatre Notebook* 13 (1958): 43–65.

———. "New Light on *Dido and Aeneas.*" In *Henry Purcell 1659–1695: Essays on His Music.* Edited by Imogen Holst. London: Oxford University Press, 1959. 14–34.

Wikander, Matthew W. "'The Duke My Father's Wrack': The Innocence of the Restoration *Tempest.*" *Shakespeare Survey* 43 (1991): 91–98.

Wilcox, John. *The Relation of Molière to Restoration Comedy.* New York: Columbia University Press, 1938.

Williams, Aubrey. "No Cloistered Virtue: or, Playwright versus Priest in 1698." *PMLA* 90 (1975): 234–46.

Williams, Gary Jay. *Our Moonlight Revels: "A Midsummer Night's Dream" in the Theatre.* Iowa City: University of Iowa Press, 1997.

Wilson, Charles. *England's Apprenticeship 1603–1763*. 2d ed. London: Longman, 1984.

Wilson, Douglas L. "Thomas Jefferson's Early Notebooks." *William and Mary Quarterly* 42 (1985): 433–52.

Wilson, John Harold. *All the King's Ladies: Actresses of the Restoration*. Chicago: University of Chicago Press, 1958.

———. "Granville's 'Stock-Jobbing Jew.'" *Philological Quarterly* 13 (1934): 1–15.

———. *The Influence of Beaumont and Fletcher on Restoration Drama*. 1928. Rpt., New York: Haskell House Publishers, 1969.

———. "More Theatre Notes from the Newdigate Newsletters." *Theatre Notebook* 16 (1961/62): 59.

———. "Theatre Notes from the Newdigate Newsletters." *Theatre Notebook* 15 (1961): 79–84.

Winn, James A. "Heroic Song: A Proposal for a Revised History of English Theater and Opera, 1656–1711." *Eighteenth-Century Studies* 30 (1996–97): 112–28.

Winton, Calhoun. "The London Stage Embattled: 1695–1710." *Tennessee Studies in Literature* 19 (1974): 9–19.

———. "Sentimentalism and Theater Reform in the Early Eighteenth Century." In *Quick Springs of Sense: Studies in the Eighteenth Century*. Edited by Larry S. Champion. Athens: University of Georgia Press, 1974. 97–112.

Wiseman, Susan. *Drama and Politics in the English Civil War*. Cambridge: Cambridge University Press, 1998.

Wood, Bruce and Andrew Pinnock. "*The Fairy Queen*: A Fresh Look at the Issues." *Early Music* 21 (1993): 45–62.

———. "'Unscarr'd by turning times'?: The Dating of Purcell's *Dido and Aeneas*." *Early Music* 20 (1992): 372–90.

Wood, Frederick T. "*The Merchant of Venice* in the Eighteenth Century." *English Studies* 15 (1933): 209–18.

Wormald, Jenny. *Court, Kirk, and Community: Scotland, 1470–1625*. Toronto: University of Toronto Press, 1981.

Worsdale, James. *A Cure for a Scold. A Ballad Farce of Two Acts*. 1735. London: Cornmarket Press, 1969.

Wright, Louis B. "The Reading of Plays during the Puritan Revolution." *Huntington Library Bulletin* 6 (1934): 73–108.

Wright, Thomas, ed. *Political Ballads: Published in England During the Commonwealth*. London: Percy Society, 1841.

Zimmerman, Franklin B. "The Court Music of Henry Purcell." In *The Age of William III and Mary II*. Edited by Robert P. Maccubbin and Martha Hamilton-Phillips. Williamsburg: College of William & Mary, 1989.

———. *Henry Purcell 1659–1695: An Analytical Catalogue of His Music*. New York: St. Martin's, 1963.

Zwicker, Steven N. *Lines of Authority: Politics and English Literary Culture, 1649–1689*. Ithaca: Cornell University Press, 1993.

Index

Achilles (Boyer), 133, 263n. 165
Acis and Galatea (Motteux/Eccles), 83, 268n. 212
Actaeon and Diana (Cox), 277n. 76
Adams, Martin, 79, 246n. 101, 247n. 116
Addison, Joseph, 127, 156–57, 251n. 29, 262n. 135, 278n. 95, 283n. 11
"Advancement and Reformation of Modern Poetry, The," (Dennis), 131
Adventures of Five Hours, The (Tuke), 31, 230n. 22
Adventures of Half an Hour, The (Bullock), 169, 178, 277n. 79
Afterpieces, 24, 151, 153–87, 271n. 25, 272n. 26, 277n. 77
Agnew, Jean-Christophe, 224n. 13
Akerby, George, 170–72, 174, 275nn. 55 and 57
Albion and Albanius (Dryden), 61, 73, 247n. 117, 255n. 69
Alchemist, The (Jonson), 101, 107, 251n. 38, 264n. 168
Alexander the Great (Lee), 114, 257n. 89
All for Love (Dryden), 284n. 17
All Mistaken (Howard), 232n. 48
Allen, B. Sprague, 224n. 16, 247nn. 109 and 118
Allen, David, 277n. 78
Alssid, Michael W., 242n. 52
Ambitious Step-mother, The (Rowe), 94, 113
Amiable humor, 98, 132, 136–39, 143, 145, 147–49
Amorous Miser, The, 181
Amphitryon (Dryden), 74
Anatomist, The (Ravenscroft), 90, 104, 255n. 67
Anderson, James: *Constitutions*, 199
Angell, Edward: as Stephano in *The Tempest*, 56
"Animadversions on Mr. Congreve's Late Answer to Mr. Collier," 101

Anne, Queen, 21, 69, 87, 135, 142, 157, 226nn. 24 and 26, 249nn. 2 and 3
Antony and Cleopatra (Sedley), 284n. 17
Antony and Cleopatra (Shakespeare), 231n. 30
Apology for the Life of Mr. Colley Cibber, An, 17, 21, 50, 52, 83, 89, 92, 93, 94, 97, 122, 123, 131, 135, 136, 153, 157–59, 250n. 21, 265nn. 181 and 182
Ariadne (Perrin), 66
Armistead, Jack, 239n. 20
Arrowsmith, Joseph: *The Reformation*, 19
Arsinoe (Clayton), 154, 155, 171, 180, 270nn. 4 and 6
Art of English Poetry, The (Bysshe), 203–4, 283n. 7, 284nn. 14, 15, and 22
Arthur, John, 123
Arviragus and Philicia (Carlell), 273n. 33
As You Find It (Boyle), 102, 114, 144, 258n. 99, 268n. 212
As You Like It (Shakespeare), 150, 175, 188, 194, 195–98, 206–9, 212, 219, 231n. 30, 273n. 33, 278n. 96, 279n. 2, 283n. 11, 286n. 40
Aston, Anthony, 122
Aston, Walter, 123
Atterbury Plot, 189, 193, 199
Auberlen, Eckhard, 53, 238n. 19
Aubrey, John, 234n.59
Audience taste, 17, 18, 22, 102, 224n. 16
Author's Farce, The (Fielding), 18, 21
Author's Triumph, The, 17
Avery, Emmett L., 213n. 34, 225n. 18, 226n. 30, 268n. 216, 271n. 19, 274n. 39

Bajazet (Racine), 273n. 33
Baker, David Erskine, 230n. 26
Baker, Henry, 212
Baker, Thomas: *The Humour of the Age*, 88, 90, 99, 257n. 89; *Tunbridge-Walks*, 90, 144

314

INDEX

Baldwin, Olive, 277n. 85, 278n. 87
Banditti, The (Durfey), 50–51
Banister, John, 55, 62, 66, 96, 239n. 22, 255n. 65
Banks, John: *The Island Queens*, 244n. 94; *Vertue Betray'd*, 17–18
Barlow, Graham, 270n. 6
Barnet, Sylvan, 272n. 29
Barnett, R. D., 259n. 110
Barry, Elizabeth, 256n. 74, 269n. 230
Bartholomew Fair (Jonson), 96, 251n. 38, 265n. 183
Bartholomew Fair, 27, 96–97, 121, 142, 174, 178, 198, 240n. 33, 251n. 30
Bartley, J. O., 234n. 64, 235n. 70
Baskervill, Charles Read, 273n. 39, 275n. 50, 276n. 72, 277nn. 74 and 76, 278n. 94
Baston, John, 125
Bate, Jonathan, 222n. 5, 284n. 21
Bath, The (Durfey), 257n. 89
Bathurst, Villiers, 135
Bawcutt, N. W., 228n. 3, 229n. 14, 264n. 171
Bear Garden, 251n. 37
Beattie, John M., 226n. 24
Beaumont, Francis, 23, 32, 83, 103, 231n. 37
Beaumont, Francis, and John Fletcher: plays adapted, 83–84, 227n. 34, 248n. 124
Beauties of Shakespear, The (Dodd), 284n. 21
Beauties Triumph (Duffett), 255n. 65
Bedford, Arthur, 109, 253n. 48
Beggar's Opera, The (Gay), 176, 220
Behn, Aphra, 218; *The Forc'd Marriage*, 52; *The Revenge*, 169; *The Roman Bride's Revenge*, 101; *The Roundheads*, 43, 164
Belanger, Terry, 282n. 2
Belvedere (Bodenham), 283n. 13
Bentley, G. E., 135, 137, 149, 231n. 30, 251n. 38, 264n. 175, 268n. 223
Bermingham, Ann, 224n. 13
Bertie, Peregrine, 45
Betterton, Thomas, 49, 66, 69, 73, 80, 84, 88, 92, 94, 98, 100–101, 105, 106, 113–15, 130, 131, 142, 145, 147, 153, 156, 157, 237n. 10, 243n. 61, 248n. 130, 254n. 62, 256n. 74, 257n. 89, 263n. 158, 264n. 173, 265n. 176, 268nn. 209 and 217; adaptation of Massinger and Fletcher's *The Prophetess*, 74, 75, 81, 83, 240n. 35, 247n. 119, 278n. 90; as Bassanio in Granville's *The Jew of Venice*, 116–19; Dorset Garden Spectaculars, 60, 92, 242n. 52; as Falstaff in *Henry IV*, 106, 135–36, 265n. 182; as possible author of *The Fairy-Queen*, 76; *The Prophetess* as revived by Rich, 84, 98; *The Rape of Europa by Jupiter*, 83
Bevis, Richard, 271n. 25, 275n. 48, 277n. 77
Bianconi, Lorenzo, 249n. 6
Bignell, Mrs., 96
Black Act, 188–200, 210, 279n. 5
Blackmore, Sir Richard, 143
Blagge, Margaret, 69
Blayney, Glenn H., 267n. 201
"Bloody Bed-roll, or Treason displayed in its Colours, The," 164–65
Blow, John: *Venus and Adonis*, 255n. 65
Bodenham, John: *Belvedere*, 283n. 13
Boheme, Anthony, 123
Bondman, The, (Massinger), 230nn. 19 and 20
Bonduca (Fletcher), 83, 84, 250n. 22
Booth, Barton, 283n. 7
Boswell, Eleanore, 69, 243n. 71
Bottom the Weaver, 26–28, 30, 37, 47, 59, 85, 186, 198, 227n. 1, 245n. 96
Boyer, Abel: *Achilles*, 133, 263n. 165
Boyle, Charles: *As You Find It*, 102, 114, 144, 258n. 99, 268n. 212
Bracegirdle, Anne, 84, 106, 150, 256n. 74, 264n. 173, 269n. 230
Bradshaw, Mrs., 145
Branam, George C., 223n. 7, 252n. 41
Braverman, Richard, 257n. 86, 258n. 103, 261n. 128
Brewer, John, 224n. 13, 225n. 22, 226n. 28
Brissenden, Alan, 222n. 3
British Enchanters, The (Granville), 50, 117, 147, 155, 258n. 101, 268n. 222
Broad, John, 194, 280n. 15
Brome, Richard, 32; *The Jovial Crew*, 96, 234n. 60
Brooks, Harold F., 245n. 94
Brown, Arthur, 282n. 3
Brown, F. C., 245n. 99
Brown, Howard Mayer, 237n. 2

Brown, Laura, 222n. 6
Brown, Tom, 120
Browne, Dr.: *Everybody Mistaken*, 184–85
Browne, Edward, 33, 229n. 15
Bruster, Douglas, 224n. 13
Buckingham, George Villiers, Second Duke of: "An Essay Upon Poetry," 102; *The Rehearsal*, 51–52, 54, 182
Budd, F. E., 144, 269n. 226, 270n. 230
Bullock, Christopher, 13, 159, 275nn. 53, 54, 55, and 57, 276n. 64. Works: *Adventures of Half an Hour*, 169, 178, 277n. 79; *The Cobler of Preston*, 13, 23, 24, 59, 108, 125, 126, 159, 160, 168–82, 185, 186, 209, 216–19, 221n. 1, 223n. 8, 248n. 126, 272nn. 28 and 29, 275nn. 57 and 58, 277n. 76, 285n. 25; *The Per-Juror*, 169, 171–72, 173; *The Slip*, 169, 275n. 58; *The Traytor*, 169; *Woman Is a Riddle*, 161, 169, 172–73, 275n. 53; *A Woman's Revenge*, 169, 174, 177
Bullock, Hildebrand, 183
Bullock, Stephen C., 281n. 36
Bullock, William, 157, 169, 170, 173, 174, 176, 182, 265n. 180
Burling, William J., 267n. 205, 273n. 33
Burnaby, William: connections with John Dennis, 143–44; *The Ladies' Visiting Day*, 113, 145, 150, 151, 195, 268n. 215, 269n. 225; *Love Betray'd*, 24, 97–98, 100, 138, 143–53, 185, 194–95, 219, 223n. 8, 252n. 42, 268nn. 212 and 223, 269nn. 226, 228, and 229, 284n. 24; *The Modish Husband*, 265n. 183; *The Reform'd Wife*, 93, 268n. 215
Burnim, Kalman A., 235n. 70
Burridge, Richard: *A Scourge for the Play-Houses*, 109
Butt, John, 282nn. 6 and 7
Button's Coffee House, 160–61, 186
Bysshe, Edmund: *The Art of English Poetry*, 203–4, 283n. 7, 284nn. 14, 15, and 22

Caelia (Johnson), 273n. 33
Cairns, Edward A., 232n. 46, 253n. 49, 254n. 58, 256n. 76
Caius Marius (Otway), 284n. 17
Calisto (Crowne), 68, 69, 104, 243nn. 57, 71, and 72, 244n. 74
Camilla (Motteux), 93
Capell, Edward, 213, 286n. 42

Careless Lovers, The (Ravenscroft), 35
Cares of Love, The (Chaves), 151
Carey, Henry, 280n. 25
Carlell, Lodowick: *Arviragus and Philicia*, 273n. 33
Carlyle, Thomas, 21
Carrington, John: *The Modern Receipt*, 212–13
Case, Arthur E., 283n. 13
Catherine and Petruchio (Garrick), 233n. 54
"Causes of the Decay and Defects of Dramatick Poetry, The," (Dennis), 263n. 153
Cave of Poverty, The (Theobald), 285n. 31
Cavendish, Margaret, 233n. 55
Centlivre, Susannah, 144, 218; Works: *The Basset-Table*, 16; *The Gamester*, 155; *The Heiress*, 268n. 212; *Love at a Venture*, 268n. 215; *Love's Contrivance*, 90, 99, 103, 252n. 45; *The Perjured Husband*, 257n. 89
Change of Crownes, The (Howard), 39
Chappell, William, 273n. 39, 277n. 74
Characters of the Times, 160
Charles I, 34, 274n. 44
Charles II, 21, 31, 44, 53, 62, 66, 132, 240n. 35, 255n. 69; support of foreign entertainers, 65–66, 73, 242n. 53
Charlett, Arthur, 135
Chaves, A.: *The Cares of Love*, 151
Cheats of Scapin, The (Otway), 146
Chetwood, William, 136, 183, 283n. 7; *The Generous Freemason*, 198
Chit-Chat (Killigrew), 252n. 43
Churchill, Sarah, Duchess of Marlborough, 280nn. 19 and 22
Cibber, Colley, 17, 137, 157, 188, 218, 258n. 101, 262n. 144; as character in Fielding's *The Author's Farce*, 21; as Jaques in Johnson's *Love in a Forest*, 197; Works: *An Apology for the Life of Mr. Colley Cibber*, 17, 21, 50, 52, 83, 89, 92–94, 97, 122, 123, 131, 135, 136, 153, 157–59, 250n. 21, 265nn. 181 and 182; *The Double Gallant*, 268n. 215; *Love Makes a Man*, 94, 101, 257n. 89; *Love's Last Shift*, 146; *The Non-Juror*, 171–172, 197, 252n. 43; *Richard III*, 206, 219, 284nn. 17 and 24; *Ximena*, 94
Cibber, Theophilus, 212
Circe (Davenant), 61

INDEX

Clark, Peter, 274n. 41
Clark, Sandra, 233n. 55
Clarke, Jeremiah, 82
Clarke, Samuel: *Scripture Doctrine of the Trinity*, 113
Clayton, Thomas: *Arsinoe*, 154, 155, 171, 180, 270nn. 4 and 6
Clinch, Mr., 95, 96, 146–47
Clive, Mrs., 212
Cobb, Samuel, 99
Cobler of Preston, The (Bullock), 13, 23, 24, 59, 108, 125, 126, 159, 160, 168–82, 185, 186, 209, 216–19, 221n. 1, 223n. 8, 248n. 126, 272nn. 28 and 29, 275nn. 57 and 58, 277n. 76, 285n. 25
Cobler of Preston, The (Johnson), 13, 23, 24, 59, 108, 126, 159, 160–73, 176, 177–82, 184–89, 193, 197, 198, 209, 216, 218, 219, 223n. 8, 272n. 29, 274n. 42, 275nn. 49, 52, 57, and 58, 276n. 68, 277n. 81, 280n. 21
Coffey, Charles: *The Merry Cobler*, 179
Coke, Thomas, 113
Coleman, Charles, 34
Coleman, William S. E., 258n. 105, 259n. 113, 260nn. 117 and 122
Coleridge, Hartley, 263n. 163
Colley, Linda, 234n. 65
Collier, Jeremy, 101, 253n. 48, 266n. 194
Collier, William, 157
Collins, Howard S., 222n. 3, 229n. 13
Collison, Robert Lewis, 225n. 19
"Colonel Huson's (Or the Cobler's) Confession, In a Fit of Despair," 164
Comedy of Errors, The (Shakespeare), 184
Comical Gallant, The (Dennis), 24, 97, 98, 100, 115–16, 126–43, 147–48, 150, 151, 152, 167, 219, 221n. 3, 252n. 42, 255n. 70, 263n. 163, 265n. 183, 266nn. 184 and 188, 267nn. 197, 201, 202, 203, and 205
Comical History of Don Quixote, The (Durfey), 147, 277n. 75
Commendatory Verses on the Author of the Two Arthurs, 143
Committee, The (Howard), 39, 42
Commonplace books, 203–5, 283n. 13
Commonwealth of Women, A (Durfey), 58–59, 239n. 32
Comparison between the French and Italian Musick, A (Raguenet), 245n. 97
Comparison Between the Two Stages, A, 20, 81, 88, 91, 92, 97, 100–101, 106–7, 133, 136, 142–43, 145, 263n. 165, 267n. 203
Complete Art of Poetry, The (Gildon) 151, 204–5, 254n. 58, 262n. 135, 284nn. 15, 21, and 22
Confederacy, The (Vanbrugh), 139
Congreve, William, 94, 114–15, 137, 154–55, 157, 218, 240n. 33, 282n. 4; epilogue to *The Loves of Ergasto*, 154. Works: *Love for Love*, 92, 123, 239n. 19; *The Mourning Bride*, 156; *The Old Batchelour*, 123, 136, 269n. 224, 278n. 94; *The Way of the World*, 141, 149, 150
Conscious Lovers, The (Steele), 265n. 183
Constant Couple, The (Farquhar), 18, 103, 105
Constant Nymph, The, 147
Consumer society, 17–22, 91, 125, 224n. 13
Cook, Henry, 34
Cook, William: *Memoirs of Charles Macklin, Comedian*, 260n. 121
Cooper, Charles W., 235n. 70
Corbett, William, 245n. 97, 269n. 229
Corman, Brian, 137, 139, 222n. 6, 240n. 36, 242n. 52, 243n. 67, 268n. 215, 269n. 224
Corneille, Pierre, 258n. 101; *Horace*, 234n. 60
Corye, John: *The Metamorphosis*, 89
Country Lasses, The (Johnson), 273n. 33, 275n. 58, 280n. 19
Country Wake, The (Doggett), 122, 250n. 13
Country Wife, The (Wycherley), 96, 239n. 19, 265n. 183, 269n. 225, 281n. 37
Courtship A-la-mode (Crauford), 106
Cowley, Abraham: *Cutter of Coleman-Street*, 31, 230n. 21
Cox, Robert, 27, 28, 46, 217; *Actaeon and Diana*, 277n. 76
Craft, Catherine A., 258n. 105, 259nn. 108 and 113
Craik, T. W., 144, 223n. 8, 268n. 210
Crauford, David: *Courtship A-la-mode*, 106
"Critical Discourse on Opera's and Musick in England," 154
Critical Remarks on the Four Taking Plays of This Season, 202, 252n. 43, 283n. 11, 284n. 25

Cromwell, Oliver, 164
Cross, Letitia, 63
Crowne, John, 258n. 101; *Calisto*, 68, 69, 104, 243nn. 57, 71, and 72, 244n. 74
Cruickshanks, Eveline, 281n. 33
Culler, A. Dwight, 284n. 14
Cure for a Scold, A (Worsdale), 179, 277n. 83
Curll, Edmund: *The Life of That Eminent Comedian Robert Wilks*, 93, 94, 113
Cutter of Coleman-Street (Cowley), 31, 230n. 21
Cymbeline (Shakespeare), 83, 231n. 30, 268n. 216
Czar of Muscovy, The (Pix), 257n. 89

Danchin, Pierre, 243n. 60, 258n. 99
Davenant, Mary, 33
Davenant, Sir William, 26, 39, 46, 47, 76, 81, 89, 91, 104, 228nn. 4 and 6, 231nn. 36 and 38, 232nn. 41 and 44, 237n. 10, 238n. 16, 253n. 49, 258n. 101. Works: *Circe*, 61; *The First Day's Entertainment at Rutland House*, 34; *The Law Against Lovers*, 24, 28–37, 46–47, 51, 53, 59, 85, 98, 107–8, 162, 195, 204, 206, 217, 218, 220, 227n. 3, 229nn. 13 and 18, 230n. 26, 231nn. 28, 29, and 37, 232n. 46, 238nn. 15 and 16, 256n. 76; *Love and Honour*, 31, 34, 230n. 21; *The Rivals*, 232n. 48, 238n. 15, 277n. 74; *The Siege of Rhodes*, 31–35, 232nn. 40 and 43, 246n. 102; *The Play-house to be Let*, 30, 31, 34, 65, 229n. 15; *The Stepmother*, 229n. 15; *The Unfortunate Lovers*, 34; *The Wits*, 31, 34
Davis, Mary (Moll), 33, 35, 54, 98, 232n. 48
Davison, Lee, 224n. 13
Dawson, Giles E., 286n. 35
De Beer, E. S., 235n. 70
Deceiver Deceived, The (Pix), 23
"Defence of an Essay of Dramatique Poesie, A" (Dryden), 21, 56
Defoe, Daniel, 133, 258n. 107; *Robinson Crusoe*, 240n. 33
DeGrazia, Margreta, 222n. 5, 284n. 18, 285n. 29
Dekker, Thomas: *The Virgin Martyr*, 239n. 23
Deloney, Thomas, 276n. 73

Dennis, John, 117–18, 144, 145, 158, 184, 258n. 101, 262n. 150; against Italian opera, 127–28, 130, 262nn. 136, 138, and 141; as critic, 126–28, 219, 261n. 134, 262n. 144, 266n. 194; concern for public taste, 128–30, 154, 156, 180, 202, 255n. 70; condemnation of actors' financial motivations, 91; condemnation of scribblers, 90; connections with Charles Gildon, 101, 253n. 50; connections with George Granville, 126, 134, 261n. 133; connections with William Penkethman, 263n. 158; defends Shakespeare's knowledge of the rules, 134, 254n. 57; influence of Wycherley, 269n. 225; on actors, 131–32; on Ben Jonson, 264n. 168; on comedy, 263n. 161, 266nn. 192 and 196; on music, 262n. 151; on the rules, 130–31, 253n. 56, 263nn. 152, 153 and 155, 264n. 166; on Shakespeare, 264n. 169. Works: "The Advancement and Reformation of Modern Poetry," 131; "The Causes of the Decay and Defects of Dramatick Poetry," 263n. 153; *The Comical Gallant*, 24, 97, 98, 100, 115–16, 126–43, 147–48, 150, 151, 152, 167, 219, 221n. 3, 252n. 42, 255n. 70, 263n. 163, 265n. 183, 266nn. 184 and 188, 267nn. 197, 201, 202, 203, and 205; "Essay on the Genius and Writings of Shakespeare," 126, 134, 187; "Essay on the Opera's," 128, 261n. 135; "The Grounds of Criticism in Poetry," 143–44; "The Impartial Critic," 264n. 166; "A Large Account of the Taste in Poetry," 129, 131, 132–33, 255n. 70, 262n. 143; *Liberty Asserted*, 131, 133, 276n. 61; *A Plot and no Plot*, 133; "Reflections Critical and Satyrical," 131; "Reflections on an Essay Upon Criticism," 128; "Remarks upon Cato," 128; *Rinaldo and Armida*, 84, 130; "The Stage Defended," 128
Dent, Edward J., 237n. 2, 243n. 71, 245n. 95, 247n. 117
Devil of a Wife, The (Jevon), 45, 178, 179, 185, 277n. 81
Devil to Pay, The, 45, 277n. 82
Diary of Mary Countess Cowper, The, 157
Dido and Aeneas (Tate/Purcell), 36, 76, 103–12, 118–19, 204, 254n. 62, 255nn.

65, 67, 68, and 70, 256nn. 78, 80, 84, and 85
"Discourse Upon Comedy, A" (Farquhar), 18, 89, 99, 100, 252n. 43
Distracted State, The (Tatham), 43
Distressed Virgin, The, 121
Dixon, Peter, 282n. 7, 284n. 19
Dobson, Michael, 100, 162, 210, 222n. 4, 223n. 9, 228n. 3, 240n. 33, 262n. 139, 263n. 163, 276n. 64, 277n. 81, 285n. 27, 286n. 40, 287n. 4
Dodd, William: *The Beauties of Shakespear*, 284n. 21
Doggett, Thomas, 23, 46, 84, 157, 264n. 173, 278n. 94; as actor at the fairs, 121–22, 123; as comic actor, 122–23, 126, 175, 201, 210; as Shylock in Granville's *The Jew of Venice*, 114, 118–24, 135, 217, 219, 259nn. 113 and 117, 260n. 122; as strolling actor, 121–22, 259n. 114; *The Country Wake*, 122, 250n. 13
Dorset Garden Theater, 24, 70, 71, 74, 75, 77, 80, 84, 85, 92, 98, 110, 114, 115, 153, 216, 240n. 34, 242nn. 50 and 52, 248n. 130
Double Distress, The (Pix), 95, 257n. 89
Double Falshood (Theobald), 210–12, 285nn. 32 and 33
Double Gallant, The (Cibber), 268n. 215
Downes, John, 31, 34, 52–53, 60, 64, 68, 70, 73, 74, 78, 83, 94, 123, 134–35, 154, 155, 198, 230n. 19, 241n. 37, 242n. 52, 260n. 120, 264nn. 171 and 173, 268n. 209
Draghi, Giovanni Baptista, 62, 63
Dramatic Records of Sir Henry Herbert, The, 234n. 57
Dryden, John, 25, 34, 48, 50, 70–71, 129, 218, 238nn. 15 and 16, 240n. 36, 248n. 126, 258n. 101; as critic of foreign entertainers, 65, 66; as possible author of *The Fairy-Queen*, 76; commendatory verses to George Granville, 95; epilogue and masque to Vanbrugh's *The Pilgrim*, 83; ghost of, 115–17. Works: *Albion and Albanius*, 61, 73, 247n. 117, 255n. 69; *All for Love*, 284n. 17; *Amphitryon*, 74; "A Defence of an Essay of Dramatique Poesie," 21, 56; *An Evening's Love*, 56; *Examen Poeticum*, 21; *The Indian Queen* (with Howard), 84, 244nn.

93 and 94, 261n. 130; *King Arthur*, 61, 75, 81, 98; *Love Triumphant*, 121; *Secret Love*, 238n. 19, 244n. 93; *The Spanish Fryar*, 155; *Troilus and Cressida*, 258n. 97, 284n. 17; *The Wild Gallant*, 35
Duchess of Malfi, The (Webster), 230n. 22
Duffett, Thomas: *Beauties Triumph*, 255n. 65; *The Mock-Tempest*, 52, 71–73; *Psyche Debauched*, 71
Duke and No Duke, A, (Tate), 155, 178
Dumb Lady, The (Lacy), 38, 45, 234n. 62, 235nn. 72 and 73
Dunciad, The (Pope), 51
Dunkin, Paul, 246n. 108
Du Perier, François, 74
Durfey, Thomas, 38, 244n. 81, 247n. 108, 258n. 101; epilogue to Robert Gould's *The Rival Sisters*, 88, 90. Works: *The Banditti*, 50–51; *The Bath*, 257n. 89; *The Comical History of Don Quixote*, 147, 277n. 75; *A Commonwealth of Women*, 58–59, 239n. 32; *The Fool Turn'd Critick*, 19; *The Marriage-Hater Match'd*, 123; *A New Opera, call'd Cinthia and Endimion*, 84; *The Old Mode and the New*, 94–95; *Wonders in the Sun*, 155
Dutch Courtezan, The (Marston), 169
Dyregrov, David, 245n. 99

Earl of Mar Marr'd, The, 167
Eccles, John, 84, 114, 269n. 229; *Acis and Galatea*, 83; *The Judgment of Paris*, 257n. 92; *Peleus and Thetis*, 118–119; music to *The Rape of Europa by Jupiter*, 83
Edmond, Mary, 231n. 38
Ellis, Frank, 276n. 73
Empress of Morocco, The (Settle), 60
English Parnassus (Poole), 283n. 13
English Theophrastus, The, 20, 90
Ephesian Matron, The (Johnson), 273n. 33
Epicoene (Jonson), 101, 107, 251n. 38, 264n. 168
Essay on Criticism (Pope), 133, 261n. 134
"Essay on the Genius and Writings of Shakespeare" (Dennis), 126, 134
"Essay on the Opera's" (Dennis), 128, 261n. 135
Estcourt, Richard, 265n. 181; epilogue to Motteux's *Camilla*, 93
Etherege, George, 218; *The Man of Mode*,

255n. 67; *She Wou'd If She Cou'd*, 125, 155
Euripides, 131
Evans, G. Blakemore, 245n. 96, 284n. 13
Evelyn, John, 33, 66, 69, 78–79, 229n. 15, 230nn. 19 and 22, 235n. 70
Evening's Love, An (Dryden), 56
Everybody Mistaken (Browne/Taverner), 184–85, 279n. 97
Examen Poeticum (Dryden), 21
Exclusion Crisis, 74, 164, 274n. 45, 277n. 78

Fair Penitent, The (Rowe), 268n. 212
Fairs, 121–22, 126. *See also* Bartholomew Fair
Fairs: influence on theaters, 79, 96–98, 247n. 115
Fairy-Queen, The, 24, 69, 72–82, 85, 97, 98, 104, 105, 140, 150, 155, 162, 182, 209, 219, 244n. 94, 245nn. 95, 98, and 101, 246nn. 102–8, 247nn. 109, 112, 116–19, 248n. 121, 279n. 2; authorship debate, 50, 76, 85–86, 245n. 99
False Friend, The (Vanbrugh), 87, 265n. 183
farce, 137–40, 143, 158, 167–68, 172, 173, 177, 210, 275n. 48, 276n. 63
Farewel Folly (Motteux), 89
Farquhar, George, 137, 156–58, 218, 250n. 23, 251nn. 28 and 32, 254n. 60; *The Constant Couple*, 18, 103, 105; "A Discourse Upon Comedy," 18, 89, 99, 100, 252n. 43; *The Inconstant*, 89, 265n. 183; *The Recruiting Officer*, 281n. 37; *Sir Harry Wildair*, 257n. 89
Fashionable Lady, The (Ralph), 23
Fatal Marriage, The (Southerne), 177
Fatal Vision, The (Hill), 101
Felsenstein, Frank, 259n. 110, 260n. 121
Female Fortune-Teller, The (Johnson), 273n. 33
Ferguson, William, 234n. 65
Fickle Shepherdess, The (Randolph), 268n. 212
Fielding, Henry, 204, 218; *The Author's Farce*, 18, 21; *The Miser*, 286n. 36
Fine, Ben, 225n. 22
Finger, Godfrey, 114
Fiorilli, Tiberio (Scaramouche), 65–66

First Day's Entertainment at Rutland House, The (Davenant), 34
Fiske, Roger, 241n. 46, 248n. 121, 270n. 1, 277nn. 82 and 83
Fitzgerald, Mrs., 176, 177
Fitzgerald, Percy, 156
Flecknoe, Richard, 67, 238n. 16
Fleisher, Jeannette, 268n. 223
Fletcher, Anthony, 274n. 41
Fletcher, John, 15, 23, 32, 82, 93, 94, 102, 103, 137, 161, 231n. 37, 258n. 101. Works: *Bonduca*, 83, 84, 250n. 22; *The Island Princess*, adapted by Motteux, 81, 82, 84, 98, 278n. 94; *The Knights of Malta*, with music by Purcell, 83; *The Mad Lover*, 83, 229n. 19, adapted by Motteux, 114; *The Maid in the Mill*, 230n. 20; *The Maid's Tragedy*, adapted by Waller, 117; *The Pilgrim*, 83, 84, 248n. 124, 248n. 126, 258n. 101; *Rule a Wife and Have a Wife*, 174, 230n. 19; *The Tamer Tam'd*, 41, 46, 233n. 55, 236nn. 76, 77, and 78; *Valentinian*, as adapted by Rochester, 73, 83, 117; *The Wild Goose Chase*, 265n. 183; Fletcher and Massinger, *The Sea-Voyage*, 57–58, 239nn. 26, 27, and 30, 240n. 32
Flora's Vagaries (Rhodes), 234n. 61
Foakes, R. A., 272n. 29
Fool Turn'd Critick, The (Durfey), 19
Forc'd Marriage, The (Behn), 52
Force of Friendship, The (Johnson), 161, 273n. 33
Foreign performers: as competition for native English drama, 64–67, 72–73, 76, 85, 93–96, 98, 146, 156–57, 181, 186, 217, 242n. 53, 243nn. 56 and 57, 251n. 29
Forfeiture, The, (Jordan), 260n. 121
Forsythe, Robert Stanley, 227n. 1
Foss, Michael, 226n. 24
Freehafer, John, 29, 232n. 41, 285n. 32
Freemasons, 198–99, 281n. 36
French Conjurer, The (Porter), 67
French Dancing Master, The (Lacy), 42
Funeral, The (Steele), 94, 174, 265n. 183
Fuzélier, Louis: *La Matron d'Ephese*, 273n. 33

Gamester, The (Centlivre), 155
Garrick, David, 25, 201, 203–5, 209–10,

INDEX

212–14, 216, 217, 241n. 38, 286nn. 41, 42 and 43; *Catherine and Petruchio*, 233n. 54; *Macbeth*, 61
Gay, John, 218; *The Beggar's Opera*, 176, 220; *Three Hours After Marriage*, 181; *The What D'Ye Call It*, 181, 182, 278n. 88
Gellert, James, 231n. 28
Generous Conquerour, The (Higgons), 265n. 183
Generous Freemason, The (Chetwood), 198
Generous Husband, The (Johnson), 273n. 33
Genest, John, 107, 136, 163, 231n. 37, 256n. 77, 275nn. 49 and 58, 279n. 97, 280n. 23
Gentleman Cully, The (Johnson), 257n. 89
George I, 157, 158, 163, 166, 189, 190, 193, 199, 226n. 24, 271n. 18, 280n. 19
Gewirtz, Arthur, 223n. 7, 227n. 34
Gibbs, Ann, 268n. 209
Gilbert, W. S. and Arthur Sullivan, 167
Gildon, Charles, 117, 127, 132, 133, 144, 248n. 126, 250n. 16, 253n. 49, 258n. 101, 272n. 31; concern for public taste, 101–2; connections with Dennis, 101, 127, 253n. 50; praise of Leveridge, 181; prologue to Boyle's *As You Find It*, 102. Works: *The Complete Art of Poetry*, 151, 204–5, 254n. 58, 262n. 135, 284nn. 15, 21, and 22; *The Laws of Poetry*, 204; *The Life of Mr. Thomas Betterton*, 130, 262n. 135, 265n. 175; *Lives and Characters of the English Dramatick Poets*, 104, 254n. 57; *Love's Victim*, 100, 101, 103, 129, 257n. 89; *Measure for Measure*, 24, 85, 97, 98, 100–115, 118, 150, 151, 182, 185, 204–5, 219, 221n. 3, 231n. 37, 253n. 47, 254n. 62, 255nn. 70 and 72, 256nn. 74, 76, 77, 78, 80, 84, and 85, 258n. 97; *The Patriot*, 101; *Phaeton*, 82, 101; *Remarks on the Plays of Shakespeare*, 102, 205, 238n. 14; *Shakespeare's Life and Works*, 187; *The Younger Brother*, 101
Gilman, Todd S., 237n. 2, 240n. 36, 242n. 52, 243nn. 56 and 67, 258n. 102, 262nn. 136 and 138, 270n. 1, 271n. 12
Glorious Revolution, 74
Goblins, The (Suckling), 58, 247n. 108
Goff, Moira, 227n. 33, 248n. 130
Goggin, L. P., 286n. 36
Goldsmith, Oliver, 204

Gondris, Joanna, 282n. 3
Goring, Sir Henry, 193
Gormon the fighter, 118
Gosnell, Mrs., 54
Gould, Robert: *The Rival Sisters*, 88, 90
Governour of Cyprus, The (Oldmixon), 95, 268n. 212
Grabu, Louis, 73
Granville, George, Lord Lansdowne, 50, 95, 258n. 100, 271n. 18; connections with Dennis, 134, 261n. 133; epilogue to Boyle's *As You Find It*, 114. Works: *The British Enchanters*, 50, 117, 147, 155, 258n. 101, 268n. 222; *The Jew of Venice*, 23, 24, 85, 97, 98, 100, 113–26, 136, 143, 150–52, 159, 185–86, 207, 218, 221n. 3, 252n. 42, 257nn. 86, 87, 94, and 95, 258nn. 102, 104–7, 259nn. 108, 110, 113, and 117, 260n. 122, 261nn. 128 and 132, 284nn. 17 and 24; *Poems upon Several Occasions*, 119; *The She-Gallants*, 114
Graphic Illustrations of Hogarth (Ireland), 275nn. 55 and 57, 276n. 69
Greber, Giacomo: *The Loves of Ergasto*, 154–55
Griffin, Benjamin, 123, 173–75; *The Humours of Purgatory*, 178; *The Masquerade*, 125; *Whig and Tory*, 280n. 20
Griffin, Dustin, 226n. 24
Griffiths, Trevor R., 245n. 95
Gross, John, 260n. 117
"Grounds of Criticism in Poetry, The" (Dennis), 143–44
Grout, Donald J., 246n. 102
Grove, The (Oldmixon), 84, 255n. 72
"Grove, or the Rival Muses, The" 83–84
Grub Street, 19
Guffey, George R., 53, 57, 239n. 29, 241n. 38, 242n. 52
Guillory, John, 224n. 16
Gurr, Andrew, 242n. 50
Gwyn, Nell, 232n. 48, 240n. 35, 269n. 230

Halio, Jay L., 261n. 132
Hall, John, 174–75
Halliwell, J. O., 277n. 73
Hamlet (Shakespeare), 33, 93, 99, 124, 211, 218, 219, 228n. 4, 230nn. 19, 20, and 22, 231n. 30, 264n. 171, 278nn. 88 and 94

322 INDEX

Hammond, Brean S., 211, 225n. 19, 285n. 33
Handasyde, Elizabeth, 258nn. 100 and 106
Harbage, Alfred, 229n. 18
Haring-Smith, Tori, 223n. 8, 233n. 54, 272n. 29, 275n. 49
Harris, Ellen T., 104, 111, 254n. 62, 255nn. 64, 65, and 70, 256n. 78
Harris, Henry, 55, 237n. 10, 239n. 22, 268n. 209
Harris, Michael, 226n. 28
Hart, James, 62
Harvey, A. D., 227n. 3
Haun, Eugene, 237n. 2
Haynes, Jo, 66, 157; as possible author of *The Fairy-Queen*, 76
Heir of Morocco, The (Settle), 17
Heiress, The (Centlivre), 268n. 212
Henry IV (Shakespeare), 101, 106, 107, 139–40, 143, 174, 199, 206, 211, 264n. 171; Betterton's version, 135–36
Henry V (Hill), 281n. 41, 284n. 17
Henry V (Shakespeare), 206, 234n. 64
Henry VI (Shakespeare), 206
Henry VIII (Shakespeare), 29, 33, 101, 107, 228n. 4, 231n. 33
Herbert, Sir Henry, 228n. 8; *The Dramatic Records of Sir Henry Herbert*, 234n. 57
Herford, C. H., 269n. 223
Herringman, Henry, 33
"Hewson Reduc'd, or, The Shoomaker return'd to his trade," 166
Hewson, Colonel John, 164–68, 274n. 44, 275n. 47, 276n. 68, 277n. 73
Heywood, Thomas: *The Royall King*, 42
Higden, Henry: *The Wary Widdow*, 147
Higgons, Bevil: *The Generous Conquerour*, 265n. 183; prologue to *The Jew of Venice*, 115–17
Highfill, Philip H., Jr., 235n. 70
Hill, Aaron, 127, 253n. 56, 283n. 7; *The Fatal Vision*, 101; *Henry V*, 281n. 41, 284n. 17; *The Walking Statue*, 125
Hitchcock, Tim, 224n. 13
"Hive: A Collection of the Most Celebrated Songs, The," 168
Hoadly, Benjamin, 274n. 42
Hogan, Charles B., 264n. 171
Hogarth, William, 204, 276n. 69
Holderness, Graham, 223n. 8, 233nn. 54 and 56, 272n. 29

Holding, Edith, 279n. 5
Holland, Peter, 223n. 11
Hook, Lucyle, 245n. 100
Hooker, Edward Niles, 252n. 44, 262n. 141, 263n. 152, 266n. 195, 273n. 33
Hooker, Helene Maxwell, 71
Hopkins, Charles: *Boadicea*, 20, 87, 90, 250n. 16
Horace (Corneille), 234n. 60
Horn-Monval, Madam, 243n. 56
Hotson, Leslie, 230n. 26
Howard, Edward: *The Change of Crownes*, 39; *The Six Days Adventure*, 35; *The Usurper*, 238n. 13; *The Womens Conquest*, 49
Howard, James: *All Mistaken*, 232n. 48
Howard, Sir Robert, 38, 99; *The Committee*, 39, 42; *The Indian Queen* (with Dryden), 244nn. 93 and 94
Howe, Elizabeth, 270n. 230
Hudson, George, 34
Hughes, Derek, 222n. 6, 228n. 3, 238n. 12, 244n. 81
Hughes, Leo, 163–64, 172, 173, 225n. 18, 234n. 63, 235n. 75, 249n. 8, 255n. 70, 272n. 25, 273n. 37, 275n. 55, 276n. 63
Humane comedy, 137, 139
Hume, Robert D., 88, 136–38, 141, 142, 144, 155, 216, 222n. 6, 223n. 11, 225n. 18, 226n. 32, 227n. 35, 229nn. 15 and 18, 230n. 25, 232n. 50, 234n. 63, 237n. 2, 238n. 12, 239n. 24, 242n. 52, 243nn. 56 and 57, 245nn. 95 and 99, 248n. 130, 249nn. 1, 3, and 5, 250n. 18, 253n. 48, 255n. 65, 257nn. 89 and 92, 259n. 114, 264nn. 171 and 173, 265nn. 176 and 183, 267nn. 201 and 205, 268n. 222, 270nn. 1, 2, and 4, 271nn. 15 and 23, 277n. 83, 279n. 4, 285n. 26, 286n. 36, 287nn. 2 and 3
Humfrey, Pelham, 62, 66, 239nn. 22 and 28
Humorists, The (Shadwell), 42
Humour of the Age, The (Baker), 88, 90, 99, 257n. 89
Humours of Purgatory, The (Griffin), 178
Hydaspes (Mancini), 278n. 95

Ibrahim (Settle), 68
"Impartial Critic, The" (Dennis), 264n. 166

INDEX

Inconstant, The (Farquhar), 89, 265n. 183
Indian Queen, The (Dryden/Howard), 84, 244nn. 93 and 94, 261n. 130
Ingratitude of a Commonwealth, The (Tate), 284n. 17
Innocent Mistress, The (Pix), 87
Iphigénie (Racine), 273n. 33
Ireland, Samuel: *Graphic Illustrations of Hogarth,* 275nn. 55 and 57, 276n. 69
Island Princess, The (Fletcher/Motteux), 81, 82, 84, 98, 278n. 94
Island Queens, The (Banks), 244n. 94
Italian opera, 81, 85

Jacob, Giles, 127
Jacob, Margaret, 281n. 36
Jacobite Rebellion, 13, 160, 162–68, 180, 186, 188, 189, 193, 198–99, 261n. 128, 274n. 42, 275n. 51, 276n. 59, 279n. 5
James II, 226n. 24
Jane Shore (Rowe), 219, 272n. 30
Jarvis, Simon, 283n. 7
Jason, Philip K., 271n. 25, 272n. 32
Jefferson, Thomas, 284n. 16
Jevon, Thomas, 66; *The Devil of a Wife*, 45, 178, 179, 185, 277n. 81
Jew of Venice, The (Granville), 23, 24, 85, 97, 98, 100, 113–26, 136, 143, 150–52, 159, 185–86, 207, 218, 221n. 3, 252n. 42, 257nn. 86, 87, 94, and 95, 258nn. 102, 104–7, 259nn. 108, 110, 113, and 117, 260n. 122, 261nn. 128 and 132, 284nn. 17 and 24
Jews as stage figures, 120–21, 259nn. 109 and 113, 260n. 122
Johnson, Charles, 104, 273nn. 35 and 37, 280n. 19. Works: *Caelia,* 273n. 33; *The Cobler of Preston*, 13, 23, 24, 59, 108, 126, 159, 160–72, 173, 176–82, 184–89, 193, 197, 198, 209, 216, 218, 219, 223n. 8, 272n. 29, 274n. 42, 275nn. 49, 52, 57, and 58, 276n. 68, 277n. 81, 280n. 21; *The Country Lasses,* 273n. 33, 275n. 58, 280n. 19; *The Ephesian Matron,* 273n. 33; *The Female Fortune-Teller,* 273n. 33; *The Force of Friendship,* 161, 273n. 33; *The Generous Husband,* 273n. 33; *The Gentleman Cully,* 257n. 89; *Love in a Chest,* 266n. 195, 273n. 33; *Love in a Forest,* 23, 24, 160, 188–201, 204, 205–9, 211–12, 213, 219, 245n. 96, 273n. 33, 279nn. 2 and 5, 280nn. 23 and 29, 281n. 37, 284n. 22; *The Masquerade,* 161–62, 273n. 33, 285n. 25; *Medæa,* 273nn. 33 and 37; *The Successful Pyrate,* 273n. 33; *The Sultaness,* 273n. 33; *The Tragedy of Medea,* 162; *The Victim,* 273n. 33, 280n. 19; *The Village Opera,* 273n. 33; *The Wife's Relief,* 161, 273n. 33
Johnson, Samuel, 19, 25, 81, 204, 225n. 19, 275n. 53
Jones, Inigo, 237n. 5
Jones, R. F., 282n. 3
Jonson, Ben, 23, 94, 101, 106–7, 131, 135, 137, 151, 156, 157, 161, 237n. 5, 265nn. 175 and 178, 268nn. 216 and 223. Works: *The Alchemist,* 101, 107, 251n. 38, 264n. 168; *Bartholomew Fair,* 96, 251n. 38, 265n. 183; *Epicoene,* 101, 107, 251n. 38, 264n. 168; *The Tale of a Tub,* 234n. 59; *Volpone,* 48, 101, 107, 156, 251n. 38, 264n. 168
Jordan, Rob, 246n. 103, 264n. 171
Jordan, Thomas: *The Forfeiture,* 260n. 121; *Royal Arbor of Loyal Poesie,* 257n. 88
Jovial Cobler, The, 179–80
Jovial Crew, The (Brome), 96, 234n. 60
Joy, William ("The English Sampson"), 92
Judgment of Paris, The (Eccles), 257n. 92
Julius Caesar (Shakespeare), 199

Kahrl, George M., 286n. 42
Kavenik, Frances M., 222n. 6, 233n. 55, 239nn. 24 and 26
Keene, Theophilus, 169
Keirn, Tim, 224n. 13
Kenny, Shirley Strum, 92, 137, 139, 224n. 15, 250n. 19, 254n. 60, 267n. 205, 268n. 217, 282n. 2
Kenyon, J. P., 274n. 42
Kern, Ronald C., 270n. 1
Kernan, Alvin, 226n. 24, 282nn. 2 and 4, 283n. 8
Kewes, Paulina, 227n. 34, 232n. 51, 250n. 11, 253n. 49, 258n. 101, 269n. 227
Killigrew, Thomas, 26, 28, 29, 35, 38, 46, 230n. 20, 232n. 42, 239n. 30; *Chit-Chat,* 252n. 43
King Arthur (Dryden), 61, 75, 81, 98
King Lear (Shakespeare), 29, 32, 117, 124, 228n. 4, 231n. 30

King Lear (Tate), 218, 219, 284n. 17
Kirkman, Francis, 27
Knapp, J. Merrill, 154, 270n. 1
Knepp, Mrs., 58
Knights of Malta, The (Fletcher), 83
Korshin, Paul J., 226n. 24
Krutch, Joseph Wood, 249n. 1, 252n. 44
Kunz, Don R., 242n. 52

Lacy, John: as comic actor, 37–38, 39–40, 46, 91, 121, 122, 175, 201, 210, 217, 234n. 60; as dancer, 39; as improviser, 39–40; as physical comedian, 40, 41; as specialist in comic dialect parts, 39, 42; triple portrait of, 235n. 70. Works: *The Dumb Lady*, 38, 45, 234n. 62, 235nn. 72 and 73; *The French Dancing Master*, 42; *The Old Troop*, 38, 40, 42, 44, 235n. 71; *Sauny the Scott*, 23, 24, 37–47, 56, 59, 97, 113, 120, 121, 143, 170, 175, 178, 186, 207, 209, 217–19, 221n. 2, 223n. 8, 231n. 31, 233nn. 53–56, 234n. 57, 235n. 70, 248n. 126, 269n. 228, 277n. 84
Ladies' Visiting Day, The (Burnaby), 113, 145, 150, 151, 195, 268n. 215, 269n. 225
Lady of Pleasure, The (Shirley), 273n. 33
Lambranzi, Gregorio: *New and Curious School of Theatrical Dancing*, 273n. 39
Lampe: *Pyramus and Thisbe*, 184
Lancashire Witches, The (Shadwell), 61, 73, 110
Langbaine, Gerard, 27, 32, 34, 37, 39, 43, 68, 72, 103, 227n. 1, 231n. 29, 232n. 51, 240n. 32
Langhans, Edward A., 235n. 70
"Large Account of the Taste in Poetry, A" (Dennis), 129, 131, 132–33, 255n. 70, 262n. 143
Law Against Lovers, The (Davenant), 24, 28–37, 46–47, 51, 53, 59, 85, 98, 107–8, 162, 195, 204, 206, 217, 218, 220, 227n. 3, 229nn. 13 and 18, 230n. 26, 231nn. 28, 29, and 37, 232n. 46, 238nn. 15 and 16, 256n. 76
Lawes, Henry, 34
Lawrence, W. J., 237n. 2, 239n. 22, 240n. 36, 242nn. 52 and 53, 246n. 107, 276n. 69
Laws of Poetry, The (Gildon), 204
Layer, Christopher, 193

Lechner, Sister Joan Marie, 283n. 13
Lee, Nathaniel, 258n. 101; *Alexander the Great*, 257n. 89; *Lucius Junius Brutus*, 101; *The Rival Queens*, 114, 244n. 94; *Theodosius*, 125
Leggatt, Alexander, 15
Lelyveld, Toby, 260n. 122, 261n. 132
Leopold, Ellen, 225n. 22
Letters of Wit, Politics, and Morality, (Dennis), 129
Leveridge, Richard, 23, 82, 125, 176, 185, 186, 233n. 53, 255n. 65, 277nn. 84 and 85, 278nn. 87, 91 and 94; *Macbeth* music, 180; *Pyramus and Thisbe*, 24, 160, 180–85, 198, 218, 219, 247n. 112, 272n. 29, 278nn. 89, 92, 93, 95, and 96, 279n. 2
Lewis, Peter Elfed, 278nn. 89, 93 and 95
Liberty Asserted (Dennis), 131, 133, 276n. 61
Licensing Act of 1737, 25, 210, 212, 216, 286n. 38, 287nn. 2 and 3
Liesenfeld, Vincent J., 287n. 2
Life and Death of Dr. Faustus, The (Mountfort), 66
Life of Mr. Thomas Betterton, The (Gildon), 130, 262n. 135, 265n. 175
Life of That Eminent Comedian Robert Wilks, The (Curll), 93, 94, 113
Like to Like (Shirley), 257n. 89
Lives and Characters of the English Dramatick Poets (Gildon), 104, 254n. 57
Locke, Matthew, 34, 48, 62, 67, 78, 241n. 47
Lockwood, Thomas, 286n. 38
Loftis, John, 195, 271n. 18, 273n. 36, 275n. 55, 276n. 59, 280nn. 20 and 26, 287n. 3
London Cuckolds, The (Ravenscroft), 96
Long, Jane, 54
Lord Hayes' Masque, The (Campion), 239n. 21
Loughrey, Bryan, 223nn. 8, 54 and 56, 272n. 29
Love, Harold, 225n. 18
Love and Honour (Davenant), 31, 34, 230n. 21
Love at a Loss (Trotter), 89, 257n. 89
Love at a Venture (Centlivre), 268n. 215
Love Betray'd (Burnaby), 24, 97–98, 100, 138, 143–53, 185, 194–95, 219, 223n. 8,

INDEX

252n. 42, 268nn. 212 and 223, 269nn. 226, 228, and 229, 284n. 24
Love for Love (Congreve), 92, 123, 239n. 19
Love in a Chest (Johnson), 266n. 195, 273n. 33
Love in a Forest (Johnson), 23, 24, 160, 188–200, 201, 204–9, 211–13, 219, 245n. 96, 273n. 33, 279nn. 2 and 5, 280nn. 23 and 29, 281n. 37, 284n. 22
Love in a Maze (Shirley), 39
Love Makes a Man (Cibber), 94, 101, 257n. 89
Love Triumphant (Dryden), 121
Love's a Jest (Motteux), 278n. 94
Love's Contrivance (Centlivre), 90, 99, 103, 252n. 45
Love's Labour's Lost (Shakespeare), 188, 195, 208, 209, 273n. 33, 279n. 2
Love's Last Shift (Cibber), 146
Love's Victim (Gildon), 100, 101, 103, 129, 257n. 89
Loves of Ergasto, The (Greber), 154–55
Loves of Mars and Venus, The (Motteux), 104, 237n. 2, 250n. 22
Lucius Junius Brutus (Lee), 101
Luckett, Richard, 237n. 2, 243n. 56, 245n. 97, 246n. 101, 255n. 65
Luttrell, Narcissus, 246n. 107

Mabbett, Margaret, 242n. 53
Macbeth (Davenant), 34, 35, 219, 232n. 46, 238nn. 15 and 16
Macbeth (Shakespeare), 228n. 4, 231n. 30, 264n. 171, 268n. 216
McDowell, Paula, 225n. 19
Mace, Nancy A., 264n. 171, 266n. 188
McGeary, Thomas, 270nn. 1 and 4
McIntosh, William, 163
McKeithan, Daniel Morley, 239n. 26
McKendrick, Neil, 225n. 22
McKerrow, R.B., 282n. 3
Macklin, Charles, 257n. 88, 260n. 122
McManaway, James, 241nn. 43 and 45, 242n. 52, 247n. 115, 283n. 13
Macready, William Charles: production of *The Tempest*, 54
Mad Lover, The (Fletcher), 83, 229n. 19; adapted by Motteux, 114, 257n. 89
Mad World My Masters, A (Middleton), 169
Maguire, Nancy Klein, 53, 228n. 3
Mahood, M. M., 259n. 113

Maid in the Mill, The (Fletcher/Rowley), 230n. 20
Maid's Tragedy, The, (Fletcher/Waller), 117
Mainwaring, Arthur, 276n. 73
Man of Mode, The (Etherege), 255n. 67
Mancini, Francesco: *Hydaspes*, 278n. 95
Mann, Francis Oscar, 276n. 73
Marlowe, Christopher: *Tamburlaine*, 156
Marriage-Hater Match'd, The (Durfey), 123
Marsden, Jean I., 222n. 5, 224n. 16, 252n. 42, 267n. 203, 279n. 99, 282n. 4
Marston, John: *The Dutch Courtezan*, 169
Marvell, Andrew, 66
Mary, Queen, 77
Masquerade, The (Griffin), 125
Masquerade, The (Johnson), 161–62, 273n. 33, 285n. 25
Massinger, Philip, 15, 32; *The Bondman*, 230nn. 19 and 20; *The Virgin Martyr*, 239n. 23
Mattick, Paul, Jr., 224n. 16
Maurer, Margaret, 234n. 78
Maus, Katharine Eisaman, 238n. 14, 244n. 77, 252n. 42
Measure for Measure (Gildon), 24, 85, 97, 98, 100–15, 118, 150, 151, 182, 185, 204–5, 219, 221n. 3, 231n. 37, 253n. 47, 254n. 62, 255nn. 70 and 72, 256nn. 74, 76, 77, 78, 80, 84, and 85, 258n. 97
Measure for Measure (Shakespeare), 24, 199, 228nn. 4, 6, and 12; as adapted in *The Law Against Lovers*, 28–37, 206
Medœa (Johnson), 273nn. 33 and 37
Memoirs of Charles Macklin, Comedian (Cooper), 260n. 121
Merchant of Venice, The (Shakespeare), 32, 113, 118, 121, 123, 126, 150, 204, 219, 231n. 30, 257n. 88
Merchant, W. Moelwyn, 246n. 101
Merry Cobler, The (Coffey), 179
Merry Wives of Windsor, The (Shakespeare), 97, 131, 133–36, 139, 142, 143, 246n. 102, 250n. 22, 257n. 88, 264nn. 171 and 172, 265nn. 175, 178, and 181, 267n. 198, 279n. 1
Metamorphosis, The (Corye), 89
Middleton, Thomas, 32, 275n. 58; *A Mad World My Masters*, 169; Middleton and Rowley, *The Spanish Gypsies*, 56
Midsummer Night's Dream, A (Shake-

speare), 24, 49, 75, 77, 79, 80, 81, 83, 123, 150, 159, 180, 182, 188, 197–99, 204, 209, 217, 227n. 1, 273n. 33, 278n. 88, 279n. 2
Miles, James, 251n. 30
Milhous, Judith, 20, 60, 87, 91, 141, 142, 144, 153, 155, 223n. 11, 225nn. 18 and 20, 229n. 14, 232n. 42, 237n. 2, 242n. 52, 243n. 57, 245n. 99, 248nn. 120 and 130, 249nn. 3, 5, and 8, 250nn. 18 and 19, 255n. 65, 256n. 74, 257n. 89, 259n. 114, 264nn. 171 and 173, 267n. 205, 268n. 222, 270nn. 1, 2, and 4, 271n. 23
Miller, James: *The Universal Passion*, 212, 215–16, 220, 286nn. 36 and 37, 287n. 1
Miller, Josias, 198
Milton, John, 165, 263n. 155, 264n. 166
Milton, William M., 242n. 52
Miser, The (Fielding), 286n. 36
Mish, Charles C., 240n. 33
Mitchell, C. J., 284n. 24
Mitchell, Louis D., 226n. 24, 249n. 2, 264n. 173
Mock Marriage, The (Scott), 99, 250n. 13
Mock-Tempest, The (Duffett), 52, 71–73
Modern Account of Scotland, A, 44
Modern Receipt, The (Carrington), 212–13
Modish Husband, The (Burnaby), 265n. 183
Molière, 229n. 18, 273n. 33, 286nn. 36 and 37; *Princess d'Elide*, 212, 287n. 1
Monod, Paul Klebér, 189, 198, 275n. 51, 281nn. 31, 32, and 33
Montagu, John, Duke of, 199
Moore, John Robert, 240n. 33
Moore, Robert Etheridge, 237n. 2, 241n. 46, 245n. 95, 248n. 119
Morley, Henry, 251n. 30
Morley, William, 113
Morris, Corbyn, 137–38
Motteux, Peter Anthony, 48, 75, 76, 77, 245n. 100, 264n. 172; epilogue to Ravenscroft's *The Anatomist*, 90, 250n. 15; prologue to Mary Pix's *The Innocent Mistress*, 87. Works: *Acis and Galatea*, 83, 268n. 212; *Camilla*, 93; *Farewel Folly*, 89; adaptation of Fletcher's *The Island Princess*, 82, 84; *Love's a Jest*, 278n. 94; *The Loves of Mars and Venus*, 104, 237n. 2, 250n. 22; adaptation of Fletcher's *The Mad Lover*, 114, 257n. 89; *The Novelty*, 89; *The Temple of Love*, 94, 155

Mountfort: *The Life and Death of Dr. Faustus*, 66
Mountfort, Mrs., 269n. 230
Mourning Bride, The (Congreve), 156
Moyle, Walter, 131
Much Ado About Nothing (Shakespeare), 188, 195, 207–9, 212, 215, 218, 228nn. 4, 6, and 12, 231n. 30, 273n. 33, 279n. 2, 284n. 23
Mueschke, Paul, 268n. 223
Muir, Kenneth, 285n. 32
Mullin, Donald C., 270n. 1
Munro, John, 283n. 13
Munsche, P. B., 280n. 7
Murphy, Avon Jack, 140, 141, 143, 265n. 176, 266nn. 194 and 196
Music: additions to dramatic texts, 34–36, 48–49, 54, 55, 57, 59, 60, 61–63, 74–75, 78–80, 82, 85, 100, 103–5, 108–12, 114, 118–19, 128, 146–47, 150, 168, 182

Nalbach, Daniel, 270n. 1
Neighbarger, Randy L., 145, 227n. 33, 246n. 107, 277n. 84, 280n. 25
Neoclassical unities, 17, 99–100, 102, 130–31, 133–34
Nethercot, Arthur H., 238n. 19
New Opera Called Brutus of Alba, A, 81, 84, 104, 254n. 62
New Opera, call'd Cinthia and Endimion, A (Durfey), 84
New Project for the Regulation of the Stage, A, 101
New Rehearsal, or Bays the Younger, A, 160
Nichols, Charles Washburn, 286n. 39
Non-Juror, The (Cibber), 171–72, 197, 252n. 43
Norris, Dicky, 157, 198
North, Roger, 48, 49, 61, 62, 74, 236n. 2, 242n. 53, 274n. 40
Novak, Maximillian A., 54–55, 70, 238nn. 12 and 16, 239n. 30, 242n. 52
Novelty, The (Motteux), 89
Noyes, Robert Gale, 227n. 34

Odell, George C.D., 215–16, 221n. 3, 222n. 3, 233n. 55
Ogden, John, 123
Old Batchelour, The (Congreve), 123, 136, 269n. 224, 278n. 94
Old Mode and the New, The (Durfey), 94–95

Old Troop, The (Lacy), 38, 40, 42, 44, 235n. 71
Oldfield, Anne, 84
Oldmixon, John, 36, 105, 127; *The Governour of Cyprus*, 95, 268n. 212; *The Grove*, 84, 255n. 72; *Reflections on the Stage*, 252n. 45
Oldys, William, 204
Oliver, H. J., 223n. 8, 233n. 54, 272n. 29
Olleson, Philip, 270n. 1
On the Genius and Writings of Shakespear (Dennis), 187
Opera, Italian, 154–56, 158, 160, 180–84
Orgel, Stephen, 285n. 29
Oroonoko (Southerne), 96, 146, 250n. 22
Osborne, Francis: *The True Tragicomedy*, 43
Othello (Shakespeare), 32, 93, 200, 219, 231n. 30, 264n. 171, 281n. 37
Otway, Thomas, 151, 210; *Caius Marius*, 284n. 17; *The Cheats of Scapin*, 146
"Out-Cry of The London Prentices for Justice, The," 165

Pack, George, 125, 144–45, 183, 277nn. 79 and 85, 278n. 94
Pate, John, 78, 82, 247n. 112
Patriot, The (Gildon), 101
Paul, Harry Gilbert, 265n. 180
Paxman, David, 227n. 34, 263n. 162
Payne, Deborah C., 213n. 36, 226n. 24
Pedicord, Harry William, 198–99, 225n. 18, 280n. 30
Peleus and Thetis (Eccles), 118–19
Pelham-Holles, Thomas, 280n. 19
Penkethman, William, 16, 46, 96, 124, 125, 146, 170, 172, 198, 263n. 158, 264n. 173, 275n. 57
Penn, William, 55
Pennington, Donald, 274n. 41
Pepys, Samuel, 30, 33, 35, 39, 40, 42, 52–59, 62, 75, 144, 145, 229n. 15, 230n. 22, 231nn. 31 and 33, 234nn. 60 and 61, 236n. 77, 237n. 10, 238n. 13, 239nn. 21, 22, and 23, 240n. 33, 243n. 71, 264n. 171, 286n. 41
Percival, Sir John, 142
Perjured Husband, The (Centlivre), 257n. 89
Per-Juror, The (Bullock), 169, 171–72, 173
Perrin, Pierre: *Ariadne*, 66
Peters, Julie Stone, 282n. 4

Petticoat Plotter, The, 159
Phaedra and Hippolitus (Smith), 94
Phaeton (Gildon), 82, 101
Philips, John: *The Pretender's Flight*, 167, 170–71, 177, 178
Pilgrim, The (Fletcher), 83, 84, 248nn. 124 and 126, 258n. 101
Pinnock, Andrew, 244n. 77, 245n. 98, 247n. 108, 255n. 65, 261n. 130
Pix, Mary: *The Czar of Muscovy*, 257n. 89; *The Deceiver Deceived*, 23; *The Double Distress*, 95, 257n. 89; *The Innocent Mistress*, 87
Plain Dealer, The (Wycherley), 149, 156, 269nn. 225 and 228
Platt, Richard, 257n. 92
Play-house to be Let, The (Davenant), 30, 31, 34, 65, 229n. 15
Plot and No Plot, A (Dennis), 133
Plumb, J. H., 22, 225n. 22, 226n. 23
Pollins, Harold, 120
Poole, Josua: *English Parnassus*, 283n. 13
Pope, Alexander, 127, 211, 283nn. 7 and 8; on Shakespeare, 202–3, 213; *The Dunciad*, 51; *Essay on Criticism*, 133, 261n. 134; *Umbra*, 160; *The Works of Shakespear*, 129, 202, 204, 206, 213, 282n. 6
Popish Plot, 164, 274n. 45
Porter, Roy, 224n. 13
Porter, Thomas: *The French Conjurer*, 67; *The Villain*, 31, 230n. 22
Powell, George, 135–36, 152, 265nn. 181 and 182; *The Treacherous Brothers*, 51, 73
Powell, Jocelyn, 235n. 70, 241n. 40
Presumptuous Love, 184
Pretender's Flight, The (Philips), 167, 170–71, 177, 178
Price, Cecil, 286n. 41
Price, Curtis A., 145, 232nn. 45 and 49, 236n. 1, 237n. 2, 241n. 40, 244n. 93, 245n. 101, 246nn. 104 and 105, 247nn. 109, 114, and 118, 251n. 28, 254n. 62, 255nn. 65 and 68, 256nn. 78, 84, and 85, 258n. 102, 270n. 1
Priest, Josias, 104, 255nn. 65 and 66
Priestly, Joseph, 202, 282n. 5
Princess d'Elide (Molière), 212, 287n. 1
Print culture, 25, 282n. 2; influence on Shakespeare, 201–14, 216, 217, 220
Prophetess, The (Betterton adaptation of

Massinger/Fletcher) 74, 75, 81, 83, 240n. 35, 247n. 119, 278n. 90; revived by Rich, 84, 98
Proposal for the Better Regulation of the Stage, A, 210
Provok'd Wife, The (Vanbrugh), 124–25
Psyche (Shadwell), 60, 61, 62, 68, 84, 92, 240n. 35, 243n. 67, 244n. 76
Psyche Debauched (Duffett), 71
Purcell, Daniel, 82, 114; music to Vanbrugh's *The Pilgrim*, 83
Purcell, Henry, 23, 36, 48, 63, 74, 83, 124, 244n. 77. Works: *Dido and Aeneas*, 36, 76, 103–5, 107–12, 118–19, 204, 254n. 62, 255nn. 65, 67, 68, and 70, 256nn. 78, 80, 84, and 85; *The Island Princess* 81; music for *Bonduca*, 83; music for *The Fairy-Queen*, 74–81, 112, 201; music for *The Indian Queen*, 244n. 93, 261n. 130; music for Fletcher's *The Knights of Malta*, 83; *A New Opera Called Brutus of Alba*, 81, 84, 254n. 62; contributions to Fletcher's *The Pilgrim*, 84; music for Betterton's adaptation of *The Prophetess*, 74; possible music for *The Tempest*, 84, 241nn. 45 and 46
Pye, Christopher, 224n. 13
Pyramus and Thisbe (Lampe), 184
Pyramus and Thisbe (Leveridge), 24, 160, 180–85, 198, 218, 219, 247n. 112, 272n. 29, 278nn. 89, 92, 93, 95, and 96, 279n. 2

Quin, James, 135, 264n. 171

Racine: *Bajazet*, 273n. 33; *Iphigénie*, 273n. 33
Raddadi, Mongi, 229n. 13, 238n. 12
Radice, Mark A., 78, 241n. 40, 241nn. 41 and 49
Raguenet, François: *A Comparison between the French and Italian Musick*, 245n. 97
Ralph, James, 225n. 23; *The Fashionable Lady*, 23
Randall, Dale B. J., 227n. 1
Randolph, Thomas: *The Fickle Shepherdess*, 268n. 212
Rape of Europa by Jupiter, The (Betterton), 83
Ravenscroft, Edward: *The Anatomist*, 90, 104, 255n. 67; *The Careless Lovers*, 35;

The London Cuckolds, 96; *Scaramouch a Philosopher*, 66
Ray, John, 198
Reading, John, 78, 247n. 112
Recruiting Officer, The (Farquhar), 281n. 37
"Reflections Critical and Satyrical" (Dennis), 131
"Reflections on an Essay Upon Criticism" (Dennis), 128
Reflections on the Stage (Oldmixon), 252n. 45
Reformation, The (Arrowsmith), 19
Reform'd Wife, The (Burnaby), 93, 268n. 215
Reggio, Pietro, 62
Rehearsal, The (Buckingham), 51–52, 54, 182
Relapse, The (Vanbrugh), 239n. 19
Remarks on the Plays of Shakespeare (Gildon), 102, 205, 238n. 14
"Remarks upon Cato" (Dennis), 128
Revenge, The (Behn), 169
Rhodes, Richard: *Flora's Vagaries*, 234n. 61
Rich, Christopher, 80, 84, 88, 97, 98, 107, 153–57, 248n. 130, 257nn. 89 and 96, 270n. 4
Rich, John, 135, 157, 158, 159, 169, 174, 180, 271n. 18, 272n. 26, 278n. 87
Richard II (Shakespeare), 188, 206–7, 209, 273n. 33, 279n. 2
Richard II (Theobald), 279n. 2
Richard III (Cibber), 206, 219, 284nn. 17 and 24
Richard III (Shakespeare), 268n. 216
Richardson, Samuel, 204
Rinaldo and Armida (Dennis), 84, 130
Riot Act of 1715, 194
Rival Queens, The (Lee), 114, 244n. 94
Rival Sisters, The (Gould), 88, 90
Rivals, The (Davenant), 232n. 48, 238n. 15, 277n. 74
Roberts, Jeanne Addison, 141, 263n. 163, 267nn. 197 and 202
Robinson Crusoe (Defoe), 240n. 33
Robinson, Robert, 247n. 118
Rochester, John Wilmot, First Earl of, 65, 248n. 125
Rogers, Jane, 171
Rogers, Pat, 225n. 19, 269n. 230
Rollins, Hyder, 276n. 73

Roman Bride's Revenge, The (Behn), 101
Romeo and Juliet (Shakespeare), 211, 228n. 4
Rose, Mark, 285n. 29
Rosenfeld, Sybil, 242n. 53, 244n. 76
Rosenthal, Laura, 227n. 34, 232n. 51
Rothstein, Eric, 222n. 6, 233n. 55, 239nn. 24 and 26
Roundheads, The (Behn), 43, 164
Rowe, Nicholas: *The Ambitious Stepmother*, 94, 113; *The Fair Penitent*, 268n. 212; *Jane Shore*, 219, 272n. 30; *Tamerlane*, 265n. 183; *The Works of Mr. William Shakespear*, 102, 123, 135, 151, 187, 202, 205, 236n. 78, 238n.14, 282n. 6
Rowley, William: *The Maid in the Mill*, 230n. 20
Royal Arbor of Loyal Poesie (Jordan), 257n. 88
Royall King, The (Heywood), 42
Rule a Wife and Have a Wife (Fletcher), 174, 230n. 19
The Rump (Tatham), 43, 164
Ruttkay, K. G., 270n. 1
Ryder, Dudley, 42, 113, 137, 272n. 28
Rymer, Thomas, 101; *A Short View of Tragedy*, 261n. 135

Sauny the Scott (Lacy), 23, 24, 37–47, 56, 59, 97, 113, 120, 121, 143, 170, 175, 178, 186, 207, 209, 217–19, 221n. 2, 223n. 8, 231n. 31, 233nn. 53, 54, 55, and 56, 234n. 57, 235n. 70, 248n. 126, 269n. 228, 277n. 84; reputation in the eighteenth century, 42, 150, 236n. 78
Savage, Richard, 275n. 53
Savage, Roger, 245n. 95, 246nn. 101 and 102, 248n. 119
Savile, Henry, 65
Sawday, Jonathan, 274n. 44
Sawyer, Paul, 272n. 26, 275n. 54, 279n. 1
Scaramouch a Philosopher (Ravenscroft), 66
Scheil, Katherine West, 232n. 50, 281n. 1
Schellinks, Will, 33, 229n. 15
Schneider, Ben Ross, Jr., 257n. 88, 258nn. 104 and 107, 259nn. 108 and 113
Schwerin, Baron von, 64
Scotland Characterised, 43
Scots Figgaries, The (Tatham), 43, 44

Scots, English stereotypes of, 38, 42–45, 120, 234nn. 65 and 66
Scott, Thomas: *The Mock Marriage*, 99, 250n. 13
Scottish characters in English drama, 234n. 64
Scourge for the Play-Houses, A (Burridge), 109
Scouten, Arthur H., 88, 144, 163–64, 225n. 18, 226n. 30, 227n. 35, 275n. 55, 279n. 1, 285n. 35, 286n. 43
Scripture Doctrine of the Trinity (Clarke), 113
Seary, Peter, 282nn. 3 and 7, 283n. 8, 285nn. 30, 31, 32, and 35
Sea-Voyage, The (Fletcher and Massinger), 57–58, 239nn. 26, 27, and 30, 240n. 32
Secret Love (Dryden), 238n. 19, 244n. 93
Sedley, Sir Charles, 117; *Antony and Cleopatra*, 284n. 17
Serious Reflections on the Scandalous Abuse and Effects of the Stage, 256n. 79
Settle, Elkanah, 99, 246n. 108; as possible author of *The Fairy-Queen*, 76, 245n. 99. Works: *The Empress of Morocco*, 60; *The Heir of Morocco*, 17; *Ibrahim*, 68; *The Siege of Troy*, 45, 178; *The Virgin Prophetess*, 115, 257n. 89; *The World in the Moon*, 81, 84, 85, 88, 247n. 109, 248n. 130, 262n. 139
Shadwell, Thomas, 243n. 67; as author of 1674 *The Tempest*, 64, 240n. 36, 242n. 52, 244n. 77. Works: *The Humorists*, 42; *The Lancashire Witches*, 61, 73, 110; "The Protestant Satire," 274n. 45; *Psyche*, 60, 61, 62, 68, 84, 92, 240n. 35, 243n. 67, 244n. 76; *The Squire of Alsatia*, 52; *The Sullen Lovers*, 49, *Timon of Athens*, 284n. 17; *The Volunteers*, 120, 121
Shakespeare Ladies' Club, 281n. 1
Shakespeare Restored (Theobald), 134, 202, 210
Shakespeare, William: eighteenth-century editions of, 282n. 3; character of Falstaff, 132, 134–43, 147–48, 174, 246n. 102, 263n. 163, 264n. 173, 265nn. 178 and 180, 266n. 194; ghost of Shakespeare, 106, 115–17; as "National Poet," 14, 16, 67, 75, 100, 162, 200, 218; in poetical commonplace books, 283n. 13; reading knowledge of,

330 INDEX

202–14; as source material, 16, 161; as writer of tragedies and histories, 16, 93, 98, 218, 219, 223n. 7, 272n. 30. Works: *Antony and Cleopatra*, 231n. 30; *As You Like It*, 150, 175, 188, 194, 195–98, 206–9, 212, 219, 231n. 30, 273n. 33, 278n. 96, 279n. 2, 283n. 11, 286n. 40 (*see also* Johnson, *Love in a Forest*); *The Comedy of Errors*, 184 (*see also* Browne/Taverner, *Everybody Mistaken*); *Cymbeline*, 83, 231n. 30, 268n. 216; *Hamlet*, 33, 93, 99, 124, 211, 218, 219, 228n. 4, 230nn. 19, 20, and 22, 231n. 30, 264n. 171, 278nn. 88 and 94; *Henry IV*, 101, 106 and 107, 264n. 171; —Betterton's version, 135–36, 139–40, 143, 174, 199, 206, 211; *Henry V*, 206, 234n. 64; *Henry VI*, 206; *Henry VIII*, 29, 33, 101, 107, 228n. 4, 231n. 33; *Julius Caesar*, 199; *King Lear*, 29, 32, 117, 124, 228n. 4, 231n. 30; *Love's Labour's Lost*, 188, 195, 208, 209, 273n. 33, 279n. 2 (*see also* Johnson, *Love in a Forest*); *Macbeth*, 228n. 4, 231n. 30, 264n. 171, 268n. 216; —1672 operatic version, 61, 104, 110, 244n. 79; —Davenant adaptation, 34, 35, 219, 232n. 46, 238nn. 15 and 16; —Leveridge music, 180; *Measure for Measure*, 24, 199, 228nn. 4, 6 and 12; —adapted as *The Law Against Lovers*, 28–37, 206 (*see also* Davenant, *The Law Against Lovers*); —adapted by Charles Gildon, 36–37, 76, 100–112 (*see also* Gildon, *Measure for Measure*); *The Merchant of Venice*, 32, 113, 118, 121, 123, 126, 150, 204, 219, 231n. 30, 257n. 88; —adapted by Charles Macklin, 126; —adapted by George Granville, 113–26 (*see also* Granville, *The Jew of Venice*); *The Merry Wives of Windsor*, 97, 131, 133–36, 139, 142, 143, 246n. 102, 250n. 22, 257n. 88, 264nn. 171 and 172, 265nn. 175, 178, and 181, 267n. 198, 279n. 1; —adapted as *The Comical Gallant*, 126–43 (*see also* Dennis, *The Comical Gallant*); *A Midsummer Night's Dream*, 24, 49, 75, 77, 79, 80, 81, 83, 123, 150, 159, 180, 182, 188, 197–99, 204, 209, 217, 227n. 1, 273n. 33, 278n. 88, 279n. 2; —adapted as *Bottom the Weaver*, 27 (*see also Bottom the Weaver*); —adapted as *The Fairy-Queen*, 74–81 (*see also* The Fairy-Queen); *Much Ado About Nothing*, 24, 188, 195, 207–9, 212, 215, 218, 228nn. 4, 6, and 12, 231n. 30, 273n. 33, 279n. 2, 284n. 23; —adapted as *The Law Against Lovers*, 28–37, 107, 206 (*see also* Davenant, *The Law Against Lovers*); *Othello*, 32, 93, 200, 219, 231n. 30, 264n. 171, 281n. 37; *Richard II*, 188, 206–7, 209, 273n. 33, 279n. 2 (*see also* Johnson, *Love in a Forest*); *Richard III*, 268n. 216; —adapted by Cibber, 206, 219, 284n. 17, 284n. 24 (*see also* Cibber, *Richard III*); *Romeo and Juliet*, 211, 228n. 4; *The Taming of the Shrew*, 13, 24, 108, 126, 159, 162, 168, 170, 173, 175, 177, 180, 185, 217–18, 223n. 8, 233nn. 54 and 56, 235n. 76, 273n. 33; —adapted as *Sauny the Scott*, 37, 39, 233n. 55 (*see also* Lacy, *Sauny the Scott*; Bullock, *The Cobler of Preston*; Johnson, *The Cobler of Preston*); *The Tempest*, 24, 49, 52–56, 59, 62–63, 75, 82, 83, 84, 150, 228n. 4, 231n. 30, 238n. 14, 239n. 26, 266n. 193; —1674 version, 52, 59–71, 74, 77, 84, 85, 92, 97–99, 107, 108, 113, 150, 151, 155, 182, 186, 201, 217, 219, 240n. 36, 241nn. 37, 38, 40, 41, 43, 45, and 46, 243n. 56, 244n. 77, 252n. 46, 253n. 48, 287n. 4; —1674 version, authorship debate, 50, 64, 76, 85–86, 242n. 52; —1674 version, burlesqued by Duffett in *The Mock-Tempest*, 71–73; —adapted by Davenant-Dryden, 34, 50, 52–59, 62, 71, 117, 217, 221n. 3, 238nn. 12, 15, and 19, 239nn. 19, 20, and 30, 240n. 33, 241n. 38, 242n. 52, 244n. 77, 247n. 108, 284n. 17, 287n. 4; —Davenant-Dryden adaptation, as compared to the 1674 version, 63–64, 69–70 (*see also The Tempest*, Dryden-Davenant version); *Timon of Athens*, 117, 124; *Titus Andronicus*, 268n. 216; *Troilus and Cressida*, 117, 211; *Twelfth Night*, 29, 33, 138, 144, 148, 149, 175, 188, 208, 212, 218, 219, 223n. 8, 228n. 4, 230nn. 20 and 22, 231n. 30 and 33, 268nn. 209 and 223, 273n. 33, 278n. 96, 279n. 2; —adapted as *Love Betray'd*, 143–50 (*see also* Burnaby, *Love Betray'd*); *The Two Gentlemen of Verona*, 212; *The Winter's Tale*, 231n. 30

INDEX

Shane, Denise Elliot, 271n. 18
Shattuck, Charles H., 228n. 12, 245n. 96
She Ventures and He Wins, 250n. 22
She Wou'd If She Cou'd (Etherege), 125, 155
She-Gallants, The (Granville), 114
Sherbo, Arthur, 282n. 3
Shirley, James, 32; *The Lady of Pleasure*, 273n. 33; *Like to Like*, 257n. 89; *Love in a Maze*, 39; *The Triumph of Beauty*, 227n. 1
Shoemaker, Robert B., 224n. 13
Short View of Tragedy, A (Rymer), 261n. 135
Shrew-taming plots, popularity of, 37, 45–46, 59, 173, 175–76, 178–80, 184–85, 217
Shudofsky, M. Maurice, 279n. 5
Siege of Rhodes, The (Davenant), 31–35, 232nn. 40 and 43, 246n. 102
Siege of Troy, The (Settle), 45, 178
Simpson, Claude M., 276n. 73
Simpson, Percy and Evelyn, 269n. 223
Sir Harry Wildair (Farquhar), 257n. 89
Sir Walter Raleigh, 158
Six Days Adventure, The (Howard), 35
Slip, The (Bullock), 169, 275n. 58
Smith, Edmund: *Phaedra and Hippolitus*, 94
Smith, John Harrington, 266n. 184
Smith, Robert, 239n. 28
Some Thoughts Concerning the Stage in a Letter to a Lady, 21, 88
Sorelius, Gunnar, 223n. 7, 227n. 34, 228n. 4, 235n. 70, 245n. 95
South Sea Bubble, 189
Southerne, Thomas: *The Fatal Marriage*, 177; *Oroonoko*, 96, 146, 250n. 22
Southwark Fair, 126, 174, 198
Spanish Fryar, The (Dryden), 155
Spanish Gypsies, The (Middleton/Rowley), 56
Spectator, The, 187, 203, 259n. 110, 262n. 135, 265n. 182, 278n. 95
Spencer, Christopher, 221n. 2, 238n. 16, 240n. 36, 242n. 52, 257n. 87, 259n. 113, 260n. 117
Spencer, Hazelton, 141, 215–16, 221n. 3, 228n. 9, 233n. 55, 245n. 95, 260n. 117, 266n. 194
Spiller, James (Jemmy), 13, 46, 169–74, 177, 178, 182, 275nn. 55 and 57, 276n. 69

Sprague, Arthur Colby, 227n. 34, 248n. 124, 260n. 117
Squire of Alsatia, The (Shadwell), 52
"Stage Defended, The" (Dennis), 128
Stamm, Rudolf, 229n. 13
Stanley, Sir John, 147
Staves, Susan, 233n. 55
Steele, Sir Richard, 20, 126, 137, 157, 178, 203, 218, 261n. 135, 271n. 18, 272n. 27, 283n. 11; *The Conscious Lovers*, 265n. 183; *The Funeral*, 94, 174, 265n. 183; *The Tender Husband*, 177
Stepmother, The (Davenant), 229n. 15
Stewart, Powell, 286n. 37
Stone, George Winchester, Jr., 203, 241n. 38, 286n. 42
Storm, The, 57–58
Successful Pyrate, The (Johnson), 273n. 33
Suckling, Sir John: *The Goblins*, 58, 247n. 108
Sullen Lovers, The (Shadwell), 49
Sultaness, The (Johnson), 273n. 33
Sutherland, James R., 22, 226n. 28
Swaen, A. E. H., 273n. 39
Swift, Jonathan, 127

Tale of a Tub, The (Jonson), 234n. 59
Tamer Tam'd, The (Fletcher), 41, 46, 233n. 55, 236nn. 76, 77, and 78
Tamburlaine (Marlowe), 156
Tamerlane (Rowe), 265n. 183
Taming of the Shrew, The (Shakespeare), 13, 24, 108, 126, 159, 162, 168, 170, 173, 175, 177, 180, 185, 217–18, 223n. 8, 233nn. 54 and 56, 235n. 76, 273n. 33
Tate, Nahum: *Dido and Aeneas*, 76, 103–12, 256n. 85; *A Duke and no Duke*, 155, 178; *The Ingratitude of a Commonwealth*, 284n. 17; *King Lear*, 218, 219, 284n. 17; *A New Opera Called Brutus of Alba*, 81, 104
Tatham, John, 42; *The Distracted State*, 43; *The Rump*, 43, 164; *The Scots Figgaries*, 43, 44
Tatler, The, 187, 203, 261n. 135
Tave, Stuart M., 132, 137, 263n. 161
Taverner, William *Everybody Mistaken*, 184–85, 279n. 97
Tempest, The (Davenant-Dryden adaptation), 34, 50, 52–59, 62, 71, 117, 217, 221n. 3, 238nn. 12, 15, and 19, 239nn. 19, 20, and 30, 240n. 33, 241n. 38,

242n. 52, 244n. 77, 247n. 108, 284n. 17, 287n. 4
Tempest, The (Shakespeare), 24, 49, 52, 53, 54, 56, 59, 62–63, 75, 82, 83, 84, 150, 228n. 4, 231n. 30, 238n. 14, 239n. 26, 266n. 193
Temple of Love, The (Motteux), 94, 155
Tender Husband, The (Steele), 177
Tenger, Zeynep, 224n. 12, 252n. 44
Terence, 131
Theobald, Lewis, 283nn. 8 and 11. Works: *The Cave of Poverty*, 285n. 31; *Double Falshood*, 210–12, 285nn. 32 and 33; *Richard II*, 279n. 2; *Shakespeare* edition, 202–3, 210–12, 285n. 30; *Shakespeare Restored*, 134, 202, 210
Theodosius (Lee), 125
Thesaurus Dramaticus, 204, 284n. 16
Thierry, Jacques, 33, 229n. 15
Thomas, Claudia, 225n. 19, 250n. 14, 255n. 72
Thomas, Keith, 274n. 41
Thompson, Ann, 223n. 8, 272n. 29
Thompson, E. P., 194
Thomson, James, 283n. 11
Thorn-Drury, G., 241n. 46
Thornhill, Sir James, 270n. 6
Thorp, Jennifer, 226n. 24, 255n. 66
Three Hours After Marriage (Gay), 181
Timon of Athens (Shadwell), 284n. 17
Timon of Athens (Shakespeare), 117, 124
Titus Andronicus (Shakespeare), 268n. 216
Tonson, Jacob, 77, 188, 211, 285n. 35
Tragedy of Medea, The (Johnson), 162
Traytor, The (Bullock), 169
Treacherous Brothers, The (Powell), 51, 73
Triumph of Beauty, The (Shirley), 227n. 1
Troilus and Cressida (Dryden), 258n. 97, 284n. 17
Troilus and Cressida (Shakespeare), 117, 211
Trolander, Paul, 224n. 12, 252n. 44
Trotter, Catharine, 252n. 44, 254n. 57; *Love at a Loss*, 89, 257n. 89; *The Unhappy Penitent*, 257n. 89
True Tragicomedy, The (Osborne), 43
Tucker, Joseph E., 286n. 36
Tuerk, Cynthia M., 233n. 55
Tuke, Samuel: *The Adventures of Five Hours*, 31, 230n. 22
Tunbridge-Walks (Baker), 90, 144

Tupper, Fred S., 262n. 150
Twelfth Night (Shakespeare), 29, 33, 138, 144, 148, 149, 175, 188, 208, 212, 218, 219, 223n. 8, 228n. 4, 230nn. 20 and 22, 231nn. 30 and 33, 268nn. 209 and 223, 273n. 33, 278n. 96, 279n. 2
Two Gentlemen of Verona, The (Shakespeare), 212

Underhill, Cave, 56, 268n. 209
Unfortunate Lovers, The (Davenant), 34
Unhappy Penitent, The (Trotter), 257n. 89
United company, 38, 73, 75, 92, 105
Universal Passion, The (Miller), 212, 215–16, 220, 286nn. 36 and 37, 287n. 1
Usurper, The (Howard), 238n. 13

Valentinian (Fletcher/Rochester), 73, 83, 117
Van Lennep, William, 229n. 15, 239n. 22, 240n. 35
Vanbrugh, Sir John, 94, 137, 153–58, 188, 249n. 1, 264n. 173, 270n. 4, 271n. 13. Works: *The Confederacy*, 139; *The False Friend*, 87, 265n. 183; *The Pilgrim*, 83; *The Provok'd Wife*, 124–25; *The Relapse*, 239n. 19
Vaughan, Virginia Mason and Alden T., 266n. 193
Venus and Adonis (Blow), 255n. 65
Verbruggen, John, 256n. 74, 258n. 97; as Antonio in Granville's *The Jew of Venice*, 116–17
Vertue Betray'd (Banks), 17–18
Vickers, Brian, 221n. 2, 282n. 4
Victim, The (Johnson), 273n. 33, 280n. 19
Victorious Love (Walker), 93
Village Opera, The (Johnson), 273n. 33
Villain, The (Porter), 31, 230n. 22
Virgil: *The Aeneid*, 104
Virgin Martyr, The (Massinger/Dekker), 239n. 23
Virgin Prophetess (Settle), 115, 257n. 89
Visser, Colin, 67
Volpone (Jonson), 48, 101, 107, 156, 251n. 38, 264n. 168
Volunteers, The (Shadwell), 120, 121

Walker, Thomas, 249n. 6
Walker, William: *Victorious Love*, 93
Walking Statue, The (Hill), 125

INDEX

Walkling, Andrew W., 243nn. 64 and 72, 244n. 74
Waller, Edmund, 258n. 100; adaptation of Fletcher's *The Maid's Tragedy*, 117
Walpole, Horace, 204
Walpole, Robert, 193
Wanton Wife, The, 155
Ward, Charles E., 242n. 52
Ward, Ned, 64, 120, 121
Wary Widow, The (Higden), 147
Waterson, Reverend Will, 19, 194
Way of the World, The (Congreve), 141, 149, 150
Webster, John: *The Duchess of Malfi*, 230n. 22
Weeks, Louise Jaquelyn, 251n. 40
Wells, Staring B., 250n. 16, 251n. 37
Wharton, Philip, Duke of, 199
What D'Ye Call It, The (Gay), 181, 182, 278n. 88
Wheeler, David, 141, 262n. 136, 266n. 184, 267n. 197
Whig and Tory (Griffin), 280n. 20
White, Eric Walter, 246n. 103
Wife's Relief, The (Johnson), 161, 273n. 33
Wikander, Matthew W., 238n. 12
Wilcox, John, 229n. 18
Wild Gallant, The (Dryden), 35
Wild Goose Chase, The (Fletcher), 265n. 183
Wilkins, W. Walker, 277n. 73
Wilks, Robert, 156, 157, 162, 171
Will's coffeehouse, 144
William and Mary, 21, 245n. 95, 247nn. 109 and 119, 256n. 85
William, King, 142, 249n. 3
Williams, Aubrey, 249n. 1
Williams, Gary Jay, 245n. 95, 246n. 108, 247nn. 109, 118, and 119
Wilson, Douglas L., 284n. 16
Wilson, John Harold, 119, 227n. 34, 240n. 32, 246n. 102, 248n. 124, 259n. 113, 260n. 117

Wilson, Thelma, 277n. 85, 278n. 87
Wilson, Thomas, 198
Winn, James A., 34, 232nn. 43 and 44
Winter's Tale, The (Shakespeare), 231n. 30
Winton, Calhoun, 226nn. 24 and 26, 253n. 48, 256n. 79, 271n. 18
Wit for Money: or, Poet Stutter, 247n. 108
Wits, The (Davenant), 31, 34
Wits, The (Kirkman), 27
Woman Is a Riddle (Bullock), 161, 169, 172–73, 275n. 53
Woman's Revenge, The (Bullock), 169, 174, 177
Womens Conquest, The (Howard), 49
Wonders in the Sun (Durfey), 155
Wood, Bruce, 245n. 98, 247n. 108, 255n. 65
Wood, Frederick T., 259n. 113
Works of Mr. William Shakespear, The (Rowe), 102, 123, 135, 151, 187, 202, 205, 236n. 78, 238n.14, 282n. 6
Works of Shakespear, The (Pope), 129, 202, 204, 206, 213, 282n. 6
World in the Moon, The (Settle), 81, 84, 85, 88, 247n. 109, 248n. 130, 262n. 139
Worsdale, James: *A Cure for a Scold*, 179, 277n. 83
Wright, Michael, 44
Wright, Thomas, 276n. 73
Wycherley, William, 151, 218; *The Country Wife*, 96, 239n. 19, 265n. 183, 269n. 225, 281n. 37; *The Plain Dealer*, 149, 156, 269nn. 225 and 228

Ximena (Cibber), 94

Younger Brother, The (Gildon), 101
Younger, Elizabeth, 281n. 37

Zimmerman, Franklin B., 226n. 31, 241n. 45, 247n. 112
Zwicker, Steven N., 274n. 42